Research Methods
for Business Students

Research Methods for Business Students

Second edition

Dr Mark N K Saunders
Dr Philip Lewis
Dr Adrian Thornhill

FINANCIAL TIMES
Prentice Hall

An imprint of **Pearson Education**

Harlow, England · London · New York · Reading, Massachusetts · San Francisco
Toronto · Don Mills, Ontario · Sydney · Tokyo · Singapore · Hong Kong · Seoul
Taipei · Cape Town · Madrid · Mexico City · Amsterdam · Munich · Paris · Milan

Pearson Education Limited

Edinburgh Gate
Harlow
Essex CM20 2JE
England

and Associated Companies around the world

Visit us on the World Wide Web at
www.pearsoneduc.com

First published in Great Britain under the Pitman Publishing imprint in 1997
Second edition published 2000

© Pearson Professional Limited 1997
© Pearson Education Limited 2000

The right of Mark Saunders, Philip Lewis and Adrian Thornhill
to be identified as Authors of this Work has been asserted by them
in accordance with the Copyright, Designs and Patents Act 1988.

ISBN 0 273 63977 3

British Library Cataloguing in Publication Data
A CIP catalogue record for this book can be obtained from the British Library.

10 9 8 7 6 5 4 3 2

Typeset by M Rules
Printed and bound in Great Britain by Ashford Colour Press Ltd., Gosport

Contents

Preface to the second edition

The second edition of *Research Methods for Business Students* has been written against a background of rapid change, and in particular the phenomenal growth in readily available computer processing power. Since the first edition, the decline in relative cost has made access to both powerful analysis software and the Internet a reality for almost all students. As in the first edition we have taken a predominantly non-software-specific approach. By doing this, we have been able to focus on the general principles needed to utilise both analysis software and the Internet effectively for research. These principles have been incorporated throughout the book, and have entailed substantial rewriting of Chapter 3, 'Critically reviewing the literature', and Chapter 7, 'Using secondary data'. We have also taken the opportunity to include tables of Internet addresses that we, and our students, have found useful.

Inevitably the body of knowledge on research methods has expanded since 1996 and we have revised the chapters accordingly. As part of this we have incorporated suggestions for the uses of on-line survey approaches into Chapter 10, 'Collecting primary data using questionnaires'. We have also taken the opportunity to update and refine existing worked examples and case studies where appropriate. New worked examples and diagrams have also been introduced where it was felt their inclusion would assist clarity.

The other most significant changes relate to the reworking of Chapter 4, 'Deciding on the research approach and choosing a research strategy'. This now distinguishes more clearly between research philosophies, research approaches and research strategies. We have included a new section that reviews both inductive and deductive approaches. The section on research strategies has also been expanded to include action research, ethnography and grounded theory.

Other minor changes and updatings have been made throughout. Needless to say, any errors of omission and commission are our responsibility.

Much of our updating has been undertaken on the basis of comments from students, colleagues and reviewers to whom we are most grateful. We would like to thank our students for their comments on all of the chapters. Thanks are also due to Professor Tom McEwan (University of Natal, South Africa), David Shuttleworth and Denise Skinner (both at Nene University College, Northampton) for their thought provoking comments and suggestions. Past and present colleagues at Cheltenham & Gloucester College of Higher Education again deserve thanks for their assistance in providing examples of research across the spectrum of business and management and in reviewing parts of this book, in particular Lynnette Bailey, Barry Baker, Tony Beasley, Fiona

Campbell (now at the University of Wolverhampton), Valerie Cowley, Huw Davies (now Planning Manager at Courtaulds Bodywear, Bristol), Sue Davis, David Dawson, Andrew Gibbons, Andy Guppy (now at the University of Middlesex), Martin Jenkins, Jim Keane, Sheila Ryan and Christine Williams.

Sadie McClelland, our commissioning editor, provided excellent support and enthusiasm throughout the process.

Finally our thanks are due to Jane, Jenny, Jan, Jemma, Ben, Andrew and Katie who have, again, allowed us the evenings, weekends and 'holiday time' to be slaves to our word processors.

MNKS
PL
AT

September 1999

Preface to the first edition

The idea for this book grew from our own experiences of undertaking and teaching business and management research. Over the past six years we have undertaken research together, taught research methods as a team and been involved in joint project supervisions at both undergraduate and postgraduate levels. These experiences have helped to develop our knowledge, understanding and skills as researchers and, in particular, our awareness of the realities of undertaking research. They have also provided numerous insights into the needs and wants of student researchers.

In our teaching and supervision we have used a number of research methods textbooks. However, none of these have fully met our students' needs or our needs as tutors. This was sometimes because of their focus on either quantitative or qualitative research, or due to relatively brief discussions in relation to particular aspects such as reviewing the literature or writing the project report. In addition, our students felt that there was sometimes a tendency to present research as a straightforward, unproblematic affair, rather than the messy process which they experienced.

Few of the textbooks we encountered made use of either case studies or examples to overcome the problems and pitfalls that are part of the process. Our students commented that few included activities which they could undertake to practise their skills and test their understanding. Clear guidelines to make the process as straightforward as possible were also rarely provided. Similarly, the application of appropriate information technology was rarely considered as an integral part of the text. Where this was considered the discussion was often software specific, rather than discussing general principles that would enable the researcher to utilise information technology most effectively. As such, we felt that the undergraduate and postgraduate student researcher was left unprepared for the realities of research.

When faced with these reservations about the suitability of existing textbooks for our purposes, we responded to the challenge set by our students. This book is that response! The book could not, however, have been written without considerable help from our students, friends, colleagues and families. They have contributed through their encouragement and ideas. Many of these ideas are reflected in the cases and worked examples used in the book, for which they kindly gave their permission.

We would like to thank our students, in particular the 1994–5 and 1995–6 cohorts of students on the management Master's research methods course, for their advice and constructive criticism on all of the chapters. Our colleagues at Cheltenham & Gloucester College of Higher Education also deserve thanks for their interest and assistance in reviewing parts of this book; in particular Lynnette Bailey, Barry Baker,

Tony Beasley, Fiona Campbell, Jacquelyn Collinson, Valerie Cowley, Huw Davies, Sue Davis, David Dawson, Brian Eaton, Andrew Gibbons, Andy Guppy (now at Liverpool John Moores University), Martin Jenkins, Jim Keane, Alison McGregor, Mike Millmore, Sheila Ryan, John Wilkin and Christine Williams.

Our thanks are also due to our head of department Paul Taylor for his support, and to our commissioning editor Kara Regan for her constructive comments and never-ending enthusiasm throughout the entire process.

Finally, our thanks to Jane, Jenny, Jan, Jemma, Benjamin, Andrew and Katie for putting up with the long hours when we were slaves to our wordprocessors. We hope you will find that it was worth the effort.

MNKS
PL
AT

September 1996

Contributors

Mark NK Saunders BA, MSc, PGCE, PhD, is Head of the Human Resource Management Research Centre at Gloucestershire Business School, Cheltenham & Gloucester College of Higher Education. He teaches research methods, quantitative methods and HRM to postgraduate, undergraduate and professional students as well as supervising research degrees. Mark has published articles on research methods, employee recruitment and mobility and downsizing. He is co-author with Phil, Adrian and Mike Millmore of *Managing Change: A Human Resource Strategy Approach*, published by Financial Times Prentice Hall, and has also co-authored a book on business statistics. He has undertaken consultancy in both public and private sectors, prior to which he was Principal Research Officer for Hereford and Worcester Social Services.

Philip Lewis BA, PhD, MSc, MIPD, PGDipM, Cert. Ed., is a Principal Lecturer in Human Resource Management (HRM) and MA Management of Human Resources course leader at Gloucestershire Business School, Cheltenham & Gloucester College of Higher Education. He teaches HRM and research methods to postgraduate, undergraduate and professional students and is involved in research degree supervision. Phil's research interests are reward management and performance management, on which he has published several articles. He is co-author with Adrian, Mark and Mike Millmore of *Managing Change: A Human Resource Strategy Approach*, published by Financial Times Prentice Hall. He has undertaken consultancy in both public and private sectors. Prior to his career in higher education Phil was a training adviser with the Distributive Industry Training Board.

Adrian Thornhill BA, PhD, PGCE, FIPD, is Head of the School of Human Resource Management at Gloucestershire Business School, Cheltenham & Gloucester College of Higher Education. He teaches HRM and research methods to postgraduate, undergraduate and professional students and is involved in research degree supervision. Adrian's main research interest is related to managing change and the management of organisational downsizing and redundancy, on which he has published several articles. He is co-author with Mark, Phil and Mike Millmore of *Managing Change: A Human Resource Strategy Approach*, published by Financial Times Prentice Hall and has also co-authored a book on downsizing and redundancy. He has undertaken consultancy in both public and private sectors.

Lynnette Bailey is a Senior Learning Advisor with a special interest in education and information technology at Cheltenham & Gloucester College of Higher Education.

Barry Baker is a Principal Lecturer in Human Resource Management with a special interest in ethics at Gloucestershire Business School, Cheltenham & Gloucester College of Higher Education.

Tony Beasley is a Senior Lecturer in Accountancy at Gloucestershire Business School, Cheltenham & Gloucester College of Higher Education.

Fiona Campbell is a Research Assistant at Wolverhampton Business School, University of Wolverhampton. She was formerly a Postgraduate Research Student at Gloucestershire Business School, Cheltenham & Gloucester College of Higher Education.

Valerie Cowley is a Senior Lecturer in Public Relations and Marketing at Gloucestershire Business School, Cheltenham & Gloucester College of Higher Education.

Huw Davies is the Planning Manager at Courtaulds Bodywear, Bristol. He was formerly a Senior Lecturer in Operations Management at Gloucestershire Business School, Cheltenham & Gloucester College of Higher Education.

David Dawson is a Lecturer in Human Resource Management at Gloucestershire Business School, Cheltenham & Gloucester College of Higher Education.

Andy Guppy is the Professor of Organisational Psychology at the University of Middlesex. He was formerly the Reader in Organisational Behaviour at Gloucestershire Business School, Cheltenham & Gloucester College of Higher Education.

Martin Jenkins is a Senior Learning Advisor with a special interest in business and management at Cheltenham & Gloucester College of Higher Education.

Jim Keane is a Senior Lecturer in Financial Services at Gloucestershire Business School, Cheltenham & Gloucester College of Higher Education.

Christine Williams is the Head of the School of Marketing and Strategy at Gloucestershire Business School, Cheltenham & Gloucester College of Higher Education.

1 The nature of business and management research and how to use this book

By the end of this chapter you should:

- be able to outline the purpose and distinct focus of management research;
- be able to place your research project on a basic–applied research continuum according to its purpose and context;
- understand the stages you will need to complete (and revisit) as part of your research process;
- have an overview of this book's purpose and structure;
- be aware of some of the ways you can use this book.

1.1 The aims of this book

This book is designed to help you to undertake a research project whether you are an undergraduate or postgraduate student of business and management or a manager. It provides a clear guide on how to undertake research as well as highlighting the realities of undertaking research, including the more common pitfalls. The book is written as an introductory text to provide you with a guide to the research process and necessary knowledge and skills to undertake a piece of research from thinking of a research topic to writing your project report. As such, you will find it useful as a manual or handbook on how to tackle your research project.

After reading the book you will have been introduced to and explored a range of approaches, strategies and methods with which you could tackle your research project. Of equal importance, you will know that there is no one best way for undertaking all research. You will be able to make an informed choice about the approaches, strategies and methods that are most suitable to your own research project and be able to justify this choice. In reading the book you will have been introduced to the more frequently used techniques for analysing different types of data, have had a chance to practise them and be able to make a reasoned choice regarding which to use. When selecting and using these techniques you will be aware of the contribution that the appropriate use of information technology can make to your research.

1.2 The nature of business and management research

People undertake research in order to find things out in a systematic way, thereby increasing their knowledge (Jankowicz, 1995). It therefore follows that business and management research is undertaking systematic research to find out things about business and management. Two phrases are important in this definition: 'systematic research' and 'to find out'. 'Systematic' suggests that research is based on logical relationships and not just beliefs (Ghauri *et al.*, 1995). As part of this your research will involve an explanation of the methods used to collect the data, will argue why the results obtained are meaningful and will explain any limitations that are associated with them. 'Finding out' suggests a multiplicity of possible purposes for your research. These may include describing, explaining, understanding, criticising and analysing (Ghauri *et al.*, 1995).

Easterby-Smith *et al.* (1991) argue that three things combine to make business and management a distinctive focus for research:

- the way in which managers (and researchers) draw on knowledge developed by other disciplines;

- the fact that managers tend to be powerful and busy people. Therefore, they are unlikely to allow research access unless they can see personal or commercial advantages;

- the requirement for the research to have some practical consequence. This means it either needs to contain the potential for taking some form of action or needs to take account of the practical consequences of the findings.

Recent discussion within the British Academy of Management has explored the status of management research. One feature, which has gained considerable support, is the *transdisciplinary* nature of such research. While this has similarities to Easterby-Smith *et al.*'s (1991) point regarding the use of knowledge from other disciplines, it also emphasises that the research 'cannot be reduced to any sum of parts framed in terms of contributions to associated disciplines' (Tranfield and Starkey, 1998: 352). Another feature of management research highlighted by the debate is the belief that it should be able to develop ideas and to relate them to practice. In particular that research should complete a *virtuous circle* of theory and practice (Tranfield and Starkey, 1998) through which research on practice informs theory that in turn informs practice. Thus, business and management research needs to engage with both the world of theory and the world of practice. Consequently, the problems addressed should grow out of interaction between these two worlds rather than either on their own.

Thus, not only does business and management research need to provide findings that advance knowledge and understanding, it also needs to address business issues and to provide a process for solving managerial problems. This is not to say that the satisfaction of your intellectual curiosity, for its own sake, is out of the question. Rather, in this pursuit you should be considering the practical implications of your findings.

Within these boundaries of advancing knowledge, solving managerial problems and addressing business issues, the purpose and the context of your research project can differ considerably. For some research projects, your purpose may be to understand and explain the impact of something, such as a particular policy. You may undertake this research within an individual organisation and suggest appropriate action on the basis of your findings. For other research projects, you may wish to explore the ways in which different organisations do things differently. In such projects, your purpose may be to discover and understand better the underlying processes in a wider context, thereby providing greater understanding for practitioners. For yet other research projects, you may wish to combine an in-depth investigation of an organisation within the context of a wider understanding of the processes that are operating.

Despite this variety, we believe that all business and management research projects can be placed on a continuum (Fig 1.1) according to their purpose and context. At one extreme of the continuum is research that is undertaken purely to understand the processes of business and management and their outcomes. This is often termed *basic, fundamental* or *academic research*. Given our earlier discussion it is unlikely that such research would fulfil our criteria for business and management research without some consideration being made of the practical consequences. Through doing this, the research would start to move towards the other end of the continuum (Fig 1.1). At this end is research that is of direct and immediate relevance to managers, addresses issues which they see as important and is presented in ways which they understand and can act on. This is termed *applied research*.

Wherever your research project lies on this basic–applied continuum, we believe that you should undertake your research with rigour. To do this you will need to pay careful attention to the entire research process.

Basic research ⟵————————————⟶ Applied research	
Purpose:	*Purpose:*
• expand knowledge of processes of business and management	• improve understanding of particular business or management problem
• results in universal principles relating to the process and its relationship to outcomes	• results in solution to problem
• findings of significance and value to society in general	• new knowledge limited to problem
	• findings of practical relevance and value to manager(s) in organisation(s)
Context:	*Context:*
• undertaken by people based in universities	• undertaken by people based in a variety of settings including organisations and universities
• choice of topic and objectives determined by the researcher	• objectives negotiated with originator
• flexible timescales	• tight timescales

Fig 1.1   **Basic and applied research**

Sources: Authors' experience; Easterby-Smith et al., 1991; Hedrick et al., 1993; Johnson, 1996.

1.3 The research process

Most research textbooks represent research as a multi-stage process that you must follow in order to undertake and complete your research project. The precise number of stages varies but they usually include formulating and clarifying a topic, reviewing the literature, choosing a strategy, collecting data, analysing data and writing up. In the majority of these the research process, although presented with rationalised examples, is described as a series of stages through which you must pass. Articles you have read may also suggest that the research process is rational and straightforward. Unfortunately, this is very rarely true and the reality is considerably messier (Saunders and Lewis, 1997). While you will need to pass through the stages outlined above, you will probably revisit all of them more than once. Each time you revisit a stage you will need to reflect on the associated issues and to refine your ideas. In addition, as highlighted by some textbooks, you will need to consider ethical and access issues during the process.

This textbook also presents the research process as a series of linked stages. At the start of this process, we believe that it is vital that you spend time formulating and clarifying your research topic. This we believe should be as one or a series of research questions your research must answer and objectives your research must address. However, we would also stress the continuing need to reflect on and to revise your ideas and the way in which you intend to progress your research. Often this will involve revisiting stages (including your research question(s) and objectives) and working through them again. There is also a need to plan ahead, thereby ensuring that the necessary preliminary work for later stages has been undertaken. This is emphasised by Fig 1.2, which also provides a schematic index to the remaining chapters of the book. Within this flow chart (Fig 1.2), the stages you will need to complete as part of your research project are emphasised in the centre of the chart. However, be warned; the process is messier than a brief glance at Fig 1.2 suggests!

1.4 The purpose and structure of this book

The purpose

As we stated earlier (Section 1.1), the overriding purpose of this book is to help you to undertake research. This means that early on in your research project you will need to be clear about what you are doing, why you are doing it and the associated implications of what you are seeking to do. You will also need to ensure that you can show how your ideas relate to research that has already been undertaken in your topic area and that you have a clear approach and strategy for collecting and analysing your data. As part of this, you will need to consider the validity and reliability of the data you intend to use along with associated ethical and access issues. The appropriateness and suitability of the analysis techniques you choose to use will be of equal importance. Finally, you will need to write your research report as clearly and precisely as possible.

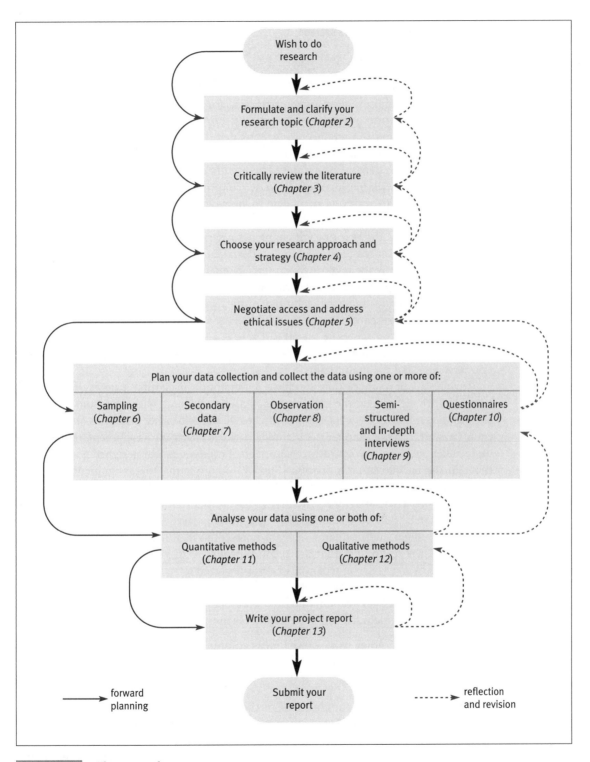

Fig 1.2 **The research process**

© *Mark Saunders, Philip Lewis and Adrian Thornhill, 2000*

The structure of each chapter

Each of the subsequent chapters deals with part of the research process outlined in Fig 1.2. The ideas, techniques and methods are discussed using as little jargon as is possible. Where appropriate you will find summaries of these using tables, checklists or diagrams. When new terms are introduced for the first time, they are shown in italics and a definition or explanation follows shortly afterwards. The application of appropriate information technology is considered, in most instances as an integral part of the text. Discussion of information technology is not software specific but is concerned with the general principles. These will enable you to utilise whatever software you have available most effectively. Chapters have been cross-referenced as appropriate and an index is provided to help you to find your way around the book.

Included within the text of each chapter is a series of *worked examples*. These are based on actual research projects, often undertaken by our students and colleagues, in which points made in the text are illustrated. In many instances these worked examples illustrate possible pitfalls you may come across while undertaking your research. These will help you to understand the technique or idea and to assess its suitability or appropriateness to your research. Where a pitfall has been illustrated, it will, it is hoped, help you to avoid making the same mistake. There is also a summary of the key points of each chapter, which you may look at before and after reading the chapter to ensure that you have digested the main points.

To enable you to check that you have understood the chapter a series of *self-check questions* are included at the end. These can all be answered without recourse to other (external) resources. Answers are provided to all the self-check questions at the end of each chapter. Each chapter also includes a research-based assignment that can be undertaken as part of your research project. *Assignments* are designed to guide you through the entire research process (Fig 1.2). Completing the assignments for each chapter will enable you to generate all the material that you will need to include in your project report. Each assignment involves you in undertaking activities that are more complex than self-check questions such as a library-based literature search or designing and piloting a questionnaire. They are presented in sufficient detail to enable you to focus on the techniques that are most appropriate to your research. However, as emphasised by Fig 1.2, you will almost certainly need to revisit and revise each assignment's answer as your research progresses.

Each chapter is also accompanied by references, further reading and a case study. *Further reading* is included for two distinct reasons:

- to direct you to other work on the ideas contained within the chapter;
- to direct you to further examples of research where the ideas contained in the chapter have been used.

The main reasons for our choice of further reading are therefore indicated.

Case studies are drawn from a variety of business and management research scenarios and have been based on the case study's authors' or their students' experiences when undertaking a research project. They have been written to highlight real issues that occur when undertaking business and management research. To help to focus your thoughts or discussion on some of the pertinent issues each case is followed by evaluative questions. A case study follows every chapter other than Chapter 1.

An outline of the chapters

The book is organised in the following way.

Chapter 2 is written to assist you in the generation of ideas, which will help you to choose a suitable research topic, and offers advice on what makes a good research topic. If you have already been given a research topic, perhaps by an organisation or tutor, you will need to refine it into one that is feasible and should still therefore read this chapter. After your idea has been generated and refined, the chapter discusses how to turn this idea into clear research question(s) and objectives. (Research questions and objectives are referred to throughout the book.) Finally, the chapter provides advice on how to write a research proposal.

The importance of the critical literature review to your research is discussed in Chapter 3. This chapter outlines what a critical review needs to include and the range of primary, secondary and tertiary literature sources available. The chapter explains the purpose of reviewing the literature, discusses a range of search strategies and contains advice on how to plan and undertake your search and to write your review. The processes of identifying key words and searching, including using on-line databases and the Internet, are outlined. It also offers advice on how to record items and to evaluate their relevance.

Chapter 4 examines different ways of approaching research. It considers differing approaches to and strategies for research, the need for a clear research strategy and, crucially, the issue of the credibility of your research findings and conclusions.

Chapter 5 explores issues related to gaining access and research ethics. It offers advice on how to gain access to both organisations and individuals. Potential ethical issues are discussed in relation to each stage of the research process and different data collection methods.

A range of the probability and non-probability sampling techniques available for use in your research is explained in Chapter 6. The chapter considers why sampling is necessary and looks at issues of sample size and response rates. Advice on how to relate your choice of sampling techniques to your research topic is given and techniques for assessing the representativeness of those who respond are discussed.

Chapters 7, 8, 9 and 10 are concerned with different methods of obtaining data. The use of secondary data is discussed in Chapter 7, which introduces the variety of data that are likely to be available and suggests ways in which they can be used. Advantages and disadvantages of secondary data are discussed and a range of techniques for locating these data is suggested. Chapter 7 also offers advice on how to evaluate the suitability of secondary data for your research.

In contrast, Chapter 8 is concerned with collecting primary data through observation. The chapter examines two types of observation: participant observation and structured observation. Practical advice on using each is offered and particular attention is given to ensuring that the data you obtain are both valid and reliable.

Chapter 9 is also concerned with collecting primary data, this time using semi-structured and in-depth interviews. The appropriateness of using these interviews in relation to your research strategy is discussed. Advice on how to undertake such interviews is offered including the conduct of group interviews. Particular attention is given to ensuring that the data collected are both reliable and valid.

Chapter 10 is the final chapter concerned with collecting data. It introduces you to the use of both self-administered and interviewer-administered questionnaires and explores their advantages and disadvantages. Practical advice is offered on the process of designing, piloting and administering questionnaires to enhance their response rates. Particular attention is again given to ensuring that the data collected are both reliable and valid.

Analysis of data is covered in Chapters 11 and 12. Chapter 11 outlines and illustrates the main issues that you need to consider when preparing quantitative data for analysis and when analysing these data by computer. Different types of data are defined and advice is given on how to create a data matrix and to code data. Practical advice is also offered on the analysis of these data. The most appropriate diagrams to explore and illustrate data are discussed and suggestions made about which statistics to use to describe data, to explore relationships and to explore trends.

Chapter 12 outlines and discusses the main approaches available to you to analyse qualitative data. The nature of qualitative data is discussed and an overview of the analysis process provided. Strategies relating to the use of predicted theoretical explanations, the use of grounded theory and quantifying qualitative data are discussed. The chapter also considers the use of computer-based text retrievers and managers.

Chapter 13 helps you with the structure, content and style of your final project report. Above all, it encourages you to see writing as an intrinsic part of the research process that should not be left until everything else is completed.

1.5 How to use this book

This book is written with a progressive logic, which means that terms and concepts are defined when they are first introduced. One implication of this is that it is sensible for you to start at the beginning and to work your way through the text and worked examples, self-check questions, case studies and case study questions. You can do this in a variety of ways depending on your reasons for using this book. However, this approach may not necessarily be suitable for your purposes and you may wish to dip into particular sections of the book. If this is true for you then you will need to use the book in a different way. Suggestions for three of the more common ways in which you might wish to use this book are given below.

As part of a research methods course or for self-study

If you are using this book as part of a research methods course or for self-study, it is probable that you will follow the chapter order quite closely. Groups of chapters within which we believe you can switch the order without affecting the logic of the flow too much are:

- those chapters associated with data collection (Chapters 7, 8, 9 and 10);
- those associated with data analysis (Chapters 11 and 12).

In addition, you might wish to read Chapter 13 on writing prior to starting to draft your critical review of the literature (Chapter 3).

As you work through the book, we would recommend that you attempt all the self-check questions and those questions associated with the case studies. Your answers to the self-check questions can be self-assessed using the answers at the end of each chapter. However, we hope that you will actually have a go at the question prior to reading the answer! If you need further information on an idea or a technique then first look at the references in the further reading section.

Appropriate assignments, when grouped together, will provide a useful *aide-mémoire* for assessed work. Such work might involve you in just planning a research project or, alternatively, planning and undertaking a small research project of your own.

As a guide through the research process

If you are intending to use this book to guide you through the research process for a research project you are undertaking, such as your dissertation, we recommend that you read the entire book quickly before starting your research. In that way you will have a good overview of the entire process including the range of techniques available and will be better able to plan your work.

After you have read the book once, we suggest that you work your way through the book again following the chapter order. This time you should attempt the self-check questions and those questions associated with each case study to ensure that you have understood the material contained in each chapter prior to applying it to your own research project. Your responses to self-check questions can be assessed using the answers at the end of each chapter.

If you are still unsure as to whether particular techniques or ideas are relevant then look in the further reading for other examples of research where these have been used. If you need further information on an idea or a technique then, again, start with the references in the further reading section.

Material in some of the chapters is likely to prove less relevant to some research topics than others. However, you should beware of choosing techniques because you are happy with them if they are inappropriate. Completion of the assignments for Chapters 2–12 will enable you to generate all the material that you will need to include in your project report. It will also help you to focus on the techniques and ideas that are most appropriate to your research. When you have also completed the assignment for Chapter 13 you will have written your project report.

As a reference source

It may be that you wish to use this book now or subsequently as a reference source. If this is the case, an extensive index will point you to the appropriate page or pages. You should also find the contents pages useful. In addition, we have tried to help you to use the book in this way by including cross-references between sections in chapters as appropriate. Do follow these up as necessary. If you need further information on an idea or a technique then begin by consulting the references in the further reading section.

1.6 Summary

- This book is designed to help you to undertake a research project whether you are an undergraduate or postgraduate student of business and management or a manager. It is designed as an introductory text and will guide you through the entire research process.

- Business and management research involves undertaking systematic research to find out things. It is transdisciplinary and should engage with both theory and practice.

- All business and management research projects can be placed on a basic–applied continuum according to their purpose and context.

- Wherever your research project lies on this continuum, you should undertake your research with rigour. To do this you will need to pay careful attention to the entire research process.

- In this book, research is represented as a multi-stage process; however, this process is rarely straightforward and will involve both reflecting on and revising stages already undertaken and forward planning.

- Each chapter contains advice with worked examples, self-check questions, an assignment and a case study with questions. Answers to all self-check questions are at the end of the appropriate chapter. Completing the assignments for Chapters 2–12 will enable you to generate all the material that you will need to include in your project report. When you have also completed the assignment for Chapter 13 you will have written your research report.

- The book can be used as part of a taught research methods course, for self-study, as a guide through the research process or for reference.

Self check Questions

1.1 Outline the features that make business and management research distinctive from research in other disciplines.

1.2 What are the key differences between basic and applied research?

1.3 Examine Fig 1.2. What does this suggest about the need to plan and to reflect on and revise your ideas?

References

Easterby-Smith, M., Thorpe, R. and Lowe, A. (1991) *Management Research: an Introduction*, London, Sage.

Ghauri, P., Grϕnhaug, K. and Kristianslund, I. (1995) *Research Methods in Business Studies: a Practical Guide*, Harlow, Prentice Hall.

Hedrick, T.E., Bickmann, L. and Rog, D.J. (1993) *Applied Research Design*, Newbury Park, CA, Sage.

Jankowicz, A.D. (1995) *Business Research Projects* (2nd edn), London, Chapman & Hall.

Johnson, G. (1996) 'The debate begins', *BAM News*, 6, 1–2.

Saunders, M.N.K. and Lewis, P. (1997) 'Great ideas and blind alleys? A review of the literature on starting research', *Management Learning*, 28:3, 283–99.

Tranfield, D. and Starkey, K. (1998) 'The nature, social organization and promotion of management research: towards policy', *British Journal of Management*, 9, 341–53.

Further reading

Easterby-Smith, M., Thorpe, R. and Lowe, A. (1991) *Management Research: an Introduction*, London, Sage. Chapter 1 provides a very clear and readable introduction to management research and why it is distinctive from other forms of research.

Tranfield, D. and Starkey, K. (1998) 'The nature, social organization and promotion of management research: towards policy', *British Journal of Management*, 9, 341–53. This paper argues for the distinctiveness of management research emphasising its applied nature and the importance of the relationship between theory and practice.

Self check   Answers

1.1 The features you outline are likely to include the:

- transdisciplinary nature of business and management research;
- development of ideas which are related to practice and in particular the requirement of the research to have some practical consequence;
- need for research to complete the virtuous circle of theory and practice;
- addressing of problems that grow out of the interaction between the worlds of theory and practice.

1.2 The key differences between basic and applied research relate to both the purpose and the context in which it is undertaken. They are summarised in Fig 1.1.

1.3 Fig 1.2 emphasises the importance of planning during your research project. Forward planning needs to occur at all stages up to submission. In addition, you will need to reflect on and to revise your work throughout the life of the research project. This reflection needs to have a wide focus. You should both consider the stage you have reached as well as revisit earlier stages and work through them again. Reflection may also lead you to amend your research plan. This should be expected, although large amendments in the later stages of your research project are unlikely.

2 Formulating and clarifying the research topic

By the end of this chapter you should be able:

- to generate ideas that will help in the choice of a suitable research topic;
- to identify the attributes of a good research topic;
- to turn research ideas into a research project which has clear research question(s) and objectives;
- to draft a research proposal.

2.1 Introduction

Before you start your research you need to have at least some idea of what you want to do. This is probably the most difficult, and yet the most important, part of your research project. Up until now most of your studies have been concerned with answering questions that other people have set. This chapter is concerned with how to formulate and clarify your research topic and your research question. Without being clear about what you are going to research it is difficult to plan how you are going to research it. This reminds us of a favourite quote in *Alice's Adventures in Wonderland*. This is part of Alice's conversation with the Cheshire Cat. In this Alice asks the Cat (Carroll, 1989:63–4):

> 'Would you tell me, please, which way I ought to walk from here?'
> 'That depends a good deal on where you want to get to,' said the Cat.
> 'I don't much care where,' said Alice.
> 'Then it doesn't matter which way you walk,' said the Cat.

Formulating and clarifying the research topic is the starting point of your research project (Ghauri *et al.*, 1995; Smith and Dainty, 1991). Once you are clear about this you will be able to choose the most appropriate research strategy and data collection and analysis techniques. The formulating and clarifying process is time-consuming and will probably take you up blind alleys (Saunders and Lewis, 1997). However, without spending time on this stage you are far less likely to achieve a successful project (Raimond, 1993).

In the initial stages of the formulating and clarifying process you will be generating and refining research ideas (Section 2.3). It may be that you have already been given a research idea, perhaps by an organisation or tutor. Even if this has happened you will still need to refine the idea into one that is feasible. Once you have done this you will need to turn the idea into research questions and objectives (Section 2.4) and to write the research proposal for your project (Section 2.5).

However, before you start the formulating and clarifying process we believe that you need to understand what makes a good research topic. For this reason we begin this chapter (Section 2.2) with a discussion of the attributes required for a good research topic.

2.2　Attributes of a good research topic

The attributes of a business and management research topic do not vary a great deal between universities (Raimond, 1993), although there will be differences in the emphasis placed on different attributes. If you are undertaking your research project as part of a course of study the most important attribute will be that it meets the examining body's requirements and, in particular, that it is at the correct level. This means that you must choose your topic with care. For example, some universities require students to collect their own data as part of their research project while others allow them to base their project on data that have already been collected. You therefore need to check the assessment criteria for your project and ensure that your choice of topic will enable you to meet these criteria. If you are unsure, you should discuss any uncertainties with your project tutor.

In addition, your research topic must be something you are capable of undertaking and one that excites your imagination. Capability can be considered in a variety of ways. At the personal level you need to feel comfortable that you have, or can develop, the skills that will be required to research the topic. We hope that you will develop your research skills as part of undertaking your project. However, some skills, for example foreign languages, may be impossible to acquire in the time you have available. As well as having the necessary skills we believe that you also need to have a genuine interest in the topic. Most research projects are undertaken over at least a six-month period. A topic in which you are only vaguely interested at the start is likely to become a topic in which you have no interest and with which you will fail to produce your best work.

Your ability to find the financial and time resources to undertake research on the topic will also affect your capability. Some topics are unlikely to be possible to complete in the time allowed by your course of study. This may be because they require you to measure the impact of an intervention over a long time period. Similarly, topics which are likely to require you to travel widely or need expensive equipment should also be disregarded unless financial resources permit.

Capability also means you must be reasonably certain of gaining access to any data you might need to collect. Gill and Johnson (1997) argue that this is usually relatively straightforward to assess. They point out that many people start with ideas where access to data will prove difficult. Certain, more sensitive topics, such as financial performance or decision making by senior managers, are potentially fascinating. However, they may present considerable access problems. You should therefore discuss this with your project tutor after reading Chapter 5.

For most topics it is important that the issues within the research are capable of being linked to theory (Raimond, 1993). Initially, theory may just be based on the reading you have undertaken as part of your study to date. However, as part of your assessment criteria you are almost certain to be asked to set your topic in context (Section 3.2). As a consequence you will need to have a knowledge of the literature and to undertake further reading as part of defining your research questions and objectives (Section 2.4).

Most project tutors will argue that one of the attributes of a good topic is clearly defined research questions and objectives (Section 2.4). These will, along with a good knowledge of the literature, enable you to assess the extent to which your research is likely to provide fresh insights on the topic. Many students believe this is going to be difficult. Fortunately, as pointed out by Phillips and Pugh (1994), there are many ways in which such insight can be defined as 'fresh' (Section 2.5).

If you have already been given a research idea (perhaps by an organisation) you will need to ensure that your questions and objectives relate clearly to the idea (Kervin, 1992). It is also important that your topic will have a *symmetry of potential outcomes*, that is your results will be of similar value whatever you find out (Gill and Johnson, 1997). Without this symmetry you may spend a considerable amount of time researching your topic only to find an answer of little importance. Whatever the outcome, you need to ensure you have the scope to write an interesting project report.

Worked example

Ensuring symmetry of potential outcomes

Karmen was a part-time student. Her initial research topic was concerned with finding out whether there was any relationship between the levels of stress experienced by social workers and the number of years they had been employed as social workers. If she established that there was a link between these factors this would be an interesting finding; if, however, she discovered no relationship the finding would be less interesting and would have no real practical relevance to her organisation.

She therefore decided to amend her topic to exploring and understanding the impact of a forthcoming stress management course on the relative levels of stress experienced by social workers before the course. The results of this research would be interesting and important whether or not the course had an impact.

Finally, it is important to consider your career goals (Creswell, 1994). If you wish to become an expert in a particular subject area or industry sector, it is sensible to use the opportunity to develop this expertise.

It is almost inevitable that the extent to which these attributes apply to your research topic will depend on your topic and the reasons for which you are undertaking the research. However, most of these attributes will apply. For this reason it is important that you check and continue to check any potential research topic against the summary checklist contained in Table 2.1.

Table 2.1	Checklist of attributes of a good research topic

✓ Does the topic fit the specifications and meet the standards set by the examining institution?

✓ Is the topic something with which you are really fascinated?

✓ Does your research topic contain issues that have a clear link to theory?

✓ Do you have, or can you develop within the project time frame, the necessary research skills to undertake the topic?

✓ Is the research topic achievable within the available time?

✓ Is the research topic achievable within the financial resources that are likely to be available?

✓ Are you reasonably certain of being able to gain access to data you are likely to require for this topic?

✓ Are you able to state your research question(s) and objectives clearly?

✓ Will your proposed research be able to provide fresh insights on this topic?

✓ Does your research topic relate clearly to the idea you have been given (perhaps by an organisation)?

✓ Are the findings for this research topic likely to be symmetrical, that is of similar value whatever the outcome?

✓ Does the research topic match your career goals?

2.3 Generating and refining research ideas

Some business and management students are expected both to generate and to refine their own research ideas. Others, particularly those on professional and post-experience courses, are provided with a research idea by an organisation or their university. In the initial stages of their research they are expected to refine this to a clear and feasible idea which meets the requirements of the examining organisation. If you have already been given a research idea we believe you will still find it useful to read the next sub-section which deals with generating research ideas. Many of the techniques which can be used for generating research ideas can be used for the refining process.

Generating research ideas

If you have not been given an initial *research idea* there is a range of techniques that can be used to find and select a topic which you would like to research. They can be thought of as those which are predominantly *rational thinking* and those which involve more *creative thinking* (Table 2.2). The precise techniques which you choose to use and the order in which you use them are entirely up to you. However, like Raimond (1993), we believe you should use both rational and creative techniques, choosing those which you believe are going to be of most use to you and which you will enjoy using. By using one or more creative techniques you are more likely to ensure that your heart as well as your head are in your research project. In our experience, it is usually better to use a variety of techniques. In order to do this you will need to have some understanding of the techniques and the ways in which they work. We therefore outline the techniques in Table 2.2 and suggest possible ways they might be used to generate research ideas. These techniques will generate one of two outcomes:

- one or more possible project ideas that you might undertake;
- absolute panic because nothing in which you are interested or which seems suitable has come to mind (Jankowicz, 1995).

In either instance, but especially the latter, we suggest that you talk to your project tutor.

Table 2.2 **More frequently-used techniques for generating and refining research ideas**

Rational thinking	Creative thinking
■ Examining your own strengths and interests	■ Keeping a notebook of ideas
■ Looking at past projects	■ Exploring personal preferences using past projects
■ Discussion	■ Relevance trees
■ Searching the literature	■ Brainstorming

Examining own strengths and interests

It is important that you choose a topic in which you are likely to do well and, if possible, already have some academic knowledge. Jankowicz (1995) suggests that one way of doing this is to look at those assignments for which you have received good grades. For most of these assignments they are also likely to be the topics in which you were interested (Table 2.1). They will provide you with an area in which to search for and find a research idea. In addition you may, as part of your reading, be able to focus more precisely on the sort of ideas about which you wish to conduct your research.

As noted in Section 2.2, there is the need to think about your future. If you plan to work in financial management it would be sensible to choose a research project in the financial management field. One part of your course that will inevitably be discussed at any job interview is your research project. A project in the same field will provide you with the opportunity to display clearly your depth of knowledge and your enthusiasm.

Looking at past project titles

Many of our students have found looking at *past projects* a useful way of generating research ideas. For undergraduate and taught masters degrees these are often called *dissertations*. For research degrees they are termed *theses*. A common way of doing this is to scan a list of past project titles (such as those in Appendix 1) for anything that captures your imagination. Titles that look interesting or which grab your attention should be noted down, as should any thoughts you have about the title in relation to your own research idea. In this process the fact that the title is poorly worded or the project report received a low mark is immaterial. What matters is the fact that you have found a topic that interests you. Based on this you can think of new ideas in the same general area which will enable you to provide fresh insights.

Scanning actual research projects may also produce research ideas. However, you need to beware. The fact that a project is in your library is no guarantee of the quality of the arguments and observations it contains. In many universities all projects are placed in the library whether they are bare passes or distinctions.

Exploring personal preferences using past projects

Another way of generating possible project ideas is to explore your *personal preferences* using past project reports from your university. To do this Raimond (1993) suggests that you:

1   Select six projects which you like.
2   For each of these six projects note down your first thoughts in response to three questions (if responses for different projects are the same this does not matter):
    a   What appeals to you about the project?
    b   What is good about the project?
    c   Why is the project good?
3   Select three projects that you do not like.
4   For each of these three projects note down your first thoughts in response to three questions (if responses for different projects are the same, or cannot be clearly expressed, this does not matter; note them down anyway):
    a   What do you dislike about the project?
    b   What is bad about the project?
    c   Why is the project bad?

You now have a list of what you consider to be excellent and what you consider to be poor in projects. This will not be the same as a list generated by anyone else. It is also very unlikely to match the attributes of a good research project (Table 2.1). However, by examining this list you will begin to understand those project characteristics that are important to you and with which you feel comfortable. Of equal importance is that you will have identified those which you are uncomfortable with and should avoid. These can be used as the parameters against which to evaluate possible research ideas.

Discussion

Colleagues, friends and university tutors are all good sources of possible project ideas. Often project tutors will have ideas for possible student projects which they will be pleased to discuss with you. In addition, ideas can be obtained by talking to practitioners and professional groups (Gill and Johnson, 1997). It is important that as well as discussing possible ideas you also make a note of them. What seemed like a good idea in the coffee shop may not be remembered quite so clearly after the following lecture!

Searching the literature

As part of your discussions, relevant literature may also be suggested. Sharp and Howard (1996) discuss types of literature which are of particular use for generating research ideas. These include:

- articles in academic and professional journals;
- reports;
- books.

Of particular use are academic *review articles*. These articles contain both a considered review of the state of knowledge in that topic area and pointers towards areas where further research needs to be undertaken. In addition you can browse recent publications, in particular journals, for possible research ideas (Section 3.5). For many subject areas your project tutor will be able to suggest possible recent review articles, or articles which contain recommendations for further work. *Reports* may also be of use. The most recently published are usually up to date and, again, often contain recommendations which may form the basis of your research idea. *Books* by contrast are less up to date than other written sources. They do, however, often contain a good overview of research that has been undertaken which may suggest ideas to you.

Searching for publications is only possible when you have at least some idea of the area in which you wish to undertake your research. One way of obtaining this is to re-examine your lecture notes and course textbooks and to note those subjects that appear most interesting (discussed earlier in this section) and the names of relevant authors. This will give you a basis on which to undertake a *preliminary search* (using techniques outlined in Sections 3.4 and 3.5). When the articles, reports and other items have been obtained it is often helpful to look for unfounded assertions and statements on the absence of research (Raimond 1993), as these are likely to contain ideas which will enable you to provide fresh insights.

Keeping a notebook of ideas

One of the more creative techniques which we all use is to keep a *notebook of ideas*. All this involves is simply noting down any interesting research ideas as you think of them and, of equal importance, what sparked off your thought. You can then pursue the idea using more rational thinking techniques later. Mark keeps a notebook by his bed so he can jot down any flashes of inspiration which occur to him in the middle of the night!

Brainstorming

The technique of *brainstorming*, taught as a problem-solving technique on many business and management courses, can also be used to generate and refine research ideas. It is best undertaken with a group of people, although you can brainstorm on your own. To brainstorm, Moody (1983) suggests that you:

1   define your problem, that is the sorts of ideas you are interested in, as precisely as possible. In the early stages of formulating a topic this may be as vague as 'I am interested in marketing but don't know what to do for my research topic';

2   ask for suggestions relating to the problem;

3   record all suggestions observing the following rules:

–   no suggestion should be criticised or evaluated in any way before all ideas have been considered,

–   all suggestions, however wild, should be recorded and considered,

–   as many suggestions as possible should be recorded;

4   review all the suggestions and explore what is meant by each;

5   analyse the list of suggestions and decide which appeal to you most as research ideas and why.

Worked example

Brainstorming

George's main interest was football. When he finished university he wanted to work in marketing, preferably for a sports manufacturer. He had examined his own strengths and discovered that his best marks were in marketing. He wanted to do his research project on some aspect of marketing, preferably linked to football, but had no real research idea. He asked three friends, all taking business studies degrees, to help him to brainstorm the problem.

George began by explaining the problem in some detail. At first the suggestions emerged slowly. He noted them down on the whiteboard. Soon the board was covered with suggestions. George counted these and discovered there were over 100.

Reviewing individual suggestions produced nothing which any of the group felt to be of sufficient merit for a research project. However, one of George's friends pointed out that combining the suggestions of Premier League football, television rights and sponsorship might provide an idea which satisfied the assessment requirements of the project.

They discussed the suggestion further and George noted the research idea as 'something about how exclusive television rights to satellite broadcasters would impact on sports sponsorship, concentrating on Premier League football'.

George arranged to see his project tutor to discuss how to refine the idea they had just generated.

Relevance trees

Relevance trees may also prove useful in generating research topics. In this instance, their use is similar to that of mind mapping (Buzan with Buzan, 1995) in which you start with a broad concept from which you generate further (usually more specific)

topics. Each of these topics forms a separate branch from which you can generate further more detailed sub-branches. As you proceed down the sub-branches more ideas are generated and recorded. These can then be examined and a number selected and combined to provide a research idea (Sharp and Howard, 1996).[1]

Refining research ideas

The Delphi technique

An additional approach which our students have found particularly useful in refining their research ideas is the *Delphi technique*. This involves using a group of people who are either involved or interested in the research idea to generate and choose a more specific research idea (Robson, 1993). To use this technique you need:

1 to brief the members of the group about the research idea (they can make notes if they wish);

2 at the end of the briefing to encourage group members to seek clarification and more information as appropriate;

3 to ask each member of the group, including the originator of the research idea, to generate independently up to three specific research ideas based on the idea that has been described (they can also be asked to provide a justification for their specific ideas);

4 to collect the research ideas in an unedited and non-attributable form and to distribute them to all members of the group;

5 a second cycle of the process (steps 2 to 4) in which individuals comment on the research ideas and revise their own contributions in the light of what others have said;

6 subsequent cycles of the process until a consensus is reached. These either follow a similar pattern (steps 2 to 4) or use discussion, voting or some other method.

This process works well, not least because people enjoy trying to help one another. In addition it is very useful in moulding groups into a cohesive whole.

Worked example

Using a Delphi group

Tim explained to the group that his research idea was concerned with understanding the decision-making processes associated with mortgage applications and loan advances. His briefing to the three other group members, and the questions which they asked him, considered aspects such as:

---

[1]This technique is discussed in more detail in Section 3.4 which also includes a worked example in which a relevance tree is used to help generate key words for a literature search.

- the influences on a potential first-time buyer to approach a specific financial institution;
- the influence of face-to-face contact between potential borrower and potential lender on decision making.

The group then moved on to generate a number of more specific research ideas, among which were the following:

- the factors that influenced potential first-time house purchasers to deal with particular financial institutions;
- the effect of interpersonal contact on mortgage decisions;
- the qualities that potential applicants look for in mortgage advisers.

These were considered and commented on by all the group members. At the end of the second cycle Tim had, with the other students' agreement, refined his research idea to:

- the way in which a range of factors influenced potential first-time buyers' choice of lending institution.

He now needed to pursue these ideas by undertaking a preliminary search of the literature.

The preliminary study

Even if you have been given a research idea, it is still necessary to refine it in order to turn it into a research project. Some authors, for example Bennett (1991), refer to this process as a *preliminary study*. For some research ideas this will be no more than a review of some of the literature. This can be thought of as the first iteration of your critical literature review (Fig 3.1). For others it may include revisiting the techniques discussed earlier in this section as well as informal discussions with people who have personal experience of and knowledge about your research ideas. In some cases *shadowing* employees who are likely to be important in your research may also provide insights. If you are planning on undertaking your research within an organisation it is important to gain a good understanding of your host organisation (Kervin, 1992). However, whatever techniques you choose the underlying purpose is to gain a greater understanding so that your research question can be refined.

At this stage you need to be testing your research ideas against the checklist in Table 2.1 and where necessary changing them. It may be that after a preliminary study, or discussing your ideas with colleagues, you decide that the research idea is no longer feasible in the form in which you first envisaged it. If this is the case do not be too downhearted. It is far better to revise your research ideas at this stage than to have to do it later, when you have undertaken far more work.

Integrating ideas

The integration of ideas from these techniques is essential if your research is to have a clear direction and not to contain a mismatch between objectives and your final research report. Jankowicz (1995:34) suggests an integrative process which our students have found most useful. This he terms 'working up and narrowing down'. It involves classifying each research idea into first its area, then its field and finally the precise aspect in which you are interested. These represent an increasingly more detailed description of the research idea. Thus your initial area, based on examining your course work, might be accountancy. After browsing some recent journals and discussion with colleagues this becomes more focused on the field of financial accounting methods. With further reading, the use of the Delphi technique and discussion with your project tutor you decide to focus on the aspect of activity-based costing.

You will know when the process of generating and refining ideas is complete as you will be able to say 'I'd like to do some research on . . .'. Obviously there will still be a big gap between this and the point when you are ready to start serious work on your research. Sections 2.4 and 2.5 will ensure that you are ready to bridge that gap.

Refining topics given by your employing organisation

If, as a part-time student, your manager gives you a topic, this may present particular problems. It may be something in which you are not particularly interested. In this case you will have to weigh the advantage of doing something useful to the organisation against the disadvantage of a potential lack of personal motivation. You therefore need to achieve a balance. Often the project your manager wishes you to undertake is larger than that which is appropriate for your course project. In such cases, it may be possible to complete both by isolating an element of the larger organisational project that you find interesting and treating this as the project for your course.

One of our students was asked to do a preliminary investigation of the strengths and weaknesses of her organisation's pay system and then to recommend consultants to design and implement a new system. She was not particularly interested in this project. However, she was considering becoming a freelance personnel consultant. Therefore, for her course project she decided to study the decision-making process in relation to the appointment of personnel consultants. Her organisation's decision on which consultant to appoint, and why this decision was taken, proved to be a useful case study against which to compare management decision-making theory.

In this event you would write a larger report for your organisation and a part of it for your project report. Section 13.4 offers some guidance on writing two separate reports for different audiences.

2.4 Turning research ideas into research projects

Writing research questions

Much is made in this book of the importance of defining clear *research questions* at the beginning of the research process. The importance of this cannot be over-emphasised.

One of the key criteria of your research success will be whether you have a set of clear conclusions drawn from the data you have collected. The extent to which you can do that will be determined largely by the clarity with which you have posed your initial research questions.

Defining the research question

Alex was a personnel officer in his first post in an advanced electronics company specialising in research. When he first joined the company he was surprised by the seeming arbitrary way in which many of the personnel policies were formulated and conducted. They seemed to bear little relation to the strategic direction the company was taking.

Alex had studied corporate strategy as part of his business studies degree. He was familiar with some of the literature which suggested that operational areas such as personnel would benefit from tying their policies to corporate strategy. It was an area in which he was very interested. He wanted to do some research on corporate strategy in his organisation and the links with personnel policies. At the same time he needed to satisfy the requirements of his Institute of Personnel and Development course.

After talking this over with his project tutor Alex decided on the following research question: 'Why do my organisation's personnel policies not reflect the corporate strategy?'

Defining research questions, rather like generating research ideas (Section 2.3), is not a straightforward matter. It is important that the question is sufficiently involved to generate the sort of project that is consistent with the standards expected of you (Table 2.1). A question which prompts a descriptive answer, for example 'what proportion of graduates from public schools enter the civil service?', is far easier to answer than: 'why are graduates from public schools more likely to enter the civil service?' More will be said about the importance of theory in defining the research question later in this section. However, beware of research questions that are too easy.

It is perhaps more likely that you fall into the trap of asking research questions that are too difficult. The question cited above, 'why are graduates from public schools more likely to enter the civil service?', is a case in point. It would probably be very difficult to gain sufficient access to the inner portals of the civil service to get a good grasp of the subtle 'unofficial' processes that go on at staff selection which may favour one type of candidate over another. Over-reaching yourself in the definition of research questions is a danger.

The pitfall that you must avoid at all costs is asking research questions that will not generate new insights (Table 2.1). This raises the question of the extent to which you have consulted the relevant literature. It is perfectly legitimate to replicate research because you have a genuine concern about its applicability to your research setting (for example, your organisation). However, it certainly is not legitimate to display your ignorance of the literature (Robson, 1993).

It is often a useful starting point in the writing of research questions to begin with one *general focus research question* which flows from your research idea. This may lead to several more detailed questions or the definition of research objectives. Table 2.3 has some examples of general focus research questions.

Table 2.3   **Examples of research ideas and their derived focus research questions**

Research idea	General focus research question
The sponsorship of county cricket clubs	What benefit do commercial organisations derive from their sponsorship of county cricket clubs?
The adoption by manufacturing companies of 'flexible workforces'	Why do manufacturing companies divide their workforces into 'core' and 'peripheral' workers?
The loss of mutuality status by building societies and the effect on the future of the industry	How will the loss of mutuality status by building societies affect the terms they offer to borrowers and savers in comparison with societies retaining mutual status?
The future of trade unions	What are the strategies that trade unions should adopt to ensure their future viability?

Writing your research questions will be, in most cases, your individual concern but it is useful to get other people to help you. An obvious source of guidance is your project tutor. Consulting your project tutor will avoid the pitfalls of the questions that are too easy or too difficult or have been answered before. Discussing your area of interest with your project tutor will lead to your research questions becoming much clearer.

Prior to discussion with your project tutor you may wish to conduct a brainstorming session with your peers or use the Delphi technique (Section 2.3). Your research questions may flow from your initial examination of the relevant literature. As outlined in Section 2.3, journal articles reporting primary research will often end with a conclusion which includes the consideration of the author of the implications for future research of the work in the article. This may be phrased in the form of research questions. However, even if it is not, it may suggest pertinent research questions to you.

Writing research objectives

Your research may begin with a general focus research question that then generates more detailed research questions or you may use your general focus research question as a base from which you write a set of *research objectives*. Objectives are more generally acceptable to the research community as evidence of the researcher's clear sense of purpose and direction. It may be that either is satisfactory. Do check whether your examining body has a preference.

| Table 2.4 | **Phrasing research questions as research objectives** |

Research question	Research objective
1 Why have organisations introduced team briefing?	1 To identify organisations' objectives for team briefing schemes.
2 How can the effectiveness of team briefing schemes be measured?	2 To establish suitable effectiveness criteria for team briefing schemes.
3 Has team briefing been effective?	3 To describe the extent to which the effectiveness criteria for team briefing have been met.
4 How can the effectiveness of team briefing be explained?	4a To determine the factors associated with the effectiveness criteria for team briefing being met.
	b To estimate whether some of those factors are more influential than other factors.
5 Can the explanation be generalised?	5 To develop an explanatory theory that associates certain factors with the effectiveness of team briefing schemes.

We contend that research objectives are likely to lead to greater specificity than research questions. Table 2.4 illustrates this point. It summarises the objectives of some research conducted by one of our students. Expression of the first research question as an objective prompted a consideration of the objectives of the organisations. This was useful because it led to the finding that there often were no clear objectives. This in itself was an interesting theoretical discovery.

The second and third objectives operationalise the matching research questions by introducing the notion of explicit effectiveness criteria. In a similar way the fourth and fifth objectives are specific about factors which lead to effectiveness in question 4. The biggest difference between the questions and objectives is illustrated by the way in which the fifth question becomes the sixth objective. They are similar but differ in the way that the objective makes clear that a theory will be developed which will make a causal link between two sets of variables: effectiveness factors and team briefing success.

This is not to say that the research questions could not have been written with a similar amount of specificity. They could. Indeed, you may find it easier to write specific research questions than objectives. However, we doubt whether the same level of precision could be achieved through the writing of research questions alone. Research objectives require more rigorous thinking which derives from the use of more formal language.

The importance of theory in writing research questions and objectives

Section 4.1 outlines the role of theory in helping you to decide your approach to research design. However, your consideration of theory should begin earlier than this. It should inform your definition of research questions and objectives.

Theory is defined by Gill and Johnson (1997:178) as 'a formulation regarding the cause and effect relationships between two or more variables, which may or may not have been tested'.

There is probably no word which is more misused and misunderstood in education than the word 'theory'. It is thought that material included in text books is 'theory' whereas what is happening in the 'real world' is practice. The citing of references in students' written work is often referred to by them as 'theory'. Students who saw earlier drafts of this book remarked that they were pleased that the book was not too 'theoretical'. What they meant was that the book concentrated on giving lots of practical advice. Yet the book is full of theory. Advising you to carry out research in a particular way (variable A) is based on the theory that this will yield effective results (variable B). This is the cause and effect relationship referred to in the definition of theory cited above.

The definition demonstrates that 'theory' has a specific meaning. It refers to situations where if A is introduced B will be the consequence. Therefore, the marketing manager may theorise that the introduction of loyalty cards by a supermarket will lead to customers being less likely to shop regularly at a competitor supermarket. That is a theory. Yet the marketing manager would probably not recognise it as such. He or she is still less likely to refer to it as a theory, particularly in the company of fellow managers. Many managers are very dismissive of any talk that smacks of 'theory'. It is thought of as something that is all very well to learn about at business school but bears little relation to what goes on in everyday organisational life. Yet the loyalty card example shows that it has everything to do with what goes on in everyday organisational life.

Section 4.1 notes that every purposive decision we take is based on theory: that certain consequences will flow from the decision. It follows from this that every managers' meeting which features a number of decisions will be a meeting which is highly *theory dependent* (Gill and Johnson, 1997). All that will be missing is a realisation of this fact. So, if theory is something that is so rooted in our everyday lives it certainly is something that we need not be apprehensive about. If it is implicit in all our decisions and actions then recognising its importance means making it explicit. In research the importance of theory must be recognised; therefore it must be made explicit.

Kerlinger (1973) reinforces Gill and Johnson's definition by noting that the purpose of examining relationships between two or more variables is to explain and predict these relationships. Gill and Johnson (1997:27) neatly tie these purposes of theory to their definition.

> . . . it is also evident that if we have the expectation that by doing A, B will
> happen, then by manipulating the occurrence of A we can begin to predict and
> influence the occurrence of B. In other words, theory is clearly enmeshed in
> practice since explanation enables prediction which in turn enables control.

In our example, the marketing manager theorised that the introduction of loyalty cards by a supermarket will lead to customers being less likely to shop regularly at a competitor supermarket. Following Gill and Johnson's (1997:27) point that 'explanation enables prediction which in turn enables control', the supermarket would be well advised to conduct research that yielded an explanation of why loyalty cards encourage loyalty. Is it a purely economic rationale? Does it foster the 'collector' instinct in all of us? Does it appeal to a sense of thrift is us which helps us cope with an ever more wasteful world? These explanations are probably complex and inter-related. Reaching a better understanding of them would help the marketing manager to predict the outcome of any changes to the scheme. Increasing the amount of points per item would be effective if the economic explanation was valid. Increasing the range of products on which extra points were offered may appeal to the 'collector' instinct. More accurate prediction would offer the marketing manager increased opportunities for control.

Phillips and Pugh (1994) distinguish between research and what they call *intelligence gathering*. The latter is the gathering of facts. For example, what is the relative proportion of undergraduates to postgraduates reading this book? What is the current spend per employee on training in the UK? What provision do small businesses make for bad debts? This is often called descriptive research (Section 4.2) and may form part of your research project. Descriptive research would be the first step in our example of supermarket loyalty card marketing. Establishing that there had been a change in customer behaviour following the introduction of supermarket loyalty cards would be the first step prior to any attempt at explanation.

Phillips and Pugh contrast such 'what' questions with 'why' questions. Examples of these 'why' questions are as follows: Why do British organisations spend less per head on training than German organisations? Why are new car purchasers reluctant to take out extended warranties on their vehicles? Why do some travellers still prefer to use cross-channel ferries as opposed to the Channel Tunnel? Such questions go 'beyond description and require analysis'. They look for 'explanations, relationships, comparisons, predictions, generalisations and theories' (Phillips and Pugh, 1994:47).

It is a short step from the 'why' research question to the testing of an existing theory in a new situation or the development of your own theory. This may be expressed as a hypothesis that is to be tested (Section 4.1) or the eventual answer to your research question may be the development or amendment of a theory.

Worked example

Writing a research question based on theory

David was a senior manager studying part time. He was worried that the many changes that had taken place in his organisation, including large-scale redundancies at all levels, meant that the nature of the relationship between the organisation and its employees was changing.

His reading led him to become fascinated by the idea of the psychological contract between the organisation and the employee: what each will give the other (e.g. security, loyalty, ambition, career progression) in return for work and employment over and above the normal terms and conditions which are part of the legal employment contract.

David's research question was: 'How are the structural changes in my organisation affecting the way in which employees think about the psychological contract they have with the organisation?'

▶

David was asked to clarify the theory underpinning his research. He did so by explaining that redundancies created in employees feelings of insecurity such that they saw the employment relationship simply as a short-term 'wage–work bargain'. This meant that they were unprepared to put in the extra commitment normally associated with building a career.

Although intelligence gathering will play a part in your research, it is unlikely to be enough. You should be seeking to explain phenomena, to analyse relationships, to compare what is going on in different research settings, to predict outcomes and to generalise; then you will be working at the theoretical level. This is a necessary requirement for most assessed research projects.

You may still be concerned that the necessity to be theory dependent in your research project means that you will have to develop a ground-breaking theory which will lead to a whole new way of thinking about management. If this is the case you should take heart from the three-fold typology of theories summarised by Creswell (1994) (see Fig 2.1). He talks of 'grand theories', usually thought to be the province of the natural scientists (e.g. Darwin and Newton). He contrasts these with 'middle-range theories' which lack the capacity to change the way in which we think about the world but are nonetheless of significance. Some of the theories of human motivation well known to managers would be in this category. However, most of us are concerned with 'substantive theories' which are 'restricted to a particular setting, group, time population or problem' (Creswell, 1994:83). For example, studying the reasons why a total quality initiative in a particular organisation failed would be an example of a substantive theory. Restricted they may be, but a host of 'substantive theories' which present similar propositions may lead to 'middle-range theories'. By developing 'substantive theories', however modest, we are doing our bit as researchers to enhance our understanding of the world about us. A grand claim, but a valid one!

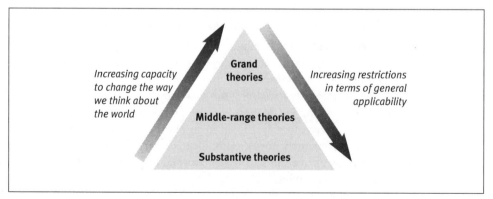

Fig 2.1   **Grand, middle-range and substantive theories**

This discussion of theory does assume that a clear theoretical position is developed prior to the collection of data (the *deductive* approach). This will not always be the case. It may be that your study is based on the principle of developing theory after the data have been collected (the *inductive* approach). This is a fundamental difference in research approach and will be discussed in detail in Section 4.1.

2.5   Writing your research proposal

At the start of all courses or modules we give our students a plan of the work they will be doing. It includes the learning objectives, the content, the assessment strategy and the recommended reading. This is our statement of our side of the learning contract. Our students have a right to expect this.

However, when we insist on a proposal for a dissertation which is often the equivalent of at least two other modules, there is often a marked reluctance to produce anything other than what is strictly necessary. This is unsatisfactory. It is unfair to your project tutor because you are not making entirely clear what it is you intend to do in your research. You are also being unfair to yourself because you are not giving yourself the maximum opportunity to have your ideas and plans scrutinised and subjected to rigorous questioning.

Writing a research proposal is a crucial part of the research process. If you are applying for research funding, or if your proposal is going before an academic research committee, then you will know that you will need to put a great deal of time into the preparation of your proposal. However, even if the official need for a proposal is not so vital it is still a process which will repay very careful attention.

The purposes of the research proposal

Organising your ideas

Section 13.1 notes that writing can be the best way of clarifying our thoughts. This is a valuable purpose of the proposal. Not only will it clarify your thoughts but it will help you to organise your ideas into a coherent statement of your research intent. Your reader will be looking for this.

Convincing your audience

However coherent your ideas and exciting your research plan, it counts for little if the proposal reveals that what you are planning to do is simply not possible. As part of our research methods course for taught postgraduate students we have a three-stage assignment, the first stage of which is to write a proposal. This is then discussed with a project tutor. What usually happens is that this discussion is about how the plans can be amended so that something more modest in scope is attempted. Often work that is not achievable in the given timescale is proposed. If your proposal has not convinced your audience that the research you have proposed is achievable, then you will have saved yourself a great deal of time and frustration.

Contracting with your 'client'

If you are asked to carry out a research project for a commercial client or your own organisation it is unthinkable that you would go ahead without a clear proposal which you would submit for approval. Acceptance of your proposal by the client would be part of the contract that existed between you. So it is with your proposal to your project tutor or academic committee. Acceptance implies that your proposal is satisfactory. While this is obviously no guarantee of subsequent success, it is something of comfort to you to know that at least you started your research journey with an appropriate destination and journey plan. It is for you to ensure that you are not de-railed!

The content of the research proposal

Title

This may be your first attempt at the title. It may change as your work progresses. At this stage it should closely mirror the content of your proposal.

Background

This is an important part of the proposal. It should tell the reader why you feel the research which you are planning is worth the effort. This may be expressed in the form of a problem which needs solving or something which you find exciting and has aroused your curiosity. The reader will be looking for evidence here that there is sufficient interest from you to sustain you over the long months (or years) ahead.

This is also the section where you will demonstrate your knowledge of the relevant literature. Moreover, it will clarify where your proposal fits into the debate in the literature. You will be expected to show a clear link between the previous work that has been done in your field of research interest and the content of your proposal. In short, the literature should be your point of departure. This is not the same as the critical literature review (Section 3.2) you will present in your final project report. It will just indicate the key literature sources from which you intend to draw.

Research questions and objectives

The background section should lead smoothly into a statement of your research question(s) and objectives. These should leave the reader in no doubt as to precisely what it is that your research seeks to achieve.

Method

This and the background sections will be the longest sections of the proposal. It will detail precisely how you intend to go about achieving your research objectives. It will also justify your choice of method in the light of those objectives. These two aims may be met by dividing your method section into two parts: research design and data collection.

In the part on research design you will explain where you intend to carry out the research. If your earlier coverage has pointed out that your research is a single-organisation issue, then this will be self-evident. However, if your research topic is more generic you will wish to explain, for example, which sector(s) of the economy you have chosen to research and why you chose these sectors. You will also need to explain the identity of your research population (for example, managers or trade union officials) and why you chose this population.

This section should also include an explanation of the general way in which you intend to carry out the research. Will it be based on a survey, interviews, examination of secondary data or a combination of methods? Here again, it is essential to explain why you have chosen your approach. Your explanation should be based on the most effective way of meeting your research objectives.

The research design section gives an overall view of the method chosen and the reason for that choice. The data collection section goes into much more detail about how specifically the data are to be collected. For example, if you are using a survey approach you should specify your population and sample size. You should also clarify how the questionnaires will be distributed and how they will be analysed. If you are using interviews you should explain how many interviews will be conducted, their intended duration, whether these will be tape recorded and how they will be analysed. In short, you should demonstrate to your reader that you have thought carefully about all the issues regarding your method and their relationship to your research objectives.

Worked example

A research time scale

As part of the final year of their undergraduate business studies degree all our students have to undertake an 8000–10 000-word research project. In order to assist them with their time management we discuss the following outline timescale with them.

Target date	Month number	Task to be achieved
Start October	1	■ Start thinking about research ideas (latest start date)
End November	2	■ Literature read ■ Objectives clearly defined with reference to literature
End December	3	■ Literature review written ■ Methodology literature read for dissertations involving secondary/primary date
End January	4	■ Secondary/primary data collected and analysed (analysis techniques linked to methodology/research literature) ■ Literature review extended further
Mid-February	5	■ Further writing up and analysis
End March	6	■ Draft completed including formatting bibliography etc.
Mid-May	8	■ Draft revised as necessary
End May	8	■ Submission

However, it is normally not necessary in the proposal to include precise detail of the method you will employ, for example the content of the observation schedule or questionnaire questions.

In addition, it may also be necessary to include a statement about how you are going to adhere to any ethical guidelines. This is particularly important in some research settings, e.g. the National Health Service.

Timescale

This will help you and your reader to decide on the viability of your research proposal. It will be helpful if you divide your research plan into stages. This will give you a clear idea as to what is possible in the given timescale. Experience has shown that however well the researcher's time is organised the whole process seems to take longer than anticipated.

Resources

This is another facet of viability (Table 2.1). It will allow you and the reader to assess whether what you are proposing can be resourced. Resource considerations may be categorised as finance, data access and equipment.

Conducting research costs money. This may be for travel, subsistence, help with data analysis, postage for questionnaires. Think through the expenses involved and ensure that you can meet these expenses.

Assessors of your proposal will need to be convinced that you have access to the data you need to conduct your research. This may be unproblematic if you are carrying out research in your own organisation. Many academic committees wish to see written approval from host organisations in which researchers are planning to conduct research. You will also need to convince your reader of the possibility of obtaining a reasonable response to any questionnaire that you send.

It is surprising how many research proposals have ambitious plans for large-scale surveys with no thought given to how the data will be analysed. It is important that you convince the reader of your proposal that you have access to the necessary computer hardware and software to analyse your data. Moreover, it is necessary for you to demonstrate that you have the necessary skill to perform the analysis or you have access to help.

References

It is not necessary to try and impress your proposal reader with an enormous list of references (Robson, 1993). A few literature sources to which you have referred in the background section and which relate to the previous work which is directly informing your own proposal should be all that is necessary.

Criteria for evaluating research proposals

The extent to which the components of the proposal fit together

Your rationale for conducting the research should include a study of the previous published research, including relevant theories in the topic area. This study should inform your research question(s) and objectives. Your proposed methodology should flow directly from these research question(s) and objectives. The time that you have allocated should be a direct reflection of the methods you employ as should the resources which you need.

> **Worked example**
>
> ### Fitting together the various components of the research proposal
>
> Karl was fascinated by the idea of men seeking what had traditionally been thought of as 'women's jobs'. He read all he could on this topic, including accounts of research that had been carried out in different countries. This helped Karl to define his research question as: 'Why may employers discriminate against men seeking what had traditionally been thought of as "women's jobs"?'
>
> He reasoned that research design based on asking employers why they discriminated would be ineffective at answering his research question. Therefore, he decided to apply for some 'women's jobs' himself and from resultant interviews to see whether he could discover first-hand what the reasons may be. He also advertised in local newspapers for men who had been in similar situations to contact him.
>
> Karl reckoned that a six-month period would allow him to apply and be interviewed for approximately 20 jobs. This would give him sufficient data from which to draw conclusions. He thought that this would also give him enough time to interview any male respondents to his advertisements.
>
> The main resource which Karl needed was acting ability. Since he was a member of the University Drama Society he possessed this in abundance!

The viability of the proposal

This is the answer to the question: 'Will this research be carried out satisfactorily within the timescale?'

The absence of pre-conceived ideas

Your research should be an exciting journey into the unknown. Do not be like the student who came to Phil to talk over a research proposal who said 'of course, I know what the answer will be'. When asked to explain the purpose of doing the research if he already knew the answer he became rather defensive and eventually looked for another supervisor and, probably, another topic.

Worked example

A written research proposal

Puvadol was a student from Thailand who returned home from the UK to complete his MA dissertation. His proposed dissertation concerned the applicability of Western methods of involving employees in decision making in Thai organisations.

An abbreviated version of Puvadol's proposal follows:

Title

The influences of Thai culture on employee involvement.

Background

Involving employees in the decision making of their employing organisations has been increasingly popular in Europe and North America in recent years. The influx of American organisations into Thailand has meant that similar approaches are being adopted. However, this assumes that Thai employees will respond to these techniques as readily as their European and American counterparts.

Doubts about the validity of these assumptions derive from studies of Thai national culture (Komin, 1990). Using Rokeach's (1979) conceptual framework, Komin characterised Thai culture in a number of ways. I have isolated those which relate to employee involvement. These are that Thais wish to:

a save face, to avoid criticism and to show consideration to others;

b exhibit gratitude to those who have shown kindness and consideration;

c promote smooth, conflict-free interpersonal relations;

d interpret 'rules' in a flexible way with little concern for principles;

e promote interdependent social relations;

f be seen to be achieving success through good social relations rather than individual success.

I intend to demonstrate in this section that these six cultural values contradict the values of employee involvement (e.g. employee involvement may involve employees in openly criticising managers which contradicts directly a above).

Research objectives

1 To examine the assumptions behind the management technique of employee involvement

2 To establish the characteristics of the Thai national culture

3 To identify the opinions of Thai employees and their managers, working in American-owned organisations in Thailand, towards values underpinning employee involvement

4 To draw conclusions about the applicability of employee involvement to Thai employees

Method

1 Conduct a review of the literatures on employee involvement and Thai national culture in order to develop research hypotheses.

2 Carry out primary research in three American-owned petrochemical and manufacturing organisations in Thailand to assess the opinions of Thai employees and their managers towards values underpinning employee involvement. Informal approval has been gained from three organisations. American-owned organisations are relevant because it is in these that employee involvement is most likely to be found and values underpinning employee involvement exhibited. Petrochemical and manufacturing organisations are chosen because the occupations carried out in these organisations are likely to be similar, thus ensuring that any differences are a function of Thai national culture rather than occupational culture.

A questionnaire will be developed with questions based on the Thai values a–f in the Background section above. Each value will lead to a hypothesis (e.g. employee involvement may not be appropriate to Thai culture because it may mean that employees openly criticise their managers. The questions in the questionnaire will seek to test these hypotheses. The questionnaire will be distributed to a sample (size to be agreed) of employees and of managers across all three organisations.

Data analysis will use the SPSS software. Statistical tests will be run to ensure that results are a function of Thai cultural values rather than values which relate to the individual organisations.

Timescale

January–March 1998: review of literature

April 1998: draft literature review

May 1998: review research methods literature and agree research strategy

June 1998: agree formal access to three organisations for collection of primary data

July–August 1998: compile, pilot and revise questionnaire

September 1998: administer questionnaire

October–November 1998: final collection of questionnaires and analysis of data

November 1998–February 1999: completion of first draft of project report

March–May 1999: final writing of project report

Resources

I have access to computer hardware and software. Access to three organisations has been negotiated, subject to confirmation. My employer has agreed to pay all incidental costs as part of my course expenses.

References

Komin, S. (1990) *Psychology of the Thai People: Values and Behavioral Patterns*, Thailand, National Institute of Development Administration (in Thai).

Rokeach, M. (1979) *Understanding Human Values: Individual and Society*, New York, The Free Press.

If it is absolutely crucial that your proposal is of the highest quality then you may wish to use an *expert system* such as 'Peer Review Emulator'. This software is available on its own and as part of the 'Methodologist's Toolchest' suite of programs. It asks you a series of questions about your proposed research. The program then critiques these answers to ensure that common research standards are achieved (Scolari Sage, 1999).

2.6　Summary

- The process of formulating and clarifying your research topic is the most important part of your research topic.

- Attributes of a research topic do not vary a great deal between universities. The most important of these is that your research topic will meet the requirements of the examining body.

- Generating and refining research ideas makes use of a variety of techniques. It is important that you use a variety of techniques including those which involve rational and those which involve creative thinking.

- The ideas generated can be integrated subsequently using a technique such as working up and narrowing down.

- Clear research questions, based on the relevant literature, will act as a focus for the research which follows.

- Research can be distinguished from intelligence gathering. Research is theory dependent.

- Writing a research proposal helps you to organise your ideas and can be thought of as a contract between you and the reader.

- The content of the research proposal should tell the reader what you want to do, why you want to do it, what you are trying to achieve and how you to plan to achieve it.

Self check　Questions

2.1　Why is it important to spend time formulating and clarifying your research topic?

2.2　You have decided to search the literature to 'try and come up with some research ideas in the area of Operations Management'. How will you go about this?

2.3　A colleague of yours wishes to generate a research idea in the area of accounting. He has examined his own strengths and interests on the basis of his assignments and read some review articles but has failed to find an idea about which he is excited. He comes and asks you for advice.

Suggest two techniques which your colleague could use and justify your choice.

2.4　You are interested in doing some research on the interface between business organisations and schools. Write three research questions which may be appropriate.

2.5 What may be the theory underpinning the decision by organisations sponsoring schools?

2.6 How would you demonstrate the influence of relevant theory in your research proposal?

Assignment 2

→ If you have not been given a research idea consider the techniques available for generating and refining research ideas. Choose a selection of those with which you feel most comfortable making sure to include both rational and creative thinking techniques. Use these to try to generate a research idea or ideas. Once you have got some research ideas, or if you have been unable to find an idea, talk to your project tutor.

→ Evaluate your research ideas against the checklist of attributes of a good research project (Table 2.1).

→ Refine your research ideas using a selection of the techniques available for generating and refining research ideas. Re-evaluate your research ideas against the checklist of attributes of a good research project (Table 2.1). Remember that it is better to revise (and in some situations to discard) ideas which do not appear to be feasible at this stage. Integrate your ideas using the process of working up and narrowing down to form one research idea.

→ Use your research idea to write a general focus research question. Where possible this should be a 'why?' or a 'how?' rather than a 'what?' question.

→ Use the general focus research question to write more detailed research questions and your research objectives.

→ Write your research proposal making sure it includes a clear title and sections on:

- the background to your research;
- your research questions and objectives;
- the method you intend to use;
- the timescale for your research;
- the resources you require;
- references to any literature to which you have referred.

References

Bennett, R. (1991) 'What is management research?', in Smith, N.C. and Dainty, P. (eds) *The Management Research Handbook*, London, Routledge, pp. 67–77.

Buzan, T. with Buzan, B. (1995) *The Mind Map Book* (revised edn), London, BBC Books.

Carroll, L. (1989) *Alice's Adventures in Wonderland*, London, Hutchinson.

Creswell, J. (1994) *Research Design: Quantitative and Qualitative Approaches*, Thousand Oaks, CA, Sage.

Ghauri. P., Grønhaug, K. and Kristianslund, I. (1995) *Research Methods in Business Studies*, Harlow, Prentice Hall.

Gill, J. and Johnson, P. (1997) *Research Methods for Managers* (2nd edn), London, Paul Chapman.

Jankowicz, A.D. (1995) *Business Research Projects* (2nd edn), London, Chapman & Hall.

Kerlinger, F. (1973) *Foundations of Behavioral Research* (2nd edn), New York, Holt Rinehart and Winston.

Kervin, J.B. (1992) *Methods for Business Research*, New York, HarperCollins.

Moody, P.E. (1983) *Decision Making: Proven Methods for Better Decisions*, Maidenhead, McGraw-Hill.

Phillips, E.M. and Pugh, D.S. (1994) *How to get a Ph.D.* (2nd edn), Milton Keynes, Open University Press.

Raimond, P. (1993) *Management Projects*, London, Chapman & Hall.

Robson, C. (1993) *Real World Research: a Resource for Social Scientists and Practitioner-Researchers*, Oxford, Blackwell.

Scolari Sage (1999) 'Research methodology and CD-ROMS' (online)(cited 16 June 1999). Available from <URL:http://www.scolari.co.uk>.

Saunders, M.N.K. and Lewis, P. (1997) 'Great ideas and blind alleys? A review of the literature on starting research', *Management Learning*, 28:3, 283–99.

Sharp, J. and Howard, K. (1996) *The Management of a Student Research Project* (2nd edn), Aldershot, Gower.

Smith, N.C. and Dainty, P. (1991) *The Management Research Handbook*, London, Routledge.

Further reading

Gill, J. and Johnson, P. (1997) *Research Methods for Managers* (2nd edn), London, Paul Chapman. Chapter 3 is a particularly clear account of the role of theory in research methods and is worth reading to gain a better understanding of this often-misunderstood area.

Raimond, P. (1993) *Management Projects*, London, Chapman & Hall. Chapter 4 contains a useful discussion of techniques for helping to identify project ideas. It is particularly good for those techniques which we have classified as creative rather than rational.

Robson, C. (1993) *Real World Research: a Resource for Social Scientists and Practitioner–Researchers,* Oxford, Blackwell. Appendix A is devoted to the writing of research proposals and is a very useful source of further information.

Case 2 **The use of internal and word-of-mouth recruitment methods**

A few years ago Mark and Phil thought it would be fun to work together on a piece of research. They also hoped it would benefit their continuing development as researchers. Mark's research background (strength) has its origins in the recruitment and subsequent mobility of labour. His research methods skills emphasise the quantitative approach although he had undertaken a variety of qualitative research projects. Phil's strength is as a mainstream HRM academic with a bias towards understanding the processes of everyday HRM. His research methods skills are mainly qualitative. Unlike many students their research area was one in which they were aware of the literature. However, despite this, they were in a similar situation to many students. They wanted to undertake a new piece of work which would excite them and be of some practical benefit to organisations.

In the early 1990s Mark had carried out a survey of recruitment methods used by local authority employers. This had built on and developed research he had undertaken as part of his doctoral thesis approximately 10 years earlier. While discussing the findings in the coffee shop Phil agreed to take a more detailed look to see whether there was anything of practical significance for managers. During discussion a few weeks later an issue which they felt was fascinating emerged. Throughout the previous decade there appeared to have been a dominance of internal and word-of-mouth recruitment. Internal recruitment is where recruitment is restricted to an organisation's existing employees. Word of mouth is where recruitment relies on the organisation's existing employees to tell other people in their social networks about the vacancies.

Through their discussion Phil and Mark developed a clear research idea which was in both their areas of academic strength. This was concerned with explaining why, given the centrality of equal opportunities to local authorities' recruitment, internal and word-of-mouth forms of recruitment were so dominant. They felt this idea was fascinating because, on the face of it, both forms of recruitment were alien to the principle of equal opportunities. Quantitative evidence from Mark's survey showed that the phenomena of internal and word-of-mouth recruitment were dominant. Mark's experience of working in local authorities supported this. They now needed to refine the idea, to develop a clear research question and objectives and to write their research proposal.

They adopted what we felt was a rational process. They both drafted outline proposals simultaneously and criticised each other's work. This led to an outline proposal which integrated their ideas and encompassed research questions and objectives.

Next they reviewed the literature to establish what work had been done on this aspect of recruitment. The overall conclusion from the empirical research, undertaken in all sectors of the economy, was that word-of-mouth and internal recruitment methods were still important. However, none of this work concentrated on local authorities. Moreover, they thought that awareness of the importance of equal opportunities would have grown since the time when the research was conducted. Their research proposal still seemed valid and the literature confirmed its relevance. In addition reading the literature had suggested possible new research questions. However, they still needed to discuss their proposal with other people.

The first discussion was with an equal opportunities officer with a London borough. He was not excited by their research idea and commented that he was not surprised by the survey findings. These he said were due to the need to re-deploy people who would otherwise be made redundant. The second discussion was with a personnel specialist from a large county authority. Her response can be paraphrased as 'well what do you expect . . . the pay for manual positions is relatively low so there are few applicants . . . we therefore have to rely on word of mouth'.

Mark and Phil were, to say the least, depressed. They thought they had a fascinating research question. Yet the first two people they had discussed their ideas with had shown them the answer was obvious. They had spent a great deal of time refining their research proposal and in searching the literature. Their immediate reaction was to abandon the research completely. However, a few days later they decided to revise their research ideas. They decided to discard the local authorities' and equal opportunities' perspectives and focus on the notification channels used by employers. Their revised research question was: 'Why do organisations use word of mouth recruitment?'

Questions

1 Do you think that Phil and Mark had good reasons for choosing the research topic initially? Give reasons for your answer.

2 Draft a possible first research question for Mark's and Phil's idea as described in the first three paragraphs of the case study.

3 What lessons can you learn from Phil's and Mark's experience?

4 To what extent do you feel that Mark's and Phil's final research question meets the criteria outlined in Table 2.1?

Self check ## Answers

2.1 There are numerous reasons you could include in your answer. Some of the more important include:

- without being clear what you are going to do it is difficult to plan your research;
- to enable you to choose the most appropriate research strategy and data collection and analysis techniques;
- to ensure that your topic meets the examining body's requirements;
- to ensure that your topic is one that you are capable of doing and excites your imagination;
- to ensure that you will have sufficient time and money resources to undertake your topic;
- to ensure that you will be able to gain access to the data you require;
- to ensure that the issues in your topic are capable of being linked to theory.

2.2 One starting point would be to ask your project tutor for suggestions of possible recent review articles or articles containing recommendations for further work which he or she has read. Another would be to browse recent editions of operations management journals such as the *International Journal of Operations & Production Management* for possible research ideas. These would include both statements of the absence of research and unfounded assertions. Recent reports held in your library may also be of use here. You could also scan one or two recently published operations management textbooks for overviews of research that has been undertaken.

2.3 From the description given it would appear that your colleague has only considered rational thinking techniques. It would therefore seem sensible to suggest two creative thinking techniques as these would hopefully generate an idea which would appeal to his heart.

One technique which you could suggest is brainstorming, perhaps emphasising the need to do it with other colleagues. Exploring past projects in the accountancy area would be another possibility. You might also suggest that he keeps a notebook of ideas.

2.4 Your answer will probably differ from that below. However, the sorts of things you could be considering include:

1 How do business organisations benefit from their liaison with schools?

2 Why do business organisations undertake school liaison activities?

3 To what degree do business organisations receive value for money in their schools liaison activities?

2.5 Undoubtedly organisations would be looking for a 'pay-off'. This may be left undefined: that it is bound to be a 'good thing' or it may be linked to a specific theory that it will create an image of the organisation as one that is community minded. This is a particularly important concept if the product or service is one that has community values, for example water or electricity.

2.6 Try including a subsection in the background section which is headed 'how the previous published research has informed my research questions and objectives'. Then show how, say, a gap in the previous research which is there because nobody has pursued a particular approach before has led to you filling that gap.

3 Critically reviewing the literature

By the end of this chapter you should:

- understand the importance and purpose of the critical literature review to your research project;
- know what you need to include when writing your critical review;
- be aware of the range of primary, secondary and tertiary literature sources available;
- be able to identify key words and to undertake a literature search using a range of paper-based and electronic methods including the Internet;
- be able to evaluate the relevance and sufficiency of the literature found;
- be able to reference the literature found accurately;
- be able to apply the knowledge, skills and understanding gained to your own research project.

3.1 Introduction

Two major reasons exist for reviewing the literature (Sharp and Howard, 1996). The first, the preliminary search which helps you to generate and refine your research ideas, has already been discussed in Section 2.3. The second, often referred to as the *critical review*, is part of your research project proper. Most research textbooks, as well as your project tutor, will argue that this critical review of the literature is necessary. Although you may feel that you already have a good knowledge of your research area, we believe that reviewing the literature is essential. Project assessment criteria usually require you to demonstrate awareness of the current state of knowledge in your subject, its limitations and how your research fits in this wider context (Gill and Johnson, 1997). In Jankowicz's (1995: 128–9) words:

> Knowledge doesn't exist in a vacuum, and your work only has value in relation to other people's. Your work and your findings will be significant only to the extent that they're the same as, or different from, other people's work and findings.

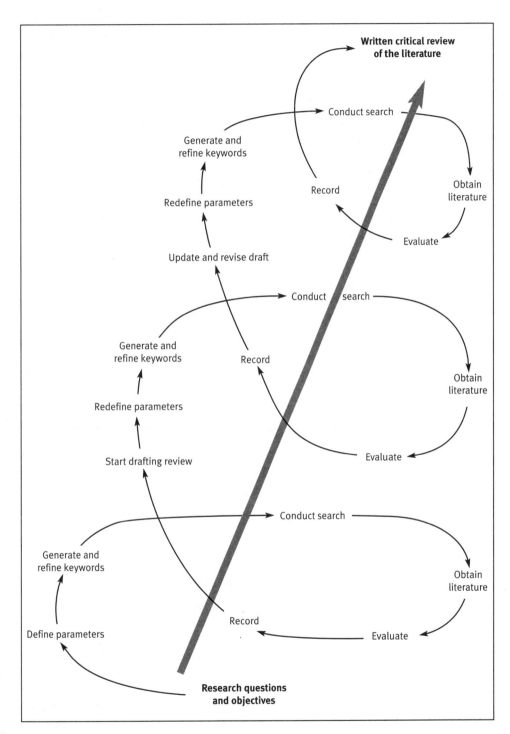

Fig 3.1   **The literature review process**

© Mark Saunders, Philip Lewis, Adrian Thornhill, Lynnette Bailey and Martin Jenkins, 2000

You therefore need to establish what research has been published in your chosen area and to try to identify any other research that might currently be in progress. The items you read and write about will enhance your subject knowledge and help you to clarify your research question(s) further. This process is called *critically reviewing the literature*.

For most research projects, your literature search will be an early activity. Despite this early start, it is usually necessary to continue searching throughout your project's life. The process can be likened to an upward spiral culminating in the final draft of a written critical literature review (Fig 3.1). In the initial stage of your literature review, you will start to define the parameters to your research question(s) and objectives (Section 3.4). After generating key words and conducting your first search (Section 3.5), you will have a list of references to authors who have published on these subjects. Once these have been obtained, you can read and evaluate them (Section 3.6), record the ideas (Section 3.7) and start drafting your review. After the initial search, you will be able to redefine your parameters more precisely and to undertake further searches keeping in mind your research question(s) and objectives. As your thoughts develop each subsequent search will be focused more precisely on material that is likely to be relevant. At the same time, you will probably be refining your research question(s) and objectives in the light of your reading (Section 2.4).

Unlike some academic disciplines, business and management research makes use of a wide range of literature. While your review is likely to include specific business disciplines such as finance, marketing and human resource management, it is also likely to include other disciplines. Those most frequently consulted by our students include economics, psychology, sociology and geography. Given this, and the importance of the review to your research, it is vital for you to be aware of what a critical literature review is and the full range of literature available before you start the reviewing process. For these reasons, we start this chapter by outlining what your critical review of the literature needs to include (Section 3.2) and the literature resources available (Section 3.3).

3.2 The critical review

The purpose of the critical review

Your critical literature review will form the foundation on which your research is built. As you will have gathered from the introduction, its main purpose is to help you to develop a good understanding and insight into relevant previous research and the trends that have emerged. You would not expect a scientific researcher inquiring into the causes of cot death to start his or her research without first reading about the findings of other cot death research. Likewise you should not expect to start your research without first reading what other researchers in your area have already found out.

The precise purpose of your reading of the literature will depend on the approach you are intending to use in your research. For some research projects you will use the literature to help you to identify theories and ideas that you will test using data. This is known as a *deductive approach* (Section 4.1) in which you develop a theoretical or conceptual framework which you subsequently test using data. For other research projects, you will be planning to explore your data and to develop theories from them that you will subsequently relate to the literature. This is known as an *inductive approach* (Section 4.1) and, although your research still has a clearly defined purpose with research question(s) and objectives, you do not start with any predetermined theories or conceptual frameworks. We believe such an approach cannot be taken without a competent knowledge of your subject area. There is, however, no need to review all of the literature before collecting your data. You do not want your own ideas to be drowned out by the ideas in the literature. If your analysis is effective, new findings and theories will emerge which neither you nor anyone else has thought about (Strauss and Corbin, 1990). Despite this, when you write your critical review, you will need to show how your findings and the theories you have developed relate to the work that has gone before.

Your review also has a number of other purposes. Many of these have been highlighted by Gall *et al.* (1996) in their book for students undertaking educational research and are, we believe, of equal relevance to business and management researchers:

■ to help you to refine further your research question(s) and objectives;

■ to highlight research possibilities that have been overlooked implicitly in research to date;

■ to discover explicit recommendations for further research. These can provide you with a superb justification for your own research question(s) and objectives;

■ to help you to avoid simply repeating work that has been done already;

■ to sample current opinions in newspapers, professional and trade journals thereby gaining insights into the aspects of your research question(s) and objectives that are considered newsworthy;

■ to discover and provide an insight into research strategies (Section 4.2) and methodologies that may be appropriate to your own research question(s) and objectives.

The content of the critical review

As you begin to find, read and evaluate the literature, you will need to think how to combine the academic theories and ideas it contains to form the critical review that will appear in your project report. This will need to discuss critically the work that has already been undertaken in your area of research and reference that work (Appendix 2). It will draw out the key points and trends (recognising any omissions and bias) and present them in a logical way. In doing this you will provide readers of your project report with the necessary background knowledge to your research question(s) and objectives and establish the boundaries of your own research. It will also enable the readers to see your ideas against the background of previous published research in the area. This does not necessarily mean that your ideas must extend, follow or approve those set out in the literature. You may be highly critical of the earlier research and seek to discredit it. However, if you wish to do this you must still review the literature, argue clearly why it is problematic and then justify your own ideas.

In writing your critical review you will therefore need:

- to include the key academic theories within your chosen area;
- to demonstrate that your knowledge of your chosen area is up to date;
- to show how your research relates to previous published research;
- to assess the strengths and weaknesses of previous work including omissions or bias and take these into account in your arguments;
- to justify your arguments by referencing previous research;
- through clear referencing, to enable those reading your project report to find the original work you cite.

In addition, by fully acknowledging the work of others you will avoid charges of *plagiarism* and the associated penalties.

The structure of the critical review

The literature review that you write for your project report should be a description and critical analysis of what other authors have written (Jankowicz, 1995). When drafting your review you need to focus on your research question(s) and objectives. One way of helping you to focus is to think of your literature review as discussing how far the literature goes in answering your research question(s). The shortfall in the literature will be addressed, at least partially, in the remainder of your project report. Another way of helping you to focus is to ask yourself how your review relates to your objectives. If it does not, or only does partially, there is a need for a clearer focus on your objectives. The precise structure of the critical review is usually your choice although you should check as your examining body may specify it. Three common structures are:

- a single chapter;
- a series of chapters;
- throughout the project report as you tackle various issues.

In all project reports, you should return to the key issues from the literature in your conclusions (Section 13.3).

Within your critical review, you will need to juxtapose different authors' ideas and to form your own opinions and conclusions based on these. Although you will not be able to start writing until you have undertaken some reading, we recommend that you start drafting your review early (Fig 3.1). What you write can then be updated and revised as you read more.

A common mistake with critical literature reviews is that they become uncritical listings of previous research. Haywood and Wragg (1982:2, cited by Bell 1999:92) describe this adeptly as:

> . . . the furniture sale catalogue, in which everything merits a one paragraph entry no matter how skilfully it has been conducted: Bloggs (1975) found this, Smith (1976) found that, Jones (1977) found the other, Bloggs, Smith and Jones (1978) found happiness in heaven.

Although there is no single structure that your critical review should take, our students have found it useful to think of the review as a funnel in which you:

1 start at a more general level before narrowing down to your specific research question(s) and objectives;

2 provide a brief overview of key ideas;

3 summarise, compare and contrast the work of the key writers;

4 narrow down to highlight the work most relevant to your research;

5 provide a detailed account of the findings of this work;

6 highlight those issues where your research will provide fresh insights;

7 lead the reader into subsequent sections of your project report, which explore these issues.

Whichever way you structure your review you must demonstrate that you have read, understood and evaluated the items you have located. The key to writing a critical literature review is therefore to link together the different ideas you find in the literature to form a coherent and cohesive argument, which set in context and justify your research. Obviously, it should relate to your research question and objectives. It should show a clear link from these as well as a clear link to the empirical work that will follow. Table 3.1 provides a checklist to help you do this. Subsequent parts of your project report (Section 13.3) must follow on from this 'seamlessly as a continuation of the argument' (Jankowicz, 1995:130).

Table 3.1	Checklist for evaluating your literature review

✓ Does your review start at a more general level before narrowing down?

✓ Does the literature covered relate clearly to your research question and objectives?

✓ Have you covered the key theories?

✓ Have you covered the key literature or at least a representative sample?

✓ Are those issues where your research will provide fresh insights highlighted?

✓ Is the literature you have included up to date?

✓ Have you been objective in your discussion and assessment of other people's work?

✓ Have you included references that are counter to your own opinion?

✓ Have you justified clearly your own ideas?

✓ Is your argument coherent and cohesive – do the ideas link together?

✓ Does your review lead the reader into subsequent sections of your project report?

Sources: Authors' experience; Higgins, 1996

A critical review of the literature

An article by Mark published in the *International Journal of Manpower* (Saunders 1993:40–1) reviewed the vacancy notification and employee mobility literature. The following extract illustrates:

- the overall structure of starting at a more general level before narrowing down;
- the provision of a brief overview of (some of) the key ideas;
- summarising, comparing and contrasting the work of key writers;
- highlighting of (some of) the most relevant work.

Employers recruit for two reasons, to replace employees (80%) and for expansion (20%) (Roper 1988). In both cases notification can be viewed as the point at which employer and job seeker labour searches interact (Dale 1987) and make contact (Watson 1989), where the employers' search for new employees links into those searching for employment within both the internal and the wider labour markets. For employees to be mobile within their company or between employers they need to be aware of vacancies. The key factor here is therefore the availability of information about job vacancies (for example Saunders 1985, Mortenson 1986). The methods adopted by an employer to search for potential new employees to fill a vacancy is based on a series of factors. Crucial to the choice of notification method is the company policy regarding filling vacancies externally or internally (Salt 1990). Subsequent to this the employer will need to decide how and when to notify the vacancy, whether or not to shortlist an applicant and whether or not to offer the post (Herriot 1989).

The importance of this initial vacancy notification to the recruiter has been emphasised, particularly in the more prescriptive (HRM) literature. For example Mondy *et al.* (1987:42) state:

> Effective employee selection depends on attracting the most qualified applicants. Time and money are wasted when the job search is conducted in the wrong place with the wrong methods.

Wheeler (1988) identified associated advertising costs of over £370 million in the UK in 1987, the vast majority of this being spent in local and regional press. This excluded all associated costs such as the brochures, leaflets as well as other below the line costs such as staff time. Thus, the HRM literature is concerned with how the employer reaches potential employees (Roper 1988). By contrast mobility and migration literature, such as Granovetter (1974), Saunders and Flowerdew (1987), have often focused on the impact on the person actively seeking a new post (the 'job seeker'), such as how choice of notification outlet directly influences applicant location. Theoretical job search and migration literature (principally North American) has been concerned with modelling this process using methods based on stopping rule models (for example Seater 1979, Mortensen 1986). In focusing on job seekers rather than all potential employees they have excluded those notification methods aimed at people not searching for a job, such as the use of head hunters.

The importance to employers of factors likely to prevent potential applicants from applying and from taking up individual posts (that is factors preventing mobility between jobs) has also been cited in the HRM literature. However, this has rarely been considered in any depth by UK textbooks on personnel management (Forster 1991a). To induce mobility employers may well offer incentives to the potential applicant(s) to overcome geographical inertia such as relocation assistance or golden handshakes for some very senior posts (Salt 1990). In the latter case the employee will usually need to move house, that is migrate. Migration specialists, in particular Geographers, have shown that wider institutional, legislative and labour market constraints are also likely to influence mobility and in particular the decision to migrate (Mondy et al. 1987). Other constraints such as those introduced by the Employment Protection Act are also likely to have an impact.

When an employer needs to go outside their organisation to find workers, they must begin by identifying sources and methods of recruitment. HRM research and the more prescriptive literature both emphasise the impact and importance of choice of vacancy notification and methods used to encouraging mobility for a company both in terms of the cost of recruitment, and equally in the cost of integrating and supporting new employees within the company (Forster and Munton 1990, Male and Clarke 1991). The crucial factor determining the subsequent stages of this process is the way in which potential applicants are made aware that a vacancy exists. To do this the most cost effective sources of recruitment and the appropriate incentives to encourage internal and external applications must be identified for each specific vacancy.

Subsequent to this, the employer will need to select the most suitable candidate. HRM writers have argued that in the future employers will be likely to demand increasing mobility from employees within their company (Forster 1991a). Migration researchers have argued that, at a more aggregate level, the implications of this are considerable. They feel that there will be a similar increase in the number of job changes between companies requiring people to move house, that is migrate (Owen and Green 1992a). HRM research points to the need to provide a range of support mechanisms for new employees who, in addition to coping with a new job, will have moved to a new area and would in many cases welcome support with the personal side of relocation (Forster 1991b).

Much of the HRM literature has therefore been concerned with the implications of the recruitment process for the employer; in particular how the employer can best manage it to ensure that quality people can be attracted to the organisation and the overall resourcing strategy met (Spellman 1992). Sisson (1989) argues that this takes two approaches; the most important of these in terms of articles published is largely prescriptive and concerned with techniques of personnel management. The latter is a critique and, whilst also from the manager's viewpoint, is concerned with the controls imposed and methods used to maximise employees' surplus value. By contrast the Migration literature has often taken the job seekers' viewpoint and considered the importance and impact of external factors. In addition the scale at which the process has been viewed has ranged from the individual to the international whilst the HRM literature has been principally concerned with the impact at the individual and company scales.

3.3   Literature sources available

An overview

The literature sources available to help you to develop a good understanding of and insight into previous research can be divided into three categories: primary (published and unpublished), secondary and tertiary (Fig 3.2). In reality these categories often overlap; for example primary literature sources including conference proceedings can appear in journals and some books also contain indexes to primary and secondary literature.

The different categories of literature resources represent the flow of information from the original source. Often as information flows from primary to secondary to tertiary sources it becomes less detailed and authoritative but more easily accessible. It is because primary sources can be difficult to trace they are sometimes referred to as *grey literature*. Recognising this information flow helps you to identify the most appropriate sources of information for your needs. Some research projects may only access secondary information sources whereas others will necessitate the use of primary sources.

Fig 3.2 also illustrates the reduced currency of secondary sources, which are utilising information already published in primary sources. Because of the time taken to publish, the information in these sources can be dated. Your literature review should reflect current thinking as far as possible, so the limitations of such sources must be recognised.

Primary literature sources (also known as grey literature) are the first occurrence of a piece of work. They include published sources such as reports and some central and local government publications such as white papers and planning documents. They also include unpublished manuscript sources such as letters, memos and committee minutes that may be analysed as data in their own right (Section 7.2).

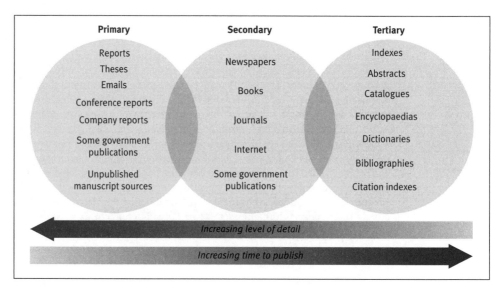

Fig 3.2   **Literature sources available**

Secondary literature sources such as books and journals are the subsequent publication of primary literature. These publications are aimed at a wider audience. They are easier to locate than primary literature as they are better covered by the tertiary literature.

Tertiary literature sources, also called *search tools*, are designed either to help to locate primary and secondary literature or to introduce a topic. They therefore include indexes and abstracts as well as encyclopaedias and bibliographies.

Your use of these literature sources will depend on your research question(s) and objectives, the need for secondary data to answer them (Section 7.3) and the time available. For some research projects you may only use tertiary and secondary literature; for others you may need to locate primary literature as well. Most research projects will make the greatest use of secondary literature and so it is this we consider first, followed by the primary literature. Tertiary literature sources are not discussed until Section 3.5 as their major use is in conducting a literature search.

Secondary literature sources

The number of secondary literature sources available to you is expanding rapidly (Easterby-Smith *et al.*, 1991). Haythornthwaite (1990) gives a good general introduction to the wide range of sources available. Many new resources have appeared since 1990 especially in *electronic form* and can be accessed via the Internet or on CD-ROM. Your university's librarians are likely to be aware of a wide range of secondary literature in business and management which can be accessed from your library and will keep themselves up to date with new resources.

The main secondary literature sources that you are likely to use, along with those primary sources most frequently used for a literature review, are outlined in Table 3.2. The most important when placing your ideas in the context of earlier research are refereed academic journals. Books are however, likely to be more important than professional and trade journals in this context.

Journals

Journals are also known as *periodicals*, *serials* and *magazines* and are published on a regular basis. At present most are printed, but they are appearing increasingly in electronic form via the Internet. Journals are a vital literature source for any research. The articles in them are easily accessible as they are well covered by tertiary literature and a good selection are kept for reference in most university libraries (Table 3.2). However, trade and some professional journals may only be covered partially by the tertiary literature (see Table 3.3). You therefore need to browse these journals regularly to be sure of finding useful items. Increasingly journals' content pages can also be browsed via the Internet (Section 3.5).

Articles in *refereed academic journals* (such as the *Journal of Management Studies*) are evaluated by academic peers prior to publication to assess their quality and suitability. These are usually the most useful for research projects as they will contain detailed reports of relevant earlier research. Not all academic journals are refereed. Most *other academic journals* will have an editor and possibly an editorial board with subject knowledge to select articles. The relevance and usefulness of such journals varies considerably and occasionally you may need to be wary of possible bias (Section 3.6).

Table 3.2 Main secondary and primary literature sources

Source	Frequency of publication	Format of publication	Coverage by abstracts and indexes (tertiary sources)	Likely availability
Refereed academic journal **Other academic journal**	Mainly monthly or quarterly	Mainly printed but increasingly available on the Internet, CD-ROM and microfiche	Well covered	Kept as reference in most university libraries. Those not available locally can usually be obtained using inter-library loans or, increasingly, via the Internet. Professional organisations may also provide access to their journals via their own web pages
Professional journal	Mainly weekly or monthly		Not as good as academic and refereed journals, will probably need to browse actual copies of journal	
Trade journal				Not as widely available in university libraries as academic and refereed journals. Can be obtained using inter-library loans
Books	Once, subsequent editions may be published	As for refereed academic journals	Well covered by abstracts and indexes. Searches can be undertaken on remote university OPACs* via the Internet	Widely available. Those not available locally can be obtained using inter-library loans
Newspapers	Mainly daily or weekly	All UK broadsheets now available on CD-ROM and increasingly via the Internet. Also available on microfilm. Many international broadsheets are available via the Internet	Specialised indexes available. CD-ROM and Internet format easy to search using key words	Home nation broadsheets kept as reference in most university libraries. Internet access to selected/current issues of national and international broadsheets often possible.

Table 3.2 *Cont.*

Source	Frequency of publication	Format of publication	Coverage by abstracts and indexes (tertiary sources)	Likely availability
Conference proceedings	Dependent on the conference, sometimes as part of a journal	As for refereed academic journals. May be published in book form	Depends on conference although often limited. Specialist indexes sometimes available	Not widely held by university libraries. May be possible to obtain using inter-library loans
Reports	Once	As for refereed academic journals	Poor compared with most secondary sources although some specialised indexes exist	
Theses	On the awarding of the research degree	Mainly printed but increasingly available on microfiche	Good for PhD and MPhil research degrees, otherwise poor	Usually obtained using inter-library loans. Often only one copy

© *Mark Saunders, Philip Lewis, Adrian Thornhill, Lynnette Bailey and Martin Jenkins, 2000*

*OPAC, Online Public Access Catalogue

Professional journals (such as *People Management*) are produced for their members by organisations such as the Institute of Personnel and Development, The Institute of Chartered Accountants and the American Marketing Association. They contain a mix of news-related items and articles that are more detailed. However, you need to exercise caution as articles can be biased towards their author's or the organisation's views. Articles are often of a more practical nature and more closely related to professional needs than those in academic journals. Some organisations will also produce newsletters or current awareness publications that you may find useful for up-to-date information. Some professional organisations now give access to selected articles in their journals via their web page (see Table 7.2 and Section 3.5). *Trade journals* fulfil a similar function to professional journals. They are published by trade organisations or aimed at particular industries or trades such as catering or mining. Often they focus on new products or services and news items. They rarely contain articles based on empirical research although some provide summaries of research.

Books

Books or *monographs* are written for a specific audience. Some are aimed at the academic market, with a theoretical slant. Others, aimed at practising professionals, may be more applied in their content. The material in books is usually presented in a more ordered and accessible manner than in journals, pulling together a wider range of topics. They are therefore particularly useful as introductory sources to help clarify your research question(s) and objectives or the research methods you intend to use. Beware, books may contain out of date material even by the time they are published.

Newspapers

Newspapers are a good source of topical events, developments within business and government and recent statistical information such as share prices. They also produce special reports such as the *Financial Times* industrial sector reports. The main broadsheet newspapers since the early 1990s are available on CD-ROM in most university libraries and increasingly selected stories can be accessed via the Internet (Table 3.2). Consequently finding items in these newspapers is quick and easy. Items in earlier issues are more difficult to access, as they are usually stored on microfilm and need to be located using printed indexes. However, you need to be careful as newspapers may contain bias in their coverage, be it political, geographical or personal. Reporting can also be inaccurate and you may not pick up any subsequent amendments. In addition the news presented is filtered depending on events at the time with priority given to more headline-grabbing stories (Stewart and Kamins, 1993).

Primary literature sources

Primary literature sources are more difficult to locate (Table 3.2). The most accessible, and those most likely to be of use in showing how your research relates to that of other people, are reports, conference proceedings and theses.

Reports

Reports include market research reports such as those produced by Mintel and Keynote, government reports and academic reports. Even if you are able to locate these, you may find it difficult to gain access to them as they are not as widely available as books (Section 7.4). Reports are not well indexed in the tertiary literature and you will need to rely on specific search tools such *British National Bibliography for Report Literature* and the British Library's *OPAC '97* (see Table 3.3).

Conference proceedings

Conference proceedings sometimes referred to as *symposia* are often published as unique titles within journals or as books. Most conferences will have a theme that is very specific but some have a wide-ranging overview. Proceedings are not well indexed by tertiary literature so as with reports you may have to rely on specific search tools such as *Index to Conference Proceedings* and the British Library's *OPAC '97* (see Table 3.3). If you do locate and are able to obtain the proceedings for a conference on the theme of your research, you will have a wealth of relevant information.

Theses

Theses are unique and so for a major research project can be a good source of detailed information; they will also be a good source of further references. Unfortunately, they can be difficult to locate and, when found, difficult to access as there may be only one copy at the awarding institution. Specific search tools are available such as *Index to Theses* and *British National Bibliography for Report Literature* (see Table 3.3). Only research degrees such as PhD and MPhil are covered well by these tertiary resources. Research undertaken as part of a taught Masters degree is not covered as systematically.

3.4 Planning the literature search

It is important that you plan this search carefully to ensure that you locate relevant and up-to-date literature. This will enable you to establish what research has been previously published in your area and to relate your own research to it. All our students have found their literature search a time-consuming process, which takes far longer than expected. Fortunately time spent planning will be re-paid in time saved when searching the literature. As you start to plan your search, you need to beware of information overload! One of the easiest ways to achieve this is to start the main search for your critical review without a clearly defined research question(s), objectives and outline proposal (Sections 2.4 and 2.5). Before commencing your literature search we suggest that you undertake further planning by:

- defining the parameters of your search;
- generating key words and search terms;
- discussing your ideas as widely as possible.

Defining parameters

For most research questions and objectives you will have a good idea of which subject matter is going to be relevant. You will, however, be less clear about the parameters within which you need to search. In particular you need to be clear about the (Bell, 1999):

- language of publication (for example English);
- subject area (for example accountancy);
- business sector (for example manufacturing);
- geographical area (for example Europe);
- publication period (for example the last 10 years);
- literature type (for example journals and books).

One way of starting to firm up these parameters is by re-examining your lecture notes and course textbooks in the area of your research question. While re-examining these we suggest you make a note of subjects that appear most relevant to your research question and the names of relevant authors. These will be helpful when generating possible key words later.

For example, if your research was on the marketing benefits of arts sponsorship to UK banking organisations you might identify the subject area as marketing and sponsorship. Implicit in this is the need to think broadly. A common comment we hear from students who have attempted a literature search is 'there's nothing written on my research topic'. This is usually because they have identified one or more of their parameters too narrowly (or chosen key words that do not match the control language, Section 3.5). We therefore recommend that if you encounter this problem you broaden one or more of your parameters to include material your narrower search would not have located.

Worked example

Defining parameters for a research question

Simon's research question was 'How have green issues influenced the way in which manufacturers advertise cars?' To be certain of finding material he defined each parameter in narrow and, in most instances, broader terms:

Parameter	Narrow	Broader
Language	UK (e.g. car)	UK and USA (e.g. car and automobile)
Subject area	Green issues	Environmental issues
	Motor industry	Manufacturing
	Advertising	Marketing
Business sector	Motor industry	Manufacturing
Geographical area	UK	Europe and North America
Publication period	Last 5 years	Last 15 years
Literature type	Academic journals and books	Journals and books

Generating key words

Undertaking reading of articles by key authors and recent review articles in your research area is also important at this stage. It will help you to define your subject matter and to suggest appropriate key words. Recent *review articles* are often helpful here. Their discussion of the current state of research for a particular topic will help you to refine your key words. In addition, they will probably contain references to other work that is pertinent to your research question(s) and objectives. If you are unsure about review articles, your project tutor should be able to point you in the right direction.

After re-reading your lecture notes and textbooks and undertaking the limited reading you will have a list of subjects that appear relevant to your research project. You now need to define precisely what is relevant to your research in terms of key words.

The identification of *key words* or *search terms* is the most important part of planning your search for relevant literature (Bell, 1999). Key words are the basic terms that describe your research question(s) and objectives and will be used to search the tertiary literature. Key words (which can include authors' surnames identified in the examination of your lecture notes and course textbooks) can be identified using one or a number of different techniques in combination. Those found most useful by our students include:

- discussion with colleagues, your project tutor and librarians;
- initial reading;
- dictionaries, thesauruses, encyclopaedias and handbooks;
- brainstorming;
- relevance trees.

Discussion

We believe you should be taking every opportunity to discuss your research. In discussing your work with others, whether face to face, by electronic mail or by letter you will be sharing your ideas, getting feedback and obtaining new ideas and approaches.

Initial reading, dictionaries, encyclopaedias, handbooks and thesauruses

To produce the most relevant key words you may need to build on your brainstorming session with support materials such as *dictionaries, encyclopaedias, handbooks* and *thesauruses*, both general and subject specific. These are also good starting points for new topics with which you may be unfamiliar and for related subject areas. Initial reading, particularly of recent review articles, may also be of help here. Project tutors, colleagues and librarians can also be useful sources of ideas.

Brainstorming

Brainstorming has already been outlined as a technique for helping you to develop your research question (Section 2.3). However, it is also helpful for generating key words. Either you individually, or as part of a group, write down all the words and short phrases that come to mind on your research topic. These are then evaluated and key words (and phrases) selected.

Worked example

Generating key words

Han's research question was 'How do the actual management requirements of a school pupil record administration system differ from those suggested by the literature?' She brainstormed this question with her peer group, all of whom were teachers in Hong Kong. The resulting list included the following key words and phrases:

> schools, pupil records, administration, user requirements, computer, management information system, access, legislation, information, database, security, UK, Hong Kong, theories

The group evaluated these and others. As a result, the following key words (and phrases) were selected:

> pupil records, management information system, computer, database, user requirement

Dictionaries and encyclopaedias were used subsequently to add to the choice of key words:

> student record, MIS, security

These were then used in combination to search the tertiary literature sources.

Relevance trees

Relevance trees provide a useful method of bringing some form of structure to your literature search and of guiding your search process (Sharp and Howard, 1996). They look similar to an organisation chart and are a hierarchical 'graph-like' arrangement of headings and subheadings. These headings and subheadings describe your research question(s) and objectives and may be key words (including authors' names) with which you can search. Relevance trees are often constructed after brainstorming. They enable you to decide either with help or on your own (Jankowicz, 1995):

- which key words are directly relevant to your research question(s) and objectives;
- which areas you will search first and which your search will use later;
- which areas are more important – these tend to have more branches.

To construct a relevance tree you:

1 start with your research question or objective at the top level;
2 identify two or more subject areas that you think are important;
3 further subdivide each major subject area into subareas which you think are of relevance;
4 further divide the subareas into more precise subareas that you think are of relevance;
5 identify those areas that you need to search immediately and those that you particularly need to focus on. Your project tutor will be of particular help here;
6 as your reading and reviewing progress add new areas to your relevance tree.

Worked example

Using a relevance tree

Lily's research question asked 'Is there a link between benchmarking and Total Quality Management?' After brainstorming her question, she decided to construct a relevance chart using the key words and phrases that had been generated:

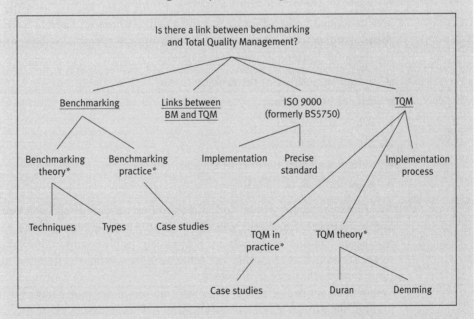

Using her relevance tree Lily identified those areas which she needed to search immediately (<u>underlined</u>) and those which she particularly needed to focus on (starred*).

3.5   Conducting the literature search

Your literature search will probably be conducted using a variety of approaches:

- searching using tertiary literature sources;
- obtaining relevant literature (Section 3.6) referenced in books and journal articles you have already read;
- scanning and browsing secondary literature in your library;
- searching using the Internet.

Eventually you will be using a variety of these in combination. However, we suggest that you start your search by obtaining relevant literature that has been referenced in books and articles you have already read. Although books are unlikely to give adequate up-to-date coverage of your research question they provide a useful starting point and usually contain some references to further reading. Reading these will enable you to refine your research question(s), objectives and the associated key words prior to searching using tertiary literature sources. It will also help you to see more clearly how your research relates to previous research and will provide fresh insights.

Tertiary literature sources

A variety of tertiary literature is available to help you in your search. Most of these publications are called indexes and abstracts and a selection will be accessible via the Internet or held by your university library. An *index* will, as its name suggests, index articles from a range of journals and sometimes books, chapters from books, reports, theses, conferences and research. The information provided will be sufficient to locate the item; for example for journal articles:

- author or authors of the article;
- date of publication;
- title of the article;
- title of the journal;
- volume and part number of the journal issue;
- page numbers of the article.

Most index searches will be undertaken to find articles using key words, including the author's name. Occasionally you may wish to search by finding those authors who have referenced (cited) a key article after it has been published. A *citation index* enables you to do this as it lists by author the other authors who have cited that author's publications subsequent to their publication.

An *abstract* provides the same information as an index but also includes a summary of the article, hence the term abstract. This abstract can be useful in helping you to assess the content and relevance of an article to your research before obtaining a copy. You should beware of using abstracts as a source of information for your research. They only contain a summary of the article and are likely to exclude much of relevance.

Indexes and abstracts are produced in printed and electronic (computerised) formats, the latter often being referred to as *databases*. This is the term we will use to refer to all electronic information sources. With the increasing amount of information available electronically, printed indexes and abstracts may be overlooked. Yet they are still a valuable resource, providing a varied and sometimes more specific range of information. Searching printed sources and databases is normally free, although some libraries may charge for printing from databases. One way round this is to take a computer disk on which to save the results of your search. This can subsequently be read into your word-processing software.

Databases held at other institutions or by publishers can be accessed via a telecommunications link or the Internet from many university libraries. Many of these will be paid for by subscription, but for pay-as-you-use databases the costs of the search may be passed on to the user. *On-line databases* provide a wealth of information and are accessed via a telecommunications link rather than the Internet. They may be updated daily or even several times during one day, an advantage over CD-ROM databases that are usually updated quarterly. It is advisable to obtain a librarian's help or to attend a training session prior to using on-line databases because of the variety of software and the volume of information. It is also vital to have planned and prepared your search in advance so your time is not wasted. With the development of the Internet, many databases can now be accessed using this technology. For some databases, access may be possible from remote sites such as home or work as well as from your university. However, you are likely to need your university's specific username and password. Another source of information via the Internet which our students have found useful is publishers' web pages. These often include journals' content pages (see Table 3.6).

Most university OPACs (library catalogues) are now accessible via the Internet (see Table 3.7). These provide a very useful means of locating resources. If you identify useful collections of books and journals, it is possible to make use of other university libraries in the vacations. The SCONUL Vacation Access Scheme gives details of access policies of the libraries in UK higher-education institutions. Details of these can be found on the Internet at http://www.sconul.ac.uk/vacation.html.

To ensure maximum coverage in your search you need to use all appropriate abstracts and indexes. One mistake many people make is to restrict their searches to one or two business and management tertiary sources rather than to use a variety. The coverage of each abstract and index differs both in geographical coverage and type of journals (Section 3.3). In addition an abstract or index may state that it indexes a particular journal yet may do so only selectively. This emphasises the importance of using a range of databases to ensure a wide coverage of available literature. Some of those more frequently used are outlined in Table 3.3. However, new databases are being developed all the time so it is worth asking a librarian for advice.

Searching using tertiary literature

Once your key words have been identified, searching using tertiary literature is a relatively straightforward process.

Table 3.3 **Tertiary literature sources and their coverage**

Name	Format	Coverage
ABI/Inform	CD-ROM, on-line	Indexes approximately 1000 international business and management journals. Also covers subjects such as engineering, law and medicine. Full text of selected articles from 500 journals may be available depending on subscription (CD-ROM updated monthly)
Anbar	CD-ROM, Internet, print	Abstracts of articles selected from more than 400 English language publications on the basis of a significant contribution to knowledge
BIDS	Internet	Includes access to a wide range of services including citation indexes, journals contents pages
British National Bibliography (BNB)	CD-ROM, print	Bibliographic information for books and serials (journals) deposited at the British Library by UK and Irish publishers since 1950
British National Bibliography for Report Literature (formerly British Reports, Translations and Theses)	Microfiche, print	Detailed listings of research and practice reports produced by non-commercial publishers, local and national government, industry, research institutions and charities. Includes UK doctoral theses since 1970
British Library OPAC '97	Internet	Gives access to British Library catalogues including reference collections and document supply collections (books, journals, reports, conferences, theses)
Business Periodicals Index	CD-ROM, print, on line	Indexes English language business periodicals (articles and book reviews). North American focus. Selection for indexing is by subscriber preference and has altered over time (since 1959)
EMERALD	Internet	80+ full text journals from MCB University Press
European Business	CD-ROM, Internet	100 journals mostly full text. Includes a mix of academic journals and business press
Global Books in Print	CD-ROM	English language bibliographic information for books in print from most of the world!
Helecon	CD-ROM	Combined indexes from seven European databases on business and management. European focus (updated three times a year)
Index to Business Reports	Print	Indexes over 800 business reports published in business journals and newspapers each year (updated half-yearly)

Table 3.3   *Cont.*

Name	Format	Coverage
Index to Conference Proceedings	CD-ROM, on line, print	Indexes all conference publications regardless of subject or language held by British Library Document Supply Centre (updated monthly – print, quarterly – CD-ROM)
Index to Theses	Internet, print	Indexes theses accepted for higher degrees by universities in Great Britain and Ireland and by the CNAA
HMSO Monthly Catalogue	Print	Lists all publications published and distributed through HMSO (includes parliamentary, government department and European)
MINTEL	CD-ROM, Internet	Mintel reports plus short business press articles used in the compilation of the reports
Research Index	Internet, print	Indexes articles and news items of financial interest which appear in the UK national newspapers, professional and trade journals (updated frequently)
Sage Publications/SRM Database of Social Research Methodology	CD-ROM	Abstracts of methodological literature published in English, German, French and Dutch since 1970
Social Science Citation Index	Internet, on line, print	Indexes 130 000 articles each year from over 1400 journals in behavioural and social sciences and selected articles from 3100 journals from physical and natural sciences
Uncover	Internet	Journals contents page service, updated daily

You need:

1 to ensure your key words match the controlled index language (unless you can use free text searching);
2 to search appropriate printed and database sources;
3 to note the full reference of relevant items found.

Printed sources

Searching printed indexes and abstracts requires a different technique to electronic databases. The coverage of printed indexes tends to be smaller and possibly more specialised than databases. Unlike databases, it is normally only possible to search by author or one broad subject heading, although some cross-references may be included. Because they are paper based each issue or annual accumulation must be searched individually, which can be time consuming.

Databases

Most databases, in contrast, allow more precise searches using combinations of key words. These key words need to match the database's *controlled index language* of pre-selected terms and phrases or *descriptors*. If your key words do not match this vocabulary, your search will be unsuccessful. Your first stage should therefore be to check your key words with the *index* or *browse* option. This is especially useful for checking how an author is indexed or whether hyphens should be used when entering terms. Some databases will also have a *thesaurus* which links words in the controlled index language to other terms. Some thesauruses will provide a definition of the term used as well as indicating other broader subject areas, more specific subject areas or subjects related to the original term. Despite using these your searches may still be unsuccessful. The most frequent causes of failure are summarised in Table 3.4 as a checklist.

Table 3.4 **Checklist for key words**

✓	Is the spelling incorrect? Behaviour is spelt with a 'u' in the UK but without in the USA
✓	Is the language incorrect? Chemists in the UK but Drug Stores in the USA
✓	Are you using incorrect terminology? In recent years some terms have been replaced by others, such as redundancy being replaced by downsizing
✓	Are you using acronyms and abbreviations? For example, UK for United Kingdom or ICI instead of Imperial Chemical Industries
✓	Are you using jargon rather than accepted terminology? For example, de-recruitment rather than redundancy
✓	Are you using a word that is not in the controlled index language?

Once individual key words have been checked, subsequent searches normally use a combination of key words linked using *Boolean logic*. This enables you to combine, limit or widen the variety of items found using *link terms* (Table 3.5). Boolean logic can also be used to construct searches using dates, journal titles and names of organisations or people. Initially it may be useful to limit your search to journal titles held by your library or accessible via the Internet. It may also be valuable to narrow your search to specific years, especially if you are finding a wealth of items and need to concentrate on the most up to date. By contrast, searching by author allows you to broaden your search to find other work by known researchers in your area.

You can also just search one or more specified fields in the database such as the author, title or abstract. This may be useful if you wish to find articles by a key author in your subject area. Alternatively, many databases allow you to search the entire database rather than just the controlled vocabulary using *free text searching*. Free text searching is increasingly common for electronic publications both on CD-ROM and accessed via the Internet, in particular broadsheet newspapers and journals. These may not have a controlled index language. There are, however, problems with using a free text search. The context of a key word may be inappropriate, leading to retrieval of irrelevant articles and information overload.

Table 3.5 **Common link terms that use Boolean logic**

Link term	Purpose	Example	Outcome
AND	Narrows search	Recruitment and interviewing and skills	Only articles containing all three key words selected
OR	Widens search	Recruitment or selection	Articles with at least one key word selected
NOT	Excludes terms from search	Recruitment not selection	Selects articles containing the key word recruitment which do not contain the key word selection
* (truncation)	Uses word stems to pick up different words	Motivat*	Selects articles with: Motivate Motivation Motivating
? (wild card)	Picks up different spellings	behavio?r	Selects articles with: Behavior Behaviour

---

Worked example

Searching printed and electronic indexes and abstracts

Matthew described his research project using the key words 'performance related pay' and 'organisational change'. As a technophobe, he decided to use printed indexes rather than electronic databases. He chose the printed versions of *Anbar* and *Business Periodicals Index*. He checked his key words against each of these tertiary sources, and found they matched with *Anbar*. However, for *Business Periodicals Index* he needed to use 'Pay for Performance'. 'Organizational change' used the American spelling, but this did not matter with the printed index. Unfortunately, he encountered problems when carrying out the search:

- there were large numbers of references under each index heading;
- many of the references were not relevant to his research;
- the search terms could not be combined to make his search more specific.

After discussing the problem, the librarian showed Matthew how to use the electronic versions of these printed tertiary sources. Using the databases' indexes, he checked his key words again. It was now crucial that he got the appropriate spelling, such as for 'organizational change'. The link term AND enabled him to combine his key words and to obtain a manageable list of references. Furthermore, he was able to print out the results of the search rather than noting them by hand.

Scanning and browsing

Any search will only find some of the relevant literature. You will therefore also need to scan and browse the literature. New publications such as journals are unlikely to be indexed immediately in tertiary literature so you will need to *browse* these publications to gain an idea of their content. In contrast *scanning* will involve you going through individual items such as a journal article to pick out points which relate to your own research. It is particularly important that you browse and scan trade and professional journals, as these are less likely to be covered by the tertiary literature.

To make browsing and scanning easier you should:

- identify when those journals that are the most relevant are published and regularly browse them;
- browse new book displays in libraries;
- scan new book reviews in journals and newspapers;
- scan publishers' new book catalogues where available;
- discuss your research with your project tutor and librarians who may be aware of other relevant literature.

Internet access to resources now allows you to browse journals that may not be held in or accessible from your university library. Some publishers make the contents pages of their journals available without charge on the web (Table 3.6) and may offer an *article alert* service where they will provide a regular email update of articles in your area of interest. Alternatively databases such as Uncover provide access to thousands of journals contents pages (Table 3.3). Professional journals may also be accessible through the web page of the professional organisation (Table 7.2). Many publishers make their current book catalogues available on the Internet and these can be accessed either directly (Table 3.6) or through the Publishers' catalogues homepage information gateway (see Table 3.7). In addition web sites of book shops such as Amazon, Blackwell and the Internet Book Shop provide access to catalogues of books in print. These can usually be searched, at least by author, title and subject (Table 3.6).

Searching the Internet

The *Internet*, sometimes described as the *information superhighway*, is a world-wide network of computers that can provide access to a vast range of literature and other resources stored on computers around the world. The places where these resources are stored are known as *sites*. The Internet is often referred to as the *world wide web* (WWW), although this is only a method for searching and browsing the Internet. Its popularity is due largely to *hypertext links* whereby pointing and clicking on the screen takes you to a new document and to colour graphics. The number of web sites is impossible to calculate, although the number of documents are said to double every 55 days (BECTA, 1997). Searching these will uncover further material, with which you can compare and contrast your ideas. Some of the resources may be of use either for your literature review or as secondary data (Chapter 7). However, you should beware as

Table 3.6	**Selected publishers' and bookshops' Internet addresses**

Name	Internet address	Contents
Publishers		
Blackwell Publishers	http://www.blackwellpublishers.co.uk	Books and journals
Cambridge University Press	http://www.cup.cam.ac.uk	Books and journals, links to other university presses and publishing related services
Pearson Education Limited	http://www.pearsoneduc.com	Business and management books for practitioners and students
The Stationery Office	http://www.hmso.gov.uk	TSO publications including full text of Statutory Instruments and Public Acts
MCB University Press	http://www.mcb.co.uk	Over 100 professional and academic management journals
Open University Press	http://www.openup.co.uk	Books and journals
Oxford University Press	http://www.oup.co.uk	Books and journals including full text online journals, a database of abstracts
Routledge	http://www.routledge.com	Books
Sage	http://www.sagepub.co.uk	Books, journals, software, CD-ROMs
Book shops		
Amazon	http://www.amazon.co.uk	Searchable database principally of books (UK site)
	http://www.amazon.com	Searchable database principally of books (USA site)
Blackwell	http://www.blackwell.co.uk/bookshops	Searchable database principally of books
Internet Book Shop	http://www.bookshop.co.uk	Searchable database principally of books

NB. All services in this table were free at the time of writing

these resources may be difficult to locate and the quality of the material is highly variable. This is emphasised by Clausen (1996: 4) who likens the Internet to:

> . . . a huge vandalized library where someone has destroyed the catalogue and removed the front matter and indexes from most of the books. In addition thousands of unorganized fragments are added daily by a myriad of cranks, sages and persons with time on their hands who launch their unfiltered messages into cyberspace.

As a student, you are likely to have access to the Internet through your university's or another organisation's computer network. Alternatively, you can connect to the Internet through a service provider using a microcomputer, modem and telephone. Once you have decided to search the Internet, there are a variety of approaches. These are summarised in Fig 3.3. Your first decision is whether to consult one of the many guidebooks. These are invaluable guides for an initial search and often contain copious lists of evaluated resources and addresses of web sites, for example Ellsworth and Ellsworth (1996), Campbell and Campbell (1995) and Branscomb (1998). However, because of the rate at which the Internet is growing and the fact that material can literally disappear overnight, these guidebooks are likely to become out of date extremely quickly.

Home pages

Access to the Internet can be through a home page. The *home page*, which can have multiple linked pages and hypertext links to other web sites, is similar to a title or contents page. Although home pages often contain publicity for a company or institution, they are an excellent way of navigating around the Internet, as they bring a selection of Internet site addresses and search tools together (Table 3.7).

Addresses

Addresses of Internet sites (such as http://www.chelt.ac.uk) can be the quickest and most direct method of accessing these resources. Addresses can be obtained from many sources, the most frequently used of which are guide books (for example: New Riders, 1997), newspaper reviews, articles in journals, librarians and lecturers. A problem with going directly to one address is that your search is constrained by other people's ideas. Similarly, hypertext links are limited by other people's ideas and the way they have linked pages.

Search tools

Search tools, often referred to as *search engines*, are probably the most important method of Internet searching for your literature review as they will enable you to locate most current and up to date items. Although normally accessed through home pages, each search tool will have its own address (Table 3.7).

Most search tools search by key words or subject trees. A *subject tree* is similar to a contents page or index. Some are in the form of alphabetical subject lists while others are in hierarchical groups of subjects which are then further subdivided with links to more narrowly focused subject groups. It is vital that you do not rely on one search tool but use a variety, evaluating each as you use them. Each search tool will have different interfaces, ways of searching and methods of displaying information. They will search different areas of the Internet and are likely to display different results. Search tools are continually being updated with the aim of becoming easier to use.

Search tools can be divided into four distinct categories (Fig 3.3, Table 3.7):

- general search engines;
- meta search engines;
- specialised search engines and information gateways;
- subject directories.

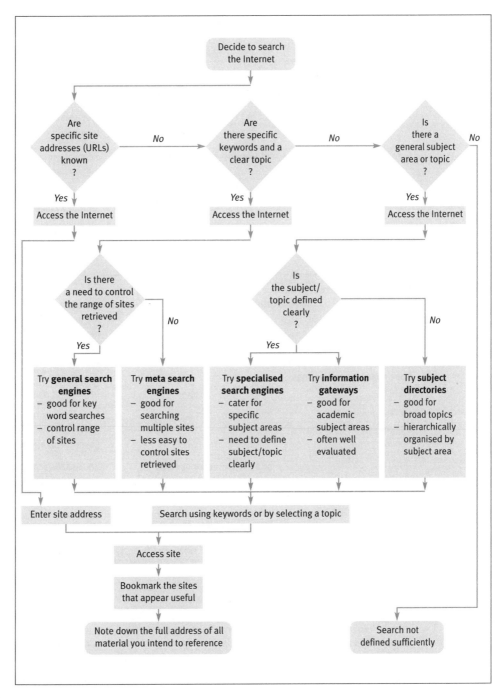

Fig 3.3 **Searching the Internet**
© Mark Saunders, Philip Lewis and Adrian Thornhill, Lynnette Bailey and Martin Jenkins, 2000

Table 3.7   **Selected Internet search tools and their coverage**

Name	Internet address	Comment
General search engines		
Alta Vista Search	http://www.altavista.com	Searches web and Usenet news groups, differentiates between simple and advanced searches and between languages
Euroferret	http://www.muscat.co.uk/ferret	Searches web, has indexed over 30 million European sites
HotBot	http://www.hotbot.com	Searches web, useful features include sorting by date and media type
Lycos	http://www.lycos.com	Searches web, gopher and ftp sites, offers both keyword and subject searching
Meta search engines		
Dogpile	http://www.dogpile.com	Searches a selection of search engines and subject directories including Yahoo, Lyco and Yellow Pages
Specialised search engines		
Bigfoot	http://www.bigfoot.com	Specialises in searching for people
UK Government, CCTA Government Information Service	http://www.open.gov.uk	Searches central and local government web sites and government agencies
Hotel Net	http://www.hotelnet.co.uk	Specialises searches for hotels and self-catering properties
Information gateways		
Biz/Ed	http://www.bized.ac.uk	Information service, links economics and business students and teachers and information providers
BUBL subject tree	http://bubl.ac.uk	Links to a vast range of Internet resources by alphabetical subject list or by class (subject) number order
Human Resource Management Resources on the Internet	http://www.nbs.ntu.ac.uk/staff/l yerj/hrm_link.htm	Annotated list of links. List split into subcategories and provides short description of content
NISS (UK Universities and Colleges OPACs)	http://www.niss.ac.uk/reference/ index.html	Links to UK university and college online public access (library) catalogues (OPACs)
Pinakes	http://www.hw.ac.uk/libWWW/irn/ pinakes/pinakes.html	Links to major information gateways to Internet resources (especially UK based)

Table 3.7	**Cont.**		

Name	Internet address	Comment
Publishers' catalogues homepage	http://www.lights.com/publisher	Links to major publishers' web sites, listed alphabetically by country
SOSIG UK Business and Industrial Management Resources	http://www.sosig.ac.uk:80/roads/ subject-listing/UK/indman.html	Detailed descriptions and links to UK business and industrial management sites
Subject directories		
Argus Clearinghouse	http://www.clearinghouse.net	Indexes specialised directories
Yahoo	http://www.yahoo.com	Subject-based directory
Yahoo UK	http://www.yahoo.co.uk	Brings the option of limiting searches to just Great Britain and Ireland
	http://dir.yahoo.com/News_and_ Media/Newspapers	Comprehensive listing of newspapers available on the Internet, world-wide
Yellow Pages UK	http://www.yell.co.uk	Telephone yellow pages with useful links to UK companies' home pages

General search engines normally search parts of the Internet using key words and Boolean logic (Table 3.5) or a phrase. Each search engine uses an automated computer process to index and search, often resulting in a very large number of sites being found. As these sites have not been evaluated by people, many are usually inappropriate or unreliable. As no two general search engines search in precisely the same way it is advisable (and often necessary) to use more than one. In contrast, *meta search engines* allow you to search using a selection of search engines at the same time, using the same interface. This makes searching easier, and the search can be faster. Unfortunately, it is less easy to control the sites that are retrieved. Consequently, meta search engines often generate more inappropriate or unreliable sites than general search engines.

Specialised search engines cater for specific subject areas. To use these it is necessary to define your general subject area prior to your search. *Information gateways* also require you to define your subject area. Information gateways are often compiled by staff from departments in academic institutions. Although the number of web sites obtained is fewer, they can be far more relevant, as each site is evaluated prior to being added to the gateway.

Subject directories are hierarchically organised indexes categorised into subject areas and are useful for searching for broad topics. As people normally compile them, their content has been partly censored and evaluated. Consequently, the number of sites retrieved is fewer but they usually provide material that is more appropriate. Most of the subject directories now offer some form of key words search and links to other search tools.

Search tools are becoming more prolific and sophisticated all the time. Be careful: their use can be extremely time consuming. Your search will probably locate a mass of resources, many of which will be irrelevant to you. It is also easy to become sidetracked to more interesting and glossy web sites not relevant to your research needs!

Bookmarking

Once you have found a useful Internet site, you need to note its address electronically. This process is termed *bookmarking* or *add to favourites* depending on your Internet software. It uses the software to note the Internet address and means that you will be able to access it again directly. The vast amount of resources available and the fact that resources, home pages and sites can be added and deleted by their producers means it is vital to keep a record of the addresses (Section 3.7). These will be needed to reference your sources when you write your critical review (Section 3.2). When sufficient sites have been bookmarked, it is possible to arrange them in whatever hierarchical way you wish.

3.6   Obtaining and evaluating the literature

Obtaining the literature

After your initial search of books and journal articles tertiary literature will provide you with details of what literature is available and where to locate it. The next stage (Fig 3.1) is to obtain these items. To do this you need:

1   to check your library catalogue to find out whether your library holds the appropriate publication. Remember many libraries now hold publications such as journals and newspapers in electronic form on CD-ROM or provide access via the Internet;

2   (for those publications that are held by your library or available via the Internet) to note their location:

    a   locate the publication and scan it to discover if it is likely to be worth reading thoroughly;

    b   browse other books and journals with similar class marks to see whether they may also be of use;

3   (for those items that are not held by your library or available via the Internet) to order the item from another library on *inter-library loan*. As Bell (1999) points out this is not a free service so make sure you really need it first. Our students have found that, in general, it is only worthwhile to inter-library loan articles from refereed journals and books.

Evaluating the literature

Two questions frequently asked by our students are 'how do I know what I'm reading is relevant?' and 'how do I know when I've read enough?' Both of these are concerned with the process of evaluation. They involve defining the scope of your review and assessing the value of the items that you have obtained in helping you to answer your research question(s). Although there are no set ways of approaching these questions our students have found the following advice helpful.

You should, of course, read all the literature that is closely related to your research question(s) and objectives. The literature that is most likely to cause problems is that which is less closely related (Gall *et al.*, 1996). For some research questions, particularly for new research areas, there is unlikely to be much closely related literature and so you will have to review more broadly. For research questions where research has been going on for some years you may be able to focus on more closely related literature.

Assessing relevance

Assessing the relevance of the literature you have collected to your research depends on your research question(s) and objectives. Remember that you are looking for relevance, not critically assessing the ideas contained within. Table 3.8 provides a checklist to help you in this process.

Remember to make notes about the relevance of each item as you read it and the reasons you came to your conclusion. You may need to include your evaluation as part of your critical review.

Table 3.8	**Checklist for evaluating the relevance of literature**

✓ How recent is the item?

✓ Is the item likely to have been superseded?

✓ Is the context sufficiently different to make it marginal to your research question(s) and objectives?

✓ Have you seen references to this item (or its author) in other items that were useful?

✓ Does the item support or contradict your arguments? For either it will probably be worth reading!

✓ Does the item appear to be biased? Even if it is it may still be relevant to your critical review

✓ What are the methodological omissions within the work? Even if there are many it still may be of relevance!

✓ Is the precision sufficient? Even if it is imprecise it may be the only item you can find and so still of relevance!

Sources: Authors' experience; Bell, 1999; Jankowicz, 1995; McNeill, 1990

Assessing sufficiency

Your assessment of whether you have read a sufficient amount is even more complex. It is impossible to read everything as you would never start to write your critical review, let alone your project report. Yet you need to be sure that your critical review discusses what research has already been undertaken and that you have positioned your research project in the wider context, citing the main writers in the field (Section 3.2). One clue that you have achieved this is when further searching provides mainly references to items you have already read. You also need to check what constitutes an acceptable amount of reading, in terms of both quality and quantity, with your project tutor.

Evaluating sites found by an Internet search

Eline's research question was reasonably defined, if somewhat broad. She wanted to assess the impact of the Euro on organisations. She decided to search the Internet using a general search engine. Her first key word 'Euro' revealed that there were over 200 000 sites and displayed the first ten, ranked in order of relevance. Of these, two appeared marginally relevant, the remainder having nothing to do with European Monetary Union. She decided to refine her search using the key word 'European Monetary Union'. Although the search engine found over 300 000 sites, the content of the first ten appeared more relevant to her research question.

Among these were:

3. **European Monetary Union and Canada**
[URL: http://www.cfp-pec.gc.ca/english/emu.htm]
European Monetary Union and Canada: Implications for Trade and
Last modified 29-Jul-1998 -Size 246K - in English [Translate]

5. **European Monetary Union - Economic Assessment - Implementation in the Companies**
[**URL**: http://www.euro.fee.be/Library/De/DEC072502a.htm]
Verband der Chemishen Industrie e.V. (Association of the Germ
Last modified 25-Feb-1998 Size 68K - in English [Translate]

6. **European Monetary Union Consultancy IBM**
[**URL**: http://www.europe.ibm.com/euro/european_monetary_
union_consultancy_bw.html]
European Monetary Union provided by IBM
Last modified 08-Apr-1998 - Size 1K - in English [Translate]

Eline looked at all these sites. At first glance number 5, 'European Monetary Union – Economic Assessment – Implementation in the Companies', appeared particularly relevant and recent, having been last modified on 25 February 1998. However, on accessing the site Eline found that the document had been written in May 1995 by the Association of the German Chemical Industry and was therefore representing their views. Thus, although it was still relevant it was not as recent as had first been thought and offered the views of an industrial association from one country.

By contrast number 3, 'European Monetary Union and Canada', appeared less relevant from the brief description. Despite this, Eline decided to access the site and found that it held the full text of an article based on a survey of Canadian companies written by an academic at St Mary's University, Halifax, Nova Scotia, in July 1997. One Section of the article discussed the impact of

European Monetary Union on these companies. The article also had a long list of recent references. She decided to print a copy of the article and to assess the ideas critically in more detail.

When Eline accessed number 6, 'European Monetary Union Consultancy IBM', she discovered that it was concerned primarily with consultancy services offered by IBM in relation to the Euro. She decided to bookmark this site just in case it was relevant, once she had refined her research question more precisely.

Eline visited the next 40 sites that had been listed by the search engine. After this, she noted that the sites were becoming, at best, marginally relevant. She therefore decided to ignore the remaining sites and to narrow her search using the refine feature of the search engine.

3.7 Recording the literature

The literature search, as you will now be aware, is a vital part of your research project, in which you will invest a great deal of time and effort. As you read each item, you need to ask yourself how it contributes to your research question(s) and objectives and to make *notes* with this focus (Bell, 1999). When doing this many students photocopy articles and pages from books to ensure that they have all the material. We believe that, even if you photocopy, you still need to make notes. The process of note making will help you to think through the ideas in the literature in relation to your research.

In addition to making notes Sharp and Howard (1996) identify three sets of information you need to record. These are:

- bibliographic details;
- brief summary of content;
- supplementary information.

Until the advent of inexpensive micro computers, it was usual to write this information on to *index cards*. Database software such as 'Access' or specialist bibliographic software such as 'Reference Manager for Windows' provide a powerful and flexible alternative method for recording the literature, although they will probably mean noting it down and later transferring it to your database. Recording can seem very tedious, but it must be done. We have seen many students frantically repeating searches for items that are crucial to their research because they failed to record all the necessary details, either in their database of references or on index cards.

Bibliographic details

For some project reports, you will be required to include a *bibliography*. Convention dictates that this should include all the relevant items you consulted for your project including those not referred to directly in the text. For others, you will only be asked to include a list of *references* for those items referred to directly in the text. The *bibliographic details* contained in both need to be sufficient to enable readers to find the original items. These are summarised in Table 3.9.

Table 3.9 **Bibliographic details required**

Journal	Book	Chapter in an edited book
■ Author(s) – surname, first name initials	■ Author(s) – surname, first name initials	■ Author(s) – surname, first name initials
■ Year of publication (in parentheses)	■ Year of publication (in parentheses)	■ Year of publication (in parentheses)
■ Title of article	■ Title and subtitle of book (underlined)	■ Title of chapter
■ Title of journal (underlined)	■ Edition	■ Author(s) of book – surname, first name initials
■ Volume	■ Place of publication	■ Title and subtitle of book (underlined)
■ Part/issue	■ Publisher	■ Edition
■ Page numbers (preceded by 'p.' for page or 'pp.' for pages)		■ Place of publication
		■ Publisher
		■ Page numbers of chapter

Table 3.10 **Supplementary information**

Information	Reason
ISBN	The identifier for any book and useful if the book has to be requested on inter-library loan
Class (Dewy decimal) number	Useful to locate books in your university's library and as a pointer to finding other books on the same subject
Quotations	Always note useful quotations in full and with the page number of the quote; if possible also take a photocopy
Where it was found	Noting where you found the item is useful especially if it is not in your university library and you could only take notes
The tertiary resource used	Useful to help identify resources for follow-up searches
Evaluative comments	Your personal notes on the value of the item to your research (Table 3.8 will help here)
When the item was consulted	Especially important for items found via the Internet as these may disappear without trace

If an item has been taken from an electronic source you need to record as much of the information in Table 3.9 as is available along with details of format (e.g. CD-ROM). If you located the item via the Internet you need to record the full address of the resource and the date you accessed the information as well (Appendix 2). This address is often referred to as the *URL* or *unique resource location*.

Most universities have a preferred *referencing style* that you must use in your project report. This will normally be prescribed in your assessment criteria. Two of the most common styles are the *Harvard system* (which we have used in this book) and the *Vancouver* or *footnotes system*. Guidelines on using these are given in Appendix 2.

Brief summary

A brief summary of the content of each item on your index card or in your reference database will help you to locate the relevant items and facilitate reference to your notes and photocopies. This can be done by annotating each record with the key words used to locate the item and the abstract. It will also help you to maintain consistency in your searches.

Supplementary information

As well as recording the details discussed earlier, other information may also be worth recording. These items can be anything you feel will be of value. In Table 3.10 we outline those that we have found most useful.

3.8 ## Summary

- A critical review of the literature is necessary to help you to develop a thorough understanding of and insight into previous research that relates to your research question(s) and objectives. Your review will set your research in context by critically discussing and referencing work that has already been undertaken, drawing out key points and presenting them in a logically argued way and highlighting those areas where you will provide fresh insights. It will lead the reader into subsequent sections of your project report.

- There is no one correct structure for a critical review, although it is helpful to think of it as a funnel in which you start at a more general level prior to narrowing down to your specific research question(s) and objectives.

- Literature sources can be divided into three categories: primary, secondary and tertiary. In reality, these categories often overlap. Your use of these resources will depend on your research question(s) and objectives. Some may use only tertiary and secondary literature. For others, you may need to locate primary literature as well.

- When planning your literature search you need:
  - to have clearly defined research question(s) and objectives;
  - to define the parameters of your search;
  - to generate key words and search terms;
  - to discuss your ideas as widely as possible.

  Techniques to help you in this include brainstorming and relevance trees.

- Your literature search will be undertaken using a variety of approaches in tandem. These will include:

  – searching using tertiary sources and the Internet;
  – following up references in articles you have already read;
  – scanning and browsing secondary literature in your library.

- Once obtained, the literature must be evaluated for its relevance to your research question(s) and objectives. This must include a consideration of each item's currency. Each item must be read and noted. Bibliographic details, a brief description of the content and appropriate supplementary information should also be recorded.

Self check Questions

3.1 The following extract and associated references are taken from the first draft of a critical literature review. The research project was concerned with the impact of direct insurers on the traditional motor insurer.

List the problems with this extract in terms of its:

a content;

b structure.

> Jackson (1995) suggests that businesses must be developed from a customer rather than a product perspective. Lindesfarne (1995) demonstrates that direct selling gives the consumer increased control as it is up to them when and if they wish to respond to adverts or direct mail. MacKenzie (1995) comments that free gifts are useful for getting responses to adverts which is ultimately what all direct insurers need. Bowen (1995) suggests that this type of company can be split into three equally important parts: marketing, insurance and information technology. Motor insurance is particularly price sensitive because of its compulsory nature and its perception by many to have no real 'value' to themselves.
>
> Bowen I (1994) Short Cut To Success *Post Magazine* 2nd July 26
>
> Jackson DR (1995) Prudential's Prudent Parochialism *Direct Marketing* April 26–29
>
> Lindisfarne I (1995) Death Of A Salesman *Post Magazine* 15th June 30–31
>
> MacKenzie G (1995) Rise Of The Freebie *Post Magazine* 2nd February 56

3.2 Outline the advice you would give a colleague on:
a how to plan her search
b which literature to search first.

3.3 Brainstorm at least one of the following research questions, either on your own or with a colleague, and list the key words that you have generated.
a How effective is profit related pay as a motivator?

b How do the opportunities available to a first time house buyer through inter-personal discussion influence the process of selecting a financial institution for the purposes of applying for a house purchase loan?

c To what extent do new methods of direct selling of financial services pose a threat to existing providers?

3.4 You are having considerable problems with finding relevant material for your research when searching databases. Suggest possible reasons why this might be so.

3.5 Rewrite the following passage as part of a critical literature review using the Harvard system of referencing:

> Most of the writers[1] I've read on the European Union's future employment needs reckon that there's going to be an increase in the need for highly qualified employees. Yet the European Commission[2] have worked out that there's going to be fewer of these people about due to technological and economic changes and because there are fewer people are entering the labour market. Now that we're all in one 'single European market' these problems are likely to get even worse as some countries have a far higher demand for such people than they can supply internally.[3]
>
> [1] for example: Atkinson J (1989) Corporate Employment Policies for the Single European Market *IMS Report No 179* Sussex, Institute of Manpower Studies; Pearson R & Pike G (1989) The Graduate Labour Market in the 1990s *IMS Report No. 167* Sussex, Institute of Manpower Studies; Werner H (1990) Free movement of labour in the Single European Market *Intereconomics* 25.2 77–81
>
> [2] Commission of the European Communities (1991) *Employment in Europe* COM (89)339
>
> [3] Walwei U and Werner H (1993) Europeanising the Labour Market: Employee Mobility and Company Recruiting Methods *Intereconomics* Feb. 3–10

Assignment 3

Critically reviewing the literature

→ Consider your research questions and objectives. Use your lecture notes, course textbooks and relevant review articles to define both narrow and broader parameters of your literature search considering language, subject area, business sector, geographical area, publication period and literature type.

→ Generate key words and search terms using one or a variety of techniques such as reading, brainstorming and relevance trees. Discuss your ideas widely, including with your project tutor and colleagues.

→ Start your search using both database and printed tertiary sources to identify relevant secondary literature. Begin with those tertiary sources that abstract and index academic journal articles and books. At the same time, obtain relevant literature that has been referenced in articles you have already read.

→ Expand your search via other sources such as the Internet and by browsing and scanning.

→ Obtain copies of relevant items, read them and make notes. Remember also to record bibliographic details, a brief description of the content and supplementary information on an index card or in your reference database.

→ Start drafting your critical review as early as possible keeping in mind its purpose.

→ Continue to search the literature throughout your research project to ensure that your review remains up to date.

References

BECTA (1997) 'Information sheet on Internet searching' (online) (cited 1 January 1999). Available from <URL:http://www.becta.org.uk/info-sheets/intsearch.html>.

Bell, J. (1999) *Doing Your Research Project* (3rd edn), Buckingham, Open University Press.

Branscomb, H.E. (1998) *Casting Your Net: a Student's Guide to Research on the Internet,* Boston, MA, Allyn and Bacon.

Campbell, D. and Campbell, M. (1995) *The Students' Guide to Doing Research on the Internet,* Reading, MA, Addison-Wesley.

Clausen, H. (1996) 'Web information quality as seen from libraries', *New Library World* 97: 1130, 4–8.

Easterby-Smith, M., Thorpe, R. and Lowe, A. (1991) *Management Research: an Introduction,* London, Sage.

Ellsworth, J.H. and Ellsworth, M.V. (1996) *The New Internet Business Book* (2nd edn), New York, Wiley.

Gall, M.D., Borg, W.R. and Gall, J.P. (1996) *Educational Research: An Introduction* (6th edn), New York, Longman.

Gill, J. and Johnson, P. (1997) *Research Methods for Managers* (2nd edn), London, Paul Chapman.

Haythornthwaite, J. (ed.) (1990) *The Business Information Maze: an Essential Guide,* London, ASLIB.

Haywood, P. and Wragg, E.C. (1982) *Evaluating the Literature: Rediguide 2,* University of Nottingham School of Education, Nottingham.

Higgins, R. (1996) *Approaches to Research: a Handbook for Those Writing a Dissertation,* London, Jessica Kingsley.

Jankowicz, A.D. (1995) *Business Research Projects* (2nd edn), London, Chapman & Hall.

McNeill, P. (1990) *Research Methods* (2nd edn), London, Routledge.

New Riders (1997) *New Riders Official Internet Directory* (revised edn), Indianapolis, IN, New Rider Publishing.

Saunders, M.N.K. (1993) 'Vacancy notification and employee mobility', *International Journal of Manpower,* 14:6, 39–57.

Sharp, J.A. and Howard, K. (1996) *The Management of a Student Research Project* (2nd edn), Aldershot, Gower.

Stewart, D.W. and Kamins, M.A. (1993) *Secondary Research: Information Sources and Methods* (2nd edn), Newbury Park, CA, Sage.

Strauss, A. and Corbin, J. (1990) *Basics of Qualitative Research,* Newbury Park, CA, Sage.

Further reading

Bell, J. (1999) *Doing Your Research Project* (3rd edn), Buckingham, Open University Press. Chapter 6 provides a good introduction to the process of reviewing the literature. The section on the critical review of the literature is especially helpful.

Branscomb, H.E. (1998) *Casting Your Net: a Student's Guide to Research on the Internet,* Boston, MA, Allyn and Bacon. This book contains a wealth of fascinating information on the Internet. However, by the time you read this book a substantial proportion will have probably changed so look for a more recent edition!

Jankowicz, A.D. (1995) *Business Research Projects* (2nd edn), London, Chapman & Hall. Chapter 8 provides a good discussion of reviewing and using the literature for business research projects.

Sharp, J.A. and Howard, K. (1996) *The Management of a Student Research Project* (2nd edn), Aldershot, Gower. Chapter 4 contains a useful in-depth discussion of the use of relevance trees in your literature search.

Case 3	**The development of discount warehouse clubs**

Jane was keen to start her research project early. She had decided on her dissertation topic – the development of discount warehouse clubs in the UK. She spent two days each week in the library over the vacation reading and noting all the articles she could find and wrote her literature review. In order to give her project tutor plenty of time to read the draft she sent it to him a week before the tutorial.

Jane arrived at her tutorial looking forward to her tutor's praise. 'Well Jane, you've obviously worked over the summer, but there's still a great deal of reading to be done . . .' Jane was crestfallen as her tutor explained the problems with her literature review. Every article was taken either from a trade magazine or from a newspaper and there was not a single mention of any academic underpinning. The review consisted almost entirely of quotations from the articles, a couple of paragraphs being devoted to each article. Although the ideas contained in the articles were summarised they were not ordered in any logical manner and the purpose was unclear.

'Why didn't you use the Internet abstract and indexes such as *Anbar*?' asked her tutor. 'I did . . .' Jane replied, '. . . but there's nothing written on the development of discount warehouse clubs in the UK.' After considerable discussion about how to search the literature and the purpose of the literature review in her project report Jane went away feeling happier. She now knew that quotations should only be used sparingly in her review. The literature she had discovered in the trade magazines was still likely to be useful. Of most importance she liked her tutor's suggestion of placing her research in the context of the spread of retailing innovation and, in particular, how innovations crossed from North America to the UK.

Over the next few months Jane diligently searched the tertiary literature and found lots of relevant items. Articles in the university library were noted. Those not available from the university library were obtained using inter-library loan. Appropriate sections from books on retailing innovation were photocopied. By February, she had two lever-arch files full of information.

Jane began to re-draft her literature review. This time she was determined to write a critical review. She made sure that her arguments flowed and that the review was focused on the transfer of retail innovations from North America to the UK. The work of different authors was clearly referenced. This time she included only two quotations, which she felt added significantly to her argument. She completed her draft, left it for a week, read it again and made further amendments. She was now ready to show it to her project tutor again.

This time Jane's project tutor seemed far more pleased. She suggested a few areas where points needed further explanation or justification, but that was all. Just as

▶

Jane was leaving she asked, 'You've got all the references together for your bibliography haven't you?' Jane responded that she was going to do that next weekend and that she had noted them all down on the items as she was collecting them.

That weekend Jane sat down at her word processor to type in her bibliography. She checked the format in the project assessment criteria and discovered that she should use the Harvard system. Working through her files she entered all the items she had read in alphabetical order, including those not directly referenced in the text. Unfortunately, she discovered three journal articles where the page numbers had been missed off by the photocopier when she had copied them. She decided to sort these out on Monday morning.

On Monday morning, the library was packed and all microcomputers with Internet access were booked solid until 8 p.m. As no machines were available Jane booked one for 8 p.m. to 9 p.m. and went to the canteen. Over her coffee, she tried to remember which databases and key words she had used for her searches. At 8 p.m., she started to recreate her searches using the *Anbar* online database. Within 20 minutes, she had found two of the three missing sets of page numbers. The third journal article did not appear to be indexed in *Anbar*. Then she remembered that she had also used *GeoAbstracts* so accessed that database and recreated her search again. Within a few minutes, she had found the missing page numbers.

In the following months Jane browsed both the current periodicals section of the library and the lists provided by Uncover on the Internet. As relevant material was published she incorporated it into her literature review. Later that year she submitted her research project. It received a good upper second class mark.

Questions

1 How might Jane have overcome the problems of only finding relevant articles in trade journals and newspapers?

2 Why did Jane type all the items she had in her files into her word processor rather than just those she had referred to directly in the text?

3 What lessons can you learn from Jane's experience?

Self check **Answers**

3.1 There are numerous problems with the content and structure of this extract. Some of the more obvious include:

   a The content consists of predominantly trade magazines, in particular *Post Magazine* and there are no references of academic substance. Some of the references to individual authors have discrepancies, for example was the article by Lindisfarne (or is it Lindesfarne?) published in 1994 or 1995?

   b The items referenced are from 1994 and 1995. It is likely that more recent items are available.

   c There is no real structure or argument in the extract. The extract is a list of what people have written with no attempt to critically evaluate or juxtapose the ideas.

3.2 This is a difficult one without knowing her research question! However, you could still advise him or her on the general principles. Your advice will probably include:

a Define the parameters of the research considering language, subject area, business sector, geographical area, publication period and literature type. Generate key words and search terms using one or a variety of techniques such as reading, brainstorming or relevance trees. Discuss his or her ideas as widely as possible including with tutor, librarians and you.

b Start the search using tertiary sources to identify relevant secondary literature. He or she should commence with those tertiary sources that abstract and index academic journal articles and books. At the same time he/she should obtain relevant literature that has been referenced in articles that he or she has already read.

3.3 There are no incorrect answers with brainstorming! However, you might like to check your key words, suitability prior to using them to search an appropriate database. We suggest that you follow the approach outlined in Section 3.5 under 'searching using the tertiary literature'.

3.4 There are a variety of possible reasons including:

● one or more of the parameters of your search are defined too narrowly;

● the key words you have chosen do not appear in the controlled index language;

● your spelling of the key word is incorrect;

● the terminology you are using is incorrect;

● the acronyms you have chosen are not used by database;

● you are using jargon rather than accepted terminology.

3.5 There are two parts to this answer: rewriting the text and using the Harvard system of referencing. Your text will inevitably differ from the answer given below due to your personal writing style. Don't worry about this too much as it is discussed in far more detail in Chapter 13.5. The references should follow the same format.

> The vast majority of writers on the European Union's (EU) future employment needs emphasise a growth in the requirements for highly qualified, specialist employees (Atkinson 1989, Pearson and Pike 1989, Werner 1990). Such employees are forecast to become a scarce resource within the EU, due to technological change, the decline in young people entering the labour market and predictions that the economic climate will improve in the latter half of the 1990s (Commission of the European Communities 1991). The completion of the Single European Market has magnified these problems. Demand for highly qualified labour in some states is forecast to be greater than supply, whereas in others the converse will be true (Walwei and Werner 1993).
>
> Atkinson J (1989) Corporate Employment Policies for the Single European Market *IMS Report No 179* Sussex, Institute of Manpower Studies
>
> Commission of the European Communities (1991) *Employment in Europe* COM (89)339
>
> Pearson R & Pike G (1989) The Graduate Labour Market in the 1990s *IMS Report No. 167* Sussex, Institute of Manpower Studies
>
> Walwei U and Werner H (1993) Europeanising the Labour Market: Employee Mobility and Company Recruiting Methods *Intereconomics* Feb. pp. 3–10
>
> Werner H (1990) Free movement of labour in the Single European Market *Intereconomics* 25.2 pp. 77–81

4 Deciding on the research approach and choosing a research strategy

By the end of this chapter you should be able:

■ to distinguish between two main approaches to research: deductive and inductive;

■ to identify the main research strategies and to explain why these should not be thought of as mutually exclusive;

■ to explain the benefits of adopting a multi-method approach to the conduct of research;

■ to explain the concepts of validity and reliability and to identify the main threats to validity and reliability;

■ to understand some of the main ethical issues implied by the choice of research strategy.

4.1 Differing approaches to research

Much of this book is concerned with the way in which you collect data to answer your research question. You are not unusual if you begin thinking about your research methodology by considering whether you should, for example, administer a questionnaire or conduct interviews. However, thoughts on this question belong in the centre of the research 'onion' by which means we have chosen to depict the issues underlying the choice of data collection methods in Fig 4.1. Before coming to this central point we argue that there are important layers of the onion that need to be peeled away.

The first of these layers raises the question of the research philosophy you adopt. The second considers the subject of your research approach that flows from that research philosophy. Thirdly, we examine what we call the research strategy and the fourth layer refers to the time horizons you apply to your research. The fifth layer, data collection methods, is dealt with in Chapters 6–10.

Research philosophy

Your research philosophy depends on the way that you think about the development of knowledge. This seems rather profound, and not something about which you would normally give much thought. Yet the way we think about the development of knowledge affects, albeit unwittingly, the way we go about doing research. Two views about the research process dominate the literature: *positivism* and *phenomenology*. They are different, if not mutually exclusive, views about the way in which knowledge is developed and both have an important part to play in business and management research.

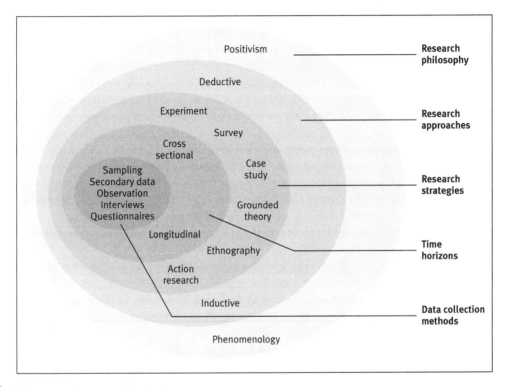

Fig 4.1 **The research process 'onion'**

© Mark Saunders, Philip Lewis and Adrian Thornhill, 2000

Positivism

If your research philosophy reflects the principles of positivism then you will probably adopt the philosophical stance of the natural scientist. You will prefer 'working with an observable social reality and that the end product of such research can be law-like generalisations similar to those produced by the physical and natural scientists' (Remenyi *et al.*, 1998:32). The researcher in this tradition assumes the role of an objective analyst, coolly making detached interpretations about those data that have been collected in an apparently value-free manner. There will be an emphasis on a highly structured methodology to facilitate replication (Gill and Johnson, 1997) and quantifiable observations that lend themselves to statistical analysis. The assumption is that 'the researcher is independent of and neither affects nor is affected by the subject of the research' (Remenyi *et al.*, 1998:33).

Phenomenology

You may be critical of the positivist tradition and argue that the social world of business and management is far too complex to lend itself to theorising by definite 'laws' in the same way as the physical sciences. Those researchers critical of positivism argue that rich insights into this complex world are lost if such complexity is reduced entirely to a series of law-like generalisations. If you sympathise with such a view your research philosophy is likely to be nearer to that of the phenomenologist.

This line of argument is persuasive in the case of business and management research. Not only are business situations complex, they are unique. They are a function of a particular set of circumstances and individuals. This immediately raises questions about the generalisability of research that aims to capture the rich complexity of social situations. However, the phenomenologist would argue that generalisability is not of crucial importance. We are constantly being told of the ever-changing world of business organisations. If we accept that the circumstances of today may not apply in three months time then some of value of generalisation is lost. Similarly, if we accept that all organisations are unique, that too renders generalisation less valuable.

However, perhaps the strongest argument the phenomenologist could mount is the necessity to discover what Remenyi *et al.* (1998:35) call 'the details of the situation to understand the reality or perhaps a reality working behind them'. Perhaps the clearest examples here are in the world of organisational behaviour. Organisational culture provides an illustration.

Schein (1992) talks of organisational culture as operating at three levels. Level one is visible symbols of what the organisation is like, such as open plan offices. Level two is espoused values such as may be found in mission statements. However, Schein argues that uncovering a third level is really necessary to understand a culture and to comprehend more completely values and behaviour. This involves discovering the underlying assumptions of which group members are often unaware but which usually influence strongly how they perceive, think and feel about issues. The phenomenologist would argue that only research methods rooted in the philosophy of phenomenology offer the opportunity of discovering this vital third level: 'the reality working behind the reality'.

It would be easy to fall into the trap of thinking that one research approach is 'better' than another. This would miss the point. They are 'better' at doing different things. As always, which is 'better' depends on the research question(s) you are seeking to answer. Of course, the practical reality is that research rarely falls neatly into the positivist and phenomenological camps as suggested in the 'onion' (Fig 4.1). Business and management research is often a mixture between the two. Indeed, later in this chapter we will be encouraging you to think in a more flexible way about the research approach and methods you adopt.

You may ask what practical use is an understanding of your philosophical position. Is it not as much use as the outer layer on a real onion, which is cast aside, with only the inner layers retained? We think that it is of practical benefit to understand the taken-for-granted assumptions that we all have about the way the world works. Only if we have such an understanding can we examine these assumptions, challenge them if we think it appropriate, and behave in a different way.

Choosing a research approach

Section 2.4 notes that your research project will involve the use of theory. That theory may or may not be made explicit in the design of the research, although it will usually be made explicit in your presentation of the findings and conclusions. The extent to which you are clear about the theory at the beginning of your research raises an important question concerning the design of your research project. This is whether your research should use the *deductive* approach, where you develop a theory and hypothesis (or hypotheses) and design a research strategy to test the hypothesis, or the *inductive* approach, where you would collect data and develop theory as a result of your data analysis. Insofar as it is useful to attach these approaches to the different research philosophies, the deductive approach owes more to positivism and the inductive approach to phenomenology, although we believe that such labelling is potentially misleading and of no practical value.

The next two sections of this chapter explain the differences between these two approaches and the implications of these differences.

Deduction: testing theory

As noted earlier, this approach to research owes much to what we would think of as *scientific* research. It involves the development of a theory that is subjected to a rigorous test. As such, it is the dominant research approach in the natural sciences where 'laws provide the basis of explanation, permit the anticipation of phenomena, predict their occurrence and therefore allow them to be controlled' (Hussey and Hussey, 1997:52).

Robson (1993:19) lists five sequential stages through which deductive research will progress:

1 Deducing a *hypothesis* (a testable proposition about the relationship between two or more events or concepts) from the theory.
2 Expressing the hypothesis in operational terms (i.e. ones indicating exactly how the variables are to be measured) which propose a relationship between two specific variables.
3 Testing this operational hypothesis. This will involve an experiment or some other form of empirical inquiry.
4 Examining the specific outcome of the inquiry. It will either tend to confirm the theory or indicate the need for its modification.
5 If necessary, modifying the theory in the light of the findings. An attempt is then made to verify the revised theory by going back to the first step and repeating the whole cycle.

There are several important characteristics of the deductive approach. First, there is the search to explain causal relationships between variables. It may be that you wish to establish the reasons for high employee absenteeism in a retail DIY store. After studying absence patterns it occurs to you that there seems to be a relationship between absence, the age of workers and length of service. Consequently you develop a hypothesis which states that absenteeism is more likely to be prevalent among younger workers who have worked for the organisation for a relatively short period of time. To test this hypothesis you utilise another characteristic, the collection of quantitative data. (This is not to say that deductive research may not use qualitative data.) It may be that there are important differences in the way work is arranged in different stores; therefore you would need to employ a further important characteristic of the deductive approach, *controls to allow the testing of hypotheses*. These controls would help to ensure that any change in absenteeism was a function of worker age and length of service rather than any other aspect of the store, for example the way in which people were managed. Your research would use a *highly structured methodology* to facilitate replication (Gill and Johnson, 1997), an important issue to ensure reliability, as we will emphasise in Section 4.4.

In order to pursue the principle of scientific rigour, the deductive approach dictates that the researcher should be independent of what is being observed. This is easy in our example because it only involves the collection of absence data. It is also unproblematic if a postal survey is being conducted, although the high level of objectivity this suggests appears less convincing when one considers the element of subjectivity in the choice of questions and the way these are phrased.

An additional important characteristic of deduction is that concepts need to be *operationalised* in a way that enables facts to be measured quantitatively. In our example above, the obvious one is absenteeism. Just what constitutes absenteeism would have to be strictly defined: an absence for a complete day would probably count, but what about absence for two hours? In addition, what would constitute a 'short period of employment' and 'younger' employees? What is happening here is that the principle of *reductionism* is being followed. This holds that problems as a whole are better understood if they are reduced to the simplest possible elements.

The final characteristic of the deductive approach is *generalisation*. In order to be able to generalise about regularities in human social behaviour it is necessary to select samples of sufficient numerical size. In our example above, research at a particular store would only allow us to make inferences about that store; it would be dangerous to predict that worker youth and short length of service lead to absenteeism in all cases.

Induction: building theory

An alternative approach to conducting research on DIY store employee absenteeism would be to go on to the shop floor and interview a sample of the employees and their supervisors about the experience of working at the store. The purpose here would be to get a feel of what was going on, so as to understand better the nature of the problem. Your task then would be to make sense of the interview data you had collected by analysing those data. The result of this analysis would be the formulation of a theory. This may be that there is a relationship between absence and relatively short periods of employment. Alternatively, you may discover that there are other competing reasons for absence that may or may not be related to worker age or length of service. You may end up with the same theory, but you would have gone about the production of that theory in an *inductive* way: theory would follow data rather than vice versa as in the deductive approach.

We noted earlier that the deductive approach has its origins in research in the natural sciences. However, the emergence of the social sciences in the 20th century led social science researchers to be wary of the deductive approach. They were critical of an approach which enabled a cause–effect link to be made between particular variables without an understanding of the way in which humans interpreted their social world. Developing such an understanding is, of course, a strength of inductive research. In our absenteeism example, we would argue it is more realistic to treat workers as humans whose attendance behaviour is a consequence of the way in which they perceive their work experience, rather than as if they were unthinking research objects who respond in a mechanistic way to certain circumstances.

Followers of the inductive approach would also criticise the deductive approach because of its tendency to construct a rigid methodology that does not permit alternative explanations of what is going on. In that sense, there is an air of finality about the choice of theory and definition of the hypothesis. Alternative theories may be suggested by the deductive approach. However, these would be within the limits set by the highly structured research design. In this respect, a significant characteristic of the absenteeism research design noted above is that of the operationalisation of concepts. As we saw in the absenteeism example, age was precisely defined. However, a less structured approach may reveal alternative explanations of the absenteeism–age relationship denied by a stricter definition of age.

Research using the inductive approach would be particularly concerned with the context in which such events were taking place. Therefore the study of a small sample of subjects may be more appropriate than a large number as with the deductive approach. As can be seen in Chapter 9, researchers in this tradition are more likely to work with qualitative data and to use a variety of methods to collect these data in order to establish different views of phenomena (Easterby-Smith *et al.*, 1991).

At this stage you may be asking yourself: so what? Why is the approach that I take to my research project important? Easterby-Smith *et al.* (1991:21) suggest three reasons. First, it enables you to take a more informed decision about your research design which is '. . . more than simply the methods by which data are collected and analysed. It is the overall configuration of a piece of research: what kind of evidence is gathered and from where, and how such evidence is interpreted in order to provide good answers to the basic research question.'

Second, it will help you to think about those research approaches that will work for you and, crucially, those that will not. For example, if you are particularly interested in understanding why something is happening rather than being able to describe what is happening, it may be more appropriate to adopt the inductive approach than the deductive.

Third, Easterby-Smith *et al.* (1991) argue that a knowledge of the different research traditions enables you to adapt your research design to cater for constraints. These may be practical, involving, say, limited access to data, or they may arise from a lack of prior knowledge of the subject. You simply may not be in a position to frame a hypothesis because you have insufficient understanding of the topic to do this.

Combining approaches to research

So far we have conveyed the impression that there are rigid divisions between the two approaches to research. This would be misleading. Not only is it perfectly possible to combine approaches within the same piece of research, but in our experience it is often advantageous to do so.

Worked example

Deductive and inductive research

Sadie decided to conduct a research project on violence at work and its effects on the stress levels of staff. She considered the different ways she would approach the work were she to adopt:

- the deductive approach;
- the inductive approach.

If she decided to adopt a deductive approach to her work she would have:

1 to start with the hypothesis that staff working with the public are more likely to experience the threat or reality of violence and resultant stress;

2 to decide to research a population in which she would have expected to find evidence of violence, for example a sizeable social security office;

3 to administer a questionnaire to a large sample of staff in order to establish the extent of violence (either actually experienced or threatened) and the levels of stress experienced by them;

4 to be particularly careful about how she defined violence;

5 to standardise the stress responses of the staff, for example days off sick or sessions with a counsellor.

On the other hand, if she decided to adopt an inductive approach she may have decided to interview some staff who had been subjected to violence at work. She may have been interested in their feelings about the events that they had experienced, how they coped with the problems they experienced and their views about the possible causes of the violence.

Either approach would have yielded valuable data about this problem. Neither approach should be thought of as better than the other. They are better at different things. It depends where her research emphasis lies.

We return to the topic of multi-method approaches in Section 4.3. At this point we summarise some of the major differences between deductive and inductive approaches to research. This is done in Table 4.1 below.

Table 4.1   **Major differences between deductive and inductive approaches to research**

Deduction emphasises	*Induction emphasises*
■ scientific principles	■ gaining an understanding of the meanings humans attach to events
■ moving from theory to data	■ a close understanding of the research context
■ the need to explain causal relationships between variables	■ the collection of qualitative data
■ the collection of quantitative data	■ a more flexible structure to permit changes of research emphasis as the research progresses
■ the application of controls to ensure validity of data	■ a realisation that the researcher is part of the research process
■ the operationalisation of concepts to ensure clarity of definition	■ less concern with the need to generalise
■ a highly structured approach	
■ researcher independence of what is being researched	
■ the necessity to select samples of sufficient size in order to generalise conclusions	

At this point you may be wondering about which research approach you should adopt. Creswell (1994) suggests a number of practical criteria. Perhaps the most important of these is the nature of the research topic. A topic on which there is a wealth of literature from which you can define a theoretical framework and a hypothesis lends itself more readily to the deductive approach. With research into a topic that is new and exciting much debate, and on which there is little existing literature, it may be more appropriate to generate data and analyse and reflect on what theoretical themes the data are suggesting.

The time you have available will be an issue. Deductive research can be quicker to complete, albeit that time must be devoted to setting up the study prior to data collection and analysis. Data collection is often based on 'one take'. It is normally possible to predict accurately the time schedules. On the other hand, inductive research can be much more protracted. Often the ideas, based on a much longer period of data collection and analysis, have to emerge gradually. This leads to another important consideration, the extent to which you are prepared to indulge in risk. The deductive approach can be a lower-risk strategy, albeit that there are risks, such as the non-return of questionnaires. With induction you have constantly to live with the fear that no useful data patterns and theory will emerge. Finally, there is the question of audience. In our experience, most managers are familiar with the deductive approach and much more likely to put faith in the conclusions emanating from this approach. You may also wish to consider the preferences of the person marking your research report. We all have our preferences about the approach to adopt. You may be wise to establish these before nailing your colours too firmly to one mast.

This last point suggests that not all the decisions about the research approach that you make should always be so practical. Hakim (1987) uses an architectural metaphor to illustrate the approach choice process. She introduces the notion of the researcher's preferred style which, rather like the architect's, may reflect '. . . the architect's own preferences and ideas . . . and the stylistic preferences of those who pay for the work and have to live with the finished result' (Hakim, 1987:1). This echoes the feelings of Buchanan *et al.* (1988:59) who argue that 'needs, interests and preferences (of the researcher) . . . are typically overlooked but are central to the progress of fieldwork'. However, a note of caution – it is important that your preferences do not lead to you changing the essence of the research question.

4.2   The need for a clear research strategy

Your *research strategy* will be a general plan of how you will go about answering the research question(s) you have set (the importance of clearly defining the research question cannot be over-emphasised). It will contain clear objectives, derived from your research question(s), specify the sources from which you intend to collect data and consider the constraints which you will inevitably have (e.g. access to data, time, location and money, ethical issues). Crucially, it should reflect the fact that you have thought carefully about why you are employing your particular strategy. It would be perfectly legitimate for your assessor to ask you why you chose to conduct your research in a particular organisation, why you chose the particular department, why you chose to talk to one group of staff rather than another. You must have valid reasons for all your research strategy decisions. The justification should always be based on your research question(s) and objectives.

At this point we should make a clear distinction between strategy and *tactics*. The former is concerned with the overall approach you adopt, the latter is about the finer detail of data collection and analysis. Decisions about tactics will involve you being clear about the different data collection methods (e.g. questionnaires, interviews, focus groups, published data) and subsequent analysis which will be dealt with in detail in subsequent chapters. At this point we are concerned with general questions of strategy.

The different research strategies

In this section we turn our attention to the research strategies you may employ. Some of these clearly belong to the deductive tradition, others to the inductive approach. However, often allocating strategies to one tradition or the other is unduly simplistic. What matters is not the label that is attached to a particular strategy, but whether it is appropriate for your particular research question(s) and objectives. We must also emphasise that these strategies should not be thought of as being mutually exclusive. The strategies that we consider here are:

- experiment;
- survey;
- case study;
- grounded theory;
- ethnography;
- action research;

- cross-sectional and longitudinal studies;
- exploratory, descriptive and explanatory studies.

Experiment

Experiment is a classical form of research that owes much to the natural sciences, although it features strongly in much social science research, particularly psychology. It will involve typically:

- the definition of a theoretical hypothesis;
- the selection of samples of individuals from known populations;
- allocation of samples to different experimental conditions;
- introduction of planned change on one or more of the variables;
- measurement on a small number of the variables;
- control of other variables.

Worked example

Using the experimental strategy

Deci (1972) studied the effect of external rewards and controls on the intrinsic motivation of individuals. He set up a laboratory study in which each subject participated in three one-hour sessions of puzzle solving. It had been established by an earlier experiment that the puzzles were intrinsically interesting. There were two participant groups: the experimental group and the control group. Both groups were asked to solve four puzzles during each of the three sessions. The only difference between the two groups is that the experimental group was paid one dollar per puzzle solved during the second session.

During each of the three sessions each group was left alone for an eight-minute 'free-choice period'. Deci reasoned that if the subjects continued puzzle solving in the 'free-choice period' (there were other activities to pursue, e.g. read magazines) then they must be intrinsically motivated to do so. In the event, the experimental group which had been given the external incentive spent less of their 'free' time puzzle solving. The result of this led to Deci theorising that the introduction of external incentives to intrinsically interesting tasks will lead to a decrease in intrinsic motivation, a theory which has interesting implications for those introducing pay incentive schemes for employees who do jobs which they find intrinsically interesting!

Survey

The survey method is usually associated with the deductive approach. It is a popular and common strategy in business and management research. Surveys are popular for some of the reasons mentioned earlier. They allow the collection of a large amount of data from a sizeable population in a highly economical way. Based most often on a questionnaire, these data are standardised allowing easy comparison. In addition, the survey method is perceived as authoritative by people in general. This is because it is easily understood. Every day a news bulletin or a newspaper reports the results of a new survey which indicates, for example, that a certain percentage of the population thinks or behaves in a particular way.

Using a survey approach should give you more control over the research process. However, much time will be spent in designing and piloting the questionnaire. Analysing the results, even with the aid of an appropriate computer package, will also be time consuming. However, it will be your time – you will be independent. Many researchers complain that their progress is delayed by their dependence on others for information.

However, the data collected by the survey method may not be as wide ranging as those collected by qualitative research methods. There is a limit to the number of questions which any questionnaire can contain if the goodwill of the respondent is not to be presumed on too much. However, perhaps the biggest drawback with the questionnaire method is, as emphasised in Section 10.2, the capacity to do it badly!

The questionnaire, however, is not the only data collection device which belongs to the survey category. Structured observation, of the type most frequently associated with organisation and methods (O & M) research, and structured interviews, where standardised questions are asked to all interviewees, also fall into this category. Observation methods are dealt with in detail in Section 8.4 and structured interviews in Section 10.5.

Case study

Robson (1993:40) defines *case study* as the 'development of detailed, intensive knowledge about a single "case", or a small number of related "cases"'. This strategy will be of particular interest to you if you wish to gain a rich understanding of the context of the research and the processes being enacted (Morris and Wood, 1991). The case study approach also has considerable ability to generate answers to the question 'why?' as well as the 'what?' and 'how?' questions (Robson, 1993:44), although 'what?' and 'how?' questions tend to be more the concern of the survey method. The data collection methods employed may be various. They may include questionnaires, interviews, observation, documentary analysis and (as if to emphasise the dangers of constructing neat boxes in which to categorise the approaches, strategies and methods) questionnaires.

You may be suspicious of conducting case study research because of the 'unscientific' feel it has. We would argue that case study can be a very worthwhile way of exploring existing theory. In addition, a simple well-constructed case study can enable you to challenge an existing theory and also provide a source of new hypotheses.

Grounded theory

Grounded theory (Glaser and Strauss, 1967) is often thought of as the best example of the inductive approach, although this conclusion would be too simplistic. It is better to think of it as 'theory building' through a combination of induction and deduction. Sections 12.4 and 12.6 go into detail about grounded theory. Here all we will do is to explain what this strategy involves.

In grounded theory, data collection starts without the formation of an initial theoretical framework. Theory is developed from data generated by a series of observations (Section 12.6 explains in some detail how data analysis is conducted to develop deductively such theory). These data lead to the generation of predictions that are then tested in further observations which may confirm, or otherwise, the predictions. Constant reference to the data to develop and test theory leads Hussey and Hussey (1997) to call grounded theory an inductive/deductive approach, theory being grounded in such continual reference to the data.

Ethnography

Ethnography is also firmly rooted in the inductive approach. It emanates from the field of anthropology. The purpose is to interpret the social world the research subjects inhabit in the way in which they interpret it. This is obviously a research process that is very time consuming and takes place over an extended time period. The research process needs to be flexible and responsive to change since the researcher will constantly be developing new patterns of thought about what is being observed.

Although not a dominant research strategy in business, ethnography may be very appropriate as we demonstrate in Section 8.2. This deals in some detail with participant observation, the research method that dominates ethnography.

Action research

Lewin first used the term '*action research*' in 1946. It has been interpreted subsequently by management researchers in a variety of ways, but there are three common themes within the literature. The first focuses on and emphasises the purpose of the research: the management of a change (Cunningham, 1995). The second relates to the involvement of practitioners in the research and in particular a close collaboration between practitioners and researchers, for example academics or external consultants. Eden and Huxham (1996: 75) argue that the findings of action research result from 'involvement with members of an organisation over a matter which is of genuine concern to them'. Therefore the researcher is part of the organisation within which the research and change process are taking place (Zuber-Skerritt, 1996).

The final theme suggests that action research should have implications beyond the immediate project; in other words it must be clear that the results could inform other contexts. For academics undertaking action research Eden and Huxham (1996) link this to an explicit concern for the development of theory. However, they emphasise that for consultants this is more likely to focus on the subsequent transfer of knowledge gained from one specific context to another. Such use of knowledge to inform other contexts we believe also applies to others undertaking action research such as practitioners.

Thus action research differs from other forms of applied research because of its explicit focus on action, in particular promoting change within the organisation (Marsick and Watkins, 1997). In addition the person undertaking the research is involved in this action for change and subsequently application of the knowledge gained elsewhere.

Cross-sectional and longitudinal studies

An important question to be asked in planning your research is 'do I want my research to be a "snapshot" taken at a particular time or do I want it to be more akin to a "diary" and be a representation of events over a given period?' (As always, of course, the answer should be 'it depends on the research question'.) The 'snapshot' approach is what we call here *cross-sectional* while the 'diary' perspective we call *longitudinal*.

We should emphasise here that these time perspectives to research design are independent of which research strategy you are pursuing. So, for example, you may be studying the change in manufacturing processes in one company over a period of a year. This would be a longitudinal case study.

Cross-sectional studies

It is probable that your research will be cross-sectional, the study of a particular phenomenon (or phenomena) at a particular time. We say this because we recognise that most research projects undertaken for academic courses are necessarily time constrained. However, the timescales on many courses do allow sufficient time for a longitudinal study, provided, of course, that you start it in plenty of time!

Cross-sectional studies often employ the survey strategy (Robson, 1993; Easterby-Smith *et al.*, 1991). They may be seeking to describe the incidence of a phenomenon (e.g. a survey of the IT skills possessed by managers in one organisation at a given point in time) or to compare factors in different organisations (e.g. the relationship between expenditure on customer care training for sales assistants and sales revenue). However, they may also use qualitative methods. Many case studies are based on interviews conducted over a short period of time.

Longitudinal studies

The main strength of longitudinal research is the capacity that it has to study change and development. Adams and Schvaneveldt (1991) point out that in observing people or events over time the researcher is able to exercise a measure of control over variables being studied, provided that they are not affected by the research process itself. One of the best known examples of this type of research comes from outside the world of business. It is the long-running television series 'Seven Up'. This has charted the progress of a cohort of people every seven years of their life. Not only is this fascinating television, but it has provided the social scientist with a rich source of data on which to test and develop theories of human development.

Even with time constraints it is possible to introduce a longitudinal element to your research. As Section 7.2 indicates, there is a massive amount of published data collected over time just waiting to be analysed! An example is the Workplace Industrial Relations Survey which was conducted in 1980, 1984, 1990 (Millward *et al.*, 1992) and 1998 (Cully *et al.*, 1999). From these surveys you would be able to gain valuable data which would give you a powerful insight into developments in personnel management and industrial relations over a period of wide-ranging change. In longitudinal studies the basic question is 'has there been any change over a period of time?' (Bouma and Atkinson, 1995:114).

Exploratory, descriptive and explanatory studies

Enquiries can be classified in terms of their purpose as well as by the research strategy used (Robson, 1993). The classification most often used is the three-fold one of exploratory, descriptive and explanatory. In the same way as you may employ more than one strategy in your research project, so you may have more than one purpose. Indeed, as Robson (1993) points out, the purpose of your enquiry may change over time.

Exploratory studies

Exploratory studies are a valuable means of finding out 'what is happening; to seek new insights; to ask questions and to assess phenomena in a new light' (Robson, 1993:42). It is a particularly useful approach if you wish to clarify your understanding of a problem. It may well be that time is well spent on exploratory research, as it may show that the research is not worth pursuing!

There are three principal ways of conducting exploratory research:

■ a search of the literature;

■ talking to experts in the subject;

■ conducting focus group interviews.

Exploratory research can be likened to the activities of the traveller or explorer (Adams and Schvaneveldt, 1991). Its great advantage is that it is flexible and adaptable to change. If you are conducting exploratory research you must be willing to change your direction as a result of new data which appears and new insights which occur to you. A quotation from the travel writer V.S. Naipaul (1989:222) illustrates this point beautifully.

> I had been concerned, at the start of my own journey, to establish some lines of enquiry, to define a theme. The approach had its difficulties. At the back of my mind was always a worry that I would come to a place and all contacts would break down . . . If you travel on a theme the theme has to develop with the travel. At the beginning your interests can be broad and scattered. But then they must be more focused; the different stages of a journey cannot simply be versions of one another. And . . . this kind of travel depended on luck. It depended on the people you met, the little illuminations you had. As with the next day's issue of fast-moving daily newspaper, the shape of the character in hand was continually being changed by accidents along the way.

Adams and Schvaneveldt (1991) reinforce this point by arguing that the flexibility inherent in exploratory research does not mean absence of direction to the enquiry. What it does mean is that the focus is initially broad and becomes progressively narrower as the research progresses.

Descriptive studies

The object of *descriptive research* is 'to portray an accurate profile of persons, events or situations' (Robson, 1993:4). This may be an extension of, or a forerunner to, a piece of exploratory research. It is necessary to have a clear picture of the phenomena on which you wish to collect data prior to the collection of the data. One of the earliest well-known examples of a descriptive survey is the Doomsday Book which described the population of England in 1085.

Often project tutors are rather wary of work that is too descriptive. There is a danger of them saying 'that's very interesting . . . but so what?' They will want you to go further and to draw conclusions from your data. They will encourage you to develop the skills of evaluating data and synthesising ideas. These are higher-order skills than those of accurate description. Description in management and business research has a very clear place. However, it should be thought of as a means to an end rather than an end in itself.

Explanatory studies

Studies which establish causal relationships between variables may be termed explanatory studies. The emphasis here is on studying a situation or a problem in order to explain the relationships between variables. You may find, for example, that a cursory analysis of quantitative data on manufacturing scrap rates shows a relationship between scrap rates and the age of the machine being operated. You could go ahead and subject the data to statistical tests such as correlation (discussed in Section 11.5) in order to get a clearer view of the relationship.

Worked example

An explanatory study

Phil studied individual performance-related pay systems for managers. He was interested in explaining the relationship between success (a concept which needed to be given a working definition) of such systems and the factors that seemed to lead to such success. This research adopted a case study approach in examining three organisations in some detail. The data collected were mainly qualitative, although some secondary quantitative data were used. What emerged was that the way in which implementing managers conducted the processes of assessing the performance of their managers and translating these assessments into rewards was more important than the design of such systems.

4.3 Multi-method approaches

These approaches and strategies obviously do not exist in isolation and therefore can be 'mixed and matched'. Not only can they, but it is often beneficial to do so. It is quite usual for a single study to combine quantitative and qualitative methods and to use primary and secondary data.

There are two major advantages to employing *multi-methods* in the same study. First, different methods can be used for different purposes in a study. You may wish to employ case study methods, for example interviews, in order to get a feel for the key issues before embarking on a survey. This would give you confidence that you were addressing the most important issues.

Worked example

Combining survey and case study methods

We conducted an employee attitude survey in a small insurance company which used three different types of method. Two of these were qualitative and one was quantitative. The research consisted of four stages:

1 In-depth interviews with senior managers in order to get a picture of the important issues we were likely to encounter in the research. This was essential contextual data.

2 Discussion groups with six to ten employees representing different grades and occupations in the company. This was to establish the types of issues that were important to staff. This would inform the content of the questionnaire.

3 A questionnaire which was administered to 100 of the 200 head office employees. We wanted to get the sort of data which would allow us to compare the attitudes of different employee groups: by age, gender, length of service, occupation and grade. This was particularly important to the company

4 Semi-structured group interviews with further representative employee groups to clarify the content of some of the questionnaire results. This was essential to get at the meaning behind some of the data.

The second advantage of using multi-method example is that it enables *triangulation* to take place. Triangulation refers to the use of different data collection methods within one study in order to ensure that the data are telling you what you think they are telling you. For example, semi-structured group interviews may be a valuable way of triangulating data collected by other means such as a questionnaire.

Each method, tool or technique has its unique strengths and weaknesses (Smith, 1975). There is an inevitable relationship between the data collection method you employ and the results you obtain. In short, the results will be affected by the method used. The problem here is that it is impossible to ascertain the nature of that effect. Since all different methods will have different effects, it makes sense to use different methods to cancel out the 'method effect'. That will lead to greater confidence being placed in your conclusions.

The question that may occur to you at this stage is: 'how do I know which method to use in which situation?' There is no simple answer. We encourage you to use your imagination and to think of research as a highly creative process. However, above all it is vital to have clear objectives for your study. It is a great temptation to think about the methods to be employed before the objectives are clarified.

> **Worked example**
>
> ### Using a multi-method approach
>
> Darren wanted to establish how new supervisors learned to do the job. In order to do this he thought it essential that he should have the clearest possible grasp of what the supervisor's job entailed.
>
> This involved him in shadowing a new supervisor for a week, talking to night shift supervisors to establish any differences in approach, sending a questionnaire to supervisors in different locations in the company and interviewing the managers to whom those supervisors reported.
>
> This gave Darren a much better grasp of the content of the supervisor's job. It also did much to enhance his credibility in the eyes of the supervisors. He was then able to draw on the valuable data he had collected to complete his main research task: to find out how new supervisors learned to do the job.

4.4 The credibility of research findings

Underpinning the above discussion on multi-method usage has been the issue of the credibility of research findings. This is neatly expressed by Raimond (1993:55) when he subjects findings to the 'how do I know?' test: '. . . will the evidence and my conclusions stand up to the closest scrutiny?' How do you know that new supervisors learn their jobs by largely informal methods? How did we know that manual employees in our electronics factory had more negative feelings towards their employer than their clerical counterparts? The answer, of course, is that in the literal sense of the question, you cannot know. All you can do is to reduce the possibility of getting the answer wrong. This is where sound research design is important. This is aptly summarised by Rogers (1961, cited by Raimond 1993:55): 'scientific methodology needs to be seen for what it truly is, a way of preventing me from deceiving myself in regard to my creatively formed subjective hunches which have developed out of the relationship between me and my material'.

Reducing the possibility of getting the answer wrong means that attention has to be paid to two particular emphases on research design: reliability and validity.

Reliability

Reliability can be assessed by posing the following two questions (Easterby-Smith *et al.*, 1991:41):

1 Will the measure yield the same results on different occasions? (deductive approach).

2 Will similar observations be made by different researchers on different occasions? (inductive approach).

Threats to reliability

Robson (1993) asserts that there may be four threats to reliability. The first of these is *subject error*. If you are studying the degree of enthusiasm employees have for their work and their employer it may be that you will find that a questionnaire completed at different times of the week may generate different results. Friday afternoons may show a different picture to Monday mornings! This should be easy to control. You should choose a more 'neutral' time when employees may be expected to be neither on a 'high', looking forward to the weekend, nor a 'low' with the working week in front of them.

Similarly, there may be *subject bias*. Interviewees may have been saying what they thought their bosses wanted them to say. This is a particular problem in organisations which are characterised by an authoritarian management style or when there is a threat of employment insecurity. Researchers should be aware of this potential problem when designing research. For example, elaborate steps can be taken to ensure the anonymity of respondents to questionnaires, as Section 10.4 indicates. Care should also be taken when analysing the data to ensure that your data are telling you what you think they are telling you.

Third, there may have been *observer error*. In one piece of research we undertook, there were three of us conducting interviews with potential for at least three different approaches to eliciting answers. Introducing a high degree of structure to the interview schedule (Section 9.2) will lessen this threat to reliability.

Finally, there may have been *observer bias*. Here, of course, there may have been three different approaches to interpreting the replies!

There is more detail on how these threats to reliability may be reduced later in the book in the chapters dealing with specific data collection methods.

Validity

Validity is concerned with whether the findings are really about what they appear to be about. Is the relationship between two variables a *causal relationship*? For example, in a study of an electronics factory we found that employees' failure to look at new product displays was not caused by employee apathy but by lack of opportunity (the displays were located in a part of the factory employees rarely visited). This potential lack of validity in the conclusions was minimised by a research design that built in the opportunity for focus groups after the questionnaire results had been analysed.

Robson (1993) has also charted the threats to validity, which provides a useful way of thinking about this important topic.

Threats to validity

History

You may decide to study the opinions that employees have about job security in a particular organisation. However, if the research is conducted shortly after a major redundancy programme this may well have a dramatic, and quite misleading, effect on the findings (unless, of course, the specific objective of the research was to find out about post-redundancy opinions).

Testing

Your research may include measuring how long it takes telesales operators to deal with customer enquiries. If the operators believed that the results of the research may disadvantage them in some way, then this is likely to affect the results.

Instrumentation

In the above example, the telesales operators may have received an instruction that they were to take every opportunity to sell new policies between the times you tested the first batch and second batch of operators. Consequently, the calls are likely to last longer.

Mortality

This refers to participants dropping out of studies. This was a major problem to one of our students who was studying the effects on the management styles of managers exposed to a year-long management development programme.

Maturation

In the earlier management development example above, it could be that other events happening during the year have an effect on their management style.

Ambiguity about causal direction

This is a particularly difficult issue. One of our part-time students was studying the effectiveness of performance appraisal in her organisation. One of her findings was that poor performance ratings of employees were associated with a negative attitude about appraisal among those same employees. What she was not clear about was whether the poor performance ratings were causing the negative attitude to appraisal or whether the negative attitude to appraisal was causing the poor performance ratings.

Generalisability

This is sometimes referred to as *external validity*. A concern you may have in the design of your research is the extent to which your research results are generalisable, that is your findings may be equally applicable to other research settings, such as other organisations. This is a particular worry if you are conducting case study research in one organisation, or a small number of organisations. It may also be important if the organisation is markedly 'different' in some way.

In such cases the purpose of your research will not be to produce a theory which is generalisable to all populations. Your task will be simply to try to explain what is going on in your particular research setting. It may be that you want to test the robustness of your conclusions by exposing them to other research settings in a follow-up study. In short, as long as you do not claim that your results, conclusions or theory can be generalised, then there is no problem.

Logic leaps and false assumptions

So far in this chapter we have shown that there are a host of decisions which need to be made in order that your research project yields sufficient data of the sort which will result in valid conclusions being drawn. Those decisions necessitate careful thought from you. However, more than just the quantity of thought is involved. It is vital that your thought processes are of high quality. Your research design will be based on a flow of logic and a number of assumptions, all of which must stand up to the closest scrutiny.

These points have been illustrated skilfully by Raimond (1993). Raimond takes the research of Peters and Waterman on 'excellent' US companies and subjects it to just such scrutiny. The ideas of Peters and Waterman (1982) have been enormously influential in the last two decades. Their book is a management 'cookbook' which gives managers eight principles to which they must adhere if their organisations are to be successful. As such, it is fairly typical of a prescriptive type of writing in management books and journals which suggest that 'this is the way it should be done'.

Raimond's (1993) analysis of Peters and Waterman can be categorised into four 'logic steps'.

Identification of the research population

This is similar to the point made about generalisability above. If the intention is to be able to generalise the conclusions across the whole population (in the Peters and Waterman case, all organisations) is the choice of population logical? If your research project is in the National Health Service, for example, it would be fanciful to assume that the findings were valid for software houses or advertising agencies.

Data collection

Is it logical to assume that the way you are collecting your data is going to yield valid data? If you interview top bosses you are likely to encounter the 'good news' syndrome. If you collect press cuttings from newspapers how can you assume there has been no political bias put on them?

Data interpretation

It is here that there is probably the greatest danger of logic leaps and false assumptions. You will need to move from a position where you have a mountain of data to one where you write a set of conclusions which are presented coherently. This is at the same time an intellectually challenging and highly creative and exciting process.

You are likely to be using a theoretical framework against which you will analyse your data. If you are working deductively (from theory to data) this framework may have given rise to the hypothesis which you are testing in your research. One of our students studied the introduction of pay bonuses assessed by performance appraisal in the police service. Her hypothesis was based on the Meyer, Kay and French (1965) hypothesis that the non-pay benefits of appraisal (e.g. improvement of job performance) will be prejudiced by the introduction of pay considerations to the process, rendering the appraisal interview little more than a salary discussion.

It is less likely that you will be working completely inductively where you collect your data and then analyse it to what theory emerges.

You may employ a hybrid approach. This could involve using an established theoretical construct to help you to make sense of your findings. For example, you may be studying the way in which different companies within the group in which you work formulate their business strategies. In order to structure your analysis you could use the categorisation of different types of organisational strategy suggested by Mintzberg and Waters (1989). This may lead you to conclude that the dominant strategy employed is a mixture of those suggested by Mintzberg and Waters.

The important point here is that in both the deductive and the hybrid cases you are making assumptions about the appropriateness of the theory that you are using. In both cases it is clear that the theory with which you are working will shape your conclusions. Therefore it is essential that you choose an appropriate theoretical framework. It is essential that you ask yourself 'why am I using this theory and not another which may be equally, or more, appropriate?'

We are making the assumption here that you will use a theory to analyse your data. For most undergraduate and postgraduate courses this is likely to be a requirement of your project tutor. Some professional courses may be more concerned with practical management reports that emphasise the importance of the report making viable recommendations which are the result of clear conclusions based on a set of findings. It is important that you clarify this point with the project tutor prior to commencing the research.

Development of conclusions

The question to ask yourself here is 'do my conclusions (or theory) stand up to the closest scrutiny?' If the declared theory in the police appraisal study is that the introduction of pay to the appraisal will lead to the appraisal process being useful for pay purposes only, does this apply to all police appraisals? Will it be true for younger as well as older police and for all grades and locations? In other words, are you asking your readers to make logic leaps?

4.5   The ethics of research design

Section 5.4 deals in more detail with the subject of research ethics. This has important implications for the negotiation of access to people and organisations and the collection of data. Here we will only address the ethical issues which you should consider when designing your research strategy.

Your choice of topic will be governed by ethical considerations. You may be particularly interested to study the consumer decision to buy flower bouquets. Although this may provide some interesting data collection challenges (who buys, for whom and why?) there are not the same ethical difficulties as will be involved in studying, say, the funeral purchasing decision. Your research design in this case may have to concentrate on data collection from the undertaker and, possibly, the purchaser at a time as distant from the death as delicacy permits. The ideal population, of course, may be the purchaser at a time as near as possible to the death. It is a matter of judgement as to whether the data collection method strategy suggested by ethical considerations will yield data which are valid. The general ethical issue here is that the research design should not subject the research population to embarrassment or any other material disadvantage.

Your research design needs to consider the extent to which you should collect data from a research population which is unaware of the fact they are the subject of research and so have not consented. There was a dispute between solicitors and the Consumers' Association (CA). Telephone enquiries were conducted by the CA with a sample of solicitors for the purpose of assessing the accuracy of legal advice given and the cost of specified work. The calls were, allegedly, made without the CA's identity, or the purpose of the research, being disclosed (Gibb, 1995). It is for you to decide whether a similar strategy adopted in your project would be ethical.

It may be quite a different matter if you are collecting data from individuals, rather than from organisations as in the above example. This may be the case if you are conducting your research while working as an employee in an organisation. It may also be so if you are working on a student placement. In this case you would be researching as a *participant observer*. If the topic you were researching was one where it may be beneficial for your research that the fact that you were collecting data on individuals was not disclosed, then this poses a similar ethical dilemma. This will be discussed in more detail when we deal with observation as a data collection method in Chapter 8.

4.6 Summary

- There are two main philosophical positions in research: positivism and phenomenology.

- The two main approaches to research are deductive and inductive. These should not be thought of as mutually exclusive. You can use both in combination on the same research project. The main influence on your choice of research approach should be your research questions and objectives.

- The main research strategies are experiment, survey, case study, grounded theory, ethnography and action research. Again, you should not think of these as discrete entities. There may be a combination of some of these in the same research project.

- Research projects may be cross-sectional or longitudinal. In addition, they may be classed as exploratory, descriptive or explanatory.

- Multi-method approaches to research mean that different purposes may be served and that triangulation of results is facilitated.

- You should take care to ensure that your results are valid and reliable.

- You should always think carefully about the ethical issues implied by the choice of your research strategy.

Questions

4.1 You have decided to undertake a project and have defined the main research question as 'What are the opinions of consumers to a 10% reduction in weight, with the price remaining the same, of "Snackers" chocolate bars?' Write a hypothesis which you could test in your project.

4.2 You are about to embark on a year-long study of customer service training for sales assistants in two supermarket companies. The purpose of the research is to compare the way in which the training develops and its effectiveness. What measures would you need to take in the research design stage to ensure that the results were valid?

4.3 You are working in an organisation which has branches throughout the UK. The managing director is mindful of the fact that managers of the branches need to talk over common problems on a regular basis. That is why there have always been monthly meetings.

However, she is becoming increasingly concerned that these meetings are not cost effective. Too many managers see them as an unwelcome intrusion. They feel that their time would be better spent pursuing their principal job objectives. Other managers see it as a 'day off': an opportunity to recharge the batteries.

She has asked you to carry out some research on the cost-effectiveness of the monthly meetings. You have defined the research question you are seeking to answer as 'What are the managers' opinions of the value of their monthly meetings?'

Your principal data collection method will be a questionnaire to all managers who attend the monthly meetings. However, you are keen to triangulate your findings. How may you do this?

4.4 You have started conducting interviews in a university with the university's hourly-paid staff (e.g. porters, gardeners, caterers). The research objective is to establish the extent to which those employees feel a sense of 'belonging' to the university. You have negotiated access to your interviewees through the head of each of the appropriate departments. In each case you have been presented with a list of interviewees.

It soon becomes apparent to you that you are getting a rather rosier picture than you expected. The interviewees are all very positive about their jobs, their managers and the university. This makes you suspicious. Are all the hourly-paid staff as positive as this? Are you only being given the employees who can be relied on to tell the 'good news'? Have they been 'got at' by their manager?

There is a great risk that your results will not be valid. What can you do?

4.5 You wish to study the way in which the job of the bank manager has changed over the past ten years. Your chosen research strategy is to have unstructured discussions with some bank managers who have been in banking for at least that ten-year period. You are asked by a small audience of peers and supervisors to explain why your chosen strategy is as valid as a questionnaire-based survey. What would be your answer?

Assignment 4

Deciding on your research strategy

→ Return to your research question(s) and objectives. Decide on whether you intend to pursue a deductive (your theory will be tested by observation) or an inductive (the collection of your data will be followed by the development of theory) approach. Explain clearly why you have decided on the approach chosen.

➡ Decide which of the research strategies is most appropriate for your research question(s) and objectives. Look at studies in the literature that are similar to your own. Which strategies have been used? What explanations do the researchers give for their choice of strategy?

➡ Prepare notes on the constraints under which your research is being conducted. Do they, for example, preclude the pursuit of longitudinal research?

➡ How may you combine different research methods in your study? Make notes on the advantages such a multi-method approach would bring.

➡ List all the threats to reliability and validity contained in your research design.

References

Adams, G. and Schvaneveldt, J. (1991) *Understanding Research Methods* (2nd edn), New York, Longman.

Bouma, G. and Atkinson, G. (1995) *A Handbook of Social Science Research: a Comprehensive and Practical Guide for Students* (2nd edn), Oxford, Oxford University Press.

Buchanan, D., Boddy, D. and McAlman, J. (1988) 'Getting in, getting on, getting out and getting back', in Bryman, A. (ed.), *Doing Research in Organisations*, London, Routledge, pp. 53–67.

Creswell, J. (1994) *Research Design: Quantitative and Qualitative Approaches,* Thousand Oaks, CA, Sage.

Cully, M., O'Reilly, A., Millward, N., Forth, J., Woodlands, S., Dix, G. and Bryson, A. (1999) *The 1998 Workplace Employment Relations Survey: First Findings* [On-line] [cited 28 July], available from <url:http://www.dti.gov.uk/emar>.

Cunningham, J.B. (1995) 'Strategic considerations in using action research for improving personnel practices', *Public Personnel Management*, 24:2, 515–29.

Deci, E.L. (1972) 'The effects of contingent and non-contingent rewards and controls on intrinsic motivation', *Organisational Behaviour and Human Performance*, 8: 217–9.

Easterby-Smith, M., Thorpe, R. and Lowe, A. (1991) *Management Research: an Introduction,* London, Sage.

Eden, C. and Huxham, C. (1996) 'Action research for management research', *British Journal of Management*, 7:1, 75–86.

Gibb, F. (1995) 'Consumer group accuses lawyers of shoddy service', *The Times*, 5 October.

Gill, J. and Johnson, P. (1997) *Research Methods for Managers,* London, Paul Chapman.

Glaser, B. and Strauss, A. (1967), *The Discovery of Grounded Theory*, Chicago, IL, Aldine.

Hakim, C. (1987) *Research Design: Strategies and Choices in the Design of Social Research*, London, Allen and Unwin.

Hussey, J. and Hussey, R. (1997) *Business Research: a Practical Guide for Undergraduate and Postgraduate Students*, Basingstoke, Macmillan Business.

Marsick, V.J. and Watkins, K.E. (1997) 'Case study research methods', in Swanson, R.A. and Holton, E.F. (eds), *Human Resource Development Research Handbook,* San Francisco, CA, Berrett-Koehler, pp. 138–57.

Meyer, H., Kay, E. and French, J. (1965) 'Split roles in performance appraisal', *Harvard Business Review*, 43:1, 123–9.

Millward, N., Stevens, M., Smart, D. and Hawes, W.R. (1992) *Workplace Industrial Relations in Transition*, Aldershot, Dartmouth.

Mintzberg, H. and Waters, J. (1989) 'Of strategies, deliberate and emergent', in Asch, D. and Bowman, C. (eds) *Readings in Strategic Management*, Basingstoke, Macmillan Education, pp. 4–19.

Morris, T. and Wood, S. (1991) 'Testing the survey method: continuity and change in British industrial relations', *Work Employment and Society*, 5:2, 259–82.

Naipaul, V.S. (1989) *A Turn in the South*, London, Penguin.

Peters, T. and Waterman, R. (1982) *In Search of Excellence,* New York, Harper & Row.

Raimond, P. (1993) *Management Projects*, London, Chapman & Hall.

Remenyi, D., Williams, B., Money, A. and Swartz, E. (1998) *Doing Research in Business and Management: an Introduction to Process and Method*, London: Sage.

Robson, C. (1993) *Real World Research*, Oxford, Blackwell.

Rogers, C.R. (1961) *On Becoming a Person*, Constable, London.

Schein, E. (1992) 'Coming to a new awareness of organisational culture', in Salaman, G., *Human Resource Strategies,* London, Sage.

Smith, H. (1975) *Strategies of Social Research: the Methodological Imagination*, Englewood Cliffs, NJ, Prentice-Hall.

Zuber-Skerritt, O. (1996) 'Emancipatory action research for organisational change and management development, in Zuber-Skerritt, O. (ed.) *New Directions in Action Research,* London, Falmer, pp. 83–105.

Further reading

Easterby-Smith, M., Thorpe, R. and Lowe, A. (1991) *Management Research: an Introduction,* London, Sage. Chapter 3 gives a comprehensive and highly readable introduction to different research approaches.

Gill, J. and Johnson, P. (1997) *Research Methods for Managers*, London, Paul Chapman. Chapters 3, 9 and 10 provide a detailed discussion on the choice of approach and strategy and the philosophical and theoretical assumptions underlying that choice.

Raimond, P. (1993) *Management Projects*, London, Chapman & Hall. Chapters 5 and 6 provide an excellent insight into the issue of validity and reliability.

Robson, C. (1993) *Real World Research*, Oxford, Blackwell. Chapters 3–7 give an excellent account of all the topics covered in this chapter. It is very readable, not least for the attractive and accessible way it is laid out. The examples are not drawn principally from management and business. However, do not let that put you off.

The effectiveness of computer-based training at Falcon Insurance Company

(The techniques used in this case may appear complicated when you first read about them. Do not worry: the case is included as an example of a research strategy not techniques. Further details on the techniques of observation, in-depth interviews and questionnaires can be found in Chapters 8, 9 and 10 respectively.)

Ingrid works for Falcon Insurance, a large UK insurance company offering insurance in the life and motor markets. As part of its training portfolio Falcon Insurance was considering the introduction of computer-based training (CBT) for junior level courses such as telephone manner. In order to make an informed decision about introducing CBT Falcon needed to answer the question, was CBT an effective training medium? After discussion with her project tutor Ingrid decided that this would make a good research project. An extensive literature review enabled her to define the term 'effective' and to generate four interrelated research questions:

■ Was CBT effective for individual learning?

■ Was CBT effective for group study?

■ Was learning in groups more effective than self study?

■ Did a match of training media to learning style improve learning?

Ingrid wanted the research to provide both quantitative results which described the outcomes of CBT in relation to other forms of training and qualitative results which explored trainees' opinions and behaviours and the meanings behind these outcomes.

In order to describe and explore the effect of CBT on learning Ingrid decided to undertake a study which examined the impact of this type of training over an extended period. The independent variable was the training medium used, the dependent variable the learning that took place. A review of the literature suggested that four distinct groups would be needed:

1 Self-study CBT: using the CBT software individually without a trainer to facilitate and provide input;

2 Group study CBT: using the same CBT medium but studying as a group of trainees without a trainer to facilitate and provide input;

3 Traditional training course: using the message and content of the CBT but applying it to a facilitated group in which no technology was used and the input was provided by a trainer;

4 Control group: where no training took place during the study period to provide a bench mark.

A representative sample of 120 of Falcon Insurance's employees was selected and 30 were allocated to each group at random. Data were collected using a combination of questionnaires, observation and unstructured interviews (Table 1).

▶

Table 1	The research strategy				
Group		Action taken			
		Immediately before training	During training	Immediately after training	Six months after training
1 **Self-study CBT**		Questionnaire and Learning Styles Questionnaire	Descriptive observation	Questionnaire and separate in-depth interview	Questionnaire
2 **Group study CBT**		Questionnaire and Learning Styles Questionnaire	Descriptive observation	Questionnaire and separate in-depth interview	Questionnaire
3 **Traditional training**		Questionnaire and Learning Styles Questionnaire	Descriptive observation	Questionnaire and separate in-depth interview	Questionnaire
4 **Control group**		Questionnaire			Questionnaire

Ingrid decided to use pre-tests and post-tests on each of the four distinct groups. These data would be collected using a questionnaire on three separate occasions: immediately before training, immediately after training and six months after training.

A confidential self-administered questionnaire, to measure quantitatively any changes in individuals' knowledge and understanding over the study period, was designed and pilot tested. Questions tested the respondents' knowledge and understanding that should have been developed by the training they would receive. The control group was also tested despite receiving no training to measure any change in knowledge and understanding due to other factors. In addition, questions were included to measure the trainees' reactions to various aspects of the training as well as attribute questions to assess the representativeness of the sample. The questionnaire was administered to all four groups for the pre-test and, with minor alterations, the post-test stages. In addition, all respondents who actually undertook some form of training were asked to complete a learning styles questionnaire.

An important part of Ingrid's research was to examine the social context of the groups studied and to provide additional data with which to compare and explore the results of the study. Descriptive observation was used to collect data on the behaviour of each of the three groups of trainees, paying particular attention to events and observed actions and behaviours. Observers were given a sheet on which they recorded this information in a structured manner using a predetermined scheme. This scheme was developed to minimise the impact of subjectivity and inconsistency on the recorded response. Observations were recorded while each of the three trainee groups was observed, the observer remaining only as an observer and not engaging with the group.

Ingrid used unstructured interviews to collect views about group learning from a stratified sample of trainees immediately after the training. In particular, she asked trainees to discuss their views on learning in a group and whether they preferred this to self-study. Trainees who had received group study CBT were asked to discuss their views on the effectiveness of the medium in the group context and about the effect of group interaction in their particular session. Trainees were asked to consider whether or not they would put their learning into practice in their jobs. Finally the trainees were asked to consider the match between their preferred learning style and the training they had received and whether it had improved their learning.

Data collected from the questionnaire, observation and unstructured interviews were subsequently analysed.

Questions

1 Which type(s) of research strategy are employed in this study?

2 What are the benefits of adding a longitudinal dimension to this research?

3 What are the benefits of using multiple methods of data collection?

4 a What threats to reliability are inherent in the research design?

   b How may these be overcome?

5 a What threats to validity are inherent in the research design?

   b How may these be overcome?

Self check **Answers**

4.1 Probably the most realistic hypothesis here would be 'consumers of "Snackers" chocolate bars did not notice the difference between the current bar and its reduced weight successor'. Doubtless that is what the Snackers' manufacturers would want confirmed!

4.2 This would be a longitudinal study. Therefore, the potential of some of the threats to validity explained in Section 4.4 is greater simply because they have longer to develop. You would need to make sure that most of these threats were controlled as much as possible. For example, you would need:

- to account for the possibility of a major event during the period of the research (wide-scale redundancies which may affect employee attitudes) in one of the companies but not the other;

- to ensure that you use the same data collection devices in both companies;

- to be aware of the 'mortality' problem. Some of the sales assistants will leave. You would be advised to replace them with assistants with similar characteristics, as far as possible.

4.3 The questionnaire will undoubtedly perform a valuable function in obtaining a comprehensive amount of data which can be compared easily, say by district or age and gender. However, you would add to the understanding of the problem if you observed managers' meetings. Who does most of the talking? What are the non-verbal behaviour patterns displayed by managers? Who turns up late, or does not turn up at all?

You could also consider talking to managers in groups or individually. Your decision here would be whether to talk to them before or after the questionnaire, or both.

In addition, you could study the minutes of the meetings to discover who contributed the most. Who initiated the most discussions? What were the attendance patterns?

4.4 There is no easy answer to this question! You have to remember that access to organisations to research is an act of goodwill on the part of managers and they do like to retain a certain amount of control. Selecting whom researchers may interview is a classic way of managers doing this. If this is the motive of the managers concerned then they are unlikely to let you have free access to their employees.

What you could do is ask to see all the employees in a particular department rather than a sample of employees. Alternatively, you could explain that your research was still uncovering new patterns of information and more interviews were necessary. This way you would penetrate deeper into the core of the employee group and may start seeing those who were rather less positive. All this assumes that you have the time to do this!

You could also be perfectly honest with the managers and confess your concern. If you did a sound job at the start of the research in convincing them that you are purely interested in academic research, and that all data will be anonymous, then you may have less of a problem.

Of course, there is always the possibility that the employees generally are positive and feel as if they really do 'belong'!

4.5 You would need to stress here that your principal interest would be in getting a deep understanding of the changes in the manager's job and the reasons why the job had changed. You would discover what the managers thought of the changes and the ways in which they had responded to the changes. In other words, you would establish what you set out to establish, and, no doubt, a good deal besides.

You will remember from Section 4.4 that validity is concerned with whether the findings are really about what they appear to be about. There is no reason why your discussions with managers should not be as valid as a questionnaire survey. However, you should ensure that you talk to managers (and others) who are in a position to speak with authority on the subject. Your questioning should be skilful enough to elicit rich responses from your interviewees (see Chapter 9). You should be sensitive to the direction in which the discussion is moving. This will mean not being too directive, while still moving the interview in the direction you as the interviewer want.

Of course, you may alleviate any fears about validity by conducting a survey and interviews so that your findings may be triangulated!

5 Negotiating access and research ethics

By the end of this chapter you should be:

■ aware of issues related to gaining access and research ethics;

■ able to evaluate a range of strategies to help you to gain access to organisations and to individual participants;

■ able to anticipate ethical issues at each stage of your research process, to help you to deal with these;

■ able to evaluate the ethical issues associated with particular data collection methods, so that you can consider these in relation to your proposed research methods.

5.1 Introduction

Access and ethics are critical aspects for the conduct of research. Many newcomers to research want to 'get on with it' once they have identified a topic area. Insufficient attention is likely to be paid to the very real problem of gaining access and even less to the likelihood of ethical concerns arising in relation to the research project and the implications of these. These are aspects that require careful attention at the outset of any research project. Without this, what seem like good ideas for research may flounder and prove impractical or problematic once you attempt to carry them out.

The next section (5.2) of this chapter defines the types and levels of access and the issues associated with these. It discusses the key issues of feasibility and sufficiency in relation to gaining access and the effect of these on the nature and content of your research question and objectives. The following section (5.3) examines a number of proven strategies to help you to gain access to organisations and to intended participants within them. The next section (5.4) is devoted to a discussion of research ethics and the types of issues that are likely to occur at the various stages of your research project and also in relation to the use of particular research methods. A summary checklist is included in relation to gaining access and also one to help you to anticipate and deal with ethical concerns. These are designed to help you during the development of a research proposal and when you conduct your research project.

5.2 Problems associated with access

Your ability to collect data will depend on gaining access to their source or to appropriate sources where there is a choice. The appropriateness of a source will of course depend on your research question, related objectives and strategy. The first level of access is *physical access* or entry (Gummesson, 1991). Gaining physical access can be difficult for a number of reasons. First, organisations or individuals may not be prepared to engage in additional, voluntary activities because of the time and resources required. Many organisations receive frequent requests for access and co-operation and would find it impossible to agree to all or even some of these. Second, the request for access and co-operation may fail to interest the person who receives it. This may be for a number of reasons, related to:

- a lack of perceived value in relation to the work of the organisation or the individual;
- the nature of the topic because of its potential sensitivity, or because of concerns about the confidentiality of the information that would be required;
- perceptions about your credibility and doubts about your competence.

Third, the organisation may find itself in a difficult situation owing to external events totally unrelated to any perceptions about the nature of the request or the person making it, so that they have no choice but to refuse access. Even where a particular organisational participant is prepared to offer access this may be overruled at a higher level in the organisation. This may result in a 'false start' and an associated feeling of disappointment (Johnson, 1975). Where you are unable to gain this type of access, you will therefore need to adopt a different case study organisation, or even to modify your research question and objectives.

However, even where you are able to negotiate entry into an organisation there are other levels of access which you will need to consider and plan for if your research strategy is to be successfully realised. Many writers see access as a *continuing* process and not just an initial or single event (Gummesson, 1991; Marshall and Rossman, 1999; Robson, 1993). This may take two forms. First, access may be an iterative process, so that you gain entry to carry out part of your research and then seek further access in order to conduct another part. You may also seek to repeat your collection of data in different parts of the organisation and therefore engage in the negotiation of access in each part (Marshall and Rossman, 1999). Second, those whom you wish to collect data from may be a different set of people from those who considered and agreed to your request for access. Physical access to an organisation will be formally granted through its management. However, it will also be necessary for you to gain informal acceptance from intended participants within the organisation in order to gain access to the data that they are able to provide (Robson, 1993).

Access may also refer to your ability to select a representative sample of organisational participants (or secondary data) in order to attempt to answer your research question and meet your objectives in an unbiased way and to produce reliable and valid data (Chapters 4 and 6). For example, we recall a well-known current affairs programme that broadcast a feature including short extracts of interviews conducted with employees of a case study organisation. All of the interviewees' responses were very positive about the organisation. However, the reporter had prefixed the showing of these extracts saying that it was the organisation that had selected all of the employees to be interviewed. The viewer was therefore left to wonder whether these very positive employees were typical of all those employed in the organisation, or whether they were providing an unreliable and untypical view of employee attitudes in this business.

We might refer to this broader meaning of access as *cognitive* access. Where you achieve this you will have gained access to the data which you need your intended participants to share with you in order for you to understand their social reality and for you to be able to address your research question and objectives. Simply obtaining physical access into an organisation will be inadequate unless you are also able to negotiate yourself into a position where you can reveal the reality of what is occurring in relation to your research question and objectives. This fundamental point requires you to consider material included throughout this book. However, there are two specific issues that we will consider now. The first of these relates to whether you have sufficiently considered, and therefore fully realised, the extent and nature of the access that you will require in order to be able to answer your research question and meet your objectives. The second point relates to whether you are able to gain sufficient access in practice to answer your research question and meet your objectives. These two points may be linked in some instances. Your clarity of thought, which should result from sufficiently considering the nature of the access which you require, may be helpful in persuading organisations to grant entry since they are more likely to be convinced about your credibility and competence.

Access is therefore likely to be a problematic area, in terms of gaining permission for physical access, maintaining that access and being able to create sufficient scope to address fully the research question and objectives which guide your work. This suggests that the *feasibility* of your research will also be an important guiding principle alongside the recognised hallmarks of good research outlined in a number of sources (Cooper and Schindler, 1998; Marshall and Rossman, 1999; Sekaran, 1992). The issue of feasibility will determine the construction or refinement of your research question and objectives and may sometimes lead to a clash with these hallmarks of good research. This has been recognised by Buchanan *et al.* (1988:53–4):

> Fieldwork is permeated with the conflict between what is theoretically desirable on the one hand and what is practically possible on the other. It is desirable to ensure representativeness in the sample, uniformity of interview procedures, adequate data collection across the range of topics to be explored, and so on. But the members of organisations block access to information, constrain the time allowed for interviews, lose your questionnaires, go on holiday, and join other organisations in the middle of your unfinished study. In the conflict between the desirable and the possible, the possible always wins.

The extent to which feasibility will affect the nature of your research, or at least the approach that you adopt, is made clear by Johnson (1975). He recognises that the reality of undertaking a research project may be to consider where you are likely to be able to gain access and to develop a topic to fit the nature of that access.

A request to undertake research may involve you seeking access to a range of participants based on an organisational sample. In order to select such a sample you will require access to organisational data, either directly or indirectly through a request which outlines precisely how you require the sample to be selected (Chapter 6). Where you wish to undertake a longitudinal study, you will require access to the organisation and your research participants on more than one occasion. The difficulty of obtaining access in relation to these more *intrusive* methods and approaches has been recognised many times in the literature (for example: Buchanan *et al.*, 1988; Johnson, 1975; Raimond, 1993).

The nature of these problems of access will vary in relation to your status as either a full-time or a part-time student. As a full-time student, approaching an organisation where you have no prior contact, you will be seeking to operate in the role of an *external researcher*. You will need to negotiate access at each level discussed above (physical, continuing and cognitive). Operating as an external researcher is likely to pose problems although it may have some benefits. Your lack of status in relation to an organisation in which you wish to conduct research will mean not only that gaining physical access is a major issue to overcome but also that this concern will remain in relation to negotiating continued and cognitive access. Goodwill on the part of the organisation and its participants is something that external researchers need to rely on at each level of access. In this role, you need to remain sensitive to the issue of goodwill and to seek to foster it at each level. The demonstration of competence and integrity will also be critical at each level of access. These are key issues of access faced by all external researchers. Where you are able to demonstrate competence (see Chapters 8–10 in particular) and integrity, your role as an external researcher may prove to be beneficial. This is because participants are willing to accept you as being objective and without a covert organisational agenda, where they see your questions as being worthwhile and meaningful. Many organisations are also well disposed to reasonable research approaches for a number of reasons, some of which are discussed in the following section.

> ### Worked example
>
> ### Researcher's organisational status
>
> Dave recalls an amusing tale of being a research student several years ago. The project involved gaining access to several employers' and trade union organisations. Having gained access to the regional office of one such organisation, Dave used various types of organisational documentation situated there over a period of a few days. During the first day Dave was located in a very nice room and frequently brought refreshments by the janitor of the building. This appeared to Dave to be very kind treatment. However, Dave did not know that a rumour had spread among some staff that he was from 'head office' and was there to 'monitor' in some way the work of the office. On attending the second day, Dave was met by the janitor and taken to a small, plain room and no more refreshments appeared for the duration of the research visit. The rumour had been corrected!

Of course, this example of the effect of the researcher's (lack of) organisational status is most unfair on the very considerable proportion of participants who treat very well those who undertake research within their organisation in full knowledge of their status. However, it illustrates the way in which some participants may react to perceptions about status.

As a part-time student or an organisational employee operating in the role of an *internal* or *participant researcher* you are still likely to face problems of access to data although these will vary in relation to those faced by external researchers. As an internal researcher you will not face the problem associated with negotiating physical or continuing access, at least where you undertake research in your 'own part' of the organisation. However, your status in the organisation may pose particular problems in relation to cognitive access. This may be related to suspicions about why you are undertaking your research project and the use that will be made of the data, perceptions about the part of the organisation for which you work and your grade status in relation to those whom you wish to be your research participants. Any such problem may be exacerbated where you are given a project to research if others are aware that this is an issue in which management would like to implement change. This is particularly likely to be the case where resulting change would be perceived as being harmful to those whom you would wish to be your research participants. This not only will provide a problem for you in terms of gaining cognitive access but may also suggest ethical concerns as well (which are discussed in Section 5.4). As an internal researcher, you will need to consider these issues and, where appropriate, to discuss them with those who wish to provide you with a project to research.

5.3   Strategies to gain access

The preceding section has outlined problems associated with gaining access and the sufficiency of any access obtained. It has stressed the need to identify a feasible research question and objectives, from the perspective of gaining access. This section will outline and discuss a number of strategies that may help you to obtain physical and cognitive access to appropriate data. The discussion in this section will be applicable to you where you wish to gain *personal entry* to an organisation. It will be less applicable where you send a self-administered, postal questionnaire to organisational participants, in situations where you do not need to gain physical access in order to identify participants. As Raimond (1993:67) recognises, 'provided that people reply to the questionnaires, the problem of access to data is solved'. Even in this case, however, some of the points which follow will still apply to the way in which you construct the pre-survey contact and the written request to complete the questionnaire (see also Chapter 10). The applicability of these strategies will also vary in relation to your status as either an internal or external researcher. Self-check question 5.3 is specifically designed to allow you to explore this aspect and

Table 5.6 offers suggestions about the use of these strategies in relation to the respective roles of internal and external researcher.

The strategies to help you to gain access are summarised in Table 5.1. These strategies will be developed in the remainder of this section of the chapter.

Table 5.1	**Summary of strategies to gain access**

- Allowing yourself sufficient time
- Using existing contacts and developing new ones
- Providing a clear account of purpose and type of access required
- Overcoming organisational concerns about the granting of access
- Identifying possible benefits to the organisation in granting you access
- Using suitable language
- Facilitating ease of reply when requesting access
- Developing your access on an incremental basis
- Establishing your credibility with intended participants

Allowing yourself sufficient time

Physical access may take weeks or even months to arrange, and in many cases the time invested will not result in access being granted (Buchanan *et al.*, 1988). An approach to an organisation will result in either a reply or no response at all. A politely worded but clearly reasoned refusal at least informs you that access will not be granted. The non-reply situation means that if you wish to pursue the possibility of gaining access to a particular organisation, you will need to allow sufficient time before sending further correspondence or making a follow-up telephone call. Easterby-Smith *et al.* (1991) report the need to make up to four telephone calls in order to gain access. Great care must be taken in relation to this type of activity so that no grounds for offence are given. Seeking access into a large, complex organisation, where you do not have existing contacts, may also necessitate several telephone calls simply to make contact with the appropriate person, in order to ensure that your request for access will be considered by the right individual. In our experience, this can take days or even a couple of weeks to achieve. You may also consider using email where you have access to this as a way of obtaining a reply.

If you are able to contact a participant directly, such as a manager, an exchange of correspondence may be sufficient to gain access. Here you should clearly set out what you require from this person and persuade him or her of the value of your work and your credibility. Even so, you will still need to allow time for your request to be received and considered and an interview meeting to be arranged at a convenient time for your research participant. This may take a number of weeks and you may have to wait for longer to schedule the actual interview.

Where you are seeking access to a range of organisational participants to conduct a number of interviews, to undertake a survey, to engage in observation or to use secondary data, your request may be passed 'up' the organisation for clearance and may be considered by a number of people. Where you are able to use a known contact in the organisation this may help since you can probably feel assured that your request is being attended to, but you will still need to allow for this process to take weeks rather than days. Where the organisation is prepared to consider granting access it is likely that you will be asked to attend a meeting to discuss this. There may also be a period of delay after this stage while the case which you have made for access is evaluated in terms of its implications for the organisation, and it may be necessary to make a number of telephone calls to pursue your request politely.

In the situation where your intended participants are not the same people who grant you physical access, you will need to allow further time to gain their acceptance. This may involve you making *pre-survey contact* by telephone calls to these intended participants, or engaging in correspondence or holding an explanatory meeting with them (discussed later). You may well need to allow a couple of weeks or more to establish contact with your intended participants and to secure their co-operation, especially given any operational constraints which restrict their availability.

Once you have gained physical access to the organisation and to your participants, you will be concerned with gaining 'cognitive access'. Whichever method you are using to gather data will involve you in a time-consuming process, although some methods will require that more of your time be spent within the organisation to understand what is happening. The use of a questionnaire will mean less time spent in the organisation compared with the use of non-standardised interviews, whereas the use of observation techniques may result in even more time being spent to gather data (Bryman, 1988). Where you are involved in a situation of 'continuing access', as outlined in the section above, there will also be an issue related to the time which is required to negotiate, or re-negotiate, access at each stage. You will need to consider how careful planning may help to minimise the possibility of any 'stop–go' approach to your research activity.

Using existing contacts and developing new ones

Other management and organisational researchers suggest that you are more likely to gain access where you are able to use *existing contacts* (Buchanan *et al.*, 1988; Easterby-Smith *et al.*, 1991; Johnson, 1975). Buchanan *et al.* (1988:56) say that 'we have been most successful where we have a friend, relative or student working in the organisation'. We have also found this to be the case. In order to request access we have approached those whom we would consider to be professional colleagues, who may also be present or past students, course advisers, external examiners, or otherwise known to us through local, regional or national networks. Their knowledge of us means that they should be able to trust our stated intentions and the assurances given about the use of any data provided. It can also be useful to start a research project by utilising these existing contacts in order to establish a track record that you can refer to in approaches which you make to other organisations where you do not have such contacts. This should help your credibility with these new contacts.

The use of known contacts will depend largely on your choice of research strategy and approach to selecting a sample, as suggested by your research question and objectives. It will undoubtedly be easier to use this approach where you are using a case study based research strategy and non-probability sampling (Section 6.3). This will certainly be the case where you undertake an in-depth study that focuses on a small, purposively selected sample. There will clearly be a high level of *convenience* in terms of gaining access through contacts who are familiar; however, these contacts may also be used as part of a quota sample, or in relation to purposive or snowball sampling (Section 6.3).

Jankowicz (1995) refers to the possibility of using your work placement organisation as a context for your research project, where this applies to your situation as a full-time undergraduate or postgraduate student. Where you have enjoyed a successful work placement, you will undoubtedly have made a number of contacts who may be able to be very helpful in terms of co-operating with you and granting access to data. You may have become interested in a particular topic because of the time that you spent in your placement organisation. Where this applies to your situation, you can spend time reading theoretical work which may be relevant to this topic, then identify a research question and objectives and plan a research project to pursue your interest within the context of your placement organisation. The combination of genuine interest in the topic and relatively easy access to organisational participants should help towards the production of a good-quality and useful piece of work.

Where you need to develop *new contacts*, consideration of the points discussed throughout this section will help you to cultivate these. In addition, you will need to be able to identify the most appropriate person to contact for help, either directly or indirectly. There may be a number of ways to seek to do this, depending on your research topic. You may consider contacting the local branch of an appropriate professional association for the names and business addresses of key employees to contact in organisations where it would be suitable for you to conduct research. You could also contact this professional association at national level, where this was more appropriate to your research question and objectives. It might also be appropriate to contact either an employers' association for a particular industry, or a trade union, at local or national level. Alternatively, it might be appropriate for you to contact one or more chambers of commerce, training and enterprise councils or other employers' networks (Jankowicz, 1995).

You may also consider making a direct approach to an organisation in an attempt to identify the appropriate person to contact in relation to a particular research project. This has the advantage of potentially providing access to organisations which you would like to include in your research project; however, great care needs to be exercised at each stage of this exercise.

Identifying the appropriate person through whom to request access

Adrian and another colleague identified a number of specific organisations that matched the criteria established for the types of business that they wished to include in a research project. Many of these were organisations where they did not have an appropriate contact, or indeed any contact at all. The different types of organisational structures in these organisations added to their difficulties in tracking down the most appropriate employee to contact in order to request access.

National directories that were available were used to identify the corporate headquarters of each organisation. This part of the organisation was contacted by telephone. In each case the name of the researcher was given and that of the institution through which they were conducting the research. A very brief explanation was provided in order to identify the name and location of that part of the organisation which dealt with the area of their research interest. This resulted in the researchers being provided with a telephone number or connected to that part of the organisation which the receptionist to whom they spoke thought was appropriate for the enquiry (see next paragraph). This initial telephone call was always ended by thanking the person for the help that had been provided.

At the next stage, the researchers again provided their name and that of the institution through which they were conducting the research. At this stage, the purpose of the research was also briefly explained to the secretary who inevitably answered the telephone. The researchers asked for the name and business address of the person whom the secretary thought would be the most appropriate person to write to. In most cases the people to whom the researchers spoke at this stage were most helpful and provided some excellent leads.

Sometimes, particularly in relation to complex organisations, the researchers found that they were not talking to someone in the appropriate part of the organisation. They therefore asked the person to help by transferring the call. Sometimes this led to a series of calls to identify the right person. They always maintained politeness and thanked the person whom they spoke to for their help. They always gave their names and organisational location to reduce the risk of appearing to be threatening in any way. It was most important to create a positive attitude in what could be perceived as a tiresome enquiry.

The researchers chose to ask for the name and business address of a hoped-for organisational 'lead'. Using this they could send a written request to this person which could be considered when it was convenient, rather than attempt to talk to them at that point in time when it may well have not been a good time to make to such a request. This process resulted in many successes and Adrian and his colleague have added a number of good contacts to their previous list. However, the key point to note is that great care needs to be exercised when using this approach.

Making this type of contact may result in identifying the person whom you wish to participate in your research. Alternatively, your reason for making contact with this person may be to ask them to grant you access to others in the organisation whom you wish to be your participants, or to secondary data. This second type of contact is sometimes referred to as a '*broker*' (Easterby-Smith *et al.*, 1991) or a '*gatekeeper*' (Gummesson, 1991). Easterby-Smith *et al.* (1991) suggest approaching an organisation's personnel manager because this person will have contacts across the organisation and can therefore be very helpful in terms of facilitating access. This type of contact may also be the functional manager or director of those staff to whom you would like access. Having identified an organisational broker or gatekeeper you will have to persuade them about your credibility, to overcome any issues they have about the sensitivity of your research project and to demonstrate the potential value of this for them.

Providing a clear account of purpose and type of access required

Providing a clear account of your requirements will allow your intended participants to be aware of what will be required from them (Robson, 1993). Asking for access and co-operation without being specific about your requirements will probably lead to a cautious attitude on their part since the amount of time which could be required might prove to be disruptive. Even where the initial contact or request for access involves a telephone call, it is still probably advisable to send a letter that outlines your proposed research and requirements. Your *introductory letter* requesting access should outline in brief the purpose of your research, how the person being contacted might be able to help and what would be required. Healey (1991) suggests that the success of this letter will be helped by the use of short and clear sentences. Its tone should be polite and it should seek to generate interest on the part of intended respondents.

Establishing your credibility will be vital in order to gain access. The use of known contacts will mean that you can seek to trade on your existing level of credibility. However, when you are making contact with a potential participant for the first time, the nature of your approach will be highly significant in terms of beginning to establish credibility – or not doing so! Any telephone call or introductory letter will need to demonstrate your clarity of thought and purpose. Any lack of preparation at this stage will be apparent and is likely to reduce the possibility of gaining access (see Section 9.4 for further consideration of these issues).

The presentation of the introductory letter will also serve to establish credibility. Healey (1991:210) says 'a well-designed and presented letter, typed on headed note paper, which is personally addressed with a hand-written signature, would seem to be a sensible way of trying to persuade . . . managers of businesses to co-operate'.

Overcoming organisational concerns to the granting of access

Organisational concerns may be placed into one of three categories. First, concerns about the amount of time or resources that will be involved in the request for access. Easterby-Smith *et al.* (1991) suggest that your request for access may be more likely to be accepted if the amount of time and resources required are kept to a minimum. As a complementary point to this, Healey (1991) reports earlier work that found that introductory letters containing multiple requests are also less likely to be successful. However, while the achievement of access may be more likely to be realised where your demands are kept to a minimum, there will still be a need to maintain honesty. For example, where you wish to conduct an interview you may be more likely to gain access if the time requested is kept within reason. However, falsely stating that it will last for only a short time and then deliberately exceeding this is very likely to upset your participant and may prevent you gaining further access.

The second area of concern is related to *sensitivity* about the topic. We have found that organisations are less likely to co-operate where the topic of the research has a negative inference. Organisations do not normally wish to present themselves in a bad light. If this is likely to be the case you will need to consider carefully the way in which your proposed research topic may be perceived by those whom you ask to grant access. In such cases you may be able to highlight a positive approach to the issue by, for example, emphasising that your work will be designed to identify individual and organisational learning in relation to the topic (a positive inference). You should avoid sending any request that appears to concentrate on aspects associated with non-achievement or failure if you are to gain access. Your request for access is therefore more likely to be favourably considered where you are able to outline a research topic which does not appear to be sensitive to the organisation (Easterby-Smith *et al.*, 1991).

The third area of concern is related to the *confidentiality* of the data that would have to be provided and the *anonymity* of the organisation or individual participants. To overcome this concern, you will need to provide clear assurances about these aspects. One advantage of using an introductory letter is to give this guarantee in writing at the time of making the request for access, when this issue may be uppermost in the minds of those who will consider your approach. Once initial access has been granted you will need to repeat the assurance about anonymity to those who act as your participants. You will also need to consider how to maintain this when you write up your work in situations where particular participants could be indirectly identified (Bell, 1999) (Section 13.5). Illustrations of this are provided in the worked example in Section 5.4 titled 'inadvertently revealing participants' identities'.

Possible benefits to the organisation of granting you access

Apart from any general interest that is generated by the subject of your proposed research, you may find that it will have some level of *applicability* to the jobs of those whom you approach for access. Practitioners often wrestle with the same subject issues as researchers and may therefore welcome the opportunity to discuss their own analysis and course of action related to such an issue, in a non-threatening, non-judgemental environment. A discussion may allow them to think through an issue and to reflect on the action that they have adopted to manage it. In our own interviews with practitioners we are pleased when told that the discussion has been of value to the interviewee, because of this reason.

For those who work in organisations where they are perhaps the only subject practitioner, this may be the first time they have had this type of opportunity. You therefore need to consider whether your proposed research topic may provide some advantage to those from whom you wish to gain access, although this does not mean that you should attempt to 'buy' your way in based on some promise about the potential value of your work. Where it is unlikely that your proposed research will suggest any advantage to those whose co-operation you seek, you will need to consider what alternative course of action to take. This may involve re-designing your research question and objectives before seeking any access.

It may also help to offer a report of your findings to those who grant access. The intention would be to provide each of your participants with something of value and to fulfil any expectations about exchange between the provider and receiver of the research data, thereby prompting some of those whom you approach to grant access (Johnson, 1975). Buchanan *et al.* (1988) suggest that this type of report should be specially designed to be of use to those who participated rather than, say, a copy of the document you need to submit for academic examination. They also suggest that feedback about this report may further help you with your research.

Where access is granted in return for supplying a report of your findings it may be important to devise a simple 'contract' to make clear what has been agreed. This should make clear the broad form of the report and the nature and depth of the analysis that you agree to include in it. This may vary from a summary report of key findings to a much more in-depth analysis. For this reason, it will be important to determine what will be realistic to supply to those who grant you access.

Using suitable language

Some researchers advise against referring to certain terms used in relation to research activity when making an approach to an organisation for access, because these may be perceived as threatening or not interesting to the potential participant (Buchanan *et al.*, 1988, Easterby-Smith *et al.*, 1991; Jankowicz, 1995). Buchanan *et al.* (1988:57) suggest using 'learn from your experience' in place of research, 'conversation' instead of interview and 'write an account' rather than publish. Easterby-Smith *et al.* (1991:77) suggest that the term 'researcher' will have greater credibility than that of 'student'.

Use of language will largely depend on the nature of the people you are contacting. Your language should be appropriate to the type of person being contacted, without any hint of being patronising, threatening or just boring. Given the vital role of initial telephone conversations or introductory letters, we would suggest allowing adequate time to consider and draft these and using someone to check through your message. You are intending to engender interest in your research project and the initial point of contact needs to convey this.

Worked example

Introductory letter

Anytown Business School

Anytown Business School
University of Anytown
Anytown
Anyshire
AN1 52PL

Tel: 01234 567890
Fax: 01234 567891

Mr Geoffrey West
Personnel Policy Manager
Utility Co plc
South Avenue
Anytown

Date: 15 November 1999

Dear Mr West

THE POSITIVE MANAGEMENT OF CHANGE

We are currently researching the above, in order to determine and share effective practices on this topical and important issue. We are both attached to the Change Management Research Centre within the University.

You have experience that would be of value to us and we would very much like to know your views on what it takes to manage change.

We are now arranging a further group of interviews with targeted practitioners who can give personal insights into specific change management programmes. We have already undertaken two groups of interviews involving senior personnel practitioners in 30 medium and large-scale organisations towards our target of 50.

An outline of the interview structure is attached, although it is not our intention to follow this slavishly. We will conduct interviews during January and February 2000 and envisage that these will take up to two hours.

▶

We are aware of the need to treat our findings with the utmost confidentiality. No source, individual or organisational, will be identified or comment attributed without the express permission of the originator.

One of our intended outputs will be a report summarising our findings and we will be sending a copy of this to each of the participants in the study.

We hope you are able to help us and should be grateful if you would return the attached pro forma. We will contact you on receipt to confirm arrangements where you are able to participate. If you prefer to talk with us to agree a suitable time and venue please call us on the following numbers:

If you require any further information please do not hesitate to get in touch.

Yours sincerely

Adrian Thornhill   **Andrew Gibbons**

Dr Adrian Thornhill and Andrew Gibbons

Facilitating ease of reply when requesting access

We have found that the inclusion of a simple pro forma for recipients of our written requests for access to use generally ensures a reply. It may not be suitable in all cases and should be designed to fit the research method being used. Nevertheless, its use is worth considering in cases where it is necessary for your recipient to draft their own letter to reply. Inclusion of a stamped or freepost, addressed envelope, or a fax number, or an email address, may also facilitate a reply.

Developing your access on an incremental basis

Reference has been made above to the strategy of achieving access by stages, as a means of overcoming organisational concerns about time-consuming, multiple requests. Johnson (1975) provides an example of developing access on an incremental basis. He used a three-stage strategy to achieve his desired depth of access. The first stage involved a request to conduct interviews. This was the minimum requirement in order to commence his research. The next stage involved negotiating access to undertake observation. The final stage was in effect an extension to the second stage and involved gaining permission to tape record the interactions being observed.

There are potentially a number of advantages related to the use of this strategy. As suggested above a request to an organisation for multiple access may be sufficient to cause them to decline entry. Using an incremental strategy at least gains you access to a certain level of data. This strategy will also allow you the opportunity to develop a

Worked example

Pro forma to facilitate replies

Variations of the following pro forma have been used successfully to facilitate replies from organisations whom we have requested to participant in research activity.

For the attention of K Thornhill, The Business School

Dear Katie and Andrew

Managing change

❑ I am able to talk to you about managing change. I can be available to meet you at the following times, date and locations . . .

Date/s   Time   Location/s

_____

_____

_____

_____

❑ Please contact me to arrange a suitable date, time and venue.

❑ I also recommend that you speak with . . .

_____

_____

❑ I am unable to talk to you about managing change.

❑ I do recommend that you speak with . . .

_____

_____

Yours sincerely,

Position:

Organisation:

Telephone:
Fax:
Email:

positive relationship with those who are prepared to grant initial access of a restricted nature. As you establish your credibility, you can develop the possibility of achieving a fuller level of access. A further advantage may follow from the opportunity that you have to design your request for further access specifically to the situation and in relation to opportunities which may become apparent from your initial level of access. On the other hand, this incremental process will be time consuming and you need to consider the amount of time that you will have for your research project before embarking on such a strategy.

Establishing your credibility with intended participants

In Section 5.2, we differentiated between physical and cognitive access. Just because you have been granted entry into an organisation, you will not be able to assume that those whom you wish to interview, survey or observe will be prepared to provide their co-operation. Indeed, assuming that this is going to happen raises an ethical issue that is considered in the next section. Robson (1993) says that gaining co-operation from these intended participants is a matter of developing relationships. This will mean repeating much of the process that you will have used to gain entry into the organisation. You will need to share with them the purpose of your research project, state how you believe that they will be able to help your study and provide assurances about confidentiality and anonymity. This may involve writing to your intended participants or talking to them individually or in a group. Which of these means you use will depend on the intended research method, your opportunity to make contact with them, the numbers of participants involved and the nature of the setting. Where your intended method may be considered intrusive, you may need to exercise even greater care and take longer to gain acceptance. This might be the case, for example, where you wish to undertake observation. The extent to which you succeed in gaining cognitive access will depend on this effort.

Worked example

A request to participate in a discussion group

20th March 2000

Dear (staff name)

Edcoll is holding a communications audit that we have been asked to undertake. In order to explore attitudes held by members of staff we will be holding a series of discussion groups. As a member of staff randomly selected by us to be invited to one of these discussion groups, your views will be important in order for us to be able to build up a clear picture of staff attitudes about internal communication. The attitudes revealed at these discussion groups will then be used by us to inform the design of a questionnaire to be sent to all members of staff.

Each discussion group should last no longer than one hour. Comments made during the discussion group will not be attributed to any individual or to the group and will only be used by us to inform the design of the questionnaire. On completion of the audit, key results will be communicated to all members of staff.

The discussion group which you have been invited to take part in will be held on:

(time; day; date; room; location)

If you will not be able to attend please can you contact one of us by (date), so that an appropriate alternative person can be invited in your place. Our telephone number is:

We very much hope that you can attend and look forward to seeing you.

(Signed in ink by the members of the research team)

Key points from the strategies that we have outlined to help you to gain access to organisations and those whom you wish to participate in your research project have been summarised as a checklist for you to use in Table 5.2.

| Table 5.2 | **Summary checklist to help to gain access** |

✓ Allow yourself plenty of time.

✓ Consider using existing contacts, at least at the start of your research project, in order to gain access and gather data.

✓ Consider using your work placement organisation, where appropriate, as a case study setting for your research project.

✓ Where you need to seek information about organisations that may be able to grant access, approach appropriate local and/or national employer or employee, professional or trade bodies to see if they can suggest contacts.

✓ Consider making a direct approach to an organisation to identify the most appropriate person to contact for access.

✓ Invest sufficient time to identify this person and be prepared to make a number of telephone calls to achieve this.

✓ Maintain politeness at all times.

▶

Table 5.2	*Cont.*

✓ Even where your initial request for access involves a telephone conversation, it is advisable to follow this with an introductory letter to confirm your requirements.

✓ Always provide a clear account of your requirements when requesting access (at least your initial requirements).

✓ Outlining the purpose of your research project and demonstrating clarity of thought should help to establish your credibility and assist the goal of gaining access.

✓ The construction, tone and presentation of an introductory letter will also assist the establishment of your credibility and the goal of gaining access.

✓ Any request for access will need to consider and address organisational concerns relating to the amount of time or resources which would be involved on the part of the organisation, sensitivity about the topic, and confidentiality and anonymity.

✓ Consider possible benefits for the organisation should they grant access to you and the offer of a report summarising your findings to enhance your chance of achieving access.

✓ Exercise care and attention in your use of language, so that it is appropriate to the person who receives it without any hint of being patronising, threatening or boring.

✓ Include a simple pro forma for recipients of your request for access to use as a means to reply, and also send a stamped or freepost, addressed envelope, or email address, plus a fax number where possible.

✓ Be prepared to attend a meeting to present and discuss your request for access.

✓ Be prepared to work through organisational gatekeepers in order to gain access to intended types of participants.

✓ Consider developing your access on an incremental basis where it is likely that a multiple request for access would be likely to lead to a refusal to gain any entry.

✓ Allow further time to contact intended participants and to develop a relationship with them in order to gain their acceptance, once physical access has been granted.

✓ Remember that some methods will require lengthy periods of your time being spent within an organisation in order to gain 'cognitive access' to data.

5.4   Research ethics

Defining research ethics

Ethical concerns will emerge as you plan your research, seek access to organisations and to individuals, collect, analyse and report your data. In the context of research, *ethics* refers to the appropriateness of your behaviour in relation to the rights of those who become the subject of your work, or are affected by it. Wells (1994:284) defines 'ethics in terms of a code of behaviour appropriate to academics and the conduct of research'. The appropriateness or acceptability of our behaviour as researchers will be affected by broader social norms of behaviour (Wells, 1994; Zikmund, 1997). A *social norm* indicates the type of behaviour that a person ought to adopt in a particular situation (Robson, 1993; Zikmund, 1997). However, as Wells (1994) recognises, the norms of behaviour that prevail will in reality allow for a range of ethical positions. You will therefore need to consider ethical issues throughout the period of your research and to remain sensitive to the impact of your work on those whom you approach to help, those who provide access and co-operation and those affected by your results.

The conduct of your research may be guided by a code of ethics, and where you are a member of an educational institution or a professional association you should seek out the existence of such guidelines (for example, Appendix 3). A *code of ethics* will provide you with a statement of principles and procedures for the conduct of your research. This will be helpful and, where followed, should ensure that you do not transgress behavioural norms established by your institution or association. However, there may well be other ethical issues that you need to consider during the conduct of your research, as we now discuss.

The nature of business and management research means that you will be dependent on other people for access, as we have seen above. This will inevitably lead to a range of ethical issues. As Wells (1994:290) puts it, 'In general, the closer the research is to actual individuals in real-world settings, the more likely are ethical questions to be raised.' Related to this, the nature of *power relationships* in business and management research will raise ethical issues that also need to be considered. Managers will be in a very powerful position in relation to researchers who request organisational access. They will remain in a powerful position in terms of the nature and extent of the access that they allow in an organisational setting. However, researchers need to be sensitive to the way in which the granting of access affects this type of relationship. Face-to-face interviews, even with managers, will place researchers in a position of some 'power', albeit for a short time, because they are able to formulate questions including probing ones which may cause levels of discomfort. In addition, as a researcher in an organisational setting you will need to remain sensitive to the fact that your presence is a temporary one, whereas the people from whom you collect data will need to work together after you depart. We will consider these ethical issues related to business and management research in the discussion that follows.

Nature and scope of ethical issues in business and management

This discussion of ethical issues is divided into four subsections. In the first subsection, we outline the range of ethical issues that affect the research process across its various stages. In the second subsection we discuss ethical issues which arise in particular during the design stage and when seeking initial access. In the third subsection, we discuss ethical issues that are prominent during the data collection stage and examine particular issues related to different methods. In the fourth subsection, we discuss ethical issues related to the analysis and reporting stages.

Ethical issues that affect the research process generally

A number of key ethical issues arise across the stages and duration of a research project. Before we embark on a discussion of these in relation to the particular stages outlined, it is worth summarising these key ethical issues. They relate to ethical issues around the:

- privacy of possible and actual participants;
- voluntary nature of participation and the right to withdraw partially or completely from the process;
- consent and possible deception of participants;
- maintenance of the confidentiality of data provided by individuals or identifiable participants and their anonymity;
- reactions of participants to the way in which you seek to collect data;
- effects on participants of the way in which you use, analyse and report your data;
- behaviour and objectivity of the researcher.

Privacy may be seen as the cornerstone of the ethical issues that confront those who undertake research. For example, consent, confidentiality, participant reactions and the effects of the way in which you use, analyse and report your data all have the capacity to affect, or are related to, the privacy of participants. Table 5.3 summarises the implications of seeking to respect privacy within the context of business and management research.

Table 5.3   **The implications of respecting privacy in business and management research**

Respecting privacy in business and management research means the right:

- not to participate;
- not to be harassed or offered inducements to participate or to extend the scope of participation beyond that freely given;
- not to be contacted at unreasonable times or at home (where the scope of the research is related to an organisational setting);
- of participants to determine, within reason, when they will participate in the data collection process;
- of participants to expect the researcher to abide by the extent of the consent given and not to find that the researcher wishes to widen the scope of the research without first seeking and obtaining permission;
- of participants not to be subject to any attempt to prolong the duration of an interview or observation beyond that previously agreed unless the participant freely proposes this as an option;
- of participants not to answer any question, or set of questions, or provide any related data where requested;
- of participants not to be subjected to questions that create stress or discomfort;
- to expect agreed anonymity and confidentiality to be observed strictly both in relation to discussions with other research or organisational participants and during the reporting of findings (including from those who gain subsequent access to data).

There may well be additional points to the ones that we list in Table 5.3, particularly in relation to specific settings or data collection methods. Indeed, this key ethical issue of privacy is explored further in the discussion of informed consent later in this section. Consideration of the points included in Table 5.3 provides sufficient evidence that this is an area that should be treated with great concern and which is likely to require continuous evaluation to help you to take appropriate action at each stage of your research.

Where you have access you may find it useful to use the 'ETHX module' of the 'Methodologist's Toolchest' (Scolari Sage, 1999). This includes a range of features that for example allow you to consider ethical issues involving human subjects and to develop an appropriate consent form.

You may also consider using the Internet in relation to your research project. This possibility will undoubtedly continue to generate a debate and evaluation about the ethical use of this particular means to collect data. The expression *netiquette* has been developed to provide a heading for the range of ethical issues that arise from using the Internet for this purpose. The Internet may allow you to contact possible participants more easily and even to do this repeatedly – a possibility that may be an invasion of their privacy in a number of ways. Forms of covert observation may also be possible which impinge on the rights of 'participants' (Cooper and Schindler, 1998). In general terms, you should apply the ethical principles that are discussed in this chapter and elsewhere in this book when considering using the Internet as a means to collect data. We offer particular advice about online surveys in Section 10.5.

Ethical issues during the design and initial access stages

A number of management researchers state that ethical problems should be anticipated and dealt with during the design stage of any research project. This should be attempted by planning to conduct the research project in line with the ethical principles outlined above and by altering the research strategy or choice of methods where this is appropriate. Evidence that these issues have been considered and evaluated at this stage, through a discussion in your research proposal, should be one of the criteria against which your research proposal is judged (Cooper and Schindler, 1998; Marshall and Rossman, 1999).

One of the key stages at which you need to consider the potential for ethical problems to arise is when you seek initial access. As referred to above, you should not attempt to apply any pressure on intended participants to grant access (Robson, 1993; Sekaran, 1992). This is unlikely to be the case where you are approaching a member of an organisation's management to request access. However, where you are undertaking a research project as an internal researcher within your employing organisation (Section 5.3), in relation to a part-time qualification, there may be a temptation to apply pressure on others (colleagues or subordinates) to co-operate. Individuals have a right to privacy (Table 5.3) which means that you will have to accept any refusal to take part (Cooper and Schindler, 1998; Robson, 1993). Privacy may also be affected by the nature and timing of any approach which you make to intended participants – say by telephoning at 'unsociable' times, or, where possible, by 'confronting' intended participants. Access to secondary data may also raise ethical problems in relation to privacy.

Where you happen to obtain access to personal data about individuals who have not consented to let you have this (through personnel or client records) you will be obliged to treat this in the strictest confidence and not to abuse it in any way.

Consent to participate in a research project is not a straightforward matter. In general terms, an approach to a potential participant is an attempt to gain consent. However, this raises a question about the scope of any consent given. Where someone agrees to participate in a particular data collection method, this does not necessarily *imply* consent about the way in which the data provided are subsequently used. Clearly, any assurances that you provide about anonymity and confidentiality will help to develop an understanding of the nature of the consent being entered into, but even this may be inadequate in terms of clarifying the nature of that consent. This suggests a continuum that ranges across a lack of consent, involving some form of deception, a lack of clarity about the nature of consent so that the researcher *implies consent* from taking part, and consent that is fully informed as well as freely given (known as *informed consent*). This is shown in Fig 5.1.

Participant consent continuum:

Lack of consent
- Participant lacks knowledge
- Researcher uses deception to collect data

Implied consent
- Participant does not fully understand her/his rights
- Researcher implies consent about use of data from fact of access or return of questionnaire

Informed consent
- Participant consent given freely and based on full information about participation rights and use of data

Fig 5.1   The nature of participant consent

Three points are described in Fig 5.1, although in reality this is likely to operate as a continuum in the proper sense that a multitude of positions are possible around the key points described. For example, research that is conducted with those who have agreed to participate can still involve an attempt to *deceive* them in some way. This may be related to deceit over the real purpose of the research (Sekaran, 1992), or in relation to some undeclared sponsorship (Zikmund, 1997) or related to an association with another organisation which will use any data gained for commercial advantage. Where this is the case, it will cause embarrassment to those who promote your request for access within their employing organisation, as well as to yourself.

There are a number of aspects to the concept of informed consent. These are detailed in Table 5.4. The extent of the detail of informed consent that you will require will depend on the nature of your research project. The nature of establishing informed consent will also vary. Correspondence may be exchanged, such as that shown in

Section 5.3, to establish informed consent. This may be supplemented by a more detailed written agreement and signed by both parties. Informed consent may also be entered into through a verbal agreement. You will also need to operate on the basis that informed consent is a continuing requirement. This, of course, will be particularly significant where you seek to gain access on an incremental basis (Section 5.3). Although you may have established informed consent through prior written correspondence, it will still be worthwhile to reinforce this at the point of collecting data. An example of this is provided in Section 9.4 in the worked example about opening a semi-structured interview. You will also need to gain informed consent from those whom you wish to be your intended participants as well as those who act as organisational gatekeepers, granting you access.

In the preceding section, we discussed possible strategies to help you to gain access. One of these was related to possible benefits to an organisation of granting you access. You should be realistic about this. Where you are anxious to gain access, you may be tempted to offer more than is feasible. Alternatively, you may offer to supply information arising from your work without intending to do this. Such behaviour would clearly be unethical and to compound this the effect of such action (or inaction) may result in a refusal to grant access to others who come after you.

Ethical issues during the data collection stage

The data collection stage is associated with a range of ethical issues. Some of these are general issues that will apply to whichever method is being used to collect data. Other issues are more specifically related to a particular method of collecting data. We will consider the issues related to all methods first and then examine issues related to particular methods of data collection.

Irrespective of method, there are a number of ethical principles to which you need to adhere. In the previous subsection, we referred to the importance of not intruding on an intended participant's privacy. This was in relation to the participant's right not to take part. Once participants have agreed to take part in your research, they still maintain their right to privacy. This means that they have the right to withdraw as participants and that they may decline to take part in a particular aspect of your research. You should not ask them to participate in anything that will intrude on their privacy where this goes beyond the scope of the access agreed. We also referred to rights in relation to deceit in the previous subsection. Once access has been granted you should remain within the aims of your research project that you shared with your intended participant(s) (Zikmund, 1997). To do otherwise, without raising this with your participant(s) and re-negotiating access, would be, in effect, another type of deceit. This would be likely to cause upset and could result in the premature termination of your data collection. There are perhaps some situations where deception may be accepted in relation to 'covert' research and we will discuss this later in this subsection.

Another general ethical principle is related to the maintenance of your *objectivity*. During the data collection stage this means making sure that you collect your data accurately and fully – that you avoid exercising subjective selectivity in what you record. The importance of this action also relates to the validity and reliability of your

Table 5.4	**Checklist of requirements for informed consent**

Organisational 'gatekeepers' (discussed earlier in Section 5.3) and intended participants need to be informed about the following aspects of the research.

About the nature of the research

✓   What is its purpose?

✓   Who is or will be undertaking it?

✓   Is it being funded or sponsored – if so, by whom and why?

✓   Who is being asked to participate – i.e. broad details about the sampling frame, sample determination and size?

✓   How far has the research project progressed?

About the requirements of taking part

✓   What type of data will be required from those who agree to take part?

✓   How will these data be collected (e.g. interview, observation or questionnaire)?

✓   How much time will be required and on how many occasions?

✓   What are the target dates to undertake the research and for participation?

About the implications of taking part and participants' rights

✓   Recognition that participation is voluntary.

✓   Recognition that participants have the right to decline to answer a question or set of questions, or to be observed in particular circumstances.

✓   Recognition that participants have control over the right to record any of their responses where use of a tape recorder is contemplated.

✓   Recognition that participants may withdraw at any time.

✓   What are the consequences of participating – possible risks, depending on the nature of the approach and purpose, and expected benefits?

✓   What assurances will be provided about participant anonymity and data confidentiality?

About the use of the data collected and the way in which it will be reported

✓   Who will have access to the data collected?

✓   How will the results of the research project be disseminated?

✓   How will assurances about anonymity and confidentiality be observed at this stage?

✓   What will happen to the data collected after the project is completed?

✓   Where data are to be preserved, what safeguards will be 'built in' to safeguard future anonymity and confidentiality of participants?

work, which is discussed in Chapters 4 and 6–10. Without objectively collected data, your ability to analyse and report your work accurately will also be impaired. We return to this as an ethical issue in the next subsection. Obviously any invention of data is also a totally unacceptable and unethical course of action.

Worked example

The ethical dilemma of dubious data

One of the most famous debates about whether research data were invented concerns some of the work of one of the most famous British psychologists, Cyril Burt. His research concerned the relationship between IQ and genetic factors. He believed that 'individual differences in IQ are caused in part by genetic factors' (Morgan, 1995).

Claims about such a relationship are politically contentious and in the mid-1970s, after Burt's death, doubts were raised about the statistical reliability of some of Burt's data and about whether two of his research assistants had really existed. Because of the significance of the implications of Burt's work a debate has continued to exist over two decades among those in his academic discipline about some of the data which he produced to justify his conclusions (see Mackintosh, 1995).

Confidentiality and *anonymity* have also been shown to be important in terms of gaining access to organisations and individuals (Section 5.3). Once promises about confidentiality and anonymity have been given it is of great importance to make sure that these are maintained. Easterby-Smith *et al.* (1991) raise the important point that, in a qualitatively based approach to primary data collection, points of significance will emerge as the research progresses and this will probably lead you to wish to explore these with other participants. However, Easterby-Smith *et al.* recognise that where you do this within an organisation it may lead to participants indirectly identifying which person was responsible for making the point which you wish to explore with them. This may result in harmful repercussions for the person whose openness allowed you to identify this point for exploration. Great care therefore needs to be exercised in maintaining each participant's right of anonymity. You will need to consider where the use of any data gained may have harmful consequences for the disclosing participant. Where you wish to get others to discuss such a potentially sensitive point you may attempt to steer the discussion to see if they will raise it without in any way you making clear that one of the other participants has already referred to it.

The ability to explore data or to seek explanations through qualitatively based methods means that there will be greater scope for ethical issues to arise in relation to this approach to research (Easterby-Smith *et al.*, 1991). The general ethical issues which we considered above (see also Zikmund, 1997) may arise in relation to the use of quantitative research. However, in qualitatively based research, the resulting personal contact, scope to use non-standardised questions or to observe on a 'face-to-face' basis, and capacity to develop your knowledge on an incremental basis mean that you will be able to exercise a greater level of control (Chapter 9). This contrasts with the use of a quantitative approach based on structured interviews or self-administered questionnaires (Chapter 10).

The relatively greater level of control associated with qualitatively based research methods should be exercised with care so that your behaviour remains within appropriate and acceptable parameters. In face-to-face *interviews*, you should avoid overzealous questioning and pressing your participant for a response. Doing so may make the situation stressful for your participant (Sekaran, 1992). You should also make clear to your interview participant that they have the right to decline to respond to any question (Cooper and Schindler, 1998). The nature of questions to be asked also requires consideration. Sekaran (1992) states that you should avoid asking questions which are in any way demeaning to your participant (Sections 9.4, 9.5 and 9.7 provide a fuller consideration of related issues). In face-to-face interviews it will clearly be necessary to arrange a time which is convenient for your participant; however, where you seek to conduct an interview by telephone (Sections 10.2 and 10.5) you should not attempt to do this at an unreasonable time of the day. In the interview situation, whether face to face or using a telephone, it would also be unethical to attempt to prolong the discussion when it is apparent that your participant needs to attend to the next part of their day's schedule (Zikmund, 1997).

The use of *observation* techniques raises its own ethical concerns (Section 8.3). The boundaries of what is permissible to observe need to be clearly drawn. Without this type of agreement the principal participants may find that their actions are being constrained (Bryman, 1988). You should also avoid attempting to observe behaviour related to your participant's private life, such as personal telephone calls and so forth. Without this, the relationship between observer and the observed will break down with the latter finding the process to be an intrusion on their right to privacy. There is, however, a second problem related to the use of this method. This is the issue of '"*reactivity*" – the reaction on the part of those being investigated to the investigator and his or her research instruments' (Bryman, 1988:112). This issue applies to a number of strategies and methods (Bryman, 1988) but is clearly a particular problem in observation.

A solution to this problem might be to undertake a *covert* study so that those being observed are not aware of this fact. In a situation of likely 'reactivity' to the presence of an observer you might use this approach in a deceitful yet benign way, since to declare your purpose at the outset of your work might lead to non-participation or problems related to validity and reliability if those being observed altered their behaviour (Bryman, 1988; Gummesson, 1991; Wells, 1994). The rationale for this choice of approach would thus be related to a question of whether 'the ends justify the means' provided that other ethical aspects are considered (Wells, 1994:284). However, the ethical concern with deceiving those being observed may prevail over any pragmatic view (Bryman, 1988; Cooper and Schindler, 1998). Indeed the problem of reactivity may be a diminishing one where those being observed adapt to your presence as declared observer (Bryman, 1988). This adaptation is known as *habituation* (Section 8.6).

Where access is denied after being requested you may have no other choice but to carry out covert observation – where this is practical (Gummesson, 1991). However, this course of action may prove to be a considerable source of irritation when revealed and you will need to evaluate this possibility very carefully. Irrespective of the reason why a deception occurred, it is widely accepted that after the observation has taken place you should inform those affected about what has occurred and why. This process is known as *debriefing*.

One group who may consider using a covert approach are those of you whom we refer to as internal or practitioner researchers (see Sections 5.3 and 8.3). There are recognised advantages and disadvantages associated with being an internal researcher (Sections 5.3 and 8.3). One of the possible disadvantages is related to your relationship with those from whom you will need to gain co-operation in order to gain cognitive access to their data. This may be related to the fact that your status is relatively junior to these colleagues, or that you are more senior to them. Any status difference may act to inhibit your intended data collection. One solution would therefore be to adopt a covert approach in order to seek to gain data. Thus you may decide to interview subordinate colleagues, organise focus groups through your managerial status, or observe interactions during meetings without declaring your research interest. The key question to consider is, will this approach be more likely to yield trustworthy data than declaring your real purpose and acting overtly? The answer will depend on a number of factors:

■ the existing nature of your relationships with those whom you wish to be your participants;

■ the prevailing managerial style within the organisation or that part of it where these people work;

■ the time and opportunity which you have to attempt to develop the trust and confidence of these intended participants in order to gain their co-operation.

Absolute assurances about the use of the data collected may also be critical to gain trust, and the time you invest in achieving this may be very worthwhile.

In comparison with the issues discussed in the preceding paragraphs, Dale *et al.* (1988:57) believe that the 'ethical problems of survey research may be rather less difficult than those of qualitative research'. This is due to the nature of structured survey questions which are clearly not designed to explore responses and the avoidance of the in-depth interview situation, where the ability to use probing questions leads to more revealing information (Dale *et al.*, 1988). Zikmund (1997) believes that the ethical issues linked with survey research are those associated with more general issues discussed earlier: privacy, deception, openness, confidentiality and objectivity. Dale *et al.* (1988) point to particular ethical issues that arise in relation to the analysis of secondary data derived from survey research, and it is to the issues associated with the analysis and reporting stages of research that we now turn.

Ethical issues related to the analysis and reporting stages

The maintenance of your objectivity will be vital during the analysis stage to make sure that you do not misrepresent the data collected. This will include not being selective about which data to report or, where appropriate, misrepresenting its statistical accuracy (Zikmund, 1997). A great deal of trust is placed in each researcher's integrity and it would clearly be a major ethical issue were this to be open to question. This duty to represent your data honestly extends to the analysis and reporting stage of your research. Lack of objectivity at this stage will clearly distort your conclusions and any course of action that appears to stem from your work.

The ethical issues of confidentiality and anonymity also come to the fore during the reporting stage of your research. Wells (1994) recognises that it may be difficult to maintain the assurances that have been given. However, it is vital to attempt to ensure that these are maintained. Allowing a participating organisation to be identified by those who can 'piece together' the characteristics which you reveal may result in embarrassment and also in access being refused to those who seek this after you. Great care therefore needs to be exercised to avoid this situation. You also have the option of requesting permission from the organisation to use their name. To gain this permission you will undoubtedly need to let them read your work to understand the context within which they will be named.

This level of care also needs to be exercised in making sure that the anonymity of individuals is maintained. Embarrassment and even harm could result from reporting data that are clearly attributable to a particular individual (Cooper and Schindler, 1998; Robson, 1993). Care therefore needs to be taken to protect those who participated in your research.

Worked example

Inadvertently revealing participants' identities

The following examples demonstrate how the identities of research participants can be inadvertently revealed because of a lack of thought on the part of researchers presenting their findings:

- reporting a comment made by a female accounts manager when in fact there is only one such person;

- referring to a comment made by a member of the sales team, when in fact the data being reported could only have come from one person.

- reporting data and comments related to a small section of staff, where it was possible to attribute the particular opinions being reported to specific individuals, or where there was a tendency on the part of other participants to seek to attribute these opinions because of the small numbers to whom these comments related.

A further ethical concern stems from the use made by others of the conclusions which you reach and any course of action which is explicitly referred to or implicitly suggested, based on your research data. How ethical will it be to use the data collected from a group of participants effectively to disadvantage them because of the decisions that are then made in the light of your research? On the other hand, there is a view that says that while the identity of your participants should not be revealed, they cannot be exempt from the way in which research conclusions are then used to make decisions (Dale *et al.*, 1988). This is clearly a very tricky ethical issue!

Where you are aware that your findings may be used to make a decision which could adversely affect the collective interests of those who were your participants, it may be ethical to refer to this possibility even though it reduces the level of access which you achieve. An alternative position is to construct your research question and objectives to avoid this possibility, or so that decisions taken as a result of your research should only have positive consequences for the collective interests of those who participate. You may find that this alternative is not open to you, perhaps because you are a part-time student in employment and your employing organisation directs your choice of research topic. If so, it will be more honest to concede to your participants that you are in effect acting as an internal consultant rather than in a (dispassionate) researcher's role.

Table 5.5 **Summary checklist to anticipate and deal with ethical issues**

✓ Attempt to recognise potential ethical issues that will affect your proposed research.

✓ Utilise your university's code on research ethics to guide the design and conduct of your research (if one is not available use Appendix 3).

✓ Anticipate ethical issues at the design stage of your research and discuss how you will seek to control these in your research proposal.

✓ Seek informed consent through the use of openness and honesty, rather than using deception.

✓ Do not exaggerate the likely benefits of your research for participating organisations or individuals.

✓ Respect others' rights to privacy at all stages of your research project.

✓ Maintain objectivity and quality in relation to the processes you use to collect data.

✓ Recognise that the nature of a qualitatively-based approach to research will mean that there is greater scope for ethical issues to arise, and seek to avoid the particular problems related to interviews and observation.

✓ Avoid referring to data gained from a particular participant when talking to others, where this would allow the individual to be identified with potentially harmful consequences to that person.

✓ Covert research should only be considered where reactivity is likely to be a significant issue or where access is denied (and a covert presence is practical). However, other ethical aspects of your research should still be respected when using this approach.

✓ Maintain your objectivity during the stages of analysing and reporting your research.

✓ Maintain the assurances that you gave to participating organisations with regard to confidentiality of the data obtained and their organisational anonymity.

✓ Protect individual participants by taking great care to ensure their anonymity in relation to anything that you refer to in your research project report, dissertation or thesis.

✓ Consider how the collective interests of your research participants may be adversely affected by the nature of the data that you are proposing to collect and alter the nature of your research question and objectives where this possibility is likely to be the case. Alternatively, declare this possibility to those who you wish to participate in your proposed research.

✓ Consider how you will use secondary data in order to protect the identities of those who contributed to its collection or who are named within it.

This discussion about the impact of research on the collective interests of those who participate brings us back to the reference made above to the particular ethical issues which arise in relation to the analysis of secondary data derived from survey research. Dale *et al.* (1988) point out that where survey results are subsequently used as secondary data the original assurances provided to those who participated in the research may be set aside with the result that the collective interests of participants may be disadvantaged through this use of data. The use of data for secondary purposes therefore also leads to ethical concerns of potentially significant proportions and you will need to consider these in the way in which you make use of this type of data.

A summary checklist on ethical issues is given in Table 5.5.

5.5   Summary

- Access and ethics are critical aspects for the conduct of research.

- Different types and levels of access have been identified which help us to understand the problem of gaining entry: physical access to an organisation; access to intended participants; continuing access in order to carry out further parts of your research or to be able to repeat the collection of data in another part of the organisation; cognitive access in order to get sufficiently close to find out valid and reliable data.

- Feasibility has been recognised to be an important determinant of what you choose to research and how you undertake the research.

- Strategies to help you to gain access to organisations and to intended participants within them have been described and discussed.

- Research ethics refer to the appropriateness of your behaviour in relation to the rights of those who become the subject of your work or are affected by the work.

- Potential ethical issues should be recognised and considered from the outset of your research and be one of the criteria against which your research proposal is judged.

- Ethical concerns are likely to occur at all stages of your research project: when seeking access, during data collection, as you analyse data and when you report them.

- Qualitative research is likely to lead to a greater range of ethical concerns in comparison with quantitative research although all research methods have specific ethical issues associated with them.

- Ethical concerns are also associated with the 'power relationship' between the researcher and those who grant access, and the researcher's role (as external researcher, internal researcher or internal consultant).

Questions

5.1 How can you differentiate between types of access, and why is it important to do this?

5.2 What do you understand by the use of the terms 'feasibility' and 'sufficiency' when applied to the question of access?

5.3 Which strategies to help to gain access are likely to apply to the following scenarios:

    a an 'external' researcher seeking direct access to managers who will be the research participants;

    b an 'external' researcher seeking access through an organisational gatekeeper/broker to her/his intended participants;

    c an internal researcher planning to undertake a research project within her/his employing organisation?

5.4 What are the principal ethical issues you will need to consider irrespective of the particular research methods which you use?

5.5 What problems may you encounter in attempting to protect the interests of participating organisations and individuals despite the assurances that you provide?

Assignment 5

Negotiating access and addressing ethical issues

➡ Consider the following aspects:

    ● Which types of data will you require in order to be able to answer sufficiently your proposed research question and objectives?

    ● Which research methods will you attempt to use to yield this data?

    ● What type(s) of access will you require in order to be able to collect data?

    ● What problems are you likely to encounter in gaining access?

    ● Which strategies to gain access will be useful to help you to overcome these problems?

➡ Depending on the type of access envisaged and your research status (i.e. as external researcher or practitioner–researcher), produce appropriate requests for organisational access, together with a return pro forma, and/or requests to intended participants for their co-operation.

➡ Describe the ethical issues that are likely to affect your proposed research project. Discuss how you may seek to overcome or control these. This should be undertaken in relation to the various stages of your research project.

➡ Note down your answers.

References

Bell, J. (1999) *Doing your Research Project* (3rd edn), Buckingham, Open University Press.

Bryman, A. (1988) *Quantity and Quality in Social Research*, London, Unwin Hyman.

Buchanan, D., Boddy, D. and McCalman, J. (1988) 'Getting in, getting on, getting out and getting back', *in* Bryman, A. (ed.), *Doing Research in Organisations*, London, Routledge, pp. 53–67.

Cooper, D.R. and Schindler, P.S. (1998) *Business Research Methods* (6th edn), Boston, MA, Irwin McGraw-Hill.

Dale, A., Arber, S. and Procter, M. (1988) *Doing Secondary Research*, London, Unwin Hyman.

Easterby-Smith, M., Thorpe, R. and Lowe, A. (1991) *Management Research: an Introduction*, London, Sage.

Gummesson, E. (1991) *Qualitative Methods in Management Research*, Newbury Park, CA, Sage.

Healey M J (1991) 'Obtaining information from businesses', *in* Healey, M.J. (ed.), *Economic Activity and Land Use*, Harlow, Longman, pp. 193–251.

Jankowicz, A.D. (1995) *Business Research Projects for Students* (2nd edn), London, Chapman & Hall.

Johnson, J.M. (1975) *Doing Field Research*, New York, Free Press.

Mackintosh, N. (ed.) (1995) *Cyril Burt: Fraud or Framed?*, Oxford, Oxford University Press.

Marshall, C. and Rossman, G.B. (1999) *Designing Qualitative Research* (3rd edn), Thousand Oaks, CA, Sage.

Morgan, M. (1995) 'The case of the dubious data', *The Guardian*, 4 August, second section, pp. 10–11.

Raimond, P. (1993) *Management Projects*, London, Chapman & Hall.

Robson, C. (1993) *Real World Research*, Oxford, Blackwell.

Scolari Sage (1999) 'Research methodology and CD-ROMS' (online)(cited 16 June 1999). Available from <URL:http://www.scolari.co.uk>.

Sekaran, U. (1992) *Research Methods for Business: a Skill-Building Approach* (2nd edn), New York, Wiley.

Wells, P. (1994) 'Ethics in business and management research', *in* Wass, V.J. and Wells, P.E. (eds), *Principles and Practice in Business and Management Research*, Aldershot, Dartmouth, pp. 277–97.

Zikmund, W.G. (1997) *Business Research Methods* (5th edn), Fort Worth, TX, Dryden Press.

Further reading

Buchanan, D., Boddy, D. and McCalman, J. (1988) 'Getting in, getting on, getting out and getting back', *in* Bryman, A. (ed.) *Doing Research in Organisations*, London, Routledge, 53–67. This provides a highly readable and very useful account of the negotiation of access. Other chapters in Bryman's book also consider issues related to access and research ethics.

Gummesson, E. (1991) *Qualitative Methods in Management Research*, Newbury Park, CA, Sage. Chapter 2 provides a very useful examination of access and researcher roles and some highly valuable means of differentiating types of access.

Miles, M.B. and Huberman, A.M. (1994) *Qualitative Data Analysis*, Thousand Oaks, CA, Sage. Chapter 11 provides a very useful examination of a range of ethical issues principally from the perspective of their implications for data analysis.

Wells, P. (1994) 'Ethics in business and management research', *in* Wass, V.J. and Wells, P.E. (eds), *Principles and Practice in Business and Management Research*, Aldershot, Dartmouth, pp. 277–98. This provides a very useful exploration of ethics in a range of subject areas as well as a discussion of a number of key issues related to business research.

Zikmund, W.G. (1997) *Business Research Methods* (5th edn), Fort Worth, TX, Dryden Press. Chapter 4 very usefully examines ethical issues associated with business research from the perspective of the rights and obligations of participants, researchers and clients.

Case 5	**The quality of service provided by the Accounts Department**

Angela had recently returned from a successful placement year working in the Marketing Department of a large manufacturing company. She had found the experience invaluable in supporting her joint degree in Marketing Management and Financial Management. She was well regarded by her line manager within the company who considered that her contribution during the year had been excellent. It is no surprise, therefore, that the company were pleased to provide her with a dissertation study opportunity.

While on placement Angela had assimilated the culture of the company and, in particular, the subculture of the Marketing Department. One of the common topics discussed regularly within the Marketing Department was the paucity and poor quality of services provided by the Accounts Department. Marketing Department staff felt that the Accounts Department could not be relied on and that the service they provided was too little too late. While she had been at the company the Marketing Director had actively canvassed support for recruiting a departmental finance 'expert'. In addition, she had noticed a growing disquiet among her colleagues as aspects of financial responsibility were devolved without additional resources.

Angela had thought hard about this and when back at college she had expressed to her tutor an interest in looking at the way internal services within organisations were marketed and perceived within organisations. Her tutor had pointed in the direction of work on service quality by Parasuraman *et al*. (1985) and a recent paper by Robinson (1999). Therefore, she formulated a dissertation proposal that aimed to compare perceptions of service quality between the host organisation's Accounts Department with those of its internal customers. This she felt would combine the marketing and finance aspects of her degree.

At her discussion with the company's Finance Director, Angela set out her research objectives and questions along with a proposed methodology. Imperative to this was a need to include the views of all the internal stakeholders for the services provided by the Accounts Department.

The research question was agreed as:

> To *what extent do Accounts Department's staff perceptions of the services they offer match those of their internal customers?*

Angela proposed a mixed method approach to data collection and suggested holding focus groups with the interested parties to elicit the concerns and issues. These were to be followed by a series of semi-structured interviews with a cross-section of managers, members of the Accounts Department and a cross-section of non-managerial employees. She suggested that a summary of her findings should be circulated to all participants with a full report readily available to all who wished to read it.

Having listened the Finance Director said that, while he 'fully supported' Angela's proposal he felt that her approach 'needed some fine tuning'. In particular:

▶

- He liked the idea of using a mixed method approach to collect data but considered the need to engage in focus groups too time consuming. He therefore felt it would be better just to interview staff.

- He felt that the sensitive nature of the topic meant that non-managerial employees should not be involved in these interviews. However, he would supply her with a list of managers across the company who would be useful to interview. Furthermore, he would write to them to let them know the purpose of her study and to inform them of their nomination as research respondents.

- He would like to be present at the interviews with members of the Accounts Department, as this was an ideal opportunity to understand the operation of that department. He went to great lengths to say that he would be unobtrusive and would not take part in the actual interview.

- He also felt that information generated in research could be sensitive. Consequently, he would like to see the report before it was published and to reserve the right to restrict circulation of the results.

Angela was worried about the stance being adopted by the Finance Director but felt powerless to influence the process. She had set out her proposal, which she had seen 'fully supported' but amended subsequently. She considered she had little real choice but to go along with the 'fine tuning', as she was unsure there would be another dissertation opportunity.

While she was on her placement she had met and become engaged to be married to Billy, a Human Resource Advisor dealing mainly with employee relations issues. While out one evening they discussed her impending research and the meeting with the Finance Director. Billy told her in confidence that he thought the Finance Director hoped that the results of her study might be used to bring about the 're-positioning' of the Accounts Department and a resultant change in 'the way the Accounts Department was managed'.

Billy went on to say that he thought the Finance Director wanted to engineer a situation through which the Accounts Department would have to be brought under the umbrella of an integrated Financial Services Department. Naturally, the staff in the Accounts Department were unlikely to be keen. However, they were currently unaware of any threat to their independent existence as an Accounts Department.

References

Parasuraman, A., Zeithaml, V.A. and Berry, L.L. (1985) 'A conceptual model of service quality and its implications for future research', *Journal of Marketing*, 49(Fall), 41–50.

Robinson, S. (1999) 'Measuring service quality: current thinking and future requirements', *Marketing Intelligence and Planning*, 17: 1, 21–32.

Questions

1 Should Angela go ahead with the study? What advice would you give her?

2 What are the likely outcomes if the research goes ahead as planned?

3 In what way have the following influenced the study directions and process?

   a Imbalance of power.

   b Sample selection and access.

   c Hidden agendas and deceit.

   d Control of the process.

   e Personal relationships/insider information.

   f Handling results and outcomes.

   g Angela's lack of assertiveness.

4 Negative impact on people can occur in research. What is the prospect of this kind of consequential impact on participants in this case?

Self check   **Answers**

5.1 The types of access which we have referred to in this chapter are physical entry or initial access to an organisational setting, continuing access which recognises that researchers often need to develop their access on an incremental basis and cognitive access where you will be concerned to gain the co-operation of individual participants once you have achieved access to the organisation they work in. We also referred to personal access, which allows you to consider whether you actually need to meet with participants in order to carry out an aspect of your research as opposed to corresponding with them or sending them a self-administered, postal questionnaire. Access is strategically related to the success of your research project and needs to be carefully planned. In relation to many research designs, it will need to be thought of as a multifaceted aspect and not a single event.

5.2 Gaining access can be problematic for researchers for a number of reasons. The concept of feasibility recognises this and suggests that in order to be able to conduct your research it will be necessary to design it with access clearly in mind. You may care to look again at the references to the work of Buchanan *et al.* (1988) and Johnson (1975) in Section 5.2, which demonstrate the relationship between research design and feasibility.

Sufficiency refers to another issue related to access. In Section 5.2, we stated that there are two aspects to the issue of sufficiency. The first of these relates to whether you have sufficiently considered and therefore fully realised the extent and nature of the access which you will require in order to be able to answer your research question and objectives. The second aspect relates to whether you are able to gain sufficient access in practice in order to be able to answer your research question and objectives.

5.3 We may consider the three particular scenarios outlined in the question through Table 5.6.

Table 5.6 **Considering access**

	Scenario A	Scenario B	Scenario C
Allowing yourself sufficient time to gain access	Universally true in all cases. The practitioner-researcher will be going through a very similar process to those who wish to gain access from the outside in terms of contacting intended participants, meeting with them to explain the research, providing assurances etc. The only exception will be related to a covert approach, although sufficient time for planning etc. will of course still be required		
Using any existing contacts	Where possible		Yes
Developing new ones	Probably necessary		This may still apply within large, complex organisations, depending on the nature of the research
Providing a clear account of the purpose of your research and what type of access you require, with the intention of establishing your credibility	Definitely necessary		Still necessary although easier to achieve (verbally or internal memo) with familiar colleagues. Less easy with unfamiliar colleagues which suggests just as much care as for external researchers
Overcoming organisational concerns in relation to the granting of access	Definitely necessary	Absolutely necessary. This may be *the* major problem to overcome since you are asking for access to a range of employees	Should not be a problem unless you propose to undertake a highly sensitive topic to the organisation! We know of students whose proposal has been refused *within* their organisation
Outlining possible benefits of granting access to you and any tangible outcome from doing so	Probably useful		Work-based research projects contain material of value to the organisation although they may largely be theoretically based
Using suitable language	Definitely necessary		Still necessary at the level of participants in the organisation
Facilitating ease of reply when requesting access	Definitely useful		Might be useful to consider in relation to certain internal participants

Table 5.6 *Cont.*

	Scenario A	**Scenario B**	**Scenario C**
Developing your access on an incremental basis	Should not be necessary, although you may wish to undertake subsequent work	Definitely worth considering	Might be a useful strategy depending on the nature of the research and the work setting
Establishing your credibility in the eyes of your intended participants	Access is not being sought at 'lower' levels within the organisation	Definitely necessary	May still be necessary with unfamiliar participants in the organisation

5.4 The principal ethical issues you will need to consider irrespective of which research methods you use are:

■ to respect intended and actual participants' rights to privacy;

■ to avoid deceiving participants about why you are undertaking the research, its purpose and how the data collected will be used;

■ maintaining your objectivity during the data collection, analysis and reporting stages;

■ respecting assurances provided to organisations about the confidentiality of (certain types of) data;

■ respecting assurances given to organisations and individuals about their anonymity;

■ considering the collective interests of participants in the way you use the data which they provide.

5.5 A number of ethical problems might emerge. These are considered in turn. You may wish to explore a point made by one of your participants but to do so might lead to harmful consequences for this person where the point was attributed to them.

It may be possible for some people who read your work to identify a participating organisation, although you do not actually name it. This may cause embarrassment to the organisation.

Individual participants may also be identified by the nature of the comments that you report, again leading to harmful consequences for them.

Your report may also lead to action being taken within an organisation which adversely affects those who were kind enough to act as participants in your research.

Finally, others may seek to re-use any survey data that you collect and this might be used to disadvantage those who provided the data by responding to your questionnaire.

6 Selecting samples

By the end of this chapter you should:

- understand the need for sampling in business and management research;
- be aware of a range of probability and non-probability sampling techniques and the possible need to combine techniques within a research project;
- be able to select appropriate sampling techniques for a variety of research scenarios and be able to justify their selection;
- be able to use a range of sampling techniques;
- be able to assess the representativeness of respondents;
- be able to apply the knowledge, skills and understanding gained to your own research project.

6.1 Introduction

Whatever your research question(s) and objectives you will need to collect data to answer them. If you collect and analyse data from every possible case or group member this is termed a *census*. However, for many research questions and objectives it will be impossible for you either to collect or to analyse all the data available to you owing to restrictions of time, money and often access. *Sampling* techniques provide a range of methods that enable you to reduce the amount of data you need to collect by considering only data from a sub-group rather than all possible cases or *elements* (Fig 6.1). Some research questions will require sample data to generalise about all the cases from which your sample has been selected. For example, if you asked a sample of consumers what they thought of a new chocolate bar and 75 per cent said that they thought it was too expensive you might infer that 75 per cent of all consumers felt that way. Other research questions may not involve such generalisations. However, even if you are undertaking case study research within a large organisation using in-depth interviews, you will still need to select your case study (sample) organisation and a group (sample) of employees and managers to interview. Techniques for selecting samples will therefore still be important.

The full set of cases from which a sample is taken is called the *population*. In sampling the term population is not used in its normal sense, as the full set of cases need not necessarily be people. For research to discover relative levels of service at burger bars throughout the country, the population from which you would select your sample

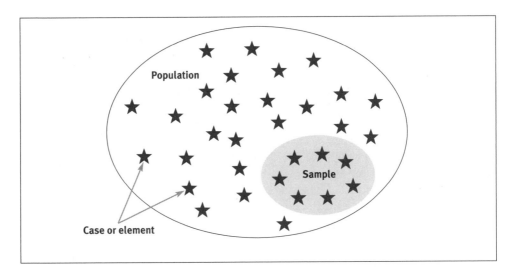

Fig 6.1 **Population, sample and individual cases**

would be all burger bars in the country. Alternatively, you might need to establish the 'life' of long life-batteries produced over the past month by a particular manufacturer. Here the population would be all the long-life batteries produced over the past month by that manufacturer.

The need to sample

For some research questions, it is possible to survey an entire population as it is of a manageable size. However, you should not assume that a census survey would necessarily provide more useful results than a well-planned sample survey. Sampling provides a valid alternative to a census when:

- it would be impracticable for you to survey the entire population;
- your budget constraints prevent surveying the entire population;
- your time constraints prevent surveying the entire population;
- you have collected all the data but need the results quickly.

For all research questions where it would be impracticable for you to survey the whole population you need to select a sample. This will be important whether you are planning to use a predominantly qualitative or quantitative research strategy. You might only be able to obtain permission to collect data from two or three organisations. Alternatively, testing an entire population of products to destruction, such as to establish the crash protection provided by cars, would be impractical for any manufacturer.

With other research questions it might be theoretically possible for you to be able to survey the whole population but the overall cost will prevent it. It is obviously cheaper for you to collect, enter (if you are analysing the data using a computer) and check data from 250 employees than from 2500, even though the cost per unit of your study (in this example employee) is likely to be higher than with a census. Your costs will be made up of new costs such as sample selection, and the fact that overhead costs such as survey design and setting up computer software for data entry are spread over a smaller number of cases.

Sampling also saves time, an important consideration when you have tight deadlines. The organisation of data collection is more manageable as fewer people are involved. As you have fewer data to enter, the results will be available more quickly. Occasionally, to save time, surveys collect data from the entire population but only analyse a sample of the data collected. For reasons of economy this procedure was adopted for hard-to-code questions, such as occupation and industry, in the United Kingdom 1991 Census. Data were collected from the total population for all questions but, for the hard-to-code questions, only 10 per cent of these data were coded using a detailed coding scheme (Section 11.2). These 10 per cent were entered into the computer and subsequently analysed (Dale, 1993).

Many researchers, for example Moser and Kalton (1986) and Henry (1990), argue that using sampling enables a higher overall accuracy than a census. The smaller number of cases for which you need to collect data means that more time can be spent designing and piloting the means of collecting this data. Collecting data from fewer cases also means that you can collect information that is more detailed. In addition, if you are employing people to collect the data (perhaps as interviewers) you can use higher-quality staff. You also can devote more time to trying to obtain data from the more difficult cases. Once your data have been collected, proportionally more time can be devoted to checking and testing the data for accuracy prior to analysis.

An overview of sampling techniques

The sampling techniques available to you can be divided into two types:

- probability or representative sampling;
- non-probability or judgmental sampling.

Those discussed in this chapter are highlighted in Fig 6.2. With *probability samples* the chance, or probability, of each case being selected from the population is known and is usually equal for all cases. This means that it is possible to answer research questions and to achieve objectives that require you to estimate statistically the characteristics of the population from the sample. Consequently, probability sampling is often associated with survey and to a lesser extent experiment research (Section 4.2). For *non-probability samples,* the probability of each case being selected from the total population is not known and it is impossible to answer research questions or to address objectives that require you to make statistical inferences about the characteristics of the population. You may still be able to generalise from non-probability samples about the population, but not on statistical grounds. For this reason non-probability sampling (other than quota sampling) is more frequently used for case study research (Section 4.2). However, with both types of sample you can answer other forms of research questions such as 'what attributes attract people to jobs?' or 'how are financial institutions adapting the services they provide to meet recent legislation?'

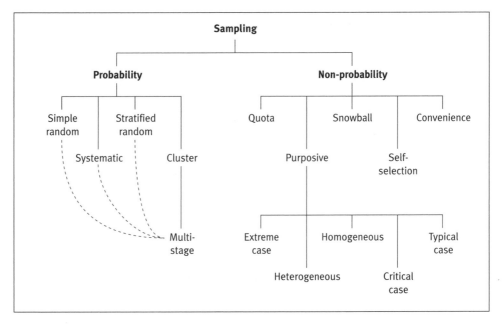

Fig 6.2   **Sampling techniques**

Subsequent sections of this chapter outline a variety of probability (Section 6.2) and non-probability (Section 6.3) sampling techniques, discuss their advantages and disadvantages and give examples of when you might use them. Although each technique is discussed separately, for many research projects you will need to use a variety of sampling techniques at different stages. This is illustrated by the case study.

6.2   Probability sampling

Probability sampling is most commonly associated with survey-based research where you need to make inferences from your sample about a population to answer your research question(s) or to meet your objectives. The process of probability sampling can be divided into four stages:

1   identify a suitable sampling frame based on your research question(s) or objectives;

2   decide on a suitable sample size;

3   select the most appropriate sampling technique and select the sample;

4   check that the sample is representative of the population.

Each of these stages will be considered in turn. However, for populations of less than 50 cases Henry (1990) advises against probability sampling. He argues that you should collect data on the entire population as the influence of a single extreme case on subsequent statistical analyses is more pronounced than for larger samples.

Identifying a suitable sampling frame

The *sampling frame* for any probability sample is a complete list of all the cases in the population from which your sample will be drawn. If your research question or objective is concerned with members of a local video club, your sampling frame will be the complete membership list for that video club. If your research question or objective is concerned with registered nursing homes in a local area your sampling frame will be a complete list of all registered nursing homes in that area. For both you then select your sample from this list. The completeness of your sampling frame is very important. An incomplete or inaccurate list means that some cases will have been excluded and so it will be impossible for every case in the population to have a chance of selection. Consequently your sample may not be representative of the total population.

Where no suitable list exists you will have to compile your own sampling frame. It is important to ensure that the sampling frame is unbiased, current and accurate. You might decide to use a telephone directory as the sampling frame from which to select a sample of typical UK householders. However, the telephone directory only covers subscribers in one geographical area who own a telephone. Your survey will therefore be biased towards householders who are telephone subscribers. Because the telephone directory is only published annually, the sampling frame will be out of date (*non-current*). As some householders choose to be ex-directory, it will be inaccurate as it does not include all those who own telephones. This means that you will be selecting a sample of telephone subscribers at the date the directory was compiled who chose not to be ex-directory!

In recent years, a number of organisations have been established which specialise in selling lists of names and addresses for surveys. These lists include a wide range of people such as company directors, chief executives, marketing managers, production managers and personnel managers, for public, private and non-profit-making organisations. They are usually in a format suitable for being read by word-processing and database computer software and can easily be merged into standard letters such as those included with questionnaires (Section 10.4). Because you pay for such lists by the case (individual address), the organisations that provide them usually select your sample. It is therefore important to establish precisely how they will select your sample as well as how the list was compiled and when it was last revised. From this, you will be able to assess the currency and accuracy of your sample and whether or not any bias is likely to exist. Table 6.1 provides a checklist against which to check your sampling frame.

Table 6.1   **Checklist for selecting a sampling frame**

✓   Are cases listed in the sampling frame relevant to your research topic, for example are they current?

✓   Does the sampling frame include all cases, in other words is it complete?

✓   Does the sampling frame exclude irrelevant cases, in other words is it precise?

✓   (For purchased lists) can you establish precisely how the sample will be selected?

Deciding on a suitable sample size

Generalisations about populations from data collected using any probability sample are based on probability. The larger your sample's size the lower the likely error in generalising to the population. Probability sampling is therefore a compromise between the accuracy of your findings and the amount of time and money you invest in collecting, checking and analysing the data. Your choice of sample size within this compromise is governed by:

■ the confidence you need to have in your data, that is the level of certainty that the characteristics of the data collected will represent the characteristics of the total population;

■ the margin of error that you can tolerate, that is the accuracy you require for any estimates made from your sample;

■ the types of analyses you are going to undertake, in particular the number of categories into which you wish to subdivide your data as many statistical techniques have a minimum threshold of data cases for each cell (for example chi square, Section 11.5);

and to a lesser extent:

■ the size of the total population from which your sample is being drawn.

Given these competing influences it is not surprising that the final sample size is almost always a matter of judgement rather than calculation (Hoinville *et al.*, 1985). For many research questions and objectives, your need to undertake particular statistical analyses (Section 11.5) will determine the threshold sample size for individual categories. These will affect the overall sample size. In such instances, *The Economist*'s (1997) advice of a minimum number of 30 for statistical analyses provides a useful rule of thumb for the smallest number in each category within your overall sample. Where the population in the category is less than 30, and you wish to undertake your analysis at this level of detail, you should normally collect data from all cases in that category. Alternatively you may have access to an *expert system* such as 'Ex-Sample'. This software uses artificial intelligence to calculate the minimum sample size required for over 60 different statistical analyses along with the maximum possible sample size, given resources such as time, money and response rates. It is available both on its own and as part of the 'Methodologist's Toolchest' suite of programs (Scolari Sage, 1999).

Researchers normally work to a 95 per cent level of certainty. This means that if your sample was selected 100 times at least 95 of these samples would be certain to represent the characteristics of the population. The margin of error describes the precision of your estimates of the population. Table 6.2 provides a rough guide to the different *minimum sample sizes* required from different sizes of population at the 95 per cent level of certainty. It assumes that data are collected from all cases in the sample (full details of the calculation for minimum sample size and adjusted minimum sample size are given in Appendix 4). For most business and management research, researchers are content to estimate the population's characteristics to within plus or minus 3–5 per cent of its true values. This means that if 45 per cent of your sample are in a certain category

155

then your estimate for the total population within the same category will be 45 per cent plus or minus the margin of error; somewhere between 42 and 48 per cent for a 3 per cent margin of error.

As you can see from Table 6.2 the smaller the sample and, to a far lesser extent, the smaller the proportion of the total population sampled, the greater the margin of error. Within this, the relative impact of sample size on the margin of error decreases for larger sample sizes. deVaus (1996) argues that it is for this reason that many market research companies limit their samples' sizes to approximately 2000. Unfortunately, for many sample surveys, a 100 per cent response rate is unlikely and so your sample will need to be larger to ensure sufficient responses for the margin of error you require.

Table 6.2 **Sample sizes for different sizes of population at a 95 per cent level of certainty (assuming data are collected from all cases in the sample)**

Population	*5%*	*3%*	*2%*	*1%*
		Margin of error		
50	44	48	49	50
100	79	91	96	99
150	108	132	141	148
200	132	168	185	196
250	151	203	226	244
300	168	234	267	291
400	196	291	434	384
500	217	340	414	475
750	254	440	571	696
1 000	278	516	706	906
2 000	322	696	1091	1655
5 000	357	879	1622	3288
10 000	370	964	1936	4899
100 000	383	1056	2345	8762
1 000 000	384	1066	2395	9513
10 000 000	384	1067	2400	9595

The importance of a high response rate

The most important aspect of a probability sample is that it represents the population. A perfect *representative sample* is one that exactly represents the population from which it is taken. If 60 per cent of your sample were small service sector companies then, provided that the sample was representative, you would expect 60 per cent of the population to be small service sector companies. You therefore need to obtain as high a response rate as possible to ensure that your sample is representative.

In reality, you are likely to have non-responses. Non-respondents are different from the rest of the population because they have refused to be involved in your research for whatever reason. Consequently, your respondents will not be representative of the total population and the data you collect may be biased. In addition, any non-responses will necessitate extra respondents being found to reach the required sample size, thereby increasing the cost of your survey.

You should therefore analyse the refusals to respond to both individual questions and entire surveys to check for bias (Section 11.2). Non-response is due to three inter-related problems:

■ refusal to respond;

■ ineligibility to respond;

■ non-contact.

The most common reason for non-response is that your respondent refuses to answer a question or be involved in your research but does not give a reason. Such non-response can be minimised by paying careful attention to the methods used to collect your data (Chapters 8, 9 and 10). Alternatively, some of your selected respondents may not meet your research requirements and so will be *ineligible* to respond. Non-contact creates a further problem; the fact that some respondents are *unreachable* means they will not be represented in the data you collect.

As part of your research report, you will need to include your *response rate*. A common way of doing this excludes ineligible respondents and those who, despite repeated attempts (Sections 9.3 and 10.5), were unreachable (deVaus, 1996):

$$\text{response rate} = \frac{\text{total number of responses}}{\text{total number in sample} - (\text{ineligible} + \text{unreachable})}$$

Even after ineligible and unreachable respondents have been included, it is probable that you will still have some non-responses. You therefore need to be able to assess how representative your data are and to allow for the impact of non-response in your calculations of sample size. These issues are explored in subsequent sections.

Estimating response rates and actual sample size required

With all probability samples, it is important that your sample size is large enough to provide you with the necessary confidence in your data. The margin of error must therefore be within acceptable limits and you must ensure that you will be able to undertake your analysis at the level of detail required. You therefore need to estimate the likely response rate, that is the proportion of cases from your sample who will respond or from which data will be collected and increase the sample size accordingly. Once you have an estimate of the likely response rate and the minimum or the adjusted minimum sample size, the *actual sample size* you require can be calculated using the following formula:

$$n^a = \frac{n \times 100}{re\%}$$

where n^a is the actual sample size required, n is the minimum (or adjusted minimum) sample size (see Table 6.2 or Appendix 4) and $re\%$ is the estimated response rate expressed as a percentage.

Worked example

Calculation of actual sample size

Jan was a part-time student employed by a large manufacturing company. He had decided to undertake a survey of customers and calculated that an adjusted minimum sample size of 439 was required. Jan estimated the response rate would be 30 per cent. From this, he could calculate his actual sample size:

$$n^a = \frac{439 \times 100}{30}$$

$$= \frac{43\,900}{30}$$

$$= 1463$$

Jan's actual sample therefore needed to be 1463 customers. Because of time and financial constraints this was rounded down to 1400 customers. The likelihood of 70 per cent non-response meant that Jan needed to include a check that his sample was representative when he designed his data collection method.

If you are collecting your sample data from a secondary source (Section 7.2) within an organisation which has already granted you access your response rate should be virtually 100 per cent. In research Mark recently undertook he established that all the data he required were available from employees' personnel files. Once access had been granted to these files by the organisation he was ensured of virtually a 100 per cent response rate. His actual sample size was therefore the same as his minimum sample size.

In contrast, estimating the likely response rate from a sample to which you will be sending a questionnaire or interviewing is more difficult. One way of obtaining this estimate is to consider the response rates achieved for similar surveys that have already been undertaken and base your estimate on these. Alternatively, you can err on the side of caution. For postal surveys a response rate of approximately 30 per cent is reasonable (Owen and Jones, 1994). For interviews you should expect a response rate of approximately 50 per cent (Kervin, 1992).

However, beware: response rates can vary considerably when collecting primary data. Research by Dillman (1978) recorded response rates of between 50 per cent and 92 per cent for questionnaire surveys and of between 73 per cent and 99 per cent for telephone interviews. More recent work by Healey (1991) also records a wide variation in response rates. He suggests lower average response rates of about 50 per cent for postal surveys and 75 per cent for face-to-face interviews. The former rate concurs with a recent questionnaire survey we undertook for a multinational organisation that had an overall response rate of 52 per cent. In our survey response rates for individual sites varied from 41 to 100 per cent, again emphasising variability. Our examination of response rates to recent business surveys reveals rates as low as 15–20 per cent for postal surveys, some authors citing respondents' questionnaire fatigue as a contributory factor! Fortunately a number of different techniques, depending on your data collection method, can be used to enhance your response rate. These are discussed with the data collection method in the appropriate sections (Sections 9.3 and 10.5).

Selecting the most appropriate sampling technique and the sample

Once you have chosen a suitable sampling frame and established the actual sample size required, you need to select the most appropriate sampling technique to obtain a representative sample. Five main techniques can be used to select a probability sample (Fig 6.2):

■ simple random;

■ systematic;

■ stratified random;

■ cluster;

■ multi-stage.

Your choice of technique depends on your research question(s) and your objectives, the structure of the sampling frame, the size of the sample you need, the geographical area of your survey and, if you are using support workers, the ease of explaining the technique. The impact of each of these is summarised in Table 6.3.

Simple random sampling

Simple random sampling involves you selecting the sample at random from the sampling frame using either random number tables (Appendix 5) or a computer. To do this you:

1 number each of the cases in your sampling frame with a unique number. The first case is numbered 0, the second 1 and so on;

2 select cases using random numbers (Table 6.4, Appendix 5) until your actual sample size is reached.

It is usual to select your first random number at random (closing your eyes and pointing with your finger is a good way!) as this ensures that the set of random numbers obtained for different samples is unlikely to be the same. If you do not you will obtain sets of numbers that are random but identical.

Starting with this number you read off the random numbers (and select the cases) in a regular and systematic manner until your sample size is reached. If the same number is read off a second time it must be disregarded as you need different cases. This means that you are not putting each case's number back into the sampling frame after it has been selected and is termed *sampling without replacement*. Alternatively, a number might be selected which is outside the range of those in your sampling frame. If this happens you simply ignore it and continue reading off numbers until your sample size is reached.

Table 6.3 Impact of various factors on choice of probability sampling techniques

Sample technique	Sampling frame required	Size of sample needed	Geographical area to which suited	Relative cost	Ease to explain to support workers	Advantages compared with simple random
Simple random	Accurate and easily accessible	Better with over a few hundred	Concentrated if face-to-face contact required, otherwise does not matter	High if large sample size or sampling frame not computerised	Relatively difficult to explain	–
Systematic	Accurate, easily accessible and not containing periodic patterns. Actual list not always needed	Suitable for all sizes	Concentrated if face-to-face contact required, otherwise does not matter	Low	Relatively easy to explain	Normally no difference
Stratified random	Accurate, easily accessible, divisible into relevant strata (see comments for simple random and systematic as appropriate)	See comments for simple random and systematic as appropriate	Concentrated if face-to-face contact required, otherwise does not matter	Low, provided that lists of relevant strata available	Relatively difficult to explain (once strata decided see comments for simple random and systematic as appropriate)	Better comparison across strata. Differential response rates may necessitate re-weighting
Cluster	Accurate, easily accessible, relates to relevant clusters not individual population members	As large as practicable	Dispersed if face-to-face contact required and geographically based clusters used	Low provided that lists of relevant clusters available	Relatively difficult to explain until clusters selected	Quick but reduced precision
Multi-stage	Initial stages: geographical. Final stage: only needed for geographical areas selected, see comments for simple random and systematic as appropriate	Initial stages: as large as practicable. Final stage: see comments for simple random and systematic as appropriate	Dispersed if face-to-face contact required, otherwise no need to use this technique!	Low as sampling frame for actual survey population only required for final stage	Initial stages: relatively difficult to explain. Final stage: see comments for simple random and systematic as appropriate	Difficult to adjust for differential response rates. Substantial errors possible!

© Mark Saunders, Philip Lewis and Adrian Thornhill, 2000

Table 6.4	**Extract from random number tables**

78	41	11	62	72	18	66	69	58	71	31	90	51	36	78	09	41	00
70	50	58	19	68	26	75	69	04	00	25	29	16	72	35	73	55	85
32	78	14	47	01	*55*	10	91	83	21	13	32	59	53	03	38	79	32
71	60	20	53	86	78	50	57	42	30	73	48	68	09	16	35	21	87
35	30	15	57	99	96	33	25	56	43	65	67	51	45	37	99	54	89
09	08	05	41	66	54	01	49	97	34	38	85	85	23	34	62	60	58
02	59	34	51	98	71	31	54	28	85	23	84	49	07	33	71	17	88
20	13	44	15	22	95												

Source: Appendix 5

You can use a computer program such as a spreadsheet to generate random numbers. However, you must ensure that the numbers generated are within your range and that if a number is repeated it is ignored and replaced. If details of the population are stored on the computer it is possible to generate a sample of randomly selected cases. For telephone interviews many market research companies now use computer-aided telephone interviewing (CATI) software to select telephone numbers at random from an existing database and to dial each respondent in turn.

Random numbers allow you to select your sample without bias. The sample selected can therefore be said to be representative of the whole population. However, the selection that simple random sampling provides is more evenly dispersed throughout the population for samples of more than a few hundred cases. The first few hundred cases selected using simple random sampling normally consist of bunches of cases whose numbers are close together followed by a gap and then further bunching. For over a few hundred cases this pattern occurs far less frequently. Because of the technique's random nature it is therefore possible that the chance occurrence of such patterns will result in certain parts of a population being over- or under-represented.

Simple random sampling is best used when you have an accurate and easily accessible sampling frame that lists the entire population, preferably stored on a computer. While you can often obtain these for employees within organisations or members of clubs or societies, adequate lists are often not available for types of organisations. If your population covers a large geographical area random selection means that selected cases are likely to be dispersed throughout the area. Consequently, this form of sampling is not suitable if you are undertaking a survey that covers a large geographical area and requires face-to-face contact owing to the associated high travel costs. Simple random sampling would still be suitable for a geographically dispersed area if you used an alternative technique of collecting data such as postal questionnaires or telephone interviewing (Chapter 10).

> **Worked example**
>
> ### Simple random sampling
>
> You have a population of 5011 supermarket customers, all of whom use the supermarket's charge card for their weekly purchases. You wish to find out why they use the charge card. There is insufficient time to interview all of them and so you decide to interview a sample. Your calculations reveal that to obtain acceptable levels of confidence and accuracy you need an actual sample size of approximately 360 customers. You decide to select them using simple random sampling.
>
> First you give each of the cases (customers) in the sampling frame a unique number. In order that each number is made up in exactly the same way you use 5011 four-digit numbers starting with 0000 through to 5010. So customer 677 is given the number 0676.
>
> The first random number you select is 55 (shown in bold and italics in Table 6.4). Starting with this number you read off the random numbers in a regular and systematic manner (in this example continuing along the line):
>
> 5510 9183 2113 3259 5303 3879 3271 6020
>
> until 360 different cases have been selected. These form your random sample. Numbers selected which are outside the range of those in your sampling frame (such as 5510, 9183, 5303 and 6020) are simply ignored.

Systematic sampling

Systematic sampling involves you selecting the sample at regular intervals from the sampling frame. To do this you:

1 number each of the cases in your sampling frame with a unique number. The first case is numbered 0, the second 1 and so on;

2 select the first case using a random number;

3 calculate the sampling fraction;

4 select subsequent cases systematically using the sampling fraction to determine the frequency of selection.

To calculate the *sampling fraction*, that is the proportion of the total population that you need to select, you use the formula:

$$\text{sampling fraction} = \frac{\text{actual sample size}}{\text{total population}}$$

If your sampling fraction is $\frac{1}{3}$ you need to select one in every three cases, that is every third case from the sampling frame. Unfortunately your calculation will usually result in a more complicated fraction. In these instances it is normally acceptable to round your population down to the nearest ten (or hundred) and to increase your minimum sample size until a simpler sampling fraction can be calculated.

On its own, selecting one in every three would not be random as every third case would be bound to be selected, whereas those between would have no chance of selection. To overcome this a random number is used to decide where to start on the sampling frame. If your sampling fraction is ⅓ the starting point must be one of the first three cases. You therefore select a random number (in this example a one-digit random number between 0 and 2) as described earlier and use this as the starting point.

Once you have selected your first case at random you then select, in this example, every third case until you have gone right through your sampling frame. As with simple random sampling you can use a computer to generate the first random and subsequent numbers that are in the sample.

In some instances it is not necessary to construct a list for your sampling frame. Research Mark undertook for a local authority required data to be collected about every tenth client of a social services department. Although these data were not held on computer they were available from each client's manual file. The files were stored in alphabetical order and, once the first file (client) was selected at random, it was easy to extract every tenth file (client) thereafter. This process had the additional advantage that it was easy to explain to social services' employees, although Mark still had to explain to inquisitive employees that he needed a representative sample and so their 'interesting' clients might not be selected!

Worked example

Systematic sampling

You have a population of approximately 1500 patients and wish to find out their attitudes to a new voucher scheme. There is insufficient time and money to collect data from all of them using a questionnaire and so you decide to send the questionnaire to a sample. Your calculation of sample size reveals that to obtain acceptable levels of confidence and accuracy you need an actual sample size of approximately 300 patients to whom you will send the questionnaire. You decide to select them using systematic sampling.

First you need to work out the sampling fraction:

$$\frac{300}{1500} = \frac{1}{5}$$

Your sampling fraction is therefore ⅕. This means that you need to select every fifth patient from the sampling frame.

You use a random number to decide where to start on the sampling frame. As your sampling fraction is ⅕ the starting point must be one of the first five patients. You therefore select a one-digit random number between 0 and 4.

Once you have selected your first patient at random you select every fifth patient until you have gone right through your sampling frame. If the random number you selected was 2, then you would select the following patient numbers:

$$2 \quad 7 \quad 12 \quad 17 \quad 22 \quad 27 \quad 32 \quad 37$$

and so on until 300 patients had been selected.

Despite the advantages you must be careful when using existing lists as sampling frames. You need to ensure that the lists do not contain periodic patterns.

A high-street bank needs you to undertake a sample survey of individual customers with joint bank accounts. A sampling fraction of ¼ means that you will need to select every fourth customer on the list. The names on the customer lists, which you intend to use as the sampling frame, are arranged alphabetically by account with males followed by females (Table 6.5). If you start with a male customer all those in your sample will be male. Conversely, if you start with a female customer all those in your sample will be female. Consequently your sample will be biased (Table 6.5). This sampling frame is therefore not suitable without re-ordering or stratifying (discussed later).

Unlike simple random sampling, systematic sampling works equally well with a small or large number of cases. However, if your population covers a large geographical area, the random selection means that the sample cases are likely to be dispersed throughout the area. Consequently systematic sampling is only suitable for geographically-dispersed cases if you do not require face-to-face contact when collecting your data.

Table 6.5   **The impact of periodic patterns on systematic sampling**

Number	Customer	Sample	Number	Customer	Sample
000	Mr L. Baker	*M*	006	Mr E. Saunders	
001	Mrs B. Baker		007	Mrs M. Saunders	*F*
002	Mr S. Davis		008	Mr J. Smith	*M*
003	Mrs P. Davis	*F*	009	Mrs K. Smith	
004	Mr J. Lewis	*M*	010	Mr J. Thornhill	
005	Mrs P. Lewis		011	Mrs A. Thornhill	*F*

M all male sample selected if start with 000, *F* all female sample selected if start with 003

Stratified random sampling

Stratified random sampling is a modification of random sampling in which you divide the population into two or more relevant and significant strata based on one or a number of attributes. In effect your sampling frame is divided into a number of subsets. A random sample (simple or systematic) is then drawn from each of the strata. Consequently stratified sampling shares many of the advantages and disadvantages of simple random and systematic sampling.

Dividing the population into a series of relevant strata means that the sample is more likely to be representative, as you can ensure that each of the strata is represented proportionally within your sample. However, it is only possible to do this if you are aware of, and can easily distinguish, significant strata in your sampling frame. In addition the extra stage in the sampling procedure means that it is likely to take longer, to be more expensive and to be more difficult to explain than simple random or systematic sampling.

In some instances, as pointed out by deVaus (1996), your sampling frame will already be divided into strata. A sampling frame of employee names which is in alphabetical order will automatically ensure that, if systematic sampling is used (discussed earlier), employees will be sampled in the correct proportion to the letter with which their name begins. Similarly membership lists which are ordered by date of joining will automatically result in stratification by length of membership if systematic sampling is used. Therefore if you are using simple random sampling or your sampling frame contains periodic patterns you will need to stratify it. To do this you:

1 choose the stratification variable or variables;

2 divide the sampling frame into the discrete strata;

3 number each of the cases within each stratum with a unique number as discussed earlier;

4 select your sample using either simple random or systematic sampling as discussed earlier.

The stratification variable (or variables) chosen should represent the discrete characteristic (or characteristics) for which you want to ensure correct representation within the sample.

Worked example

Stratified random sampling

In the survey of joint bank account holders we discussed earlier an important stratum would be each account customer's gender and so the sampling frame is divided into two discrete strata: females and males. Within each stratum the individual cases are numbered:

Female stratum			Male stratum		
Number	Customer	Selected	Number	Customer	Selected
000	Mrs B. Baker		000	Mr L. Baker	
001	Mrs P. Davis	✓	001	Mr S. Davis	
002	Mrs P. Lewis		002	Mr J. Lewis	
003	Mrs M. Saunders		003	Mr E. Saunders	✓
004	Mrs K. Smith		004	Mr J. Smith	
005	Mrs A. Thornhill	✓	005	Mr J. Thornhill	
005	Mrs D. Woollons		006	Mr J. Woollons	
007	Mrs P. Wordden		007	Mr F. Wordden	✓

You decide to select a systematic sample. A sampling fraction of ¼ means that you will need to select every fourth customer on the list. As indicated by the ticks (✓) random numbers select the first case in the female (1) and male (3) strata. Subsequently every fourth customer in each stratum is selected.

Samples can be stratified using more than one characteristic. You may wish to stratify a sample of an organisation's employees by both department and salary grade. To do this you would:

1 divide the sampling frame into the discrete departments;

2 within each department divide the sampling frame into discrete salary grades;

3 number each of the cases within each salary grade within each department with a unique number as discussed earlier;

4 select your sample using either simple random or systematic sampling as discussed earlier.

In some instances the relative sizes of different strata mean that, in order to have sufficient data for analysis, you need to select larger samples from the strata with smaller populations. Here the different sample sizes must be taken into account when aggregating data from each of the strata to obtain an overall picture. The more sophisticated statistical analysis software packages enable you to do this by differentially weighting the responses for each stratum (Section 11.2).

Cluster sampling

Cluster sampling is, on the surface, similar to stratified sampling as you need to divide the population into discrete groups prior to sampling (Henry, 1990). The groups are termed *clusters* in this form of sampling and can be based on any naturally occurring grouping. For example you could group your data by type of manufacturing firm or geographical area.

For cluster sampling your sampling frame is the complete list of clusters rather than a complete list of individual cases within the population. You then select a few clusters, normally using simple random sampling. Data are then collected from every case within the selected clusters. The technique has three main stages:

1 choose the cluster grouping for your sampling frame;

2 number each of the clusters with a unique number. The first cluster is numbered 0, the second 1 and so on;

3 select your sample using some form of random sampling as discussed earlier.

Selecting clusters randomly makes cluster sampling a probability sampling technique. However, the technique normally results in a sample that represents the total population less accurately than stratified random sampling. Restricting the sample to a few relatively compact geographical sub-areas (clusters) maximises the number of interviews you can undertake within the resources available. However, it may also reduce the representativeness of your sample. For this reason you need to maximise the number of sub-areas to allow for variations in the population within the available resources. Your choice is between a large sample from a few discrete sub-groups and a smaller sample distributed over the whole group. It is a trade-off between the amount of precision lost by using a few sub-groups and the amount gained from a larger sample size.

Worked example

Cluster sampling

Ceri needed to select a sample of firms to undertake an interview-based survey about the use of photocopiers. As she had limited resources with which to pay for travel and other associated data collection costs she decide to interview firms in four geographical areas selected from a cluster grouping of local authority areas. A list of all local authority areas formed her sampling frame. Each of the local authority areas (clusters) was given a unique number, the first being 0, the second 1 and so on. The four sample clusters were selected from a sampling frame of local authority areas using simple random sampling.

Ceri's sample was all firms within the selected clusters. She decided that the appropriate telephone directories would probably provide a suitable list of all firms in each cluster.

Multi-stage sampling

Multi-stage sampling, sometimes called *multi-stage cluster sampling*, is a development of cluster sampling. It is normally used to overcome problems associated with a geographically dispersed population when face-to-face contact is needed or where it is expensive and time consuming to construct a sampling frame for a large geographical area. However, like cluster sampling you can use it for any discrete groups including those that are not geographically based. The technique involves taking a series of cluster samples, each involving some form of random sampling. This aspect is represented by the dotted lines in Fig 6.2. It can be divided into four phases. These are outlined in Fig 6.3.

Because multi-stage sampling relies on a series of different sampling frames you need to ensure that they are all appropriate and available. In order to minimise the impact of selecting smaller and smaller sub-groups on the representativeness of your sample you can apply stratified sampling techniques (discussed earlier). This technique can be further refined to take account of the relative size of the sub-groups. It is discussed in greater detail by Hoinville *et al.* (1985). As you have selected your sub-areas using different sampling frames you only need a sampling frame which lists all the members of the population for those sub-groups you finally select. This provides considerable savings in time and money.

Worked example

Multi-stage sampling

A market research organisation needs you to interview a sample of 400 households in England and Wales. The electoral register provides a possible sampling frame. Selecting 400 households using either systematic or simple random sampling would probably result in these 400 households being dispersed throughout England and Wales. The time and cost of travelling to and interviewing your ▶

sample would be enormous. By using multi-stage sampling these problems can be overcome.

In the first stage the geographical area (England and Wales) is split into discrete sub-areas (counties). These form the sampling frame. After numbering, a small number of counties are selected using simple random sampling. Since each case (household) is located in a county each has an equal chance of being selected for the final sample.

As the counties selected are still too large the selected counties are subdivided into smaller geographically discrete areas (electoral wards) which form the next sampling frame (stage 2). Another simple random sample is selected. A larger number of wards are selected to allow for likely important variations in households between wards.

A sampling frame is generated for each ward using a combination of the electoral register and the UK Post Office's postcode address file. The cases (households) which will be interviewed are then selected using either simple random or systematic techniques.

Phase 1

- Choose sampling frame of relevant discrete groups
- Number each group with a unique number. The first is numbered 0, the second 1 and so on
- Select a small sample of relevant discrete groups using some form random sampling

Phase 2

- From these relevant discrete groups choose a sampling frame of relevant discrete sub-groups
- Number each sub-group with a unique number as described in phase 1
- Select a small sample of relevant discrete sub-groups using some form of random sampling

Phase 3

- *Repeat phase 2 if necessary*

Phase 4

- From these relevant discrete sub-groups choose a sampling frame of relevant discrete sub-sub-groups
- Number each sub-sub-group with a unique number as described in phase 1
- Select your sample using some form of random sampling

Fig 6.3 **Phases of multi-stage sampling**

Checking the sample is representative

Often it is possible to compare data you collect from your sample with data from another source for the population. For example you can compare data on the age and socio-economic characteristics of respondents in a marketing survey with these characteristics for the population in that country as recorded by the latest national census of population. If there is no statistically significant difference then the sample is representative with respect to these characteristics.

When working within an organisation comparisons can also be made. In a recent survey we undertook of all types of employees in a multinational organisation we asked closed questions about salary grade, gender, length of service and place of work. Possible responses to each question were designed to provide sufficient detail to compare the characteristics of our sample with the characteristics of the entire population of employees as recorded by the organisation's computerised personnel system. At the same time we kept the categories sufficiently broad to preserve, and to be seen to preserve, the confidentiality of individual respondents. The two questions on length of service and salary grade from a recent questionnaire we developed illustrate this:

58   How long have you worked for *Organisation's name*?

up to 3 years   ❑   over 3 years to 10 years   ❑   over 10 years

59   Which one of the following best describes your job?

Technical/clerical (grades 1–3)   ❑   Senior Management (grades 12–14)   ❑

Supervisor (grades 4–5)   ❑   Directorate (grades 15–17)   ❑

Professional (grades 6–8)   ❑   Other (please say)   ❑

Management (grades 9–11)   ❑   ....

Using the Kolmogorov–Smirnov one-sample test (Section 11.5) we found there was no statistically significant difference between the proportions of respondents in each of the length of service groups and the data obtained from the computerised personnel database. This meant that our sample was representative of all employees with respect to length of service. However, those responding were (statistically) significantly more likely to be in professional and managerial grades than in technical, clerical or supervisory grades. We therefore added a note of caution about the representativeness of our findings.

You can also assess the representativeness of samples for longitudinal studies. Obviously it is still possible to compare respondent characteristics with data from another source. In addition the characteristics of those who responded can be compared for different data collection periods. For example you could compare the characteristics of those in your sample who responded to a survey at the start of a research project with those who responded to a survey six months later. We would like to add a note of caution here. Such a comparison will enable you to discuss the extent to which the groups of respondents differed for these characteristics over time. However, depending on your choice of characteristics, these differences might be expected owing to some form of managerial intervention or change between the data collection periods.

6.3 Non-probability sampling

The techniques for selecting samples discussed earlier have all been based on the assumption that your sample will be statistically chosen at random. Consequently, it is possible to specify the probability that any case will be included in the sample. However, within business research, such as market surveys and case study research, this is often not possible and so your sample must be selected some other way. Non-probability sampling provides a range of alternative techniques based on your subjective judgement. In the exploratory stages of some research projects, such as a pilot survey, a non-probability sample may be the most practical although it will not allow the extent of the problem to be determined. Subsequent to this, probability-sampling techniques may be used. For other business and management research projects your research question(s), objectives and choice of research strategy (Sections 4.1–4.3) may dictate non-probability sampling. To answer your research question(s) and to meet your objectives you may need to undertake an in-depth study that focuses on a small, perhaps one, sample selected purposively. This would provide you with an information-rich case study in which you explore your research question. Alternatively, limited resources or the inability to specify a sampling frame may dictate the use of one or a number of non-probability sampling techniques.

Selecting the most appropriate sampling technique and the sample

A range of non-probability sampling techniques are available which should not be discounted as they can provide sensible alternatives to select cases to answer your research question(s) and to address your objectives (Fig 6.2). At one end of this range is quota sampling which, like probability samples, tries to represent the total population. Quota sampling has similar requirements for sample size as probabilistic sampling techniques.

At the other end are techniques based on the need to obtain a sample as quickly as possible where you have little control over the content and there is no attempt to obtain a representative sample. These include convenience and self-selection sampling techniques. Purposive sampling and snowball sampling techniques lie between these extremes (Table 6.6). For these techniques the issue of sample size is ambiguous. Unlike quota and probability samples there are no rules. Rather it depends on your research question(s) and objectives; in particular what you need to find out, what will be useful, what will have credibility and what can be done within your available resources (Patton 1990). This is particularly so where you are intending to collect qualitative data. The validity and understanding that you will gain from your data will be more to do with your data collection and analysis skills than the size of your sample (Patton, 1990). As such it is the logic behind your sample selection that is important.

| Table 6.6 | Impact of various factors on choice of non-probability sample techniques | | | |

Sample type	Likelihood of sample being representative	Types of research in which useful	Relative costs	Control over sample contents
Quota	Reasonable to high although dependent on selection of quota variables	Where costs constrained/ data needed very quickly so an alternative to probability sampling needed	Moderately high to reasonable	Relatively high

Purposive	Low although dependent on researcher's choices:
	    extreme case
	    heterogeneous
	    homogeneous
	    critical case
	    typical case
		Where working with very small samples
		focus: unusual or special
		focus: key themes
		focus: in-depth
		focus: importance of case
		focus: illustrative
			Reasonable	Reasonable

Snowball	Low but cases will have characteristics desired	Where difficulties in identifying cases	Reasonable	Quite low
Self-selection	Low but cases self-selected	Where exploratory research needed	Low	Low
Convenience	Very low	Where very little variation in population	Low	Low

Developed from: Kervin, 1992; Patton, 1990.

Quota sampling

Quota sampling is entirely non-random and is normally used for interview surveys. It is based on the premise that your sample will represent the population as the variability in your sample for various quota variables is the same as that in the population. Quota sampling is therefore a type of stratified sample in which selection of cases within strata is entirely non-random (Barnett, 1991). To select a quota sample you:

1   divide the population into specific groups;
2   calculate a quota for each group based on relevant and available data;
3   give each interviewer an *assignment*, which states the number of cases in each quota from which they must collect data;
4   combine the data collected by interviewers to provide the full sample.

Quota sampling has a number of advantages over the probabilistic techniques. In particular it is less costly and can be set up very quickly. If, as with television audience research surveys, your data collection needs to be undertaken very quickly then quota sampling may be the only possibility. In addition it does not require a sampling frame and may therefore be the only technique you can use if one is not available.

Quota sampling is normally used for large populations. For small populations it is usually possible to obtain a sampling frame. Decisions on sample size are governed by the need to have sufficient responses in each quota to enable subsequent statistical analyses to be undertaken. This normally necessitates a sample size of between 2000 and 5000.

Calculations of quotas are based on relevant and available data and are usually relative to the proportions in which they occur in the population. Without sensible and relevant quotas data collected may be biased. For many market research projects quota are derived from census data. Your choice of quota is dependent on two main factors:

- usefulness as a means of stratifying the data;
- ability to overcome likely variations between groups in their availability for interview.

Where pensioners are likely to have different opinions to working couples a quota which does not ensure that these differences are captured may result in the data being biased as it would probably be easier to collect the data from pensioners. Quotas used in market research surveys usually include measures of age, gender and socio-economic status or social class. These may be supplemented by additional quotas dictated by the research question(s) and objectives.

Once you have given each interviewer their particular assignment they decide whom to interview until they have completed their quota. You then combine the data from this assignment with those collected by other interviewers to provide the full sample. Because the interviewer can choose within quota boundaries whom he/she interviews

Worked example

Devising a quota sample

A market research survey requires you to interview a sample of people representing those aged 20–64 who are in employment. No sampling frame is available. You wish to disaggregate your findings into groups dependent on respondents' age and type of employment. Previous research suggests that gender will also have an impact on responses and so you need to make sure that those interviewed in each group also reflect the proportions of males and females in the population. Fortunately the national census of population contains a breakdown of the number of people in employment by gender, age and socio-economic status. These form the basis of the categories for your quotas:

gender	× age group	× socio-economic status
male	20–29	professional
female	30–34	managers/employers
	45–64	intermediate and junior non-manual
		skilled manual
		semi-skilled manual
		unskilled manual

As you wish to analyse the data for individual age and socio-economic status groups it is important that each of these categories has sufficient respondents (at least 30) to enable meaningful statistical analyses. You calculate that a 5 per cent quota for each of the groups will provide sufficient numbers for all groups, providing your analyses are not also disaggregated by gender. This gives you the following quotas:

Gender	Age group	Socio-economic status	Population	Quota
Male	20–29	Professional	1121	56
		Managers/employers	798	40
		Intermediate and junior non-manual	910	43
		Skilled manual	1611	79
		Semi-skilled manual	1260	63
		Unskilled manual	503	25
	30–44	Professional	2143	107
		Managers/employers	2327	116
		Intermediate and junior non-manual	799	40
		Skilled manual	2141	107
		Semi-skilled manual	1924	96
		Unskilled manual	498	25
	45–64	Professional	1661	83
		Managers/employers	2397	120
		Intermediate and junior non-manual	999	49
		Skilled manual	2001	100
		Semi-skilled manual	1761	88
		Unskilled manual	576	29
Female	20–29	Professional	881	44
		Managers/employers	678	34
		Intermediate and junior non-manual	2158	108
		Skilled manual	175	9
		Semi-skilled manual	963	48
		Unskilled manual	357	18
	30–44	Professional	1638	82
		Managers/employers	976	49
		Intermediate and junior non-manual	2842	142
		Skilled manual	221	11
		Semi-skilled manual	1180	59
		Unskilled manual	879	41
	45–64	Professional	882	44
		Managers/employers	784	39
		Intermediate and junior non-manual	2197	110
		Skilled manual	157	8
		Semi-skilled manual	942	47
		Unskilled manual	816	41
Total sample			44 156	2200

These are then divided into assignments of 50 people for each interviewer.

your quota sample may be subject to bias. Interviewers tend to choose respondents who are easily accessible and who appear willing to answer the survey. Clear controls may therefore be needed. In addition it has been known for interviewers to fill in quotas incorrectly. This is not to say that your quota sample will not produce good results; they can and often do! However, you cannot measure the level of certainty or margins of error as the sample is not probability based.

Purposive sampling

Purposive or *judgemental sampling* enables you to use your judgement to select cases that will best enable you to answer your research question(s) and to meet your objectives. This form of sample is often used when working with very small samples such as in case study research and when you wish to select cases that are particularly informative (Neuman, 1997). Purposive sampling may also be used by researchers following the grounded theory approach. For such research, findings from data collected from your initial sample inform the way you extend your sample into subsequent cases (Section 12.6). Such samples cannot, however, be considered to be statistically representative of the total population. The logic on which you base your strategy for selecting cases for a purposive sample should be dependent on your research question(s) and objectives. The more common strategies were outlined in Fig 6.2 and are discussed below:

- *Extreme case* sampling focuses on unusual or special cases on the basis that the data collected about these unusual or extreme outcomes will enable you to learn the most and to answer your research question(s) and to meet your objectives most effectively. This is often based on the premise that findings from extreme cases will be relevant in understanding or explaining more typical cases (Patton, 1990). Peters and Waterman's research (1982) on excellent companies was based on a purposive sample of extreme (excellent) companies.

- *Heterogeneous* or *maximum variation* sampling enables you to collect data to describe and explain the key themes that can be observed. Although this might appear a contradiction, as a small sample may contain cases that are completely different, Patton (1990) argues that this is in fact a strength. Any patterns that do emerge are likely to be of particular interest and value and represent the key themes. In addition the data collected should enable you to document uniqueness. To ensure maximum variation within a sample Patton (1990) suggests you identify your diverse characteristics (sample selection criteria) prior to selecting your sample.

- In direct contrast to heterogeneous sampling, *homogeneous* sampling focuses on one particular sub-group in which all the sample members are similar. This enables you to study the group in great depth.

- *Critical case* sampling selects critical cases on the basis that they can make a point dramatically or because they are important. The focus of data collection is to understand what is happening in each critical case so that logical generalisations can be made. Patton (1990) outlines a number of clues that suggest critical cases. These can be summarised by the questions:

- If it happens there, will it happen everywhere?
- If they are having problems, can you be sure that everyone will have problems?
- If they cannot understand the process, is it likely that no one will be able to understand the process?

■ In contrast *typical case* sampling is usually used as part of a research project to provide an illustrative profile using a representative case. Such a sample enables you to provide an illustration of what is 'typical' to those who will be reading your research report and may be unfamiliar with the subject matter. It is not intended to be definitive.

Worked example

Purposive sampling

Phil was undertaking case study research in three organisations in the financial sector. He needed to interview managers to discover their organisations' objectives for a particular pay system and the extent to which the system seemed to be successful. He decided to talk to three homogeneous samples of managers:

■ senior general managers and personnel directors (the policy designers), to establish pay objectives and the extent to which they felt these had been achieved;

■ line managers (the policy operators), to establish their views on the pay system's objectives and the level of success being achieved;

■ middle and junior managers reporting directly to these line managers (the policy recipients), to test their perceptions of the pay system's objectives and the extent to which they considered it successful. Where appropriate Phil also interviewed trade union officials.

Snowball sampling

Snowball sampling is commonly used when it is difficult to identify members of the desired population, for example people who are working while claiming unemployment benefit. You therefore need:

1 to make contact with one or two cases in the population;
2 to ask these cases to identify further cases;
3 to ask these new cases to identify further new cases (and so on).

The main problem is making initial contact. Once you have done this, these cases identify further members of the population who then identify further members and so the sample snowballs. For such samples the problems of representativeness are huge as respondents are most likely to identify other potential respondents who are similar to themselves. The next problem is to find these new cases. However, for populations that are difficult to identify snowball sampling may provide the only possibility.

Snowball sampling

Steve was a part-time student. His project was concerned with the career paths of managing directors of large companies. As part of this Steve needed to interview managing directors. He arranged his first interview with the managing director of his own company. Towards the end of the interview the managing director asked Steve whether he could be of further assistance. Two other managing directors that Steve could interview were suggested. Steve's managing director offered to 'introduce' Steve to them and provided him with contact telephone numbers and the names of their personal assistants. Steve's sample had started to snowball!

Self-selection sampling

Self-selection sampling occurs when you allow a case, usually an individual, to identify their desire to take part in the research. You therefore:

1 publicise your need for cases either by advertising through appropriate media or asking them to take part;

2 collect data from those who respond.

Cases that self-select often do so because of their feelings or opinions about the research question(s) or stated objectives. In some instances, as in research undertaken by Adrian and colleagues on the positive management of redundancy, this is exactly what the researcher wants. In this research a letter in the personnel trade press generated a list of self-selected organisations that were interested in the research topic, considered it important and were willing to devote time to being interviewed.

Self-selection sampling

Siân's research was concerned with teleworking. She had decided to administer her questionnaire using the Internet. She publicised her research on a range of bulletin boards and through the teleworkers' association asking for volunteers to fill in a questionnaire. Those who responded were sent a short questionnaire by email.

Convenience sampling

Convenience sampling involves selecting those cases that are easiest to obtain for your sample. The sample selection process is continued until your required sample size has been reached. Although this technique of sampling is widely used it is prone to bias and influences that are beyond your control as the cases only appear in the sample because of the ease of obtaining them. Often the sample is intended to represent the total population, for example managers taking an MBA course as a surrogate for all managers! In such instances the choice of sample is likely to have biased the sample meaning that subsequent generalisations are likely to be at best flawed. These problems are less important where there is little variation in the population and such samples often serve as pilots to studies using more structured samples.

6.4 Summary

- Your choice of sampling techniques is dependent on the feasibility and sensibility of collecting data to answer your research question(s) and to address your objectives from the entire population. For populations of under 50 it is usually more sensible to collect data from the entire population where you are considering using probability sampling.

- Choice of sampling technique or techniques is dependent on your research question(s) and objectives:
  - research question(s) and objectives which need you to estimate statistically the characteristics of the population from a sample require probability samples;
  - research question(s) and objectives that do not require such generalisations can make use of non-probability sampling techniques.

- Factors such as the confidence that is needed in the findings, accuracy required and likely categories for analyses will affect the size of the sample that needs to be collected:
  - statistical analyses usually require a minimum sample size of 30;
  - research question(s) and objectives, which do not require statistical estimation, may need far smaller samples.

- Sample size and the technique used are also influenced by the availability of resources, in particular financial support and time available to select the sample and to collect, to enter into a computer and to analyse the data.

- Probability sampling techniques all necessitate some form of sampling frame so they are often more time consuming than non-probability techniques.

- Where it is not possible to construct a sampling frame you will need to use non-probability sampling techniques.

- Non-probability sampling techniques also provide you with the opportunity to select your sample purposively and to reach difficult to identify members of the population.

- For many research projects you will need to use a combination of different sampling techniques.

- All your choices will be dependent on your ability to gain access to organisations. The considerations summarised earlier must therefore be tempered with an understanding of what is practically possible.

Questions

6.1 Identify a suitable sampling frame for each of the following research questions:

  a How do company directors of manufacturing firms of over 500 employees think a specified piece of legislation will affect their companies?

  b Which factors are important in accountants' decisions regarding working in mainland Europe?

  c How do employees at Cheltenham Gardens Ltd think proposed introduction of compulsory Saturday working will affect their working lives?

6.2 You have been asked to select a sample of manufacturing firms using the sampling frame below. This also lists the value of their annual output in tens of thousands of pounds over the past year. To help you in selecting your sample the firms have been numbered from 0 to 99.

Output		Output		Output		Output		Output	
0	1163	20	1072	40	1257	60	1300	80	1034
1	10	21	7	41	29	61	39	81	55
2	57	22	92	42	84	62	73	82	66
3	149	23	105	43	97	63	161	83	165
4	205	24	157	44	265	64	275	84	301
5	163	25	214	45	187	65	170	85	161
6	1359	26	1440	46	1872	66	1598	86	1341
7	330	27	390	47	454	67	378	87	431
8	2097	28	1935	48	1822	68	1634	88	1756
9	1059	29	998	49	1091	69	1101	89	907
10	1037	30	1298	50	1251	70	1070	90	1158
11	59	31	10	51	9	71	37	91	27
12	68	32	70	52	93	72	88	92	66
13	166	33	159	53	103	73	102	93	147
14	302	34	276	54	264	74	157	94	203
15	161	35	215	55	189	75	168	95	163
16	1298	36	1450	56	1862	76	1602	96	1339
17	329	37	387	57	449	77	381	97	429
18	2103	38	1934	58	1799	78	1598	98	1760
19	1061	39	1000	59	1089	79	1099	99	898

a Select two simple random samples, each of twenty firms, and mark those firms selected for each sample on the sampling frame.

b Describe and compare the pattern on the sampling frame of each of the samples selected.

c Calculate the average (mean) annual output in tens of thousands of pounds over the past year for each of the samples selected.

d Given that the true average annual output is £6 608 900 is there any bias in either of the samples selected?

6.3 You have been asked to select a 10 per cent sample of firms from the sampling frame used for self-check question 6.2.

a Select a 10 per cent systematic sample and mark those firms selected for the sample on the sampling frame.

b Calculate the average (mean) annual output in tens of thousands of pounds over the past year for your sample.

c Given that the true average annual output is £6 608 900 why does systematic sampling provide such a poor estimate of the annual output in this case?

6.4 You need to undertake a face-to-face interview survey of managing directors of small to medium-sized organisations. From the data you collect you need to be able to generalise about the attitude of such managing directors to recent changes in government policy towards these firms. Your generalisations need to be accurate to within plus or minus 5 per cent. Unfortunately you have limited resources to pay for interviewers, travelling and other associated costs.

a How many managing directors will you need to interview?

b You have been given the choice between cluster and multi-stage sampling. Which technique would you choose for this research? You should give reasons for your choice.

6.5 You have been asked to undertake a survey of residents' opinions regarding the siting of a new supermarket in an inner city suburb (estimated catchment population 111 376 at the last census). The age and gender distribution of the catchment population at the last census is listed below:

Gender	Age group							
	0–4	5–15	16–19	20–29	30–44	45–59/64*	60/65#–74	75+
Males	3498	7106	4884	7656	9812	12892	4972	2684
Females	3461	6923	6952	9460	8152	9152	9284	4488

*59 females, 64 males, #60 females, 65 males

a Devise a quota for a quota sample using these data.

b What other data would you like to include to overcome likely variations between groups in their availability for interview and replicate the total population more precisely? Give reasons for your answer.

c What problems might you encounter in using interviewers?

6.6 For each of the following research questions it has not been possible for you to obtain a sampling frame. Suggest the most suitable non-probability sampling technique to obtain the necessary data giving reasons for your choice.

a What support do people sleeping rough believe they require from social services?

b Which television advertisements do people remember watching last weekend?

c How do employers' opinions vary regarding the impact of European Community legislation on employee recruitment?

d How are manufacturing companies planning to respond to the introduction of road tolls?

e Would users of the squash club be prepared to pay a 10 per cent increase in subscriptions to help fund two extra courts (answer needed by tomorrow morning!)?

Assignment 6

Using sampling as part of your research

→ Consider your research question(s) and objectives. You need to decide whether you will be able to collect data on the entire population or will need to collect data from a sample.

→ If you decide that you need to sample you must establish whether your research question(s) and objectives require probability sampling. If they do, make sure that a suitable sampling frame is available or can be devised and calculate the actual sample size required taking into account likely responses rates. If your research question(s) and objectives do not require probability sampling or you are unable to obtain a suitable sampling frame you will need to use non-probability sampling.

→ Select the most appropriate sampling technique or techniques after considering the advantages and disadvantages of all suitable techniques and undertaking further reading as necessary.

→ Select your sample or samples following the technique or techniques as outlined in this chapter.

→ Remember to note down the reasons for your choices when you make them as you will need to justify your choices when you write about your research methodology.

References

Barnett, V. (1991) *Sample Survey Principles and Method*, London, Edward Arnold.

Dale, A. (1993) 'Fieldwork and data processing', in Dale, A. and Marsh, C. (eds), *The 1991 Census User's Guide*, London, HMSO, pp. 84–110.

Dillman, D.A. (1978) *Mail and Telephone Surveys: the Total Design Method*, New York, Wiley.

Economist, The (1997) *The Economist Numbers Guide: the Essentials of Business Numeracy* (3rd edn), London, Profile Books.

Healey, M.J. (1991) 'Obtaining information from businesses', *in* Healey, M.J. (ed.), *Economic Activity and Land Use: the Changing Information Base for Local and Regional Studies*, Harlow, Longman, pp. 193–250.

Henry, G.T. (1990) *Practical Sampling*, Newbury Park, CA, Sage.

Hoinville, G., Jowell, R. and Associates (1985) *Survey Research Practice*, Aldershot, Gower.

Kervin, J.B. (1992) *Methods for Business Research*, New York, HarperCollins.

Moser CA and Kalton G (1986) *Survey Methods in Social Investigation* (2nd edn), Aldershot, Gower.

Neuman, W.L. (1997) *Social Research Methods* (2nd edn), London, Allyn and Bacon.

Owen, F. and Jones, R. (1994) *Statistics* (4th edn), London, Pitman Publishing.

Patton, M.Q. (1990) *Qualitative Evaluation and Research Methods* (2nd edn), Newbury Park, CA, Sage.

Peters, T. and Waterman, R. (1982) *In Search of Excellence*, New York, Harper & Row.

Scolari Sage (1999) 'Research methodology and CD-ROMS' (online)(cited 16 June 1999). Available from <URL:http://www.scolari.co.uk>.

deVaus, D.A. (1996) *Surveys in Social Research* (4th edn), London, UCL Press.

Further reading

Barnett, V. (1991) *Sample Survey Principles and Method*, London, Edward Arnold. Chapters 2, 5 and 6 provide an explanation of statistics behind probability sampling and quota sampling as well as the techniques.

Diamantopoulos, A. and Schlegelmilch, B.B. (1997) *Taking the Fear Out of Data Analysis*, London, Dryden Press. Chapter 2 contains a clear humorous discussion of both probability and non-probability sampling.

Hoinville, G., Jowell, R. and Associates (1985) *Survey Research Practice*, Aldershot, Gower. Chapter 4 provides a useful discussion of the practical aspects of probability sampling techniques, although it is very limited on non-probability sampling techniques.

Moser, C.A. and Kalton, G. (1986) *Survey Methods in Social Investigation* (2nd edn), Aldershot, Gower. This is one of the definitive texts on survey methods. Chapters 4–8 inclusive are particularly useful for its discussion on the impact of sample size, probability sampling and quota sampling and discussion of the problem of non-response.

Patton, M.Q. (1990) *Qualitative Evaluation and Research Methods* (2nd edn), Newbury Park, CA, Sage. Chapter 9 contains a useful discussion of non-probability sampling techniques with examples.

deVaus, D.A. (1996) *Surveys in Social Research* (4th edn), London, UCL Press. Chapter 5 provides a useful overview of both probability and non-probability sampling techniques.

Wass, V.J. (1994) 'Minimizing and managing bias in a mail survey: a study of redundant miners', *in* Wass, V.J. and Wells, P.E., *Principles and Practice in Business and Management Research*, Aldershot, Dartmouth, pp. 91–121. This includes a useful account of the realities of sample selection for a postal questionnaire survey.

Case 6   ## Change management at Hattersley Electrics

Hattersley Electrics is a division of the Hattersley Group PLC, a United Kingdom based manufacturing conglomerate whose main markets were, until recently, the high-tech aerospace and the defence industries. In recent years both the recession in the airline industry and the contraction in defence spending by European governments have hit the division. In order to overcome these Hattersley Electrics has embarked on the process of repositioning itself within the electronics marketplace niche of advanced civilian communications equipment. As part of this it has changed its manufacturing foci and chosen to downsize and restructure its workforce.

▶

Initially the workforce was not resistant to change owing to the extensive efforts made by management to keep them involved and informed at all stages. This involved restructuring the division (Fig 1) into cells and reducing the workforce from 380 to 250. After this restructuring the works council informed the division's management team that the workforce were concerned about the longer-term effects of these changes. In particular they highlighted possible loss of employment, future job security, a lack of division identity, a lack of direction from senior management and a lack of employee involvement in recent decisions.

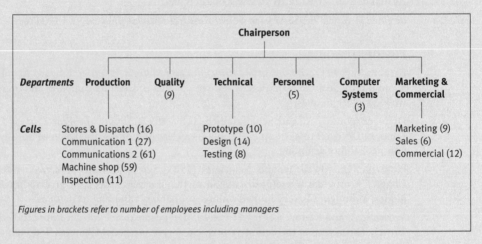

Fig 1   **Organisational structure of Hattersley Group PLC Electrics Division**

A consultancy group was hired by the management team and set three objectives to be achieved (at a 95 per cent level of certainty) within a fixed budget and a timescale of 10 weeks from start to finish. These were to establish:

1 the views of the division's managers and employees about the effectiveness of change at Hattersley Electrics;

2 general perceptions of the division's managers and staff about general aspects of the experience of the changes at Hattersley Electrics;

3 whether there were any differences in general perceptions between departments and between managers and employees.

The agreed methodology involved three stages of data collection. In the first stage interviews were undertaken with the division's chairperson and six managers and a sample of employees. One employee was selected at random from each cell. These interviews were to enable the consultants to understand the background to the changes and to establish the full variety of opinions regarding its effectiveness. In addition they covered a range of other issues associated with general aspects of the experience of the changes.

In the second stage a questionnaire was distributed, which reflected the issues generated by interviews in the first stage, to 50 per cent of company managers and employees. This sample was selected from a sampling frame generated from the personnel department's staff database and was stratified by department and cell. Within each cell employees were listed in order of seniority. All employees other than those in the production department received a questionnaire; 28 per cent of those employees in the production department received a questionnaire. The numbers sampled in each cell are given in Fig 2. Overall there was a 97.6 per cent response rate to the questionnaire, two non-responses coming from the computer systems department and one from the production department.

After the analysis of the questionnaire, three follow-up group interviews were undertaken, each group consisting of five or six people (stage 3). One group consisted of production employees, another of managers from all departments and a third of employees from all departments other than production. In the interviews issues that had arisen during the analysis of the questionnaire were probed and clarified.

Production	Quality (9)	Technical	Personnel (5)	Computer Systems (3)	Marketing & Commercial
Stores & Dispatch (4)		Prototype (10)			Marketing (9)
Communication 1 (7)		Design (14)			Sales (6)
Communications 2 (18)		Testing (8)			Commercial (12)
Machine shop (17)					
Inspection (3)					

Fig 2 **Number of managers and employees in each cell who received a questionnaire**

Questions

1 **a** Name the sampling techniques used at each of the three stages.

  b List possible reasons for the choice of each of these techniques.

2 Given the quoted response rate of 97.6 per cent what is the accuracy (margin of error) of the questionnaire results for the division likely to have been?

3 **a** What issues will need to be taken into account when generalising from the questionnaire results to:

  i   all employees in each department of the Electrics division?

  ii all employees in the Electrics division?

  b Give reasons for your answers.

4 **a** Would it be possible to use the results from the three sample surveys outlined in this case to generalise about the management of change in the Hattersley PLC group?

  b Give reasons for your answer.

Answers

6.1 a A complete list of all directors of large manufacturing firms could be purchased from an organisation which specialised in selling such lists to use as the sampling frame. Alternatively a list which only contained those selected for the sample could be purchased to reduce costs. These data are usually in a format suitable for being read by word-processing and database computer software and so they could easily be merged into standard letters such as those included with questionnaires.

b A complete list of accountants, or one that only contained those selected for the sample, could be purchased from an organisation that specialised in selling such lists. Care would need to be taken regarding the precise composition of the list to ensure that it included those in private practice as well as those working for organisations. Alternatively if the research was only interested in qualified accountants then the professional accountancy bodies' yearbooks, which list all their members and their addresses, could be used as the sampling frame.

c The personnel records or payroll of Cheltenham Gardens Ltd could be used. Either would provide an up to date list of all employees with their addresses.

6.2 a Your answer will depend on the random numbers you selected. However, the process you follow to select the samples is likely to be similar to that outlined. Starting at randomly selected points two sets of 20 two-digit random numbers are read from the random number tables (Appendix 3). If a number is selected twice it is disregarded. Two possible sets are:

Sample 1: 38 41 14 59 53 03 52 86 21 88 55 87 85 90 74 18 89 40 84 71
Sample 2: 28 00 06 70 81 76 36 65 30 27 92 73 20 87 58 15 69 22 77 31

These are then marked on the sampling frame (sample 1 is enclosed by a box, sample 2 is shaded) as shown below (see p. 185):

0	1163	20	1072	40	1257	60	1300	80	1034
1	10	21	7	41	29	61	39	81	55
2	57	22	92	42	84	62	73	82	66
3	149	23	105	43	97	63	161	83	165
4	205	24	157	44	265	64	275	84	301
5	163	25	214	45	187	65	170	85	161
6	1359	26	1440	46	1872	66	1598	86	1341
7	330	27	390	47	454	67	378	87	431
8	2097	28	1935	48	1822	68	1634	88	1756
9	1059	29	998	49	1091	69	1101	89	907
10	1037	30	1298	50	1251	70	1070	90	1158
11	59	31	10	51	9	71	37	91	27
12	68	32	70	52	93	72	88	92	66
13	166	33	159	53	103	73	102	93	147
14	302	34	276	54	264	74	157	94	203
15	161	35	215	55	189	75	168	95	163
16	1298	36	1450	56	1862	76	1602	96	1339
17	329	37	387	57	449	77	381	97	429
18	2103	38	1934	58	1799	78	1598	98	1760
19	1061	39	1000	59	1089	79	1099	99	898

b Your samples will probably produce patterns that cluster around certain numbers in the sampling frame although the amount of clustering may differ as illustrated by samples 1 and 2 above.

c The average (mean) annual output in tens of thousands of pounds will depend entirely upon your sample. For the two samples selected the averages are:

sample 1 (boxed): £6 752 000
sample 2 (shaded): £7 853 500

d There is no bias in either of the samples as both have been selected at random. However the average annual output calculated from sample 1 represents the total population more closely than that calculated from sample 2, although this has occurred entirely at random.

6.3 a Your answer will depend on the random number you select as the starting point for your systematic sample. However, the process you followed to select your sample is likely to be similar to that outlined. As a 10 per cent sample has been requested the sampling fraction is $\frac{1}{10}$. Your starting point is selected using a random number between 0 and 9, in this case 2. Once the firm numbered 2 has been selected, every tenth firm is selected:

2 12 22 32 42 52 62 72 82 92

These are marked with a box on the sampling frame and will result in a regular pattern whatever the starting point:

0	1163	20	1072	40	1257	60	1300	80	1034
1	10	21	7	41	29	61	39	81	55
2	57	22	92	42	84	62	73	82	66
3	149	23	105	43	97	63	161	83	165
4	205	24	157	44	265	64	275	84	301
5	163	25	214	45	187	65	170	85	161
6	1359	26	1440	46	1872	66	1598	86	1341
7	330	27	390	47	454	67	378	87	431
8	2097	28	1935	48	1822	68	1634	88	1756
9	1059	29	998	49	1091	69	1101	89	907
10	1037	30	1298	50	1251	70	1070	90	1158
11	59	31	10	51	9	71	37	91	27
12	68	32	70	52	93	72	88	92	66
13	166	33	159	53	103	73	102	93	147
14	302	34	276	54	264	74	157	94	203
15	161	35	215	55	189	75	168	95	163
16	1298	36	1450	56	1862	76	1602	96	1339
17	329	37	387	57	449	77	381	97	429
18	2103	38	1934	58	1799	78	1598	98	1760
19	1061	39	1000	59	1089	79	1099	99	898

b The average (mean) annual output of firms for your sample will depend upon where you started your systematic sample. For the sample selected above it is £757 000.

c Systematic sampling has provided a poor estimate of the annual output because there is an underlying pattern in the data which has resulted in firms with similar levels of output being selected.

6.4 a If you assume that there are at least 100 000 managing directors of small to medium-sized organisations from which to select your sample you will need to interview approximately 380 to make generalisations which are accurate to within plus or minus 5 per cent (table 6.1).

b Either cluster or multi-stage sampling could be suitable; what is important is the reasoning behind your choice. This choice between cluster and multi-stage sampling is dependent on the amount of limited resources and time you have available. Using multi-stage sampling will take longer than cluster sampling as more sampling stages will need to be undertaken. However, the results are more likely to be representative of the total population owing to the possibility of stratifying the samples from the sub-areas.

6.5 a Prior to deciding on your quota you will need to consider the possible inclusion of residents who are aged less than 16 in your quota. Often in such research projects residents aged under 5 (and those aged 5–15) are excluded. You would need a quota of between 2000 and 5000 residents to obtain a reasonable accuracy. These should be divided proportionally between the groupings as illustrated in the possible quota below:

Gender	Age group					
	16–19	20–29	30–44	45–59/64	60/65–74	75+
Males	108	169	217	285	110	59
Females	154	209	180	203	205	99

b Data on social class, employment status, socio-economic status or car ownership could also be used as further quotas. These data are available from the census and are likely to affect shopping habits.

c Interviewers might choose respondents who were easily accessible or appeared willing to answer the questions. In addition they might fill in their quota incorrectly or make up the data.

6.6 a Either snowball sampling as it would be difficult to identify members of the desired population or, possibly, convenience sampling because of initial difficulties in finding members of the desired population.

b Quota sampling to ensure that the variability in the population as a whole was represented.

c Purposive sampling to ensure that the full variety of responses are obtained from a range of respondents from the population.

d Self-selection sampling as it requires people who are interested in the topic.

e Convenience sampling owing to the very short timescales available and the need to have at least some idea of members' opinions.

7 Using secondary data

By the end of this chapter you should be able:

- to identify the wide variety of secondary data that are available;

- to appreciate ways in which secondary data can be utilised to help to answer research question(s) and to meet objectives;

- to understand the advantages and disadvantages of using secondary data in research projects;

- to use a range of techniques , including published guides and the Internet, to locate secondary data;

- to evaluate the suitability of secondary data for answering research question(s) and meeting objectives in terms of coverage, validity, reliability and measurement bias;

- to apply the knowledge, skills and understanding gained to your own research project.

7.1 Introduction

When considering how to answer their research question(s) or to meet their objectives, few researchers consider the possibility of re-analysing data that have already been collected for some other purpose (Hakim, 1982). Such data are known as *secondary data*. Most automatically think in terms of collecting new (*primary*) *data* specifically for that purpose. Yet, despite this, such secondary data can provide a useful source from which to answer, or to begin to answer, your research question(s).

Secondary data include both raw data and published summaries. Most organisations collect and store a variety of data to support their operations; for example, payroll details, copies of letters, minutes of meetings and accounts of sales of goods or services. Broadsheet daily newspapers contain a wealth of data including reports about take-over bids and companies' share prices. Government departments undertake surveys and publish official statistics covering social, demographic and economic topics. Consumer research organisations collect data that are used subsequently by different clients. Trade organisations survey their members on topics such as sales that are subsequently aggregated and published.

Some of these data, in particular documents such as company minutes, are only available from the organisations which produce them and so access will need to be negotiated (Section 5.3). Others, including government surveys such as the population census, are widely available in published form and on CD-ROM in university libraries. An increasing variety has been deposited in and is available from data archives (Dale *et al.*, 1988). In addition a rapidly increasing number of companies and professional organisations have their own Internet sites from which data may be obtained. On-line computer databases containing company information can be accessed via the Internet through information gateways such as Biz/Ed (Table 3.7).

For certain types of research project, such as those requiring national or international comparisons, secondary data will probably provide the main source to answer your research question(s) and to address your objectives. However, if you are undertaking your research project as part of a course of study, we recommend that you check the examination regulations before deciding to rely entirely on secondary data. You may be required to collect primary data for your research project. Most research questions are answered using some combination of secondary and primary data. Where limited appropriate secondary data are available you will have to rely mainly on data you collect yourself.

In this chapter we examine the different types of secondary data that are likely to be available to help you to answer your research question(s) and meet your objectives, how you might use them (Section 7.2) and a range of methods, including published guides, for locating these data (Section 7.3). We then consider the advantages and disadvantages of using secondary data (Section 7.4) and discuss ways of evaluating their validity and reliability (Section 7.5). We do not attempt to provide a comprehensive list of secondary data sources, as this would be an impossible task within the space available.

7.2 ■ Types of secondary data and uses in research

Secondary data include both quantitative and qualitative data and can be used in both descriptive and explanatory research. The data you use may be *raw data* where there has been little if any processing or *compiled data* that have received some form of selection or summarising (Kervin, 1999). Within business and management research, such data are mostly used in case study and survey-type research. However, there is no reason not to include secondary data in experimental research.

Different researchers (for example Bryman, 1989; Dale *et al.*, 1988; Hakim, 1982; Robson, 1993) have generated a variety of classifications for secondary data. These classifications do not, however, capture the full variety of data. We have therefore built on their ideas to create three main sub-groups of secondary data: documentary data, survey-based data and those compiled from multiple sources (Fig 7.1).

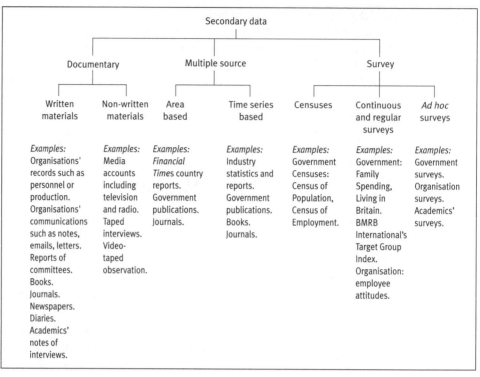

Fig 7.1   **Types of secondary data**

© Mark Saunders, Philip Lewis and Adrian Thornhill, 2000

Documentary secondary data

Documentary secondary data are often used in research projects that also use primary data collection methods. However, you can also use them on their own or with other sources of secondary data, in particular for historical research. Research based almost exclusively on documentary secondary data is termed *archival research* and, although this term has historical connotations, it can refer to recent as well as historical documents (Bryman, 1989). Documentary secondary data includes *written documents* such as notices, correspondence, minutes of meetings, reports to shareholders, diaries, transcripts of speeches and administrative and public records. Written documents can also include books, journal and magazine articles and newspapers. These can be important raw data sources in their own right, as well as a storage medium for compiled data. You could use written documents to provide qualitative data such as managers' espoused reasons for decisions. They could also be used to generate statistical measures such as data on absenteeism and profitability derived from company records (Bryman, 1989). Documentary secondary data also includes *non-written documents* (Fig 7.1) such as tape and video recordings, pictures, drawings, films and television programmes (Robson, 1993). These data can be analysed both quantitatively and qualitatively. In addition, they can be used to help to triangulate findings based on other data such as written documents and primary data collected through observation, interviews or questionnaires (Chapters 8, 9 and 10).

For your research project the documentary sources you have available will depend on whether you have been granted access to an organisation's records as well as your success in locating library, data archive and commercial sources (Section 7.4). Access to an organisation's data will be dependent on gatekeepers within that organisation (Section 5.3). In our experience, those research projects that make use of documentary secondary data often do so as part of a within-company research project or a case study of a particular organisation.

Worked example

Using documentary secondary data

You are interested in the impact of private sector values on the organisational culture of United Kingdom (UK) local authorities. As part of this research, you wish to discover whether there has been a shift from recruiting people with only public sector experience to recruiting those with at least some private sector experience. To provide quantitative data about changes you have gained access to individual employees' personnel records (documentary secondary data) over a fifteen-year period in the local authority where you undertook your work placement. Fortunately, this authority has not been affected by local government reorganisation. The records contain the date that each vacancy was filled, how it was notified, and the age, gender, qualifications and previous occupation of the successful applicant.

Your next stage will be to abstract data for each externally notified vacancy and to match these with data from vacancy advertisement invoice instructions (also documentary secondary data). The latter will enable you to obtain a complete list of all notification outlets used for each vacancy. Once your data have been combined you will be able to analyse these data quantitatively.

Survey-based secondary data

Survey-based secondary data refers usually to data collected by questionnaires (Chapter 10) which have already been analysed for their original purpose. Such data can refer to organisations, people or households (Hakim, 1982). They are made available as compiled data tables or as a computer-readable matrix of raw data (Section 11.2) for secondary analysis.

Survey-based secondary data will have been collected through one of three distinct types of survey: censuses, continuous/regular surveys or *ad hoc* surveys (Fig 7.1). *Censuses* are usually carried out by governments and are unique because, unlike surveys, participation is obligatory (Hakim, 1982). Consequently, they provide very good coverage of the population surveyed. They include population censuses, which have been carried out every ten years in the UK since 1801 with the exception of 1941 (Marsh, 1993), and others such as the UK Annual Employment Survey. This replaced the Census of Employment and has been carried out annually since September 1995

(Partington and Mayell, 1998). The data from censuses conducted by many governments are intended to meet the needs of government departments as well as local government. As a consequence they are usually clearly defined, well documented and of a high quality. Such data are easily accessible in compiled form and widely used by other organisations and individual researchers.

Continuous and regular surveys are those surveys, excluding censuses, which are repeated over time (Hakim, 1982). They include surveys where data are collected throughout the year, such as the UK's General Household Survey (Thomas *et al.*, 1998), and those repeated at regular intervals. The latter includes the Labour Force Survey, which is undertaken annually by member states throughout the European Union with a core set of questions. This means that some comparative data are available for member states, although access to these data is limited by European and individual countries' legislation (Dale *et al.*, 1988). Non-governmental bodies also carry out regular surveys. These include general-purpose market research surveys such as BMRB International's Target Group Index. Because of the Target Group Index's commercial nature, the data are very expensive. However, BMRB International has provided copies of reports (usually over three years old) to between 20 and 30 UK university libraries. Many large organisations undertake regular surveys, a common example being the employee attitude survey. However, because of the sensitive nature of such information it is often difficult to gain access to such survey data, especially in its raw form.

Census and continuous and regular survey data provide a useful resource with which to compare or set in context your own research findings. Aggregate data are often available on CD-ROMs or in published form in libraries (Section 7.3), in particular for government surveys. When using these data you need to check when they were collected as it often takes at least two years for publication to occur! If you are undertaking research in one UK organisation you could use these data to place your case study organisation within the context of its industry group or division using the Census of Employment. Aggregated results of the Census of Employment can be found in *Labour Market Trends* (formerly the *Employment Gazette*). Alternatively, you might explore issues already highlighted by data from an organisation survey through in-depth interviews.

Survey secondary data may be available in sufficient detail to provide the main data set from which to answer your research question(s) and to meet your objectives. Alternatively, they may be the only way in which you can obtain the required data. If your research question is concerned with national variations in consumer spending it is unlikely that you will be able to collect sufficient data. You will therefore need to rely on secondary data such as those contained in *Family Spending* (formerly the Family Expenditure Survey (King, 1996)). For some research questions and objectives suitable data will be available in published form. For others, you may need more disaggregated data. This may be available on CD-ROM, via the Internet (Section 3.4) or from archives (Section 7.3). We have found that for most business and management research involving secondary data you are unlikely to find all the data you require from one survey. Rather, your research project is likely to involve detective work in which you build your own multiple-source data set using different data items from a variety of surveys and other secondary data sources. Like all detective work, finding data that help to answer a research question or meet an objective is immensely satisfying.

Ad hoc surveys are usually one-off surveys and are far more specific in their subject matter. They include data from questionnaires that have been undertaken by independent researchers as well as surveys undertaken by organisations and governments. Because of their *ad hoc* nature, you will probably find it more difficult to discover relevant surveys. However, it may be that an organisation in which you are undertaking research has conducted its own questionnaire, on an issue related to your research. Some organisations will provide you with a report containing aggregated data; others may be willing to let you re-analyse the raw data from this *ad hoc* survey. Alternatively, you may be able to gain access and to use raw data from an *ad hoc* survey that has been deposited in an archive (Section 7.3).

Worked example

Integrating secondary and primary data

Sue's research was on the impact of European Union legislation on employee mobility between member states. In particular she was interested in how legislation relating to the mutual recognition of qualifications had affected those working in the accountancy profession. This legislation should mean that an accountant who has qualified in any European Union state can, after an aptitude test and a period of adaptation, apply to have that qualification recognised by another member state.

As part of her research, Sue undertook a series of in-depth interviews with UK accountants at different stages of their careers. These explored their attitudes to working elsewhere in the European Union. Within the interviews, Sue concentrated on the importance of mutual recognition of qualifications relative to other factors such as the accountants' need to move their families and their foreign language ability.

Sue's own data were set in context by analysing a variety of published secondary data. Published tables from the International Passenger Survey were re-analysed to ascertain the level of professional migration out of and into the UK. These aggregate data were also used to ascertain the proportion of professional migrants whose families move with them when they migrate. Secondary data were used to explore the frequency of applications for mutual recognition of qualifications in the UK. Unpublished tables, obtained from the Department of Trade and Industry, provided details regarding how many accountants and other professionals have applied to have their qualifications recognised by UK professions (see Davis and Saunders, 1997).

Multiple source secondary data

Multiple-source secondary data can be based entirely on documentary or on survey data or can be an amalgam of the two. The key factor is that different data sets have been combined to form another data set prior to you accessing the data. One of the more common types of multiple-source data that you are likely to come across in document form is various compilations of company information such as *The Times 1000, 1998* (Barrow, 1998). This contains comparable quantitative and qualitative data on the top 1000 UK and European companies and top 100 companies for other regions of the world. Others multiple-source secondary data include the various share price listings for different stock markets in the financial pages of broadsheet newspapers. These are available in most university libraries including back copies on microfilm or CD-ROM. However, you need to beware of relying on CD-ROM copies for tabular data or diagrams as some only contain the text of articles.

The way in which a multiple-source data set has been compiled will dictate the sorts of research question(s) or objectives with which you can use it. One method of compilation is to extract and combine selected comparable variables from a number of surveys or from the same survey that has been repeated a number of times to provide a *time-series* of data. For short research projects, this is one of the few ways in which you will be able to get data over a long period to undertake a *longitudinal* study. Other ways of obtaining time-series data are to use a series of company documents such as appointment letters or public and administrative records to create your own longitudinal secondary data set. Examples include the UK Employment Department's stoppages at work data held by the Data Archive based at the University of Essex and those derived by researchers from 19th century population census returns which, in the UK, are accessible to the public after 100 years.

Data can also be compiled for the same population over time using a series of 'snap-shots' to form *cohort studies*. Such studies are relatively rare owing to the difficulty of maintaining contact with members of the cohort from year to year. An example is the television series *Seven Up* (already mentioned in Section 4.2) which has followed a cohort since they were school children at seven-year intervals for over 40 years.

Secondary data from different sources can also be combined if they have the same geographical basis to form *area-based* data sets (Hakim, 1982). Such data sets usually draw together quantifiable information and statistics and are commonly produced by governments for their country. Area-based multiple-source data sets are usually available in published form for the countries and their component standard economic planning regions. The more widely used by our students include the UK's *Annual Abstract of Statistics* (Wisniewski, 1998), *Regional Trends* (Office of National Statistics, 1996; Pullinger, 1998) and the journal *Labour Market Trends*. Area-based multiple-source data sets are also available from data archives. These include data such as the Labour Force Survey (Data Archive, 1999).

7.3 Locating secondary data

Unless you are approaching your research project with the intention of analysing one specific secondary data set which you already know well, your first step will be to ascertain whether the data you need are available. Your research question(s), objectives and the literature you have reviewed will guide this. For many research projects you are likely to be unsure as to whether the data you require are available as secondary data. Fortunately, there are a number of pointers to the sorts of data that are likely to be available.

The breadth of data discussed in the previous sections only serves to emphasise the variety of possible locations in which such data may be found. Finding relevant secondary data requires detective work, which has two interlinked stages:

1 establishing that the sort of data you require are likely to be available as secondary data;

2 locating the precise data you require.

The availability of secondary data

There are a number of clues to whether the secondary data you require are likely to be available. As part of your literature review, you will have already read books and journal articles on your chosen topic. Where these have made use of secondary data, they will provide you with an idea of the sort of data that are available. In addition, these books and articles should contain full references to the sources of the data. Where these refer to published secondary data such as multiple-source or survey reports it is usually relatively easy to track down the original source.

References for unpublished and documentary secondary data are often less specific, referring to 'unpublished survey results' or an 'in-house company survey'. Although these may be insufficient to locate or access the actual secondary data they still provide useful clues about the sort of data that might be found within organisations and which might prove useful. Textbooks which discuss data likely to be held on organisations' management information systems, such as Kingsbury's (1997) *IT Answers to HR Questions*, can provide you with valuable clues about the sort of documentary secondary data that are likely to exist within organisations.

Tertiary literature such as indexes and catalogues can also help you to locate secondary data (Sections 3.2–3.4). Data archive catalogues, in particular the Data Archive at the University of Essex, may prove a useful source of the sorts of secondary data available.[1] This archive holds over 5000 computer-readable social science and humanities data sets for further analysis by the research community (Data Archive, 1999). These data have been acquired from academic, commercial and government sources and relate mainly to post-war Britain. The complete catalogue of these can be accessed and searched via the Internet (Section 3.5) through the Archive's home page (see Table 7.2). However, it should be remembered that the supply of data and documentation for all of the Data Archive's data sets is charged at cost and there may be additional administrative and royalty charges.

Informal discussions are also often a useful source. Acknowledged experts, colleagues, librarians or your project advisor may well have knowledge of the sorts of data that might be available (Stewart and Kamins, 1993). In addition, there is a range of published guides to secondary data sources. Those business and management guides that we, and our students, have found most useful are outlined in Table 7.1. However, there are also more subject-specific guides that provide more detail on sources for specific subject areas such as marketing and finance.

---

[1]There are numerous other data archives in Europe and the USA. The Data Archive has access to data held in many European archives through its membership of the Council for European Social Science Data Archive. The central repository for data archives in the USA is the Inter-University Consortium for Political and Social Research (ICPSR) at the University of Michigan. Copies of the ICPSR catalogue are obtainable from the Data Archive (ESRC Data Archive, 1995).

Table 7.1	Published guides to possible secondary data sources

Guide	Coverage
Central Statistical Office (1996) *Guide to Official Statistics,* London, HMSO	Official statistics produced by UK government
Croner (no date) *A–Z of Business Information Sources,* Kingston, Croner Publications	Loose-leaf regularly updated. Alphabetical list of subjects showing relevant sources including trade associations and institutional sources; UK focus
Smith G. (ed.) (annual) *Business Information Yearbook,* Headland, Headland Press	Annual survey. Covers company and market information, on-line business information, and a who's who in business information
Mort, D. (1992) *UK Statistics – a Guide for Business Users,* Aldershot, Ashgate	Official statistics collected by UK government; unofficial statistics such as those collected by major survey organisations; who produces these data
Mort, D. (1992) *European Market Information: a Handbook for Managers*, London, Pitman	General unofficial and official statistical publications on a country-by-country basis; lists of who produces these data
Mort, D. (1997) *Sources of Unofficial UK Statistics* (3rd edn), Aldershot, Gower	Unofficial UK statistics collected by major survey organisations; lists of who produces these data
Library Association (1997) *Libraries in the United Kingdom and Republic of Ireland*, London, Library Association	Lists of 2500 libraries in the UK and Eire
Dale, P. (1992) *Guide to Libraries and Information Units in Government Departments and Other Organisations* (30th edn), London, British Library	List libraries and information services in UK Government departments and related agencies
Dale, P. (1993) *Guide to Libraries in Key UK Companies,* London, British Library	Lists libraries in UK companies which are prepared to accept serious enquiries from outside
Patzer, G.L. (1996) *Using Secondary Data in Marketing Research: United States and World-wide,* Westport, CT, Quorum Books	Includes lists of sources specific to marketing, global information sources, US Census data, and more general business-related sources
McGuinness, K. and Short, T. (1998) *Research on the Net,* London, Old Bailey Press	Lists over 4000 Internet sites that offer information of research value. Chapters include accounting and finance, business, industry and labour as well as country-by-country information

Finding secondary data

Once you have ascertained that secondary data are likely to exist, you need to find their precise location. For secondary data published by governments this will be quite easy. Precise references are often given in published guides (Table 7.1) and, where other researchers have made use of them, a full reference should exist. Locating published secondary data that are likely to be held by libraries or secondary data held in archives is relatively straightforward. Specialist libraries with specific subject collections such as market research reports can usually be located using the Library Association's (1997) publication or guides by Dale (1992, 1993) (Table 7.1). If you are unsure where to start confess your ignorance and ask a librarian. This will usually result in a great deal of helpful advice, as well as saving you time. Once the appropriate abstracting tool or catalogue has been located and its use demonstrated, it can be searched for using similar techniques to those employed in your literature search (Section 3.5).

Data that are held by organisations are more difficult to locate. For within-organisation data, we have found that the information or data manager within the appropriate department is most likely to know the precise secondary data that are held. This is the person who will also help or hinder your eventual access to the data and can be thought of as the *gatekeeper* to the information (Section 5.3).

Data on the Internet can be located using site guides such as McGuinness and Short (1998, see Table 7.1) and *search tools* where you search for all possible locations that match key words associated with your research question(s) or objectives (Section 3.5). In some cases data will be located at sites hosted by companies and professional organisations such as those listed in Table 7.2. A good way of finding an organisation's home page is to use a general search engine (Table 3.7) or, in the case of UK-based companies, the links provided by the Yellow Pages UK subject directory (Table 3.7). However, although the amount of data on the Internet is increasing rapidly, much of it is, in our experience, of dubious quality. In addition, searching for relevant data is often very time consuming.

Table 7.2 **Selected secondary data sites on the Internet**

Name	Internet address	Comment
Business Zone	http://www.businesszone.co.uk	Up-to-date resource. Browsable library of research findings in condensed format
Data Archive	http://dawww.essex.ac.uk	Catalogue for over 5000 computer-readable social science and humanities data sets
FT Info	http://www.info.ft.com/companies	Company information on 11 000 companies including financial performance
Hoover's Online	http://www.hoovers.com	Company information on 12 000 US and international companies with links to CNN and *Washington Post*
Statbase	http://www.statistics.gov.uk/statbase/mainmenu.asp	UK national statistics
UK Equities Direct	http://194.200.168.251/equities/index.htm	Hemmington Scott's guide to companies and investment trusts, report service and market activity analysis
Organisations	http://www.adassoc.org.uk	Advertising Association
	http://www.asa.org.uk	Advertising Standards Authority

▶

Table 7.1	Cont.	

Name	Internet address	Comment
Organisations Cont.	http://www.acas.org.uk	Advisory Conciliation and Arbitration Service
	http://www.ama.org	American Marketing Association
	http://www.acca.co.uk	Association of Chartered Certified Accountants
	http://www.businesslink.co.uk	Business Link
	http://www.cbi.org.uk	Confederation of British Industry (CBI)
	http://www.cib.org.uk	Chartered Institute of Bankers
	http://www.cima.org.uk	Chartered Institute of Management Accountants
	http://www.cim.co.uk	Chartered Institute of Marketing (CIM)
	http://www.indsoc.co.uk	Industrial Society
	http://www.iod.co.uk	Institute of Directors
	http://www.inst-mgt.org.uk	Institute of Management
	http://www.ipd.co.uk	Institute of Personnel and Development
	http://www.ipa.co.uk	Institute of Practitioners in Advertising (IPA)
	http://www.kpmg.co.uk	KPMG UK
	http://www.sets.co.uk	London Stock Exchange
	http://www.tuc.org.uk	Trade Union Congress (TUC)

Once you have located a possible secondary data set, you need to be certain that it will meet your needs. For documentary data or data in a published form the easiest way is to obtain and evaluate a sample copy. For survey data that are available in computer-readable form, this is likely to involve some cost. One alternative is to obtain and evaluate detailed variable definitions for the data set (which include how they are coded (Section 11.2)) and the documentation that describes how the data were collected. This evaluation process is discussed in Section 7.5.

Worked example

Establishing that the secondary data you require are available

Dunkerley (1988) undertook a three-year historical research project on the naval dockyard in the Devonport area of the city of Plymouth, UK. The proposed research strategy used interviews with dockyard workers as well as secondary data sources including:

- enumerators' books for population censuses from 1851;
- records relating to dockyard employment, labour relations and skills;
- Admiralty and Treasury papers;

■ Poor Law records;

■ a sample of local newspapers.

Initially it had been assumed that these secondary data would be readily available. Unfortunately, much of the secondary data that it had been assumed were available locally had been destroyed during enemy action in the Second World War. In addition, data that still existed had been obscurely catalogued in the Public Records Office at Kew, London. This made these data difficult to find.

Although copies of enumerators' books for the population censuses were available locally the use of census material 'proved more difficult than had been imagined' (Dunkerley, 1988:86). Data collected differed between successive censuses. In addition, the 100-year confidentiality rule meant that the enumerators' books were not available for more recent censuses.

Because of these and other problems, a re-think of the aims and methods of the research was undertaken prior to proceeding further.

7.4 Advantages and disadvantages of secondary data

Advantages

May have fewer resource requirements

For many research questions and objectives the main advantage of using secondary data is the enormous saving in resources, in particular your time and money (Ghauri *et al.*, 1995). In general, it is much less expensive to use secondary data than to collect the data yourself. Consequently, you may be able to analyse far larger data sets such as those collected by government surveys. You will also have more time to think about theoretical aims and substantive issues as your data will already be collected and subsequently to be able to spend more time, and effort, analysing and interpreting the data.

Unobtrusive

If you need your data quickly, secondary data may be the only viable alternative. In addition, they are likely to be higher-quality data than could be obtained by collecting your own (Stewart and Kamins, 1993). Using secondary data within organisations may also have the advantage that, because they have already been collected, they provide an unobtrusive measure. Cowton (1998) refers to this advantage as *eavesdropping*, emphasising its benefits for sensitive situations.

Longitudinal studies may be feasible

For many research projects time constraints mean that secondary data provide the only possibility of undertaking longitudinal studies. This is possible either by creating your own or by using an existing multiple-source data set (Section 7.2). Comparative research may also be possible if comparable data are available. You may find this to be of particular use for research questions and objectives that require regional or international comparisons. However, you need to ensure that the data you are comparing were collected and recorded using methods that are comparable. Comparisons relying on unpublished data such as those from a census are likely to be expensive, as tabulations will have to be specially prepared. In addition, your research is dependent on access being granted by the owners of the data, principally governments (Dale *et al.*, 1988).

Can provide comparative and contextual data

Often it can be useful to compare data that you have collected with secondary data. This means that you can place your own findings within a more general context or, alternatively, triangulate your findings (Section 4.3). If you have undertaken a sample survey perhaps of potential customers, secondary data such as the census can be used to assess the generalisability of findings, in other words how representative these data are of the total population (Section 6.2).

Can result in unforeseen discoveries

Re-analysing secondary data can also lead to unforeseen or unexpected new discoveries. Dale *et al.* (1988) cite establishing the link between smoking and lung cancer as an example of such a serendipitous discovery. In this example, the link was established through secondary analysis of medical records that had not been collected with the intention of exploring any such relationship.

Permanence of data

Unlike data that you collect yourself secondary data generally provide a source of data which is both permanent and available in a form that may be checked relatively easily by others (Denscombe, 1998). This means that the data and your research findings are more open to public scrutiny.

Disadvantages

May be collected for a purpose which does not match your need

Data which you collect yourself will be collected with a specific purpose in mind: to answer your research question(s) and to meet your objectives. Unfortunately, secondary data will have been collected for a specific purpose which differs from your research question(s) or objectives (Denscombe, 1998). Consequently, the data you are considering may be inappropriate to your research question (Table 7.1). If this is the case then you need to find an alternative source or to collect the data yourself! More probably, you will only be able to answer your research question or address your objective partially. A common reason for this is that the data were collected a few years earlier and so are not current. Where this is the case, such as in a research project that is examining an issue within an organisation, you are likely to have to combine secondary and primary data.

Access may be difficult or costly

Where data have been collected for commercial reasons, gaining access may be difficult or costly. Market research reports, such as those produced by Mintel or Keynote, may cost hundreds of pounds. If the report(s) that you require are not available in your library they can rarely be borrowed on inter-library loan and you will need to identify (Section 7.3) and to visit the library that holds that collection.

Worked example

Changing definitions

A report in *Labour Market Trends* (Fenwick and Denman, 1995) details 31 changes which could have affected the comparability of the UK's monthly count of unemployment claimants between 1979 and 1994. Of these, Employment Department statisticians calculate that nine had a significant numerical impact on comparisons over time:

Date	Change	Effect on count (+ increase, – decrease)
October 1979	Weekly attendance for registration replaced by fortnightly attendance.	+20 000
November 1981	Older men who received long-term rate of supplementary benefit no longer required to sign as available for work.	–37 000
October 1982	Basis of count altered from registering unemployed to claiming benefits.	–190 000
April 1983*	Men aged 60+ no longer required to sign on to receive national insurance credits.	–108 000
June 1983*	Men aged 60+ who received long-term rate of supplementary benefit no longer required to sign on.	–54 000
July 1985	Corrective action due to discrepancies in figures for Northern Ireland.	–5 000
March 1986	Compilation and publication of figures delayed to correct for previous over-recording.	–50 000
September 1988	16- and 17-year-old people no longer entitled to unemployment benefit.	–40 000
July 1989	Men covered by Redundant Mineworkers Scheme no longer required to sign on.	–15 500
February 1994	Northern Ireland benefits system fully integrated with rest of UK.	–1 500

Source: Labour Market Trends, 1995. *Crown Copyright © 1995. Reproduced by permission of the Controller of HMSO and the Office of National Statistics*

*Fenwick and Denman (1995) argue that these should be treated as one change as both are the effect of the 1983 budget.

Aggregations and definitions may be unsuitable

The fact that secondary data were collected for a particular purpose may result in other, including ethical (Section 5.4), problems. Much of the secondary data you use are likely to be in published reports. As part of the compilation, process data will have been aggregated some way. These aggregations, while meeting the requirements of the original research, may not be quite so suitable for your research. The definitions of data variables may not be the most appropriate for your research question(s) or objectives. In addition, where you are intending to combine data sets, definitions may differ markedly or have been revised over time. Alternatively the documents you are using may represent the interpretations of those who produced them, rather than offer an objective picture of reality.

Initial purpose may affect how data are presented

When using data which are presented as part of a report you also need to be aware of the purpose of that report and the impact that this will have on the way the data are presented. This is especially so for internal organisational documents and external documents such as published company reports and newspaper reports. Reichman (1962; cited by Stewart and Kamins, 1993) emphasises this point referring to newspapers, although the sentiments apply to many documents. He argues that newspapers select what they consider to be the most significant points and emphasise these at the expense of supporting data. This, Reichman states, is not a criticism as the purpose of the reporting is to bring these points to the attention of readers rather than to provide a full and detailed account. For these reasons you must carefully evaluate any secondary data you intend to use. Possible ways of doing this are discussed in the next section.

7.5 Evaluating secondary data sources

Secondary data must be viewed with the same caution as any primary data that you collect. You need to be sure that:

- it will enable you to answer your research question(s) and to meet your objectives;
- the benefits associated with its use will be greater than the costs;
- you will be allowed access to the data (Section 5.3).

Secondary sources, which appear relevant at first, may not on closer examination be appropriate to your research question(s) or objectives. It is therefore important to evaluate the suitability of secondary data sources for your research.

Stewart and Kamins (1993) argue that, if you are using secondary data, you are at an advantage compared with researchers using primary data. Because the data already exist you can evaluate them prior to use. The time you spend evaluating any potential secondary data source is time well spent as rejecting unsuitable data earlier can save much wasted time later! Such investigations are even more important when you have a number of possible secondary data sources you could use. Most authors suggest a range of validity and reliability (Section 4.4) criteria against which you can evaluate potential secondary data. These, we believe, can be incorporated into a three-stage process (Fig 7.2).

Fig 7.2   **Evaluating potential secondary data sources**

Alongside this process, you also need to consider the accessibility of the secondary data. For some secondary data sources, in particular those available in your library, this will not be a problem. It may, however, necessitate long hours working in the library if the sources are 'for reference only'. For other data sources, such as those within organisations, you need to obtain permission prior to gaining access. This will be necessary even if you are working for the organisation. These issues are discussed in Section 5.3 so we can now consider the evaluation process in more detail.

Overall suitability

Measurement validity

One of the most important criteria for the suitability of any data set is *measurement validity*. Secondary data that fail to provide you with the information that you need to answer your research question(s) or to meet your objectives will result in invalid answers (Kervin, 1999). Often when you are using secondary survey data you will find that the measures used do not quite match those which you need (Jacob, 1994). For example, a manufacturing organisation may record monthly sales whereas you are interested in monthly orders. This may cause you a problem when you undertake your analyses believing that you have found a relationship with sales whereas in fact your relationship is with the number of orders. Alternatively, you may be using minutes of company meetings as a proxy for what actually happened in those meetings. These are likely to reflect a particular interpretation of what happened, the events being recorded from a particular viewpoint, often the chairperson's. You therefore need to be cautious before accepting such records at face value (Denscombe, 1998).

Unfortunately, there are no clear solutions to problems of measurement invalidity. All you can do is try to evaluate the extent of the data's validity and to make your own decision. A common way of doing this is to examine how other researchers have coped with this problem for a similar secondary data set in a similar context. If they found that the measures, while not exact, were suitable then you can be more certain that they will be suitable for your research question(s) and objectives. If they had problems then you may be able to incorporate their suggestions as to how to overcome them. Your literature search (Sections 3.4 and 3.5) will probably have identified other such studies already.

Coverage and unmeasured variables

The other important suitability criterion is *coverage*. You need to be sure that the secondary data cover the population about which you need data, for the time period you need, and contains data variables that will enable you to answer your research question(s) and to meet your objectives. For all secondary data sets coverage will be concerned with two issues:

- ensuring that unwanted data are or can be excluded;
- ensuring that sufficient data remain for analyses to be undertaken once unwanted data have been excluded (Hakim, 1982).

When analysing secondary survey data you will need to exclude those data that are not relevant to your research question(s) or objectives. Service companies for example need to be excluded if you are only concerned with manufacturing companies. However, in doing this it may be that insufficient data remain for you to undertake the quantitative analyses you require (Sections 11.4 and 11.5). For documentary sources you will need to ensure that the data contained relate to the population identified in your research. For example, check that the minutes are of board meetings and that they cover the required time period. Where you are intending to undertake a longitudinal study, you also need to ensure that the data are available for the entire period in which you are interested.

Some secondary data sets, in particular for survey data, may not include variables you have identified as necessary for your analysis. These are termed *unmeasured variables*. Their absence may not be particularly important if you are undertaking descriptive research. However, it could drastically affect the outcome of explanatory research as a potentially important variable has been excluded.

Precise suitability

Reliability and validity

The *reliability* and *validity* (Section 4.4) you ascribe to secondary data is a function of the method by which the data were collected and the source. You can make a quick assessment by looking at the source of the data. Survey data from large well-known organisations such as those found in Mintel and Keynote market research reports are likely to be reliable and trustworthy. The continued existence of such organisations is dependent on the credibility of their data. Consequently, their procedures for collecting and compiling the data are likely to be well thought through and accurate. Survey data from government organisations are also likely to be reliable for similar reasons. However, you will probably find the validity of documentary data such as organisations' records more difficult to assess. While organisations may argue that their records are reliable, there are often inconsistencies and inaccuracies. You therefore need to examine the method by which the data were collected and try to ascertain the precision needed by the original (primary) user.

For all secondary data, a detailed assessment of the validity and reliability will involve you in an assessment of the method or methods used to collect the data (Dale *et al.*, 1988). These are usually discussed in the methodology section of the report. Your assessment will involve looking at who were responsible for collecting or recording the information and examining the context in which the data were collected. From this, you should gain some feeling regarding the likelihood of potential errors or biases. In addition, you need to look at the process by which the data were selected and collected or recorded. Where sampling has been used to select cases (usually for surveys) the sampling procedure adopted and the associated sampling error and response rates (Section 6.2) will give clues to validity. Secondary data collected through a survey with a high response rate are also likely to be more reliable than from that with a low response rate. However, commercial providers of high-quality reliable data sets may be unwilling to disclose details about how data were collected. This is particularly the case where these organisations see the methodology as important to their competitive advantage.

For some documentary sources such as diaries, transcripts of interviews or meetings, it is unlikely that there will be a formal methodology describing how the data were collected. The reliability of these data will therefore be difficult to assess, although you may be able to discover the context in which the data were collected. For example, letters and memos contain no formal obligation for the writer to give a full and accurate portrayal of events. Rather they are written from a personal point of view and expect the recipient to be aware of the context (Denscombe, 1998). This means that these data are more likely to be useful as a source of the writer's perceptions and views than as an objective account of reality. The fact that you did not collect and were not present when these data were collected will also affect your analyses. Dale *et al.* (1988) argue that full analyses of in-depth interview data require an understanding derived from participating in social interactions that cannot be fully recorded on tape or by transcript.

Validity and reliability of collection methods for survey data will be easier to assess where you have a clear explanation of the methodology used to collect the data. This needs to include a clear explanation of any sampling techniques used and response rates (discussed earlier) as well as a copy of the survey instrument, which will usually be a questionnaire. By examining the questions by which data were collected, you will gain a further indication of the validity.

Where data have been compiled, such as in a report, you need to pay careful attention to how these data were analysed and how the results are reported. Where percentages (or proportions) are used without actually giving the totals on which these figures are based you need to examine the data very carefully. For example a 50 per cent increase in the number of clients from two to three for a small company may be of less relevance than the 20 per cent increase in the number of clients from 1000 to 1200 for a larger company in the same market! Similarly, where quotations appear to be used selectively without other supporting evidence you should beware as the data may be unreliable. Remember, the further away you are from the original data, the more difficult it will be to judge their quality (Patzer, 1996).

Worked example

Graphical distortion of data

Pamela examined the use of diagrams and tables in company reports as part of her dissertation. Based on a sample of 47 companies' reports she found that 68 per cent of companies used at least one form of graph and all companies used tables.

Of considerable interest was the finding that 47 per cent of diagrams used to present key financial information had distorted the data. This was done by either overstating or understating the size of the bar or graphic that represented each value in some way. One of the more frequently used techniques, not starting the value axis at zero, is illustrated below:

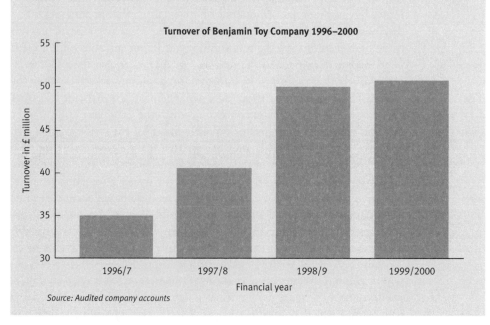

Source: Audited company accounts

Measurement bias

Measurement bias can occur for two reasons (Kervin, 1999):

■ deliberate or intentional distortion of data;

■ changes in the way data are collected.

Deliberate distortion occurs when data are recorded inaccurately on purpose and is most common for secondary data sources such as organisational records. Managers may deliberately fail to record minor accidents to improve safety reports for their departments. Data which have been collected to further a particular cause or the interests of a particular group are more likely to be suspect as the purpose of the study may be to reach a predetermined conclusion (Jacob, 1994). Reports of consumer satisfaction surveys may deliberately play down negative comments to make the service appear better to their target audience of senior managers and shareholders.

Other distortion may be deliberate but not intended for any advantage. Employees keeping time diaries may only record the approximate time spent on their main duties rather than accounting precisely for every minute. People responding to a structured interview (questionnaire) may adjust their responses to please the interviewer (Section 10.2).

Unfortunately, measurement bias resulting from deliberate distortion is difficult to detect. While we believe that you should adopt a neutral stance about the possibility of bias you still need to look for pressures on the original source which might have biased the data. For written documents such as minutes, reports and memos the intended target audience may suggest possible bias as indicated earlier in this section. Therefore, where possible you will need to triangulate the findings with other independent data sources. This is sometimes referred to as a *cross-check verification* (Patzer, 1996). Where data from two or more independent sources suggest similar conclusions, you can have more confidence that the data on which they are based are not distorted. Conversely, where data suggest different conclusions you need to be more wary of the results.

Changes in the way in which data were collected can also introduce changes in measurement bias. Provided that the method of collecting data remains constant in terms of the people collecting it and the procedures used the measurement biases should remain constant. Once the method is altered, perhaps through a new procedure of taking minutes or a new data collection form, then the bias also changes. This is very important for longitudinal data sets such as the UK's Retail Price Index where you are interested in trends rather than actual numbers. Your detection of biases is dependent on discovering that the way data are recorded has changed. Within-company sources are less likely to have documented these changes than government-sponsored sources.

Costs and benefits

Kervin (1999) argues that the final criterion for assessing secondary data is a comparison of the costs of acquiring them with the benefits they will bring. Costs include both time and financial resources that you will need to devote to obtaining the data. Some

Worked example: assessing the suitability of published data

As part of your research project, you wish to establish how the cost of living has altered over the last 15 years for medium-income households. Other research that you have read as part of your literature review has utilised the UK Office for National Statistics' Retail Price Index. Searching through the 1997 edition of *Economic Trends* (Lewin, 1997), you come across Table 2.1 – Prices. You decide to assess the suitability of this data, an extract of which follows:

Extract from Table 2.1 – Prices

Year	General index of retail prices[1]	
	All items	Total food
1980	70.7	76.1
1981	79.1	82.5
1982	85.9	89.0
1983	89.8	91.8
1984	94.3	97.0
1985	100.0	100.0
1986	103.4	103.3
1987	107.7	106.4
1988	113.0	110.1
1989	121.8	116.4
1990	133.3	125.7
1991	141.1	132.2
1992	146.4	135.0
1993	148.7	137.5
1994	152.4	138.9
1995	157.6	144.2
1996	161.4	148.9

[1]The index numbers given here are for comparative purposes only and should not be regarded as accurate to the last digit shown. The official Retail Price Index is shown in Table 2.2.

Source: Economic Trends *1997 Crown Copyright © 1997. Reproduced by permission of the Controller of HMSO and the Office for National Statistics*

Initial examination of the data's overall suitability reveals two problems:

■ the data refer to the General Index of Retail Prices rather than the Retail Price Index. This means that they may not be the precise data referred to in the literature. The note 1 confirms that the data do not meet your requirements and directs you to Table 2.2;

■ the data are not sufficiently up to date, 1996 being the most recent year.

For these reasons, you decide not to use the data in this table but consult the equivalent of Table 2.2 in a more recent edition.

Examination of the appendices in the more recent edition provides you with detail about how the Retail Price Index is calculated. The data source is credible having been compiled by the UK Government's Office for National Statistics. However, the appendix states that changes in prices are measured with the exception of certain income households. These are those within the top 4 per cent of incomes and those of retired persons mainly on state benefit. You conclude that the index is therefore suitable for medium-income households.

In addition, the methodology for calculating the index is clearly described and suggests that it will be precisely suitable. The one problem you have is that the appendix states that the data measure changes in prices and are not a cost of living index. However, because other researchers have shown that the Retail Price Index provides a reasonable surrogate for cost of living you decide to use the data from the more recent edition.

data will be available in your local library and so will be free, although you will have to pay for any photocopying you need. Other data will require lengthy negotiations before access is granted (Section 5.3). Even then, the granting of access may not be certain (Stewart and Kamins, 1993). Data from market research companies or special tabulations from government surveys will have to be ordered specially and will normally be charged for; consequently, these will be relatively costly.

Benefits from data can be assessed in terms of the extent to which they will enable you to answer your research question(s) and to meet your objectives. You will be able to form a judgement on the benefits from your assessment of the data set's overall and precise suitability (discussed earlier in this section). This assessment is summarised as a checklist of questions in Table 7.3. An important additional benefit is the form in which you receive the data. If the data are already in computer-readable form this will save you considerable time as you will not need to re-enter the data prior to analysis (Sections 11.2 and 12.8). However when assessing the costs and benefits you must remember that data which are not completely reliable and contain some bias are better than no data at all, if they enable you to start to answer your research question(s) and to achieve your objectives.

Table 7.3	Checklist to evaluate secondary data sources

Overall suitability

✓ Does the data set contain the information you require to answer your research question(s) and meet your objectives?

✓ Do the measures used match those you require?

✓ Is the data set a proxy for the data you really need?

✓ Does the data set cover the population that is the subject of your research?

✓ Can data about the population that is the subject of your research be separated from unwanted data?

✓ Are the data sufficiently up to date?

✓ Are data available for all the variables you require to answer your research question(s) and meet your objectives?

Precise suitability

✓ How reliable is the data set you are thinking of using?

✓ How credible is the data source?

✓ Is the methodology clearly described?

    ✓ If sampling was used what was the procedure and what were the associated sampling errors and response rates?

    ✓ Who were responsible for collecting or recording the data?

    ✓ (For surveys) is a copy of the questionnaire or interview checklist included?

    ✓ (For compiled data) are you clear how the data were analysed and compiled?

✓ Are the data likely to contain measurement bias?

    ✓ What was the original purpose for which the data were collected?

    ✓ Who was the target audience and what was their relationship to the data collector or compiler (were there any vested interests)?

    ✓ Have there been any documented changes in the way the data are measured or recorded including definition changes?

    ✓ How consistent are the data obtained from this source when compared with data from other sources?

✓ Are you happy that the data have been recorded accurately?

Costs and benefits

✓ What are the financial and time costs of obtaining these data?

✓ Have the data already been entered into a computer?

✓ Do the overall benefits of using these secondary data sources outweigh the associated costs?

Sources: Authors' experience; Dale et al., 1988;, Jacob, 1994; Kervin, 1999; Stewart and Kamins, 1993

7.6 Summary

- Data that have already been collected for some other purpose, perhaps processed and subsequently stored, are termed secondary data. There are three main types of secondary data: documentary, survey and those from multiple sources.

- Most research projects require some combination of secondary and primary data to answer your research question(s) and to meet your objectives. You can use secondary data in a variety of ways. These include:

  - to provide your main data set;

  - to provide longitudinal (time-series data);

  - to provide area-based data;

  - to compare with, or set in context, your own research findings.

- Any secondary data you use will have been collected for a specific purpose. This purpose may not match that of your research. In addition, the secondary data are likely to be less current than any data you collect yourself.

- Finding the secondary data you require is a matter of detective work. This will involve you in:

  - establishing whether the sort of data that you require are likely to be available;

  - locating the precise data.

- Once located you must assess secondary data sources to ensure their overall suitability for your research question(s) and objectives. In particular you need to pay attention to the measurement validity and coverage of the data.

- You must also evaluate the precise suitability of the secondary data. Your evaluation should include both reliability and any likely measurement bias. You can then make a judgement on the basis of the costs and benefits of using the data in comparison with alternative sources.

- When assessing costs and benefits you need to be mindful that secondary data which are not completely reliable and contain some bias are better than no data at all if they enable you partially to answer your research question(s) and to meet your objectives.

Self check Questions

7.1 Give three examples of different situations where you might use secondary data as part of your research.

7.2 You are undertaking a research project as part of your course. Your initial research question is 'How has the UK's import and export trade with other countries altered since its entry into the European Union?'

List the arguments that you would use to convince someone of the suitability of using secondary data to answer this research question.

7.3 Suggest possible secondary data that would help you answer the following research questions. How would you locate these secondary data?

   a To what extent do organisations' employee relocation policies meet the needs of employees?

   b How have consumer-spending patterns in the UK altered in the last 10 years?

   c How have governments' attitudes to the public sector altered since 1979?

7.4 As part of case study research based in a manufacturing company with over 500 customers you have been given access to an internal market research report. This was undertaken by the company's marketing department. The report presents the results of a recent customer survey as percentages. The section in the report which describes how the data were collected and analysed is reproduced below:

> Data were collected from a sample of current customers selected from our customer database. The data were collected using a telephone questionnaire administered by marketing department staff. 25 customers responded resulting in a 12.5 per cent response rate. These data were analysed using the SNAP computer software. Additional qualitative data based on in-depth interviews with customers were also included.

   a Do you consider these data are likely to be reliable?

   b Give reasons for your answer.

Assignment 7

Assessing the suitability of secondary data for your research

→ Consider your research question(s) and objectives. Decide whether you need to use secondary data or a combination of primary and secondary data to answer your research question. (If you decide that you need only to use secondary data and you are undertaking this research as part of a course of study check your course's examination regulations to ensure that this is permissible.)

→ If you decide that you need to use secondary data make sure that you are clear why and how you intend to use these data.

→ Locate the secondary data that you require and make sure that permission for them to be used for your research is likely to be granted. Evaluate the suitability of the data for answering your research question and make your judgement based on assessment of its suitability, other benefits and the associated costs.

→ Note down the reasons for your choices, including the possibilities and limitations of the data. You will need to justify your choices when you write your research methodology.

References

Barrow, M. (1998) *The Times 1000 1998*, London, Times Books.

Bryman, A. (1989) *Research Methods and Organisation Studies*, London, Unwin Hyman.

Cowton, C.J. (1998) 'The use of secondary data in business ethics research', *Journal of Business Ethics*, 17:4 423–34.

Dale, A., Arber, S. and Proctor, M. (1988) *Doing Secondary Analysis,* London, Unwin Hyman.

Davis, S.M. and Saunders, M.N.K. (1997) 'Freedom of movement for professionals: an assessment of the European Union policy and the barriers that remain', *Journal of Applied Management Studies,* 6:2, 199–218.

Data Archive (1999) 'Data Archive' [online] [cited 6 April] available from <URL: http://dawww.essex.ac.uk>.

Denscombe, M. (1998) *The Good Research Guide,* Buckingham, Open University Press.

Dunkerley, D. (1988) 'Historical methods and organizational analysis', *in* Bryman A (ed.), *Doing Research in Organisations* London, Routledge, pp. 82–95.

ESRC Data Archive (1995) *The ESRC Data Archive: Sharing and Preserving Research Data,* Colchester, ESRC Data Archive.

Fenwick, D. and Denman, J. (1995) 'The monthly claimant unemployment count: change and consistency', *Labour Market Trends,* November, 397–400.

Ghauri ,P., Grønhaugh, K. and Kristianslund, I. (1995) *Research Methods in Business Studies: a Practical Guide,* London, Prentice Hall.

Hakim, C. (1982) *Secondary Analysis in Social Research,* London, Allen & Unwin.

Jacob, H. (1994) 'Using published data: errors and remedies', *in* Lewis-Beck, M.S., *Research Practice,* London, Sage and Toppan Publishing, pp. 339–89.

Kervin, J.B. (1999) *Methods for Business Research* (2nd edn), New York, HarperCollins.

King, J. (ed.) (1996) *Family Spending – a Report on the 1995–96 Family Expenditure Survey,* London, Stationery Office.

Kingsbury, P. (1997) *IT answers to HR questions,* London, Institute of Personnel and Development.

Lewin, P. (1997) *Economic Trends Annual Supplement* (1997 edn), London, Stationery Office.

Marsh, C. (1993) 'An overview', *in* Dale, A. and Marsh, C. (eds), *The 1991 Census User's Guide,* London, HMSO, pp. 1–15.

McGuinness, K. and Short, T. (1998) *Research on the Net,* London, Old Bailey Press.

Office for National Statistics (1996) *30 Years of Regional Trends,* London, Stationery Office.

Patzer, G.L. (1996) *Using Secondary Data in Market Research: United States and World-wide,* Westport, CT, Quorum Books.

Partington, J. and Mayell, C. (1998) 'Revision of the annual employment survey results for 1995 and 1996', *Labour Market Trends,* 106:7, 387–97.

Pullinger, J. (ed.) (1998) *Regional Trends 33* (1998 edn), London, Stationery Office.

Reichman, C.S. (1962) *Use and Abuse of Statistics,* New York, Oxford University Press.

Robson, C. (1993) *Real World Research*, Oxford, Blackwell.

Stewart, D.W. and Kamins, M.A. (1993) *Secondary Research: Information Sources and Methods* (2nd edn), Newbury Park, CA, Sage.

Thomas, M., Walker, A., Wilmot, A. and Bennett, N. (1998) *Living in Britain: Results from the 1996 General Household Survey,* London, Stationery Office.

Wisniewski, D. (ed.) (1998) *Annual Abstract of Statistics 1998,* London, Stationery Office.

Further reading

Bryman, A. (1989) *Research Methods and Organisation Studies,* London, Unwin Hyman. Chapter 9 contains a good discussion with a series of examples of how archival research and secondary analysis of survey data have been used in management and business research.

Dunkerley, D. (1988) 'Historical methods and organizational analysis', *in* Bryman, A. (ed.), *Doing Research in Organisations*, London, Routledge, pp. 82–95. This chapter provides an open and honest account of the realities of doing historical research on an organisation using secondary data.

Levitas, R. and Guy, W. (eds) (1996) *Interpreting Official Statistics*, London, Routledge. This book provides a fascinating insight into UK published statistics. Of particular interest are Chapter 1, which outlines the changes in UK statistics since the 1980 Raynor review, Chapter 3, which looks at the measurement of unemployment, the discussion in Chapter 6 of the measurement of industrial injuries and their limitations and Chapter 7 which examines gender segregation in the labour force utilising data from the Labour Force Survey.

Stewart, D.W. and Kamins, M.A. (1993) *Secondary Research: Information Sources and Methods* (2nd edn), Newbury Park, CA, Sage. This provides a good discussion on the evaluation of secondary data (Chapter 2). It also provides a wealth of information on American government and non-government data sets and their acquisition.

Case 7	**The involvement of auditors in preliminary profit announcements**

Each year UK companies publish and issue an annual report and audited accounts, which are sent to numerous shareholders and other users. The process may take as long as three months from the end of the companies' accounting period. This delay could create problems: investors would be without up-to-date information and the probability of insider trading is therefore increased the longer the delay between the data being prepared and the accounts being published.

For these two reasons the London Stock Exchange requires listed companies to issue Preliminary Profit Announcements or 'Prelims'. Prelims are brief (usually only about four pages long) announcements, made by companies to the financial markets. They give estimates of the financial performance of the company during the year, and should, in principle at least, represent a summary of the information to be included in the subsequent full annual report and accounts.

Tony and Jim had a good knowledge of the literature. Previous research had shown that the release of Prelims had a significant impact on the share price of a company and that stock market analysts ranked Prelims as their most important source of information. Yet, despite this, Prelims were relatively lightly regulated by the stock market.

They hypothesised that the content of Prelims was more likely to differ from that in the annual accounts the greater the time period between the time that they were released and the publication of the annual accounts. A large sample survey of current company practice was therefore planned.

Companies have to issue their Prelims through the Stock Exchange Regulatory News Service (RNS) which controls the dissemination of price-sensitive information to the financial markets. Many large financial institutions have on-line real-time access to the RNS. Using a contact in one of these companies Tony and Jim were able to negotiate (for a nominal fee) access to an RNS terminal for a few days. This enabled them to collect the relevant data on their sample of Prelims. Luckily, the RNS system allows users to print out the various data, so they were also able to obtain paper copies that they were able to take away and analyse later. Data were collected on the release dates of 178 Prelims and copies of 166 of these were obtained. Unfortunately, it was only possible to obtain the corresponding subsequent annual report and audited accounts for 148 of these companies. Data were then compared between the 148 Prelims and their related full annual reports (which were issued subsequently) and differences in financial data noted, as well as the time lag between the Prelims being released and the accounts being published.

In collecting the data Tony and Jim were interested in the fact that some companies specifically mentioned that their Prelims had been issued after the audit of the full accounts had been completed and others did not. In practice, most companies made no mention of the audit. A substantial minority said that the audit had not been completed and 32 per cent said that it had been finished and that the auditors had signed their audit report.

Tony and Jim were aware of several reports that discussed the issues involved with Prelims that made recommendations for improving their regulation. These reports actually asserted that, when the majority of Prelims were released, the audit of the accounts was incomplete. These reports also suggested that some companies were disclosing that they were releasing their Prelims after the final audit had been completed. Tony and Jim knew that these assumptions could be tested. If it was found that these reports were based on incorrect assumptions, this could significantly undermine the validity of many of the recommendations they were making.

They decided to re-examine the data to see whether they could find more specific evidence about the extent to which Prelims were audited. Although the Prelims contained very little mention of the audit, the associated (and subsequent) full annual report and accounts included the date on which the audit had been signed off. This represented the end of the audit work. Since they already had the date of the release of the Prelims, they simply had to go back and compare this date with the date the audit report was signed.

They found that the majority (56 per cent) of Prelims had been issued after the audit report had been signed. This appeared to be fairly strong evidence that the assumption that the audit of the accounts was incomplete when the majority of Prelims were released was not correct.

Questions

1 a Identify data sources used by Tony and Jim in this research.

  b Which of these are secondary data and which are primary data?

  c Give reasons for your answers.

2 a What other methods (if any) do you think Tony and Jim could have used to obtain the data they needed to test their hypothesis?

  b Give reasons for your answer.

3 What were the problems faced by Tony and Jim in using these secondary data?

4 What lessons can you learn from Tony and Jim's experience?

Self check **Answers**

7.1 Although it would be impossible to list all possible situations, the key features that should appear in your examples are listed below:

- to compare findings from your primary data;
- to place findings from your primary data in a wider context;
- to triangulate findings from other data sources;
- to provide the main data set where you wish to undertake research over a long period, to undertake historical research or to undertake comparative research on a national or international scale with limited resources.

7.2 The arguments you have listed should focus on the following issues:

- The study suggested by the research question requires historical data so that changes, which have already happened, can be explored. These data will, by definition, have already been collected.
- The timescale of the research (if part of a course) will be relatively short term. One solution for longitudinal studies in a short time frame is to use secondary data.
- The research question suggests an international comparative study. Given your likely limited resources secondary data will provide the only feasible data sources.

7.3 a The secondary data required for this research question relate to organisations' employee relocation policies. The research question assumes that these sorts of data are likely to be available from organisations. Textbooks, research papers and informal discussions would enable you to confirm that these data were likely to be available. Informal discussions with individuals responsible for the personnel function in organisations would also confirm the existence and availability for research of such data.

b The secondary data required for this research question relates to consumer spending patterns in the UK. As these appear to be the sort of data in which the government would be interested they may well be available in published form. Examination of various published guides (both governmental and non-governmental sources) would reveal that these data were collected by the annual Family Expenditure Survey and summary results of which are published (for example King, 1996). These reports could then be borrowed either from your library or by using interlibrary loan. In addition, the ESRC Data Archive Catalogue could be searched. This would reveal that data from the survey had been deposited with the archive.

c The secondary data required for this research question are less clear. What you require is some source from which you can infer past and present government attitudes. Transcripts of ministers' speeches (such as in Hansard) and newspaper reports might prove useful. However, to establish suitable secondary sources for this research question you would need to pay careful attention to those used by other researchers. These would be outlined in research papers and textbooks. Informal discussions could also prove useful.

7.4 a The data are unlikely to be reliable.

   b Your judgement should be based on a combination of the following reasons:

- Initial examination of the report reveals that it is an internally conducted survey. As this has been undertaken by the marketing department of a large manufacturing company, you might assume that those undertaking the research had considerable expertise. Consequently, you might conclude the report contains credible data. However:

- The methodology is not clearly described, in particular:
  - the sampling procedure and associated sampling errors are not given;
  - it does not appear to contain a copy of the questionnaire. This means that it is impossible to check for bias in the way that questions were worded;
  - the methodology for the qualitative in-depth interviews is not described.

- In addition, the information provided in the methodology suggests that the data may be unreliable:
  - the reported response rate of 12.5 per cent is very low for a telephone survey (Chapter 6, Section 6.2);
  - responses from 25 people means that all tables and statistical analyses in the report are based on a maximum of 25 people. This may be too few for reliable results (Chapters 6 and 11, Sections 6.2 and 11.5).

8 Collecting primary data through observation

By the end of this chapter you should be able:

- to understand the role that observation may play as a data collection method in your research design;
- to identify two types of observation, participant observation and structured observation, and their differing origins and applications;
- to adopt particular approaches to data collection and analysis for both participant observation and structured observation;
- to identify threats to validity and reliability faced by the two types of observation.

8.1 Introduction to observation

If your research question(s) and objectives are concerned with what people do, an obvious way in which to discover this is to watch them do it. This is essentially what *observation* involves: the systematic observation, recording, description, analysis and interpretation of people's behaviour.

The two types of observation examined in this chapter are very different. *Participant observation* is qualitative and derives from the work of social anthropology earlier in this century. Its emphasis is on discovering the meanings which people attach to their actions. By contrast, *structured observation* is quantitative and is more concerned with the frequency of those actions.

A common theme in this book is our effort to discourage you from thinking of the various research methods as the sole means which you should employ in your study. This is also true of observation methods. It may meet the demands of your research question(s) and objectives to use both participant and structured observation in your study either as the main methods of data collection or to supplement other methods.

Participant observation: an introduction

What is participant observation?

If you have studied sociology or anthropology in the past you are certain to be familiar with *participant observation*. This is where 'the researcher attempts to participate fully in the lives and activities of subjects and thus becomes a member of their group, organisation or community. This enables the researcher to share their experiences by not merely observing what is happening but also feeling it' (Gill and Johnson, 1997:113). It has been used extensively in these disciplines to attempt to get to the root of 'what is going on' in a wide range of social settings.

Participant observation has its roots in social anthropology but it was the Chicago school of social research that encouraged its students to study by observation the constantly changing social phenomena of Chicago in the 1920s and 1930s.

Participant observation has been used much less in management and business research. However, this does not mean to say that it has limited value for management and business researchers. Indeed, it can be a very valuable tool, usually as the principal research method, but possibly in combination with other methods.

Delbridge and Kirkpatrick (1994:37) note that participant observation implies a research strategy of 'immersion [by the researcher] in the research setting, with the objective of sharing in peoples' lives while attempting to learn their symbolic world'. It is worth dwelling on this explanation. Whichever role you adopt as the participant observer (the choices open to you will be discussed later), there will be a high level of immersion. This is quite different to data collection by means of questionnaire where you probably will know little of the context in which the respondents' comments are set or the delicate nuances of meaning with which the respondents garnish their responses. In participant observation the purpose is to discover those delicate nuances of meaning. As Delbridge and Kirkpatrick (1994:39) state, 'in the social sciences we cannot hope to adequately explain the behaviour of social actors unless we at least try to understand their meanings'.

This last comment gives a clue to the point Delbridge and Kirkpatrick make about 'attempting to learn the [respondents'] symbolic world'. Some understanding of this point is vital if you are to convince yourself and others of the value of using participant observation.

The symbolic frame of reference is located with the school of sociology known as *symbolic interactionism*. In symbolic interactionism the individual derives a sense of identity from his/her interaction and communication with others. Through this process of interaction and communication he/she responds to others and adjusts his/her understandings and behaviour as he/she 'negotiates' a shared sense of order and reality with others. Central to this process is the notion that people continually change in the light of the social circumstances in which they find themselves. The transition from full-time student to career employee is one example of this. (How often have you heard people say 'she's so different since she's worked at that new place'?) The individual's sense of identity is constantly being constructed and reconstructed as he/she moves through differing social contexts and encounters different situations and different people.

This is a necessarily brief explanation of symbolic interactionism. However, we hope that you can see why Delbridge and Kirkpatrick (1994:37) think that participant observation is about 'attempting to learn the (respondents') symbolic world'. It is a quest for understanding the identity of the individual, but, more importantly, it is about trying to get to the bottom of the processes by which the individual constantly constructs and reconstructs his/her identity.

Worked example

Discovering the meanings respondents convey in their responses

The head office of a large company operating in a town with a world-famous horse-racing festival was plagued annually by some of the more junior staff going sick at the time of the festival. Over the years there had been attempts to cure the problem by 'making examples' of particular employees. However, nothing had succeeded. It seemed that the absentees always had a valid reason for their absence. Yet managers were convinced that many absentees attended the horse-racing festival.

Sarah was intrigued to discover why this phenomenon was occurring. Discovering the answer to this research question would heighten considerably Sarah's knowledge and understanding of employee absenteeism.

Answering the research question entailed Sarah working in the sections which were staffed mainly by junior employees. Sarah needed to 'become one of them' (as far as it was possible to do this). She needed to immerse herself in the social context of the junior employees' work.

A period of immersion as the participant observer enabled Sarah to unravel the complicated social processes by which junior staff 'negotiated' with one another to cover the work of absentees. Sarah also learned that staff consider taking time off work as a 'legitimate perk'. Often in their past schools, colleges and employers 'turned a blind eye' to this practice.

NB: It may have occurred to you that this example may be thought of as ethically rather dubious research. The ethical implications of participant observation are discussed in Section 8.3.

Situations in which participant observation has been used

One of the most famous examples of participant observation is that of Whyte (1955) who lived among a poor American–Italian community in order to understand 'street corner society'. A celebrated business example is the work of Roy (1952). Roy worked in a machine shop for ten months as an employee. He wanted to understand how and why his 'fellow workers' operated the piecework bonus system. Rather more colourfully, Rosen (1991) worked as a participant observer in a Philadelphia advertising agency. Rosen was working within the theoretical domain of dramaturgy. He wanted to understand how organisations used social drama to create and sustain power relationships and social structures.

These may strike you as rather elaborate examples which suggest little relevance to you as you contemplate your own research project. Yet this would be a disappointing conclusion. You may already be a member of an organisation which promises a fertile territory for research. This may be your employing organisation or a social body of which you are a member. One of Phil's students undertook research in his church community. He was a member of the church council and conducted observational research on the way in which decisions were reached in council meetings. A more specific focus was adopted by another of our students. She was a member of a school governing body. Her specific hypothesis was that the head teacher possessed the decision-making power. Her study confirmed this hypothesis. All the significant decisions were in effect taken prior to governors' meetings as a consequence of the head teacher canvassing the support of those committee members whom he defined as 'influential'.

So, adopting the participant observer role as an existing member of an organisation does present opportunities to you. However, it also has its dangers. We will deal with these later.

8.3 Participant observation: researcher roles

We have explained what participant observation is, but we have not explained clearly what participant observers do. A number of questions may have occurred to you. For example, should the participant observer keep his/her purpose concealed? Does the participant observer need to be an employee or an organisational member, albeit temporary? Can the participant observer just observe? The answers here are not straightforward. The role you play as participant observer will be determined by a number of factors. However, before examining those factors, we need to look at the different roles in which the participant observer may be cast.

Gill and Johnson (1997) develop a four-fold categorisation (Fig 8.1) of the role the participant observer can adopt. The roles are:

- complete participant;
- complete observer;
- observer as participant;
- participant as observer.

The first two of these roles, complete participant and the complete observer, involve you as the researcher in concealing your identity. This has the significant advantage of you not conditioning the behaviour of the research subjects you are studying. The second two, observer as participant and participant as observer, entail you revealing your purpose to those with whom you are mixing in the research setting. Ethically, the latter two roles are less problematic.

Complete participant

The *complete participant* role sees you as the researcher attempting to become a member of the group in which you are performing research. You do not reveal your true purpose to the group members. You may be able to justify this role on pure research grounds in the light of your research questions and objectives. For example, you may be interested to know the extent of lunchtime drinking in a particular work setting. You would probably be keen to discover which particular employees drink at lunchtimes, what they drink and how much they drink and how they explain their drinking. Were you to explain your research objectives to the group you wished to study it is rather unlikely that they would co-operate since employers would usually discourage lunchtime drinking. In addition, they may see your research activity as prying.

This example raises questions of ethics. You are in a position where you are 'spying' on people who have probably become your friends as well as colleagues. They may have learned to trust you with information, which they would not share were they to know your true purpose. On these grounds alone you may agree with us that this is a role that the researcher should not adopt.

There are also objections on pure research grounds. You may work so hard at gaining the trust of your 'colleagues' and value that trust when it is gained that you lose sight of your research purpose. The objective, detached perspective all researchers need will be lost.

Complete observer

Here too you would not reveal the purpose of your activity to those you were observing. However, unlike the complete participant role, you do not take part in the activities of the group. For example, the *complete observer* role may be used in studying consumer behaviour in supermarkets. Your research question may concern your wish to observe consumers at the checkout. Which checkouts do they choose? How much interaction is there with fellow shoppers and the cashier? How do they appear to be influenced by the attitude of the cashier? What level of impatience is displayed when delays are experienced? This behaviour may be observed by the researcher being located near the checkout in an unobtrusive way. The patterns of behaviour displayed may be the precursor to research by structured observation (Section 8.5). This would be the exploratory stage of this research.

Observer as participant

You may adopt the role of *observer as participant* in an outward-bound course to assist team building if you were attending to observe without taking part in the activities in the same way as the 'real' candidates. In other words, you would be a 'spectator'. However, your identity as a researcher would be clear to all concerned. They would know your purpose, as would the trainers running the course. This would present the advantage of you being able to focus on your researcher role. For example, you would be able to jot down insights as they occurred to you. You would be able to concentrate on your discussions with the participants. What you would lose, of course, would be the emotional involvement: really knowing what it feels like to be on the receiving end of the experience.

Participant as observer

In the role of *participant observer* you reveal your purpose as a researcher. Both you and the subjects are aware of the fact that it is a fieldwork relationship (Ackroyd and Hughes, 1992). You are particularly interested to gain the trust of the group. This was the role adopted by the sociologist Punch (1993) in his study of police work in Amsterdam. Because of the trust developed by Punch with police officers whom he was researching he was able to gain admission to activities which otherwise would have been 'out of bounds' to him. Because his identity as researcher was clear he could ask questions of his subjects to enhance his understanding. Robson (1993:197) argues that this leads to another advantage of this role. This is that key informants are likely to adopt a perspective of *analytic reflection* on the processes in which they are involved.

Fig 8.1 **Typology of participant observation researcher roles**

Worked example

Adopting the participant as observer role

Your research project is concerned with you wishing to understand what the experience of a one-day assessment centre is like for the graduates who attend these as prospective employees.

You decide that there is no better way of doing this than 'getting in on the action' and being a guinea-pig. You negotiate access with the company managers who are running the assessment centre. You also explain your research to the graduates who are there 'for real'. You become involved in all the activities and speak to as many of your fellow graduates as possible in order to discover their feelings about the experience. At the end of the day you are utterly exhausted!

Practitioner–researcher

This may be the participant observer role you are most likely to adopt. If you are a part-time student, or if you are undertaking research as part of your job, you will be surrounded by exciting opportunities to pursue business and management research. You are unlikely to encounter one of the most difficult hurdles which the participant observer has to overcome: that of negotiating research access. Indeed, like many people in such a position, you may be asked to research a particular problem by your employer which lends itself to this methodological approach.

Another advantage is your knowledge of the organisation and all this implies about understanding the complexity of what goes on in that organisation. It just is not necessary to spend a good deal of valuable time in 'learning the context' in the same way as the outsider does. However, that advantage carries with it a significant disadvantage. You must be very conscious of the assumptions and preconceptions that you carry around with you. This is an inevitable consequence of knowing the organisation well. It can prevent you from exploring issues which would enrich the research.

Familiarity has other problems. When we were doing case study work in a manufacturing company, we found it very useful to ask 'basic' questions revealing our ignorance about the industry and the organisation. These 'basic' questions are ones which as the practitioner–researcher you would be less likely to ask because you would feel that you should know the answers already.

There is also the problem of status. As a junior employee you may feel that working with more senior colleagues inhibits your interactions as researcher–practitioner. The same may be true if you are more senior than your colleagues.

A more practical problem is that of time. Combining two roles at work is obviously very demanding, particularly as the participant–observer role may involve you in much data recording 'after hours'. This activity is hidden from those who determine your workload. They may not appreciate the demands which your researcher role is making on you. For this reason, Robson (1993) makes much of practitioner–researchers negotiating a proportion of their 'work time' to devote to their research.

There are no easy answers to these problems. All you can do is to be aware of the threats to the quality of your data by being too close to your research setting. However, it is a problem which besets much participant–observer research. As will now be obvious to you, all methods have their strengths and weaknesses.

Factors which will determine the choice of participant observer role

The purpose of your research

You should always be guided by the appropriateness of the method for the research question(s) and objectives. A research question about developing an understanding of a phenomenon about which the research subjects would be naturally defensive is one that lends itself to the complete participant role. Discovering what it is like to be a participant on a particular training course is more appropriate to the participant as observer role.

The time you have to devote to your research

Some of the roles covered above may be very time consuming. If you are really to develop a rich and deep understanding of an organisational phenomenon it will need much careful study. A period of attachment to the organisation will often be necessary. However, many full-time courses have placement opportunities which may be used for this purpose. In addition, most full-time students now have part-time jobs which provide wonderful opportunities to understand the 'meanings' which their fellow employees, for whom the work is their main occupation, attach to a variety of organisational processes. What is needed is a creative perspective on what constitutes research and research opportunities. The possibilities are endless.

The degree to which you feel suited to participant observation

Delbridge and Kirkpatrick (1994) note that not everybody is suited to this type of research. Much of it relies on the building of relationships with others. A certain amount of personal flexibility is also needed. As the participant–observer you have to be 'all things to all people'. Your own personality must be suppressed to a greater extent. This is not something with which you may feel comfortable.

Organisational access

This may present a problem for some researchers. It is obviously a key issue. More is said about gaining access to organisations for research in Section 5.3.

Ethical considerations

The degree to which you reveal your identity as the researcher will be dictated by ethical considerations. The topic of ethics in research is dealt with in detail in Section 5.4.

8.4 Participant observation: data collection and analysis

Delbridge and Kirkpatrick (1994) categorise the types of data generated by participant observation as 'primary', 'secondary' and 'experiential'.

Primary observations are those where you would note what happened or what was said at the time. Keeping a diary is a good way of doing this.

Secondary observations are statements by observers of what happened or was said. This necessarily involves those observers' interpretations.

Experiential data are those data on your perceptions and feelings as you experience the process you are researching. Keeping a diary of these perceptions proves a valuable source of data when the time comes to write up your research. This may also include notes on how you feel that your values have intervened, or changed, over the research process.

Finally, you will also collect data on factors material to the research setting, for example roles played by key participants and how these may have changed, organisational structures and communication patterns.

Data collection

What will be clear from the types of data you will collect as the participant observer is that formal set-piece interviewing is unlikely to take place. Such 'interviewing' that does take place is likely to be informal discussion. It will be part of the overall approach of asking questions which should be adopted in this research method. These questions are of two types (Robson, 1993): first, to informants to clarify the situations you have observed and, second, to yourself to clarify the situation and the accounts given of the situation.

Worked example

A diary account

For a period of ten months between 1944 and 1945 Donald Roy worked on the factory floor as a production operative in order to study how workers restricted production. He kept a diary, an extract of which is reproduced below as an example of a narrative account. The 'technical' content of the piece is irrelevant. What is important is to get a feel for narrative account.

On April 7 I was able to enjoy four hours of 'free time'.

I turned out 43 pieces in the four hours from 3 to 7, averaging nearly 11 an hour or $2.085 per hour). At 7 o'clock there were only 23 pieces left in the lot, and I knew there would be no point in building up a kitty for Monday if Joe punched off the job before I got to work. I could not go ahead with the next order . . . because the new ruling made presentation of a work order to the stock-chaser necessary before material could be brought up. So I was stymied and could do nothing for the rest of the day. I had 43 pieces plus 11 from yesterday's kitty to turn in for a total of 54.

Source: Roy, 1952:432

Of course, the data that you collect depend on your research question(s) and objectives which have given a particular focus to your observation. Robson (1993) suggests that your data may well be classed as *descriptive observation* and *narrative account*. In descriptive observation you may concentrate on observing the physical setting, the key participants and their activities, particular events and their sequence and the attendant processes and emotions involved. This description may be the basis for your writing of a narrative account, in much the same way as an investigative journalist would write one. However, Robson (1993) makes the point forcefully that the researcher must go much further than the journalist. Your job as the researcher is to go on and develop a framework of theory which will help you to understand, and to explain to others, what is going on in the research setting you are studying.

How you record your data will depend to a great extent on the role you play as the participant observer. The more 'open' you are the more possible it will be for you to make notes at the time the event is being observed or reported. In any event, there is one golden rule: recording must take place on the same day as the fieldwork in order that you do not forget valuable data. The importance placed in this by one complete participant observer, working in a bakery, is evident from the following quotation:

> Right from the start I found it impossible to keep everything I wanted in my head until the end of the day . . . and had to take rough notes as I was going along. But I was 'stuck on the line', and had nowhere to retire to privately to note things down. Eventually, the wheeze of using innocently provided lavatory cubicles occurred to me. Looking back, all my notes for that third summer were on Bronco toilet paper! Apart from the awkward tendency for pencilled notes to be self-erasing from hard toilet paper...my frequent requests for 'time out' after interesting happenings or conversations in the bakehouse and the amount of time that I was spending in the lavatory began to get noticed . . .
>
> Ditton (1977), cited in Bryman (1989:145)

Data analysis

We deal with this in more depth in Chapters 11 and 12. However, you should bear in mind that in participant observation research your data collection and analysis activity may be part of the same process. That is, you will be carrying out analysis and collection of data simultaneously. Let us say you were acting as the complete participant observer in attempting to establish 'what is going on' in terms of sex discrimination at the workplace in which you were researching. You would observe informal banter, hear conversations of a discriminatory nature, talk to those who 'approved' and 'disapproved' of the activity. All this would be part of your everyday work. You may mix socially with colleagues in situations where discriminatory attitudes and behaviour may be evident. All these events would yield data which you would record, as far as possible, on the spot, or at least write up soon afterwards. You would turn these rough notes into something rather more systematic along the lines of the procedures suggested in Section 12.4. What would be emerging is what the investigative journalist may call 'promising lines of enquiry' which you may wish to follow up in your continued observation. However, remember that the journalist is interested in the story, while you are interested in generating a theory to help you understand 'what is going on'. This will lead you to adopt the researcher's equivalent of 'promising lines of enquiry'. A common approach to this is what is called *analytic induction*.

Threats to reliability and validity

Participant observation is very high on *ecological validity* because it involves studying social phenomena in their natural contexts. Nonetheless, participant observation is subject to the same threats to validity as noted in Section 4.4 (e.g. history and maturation) although the fact that your study is likely to be over an extended time period will overcome most of these.

> **Worked example**
>
> ### Using analytic induction
>
> As a result of data already collected you form an initial hypothesis that pilfering at the workplace at which you were researching was restricted to a group of employees who mixed socially outside work and they defined this as an extension of their social activities. You search for further evidence to support this hypothesis.
>
> You find that the pilfering group included colleagues who do not mix socially although these 'new' pilferers do define this as an extension of their own individual social activities.
>
> You redefine your hypothesis to state that pilferers at your workplace define their workplace pilfering as an extension of their social activities, i.e. they make no distinction in this respect between work and non-work situations.
>
> Further data collection supports this refined hypothesis.
>
> NB: This worked example is a simplified version of analytic induction. It only involves *one* re-definition of the hypothesis whereas several may be involved. Moreover, an alternative to the re-defining of the hypothesis is re-defining the phenomenon to be explained so that the particular instance which casts doubt on the hypothesis is excluded (Denzin, 1989).

The greatest threat to the reliability of your research conclusions produced as a result of a participant observation study is that of *observer bias*. As Delbridge and Kirkpatrick (1994:43) note, 'because we are part of the social world we are studying we cannot detach ourselves from it, or for that matter avoid relying on our common sense knowledge and life experiences when we try to interpret it'.

The propensity that we all have for our own perceptions to colour our interpretation of what we believe to be 'true' is well known. What we advocate here is that we cannot avoid observer bias. All we can do is to be aware of the threat to reliability it poses and to seek to control it.

The first way this may be done is to revert to the process of asking yourself questions about your conclusions: did she really mean that? What other interpretations could I have put on this? The second way is that adopted by our student who was researching decision-making power in a school governing body. Her approach was to use *informant verification*. After each of her informal discussions with fellow PTA members she wrote these up, including her own conclusions as to the meanings of the discussions in the light of her research hypothesis. She then presented the written accounts to her informants for them to verify the content. Not only is this a form of *triangulation*, but it can be a source of new interpretations which have not occurred to the researcher. This method of triangulation is also one that can be used with more formal interview results.

Advantages and disadvantages of participant observation

Before leaving the subject of participant observation, we summarise some of the advantages and disadvantages of this method.

Advantages of participant observation

- It is good at explaining 'what is going on' in particular social situations.
- It heightens the researcher's awareness of significant social processes.
- It is particularly useful for researchers working within their own organisations.
- Some participant observation affords the opportunity for the researcher to experience 'for real' the emotions of those who are being researched.
- Virtually all data collected are useful.

Disadvantages of participant observation

- It can be very time consuming.
- It can pose difficult ethical dilemmas for the researcher.
- There can be high levels of role conflict for the researcher (e.g. 'colleague' versus researcher).
- The closeness of the researcher to the situation being observed can lead to significant observer bias.
- The participant observer role is a very demanding one to which not all researchers will be suited.
- Access to organisations may be difficult.
- Data recording is often very difficult for the researcher.

8.5 Structured observation: an introduction

So far this chapter might have given you the impression that research using observational techniques is unsystematic and unstructured. This need not be the case. A sound research design based on clear research questions and objectives using participant observation should be highly systematic. However, it would be true to say that the degree of predetermined structure in participant observation may not be that high. After all, one of the strengths of this method is its responsiveness.

In contrast, structured observation is systematic and has a high level of predetermined structure. If you use this method in your data collection strategy you will be adopting a more detached stance. Your concern would be in quantifying behaviour. As such, structured observation may form only a part of your data collection approach because its function is to tell you how often things happen rather than why they happen. Once again we see that all research methods have their place in an overall research strategy. What is important is choosing the method which meets the research questions and objectives.

Using self-completion diaries

As part of a review of staffing levels in residential homes for elderly people Mark needed to establish:

- how much time care assistants actually spent on various caring activities;
- how the pattern of caring activities varied throughout a 24-hour day;
- how much time care assistants felt that they needed to undertake their caring activities adequately.

Ideally this would have involved structured observation of each care assistant throughout their working day. Unfortunately there were insufficient resources and so, in consultation with care assistants and their managers, a self-completion diary form was devised. In the extract below 'act.' refers to actual time spent on each activity; 'adeq.' refers to the amount of time that care assistants felt they needed to undertake their caring activities adequately.

Care Assistant's name:

Residential home:

Date: Time started work: a.m. / p.m.

hour ▶	1		2		3		4	
minutes taken ▶	act.	adeq.	act.	adeq.	act.	adeq.	act.	adeq.
activity ▼								
washing / bathing								
dressing / undressing								
eating / drinking								
continence / toiletting								
personal hygiene								
mobility / lifting								
medication								
counselling								
social interaction								

After pilot testing of the diary form, care assistants received training on its completion. This focused on the importance of being honest, precise definitions of activities and how to fill in the form. A definition of each activity was also provided. Data were subsequently collected from ten residential homes over a two-week period.

Situations in which structured observation may be used

The most powerful image which occurs to many people when they think of structured observation is that of the 'time-and-motion' study expert. This inscrutable figure stalked the factory floor, complete with clipboard and pencil, making notes on what tasks machine operators were performing and how long these tasks took. This may seem to you a long way from the definition of 'research' that we have assumed in this book. Is it not simply fact-finding? Yes it is, but establishing straightforward facts may play an important role in answering your research questions and meeting your objectives. This is straightforward descriptive research, as we noted in Section 4.2.

One of the best-known examples of managerial research which used structured observation as part of its data collection approach was the study of the work of senior managers by Mintzberg (1973). This led to Mintzberg casting doubt on the long-held theory that managerial work was a rational process of planning, controlling and directing. Mintzberg studied what five chief executives actually did during one of each of the executives' working weeks. He did this by direct observation and the recording of events on three predetermined coding schedules. This followed a period of 'unstructured' observation in which the categories of activity which formed the basis of the coding schedules he used were developed. So Mintzberg 'grounded' (see Section 12.6 for an explanation of grounded theory) his structured observation on data collected in the period of participant observation.

Of course, studying what job-holders of the type not normally 'observed' actually do in their everyday lives lends itself to approaches other than observation. Self-completion of diaries is one approach that is often used. However, involvement of the researcher in the process is one that lends a degree of impartiality and thoroughness. This has benefits for reliability and validity that may not be evident when the job-holder is the 'observer'.

Advantages and disadvantages of structured observation

As with other research methods, structured observation has its advantages and disadvantages.

Advantages of structured observation

■ It can be used by anyone after suitable training in the use of the measuring instrument. Therefore, you could delegate this extremely time-consuming task. In addition, structured observation may be carried out simultaneously in different locations. This would present the opportunity of comparison between locations.

■ It should yield highly *reliable* results by virtue of its replicability. We will deal with threats to reliability in Section 8.6 but suffice it to say here that the easier the observation instrument to use and understand, the more reliable the results will be.

■ Structured observation is capable of more than simply observing the frequency of events. It is also possible to record the relationship between events. For example, is the visit to the retail chemist's counter to present a prescription preceded by an examination of merchandise unrelated to the prescription transaction?

- The method allows the collection of data at the time they occur in their natural setting. Therefore there is no need to depend on 'second-hand' accounts of phenomena from respondents who put their own interpretation on events.

- Structured observation secures information which most participants would ignore because to them it was too mundane or irrelevant.

Disadvantages of structured observation

- The observer must be in the research setting when the phenomena under study are taking place.

- Research results are limited to overt action or surface indicators from which the observer must make inferences.

- Data are slow and expensive to collect.

8.6   Structured observation: data collection and analysis

Using coding schedules to collect data

One of the key decisions you will need to make before undertaking structured observation is whether you use an 'off-the-shelf' coding schedule or design your own. You will hardly be surprised to hear us say that this should depend on your research questions and objectives. What follows are two sets of guidelines for assessing the suitability of existing tailor-made coding schedules.

Choosing an 'off-the-shelf' coding schedule

There are a number of questions you should ask yourself when choosing an 'off-the-shelf' coding schedule. These are detailed in Table 8.1.

Table 8.1   **Checklist of questions to ask when choosing an 'off-the-shelf' coding schedule**

✓   For what purpose was the coding schedule developed? Is it consistent with your research question(s) and objectives? (It should be.)

✓   Is there overlap between the behaviours to be observed? (There should not be.)

✓   Are all behaviours in which you are interested covered by the schedule? (They should be.)

✓   Are the behaviours sufficiently clearly specified so that all observers will place behaviours in the same category? (They should be.) Is any observer interpretation necessary? (It should not be.)

✓   Are codes to be used indicated on the recording form to avoid the necessity for memorisation by the observer? (They should be.)

✓   Will the behaviours to be observed be relevant to the inferences you make? (They should be.)

✓   Have all sources of observer bias been eliminated? (They should have been.)

Source: Developed from Walker, 1985

One of the most frequent uses of established coding schedules in management and business is for recording inter-personal interactions in social situations such as meetings or negotiations. This lends itself to structured observation particularly well. Fig 8.2 is an example of just such an 'off-the-shelf' coding schedule which may be used for this purpose.

We would encourage you to use an 'off-the-shelf' coding schedule if you can find one that is suitable. Not only will it save you a lot of time, but it will be tried and tested. Therefore, it should make your results and conclusions more reliable and valid.

However, you may decide that no 'off-the-shelf' coding schedule is suitable for your purposes. In this case you will need to develop your own schedule. Table 8.2 contains useful guidelines for this activity. The observation categories in your schedule should be devised to be consistent with your research question(s) and objectives. To ensure ease of use and reliability the categories should reflect the attributes shown in Table 8.2.

Table 8.2   **Guidelines for developing your own coding schedule**

Attribute	Comment
Focused	Do not observe and record all that is going on. Only concern yourself with what is strictly relevant
Unambiguous	Therefore requiring the absolute minimum of observer interpretation
Non-context dependent	The observer's job is more difficult if the coding of behaviours is dependent on the context in which the behaviour occurs. It may be essential for your research question(s) and objectives to record contextual data, but this should be kept to a minimum
Explicitly defined	Provide examples for the observer (even if this is you) of behaviours which fall into each category and those that do not
Exhaustive	Ensure that it is always possible to make a coding for those behaviours you wish to observe
Mutually exclusive	Ensure that there is no overlap between behaviour categories
Easy to record	The observer must be able to tick the correct box quickly without having to memorise appropriate categories

Source: Developed from Robson, 1993

An alternative to the use of an 'off-the-shelf' coding schedule or the development of your own may be a combination of the two. If this is the option that seems most appropriate in the light of your research question(s) and objectives, we recommend that you still use the checklist in Table 8.1 and the guidelines in Table 8.2 to ensure that your schedule is as valid and reliable as possible.

	Nature of group:						
	Nature of activity:						
	Date Name of observer:						
	Initial arrangement of group:						

Initial arrangement of group:

         C   D
     B   E
  A   F

	Name of group members (or reference letters)					
	A	B	C	D	E	F
Taking initiative – e.g. attempted leadership, seeking suggestions, offering directions.						
Brainstorming – e.g. offering ideas or suggestions however valid						
Offering positive ideas – e.g. making helpful suggestions, attempting to problem-solve						
Drawing in others – e.g. encouraging contributions, seeking ideas and opinions						
Being responsive to others – e.g. giving encouragement and support, building on ideas						
Harmonising – e.g. acting as peacemaker, calming things down, compromising						
Challenging – e.g. seeking justification, showing disagreement in a *constructive* way						
Being obstructive – e.g. criticising, putting others down, blocking contributions						
Clarifying/summarising – e.g. linking ideas, checking progress, clarifying objectives/proposals						
Performing group roles – e.g. spokesperson, recorder, time-keeper, humorist						
Other comments						

Fig 8.2   **Recording sheet for observing behaviour in groups**

Source: Mullins, L.J. (1999) Management and Organisational Behaviour, 5th edn, Financial Times Pitman Publishing, p. 498.
© L.J. Mullins 1999. Reprinted with permission.

Data analysis

The complexity of your analysis will depend on your research question(s) and objectives. It may be that you are using Fig 8.2 to establish the amount of interactions by category in order to relate the result to the output of the meeting. This may enable you to conclude that 'positive' behaviours (e.g. brainstorming) may be more strongly associated with meetings which make clear decisions than 'negative' behaviours (e.g. being obstructive). Simple manual analysis may be sufficient for this purpose.

Alternatively, you may be using Fig 8.2 to see what patterns emerge. It may be that the amount of interactions varies by the nature of the group or its activity, or that seating position is associated with the amount of contributions. Patterns reflecting relationships between amounts of interaction categories may become evident (for example when 'drawing in others' was high 'clarifying/summarising' was also high). This level of analysis is obviously more complex and will need computer software to calculate the cross-classifications. Chapter 11, Section 11.2 contains guidance on preparing data for quantitative analysis by computer.

Threats to validity and reliability

The main threats here are ones of reliability. This section deals with three of these: subject error, time error and observer effects.

Subject error

Subject error may cause your data to be unreliable. You may be concerned with observing the output of sales administrators as measured by the amount of orders they process in a day. Subject error may be evident if you chose administrators in a section which was short staffed owing to illness. This may mean that they were having to spend more time answering telephones, and less time processing orders, as there were fewer people available to handle telephone calls. The message here is clear: choose subjects who in as many respects as possible are 'normal' examples of the population under study.

Time error

Closely related to the issue of subject error is that of *time error*. It is essential that the time at which you conduct the observation does not provide data which are untypical of the total time period in which you are interested. So the output of the insurance administrators may be less in the immediate hour before lunch as their energy levels are lower. If you were interested in the amount of customers using a retail shop you would need to conduct observations at different times of the day and week to provide a valid picture of total customer flow.

Observer effect

One of the most powerful threats to the validity and reliability of data collected through observation is that of *observer effect*. This is quite simply that the process of the observer's observation of behaviour changes the nature of that behaviour owing to the fact that the subject is conscious of being observed. The simplest way to overcome this effect is for the observation to take place in secret. However, this is often not possible, even if it were ethically sound to do so.

Robson (1993) notes two strategies for overcoming observer effect. The first, *minimal interaction*, means that the observer tries as much as possible to 'melt into the background' – having as little interaction as possible with the subjects of the observation. This may involve sitting in an unobtrusive position in the room and avoiding eye contact with those being observed. The second strategy is *habituation* where the subjects being observed become familiar with the process of observation so that they take it for granted. Those of you who use a tape-recorder to record discussions may notice that initially the respondent is very wary of the machine, but after a short period this apprehension wears off and the machine is not noticed.

Adopting a strategy of habituation to reduce observer effect may mean that several observation sessions are necessary in the same research setting with the same subjects. As the observer effect diminishes, so the pattern of interaction will settle down into a predictable pattern.

8.7   Summary

- Participant observation is a method in which the researcher participates in the lives and activities of those whom they are studying. It is used to attempt to get to the root of 'what is going on' in a wide range of social settings.

- You may use the participant observation method in a student placement or you may already be a member of an organisation which will enable you to adopt the role of the practitioner–researcher.

- Participant observation means that you adopt a number of potential roles differentiated by the degree to which your identity is concealed from the subjects of the research and the degree to which you participate in the events you are studying.

- Participant observation must avoid the trap of mere story telling. The purpose is to develop theory.

- A prevalent form of data analysis used in participant observation is analytic induction. This may lead to an initial hypothesis being re-developed more than once.

- Structured observation is concerned with the frequency of events. It is characterised by a high level of predetermined structure and quantitative analysis.

- A choice may be made between 'off-the-shelf' coding schedules and a schedule which you design for your own purpose. Alternatively you may decide to use a 'hybrid'.

- The main threats to reliability and validity inherent in structured observation are subject error, time error and observer effects.

Self check ## Questions

8.1 You have been asked to give a presentation to a group of managers at the accountancy firm in which you are hoping to negotiate access for research. You wish to pursue the research question, 'What are the informal rules which govern the way in which trainee accountants work and how do they learn these rules?'

You realise that talk of 'attempting to learn the trainee accountants' symbolic world' would do little to help your cause with this group of non-research-minded business people. However, you wish to point out some of the benefits to the organisation which your research may yield. Outline what you believe these would be.

8.2 You are a building society branch manager. You feel your staff are too reluctant to generate sales 'leads' from ordinary investors and borrowers which may be passed on to the society's consultants in order that they can attempt to sell life insurance policies, pensions and unit trusts. You would like to understand the reasons for their reluctance. As the participant observer, how would you go about this?

8.3 You are conducting your research project on the extent to which staff become involved in the decision-making processes conducted by a newly privatised regional electricity supplier. Staff 'involvement' is a new thing in the company and senior managers want to get some idea of 'how it is working'.

A main part of the involvement strategy is to have regular team meetings where staff can have their 'say'. You have been given access to these meetings. You decide that you will observe the meetings to get some feel for how they are working.

How would you record your observations?

8.4 Look again at Fig 8.2 and Table 8.1. Ask the questions contained in Table 8.1 of the coding schedule in Fig 8.1. How well does it match?

Assignment 8

Deciding on the appropriateness of observation

→ Return to your research question(s) and objectives. Decide on how appropriate it would be to use observation as part of your research strategy.

→ If you decide that this is appropriate, explain the relationship between your research question(s) and objectives and observation. If you decide that using observation is not appropriate, justify your decision.

→ Look again at the previous paragraph and ensure that you have responded for both participant observation and structured observation *separately*.

→ If you decide that participant observation is appropriate, what practical problems do you foresee? Are you likely to be faced with any moral dilemmas? How may you overcome both sets of problems?

→ If you decide that participant observation is appropriate, what threats to validity and reliability are you likely to encounter? How may you overcome these?

→ If you decide that structured observation is appropriate, what practical problems do you foresee? How may you overcome these?

→ If you decide that structured observation is appropriate, what threats to validity and reliability are you likely to encounter? How may you overcome these?

→ If you decide that structured observation is appropriate, design your own research instrument.

References

Ackroyd, S. and Hughes, J. (1992) *Data Collection in Context* (2nd edn), London, Longman.

Bryman, A. (1989) *Research Methods and Organisation Studies*, London, Unwin Hyman.

Delbridge, R. and Kirkpatrick, I. (1994) 'Theory and practice of participant observation', *in* Wass, V. and Wells, P. (eds), *Principles and Practice in Business and Management Research*, Aldershot, Dartmouth, pp. 35–62.

Denzin, N. (1989) *The Research Act a Theoretical Introduction to Sociological Methods* (3rd edn), Englewood Cliffs, NJ, Prentice-Hall.

Ditton, J. (1977) *Part-Time Crime: an Ethnography of Fiddling and Pilferage*, London, Macmillan.

Gill, J. and Johnson, P. (1997) *Research Methods for Managers* (2nd edn), London, Paul Chapman.

Mintzberg, H. (1973) *The Nature of Managerial Work*, New York, Harper and Row.

Mullins, L. (1999) *Management and Organisational Behaviour* (5th edn), London, Financial Times Pitman Publishing.

Punch, M. (1993) 'Observation and the police the research experience', *in* Hammersley, M., *Social Research Philosophy Politics and Practice*, London, Sage, pp. 181–99.

Robson, C. (1993) *Real World Research*, Oxford, Blackwell.

Rosen, M. (1991) 'Breakfast at Spiro's dramaturgy and dominance', *in* Frost, P., Moore, L., Louis, M., Lundberg, C. and Martin, J. (eds), *Reframing Organisational Culture*, Newbury Park, CA, Sage, pp. 77–89.

Roy, D. (1952) 'Quota restriction and goldbricking in a machine shop', *American Journal of Sociology*, 57:427–42.

Walker, R.(1985) *Doing Research: a Handbook for Teachers*, London, Methuen.

Whyte, W. (1955) *Street Corner Society* (2nd edn), Chicago, IL, University of Chicago Press.

Further reading

Ackroyd, S. and Hughes, J. (1992) *Data Collection in Context* (2nd edn), London, Longman. Chapter 6 contains a helpful analysis of the origins of and problems with participant observation. It also has a full analysis of symbolic interactionism.

Hammersley, M. and Atkinson, P. (1995) *Ethnography Principles in Practice* (2nd edn), London, Routledge. Chapters 4 and 8 on field relations and data analysis in participant observation are well worth reading.

Mintzberg, H. (1973) *The Nature of Managerial Work*, New York, Harper and Row. Appendix C has a full account of the methodology Mintzberg employed. You will be struck how such a seemingly simple methodology can lead to such important conclusions.

Punch, M. (1993) 'Observation and the police the research experience', *in* Hammersley, M. (ed.), *Social Research Philosophy Politics and Practice*, London, Sage, pp. 181–99. An absorbing account of fieldwork experience with the Amsterdam police which makes riveting reading, particularly good at the process of negotiating relationships with fellow participants.

Robson, C. (1993) *Real World Research*, Oxford, Blackwell. Chapter 8 is a most thorough and practical guide to observational methods. There is an interesting section at the end of the chapter on inter-observer reliability which you should look at if you intend to use a number of observers.

Taylor, S. and Bogdan, R. (1984*) Introduction to Qualitative Research Methods: a Guidebook and Resource*, New York, Wiley. Chapters 2 and 3 are very practical accounts of how to approach and conduct participant observation.

Case 8   Manufacturing strategy change in a textile company

Huw was a part-time student who combined his studies with his work as a free-lance consultant and writer. After graduating from business school a number of contracts arose that enabled him to become self-employed. He had developed a passionate interest in manufacturing at university and was keen to research the then developing field of manufacturing strategy, in particular the aspects of change associated with this. This he believed would also strengthen his position as a consultant.

Within six months Huw had the chance to join a team of consultants hired to develop a manufacturing strategy. The company involved manufactured textiles for export in the North of England and employed approximately 400 people. It had a traditional management style and was heavily unionised. When a new managing director was appointed he quickly became concerned about the production func-tion's ability to respond to the changing requirements of the marketplace. Different consultants were invited to tender for a contract to help the company to develop and implement a new manufacturing strategy. A chief factor in the appointment of the successful consulting team was the emphasis placed on facilitating the existing management team to develop their own manufacturing strategy. The consultant team was involved for 24 months, initially for three days a week, reducing gradu-ally to one day a week after 12 months. The team comprised a senior academic consultant with extensive industrial experience, a freelance consultant with interests in organisational change and Huw.

The consulting contract represented an ideal opportunity for Huw to engage in participant-observation research, although this was not part of his original plan. The other consultants in the team also had research interests and they were all com-fortable with each other pursuing individual research interests. This was cleared with the managing director on the condition that the company was disguised in research outputs. The team spent several weeks gaining a thorough understanding of the organisation, meeting with managers at all levels, listening to them and prob-ing key issues. Consequently managers were trained and helped to develop and implement their own strategy. Simultaneously the team became involved in meetings over several months helping to resolve short-term issues facing the company. This gained the team significant credibility and helped with access to data; they were readily provided with a wide range of reports, memos and strategic documents.

Huw recorded observations in his notebook throughout the meetings. On the right-hand page he would record observations regarding his participant role and on the left his reflections as an observer. The observer reflections were noted during meetings afterwards in the hotel and at home. This was an onerous task. The consulting team spent much time preparing for meetings and reviewing how they went; because all the team had research interests, this was a great stimulus for reflection.

Analytic induction was ongoing and iterative but took the following underlying logic:

- a list of 'activities' in which the team were involved in their consulting role was developed, e.g. understanding the organisation, education, various change activities and team preparation and review time. The duration of these activities was also mapped out using diary records of when meetings took place;
- the role the consultants played in each activity was described from notes, memos, reports and a handful of interviews with the other team members where gaps were evident;
- 'observations' were noted for each activity. This was often an intuitive approach noting points based on gut feel and interest;
- a set of 'reflections' then emerged which drew out unifying themes across the set of observations;
- 'conceptualisation' then took place where links were made between the different reflections, and between the reflections and literature.

As a result of the research Huw gained a much deeper understanding of the change process that took place. This helped him to forge a link between models of manufacturing strategy in the literature and models of change theory.

Questions

1 Describe the type of participant-observation role adopted.
2 What were the advantages/disadvantages of Huw's approach?
3 What are the merits of Huw's approach to recording data?
4 What were the strengths of Huw's approach to analytic induction?

Self check   **Answers**

8.1 The research question is very broad. It allows you plenty of scope to discover a host of interesting things about the world of the trainee accountant. Without doubt, one of the things you will emerge with a clear understanding about is what they like about their work and what they do not like. This has practical implications for the sort of people that the firm ought to recruit, how they should be trained and rewarded. You may learn about some of the short cuts practised by all occupations which may not be in the interest of the client. By the same token you will probably discover aspects of good practice which managers can disseminate to other accountants. The list of practical implications is endless.

All this assumes, of course, that you will supply the managers with some post-research feedback. This does raise issues of confidentiality which you must have thought through beforehand.

8.2 This is a difficult one. The question of status may be a factor. However, this would depend on your relationship with the staff. If you are, say, of similar age and have an open, friendly, 'one of the team' relationship with them, then it may not be too difficult. The element of threat which would attend a less open relationship would not be present.

You could set aside a time each day to work on the counter in order really to get to know what life is like for them. Even if you have done their job, you may have forgotten what it is like! It may have changed since your day. Direct conversations about lead generation would probably not feature in your research times. However, you would need to have a period of reflection after each 'research session' to think about the implications for your research question of what you have just experienced.

8.3 You may start your meetings attendance with an unstructured approach where you simply get the 'feel' of what is happening. Analysis of the data you have collected will allow you to develop an observational instrument that can be used in further meetings you attend. This instrument would be based on a coding schedule which allowed you to record, among other things, the amount of contributions by each person at the meeting and the content of that contribution.

You would need to make sure that all those attending the meetings understand fully the purpose of your research. You would also be well advised to ensure that your findings are communicated to them.

8.4 Clearly there are some question marks about the coding schedule in Fig 8.1. There does appear to be some overlap in the behavioural categories covered in the schedule. For example, it could be difficult to distinguish between what is 'offering directions' (taking initiative) and 'offering ideas' (brainstorming). It may be even more difficult to draw a distinction between 'offering suggestions' (brainstorming) and 'making helpful suggestions' (offering positive ideas). Similarly, there does not appear to be much difference between the behaviours in 'drawing in others' and 'being responsive to others'. You may argue that the first is defined by *invitation*, the second by *response*. But making the distinction when the interactions are coming thick and fast in the research setting will be much less easy.

The point about all these potential confusions is that different observers may make different estimations. This obviously has potentially harmful implications for the reliability of the coding schedule.

A much smaller point is how does the observer indicate on the schedule the occurrence of a particular interaction?

Collecting primary data using semi-structured and in-depth interviews

By the end of this chapter you should be:

- able to classify research interviews in order to help you to understand the purpose of each type;

- aware of research situations favouring the use of semi-structured and in-depth interviews, and their limitations;

- able to analyse potential data quality issues and evaluate how to overcome these;

- able to consider the development of your competence to undertake semi-structured and in-depth interviews, and the logistical and resource issues that affect their use;

- aware of particular issues and advantages associated with the use of group interviews and those conducted by telephone.

9.1 Introduction

An interview is a purposeful discussion between two or more people (Kahn and Cannell, 1957). The use of interviews can help you to gather valid and reliable data that are relevant to your research question(s) and objectives. Where you have not yet formulated such a research question and objectives, an interview(s) may help you to achieve this. In reality, the research interview is a general term for several types of interview. This fact is significant since the nature of any interview should be consistent with your research question(s) and objectives, the purpose of your research and the research strategy that you have adopted. We define types of interview in the next section of this chapter (Section 9.2) and show how these are related to particular research purposes. In order to provide a typology of research interviews we briefly outline all types in the next section, although the chapter will be concerned with those that we refer to as semi-structured and in-depth interviews.

Section 9.3 considers situations favouring the use of semi-structured and in-depth interviews. The following three sections examine issues associated with the use of these types of interview. Section 9.4 identifies data quality issues associated with their use and discusses how to overcome them. Section 9.5 considers the areas of competence that you will need to develop. Section 9.6 discusses logistical and resource issues and how to manage these. Throughout the discussion of issues related to the use of semi-structured and in-depth interviews the focus is centred on what you will need to consider in order to be able to conduct these interviews. To draw this consideration together, a checklist is presented in Section 9.7 which offers you advice about how to conduct these types of research interview. Finally, Section 9.8 considers the particular advantages and issues associated with the use of group interviews and those conducted by telephone.

9.2 Types of interview and their link to the purposes of research and research strategy

Types of interview

Interviews may be highly formalised and structured, using standardised questions for each respondent (Section 10.2), or they may be informal and unstructured conversations. In between there are intermediate positions. One typology that is commonly used is thus related to the level of formality and structure, whereby interviews may be categorised as one of:

- structured interviews (Section 10.2);
- semi-structured interviews;
- unstructured interviews.

Another typology (Healey, 1991; Healey and Rawlinson, 1993; Healey and Rawlinson, 1994) differentiates between:

- standardised interviews;
- non-standardised interviews.

Robson (1993), based on the work of Powney and Watts (1987), refers to a different typology:

- respondent interviews;
- informant interviews.

There is overlap between these different typologies, although consideration of each typology adds to our overall understanding of the nature of research interviews.

Structured interviews use questionnaires based on a predetermined and *standardised* or identical set of questions (Section 10.2). You read out each question and then record the response on a standardised schedule, usually with pre-coded answers (Sections 10.4 and 11.2). While there is social interaction between you and the respondent, such as explanations which you will need to provide, you should read out the questions in the same tone of voice so that you do not indicate any bias.

By comparison, semi-structured and unstructured interviews are *non-standardised*. In *semi-structured interviews,* the researcher will have a list of themes and questions to be covered although these may vary from interview to interview. This means that you may omit some questions in particular interviews, given the specific organisational context which is encountered in relation to the research topic. The order of questions may also be varied depending on the flow of the conversation. On the other hand, additional questions may be required to explore your research question and objectives given the nature of events within particular organisations. The nature of the questions and the ensuing discussion mean that data will be recorded by note taking, or perhaps by tape recording the conversation (Section 9.5).

Unstructured interviews are informal. You would use these to explore in depth a general area in which you are interested. We therefore refer to these as *in-depth interviews* in this chapter and elsewhere in the book. There is no predetermined list of questions to work through in this situation, although you need to have a clear idea about the aspects you want to explore. The interviewee is given the opportunity to talk freely about events, behaviour and beliefs in relation to the topic area, so that this type of interaction is sometimes called *non-directive*. It has been labelled as an *informant interview* since it is the interviewee's perceptions that guide the conduct of the interview. In comparison, a *respondent interview* is one where the interviewer directs the interview and the interviewee responds to the questions of the researcher (Easterby-Smith *et al.*, 1991; Ghauri *et al.*, 1995; Healey and Rawlinson, 1994; Robson, 1993).

We may also differentiate between types of interview related to the form of interaction that is established between the researcher and those who participate in this process. Interviews may be conducted on a one-to-one basis, between you and a single participant. Such interviews are most commonly conducted by meeting your participant 'face to face', but there may be some situations where you conduct an interview by telephone. There may be other situations where you conduct a semi-structured or in-depth interview on a group basis, where you meet with a small number of participants to explore an aspect of your research through a group discussion that you facilitate. These forms of interview are summarised in Fig 9.1. The discussion throughout most of this chapter applies to each of these forms. However, the final section (Section 9.8) includes specific consideration of the issues and advantages related to the use of a telephone interview as a substitute for a 'face-to-face' meeting and to the use of group interviews.

Fig 9.1   **Forms of qualitative interview**

Links to the purpose of research and research strategy

Each type of interview outlined above has a different purpose. Structured or standardised interviews can be used in survey research to gather data, which will then be the subject of quantitative analysis (Sections 11.3–11.5). Semi-structured and in-depth, or non-standardised, interviews are used in qualitative research in order to conduct exploratory discussions not only to reveal and understand the 'what' and the 'how' but also to place more emphasis on exploring the 'why'.

In Chapter 4, we outlined various ways in which your research can be classified. One classification is related to exploratory, descriptive and explanatory studies (Section 4.2). By examining the categories within this classification, we can see how the various types of interview may be used to gather information for, and assist the progress of, each kind of study:

■ in an exploratory study in-depth interviews can be very helpful to 'find out what is happening [and] to seek new insights' (Robson, 1993:42). Semi-structured interviews may also be used in relation to an exploratory study;

■ in descriptive studies structured interviews can be used as a means to identify general patterns;

■ in an explanatory study, semi-structured interviews may be used in order to understand the relationships between variables, such as those revealed from a descriptive study (Section 4.2). Structured interviews may also be used in relation to an explanatory study, in a statistical sense (Section 11.5).

This is summarised in Table 9.1.

Table 9.1   **Uses of different types of interview in each of the main research categories**

	Exploratory	Descriptive	Explanatory
Structured		✓✓	✓
Semi-structured	✓		✓✓
In depth	✓✓		

✓✓ = more frequent, ✓ = less frequent

Your research may incorporate more than one type of interview. In a quantitative approach to research, for example, you may decide to use in-depth or non-standardised interviews initially to identify variables. The data that you gather from such exploratory interviews will be used in the design of your questionnaire or structured interview (Section 4.2). Semi-structured interviews may be used to explore and explain themes that have emerged from the use of your questionnaire (Wass and Wells, 1994). In addition to this staged approach, Healey and Rawlinson (1994:130) state that a combination of styles may be used within one interview: 'one section of an interview may ask a common set of factual questions . . . while in another section a semi-structured qualitative approach may be used to explore [responses]'. Wass and Wells (1994) make the point that interviews, presumably semi-structured or in-depth ones, may also be used as a means to validate findings from the use of questionnaires. We can therefore see that the various types of interview have a number of potentially valuable uses in terms of undertaking your research project. The key point for you to consider is the need for consistency between the research question and objectives, the strategy to be employed and the methods of data collection used – their fitness for purpose.

Worked example

Using interviews in a research project

During a research project to survey employee attitudes in a public sector organisation, the use of interviews was considered for each stage of this undertaking. The first stage of data collection consisted of a series of in-depth interviews, which were undertaken with a representative cross-section of employees, to reveal variables to be tested empirically at the second stage of the research project. A number of decisions were made about these in-depth interviews during the initial planning phase:

■ to obtain personnel data relating to job categories and grades, gender, age and length of service in order to select a representative sample;

■ to combine similar employee categories and to use group interviews in order to overcome time constraints and assist the researcher's capacity to handle the data to be collected. As a result six group interviews were arranged, consisting of about ten participants in each group, in order to cover all employee categories;

■ not to mix managerial and non-managerial participants within a group because this could have meant that non-managerial employees would be reluctant to take part.

At the next stage of the research project a decision had to be taken about whether to use a questionnaire or structured and standardised interviews. Because the number of employees in the organisational sample to be surveyed exceeded 30, it was decided that it would be more efficient to use a questionnaire rather than interviews (Wass and Wells, 1994).

After the analysis of the questionnaire data a further stage used a series of semi-structured interviews in order to explore and explain the findings obtained through the survey. These were also conducted as group interviews. Care was again needed in relation to the representativeness, size and composition of each group as well as the setting for the discussion to occur.

9.3 Situations favouring interviews

There are many situations in which the use of interviews as a method of data collection may be advantageous, taking into account the points made in the previous section. These situations may be grouped into four categories:

- the nature of the approach to research;
- the significance of establishing personal contact;
- the nature of the data collection questions;
- length of time required and completeness of the process.

These are examined in turn.

The nature of the approach to research

We have discussed the way in which research can be classified according to its purpose. Where you are undertaking an exploratory study, or a study that includes an exploratory element, it is likely that you will include interviews in your approach (Cooper and Schindler, 1998). Similarly, an explanatory study is also likely to include interviews in order for the researcher to be able to infer causal relationships between variables (Sections 4.2 and 10.4). Essentially, where it is necessary for you to understand the reasons for the decisions which your research participants have taken, or to understand the reasons for their attitudes and opinions, it will be necessary for you to conduct an in-depth interview.

Semi-structured and in-depth interviews also provide you with the opportunity to 'probe' answers, where you want your interviewees to explain, or build on, their responses. This is important if you are adopting a phenomenological approach, where you will be concerned to understand the meanings which respondents ascribe to various phenomena (Section 4.1). Interviewees may use words or ideas in a particular way and the opportunity to probe these meanings will add significance and depth to the data obtained. It may also lead the discussion into areas which you had not previously considered but which are significant for your understanding, and which help you to address your research question and objectives, or indeed to help you formulate such a question. It also affords the interviewee an opportunity to hear herself/himself 'thinking aloud' about things she or he may not have previously thought about. The result should be that you are able to collect a rich set of data.

The significance of establishing personal contact

We have found that managers are more likely to agree to be interviewed, rather than complete a questionnaire, especially where the interview topic is seen to be interesting and relevant to their own current work. An interview provides them with an opportunity to reflect on events without needing to write anything down. Other researchers report similar conclusions, where participants prefer to be interviewed rather than fill in a questionnaire (North et al., 1983, cited in Healey, 1991). This situation also provides the opportunity for interviewees to receive feedback and personal assurance about the way in which information will be used.

Potential research participants who receive a questionnaire through the post may be reluctant to complete it for a number of reasons. They may feel that it is not appropriate to provide sensitive and confidential information to someone they have never met. They may also not completely trust the way in which the information provided is to be used. They may be reluctant to spend time providing written explanatory answers, where these are requested, especially if the meaning of any question is not entirely clear. The use of personal interviews, where appropriate, may therefore achieve a higher response rate than using questionnaires. Healey (1991:206) also makes the point that 'the interviewer . . . has more control over who answers the questions' in comparison with a questionnaire which may be passed from one person to another.

The nature of the questions

An interview will undoubtedly be the most advantageous approach to attempt to obtain data in the following circumstances (Easterby-Smith *et al.*, 1991; Healey, 1991; Jankowicz, 1995):

- where there are a large number of questions to be answered;
- where the questions are either complex or open-ended;
- where the order and logic of questioning may need to be varied.

A semi-structured or in-depth interview will be most appropriate for the latter two types of situation.

Worked example

The need to vary the order and logic of questioning

Adrian undertook a series of interviews, along with another colleague, into the management of redundancy in 40 organisations. It soon became evident that it would not be meaningful to ask exactly the same questions in each organisation. For example, some organisations only made employees redundant through a compulsory approach, whereas some other organisations relied on obtaining volunteers for redundancy. Another significant variable was associated with whether the organisation recognised trade unions in respect of any category of employees or whether it was non-unionised.

The impact of these and other variables meant that it was meaningless to ask exactly the same questions at each interview, even though many questions remained applicable in all cases and the underlying intention was to ensure consistency between interviews. It was not until each interview had started that they were able to learn which of these different variables operated within the particular organisation. This illustrates that a semi-structured or in-depth interview can allow for the flexibility that may well be required.

Length of time required and completeness of the process

Apart from the difficulty of trying to design a viable questionnaire schedule to cope with questions which are complex, or open-ended, or large in number, the time needed to obtain the required data may mean that an interview is in any case the best or only alternative. In our experience, where expectations have been clearly established about the length of time required, and participants understand and agree with the objectives of the research interview, they have generally been willing to agree to be interviewed. Some negotiation is, in any case, possible and the interview can be arranged at a time when the interviewee will be under least pressure. We have found that our respondents tend to be generous with their time, and sometimes when interviews have been arranged to start at mid-morning they often arrange for lunch which can allow the discussion and exploration of issues to continue. However, for those of you who fancy a free lunch, we do not want to raise your expectations falsely and the start time for an interview should not be set with this in mind!

Your aim will be to obtain answers to all of the questions which you ask, allowing for the right of participants to decline to respond to any question, and where you skilfully conduct the event an interview is more likely to achieve this than the use of a self-administered or telephone questionnaire. Where your respondent does not provide an answer to a particular question or questions in an interview, you should be able to form some indication of why a response could not be provided. This may even lead you to modify the question or to compose another where this would be appropriate. Section 5.4 provides a consideration of the ethical issues associated with seeking to obtain answers.

While there are a number of situations favouring the use of interviews, there are also a number of issues associated with them. The next three sections will describe issues associated with semi-structured and in-depth interviews, and discuss how you can manage them, under the following headings:

- data quality issues;
- the researcher's interviewing competence;
- logistical and resource issues.

9.4   Data quality issues and how to overcome them

Data quality issues

A number of data quality issues can be identified in relation to the use of semi-structured and in-depth interviews, related to:

- reliability,
- forms of bias,
- validity and generalisability.

These are discussed in turn.

The lack of standardisation in these interviews may lead to concerns about *relia-bility* (Robson, 1993). In relation to these interviews, reliability is concerned with whether alternative interviewers would reveal similar information (Easterby-Smith *et al.*, 1991; Healey and Rawlinson, 1994). The concern about reliability in these types of interviews is also related to issues of bias. There are various types of bias to consider. The first of these is related to *interviewer bias*. This is where the comments, tone or non-verbal behaviour of the interviewer creates bias in the way that interviewees respond to the questions being asked. This may be where you attempt to impose your own beliefs and frame of reference through the questions that you ask. It is also possible that you will demonstrate bias in the way you interpret responses (Easterby-Smith *et al.*, 1991). Where you are unable to develop the trust of the interviewee, or perhaps where your credibility is seen to be lacking, the value of the information given may also be limited, raising doubts about its validity and reliability.

Related to this is *interviewee* or *response bias*. This type of bias may be caused by perceptions about the interviewer, as referred to above, or in relation to perceived interviewer bias. However, the cause of this type of bias is not necessarily linked to any perception related to the interviewer. Taking part in an interview is an intrusive process. This is especially true in the case of in-depth or semi-structured interviews where your aim will be explore events or to seek explanations. The interviewee may, in principle, be willing to participate but may nevertheless be sensitive to the in-depth exploration of certain themes. Interviewees may therefore choose not to reveal and discuss an aspect of the topic which you wish to explore because this would lead to probing questions which would intrude on sensitive information which they do not wish, or are not empowered, to discuss with you. The outcome of this may be that the interviewee provides a partial 'picture' of the situation which casts himself or herself in a 'socially desirable' role, or the organisation which they work for in a positive or even negative fashion.

Bias may also result from the nature of the individuals or organisational participants who agree to be interviewed. The time-consuming requirements of the interview process may result in a reduction in willingness to take part on behalf of some of those to whom you would like to talk. This may bias your sample from whom data are collected (Robson, 1993). This is an issue that you will need to consider carefully and to attempt to overcome through the approach taken to sampling (Sections 6.2 and 6.3).

There is also likely to be an issue about the generalisability of the findings from qualitatively based interview studies, although the validity of such studies is not raised as an issue. If we consider *validity* first, this refers to the extent to which 'the researcher [has] gained full access to the knowledge and meanings of informants' (Easterby-Smith *et al.*, 1991:41). The high level of validity that is possible in relation to carefully conducted qualitative interviews is made clear by the following quotation:

> the main reason for the potential superiority of qualitative approaches for obtaining information is that the flexible and responsive interaction which is possible between interviewer and respondent(s) allows meanings to be probed, topics to be covered from a variety of angles and questions made clear to respondents.
>
> (Sykes, 1991:8, cited in Healey and Rawlinson, 1994:132)

However, qualitative research using semi-structured or in-depth interviews will not be able to be used to make *generalisations* about the entire population (whatever this may relate to in the context of the research topic) where this is based on a small and unrepresentative number of cases. This will be the situation in a case study approach (Yin, 1994).

Overcoming data quality issues

Reliability

One response to the issue of reliability is that the findings from using non-standardised research methods are not necessarily intended to be repeatable since they reflect reality at the time they were collected, in a situation which may be subject to change (Marshall and Rossman, 1999). The assumption behind this type of research is that the circumstances to be explored are complex and dynamic. The value of using this non-standardised approach is derived from the flexibility that you may use to explore the complexity of the topic. Therefore, an attempt to ensure that qualitative, non-standardised research could be replicated by other researchers would not be realistic or feasible without undermining the strength of this type of research. Marshall and Rossman (1999) suggest that researchers using a qualitative, non-standardised approach need to make this clear – perhaps to transform an aspect perceived to be a weakness by some into a strength based on realistic assumptions about the ability to replicate research findings.

However, they suggest that where you use this approach you should make and retain notes relating to the design of the research, the reasons underpinning the choice of strategy and methods, and the data obtained. Justification of the choice of your research strategy and methods should initially be discussed in your research proposal. These records can be referred to by other researchers in order to understand the processes that you used and to enable them to re-use the data that you collected. The use of a qualitative approach should not lead to a lack of rigour in relation to the research process – if anything greater rigour is required to overcome the views of those who may be wedded to the value of quantitative research to the exclusion of any other approach.

Interviewer and interviewee bias

Overcoming these forms of bias is integral to the way in which the interview is conducted. In order to attempt to avoid the sources of bias discussed earlier, you need to consider the points in Table 9.2.

The relationship between these aspects in Table 9.2 and the management of interviewer and interviewee bias will be explored in the discussion that follows. The aim in relation to each of these aspects will be to demonstrate your credibility and to obtain the confidence of the interviewee.

Preparation and readiness for the interview

You need to be knowledgeable about the organisational or situational context. A prior search in your university library (Sections 3.4 and 3.5) may reveal journal

Table 9.2	Key measures to overcome bias in qualitative interviews

You will need to consider the following points in order to attempt to avoid sources of bias in qualitative interviews:

- your own preparation and readiness for the interview;
- the level of information supplied to the interviewee;
- the appropriateness of your appearance at the interview;
- the nature of the opening comments to be made when the interview commences;
- your approach to questioning;
- the impact of your behaviour during the course of the interview;
- your ability to demonstrate attentive listening skills;
- your scope to test understanding;
- your approach to recording information.

articles written by senior employees of the organisation that is participating in your research. There may also be other material about the organisation and this is particularly likely to be found in the 'trade' press and the quality newspapers. It may also be appropriate to look at company reports and other publications, or financial data relating to the organisation. The ability to draw on this type of knowledge in the interview should help to demonstrate your credibility and thereby encourage the interviewee to offer a more detailed account of the topic under discussion. A further benefit of this is made clear by Healey and Rawlinson (1994:136): 'A well informed interviewer has a basis for assessing the accuracy of some of the information offered.'

Your level of knowledge about your research question and objectives should also help you to establish credibility in the view of your research participant. This knowledge may be gleaned through the review of the literature associated with the research. As you undertake a number of interviews, you will also be able to draw on the initial analysis which you make of data previously collected.

Level of information supplied to the interviewee

Credibility may also be promoted through the supply of relevant information to participants before the interview. Providing participants with a list of the interview themes before the event, where this is appropriate, should help this aim and also to promote validity and reliability through enabling the interviewee to consider the information being requested and allowing them the opportunity to assemble supporting organisational documentation from their files. We can testify to this approach and the value in allowing participants to prepare themselves for the discussion in which they are to engage. Access to organisational documentation also allows for triangulation of the data provided (Sections 7.2 and 7.3). Our experience is that participants are generally willing to supply a photocopy of such material, although of course it is sometimes necessary to conceal confidential or personal details.

Worked example

Interview themes

You have been asked to undertake semi-structured interviews with a number of employees to ascertain their views about the nature and efficiency of internal communication within an organisation. This subject is felt to be significant in relation to both customer service and employee commitment perspectives. You have been requested to provide a list of themes that you wish to explore with interviewees. After some deliberation and reading you come up with the following list of themes which you wish to explore during the course of these interviews:

- what interviewees understand by the term internal communication;

- nature and sources of internal communications received;

- perceptions about the channels used for internal communication and their impact on its intended purpose;

- value of internal communication in providing information about performance (of the organisation and more locally) and strategic direction;

- use and impact of internal communication on the work of the interviewee's department;

- effect of internal communication on the work of the interviewee;

- scope for upward communication;

- impact of upward communication on organisational procedures and practices;

- perceptions about improving the processes, content and efficiency of internal communication in relation to the twin foci of the research.

These can be used as your guide through the substantive part of the interview.

Interview themes may be derived from the literature that you read, the theories that you consider, your experience of a particular topic, common sense, discussion with co-workers, fellow students, tutors and research participants, or some combination of these approaches. You will need to have some notion of the themes which you wish to discuss with your participants even if you intend to commence with exploratory, in-depth interviews and adopt a grounded theory approach to your research project (Section 12.6). Without some focus, your work will clearly lack a sense of direction and purpose. It will be necessary for you to formulate a focus if your work is to make progress. You should therefore commence with a set of themes that reflect the variables being studied, which you can explore to see whether you can identify and test relationships between them.

Appropriateness of the researcher's appearance at the interview
Your appearance may affect the perception of the interviewee. Where this has an adverse affect on your credibility in the view of the interviewee, or results in a failure

to gain their confidence, the resulting bias may affect the reliability of the information provided. Robson (1993) advises researchers to adopt a similar style of dress to those to be interviewed. Essentially, you will need to wear clothing that will be generally acceptable for the setting within which the interview is to occur.

Checking out the dress code

Phil and Adrian arranged to visit the administration centre of a large financial services organisation on a Friday to conduct a group interview with staff drawn from one of its operating divisions and two one-to-one interviews with senior managers. They felt that it was appropriate to wear fairly 'formal' clothes to match what they thought would be the dress code of the organisation. Indeed, for four days of the working week this assumption would have been appropriate. However, the organisation had recently introduced the practice of not wearing such formal work clothes on Fridays. Thus, they found themselves the only ones to be formally dressed in the organisation on the day of their visit. Taking lunch proved to be a memorable experience, as they intermingled with everyone else dressed in jeans and tee shirts etc. Their 'mistake' proved to be an amusing opening at the start of each interview rather than a barrier to gaining access to participants' data. Indeed it may not have been appropriate for visitors such as Phil and Adrian to match too closely the 'dress-down' style of participants. Nevertheless, it did provide a useful example about the way in which expectations about appearance are likely to be noticed.

Nature of the opening comments to be made when the interview commences
Where the interviewee has not met you before, the first few minutes of conversation may have a significant impact on the outcome of the interview – again related to the issue of your credibility and the level of the interviewee's confidence. The interview is likely to occur in a setting that is unfamiliar to you, but it will nevertheless be your responsibility to shape the start of the discussion. You will need to establish your credibility and gain the interviewee's confidence. The interviewee may have some uncertainties about sharing information and the manner in which these data may be used. Alternatively, they may still need clarification about the exact nature of the data that you wish to obtain. There may also be a degree of curiosity on the part of the interviewee and probably a genuine level of interest in the research, related to the reason why the request to participate was accepted. This curiosity and interest will offer an opening for both parties to start a conversation, probably before the 'intended discussion' commences. You may find it appropriate to follow up by demonstrating interest in the interviewee by asking about their role within the host organisation (Ghauri *et al.*, 1995). However, you need to make sure that these opening moves to demonstrate

credibility and friendliness, and to relax and develop a positive relationship, are not over-stated, so that too much time is used and the interviewee starts to become bored or restive.

The commencement of the intended discussion needs to be shaped by you. This will be your opportunity to allay, wherever possible, the interviewee's uncertainties about providing information. The following example provides a structure that might be appropriate to commence an interview and to fulfil this purpose.

Worked example

Opening a semi-structured interview

As part of a research project a series of semi-structured interviews were undertaken with participants from a range of organisations. In order to raise, and where necessary to discuss, a number of aspects felt to be important, the following points were covered at the start of each interview:

- the participant was thanked for considering the request for access and agreeing to the meeting;

- the purpose of the research, its funding and progress to date were briefly outlined;

- the previously agreed right to confidentiality and anonymity was reiterated by stating that nothing said by the participant would be attributed to her or him or their employing organisation without first seeking and obtaining permission;

- the participant's right not to answer any question was carefully emphasised and that the interview would be stopped if they wished;

- the participant was told about the nature of the outputs to which the research was intended to lead and what would happen to the data collected during and after the project;

- the offer of any written documentation to the interviewee was also re-stated and when this was intended to occur;

- before the substantive discussion got under way the final points were to ask permission about the way in which the interviewer wished to conduct the meeting, to state the themes to be covered and to confirm the amount of time available.

All of these points were generally dealt with in a couple of minutes.

Healey and Rawlinson (1994) say that an assurance from you that confidential information is not being sought should make interviewees more relaxed and open in the information that they are willing to discuss. Combined with assurances about anonymity, this should increase the level of confidence in your trustworthiness and reduce the possibility of interviewee or response bias. You may also demonstrate your commitment to confidentiality by not naming other organisations who have participated in your research or by talking about the data you obtained from them.

Approach to questioning

When conducted appropriately, your approach to questioning should reduce the scope for bias during the interview and increase the reliability of the information obtained. Your questions need to be clearly phrased, so that the interviewee can understand them, and you should ask them in a neutral tone of voice. Easterby-Smith *et al.* (1991) point out that the use of open questions (Section 9.5) should help to avoid bias. These can then be followed up by the use of appropriately worded probing questions (Section 9.5) which will help you to explore the topic and to produce a fuller account. Conversely, questions that seek to lead the interviewee or which indicate bias on your part should be avoided. Perceived interviewer bias may well lead to interviewee or response bias. Long questions or those that are really made up of two or more questions should also be avoided if you are to obtain a response to each aspect that you are interested to explore (Robson, 1993).

Questions should also avoid too many theoretical concepts or jargon since your understanding of such terms may vary from that of your interviewees. Where theoretical concepts or specific terminology need to be used, you will have to ensure that the interviewee understands your intended meaning (Easterby-Smith *et al.*, 1991; Ghauri *et al.*, 1995).

> **Worked example**
>
> ## (Mis)understanding terminology
>
> When Adrian and Andrew conducted interviews about the 'survivors' of redundancies, one participant initially thought that this referred to those made redundant but who had managed to overcome and 'survive' the experience – which is a very understandable interpretation. In fact, the meaning was intended to relate to employees who remained in the organisation! The term 'survivor syndrome' has now become accepted jargon by those interested in this area. However, many people would not specifically relate it to those who stay in employment. You will therefore need to exercise great care in the way that you use similar bits of jargon that you take for granted but which others do not.

Healey and Rawlinson (1994:138) suggest that 'it is usually best to leave sensitive questions until near the end of an interview because this allows a greater time for the respondent to build up trust and confidence in the researchers.' They report cases where the first part of an interview is used by participants to assess the level of trust that can be placed in the researcher. Others have witnessed this experience, as the following example illustrates, affecting the nature of the questions that may be asked during the early part of an interview.

> **Worked example**
>
> ## Establishing trust and asking sensitive questions
>
> Sam recalls an occasion when this type of treatment was particularly noticeable: for the first hour of a two-hour interview it appeared to her that the participants were convinced that she was really there to offer them a consultancy service. When they accepted that she was not about to try to sell them something, the mood of the meeting changed and they became much more relaxed and responsive to the questions that Sam wished to ask. It was at this point that she was able to ask and pursue more sensitive questions that could have led to the interview being terminated during the period when the participants mistrusted her motives.

Once this position of trust has been reached and you wish to seek responses to potentially sensitive questions, Ghauri *et al.* (1995) point out that the wording of these deserves very particular attention in order to avoid any negative inferences related to, for example, responsibility for failure or error. Care taken over the exploration of sensitive questions should help towards the compilation of a fuller and more reliable account.

Nature and impact of the interviewer's behaviour during the course of the interview
Appropriate behaviour by the researcher should also reduce the scope for bias during the interview. Comments or non-verbal behaviour, such as gestures, which indicate any bias in your thinking should be avoided. A neutral (but not an uninterested) response should be projected to the interviewee's answers in order not to provide any lead that may result in bias. Robson (1993) says that you should enjoy the opportunity, or at least appear to do so. An appearance of boredom on your part is hardly likely to encourage your interviewee!

Your posture and tone of voice may also encourage or inhibit the flow of the discussion. You should sit slightly inclined towards the interviewee and adopt an open posture, avoiding folded arms. This should provide a signal of attentiveness to your interviewee (Torrington, 1991). Tone of voice can also provide signals to the interviewee. You need to project interest and enthusiasm through your voice, avoiding any impression of anxiety, disbelief, astonishment or other negative signals.

Demonstration of attentive listening skills
The purpose of a semi-structured or in-depth interview will be to understand the participant's explanations and meanings. This type of interaction will not be typical of many of the conversations that you normally engage in, where those involved often compete to speak rather than concentrate on listening. You therefore need to recognise that different skills will be emphasised in this kind of interaction. Torrington (1991:43) says that listening involves people being 'on the look-out for signals and willing to spend the time needed to listen and build understanding, deliberately holding back our own thoughts, which would divert or compete with the other's.'

It will be necessary for you to explore and probe explanations and meanings but you must also provide the interviewee with reasonable time to develop their responses, and you must avoid projecting your own views (Easterby-Smith *et al.*, 1991; Ghauri *et al.*, 1995; Robson, 1993). Careful listening should allow you to identify comments that are significant to the research topic and to explore these with the interviewee (Torrington, 1991).

Scope to test understanding

You may test your understanding by summarising an explanation provided by the interviewee. This will allow the interviewee to 'evaluate the adequacy of the interpretation and correct where necessary' (Healey and Rawlinson, 1994:138). This can be a powerful tool for avoiding a biased or incomplete interpretation. It may also act as a means to explore and probe the interviewee's responses further.

In addition to this opportunity to test understanding at the interview, you may also ask the interviewee to read through the factual account that you need to produce of the interview. Where the interviewee is prepared to undertake this, it will provide a further opportunity for you to test your understanding and for the interviewee to add any further points of relevance that may occur to them.

Approach to recording data

A full record of the interview should be compiled as soon as possible after it has taken place (Healey, 1991; Healey and Rawlinson, 1994; Robson, 1993). Where you do not do this, the exact nature of explanations provided may be lost as well as general points of value. There is also the possibility that you may mix up data from different interviews, where you carry out several of these within a short period of time and you do not complete a record of each one at the time it takes place (Ghauri *et al.*, 1995). Either situation will clearly lead to an issue about the trustworthiness of any data. You therefore need to allocate time to write up a full set of notes soon after the event. Recording information is considered further in Section 9.5.

As a final note to this particular discussion, we need to recognise that it is often difficult to attempt to control bias in all cases. Other factors may become significant. For example, there may be misinterpretation of responses because of cultural differences between the interviewee and the interviewer (Marshall and Rossman, 1999). This issue is not exclusively related to interviews and can be associated with a number of data collection methods. For example, we encountered it in relation to the interpretation of the data produced from a cross-national survey. An in-depth interview at least offers the opportunity to explore meanings, including those which may be culturally specific, but you will need to be aware of cultural differences and their implications (see, for example, Hofstede, 1991).

Generalisability

In the previous section which described data quality issues relating to semi-structured and in-depth interviews, we stated that there is likely to be a concern surrounding the generalisability of findings from qualitative research, based on the use of a small and unrepresentative number of cases. However, two arguments have been advanced which seek to clarify and modify the approach often adopted to the generalisability or transferability of qualitative research. The first of these relates to the situation where a single case study is used because of the in-depth nature of the research. Bryman (1988:90) states that 'within a case study a wide range of different people and activities are invariably examined so that the contrast with survey samples is not as acute as it appears at first glance'. The single case may in fact encompass a number of settings, where for example it involves a study in a large organisation with sites across the country, or even around the world. By comparison, Bryman (1988) points out that many survey samples may be restricted to one particular locality. A well-completed and rigorous case study is thus more likely to be useful in other contexts than one that lacks such rigour.

The second argument with the approach which questions the generalisability of qualitative research or a case study is related to the significance of this type of research to theoretical propositions (Bryman, 1988; Yin, 1994). Where you are able to relate your research project to existing theory you will be in a position to demonstrate that your findings will have a broader significance than the case or cases which form the basis of your work (Marshall and Rossman, 1999). It will clearly be up to you to establish this relationship to existing theory in order to be able to demonstrate the broader significance of your particular case study findings.

This relationship will allow your study to test the applicability of existing theory to the setting(s) that you are examining and where this is found wanting to suggest why. It will also allow theoretical propositions to be advanced that can then be tested in another context. However, as Bryman (1988) points out, this also has implications for the relationship between theory and research, since the identification of existing theory and its application will be necessary before the researcher embarks on the collection of data (Section 12.4).

9.5 The researcher's interviewing competence

There are several areas where you need to develop and demonstrate competence in relation to the conduct of semi-structured and in-depth research interviews. These areas are:

- opening the interview;
- using appropriate language;
- questioning;
- listening;
- testing and summarising understanding;
- behavioural cues;
- recording data.

Most of these competency areas have been discussed in relation to overcoming interviewer and interviewee bias in Section 9.4. A list of competencies is also contained in Table 9.4. However, there is scope to discuss further approaches to questioning and recording information in order to be able to develop your competence.

Questioning

Even in an in-depth interview, as well as in a semi-structured one, you will need to consider your approach to questioning. Allowing the interviewee to talk freely throughout an in-depth interview is unlikely to lead to a clearly focused discussion on issues relevant to the research topic (Easterby-Smith *et al.*, 1991; Robson, 1993), unless the purpose is simply to discover important concerns relating to the topic at a given time. It will therefore be necessary to devise relevant interview themes (Section 9.4), even though you can adopt a flexible approach about the way these are dealt with during the interview. The use of this approach demands a significant level of competence on your part. Formulating appropriate questions to explore areas in which you are interested will be critical to achieving success in this type of interviewing. We will now discuss the types of questions that you will use during semi-structured and in-depth interviews.

Open questions

The use of *open questions* will allow participants to define and describe a situation or event. An open question is designed to encourage the interviewee to provide an extensive and developmental answer and may be used to reveal attitudes or obtain facts (Grummitt, 1980). They encourage the interviewee to reply as they wish. An open question is likely to start with, or include, one of the following words: 'what', 'how' or 'why'. Examples of open questions include:

'Why did the organisation introduce its marketing strategy?'

'What methods have been used to make employees redundant?'

'How has corporate strategy changed over the past five years?'

Probing questions

Probing questions can be used to explore responses that are of significance to the research topic. They may be worded like open questions but request a particular *focus* or direction. Examples of this type of question include:

'How would you evaluate the success of this new marketing strategy?'

'Why did you choose a compulsory method to make redundancies?'

'What external factors caused the corporate strategy to change?'

These questions may be prefaced with, for example, 'That's interesting . . .' or 'Tell me more about . . .'.

Probing questions may also be used to seek an *explanation* where you do not understand the interviewee's meaning or where the response does not reveal the reasoning involved. Examples of this type of question include:

'What do you mean by "bumping" as a means to help to secure volunteers for redundancy?'

'What is the relationship between the new statutory requirements which you referred to and the organisation's decision to set up its corporate affairs department?'

Use of *reflection* may also help you to probe a theme. This is where you will 'reflect' a statement made by the interviewee by paraphrasing their words. An example of this might be:

'Why don't you think that the employees understand the organisation's mission statement?'

The intention will be to encourage exploration of the point made without offering a view or judgement on your part.

Where an open question does not reveal a relevant response, you may also probe the area of interest by using a *supplementary* question that finds a way of rephrasing the original question (Torrington, 1991).

Specific and closed questions

These types of questions may be used to obtain specific information or to confirm a fact or opinion and are more generally used in questionnaires (Section 10.4). Examples of these types of questions include:

'How many people responded to the customer survey?'

This question is designed to obtain a specific piece of data.

'Did I hear you say that the new warehouse opened on the 25th March?'

This is a closed question seeking a yes or no answer.

In phrasing questions, remember that you should avoid using leading or proposing types of questions in order to control any bias that may result from their use (Section 9.4).

Recording information

The need to create a full record of the interview soon after its occurrence was identified in Section 9.4 as one of the means to control bias and to produce reliable data for analysis. This particular discussion looks briefly at the need to develop the skill of making notes during the interview and evaluates the use of tape recorders. Most people have their own means of making notes, which may range from an attempt to create a verbatim account to a diagrammatic style which records key words and phrases, or perhaps some combination of these styles. The task of note making in this situation will be a demanding one. As you seek to test your understanding of what your interviewee has told you, this will allow some time to complete your notes concurrently in relation to the particular aspect being discussed. Most interviewees recognise the demands of the task and act accordingly. However, the interview will not be the occasion to perfect your style and you may be advised to practise in a simulated situation; for example, by watching an interview on television and attempting to produce a set of notes.

One option is to tape record the interview. However, the disadvantages of doing so may outweigh the advantages. These are considered in Table 9.3.

Table 9.3	Advantages and disadvantages of tape recording the interview

Advantages	Disadvantages
■ Allows interviewer to concentrate on questioning and listening	■ May adversely affect the relationship between interviewee and interviewer (possibility of 'focusing' on the recorder)
■ Allows questions formulated at an interview to be accurately recorded for use in later interviews where appropriate	■ May inhibit some interviewee responses and reduce reliability
■ Can re-listen to the interview	■ Possibility of a technical problem
■ Accurate and unbiased record provided	■ Disruption to discussion when changing tapes
■ Allows direct quotes to be used	■ Time required to transcribe the tape
■ Permanent record for others to use	

Sources: Authors' experience; Easterby-Smith et al., 1991, Ghauri et al., 1995; Healey and Rawlinson, 1994

Permission should always be sought to tape record an interview. Healey and Rawlinson (1994) report an earlier study that advises that you should explain why you would prefer to use a recorder rather than simply requesting permission. Where it is likely to have a detrimental effect, it is better not to use a recorder. However, some interviewees may adapt quickly to the use of the recorder.

Where a recorder is used, it will still be necessary for you to continue to listen attentively. You are advised to make notes even when using a tape recorder in order to maintain your concentration and focus (Ghauri *et al.*, 1995). It is more ethical to allow your interviewee to maintain control over the tape recorder so that if you ask a question which they are prepared to respond to, but only if their words are not tape recorded, they have the option to switch it off (see the discussion of ethical issues in Section 5.4). It will therefore be necessary to make notes in this situation.

9.6 Logistical and resource issues and how to manage these

Logistical and resource issues

Interviewing is a time-consuming process. Where the purpose of the interview is to explore themes or to explain findings, the process may call for a fairly lengthy discussion. In such cases, the time required to obtain data is unlikely to be less than one hour and could easily exceed this, perhaps taking two hours or longer. This may have an adverse impact on the number and representativeness of those who are willing to be interview participants, as we discussed above. Where managers or other potential participants receive frequent requests to participate in research projects, they will clearly need to consider how much of their time they may be willing to devote to such activities. This issue may arise in relation to either the completion of a questionnaire or participation in an interview. However, there will be more flexibility about when and where to fill in a questionnaire. It is therefore incumbent on you to establish credibility with, and to engender the interest of, potential interviewees.

Your choice of an approach that involves data collection through interviewing will have particular resource issues. Conducting interviews may become a costly process where it is necessary to travel to the location of participants, although this can be kept to a minimum by cluster sampling (Section 6.2). Interviews are almost certainly likely to be more expensive than using self-administered or telephone questionnaires to collect data. Choice of method should be determined by the nature of the research question and objectives and not by cost considerations. This highlights the need to examine the feasibility of the proposed question and research strategy in relation to resources constraints, including time available and expense, before proceeding to the collection of data. Where your research question and objectives require you to undertake semi-structured or in-depth interviews, you need to consider the logistics of scheduling interviews. Thought needs to be given to the number of interviews to be arranged within a given period, the time required to compose notes and/or to transcribe tape recordings of each one and to undertake an initial analysis of the data collected (Section 12.3).

Managing logistical and resource issues

In the preceding subsection, the issue of time required to collect data through interviewing was raised. You need to consider very carefully the amount of time that will be required to conduct an interview. In our experience, the time required to undertake research interviews is usually underestimated. The likely time required should be clearly referred to in any initial contact and it may be better to suggest that interviews are envisaged to last up to, say, one, one and a half, or two hours, so that a willing participant sets aside sufficient time. They may then be in a position to recoup time not required from a shorter interview should this be the case. Some negotiation is any case possible with an interested participant who feels unable to agree to a request for say two hours but who is prepared to agree to a briefer meeting. The interview can also be arranged at a time when the interviewee will be under least pressure.

Another possible strategy is to arrange two or more shorter interviews in order to explore a topic thoroughly. This might have the added advantage of allowing participants to reflect on the themes raised and questions being asked, and therefore to provide a fuller account and more accurate set of data. In order to establish this option it may be beneficial to arrange an initial meeting with a potential participant to discuss this request, where you will be able to establish your credibility. A series of exploratory interviews may then be agreed.

Consideration also needs to be given to the number of interviews that may be undertaken in a given period. It is easy to overestimate what is practically possible, as the following worked example on p. 264 demonstrates.

These are all factors that need to be considered in the scheduling of semi-structured and in-depth interviews. Where you are involved in a study at one establishment, it may be more practical to undertake a number of interviews in one day, although there is still a need to maintain concentration, to make notes and write up information and to conduct your initial analysis. Phil found that undertaking three interviews per day in this type of study was enough.

> **Worked example**
>
> ### Calculating the number of qualitative interviews to be undertaken in one day
>
> Feroz arranged two interviews in London during the course of a day, which involved travelling some miles across the city during the lunch hour. Two interviews appeared to be a reasonable target. However, a number of logistical issues were experienced even in relation to the plan to undertake two such interviews in one day. These issues included the following: the total travelling time to and from London; the time to find the appropriate buildings; the transfer time during a busy period; the time to conduct the interviews; the need to maintain concentration, to probe responses, to make initial notes and then to write these up without too much time elapsing. Because of his experience, Feroz took a decision not to conduct more than one interview per day where significant travel was involved, even though this necessitated more journeys and greater expense.

The nature of semi-structured or in-depth interviews also has implications for the management of the time available during the meeting. The use of open-ended questions and reliance on informant responses mean that while you must remain responsive to the objectives of the interview and the time constraint, interviewees need the opportunity to provide developmental answers. You should avoid making frequent interruptions but will need to cover the themes and questions indicated and probe responses in the time available (Ghauri *et al.*, 1995). The intensive nature of the discussion and the need to optimise one's understanding of what has been revealed means that time must be found to write up notes as soon as possible after an interview. Where a tape recorder has been used time will be required to produce a transcription and Robson (1993) states that a one-hour recording may take up to ten hours to transcribe.

9.7 A checklist for using semi-structured and in-depth interviews

Following the discussion about types of research interview (Section 9.2), this chapter has considered situations favouring their use (Section 9.3) and issues relating to data quality (Section 9.4), the level of competence required by the researcher (Section 9.5) and resources (Section 9.6). Throughout this discussion the focus has been centred on what you will need to consider in order to be able to conduct semi-structured or in-depth interviews. The checklist contained in Table 9.4 brings together the key points from the discussion above in order to help you to think about when and how to conduct these types of research interviews. You may use the checklist as a means to test your understanding of the points included in the table, to indicate where you need to return to a section of the text above to reinforce this.

| Table 9.4 | **Checklist for the use of semi-structured and in-depth interviews** |

Deciding whether to use these types of interviews

✓ Does the purpose of your research suggest using semi-structured and/or in-depth interviews?

✓ Will it help to seek personal contact in terms of gaining access to participants and their data?

✓ Are your data collection questions large in number, complex or open ended, or will there be a need to vary the order and logic of questioning?

✓ Will it help to be able to probe interviewees' responses to build on or to seek explanation of their answers?

✓ Will the data collection process with each individual involve a relatively lengthy period?

Aspects to consider before conducting a semi-structured or in-depth interview

✓ How will you seek to minimise issues related to the reliability of your data collection and its usefulness for other researchers?

✓ How will you seek to minimise forms of interviewer bias (related to your role and conduct), interviewee bias (the level of access which you gain to the data of those whom you interview) and sampling bias?

✓ What is the aim of your research interview? How can you prepare yourself to gain access to the data that you hope your participants will be able to share with you?

✓ What is the focus of your in-depth interview or what are the themes which you wish to explore or seek explanations for during a semi-structured interview?

✓ What type of information, if any, will it be useful to send to your interviewee prior to the interview?

✓ What did you agree to supply to your interviewee when you arranged the interview? Has this been supplied?

✓ How will your appearance during the interview affect the willingness of the interviewee to share data?

✓ How will your level of preparation and knowledge (in relation to the research context and your research question) affect the willingness of the interviewee to share data?

✓ How would you like to record the data that are revealed to you during the interview? Where this involves using a tape recorder have you raised this as a request and provided a reason why it would help you to use this technique?

Opening the interview

✓ How will you prepare yourself to be able to commence the interview with confidence and purpose?

✓ What will you tell your interviewee about yourself, the purpose of your research, its funding and your progress?

✓ What concerns, or need for clarification, may your interviewee have?

✓ How will you seek to overcome these concerns or provide this clarification?

✓ In particular, how do you intend to use the data to which you are given access, ensuring, where appropriate, its confidentiality and your interviewee's anonymity?

✓ What will you tell your interviewee about their right not to answer particular questions and to end the interview should they wish?

✓ How do you intend to record the data that are shared with you? What rights will your interviewee have in relation to the use of a tape recorder where they have agreed in principle to let you use one? ▶

Table 9.4   *Cont.*

✓   What reference do you need to make about sending your interviewee an output from your data analysis and when this is due to occur?

✓   How long will you have to conduct the interview?

✓   How do you wish to conduct (or structure) the interview?

Conducting the interview

How will you prepare yourself to be able:

✓   to use appropriate language and tone of voice, and avoid jargon when asking questions or discussing themes?

✓   to ask appropriately worded open questions to obtain relevant data?

✓   to ask appropriately worded probing questions to build on, clarify or explain your interviewee's responses?

✓   to avoid asking leading questions that may introduce forms of bias?

✓   to devise an appropriate order for your questions, where the early introduction of sensitive issues may introduce interviewee bias?

✓   to avoid over-zealously asking questions and pressing your interviewee for a response where it should be clear that they do not wish to provide one?

✓   to listen attentively and to demonstrate this to your interviewee?

✓   to test and summarise your understanding of the data which are shared with you in order to ensure their accuracy?

✓   to allow your interviewee to maintain control over the use of a tape recorder, where used, where they may wish to exercise this?

✓   to carry out a number of tasks at the same time, including listening, note taking and the identification of probes?

✓   to identify actions and comments made by your interviewee which indicate an aspect of the discussion which should be explored in order to reveal the reason for the response?

✓   to avoid projecting your own views or feelings through your actions or comments?

✓   to maintain a check on the interview themes which you intend to cover and to steer the discussion where appropriate to raise and explore these aspects?

✓   to draw the interview to a close within the agreed time limit and to thank the interviewee for their time and the data they have shared with you?

Recording the information

✓   How will you prepare your approach to note making so that you may recall the interviewee's responses for long enough to make an accurate and more permanent record?

✓   Has your schedule of work been formulated to permit you to find sufficient time in order to write up your notes and to analyse them before undertaking further data collection?

✓   How will you organise your material so that you retain a copy of your original notes, an extended version of your notes after writing them up or a transcript of relevant material, and a set of additional notes or memos relating to the interview and your learning from that particular experience (see Chapter 12 for further discussion)?

9.8   A final word about telephone and group interviews

Most qualitative interviews occur on a one-to-one, face-to-face basis. However, one-to-one interviews may also be conducted by telephone in particular circumstances. Qualitative interviews may also be conducted on a group basis, where the interviewer facilitates a group discussion involving a small number of participants. Fig 9.1 summarised these variations earlier in this chapter. While the discussion in this chapter relates to both one-to-one and group interviews, the use of telephone and group interviews poses particular problems as well as providing advantages in certain circumstances. We will consider each category in turn and provide a brief evaluation of their effectiveness.

Telephone interviews

Attempting to conduct qualitative interviews by telephone may lead to advantages associated with access, speed and lower cost. This method may allow you to make contact with participants with whom it would be impractical to conduct an interview on a face-to-face basis because of the distance involved and prohibitive costs and time required. Even where 'long-distance' access is not an issue, conducting interviews by telephone may still offer advantages associated with speed of data collection and lower cost. In other words, this approach may be seen as more convenient.

However, there are a number of significant issues that mitigate against attempting to collect qualitative data by telephone contact. We have already discussed the importance of establishing personal contact in this type of interviewing. The intention of qualitative interviewing is to be able to explore the participant's responses. This is likely to become more feasible once a position of trust has been established, as discussed earlier. This situation, of establishing trust, will become particularly important where you wish to ask sensitive questions. For these reasons, seeking to conduct qualitative interviews by telephone may lead to issues of (reduced) reliability, where your participants are less willing to engage in an exploratory discussion, or even a refusal to take part.

There are also some other practical issues that would need to be managed. These would relate to your ability to control the pace of the interview and to record any data that were forthcoming. Conducting an interview by telephone and recording data is a difficult process. The normal visual cues that allow your participant to control the flow of the data that they share with you would be absent. Indeed, you would lose the opportunity to witness the non-verbal behaviour of your participant through use of this means, which may adversely affect your interpretation about how far to pursue a particular line of questioning. Your participant may be less willing to provide you with as much time to talk to them in comparison with a face-to-face interview. You may also encounter difficulties in developing more complex questions in comparison with a face-to-face interview situation. Finally, attempting to gain access through a telephone call may lead to ethical issues as we discussed in Section 5.4.

For these reasons, we believe that qualitative interviewing by telephone is only likely to be appropriate in particular circumstances. It may be appropriate to conduct a short, follow-up telephone interview to clarify the meaning of some data, where you have already undertaken a face-to-face interview with a participant, with whom you have been able to establish your integrity and to demonstrate your competence. It may also be appropriate where access would otherwise be prohibited because of long distance and you have been able to establish your credibility through prior contact, perhaps through correspondence, and made clear that your requirements are reasonable and guided by ethical principles. Where this situation involves a request to undertake a telephone interview with a participant from another country, you will need to be aware of any cultural norms related to the conduct and duration of telephone conversations.

Group interviews

In a *group interview,* you will act as a facilitator and manager of the discussion. The interview is likely be relatively unstructured and to be fairly free-flowing (Zikmund, 1997), although of course where you use this method you will have particular themes which you wish to explore. The onus will be placed firmly on you to explain its purpose, to encourage participants to relax and to initiate the discussion (Easterby-Smith *et al.*, 1991), although the opportunity for you to develop the level of rapport that is possible in one-to-one interviews will not be present. Once established the discussion will need to be managed, in order to encourage involvement by all members of the group and to maintain its intended focus. A high level of skill will therefore be required from you in order for you to be able to conduct this type of discussion successfully.

Despite these difficulties, there are distinct advantages. Because of the presence of several participants, this type of situation allows a variety of points of view to emerge and for the group to respond to and to discuss these views. A dynamic group can generate or respond to a number of ideas and evaluate them, thus helping you to explain or explore concepts. They can also generate numbers of key themes that become the subject of a survey. For example, in an attitude survey the initial use of focus group interviews, as these are often referred to, can lead to a 'bottom-up' generation of concerns and issues which helps to establish the survey and also to help to involve those who will be asked to provide the data which will be vital for its success. Focus group interviews are also used in market research to test reactions to products and in a range of other contexts. Their use may allow you to adopt an interview-based strategy that can more easily be related to a representative sample, particularly where the research project is being conducted within a specific organisation or in relation to a clearly defined population. This may help to establish the credibility of this research where an attempt is made to overcome issues of bias associated with interviews in general and this type in particular.

If you are thinking about using group interviews, consideration of the following specific issues may help.

- Where your research project (or part of it) occurs within an organisation the request to participate in a group interview may be received by individuals as an instruction rather than something that they may exercise choice about. This may be the case where an organisation is acting as a host for your research and the request is sent out on official notepaper or in the name of a manager, or where you work in the organisation. In our experience participants often welcome the chance to 'have their say'. However, where any request may be perceived as indicating lack of choice, to gain their confidence you will need to exercise care over the wording to be used and in your introduction to the group when the interview occurs in order to provide a clear assurance about confidentiality.

- The effect of gathering people together may be to inhibit possible contributions. This may be related to lack of trust, perceptions about status differences or because of the dominance of certain individuals. The nature and selection of each group will affect the first two elements. We would advise using a '*horizontal slice*' through an organisation to select a sample of people who have a similar status and similar work experiences. (Using a *vertical slice* would introduce perceptions about status differences and variations in work experience.) In this way, group interviews can be conducted at a number of levels within an organisation. A reference may be made about the nature of the group to provide reassurance and you may consider asking people to introduce themselves by their first name without referring to their exact job.

- Where one or two people dominate the discussion, you should carefully seek to reduce their contributions and bring others in. Torrington (1991) suggests that this may be attempted in a general way:

   'What do you think, Barry?'

   'What do other people think about this?'

   Alternatively, more specifically:

   'How does Sally's point relate to the one which you raised, Sheila?'

   A question posed to other group members should also have the effect of inhibiting the contribution of a dominant member:

   'What do you think about John's suggestion?'

- You will need to ensure that participants understand each other's contributions and that you develop an accurate understanding of the points being made. Asking a participant to clarify the meaning of a particular contribution, where it has not been understood, and testing understanding through summarising should help to ensure this.

- You will need to consider the location and setting for a group interview. It is advisable to conduct the interview in a neutral setting rather than, say, in a manager's office, where participants may not feel relaxed. There should be no likelihood of interruption or being overheard. You should consider the layout of the seating in the room where the interview is to be held. Arrange the seating in a circular fashion so that everyone will be facing inward and so that they will be an equal distance from the central point of this circle.

- The demands of conducting this type of interview and the potential wealth of ideas which may flow from it mean that it may be difficult to manage the process and note key points at the same time. We have managed to overcome this by using two interviewers, where one person facilitates the discussion and the other person makes notes. Where you cannot use this approach, you need to write up notes almost immediately after undertaking this type of interview so as not to lose data. We would not advise one person to undertake interviews like this 'back to back' because of the danger of losing or confusing data.

9.9 ▨ Summary

- In-depth interviews are difficult to conduct properly.

- Interviews can be differentiated according to the level of structure and standardisation adopted. Different types of interviews are useful for different research purposes.

- You can use in-depth and semi-structured interviews to explore topics and explain other findings.

- Your research design may incorporate more than one type of interview.

- In-depth and semi-structured interviews can be used in quantitative as well as qualitative research.

- There are situations favouring in-depth interviews that will lead you to use this method. Apart from the nature of your research strategy, these are related to the significance of establishing personal contact, the nature of your data collection questions and the length of time required from those who provide data.

- Data quality issues, your level of competence and logistical and resource matters will all need to be considered when you use in-depth and semi-structured interviews.

- Apart from one-to-one interviews conducted on a face-to-face basis, you may consider conducting such an interview by telephone in particular circumstances. In addition, you may consider using group interviews. There may be particular advantages associated with group interviews, but these are considerably more difficult to manage than one-to-one interviews.

Self check Questions

9.1 What type of interview would you use in each of the following situations:

    a a market research project?

    b a research project seeking to understand whether trade union attitudes have changed?

    c following the analysis of a questionnaire?

9.2 What are the advantages of using semi-structured and in-depth interviews?

9.3 During a presentation of your proposal to undertake a research project, which will be qualitatively based using semi-structured or in-depth interviews, you feel that you have dealt well with the relationship between the purpose of the research and the proposed methodology when one of the panel leans forward and asks you to discuss the trustworthiness and usefulness of your work for other researchers. This is clearly a challenge to see whether you can defend such a qualitative approach. How do you respond?

9.4 Having quizzed you about the trustworthiness and usefulness of your work for other researchers, the panel member decides that one more testing question is in order. He explains that qualitatively based work isn't an easy option. 'It is not an easier alternative for those who want to avoid quantitative work,' he says. 'How can we be sure that you're competent to get involved in interview work, especially where the external credibility of this organisation may be affected by the impression which you create in the field?' How will you respond to this concern?

9.5 What are the key issues to consider when planning to use semi-structured or in-depth interviews?

9.6 What are the key areas of competence that you need to develop in order to conduct an interview successfully ?

Assignment 9

Using semi-structured or in-depth interviews in your research

→ Review your research question(s) and objectives. How appropriate would it be to use qualitative interviews to collect data? Where it is appropriate, explain the relationship between your research question(s) and objectives, and the use of such interviews. Where this type of interviewing is not appropriate, justify your decision.

→ If you decide that semi-structured or in-depth interviews are appropriate, what practical problems do you foresee? How may you attempt to overcome these practical problems?

→ What threats to the trustworthiness of the data collected are you likely to encounter? How may you overcome these?

→ Draft a list of interview themes to be explored and thoroughly compare these with your research question(s) and objectives.

→ Ask your project tutor to comment on your judgement about the use of qualitative interviews, the issues and threats which you have identified, your suggestions to overcome these and the fit between your interview themes and the research question(s) and objectives.

References

Bryman, A. (1988) *Quantity and Quality in Social Research*, London, Unwin Hyman.

Cooper, D.R. and Schindler, P.S. (1998) *Business Research Methods* (6th edn), Boston, MA, Irwin McGraw-Hill.

Easterby-Smith, M., Thorpe, R. and Lowe, A. (1991) *Management Research: an Introduction*, London, Sage.

Ghauri, P.N., Grønhaug, K. and Kristianslund, I. (1995) *Research Methods in Business Studies: a Practical Guide*, London, Prentice Hall.

Grummitt, J. (1980) *Interviewing Skills*, London, Industrial Society.

Healey, M.J. (1991) 'Obtaining information from businesses', *in* Healey, M.J. (ed.), *Economic Activity and Land Use,* Harlow, Longman, pp. 193–251.

Healey, M.J. and Rawlinson, M.B. (1993) 'Interviewing business owners and managers: a review of methods and techniques', *Geoforum* 24:3, 339–55.

Healey, M.J. and Rawlinson, M.B. (1994) 'Interviewing techniques in business and management research', *in* Wass, V.J. and Wells, P.E., *Principles and Practice in Business and Management Research,* Aldershot, Dartmouth, pp. 123–46.

Hofstede, G. (1991) *Cultures and Organisations,* London, McGraw-Hill.

Jankowicz, A.D. (1995) *Business Research Projects for Students* (2nd edition) London, Chapman & Hall.

Kahn, R. and Cannell, C. (1957) *The Dynamics of Interviewing,* New York and Chichester, Wiley.

Marshall, C. and Rossman, G.B. (1999) *Designing Qualitative Research* (3rd edn), Thousand Oaks, CA, Sage.

North, D.J., Leigh, R. and Gough, J. (1983) 'Monitoring industrial change at the local level: some comments on methods and data sources', *in* Healey, M.J. (ed.) *Urban and Regional Industrial Research: the Changing UK Data Base,* Norwich, Geo Books, pp. 111–29.

Powney, J. and Watts, M. (1987) *Interviewing in Educational Research*, London, Routledge and Kegan Paul.

Robson, C. (1993) *Real World Research*, Oxford, Blackwell.

Sykes, W. (1991) 'Taking stock: issues from the literature in validity and reliability in qualitative research', *Journal of Market Research Society* 33:3–12.

Torrington, D. (1991) *Management Face to Face*, London, Prentice Hall.

Wass, V. and Wells, P. (1994) 'Research methods in action: an introduction', *in* Wass, V.J. and Wells, P.E., *Principles and Practice in Business and Management Research*, Aldershot, Dartmouth, pp. 1–34.

Yin, R.K. (1994) *Case Study Research: Design and Methods* (2nd edn), Beverly Hills, CA, Sage.

Zikmund, W.G. (1997) *Business Research Methods* (5th edn), Fort Worth, TX, Dryden Press.

Further reading

Easterby-Smith, M., Thorpe, R. and Lowe, A. (1991) *Management Research: an Introduction,* London, Sage. Chapter 5 provides very useful and highly readable overview of qualitative methods. This includes in-depth interviews and other methods to supplement them.

Healey, M.J. and Rawlinson, M.B. (1994) 'Interviewing techniques in business and management research', *in* Wass, V.J. and Wells, P.E., *Principles and Practice in Business and Management Research,* Aldershot, Dartmouth, pp. 123–46. This is an excellent contribution and a 'must' for those of you intending to use qualitative research and interviews.

Krueger, R.C. (1994) *Focus Groups: a Practical Guide for Applied Research* (2nd edn), London, Sage. A very useful work for those considering the use of this method.

Marshall, C. and Rossman, G.B. (1999) *Designing Qualitative Research* (3rd edn), Thousand Oaks, CA, Sage This provides many excellent insights into the design of qualitative research and the methods associated with it.

Case 9   **The practices and styles of public relations practitioners**

Public relations (PR) practitioners are a significant and growing group in the UK. Some of them operate internationally with great sophistication to improve their companies' profiles and stock exchange status. Some peddle sex stories to the tabloid press. Another group in politics, known as 'spin doctors', are hired to make political moves more acceptable. However, in the UK there has been very little substantive research into PR practices and styles. This is partly because of the lack of a UK journal dedicated to research in PR and partly because PR has traditionally been subsumed within the discipline of marketing.

Valerie designed a case study that sought to examine the practices and styles of PR practitioners. However, it was recognised that this group included a wide range of people from the likes of publicity technicians to corporate communications professionals. The first stage of the research project was designed to examine the practices and styles of PR practitioners through the eyes of those they interact with most frequently – namely journalists. The second stage was designed to gauge PR practitioners' own assessments of the way they operate.

A theoretical basis for this study was established by using the model devised by Grunig and Hunt (1984). This identified a number of PR styles based on research conducted in the USA:

- Press agency – little research, main aim to get firm/product mentions in the media, truth not vital. Emphasis on one-way communication.

- Public information – some research, main aim to get media exposure, truth matters. Emphasis on one-way communication.

- Two way asymmetric – founded on research, aim to seek behaviour change, can be manipulative.

- Two-way symmetric – held to be the most ethical, sophisticated and far-reaching in that there are dialogue, negotiation and compromise to try to achieve understanding.

This research project, therefore, was exceedingly ambitious in seeking to recognise and verify the existence of such styles and relationships in the context of PR practices in the UK. It also faced potential barriers of cultural misunderstanding, based as it was in an unfamiliar area of analysis. Degree-level courses in PR, which have progressed from the practical to the academic, have only been running at UK universities for the past few years. Graduates with knowledge of Grunig and Hunt's and others key theories are only beginning to percolate into a few PR consultancies and in-house departments. The majority of PR people have only a general degree or CAMS certificate or are promoted from secretaries and assistants. Grunig and Hunt's model is, however, seminal to judging PR as either a craft, using technician-level thinking, or as something one could rightly call a profession. Because the terminology of the study was not familiar to many people it was decided that semi-structured interviews would be the best mode of approach in order to overcome these barriers by providing interpretation and clarification as necessary.

However, the selection of interview subjects posed equal problems:

- there were time constraints to this research project;

- PR practitioners interact with all the media, using slightly different techniques with each;

- PR consultancies in certain locations such as London practise internationally and at a higher level of sophistication than others;

▶

- Tunstall's (1972) important work on journalistic practice in the UK indicated there were great differences too in the standards and approach of journalists working for different specialist areas.

The decision was taken to concentrate the first part of the research on newspaper journalists and to follow this up with journalists from radio and television. The journalists would be drawn half from national publications in London and half from the regional press, and four different specialisms would be covered, namely general news, women's interest pages, business pages and political journalism. A major factor in this decision was Valerie's background in newspapers as well as in PR, since it was important that, in seeking out subjects, the interviewer could be seen to have a background that was relevant and credible.

The choice of specialisms was made for the following reasons. The news section receives the widest variety of PR news releases and personal contacts. The women's pages receive the most concentrated approaches from PR practitioners in the consumer goods areas. The business pages receive the most sophisticated forms of PR aimed at enhancing credibility, image and stock market standing of major firms. The political journalists receive the most intensive PR pressures of a governmental, party political and general lobby type.

The ideal targets to select, however, are rarely the simplest. The journalists who would best be able to illustrate the type and level of PR approaches they received would of necessity be working long anti-social hours, would have very busy and often unpredictable diaries, could frequently be protected by filter-style secretaries and might possibly self-select because of polarised views about PR practice.

It therefore took approximately eight months to make appointments with 25 journalists who constituted the right spectrum and balance – 25 who agreed to be interviewed out of some 120 contacted overall. However, a random element entered the selection, in that if a first phone call to a certain newspaper asking for a named person was unsuccessful, the caller would always ask whether a second name from that specialism was there, or, failing that, whether any of the journalists from an alternative specialism would be prepared to take the call. If a journalist agreed to help with the study, a confirmatory letter would be sent, and the appointment double checked.

The use of tape recorders during each interview did not prove an obstacle, since all of the subjects were well used to this interview format themselves and appeared quickly able to ignore a very discreet form of this technology. They were also promised anonymity.

In a pilot test interview it had been found that a broad approach to the topic – 'What do you consider to be the style of relationship between journalists and PR officers?' – worked best, followed by questions on what they perceived the role of PR practitioners to be. Many answers were reflected back to test understanding and to clarify what the journalists felt to be the most important factors of certain interactive processes between them and PR practitioners. However, the most successful ingredient of all was the critical incident technique: in recounting what they felt to be the best and the worst examples of treatment by PR practitioners they had experienced, the journalists usually became much more expansive and revealing. These questions were posed at a later stage in the meeting when some rapport had been established and often acted as a corrective to one or two somewhat guarded initial statements.

Both the interviewer and interviewees appreciated the dangers of generalising from the particular. Yet it was easier than Valerie had expected to delineate differences between reported approaches of PR practitioners as press agents and those who had a more sophisticated and more long-term approach to the building of positive media coverage and relationships. In the majority of cases it was the journalists who volunteered the information about when and how far they had ever felt in the position of being manipulated by PR practitioners. However, those few who had to be asked whether they had ever had this experience were not resentful of the implication and appeared to accept the existence of manipulative practice as a recognised by-product of PR.

References

Grunig, J. and Hunt, T. (1984) *Managing Public Relations*, New York, Reinhart and Winston.

Tunstall, J. (1972) 'News organisation goals and specialist news gathering journalists', *in* McQuail, D., *Sociology of Mass Communications*, London, Penguin , pp. 259–80.

Questions

1   What are the strengths of the design of this research project? Give reasons for your answer.

2   What are the weaknesses of the design of this research project? Give reasons for your answer. How would you seek to overcome them?

3   What reasons would you advance for using semi-structured or in-depth interviews in relation to this research project?

4   What data quality issues are evident in relation to the conduct of this research project?

5   How were these data quality issues managed during the period of the research project referred to above?

6   What logistical and resource issues are associated with the research project and what are the implications of these for its conduct?

Self check   **Answers**

9.1 The type of interview that is likely to be used in each of these situations is:

a   a standardised and structured interview where the aim is to develop response patterns from the views of people. The interview schedule might be designed to combine styles so that comments made by interviewees in relation to specific questions could also be recorded;

b the situation outlined suggests an exploratory approach to research and therefore an in-depth interview would be most appropriate;

c the situation outlined here suggests that an explanatory approach is required in relation to the data collected and in this case a semi-structured interview is likely to be appropriate.

9.2 Reasons that suggest the use of interviews include:

- the exploratory or explanatory nature of your research;
- situations where it will be significant to establish personal contact, in relation to interviewee sensitivity about the nature of the information to be provided and the use to be made of this;
- situations where the researcher needs to exercise control over the nature of those who supply data;
- situations where there are a large number of questions to be answered;
- situations where questions are complex or open ended;
- situations where the order and logic of questioning may need to be varied.

9.3 Certainly politely! Your response needs to show that you are aware of the issues relating to reliability, bias and generalisability which might arise. It would be useful to discuss how these might be overcome through the following: the design of the research; the keeping of records or a diary in relation to the processes and key incidents of the research project as well as the recording of data collected; attempts to control bias through the process of collecting data; the relationship of the research to theory.

9.4 Perhaps it will be wise to say that you understand his position. You realise that any approach to research calls for particular types of competence. Your previous answer touching on interviewee bias has highlighted the need to establish credibility and to gain the interviewee's confidence. While competence will need to be developed over a period of time, allowing for any classroom simulations and dry runs with colleagues, probably the best approach will be your level of preparation before embarking on interview work. This relates firstly to the nature of the approach made to those whom you would like to participate in the research project and the information supplied to them, secondly to your intellectual preparation related to the topic to be explored and the particular context of the organisations participating in the research and thirdly to your ability to conduct an interview. You also recognise that piloting the interview themes will be a crucial element in building your competence.

9.5 Key issues to consider include the following:

- planning to minimise the occurrence of forms of bias where these are within your control, related to interviewer bias, interviewee bias and sampling bias;
- considering your aim in requesting the research interview and how you can seek to prepare yourself in order to gain access to the data that you hope your participants will be able to share with you;
- devising interview themes which you wish to explore or seek explanations for during the interview;
- sending a list of your interview themes to your interviewee prior to the interview, where this is considered appropriate;

- requesting permission and providing a reason where you would like to use a tape recorder during the interview;

- making sure that your level of preparation and knowledge (in relation to the research context and your research question and objectives) is satisfactory in order to establish your credibility when you meet your interviewee;

- considering how your intended appearance during the interview will affect the willingness of the interviewee to share data.

9.6 There are several areas where you need to develop and demonstrate competence in relation to the conduct of semi-structured and in-depth research interviews. These areas are:

- opening the interview;
- using appropriate language;
- questioning;
- listening;
- testing and summarising understanding;
- behavioural cues;
- recording data.

10 Collecting primary data using questionnaires

By the end of this chapter you should:

- understand the advantages and disadvantages of questionnaires as a data collection method;
- be aware of a range of self-administered and interviewer-administered questionnaires;
- be aware of the possible need to combine techniques within a research project;
- be able to select and justify the use of appropriate questionnaire techniques for a variety of research scenarios;
- be able to design, pilot and administer a questionnaire to answer research questions and to meet objectives;
- be able to take appropriate action to enhance response rates and to ensure the validity and reliability of the data collected;
- be able to apply the knowledge, skills and understanding gained to your own research project.

10.1 Introduction

The greatest use of questionnaires is made by the survey strategy (Section 4.2). However, both experiment and case study research strategies can make use of these techniques. There are various definitions of the term questionnaire (Oppenheim, 1992). Some authors (for example Kervin, 1999) reserve it exclusively for surveys where the person answering the question actually records their own answers. Others (for example Bell, 1999) use it as a more general term to include interviews that are administered either face to face or by telephone.

In this book we use *questionnaire* as a general term to include all techniques of data collection in which each person is asked to respond to the same set of questions in a predetermined order (deVaus, 1996). It therefore includes both structured interviews and telephone questionnaires as well as those in which the questions are answered without an interviewer being present. The range of techniques which fall under this broad heading are outlined in the next section (10.2), along with their relative advantages and disadvantages.

The use of questionnaires is discussed in many research methods texts. These range from those which devote a few pages to those which specify precisely how you should construct and use them such as Dillman's (1978) *total design method*. Perhaps not surprisingly, the questionnaire is one of the most widely used survey data collection techniques. Because each person (*respondent*) is asked to respond to the same set of questions, it provides an efficient way of collecting responses from a large sample prior to quantitative analysis (Chapter 11). However, before you decide to use a questionnaire we would like to include a note of caution. Many authors (for example Bell, 1999; Oppenheim, 1992) argue that it is far harder to produce a good questionnaire than you might think. You need to ensure that it will collect the precise data that you require to answer your research question(s) and achieve your objectives. This is of paramount importance as you are unlikely to be able to go back to people and to collect additional data using another questionnaire. These issues are discussed in Section 10.3.

The design of your questionnaire will affect the response rate and the reliability and validity of the data you collect. Response rates, validity and reliability can be maximised by:

■ careful design of individual questions;

■ clear layout of the questionnaire form;

■ lucid explanation of the purpose of the questionnaire;

■ and pilot testing.

Together these form Section 10.4 in which we discuss designing your survey. Administering the actual questionnaire is considered in Section 10.5 along with actions to help ensure high response rates.

10.2 An overview of questionnaire techniques

When to use questionnaires

We have found that many people use a questionnaire to collect data without considering other methods such as examination of secondary sources (Chapter 7), observation (Chapter 8), semi-structured or in-depth interviews (Chapter 9). Our advice is to evaluate all possible data collection methods and to choose those most appropriate to your research question(s) and objectives. Questionnaires are not particularly good for exploratory or other research that requires large numbers of open-ended questions (Sections 9.2 and 9.3). They work best with standardised questions which you can be confident will be interpreted the same way by all respondents (Robson, 1993).

Questionnaires can therefore be used for descriptive or explanatory research. *Descriptive research,* such as that undertaken using attitude and opinion questionnaires and questionnaires of organisational practices, will enable you to identify and describe the variability in different phenomena. In contrast, *explanatory* or *analytical research* will enable you to examine and explain relationships between variables, in particular cause-and-effect relationships. These two purposes have different research design requirements (Gill and Johnson, 1997) which we will discuss later (Section 10.3).

Although questionnaires may be used as the only data collection method, it is usually better to link them with other methods in a *multi-method* approach (Chapter 4, Section 4.3). For example, a questionnaire to discover customers' attitudes can be complemented by in-depth interviews to explore and understand these attitudes (Chapter 9, Section 9.3). In addition questionnaires, if worded correctly, normally require less skill and sensitivity to administer than semi-structured or in-depth interviews (Jankowicz, 1995).

Types of questionnaire

The design of a questionnaire differs according to how it is administered, in particular the amount of contact you have with the respondents (Fig 10.1). *Self-administered questionnaires* are usually completed by the respondents. Such questionnaires are delivered and returned electronically using either email or the Internet (*on-line questionnaires*), posted to respondents who return them by post after completion (*postal* or *mail questionnaires*) or delivered by hand to each respondent and collected later (*delivery and collection questionnaires*). Responses to *interviewer-administered questionnaires* are recorded by the interviewer on the basis of each respondent's answers. A growing number of surveys, particularly in the area of market research, contact respondents and administer questionnaires using the telephone. These are known as *telephone questionnaires*. The final category, *structured interviews* (sometimes known as *interview schedules*), refers to those questionnaires where interviewers physically meet respondents and ask the questions face to face. These differ from semi-structured and in-depth interviews (Chapter 9, Section 9.2), as there is a defined schedule of questions from which interviewers should not deviate.

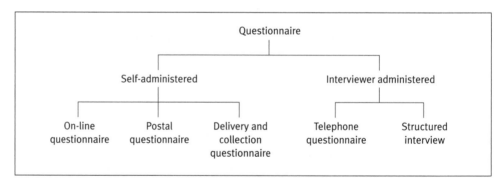

Fig 10.1 **Types of questionnaire**

The choice of questionnaire

Your choice of questionnaire will be influenced by a variety of factors related to your research question(s) and objectives (Table 10.1), in particular the:

- characteristics of the respondents from which you wish to collect data;
- importance of reaching a particular person as respondent;

- importance of respondents' answers not being contaminated or distorted;
- size of sample you require for your analysis, taking into account the likely response rate;
- types of questions you need to ask to collect your data;
- number of questions you need to ask to collect your data.

These factors will not apply equally to your choice of questionnaire, and for some research questions or objectives may not apply at all. The type of questionnaire you choose will dictate how sure you can be that the respondent is the person whom you wish to answer the questions and thus the reliability of responses (Table 10.1). Even if you address a postal questionnaire to a company manager by name, you have no way of ensuring that she or he will be the respondent. Her/his assistant or someone else could complete it! Email offers greater control because most users read and respond to their own mail at their personal computer (Witmer *et al.*, 1999). With delivery and collection questionnaires, you can sometimes check who has answered the questions at collection. By contrast, interviewer-administered questionnaires enable you to ensure that the respondent is whom you want. This improves the reliability of your data. In addition you can record who were non-respondents, thereby avoiding unknown bias caused by refusals.

Any *contamination* of respondents' answers will reduce your data's reliability (Table 10.1). Sometimes, if they have insufficient knowledge or experience they may deliberately guess at the answer, a tendency known as *uninformed response*. This is particularly likely when the questionnaire has been incentivised (Section 10.5). Respondents to self-administered questionnaires are relatively unlikely to answer to please you or because they believe certain responses are more *socially desirable* (Dillman, 1978). They may, however, discuss their answers with others, thereby contaminating their response. Respondents to telephone questionnaires and structured interviews are more likely to answer to please owing to contact with you, although the impact of this can be minimised by good interviewing technique (Section 9.5). Responses can also be contaminated or distorted when recorded. In extreme instances, interviewers may invent responses. For this reason, random checks of interviewers are often made by survey organisations.

The type of questionnaire you choose will affect the number of people who respond (Section 6.2). Interviewer-administered questionnaires will usually have a higher response rate than self-administered questionnaires (Table 10.1). The size of your sample and the way in which it is selected will have implications for the confidence you can have in your data and the extent to which you can generalise (Section 6.2).

Longer questionnaires are best presented as a structured interview. In addition, they can include more complicated questions than telephone questionnaires or self-administered questionnaires (Oppenheim, 1992). The presence of an interviewer means that it is also easier to route different sub-groups of respondents to answer different questions using a filter question (Section 10.4). The suitability of different types of question also differs between techniques.

Your choice of questionnaire will also be affected by the resources you have available (Table 10.1), in particular the:

Table 10.1 Main attributes of questionnaires

Attribute	On line	Postal	Delivery and collection	Telephone	Structured interview
Population's characteristics for which suitable	Literate individuals who can be contacted by email or Internet	Literate individuals who can be contacted by post; selected by name, household or organisation etc.		Individuals who can be telephoned; selected by name, household or organisation etc.	Any; selected by name, household, organisation, in the street etc.
Confidence that right person has responded	High if using email	Low	Low but can be checked at collection	High	
Likelihood of contamination or distortion of respondent's answer	Low	May be contaminated by consultation with others		Occasionally distorted or invented by interviewer	Occasionally contaminated by consultation or distorted/invented by interviewer
Size of sample	Large, can be geographically dispersed		Dependent on number of field workers	Dependent on number of interviewers	
Likely response rate*	Variable, 30% reasonable within organisations, Internet 10% or lower	Variable, 30% reasonable	Moderately high, 30–50% reasonable	High, 50–70% reasonable	
Feasible length of questionnaire	Conflicting advice; however, fewer 'screens' probably better	6–8 A4 pages		Up to half an hour	Variable depending on location
Suitable types of question	Closed questions but not too complex, complicated sequencing fine if uses IT, must be of interest to respondent	Closed questions but not too complex, only simple sequencing, must be of interest to respondent		Open and closed questions, but only simple questions, complicated sequencing fine	Open and closed questions, including complicated questions, complicated sequencing fine
Time taken to complete collection	2–6 weeks from distribution (dependent on number of follow ups)	4–8 weeks from posting (dependent on number of follow ups)	Dependent on sample size, number of field workers etc.	Dependent on sample size, number of interviewers etc but slower than self-administered for same sample size	
Main financial resource implications	World wide web page design	Outward and return postage, photocopying, clerical support, data entry	Field workers, travel, photocopying, clerical support, data entry	Interviewers, telephone calls, clerical support. Photo-copying and data entry if not using CATI$. Programming, software and computers if using CATI	Interviewers, travel, clerical support. Photocopying and data entry if not using CAPI£. Programming, software and computers if using CAPI
Role of the interviewer/field worker	None		Delivery and collection of questionnaires, enhancing respondent participation	Enhancing respondent participation, guiding the respondent through the questionnaire, answering respondents' questions	
Data input#	May be automated	Closed questions can be designed so that responses can be entered using optical mark readers after questionnaire has been returned		Response to all questions entered at time of collection using CATI$	Response to all questions can be can be entered at time of collection using CAPI£

*Discussed in Chapter 6 #Discussed in Section 11.2 $Computer-aided telephone interviewing £Computer-aided personal interviewing
Sources: Authors' experience; Dillman, 1978; Oppenheim, 1992; deVaus, 1996; Witmer et al., 1999

- time available to complete the data collection;
- financial implications of data collection and entry;
- availability of interviewers and field workers to assist;
- ease of automating data entry.

Time needed for data collection increases markedly for delivery and collection questionnaires and structured interviews where the samples are geographically dispersed (Table 10.1). One way you can overcome this constraint is to select your sample using cluster sampling (Section 6.2). Unless *computer-aided personal interviewing (CAPI)* or *computer-aided telephone interviewing (CATI)* is used you will need to consider the costs of reproducing the questionnaire, clerical support and entering the data for computer analysis. For postal and telephone questionnaires, costs estimates for postage and telephone calls will need to be included. If you are working for an organisation postage costs may be reduced by using *freepost* for questionnaire return. This means that you pay only postage and a small handling charge for those questionnaires that are returned by post. However, use of freepost rather than a stamp may adversely affect your response rates (see Table 10.7).

Virtually all data collected by questionnaires will be analysed by computer. Some packages (for example 'Snap' and 'SphinxSurvey') allow you both to design your questionnaire and to enter and analyse the data within the same software. Once your data have been coded and entered into the computer you will be able to explore and analyse them far more quickly and thoroughly than by hand (Section 11.2). As a rough rule, you should analyse questionnaire data by computer if they have been collected from 30 or more respondents. For larger surveys, you may wish to automate the input of data. For self-administered questionnaires, this can be done for closed questions where respondents select and mark their answer from a prescribed list.

Worked example

Closed question designed for an optical mark reader

The following question is typical of those used for large-scale market research. Similar questions can be found in many postal questionnaires. Respondents are given clear instructions on how to mark their responses on the questionnaire:

Please use a pencil to mark your answer as a solid box like this: [▬]
If you make a mistake use an eraser to rub out your answer.

1 Please mark all the types of music which you regularly listen to:		
	Pop/Rock	[ ]
	Reggae	[ ]
	New Age	[ ]
	Jazz	[ ]
	Classical	[ ]
	Easy listening	[ ]
	Other	[ ]
	(please describe):	

....

The mark is read using an *optical mark reader* which recognises and converts marks into data at rates often exceeding 200 pages a minute. Data for interviewer-administered questionnaires can be entered directly into the computer at the time of interview using CATI or CAPI software. With both types of software you read the questions to the respondent from the screen and enter their answers directly into the computer. Because of the costs of computers, software and pre-survey programming, CATI and CAPI are only financially viable for very large surveys or where repeated use of the computers and software will be made.

In reality, you are almost certain to have to make compromises in your choice of questionnaire. These will be unique to your research. This is emphasised by Salant and Dillman (1994). They argue that the question of which type of questionnaire is most suitable cannot be answered in isolation from your research question(s) and objectives and the population that you are surveying.

10.3   Deciding what data need to be collected

Research design requirements

Unlike in-depth and semi-structured interviews (Chapter 9), the questions you ask in questionnaires need to be defined precisely prior to data collection. Whereas you can prompt and explore issues further with in-depth and semi-structured interviews, this will not be possible for questionnaires. In addition, the questionnaire offers only one chance to collect the data, as it is often difficult to identify respondents or to return to collect additional information. This means that the time you spend planning precisely what data you need to collect, how you intend to analyse them (Chapter 11) and designing your questionnaire to meet these requirements is crucial if you are to answer your research question(s) and to meet your objectives.

For most management and business research, the data you collect using questionnaires will be used for either descriptive or explanatory purposes. For questions where the main purpose is to describe the population's characteristics either at a fixed time or at a series of times to enable comparisons, you will normally need to administer your questionnaire to a sample. The sample needs to be as representative and accurate as possible where it will be used to generalise about the total population (Sections 6.1–6.3). You will also probably need to relate your findings to earlier research. It is therefore important that you select the appropriate characteristics to answer your research question(s) and to address your objectives. You therefore need to have:

- reviewed the literature carefully;
- discussed your ideas with colleagues, your project tutor and other interested parties.

For research involving organisations, we have found it essential to understand the organisations in which we are undertaking the research. Without this it is easy to make mistakes, such as using the wrong terminology, and to collect useless data. For many research projects, an understanding of relevant organisations can be achieved through browsing company publications or their Internet sites (Section 7.3), observation (Chapter 8) and in-depth and semi-structured interviews (Chapter 9).

Explanatory research requires data to test a theory or theories. This means that, in addition to those issues raised for descriptive research, you need to define the theories you wish to test as relationships between variables prior to designing your questionnaire. You therefore need to have reviewed the literature carefully, discussed your ideas widely and conceptualised your own research clearly prior to designing your questionnaire (Ghauri *et al.*, 1995). In particular you need to be clear about which:

- relationships you think are likely to exist between variables;
- variables are *dependent*, that is change in response to changes in other variables;
- variables are *independent*, that is cause changes in dependent variables;
- variables are *extraneous*, that is might also cause changes in dependent variables thereby providing an alternative explanation to your independent variables.

Worked example

Defining theories in terms of relationships between variables

As part of her research Han wished to test the theory that the incidence of repetitive strain injury (RSI) was linked to the number of rest periods that keyboard operators took each working day.

The relationship that was thought to exist between the variables was that the incidence of RSI was higher when fewer or no rest periods were taken each day. The dependent variable was the incidence of RSI and the independent variable was the number of rest periods taken each day. Han thought that extraneous variables such as the use of proper seating and wrist rests might also influence the incidence of RSI. Data were therefore collected on these variables as well.

As these relationships are likely to be tested through statistical analysis (Section 11.5) of the data collected by your questionnaire you need to be clear about the way they will be measured at the design stage. Where possible you should ensure that measures are compatible with those used in other relevant research so that comparisons can be made (Section 11.2).

Types of variable

Dillman (1978) has grouped the sorts of data that can be collected through questionnaires into four distinct types of variable:

- attitude;
- belief;
- behaviour;
- attribute.

These distinctions are important, as they will influence the way your questions are worded. *Attitude* variables record how respondents feel about something. They differ from those about *belief* variables which record what respondents think or believe is true or false. Consequently questions about belief should imply neither good nor bad, only an assessment of what the respondent thinks. Although these two sorts of data can appear similar, it is important to specify precisely which you need to ensure your questions collect the data you need.

In contrast, data on behaviours and attributes are more straightforward to collect (Robson, 1993). When recording what respondents do, you are recording their *behaviour*. This differs from respondents' beliefs because you are recording a concrete experience. Behavioural variables contain data on what people (or their organisations) did in the past, do now or will do in the future. By contrast, *attribute* variables contain data about the respondents' characteristics. Attributes are best thought of as things a respondent possesses, rather than things a respondent does (Dillman, 1978). They are used to explore how attitudes, beliefs and behaviour differ between respondents as well as to check that the data collected are representative of the total population (Section 6.2). Attributes include characteristics such as age, gender, marital status, education, occupation and income.

Worked example

Attitude, belief, behaviour and attribute questions

You have been asked to undertake an anonymous survey of financial advisors' ethical values. In particular your sponsors are interested in the advice given to clients. After some deliberation you come up with three questions that address the issue of putting clients' interests before their own:

2 How do you feel about the following statement? 'Financial advisors should place their clients' interest before their own.'

	strongly agree	❑
	mildly agree	❑
(please tick the appropriate box)	neither agree or disagree	❑
	mildly disagree	❑
	strongly disagree	❑

3 In general, do financial advisors place their clients' interests before their own?

	always yes	❑
	usually yes	❑
(please tick the appropriate box)	sometimes yes	❑
	seldom yes	❑
	never yes	❑

4   How often do you place your clients' interests before your own?

	80–100% of my time	❑
	60–79% of my time	❑
(please tick the appropriate box)	40–59% of my time	❑
	20–39% of my time	❑
	0–19% of my time	❑

Your choice of question or questions to include in your questionnaire will depend on whether your need to collect data on financial advisors' attitudes, beliefs or behaviours. Question 2 is designed to collect data on respondents' attitudes to financial advisors placing their clients' interest before their own. It therefore asks respondents how they feel. In contrast, question 3 asks respondents whether financial advisors in general place their clients' interests before their own. It is therefore concerned with their individual beliefs. Question 4 focuses on how often the respondent actually places their clients' interests before their own. Unlike the previous questions it is concerned with their actual behaviour rather than what they believe or their attitudes.

To answer your research questions and to meet your objectives you also need to collect data to explore how ethical values differ between sub groupings of financial advisors. One theory you have is that ethical values are related to age. To test this you need to collect data on the attribute age. After further deliberation you come up with question 5:

5   How old are you?

	less than 30 years	❑
	30 to less than 40 years	❑
(please tick the appropriate box)	40 to less than 50 years	❑
	50 to less than 60 years	❑
	60 years or over	❑

Ensuring that essential data are collected

A problem experienced by many students and organisations we work with is how to ensure that the data collected will enable the research question(s) to be answered and the objectives achieved. Although no method is infallible, one way is to create a data requirements table (Table 10.2). This summarises the outcome of a process:

1   decide whether the main outcome of your research is descriptive or explanatory;

2   subdivide each research question or objective into more specific investigative questions about which you need to gather data;

3   repeat the second stage if you feel that the investigative questions are not sufficiently precise;

4 identify the variables about which you will need to collect data to answer each investigative question;

5 establish how to measure the data for each variable.

Table 10.2   **Data requirements table**

Research question/objective:			
Type of research:			
Investigative questions	Variable(s) required	Detail in which data measured	Check included in questionnaire✓

Investigative questions are the questions that you need to answer in order to address satisfactorily each research question and to meet each objective (Cooper and Schindler, 1998). They need to be generated with regard to your research question(s) and objectives. For some investigative questions you will need to subdivide your first attempt into more detailed investigative questions. For each you need to be clear whether you are interested in respondents' attitudes, beliefs, behaviour or attributes (discussed earlier) as what appears to be a need to collect one sort of variable frequently turns out to be a need for another (Salant and Dillman, 1994). We have found the literature review, discussions with interested parties and pilot studies to be of help here.

You then need to identify the variables about which you need to collect data to answer each investigative question and to decide the detail at which these are measured. Again, the review of the literature and associated research can suggest possibilities. However, if you are unsure about the detail needed you should measure at the more precise level. Although this is more time consuming, it will give you flexibility in your analyses. In these you will be able to use computer software to group or combine data (Section 11.2).

Once your table is complete, it must be checked to make sure that all data necessary to answer your investigative questions are included. When checking you need to be disciplined and to ensure that only data that are essential to answering your research question(s) and meeting your objectives are included. We added the final column to remind us to check that our questionnaire actually includes a question that collects the data!

10.4   Designing the questionnaire

The validity and reliability of the data you collect and the response rate you achieve depend, to a large extent, on the design of your questions, the structure of your questionnaire and the rigour of your pilot testing (all discussed in this section). A valid

Worked example

Data requirements table

Sarah was asked to discover staff attitudes to the possible introduction of a no smoking policy at her workplace. Discussion with senior management and colleagues and reading relevant literature helped her to firm up her objective and investigative questions. A selection of these is included in the extract from her table of data requirements:

Research question/objective: *To establish employees' attitudes to the possible introduction of a no-smoking policy at their workplace*			
Type of research: *Predominantly descriptive, although wish to examine differences between employees*			
Investigative questions	**Variable(s) required**	**Detail in which data measured**	**Check included in questionnaire ✓**
Do employees feel that they should be able to smoke in their office if they want to as a right? (attitude)	*Attitude of employee to smoking in their office as a right*	*Feel . . . should be allowed, should not be allowed, no strong feelings*	
Do employees feel that the employer should provide a smoking room for smokers if smoking in offices is banned? (attitude)	*Attitude of employee to the provision of a smoking room for smokers*	*Feel . . . very strongly that it should, quite strongly that it should, no strong opinions, quite strongly that it should not, very strongly that it should not*	
Would employees accept a smoking ban at work if the majority of people agreed to it? (behaviour)	*Likely behaviour of employee regarding the acceptance of a ban*	*Would . . . accept with no preconditions, accept if a smoking room was provided, not accept without additional conditions (specify conditions), would not accept whatever the conditions*	
Do employee attitudes differ depending on:	*(Attitude of employee – outlined above)*	*(Included above)*	
● age? (attribute) *● whether or not a smoker? (behaviour)*	*● Age of employee* *● Smoker*	*To nearest 5-year band (youngest 16, oldest 65)* *Non-smoker, smokes but not in office, smokes in office*	
How representative are the responses? (attributes)	*Age of employee* *Gender of employee* *Job*	*(Included above)* *Male, female* *Senior management, management, supervisory, other*	✓

question will enable accurate data to be collected while one which is reliable will mean that these data are collected consistently. Foddy (1994:17) discusses this in terms of the questions and answers making sense. In particular he emphasises that 'the question must be understood by the respondent in the way intended by the researcher and the answer given by the respondent must be understood by the researcher in the way intended by the respondent'. This means that there are at least four stages that must occur if the question is to be valid and reliable (Fig 10.2). It also means that the design stage is likely to involve you in substantial rewriting in order to ensure that the respondent decodes the question in the way you intended. We therefore recommend that you use a word processor or survey design software such as 'Snap' or 'SphinxSurvey'.

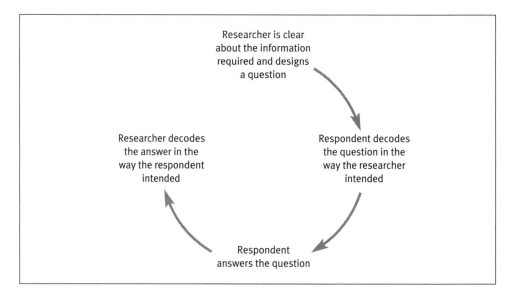

Fig 10.2 **Stages that must occur if a question is to be valid and reliable**
Source: Developed from Foddy, 1994

Designing individual questions

The design of each question should be determined by the data you need to collect (Section 10.3). When designing individual questions researchers do one of three things (Bourque and Clark, 1994):

- adopt questions used in other questionnaires;
- adapt questions used in other questionnaires;
- develop their own questions.

Adopting or adapting questions may be necessary if you wish to replicate, or to compare your findings with, another study. This can allow reliability to be assessed. It is also more efficient than developing your own questions provided that you can still collect the data you need to answer your research question(s) and to meet your objectives. Some survey design software includes questions that you may use. Alternatively, you may find questions and coding schemes that you feel will meet your needs in existing surveys or in *question banks* such as the ESRC's Question Bank.[1] However, before you adopt questions, beware! There are a vast number of poor questions in circulation, so always assess each question carefully. In addition, you need to check whether they are under copyright. If they are, you need to obtain the author's permission to use them. Even where there is no formal copyright you should note where you obtained the questions and give credit to their author.

Initially you only need to consider the type and wording of individual questions rather than the order that they will appear on the form. Clear wording of questions using terms that are likely to be familiar to, and understood by, respondents can improve the validity of the questionnaire. Most types of questionnaire include a combination of open and closed questions. *Open questions* allow respondents to give answers in their own way (Fink, 1995a). *Closed questions*, sometimes referred to as *close-ended questions* (Salant and Dillman, 1994), provide a number of alternative answers from which the respondent is instructed to choose (deVaus, 1996). The latter are usually quicker and easier to answer, as they require minimal writing. Responses are also easier to compare as they have been predetermined. However, if these responses cannot be easily interpreted then these benefits are, to say the least, marginal (Foddy, 1994). Youngman (1986, cited in Bell, 1999) identifies six types of closed questions that we discuss later:

- list where the respondent is offered a list of items, any of which may be selected;
- category where only one response can be selected from a given set of categories;
- ranking where the respondent is asked to place something in order;
- scale in which a scaling device is used to record responses;
- quantity to which the response is a number giving the amount;
- grid where responses to two or more questions can be recorded using the same matrix.

Prior to data analysis, you will need to group and code responses to each question. Detailed coding guidance is given in Section 11.2. You are strongly advised to read the entire chapter prior to designing your questions.

Open questions

Open questions are used widely in in-depth and semi-structured interviews (Section 9.5). In questionnaires they are useful if you are unsure of the response such as in exploratory research, when you require a detailed answer or when you want to find out what is uppermost in the respondent's mind. An example of an open question (from a self-administered questionnaire) is:

6 Please list up to **three** things you like about your job:

    1..

    2..

    3..

---

[1] The Internet address for the ESRC Question Bank is http://kennedy.soc.surrey.ac.uk/qb1/nav4/fr_home.htm

With open questions, the precise wording of the question and the amount of space partially determine the length and fullness of response. However, if you leave too much space the question becomes offputting. Question 6 collects data about what each respondent believes they like about their job. Thus if salary had been the reason uppermost in their mind this would probably have been recorded first. Unfortunately, for large-scale questionnaire surveys responses to open questions are extremely time consuming to code (Section 11.2). For this reason, it is usually advisable keep their use to a minimum.

List questions

List questions offer the respondent a list of responses any of which they can choose. Such questions are useful when you need to be sure that the respondent has considered all possible responses. However, the list of responses must be defined clearly and meaningfully to the respondent. For structured interviews, it is often helpful to present the respondent with a *prompt card* listing all responses. The response categories you can use vary widely and include 'yes/no', 'agree/disagree' and 'applies/does not apply' along with 'don't know' or 'not sure'. If you intend to use what you hope is a complete list you may wish to add a catch-all category of 'other'. This has been included in question 7 to illustrate this point although, in reality, the question does not contain a complete list of services.

7   Please tick ☑ the box in the provided column for services you provided as a home care assistant for this client in the past month.

   If you have not provided a particular service, please leave the box blank.

service	provided
cleaning rooms	☑
shopping	☑
bed making	☐
laundry	☐
other	☐

   (please describe:)...

Question 7 collects data on the behaviour of the home care assistant, in this instance the services he/she provided for a particular client. In this list question, the common practice of omitting negative response boxes has been adopted. Consequently, negative responses are inferred from each unmarked response. If you choose to do this, beware; non-response could also indicate uncertainty or, for some questions, that an item does not apply!

Category questions

In contrast, *category questions* are designed so that each respondent's answer can fit only one category. Such questions are particularly useful if you need to collect data about behaviour or attributes. The number of categories that you can include without affecting the accuracy of responses is dependent on the type of questionnaire. Self-administered questionnaires and telephone questionnaires should usually have no more than five response categories (Fink, 1995a). Structured interviews can have more categories provided that *prompt card* is used or, as in question 8, the interviewer categorises the responses.

8   How often do you visit this shopping centre?

Interviewer: listen to the respondent's answer and tick ☑ *as appropriate.*

☐ first visit   2 or more times a week ☑

☐ once a week   less than once a week to fortnightly ☐

☐ less than fortnightly to once a month   less often ☐

Worked example

Use of a prompt card as part of a structured interview

As part of a market research questionnaire, interviewers asked the following question:

Which of the following daily newspapers have you read during the past month?

Show respondent card 3 with the names of the newspapers. Read out names of the newspapers one at a time. Record their response with a ☑ *in the appropriate box.*

	read	not read	don't know
The Daily Telegraph	☐	☐	☐
The Times	☐	☐	☐
The Express	☐	☐	☐
The Sun	☐	☐	☐
The Mirror	☐	☐	☐
The Guardian	☐	☐	☐
Daily Mail	☐	☐	☐
Financial Times	☐	☐	☐
Star	☐	☐	☐

▶

Card 3 was given to the respondent prior to reading out newspaper names and collected back after the question had been completed:

3

The Daily Telegraph

THE TIMES

THE EXPRESS

The Sun

The Mirror

The **Guardian**

Daily Mail

FINANCIAL TIMES

Daily Star

You should arrange responses in a logical order so that it is easy to locate the response category that corresponds to each respondent's answer. Your categories should be *mutually exclusive* (not overlap) and cover all possible responses. The layout of your questionnaire should make it clear which boxes refer to which response category by placing them close to the appropriate text.

Ranking questions

A *ranking question* asks the respondent to place things in rank order. This means that you can discover their relative importance to the respondent. In question 9, taken from a postal questionnaire, the respondents are asked their beliefs about the relative importance of a series of features when choosing a new car. The catch-all feature of 'other' is included to allow respondents to add one other feature.

9 Please number each of the factors listed below in order of importance to you in your choice of a new car. Number the most important 1, the next 2 and so on. If a factor has no importance at all, please leave blank.

factor	importance
acceleration	⌷
boot size	⌷
depreciation	⌷
safety features	⌷
fuel economy	⌷
price	⌷
driving enjoyment	⌷
other	⌷

.... (⇦ please describe)

With such questions, you need to ensure that the instructions are clear and will be understood by the respondent. In general, respondents find that ranking more than seven or eight items takes too much effort so you should keep your list to this length or shorter (Kervin, 1999). Respondents can rank accurately only when they can see or remember all items. This can be overcome with face-to-face questionnaires by using prompt cards on which you list all of the features to be ranked. However, telephone questionnaires should only ask respondents to rank a maximum of three or four items, as the respondent will need to rely on their memory (Kervin, 1999).

Scale questions

Scale or *rating* questions are often used to collect attitude and belief data. The most common approach is the *Likert-style* rating scale in which you ask the respondent how strongly they agree or disagree with a statement or series of statements, usually on a four- or five-point scale. If you intend to use a series of statements, you should keep the same order of response categories to avoid confusing respondents (Kervin, 1999). You should, however, include both positive and negative statements so as to ensure that the respondent reads each one carefully and thinks about which box to tick.

10 For the following statement please tick ✔ the box which matches your view most closely.

	agree	tend to agree	tend to disagree	disagree
I feel that employees' views have influenced the decisions taken by management.	❏	❏	❏	❏

Question 10 has been taken from a delivery and collection questionnaire to employees in an organisation and is designed to collect attitude data. In this question, a four-point scale has been used to force the respondent to express their feelings towards an implicitly positive statement. By contrast question 11, also from a delivery and collection questionnaire, contains an implicitly negative statement and allows the respondent to 'sit on the fence' by ticking the 'not sure' category. The phrase 'not sure' is used here as it is less threatening to the respondent than admitting they do not know. This question is designed to collect data on what employees believe to be the situation now.

11 For the following statement please tick ✔ the box which matches your view most closely.

	agree	tend to agree	not sure	tend to disagree	disagree
I believe there are 'them and us' barriers to communication in the company *now*.	❏	❏	❏	❏	❏

You can expand this form of question further to record finer shades of attitudes and beliefs. However, respondents to telephone questionnaires find it difficult to distinguish between values on scales of more than a five points plus 'don't know'.

In question 12, the respondent's attitude is captured on a 10-point *numeric scale*. In such questions, it is important that the numbers reflect the feeling of the respondent. Thus, 1 reflects poor value for money and 10 good value for money. These end categories (and sometimes the middle) are labelled. As in this question, graphics may also be used to reflect the scale visually, thereby aiding the respondent's interpretation. An additional category of 'not sure' or don't know' can be added and should be slightly separated from the scale.

12 For the following statement please circle ◯ the number which matches your view most closely.

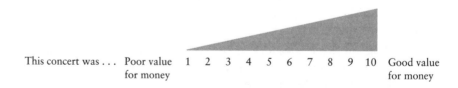

This concert was . . . Poor value for money   1 2 3 4 5 6 7 8 9 10   Good value for money

Another variation is the *semantic differential scale*. These are often used in consumer research to determine underlying attitudes. The respondent is asked to rate a single object or idea on a series of bi-polar scales. Each *bi-polar scale* is described by a pair of opposite adjectives (question 13) designed to capture respondents' attitudes towards service. For these scales, you should vary the position of positive and negative adjectives from left to right to reduce the tendency to read only the adjective on the left (Kervin, 1999).

13 On each of the lines below place a X to show how you feel about the service you received at our restaurant.

You can combine individual scaling questions to build a scale to measure a concept such as customers' loyalty. A detailed explanation of scaling techniques (including those by Likert, Guttman and Thurstone) can be found in Foddy (1994).

Quantity questions

Responses to *quantity questions* are a number, which gives the amount of a characteristic. For this reason, they tend to be used to collect behaviour or attribute data. A common quantity question, which collects attribute data, is:

14 What is your year of birth? | 1 | 9 | | |

(for example for 1974 write:) | 1 | 9 | 7 | 4 |

Because the data collected by this question could be entered into the computer without coding the question can also be termed a *self-coded* question.

Grid

A *grid* or *matrix* enables you to record the responses to two or more similar questions at the same time. The 1991 UK census form was designed using a matrix format. Questions were listed down the left-hand side of the page and each household member was listed across the top. The response to each question for each household member was then recorded in the cell where the row and column met. Although using a grid saves space, research cited by Collins and White (1995) suggests that respondents have difficulties comprehending these designs and that they are a barrier to response.

Question wording

The wording of each question will need careful consideration to ensure that the responses are valid, that is measure what you think they do. Your questions will need to be checked within the context for which they were written rather than in abstract. Given this, the checklist in Table 10.3 should help you to avoid the most obvious problems associated with wording which threaten the validity of responses.

Table 10.3	**Checklist for question wording**

✓ Does your question collect data at the right level of detail to answer your investigative question as specified in your data requirements table?

✓ Will respondents have the necessary knowledge to answer your question? A question on the implications of a piece of European Community legislation would yield meaningless answers from those who were unaware of that legislation.

✓ Does your question talk down to respondents? It should not!

✓ Are the words used in your question familiar and will all respondents understand them in the same way? In particular you should use simple words and avoid jargon, abbreviations and colloquialisms.

✓ Are there any words that sound similar and might be confused with those used in your question? This is a particular problem with interviewer-administered questionnaires.

✓ Are there any words in your question that might cause offence? These might result in biased responses or a lower response rate.

✓ Can your question be shortened? Long questions are often difficult to understand, especially in interviewer-administered questionnaires, as the respondent needs to remember the whole question. Consequently, they often result in no response at all.

✓ Are you asking more than one question at the same time? The question 'How often do you visit your mother and father?' contains two separate questions, one about each parent, so responses would probably be impossible to interpret.

✓ Does your question include a negative or double negative? Questions that include the word 'not' are sometimes difficult to understand. The question 'Would you rather not use a non-medicated shampoo?' is far easier to understand as 'Would you rather use a medicated shampoo?'

✓ Is your question unambiguous? This can arise from poor sentence structure, using words with several different meanings or having an unclear investigative question. If you ask 'When did you leave school?' some respondents might state the year, others might give their age, while those still in education might give the time of day! Ambiguity can also occur in category questions. If you ask employers how many employees they have on their payroll and categorise their answers into three groups (up to 100, 100–250, 250 plus) they will not be clear which group to choose if they have 100 or 250 employees.

✓ Does your question imply that a certain answer is correct? If it does the question is biased and will need to be reworded such as with the question 'Many people believe that too little money is spent on our Health Service. Do you believe this to be the case?' For this question, respondents are more likely to answer 'yes' to agree with and please the interviewer.

✓ Does your question prevent certain answers from being given? If it does the question is biased and will need to be reworded. The question 'Is this the first time you have pretended to be sick?' implies that the respondent has pretended to be sick whether they answer yes or no!

✓ Is your question likely to embarrass the respondent? If it is then you need either to reword it or to place it towards the end of the survey when you will, it is to be hoped, have gained the respondent's confidence. Questions on income can be asked as either precise amounts (more embarrassing) using a quantity question or income bands (less embarrassing) using a category question.

✓ Have you incorporated advice appropriate for your type of questionnaire (such as the maximum number of categories) outlined in the earlier discussion of question types?

✓ Are answers to closed questions written so that at least one will apply to every respondent?

✓ Are the instructions on how to record each answer clear?

Question coding

If you are planning to analyse your data by computer, they will need to be coded prior to entry. For quantity questions, actual numbers can be used as codes. For other questions, you will need to design a coding scheme. Whenever possible you should establish the coding scheme prior to collecting data and incorporate it into your questionnaire. This should take account of relevant existing coding schemes to enable comparisons with other data sets (Section 11.2).

For most closed questions, you should be able to add codes to response categories. These can be printed on the questionnaire thereby *pre-coding* the question and removing the need to code after data collection. Two ways of doing this are illustrated by questions 15 and 16, which collect data on the respondents' beliefs.

15 Is the service you receive?

	Excellent	Good	Reasonable	Poor	Awful
(please circle ◯ the number)	5	4	3	2	1

16 Is the service you receive?

	Excellent	Good	Reasonable	Poor	Awful
(please tick ✔ the box)	☐5	☐1	☐3	☐2	☐4

The codes allocated to response categories will affect your analyses. In question 15 an ordered scale of numbers has been allocated to adjacent responses. This will make it far easier to aggregate responses using a computer (Section 11.2) to 'satisfactory' (5, 4 or 3) and 'unsatisfactory' (2 or 1) compared with the codes in question 16. We therefore recommend that you do not allocate codes as in question 16.

For open questions, you will need to reserve space on your data collection form to code responses after data collection. Question 17 has been designed to collect attribute data in a sample survey of 5000 people. Theoretically there could be hundreds of possible responses and so sufficient spaces are left in the 'for Office use only' box.

17 In what country were you born? ....

for Office use only
☐☐☐

Open questions which generate lists of responses are likely to require more complex coding using either the multiple-response or the multiple-dichotomy method. These are discussed in Section 11.2 and we recommend that you read this prior to designing your questions.

Designing the survey form

The order and flow of questions

When constructing your questionnaire it is a good idea to spend time considering the order and flow of your questions. These should be logical to the respondent (and interviewer) rather than follow the order in your data requirements table (Table 10.2). To assist the flow of the survey it may be necessary to include *filter questions*. These identify those respondents for whom the following question or questions are not applicable, so they can skip those questions. You should beware of using more than two or three filter questions in self-administered questionnaires, as respondents tend to find having to skip questions annoying. Filter questions can also can be programmed into CAPI and CATI software so that skipped questions are never displayed on the screen and as a consequence never asked (Saris, 1994). In such situations, the respondent is unlikely to be aware of the questions that have been skipped. The following example uses the answer to question 18 to determine whether questions 19 to 23 will be answered. (Questions 18 and 19 both collect data on attributes.)

18 Are you currently registered as unemployed?   Yes ☐₁

No ☐₂

If 'no' go to question 24

19 How long have you been registered
   as unemployed? |__|__| years |__|__| months

(for example for no years and six months write:) |__| 0 | years |__| 6 | months

Where you need to introduce new topics, phrases such as 'the following questions refer to . . .' or 'I am now going to ask you about . . .' are useful. And when wording your questions, you should remember the particular population for whom your questionnaire is designed. For interviewer-administered questionnaires, you will have to include instructions for the interviewer. The checklist in Table 10.4 should help you to avoid the most obvious problems associated with question order and flow. For some questionnaires, the advice contained may be contradictory. Where this is the case, you need to decide what is most important for your particular population.

Table 10.4   **Checklist for question order**

✓   Are questions at the beginning of your questionnaire more straightforward and ones the respondent will enjoy answering? Questions about attributes and behaviours are usually more straightforward to answer than those collecting data on attitudes or beliefs.

Table 10.4   *Cont.*

✓ Are questions at the beginning of your questionnaire obviously relevant to the stated purpose of your questionnaire? For example, questions requesting contextual information may appear irrelevant.

✓ Are questions and topics that are more complex placed towards the middle of your questionnaire? By this stage most respondents should be completing the survey with confidence but not yet bored or tired.

✓ Are personal and sensitive questions towards the end of your questionnaire, and is their purpose clearly explained? On being asked these a respondent may refuse to answer; however, if they are at the end of an interviewer-administered questionnaire you will still have the rest of the data!

✓ Are filter questions and routeing instructions easy to follow so that there is a clear route through the questionnaire?

✓ (For interviewer-administered questionnaires) are instructions to the interviewer easy to follow?

✓ Are questions grouped into obvious sections which will make sense to the respondent?

✓ Have you re-examined the wording of each question and ensured it is consistent with the position in the questionnaire as well as the data you require?

Worked example

Introducing a series of scale questions in a telephone questionnaire

As part of a telephone questionnaire, you need to collect data on respondents' attitudes to motorway service stations. To do this you ask respondents to rate a series of statements on a Likert-type scale. Because the survey will be conducted by telephone the scale has been restricted to four categories: strongly agree, agree, disagree, strongly disagree.

In order to make the questionnaire easy for the interviewer to follow, instructions are in italics and the words that need to be read to the respondent in bold. An extract is given below:

Now I'm going to read you several statements. Please tell me whether you strongly agree, agree, disagree or strongly disagree with each.

Interviewer: read out statements 20 to 29 one at a time and after each ask . . .

Do you strongly agree, agree, disagree or strongly disagree?
Record respondent's response with a tick ✓

	strongly agree	agree	disagree	strongly disagree
20 I wish there were a greater number of service stations on motorways	□4	□3	□2	□1

21

The layout of the questionnaire

Layout is important for both self-administered and interviewer-administered question-naires. Interviewer-administered questionnaires should be designed to make reading questions and filling in responses easy. The layout of self-administered questionnaires should, in addition, be attractive to encourage the respondent to fill it in and to return it, while not appearing too long. However, where the choice is between an extra page and a cramped questionnaire the former is likely to be more acceptable to respondents (Salant and Dillman, 1994). Survey design and analysis software such as 'Snap' and 'SphinxSurvey' contain a series of style templates for typefaces, colours and page layout which are helpful in producing a professional-looking questionnaire more quickly (Mercator, 1999; Scolari Sage, 1999). For paper-based surveys, use of colour will increase the printing costs.

The length of your questionnaire will affect your response rate. deVaus (1996) argues that optimal length will depend on your population, your research question(s) and your objectives. The more specialised the population and the more relevant the topic the longer your questionnaire can be. Although the general rule is to keep ques-tionnaires as short as possible, we have found that for within-organisation self-administered questionnaires an optimal length is six to eight A4 pages. Telephone questionnaires can last up to half an hour, whereas structured interviews vary from only a few minutes in the street to far longer in a more comfortable environment (Section 9.6).

One way you can reduce length without reducing legibility is to record answers to questions with the same set of possible responses as a table. Usually you place questions in the rows and responses in the columns. Instructions on how to answer the question and column headings are given prior to the table and on each subsequent page as illus-trated by questions 22 and 23. These were designed to collect data on respondents' behaviour using a delivery and collection questionnaire.

For each of the following statements please tick the box which most closely matches your ex-perience . . .

	monthly	every 3 months	every 6 months	less often	never
22 I receive a company site newsletter . . .	☐	☐	☐	☐	☐
23 I receive other company publications . . .	☐	☐	☐	☐	☐

Table 10.5 summarises the most important layout issues as a checklist.

Table 10.5	**Checklist for questionnaire layout**

✓ (For self-administered questionnaires) do questions appear squashed on the page? This will put the respondent off reading it and reduce the response rate. Unfortunately, a thick questionnaire is equally off-putting!

✓ (For self-administered questionnaires) is the questionnaire going to be printed on good-quality paper? This will imply that the survey is important.

✓ (For self-administered questionnaires) is the questionnaire going to be printed on warm-pastel-coloured paper? Warm pastel shades such as yellow and pink generate more responses than cool colours such as green or blue. White is a good neutral colour but bright or fluorescent colours should be avoided.

✓ (For structured interviews) will the questions and instructions be printed on one side of the paper only? You will find it difficult to read the questions on back pages if you are using a questionnaire attached to a clipboard!

✓ Is your questionnaire easy to read? Questionnaires should be typed in 12 point or 10 point using a plain font. Excessively long and excessively short lines reduce legibility. Similarly, respondents find CAPITALS and *italics* more difficult to read.

✓ Is your questionnaire laid out in a format that respondents are accustomed to reading? Research has shown that many people skim-read questionnaires (Collins and White, 1995). Instructions that can be read one line at a time from left to right moving down the page are therefore more likely to be followed correctly.

Explaining the purpose of the questionnaire

The covering letter

Most self-administered questionnaires are accompanied by a *covering letter*, which explains the purpose of the survey. This is the first part of the questionnaire that a respondent should look at. Unfortunately some of your sample will ignore it, while others use it to decide whether to answer the accompanying questionnaire.

Research by Dillman (1978) and others has shown that the messages contained in a self-administered questionnaire's covering letter will affect the response rate. The results of this research are summarised in Table 10.6.

Table 10.6	**Structure of a covering letter**

Type of paper:	good quality, official letterhead, including telephone number
Maximum length of letter:	one side (12 point font size if possible)
Salutation:	use recipient's title and name (if possible)
First set of messages:	what research is about, why it is useful
Second set of messages:	why recipient is important, how long it will take to complete
Third set of messages:	promises of confidentiality or anonymity
Fourth set of messages:	how results will be used; token reward or charity donation for participation (if any)
Final set of messages:	whom to contact if have any queries
Closing remarks:	thank recipient for their help
Signature:	yours, by hand, in blue
Name and title:	yours including forename and surname

Source: Developed from Dillman, 1978

For some research projects, you may also send a letter prior to administering your questionnaire. This will be used by the respondent to decide whether to grant you access. Consequently, it is often the only opportunity you have to convince the respondent to participate in your research. Ways of ensuring this are discussed in Section 5.4.

Introducing the questionnaire

At the start of your questionnaire, you need to explain clearly and concisely why you want the respondent to complete the survey. Salant and Dillman (1994) argue that, to achieve as high a response rate as possible, this should be done on the first page of the questionnaire in addition to the covering letter. They suggest that in addition to a summary of the main messages in the covering letter (Table 10.6) you include a:

- clear unbiased title which conveys the topic of the questionnaire and makes it sound interesting;

- sub-title which conveys the research nature of the topic (optional);

- neutral graphic illustration or logo to add interest and to set the questionnaire apart (self-administered questionnaires).

In addition, it is helpful to include the return name and address at the end of the questionnaire.

Interviewer-administered questionnaires will require this information to be phrased as a short introduction which the interviewer can read to each respondent. A template for this (developed from deVaus, 1996:122) is given in the next paragraph:

> **Good morning / afternoon / evening. My name is (your name) from (your organisation). We are doing a research project to find out (brief description of purpose of the research). Your telephone number was drawn at random. The questions I need to ask will take about (number) minutes. If you have any queries, I will be happy to answer them. (Pause). Please can I ask you the questions now?**

Worked example

Introducing a self-administered questionnaire

Dave and Mark were researching which job attributes attracted people to junior non-manual vacancies in a local labour market. As part of this research, 10 local employers agreed to include a questionnaire with each job application form they sent to prospective applicants.

The employers requested that the introduction to the questionnaire emphasised that responses were confidential and would not be passed on to the employing organisation.

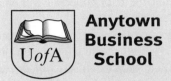

JOB SEEKER QUESTIONNAIRE

What influences your search for a job?

This survey is part of a research project to understand better what influences people such as you in your search for a job. Please answer the questions freely. You cannot be identified from the information you provide. The project is not attached to the employing organisation and your responses will not be given to that organisation.

ALL THE INFORMATION YOU PROVIDE WILL BE TREATED IN THE STRICTEST CONFIDENCE

The questionnaire should take you about five minutes to complete. Please answer the questions in the space provided. Try to complete the questions at a time when you are unlikely to be disturbed. Also, do not spend too long on any one question. Your first thoughts are usually your best!

Even if you feel the items covered may not apply directly to you in your search for a job please do not ignore them. Your answers are essential in building an accurate picture of what people find important when looking for a job.

WHEN YOU HAVE COMPLETED THE QUESTIONNAIRE PLEASE RETURN IT TO US IN THE ENCLOSED FREEPOST ENVELOPE

We hope you find completing the questionnaire enjoyable, and thank you for taking the time to help us. If you have any queries or would like further information about this project, please call us on 01234-5678910.

Thank you for your help.

David Dawson and Mark Saunders
Human Resource Management Research Centre
Anytown Business School
University of Anytown

Pilot testing and assessing validity

Prior to using your questionnaire to collect data it should be pilot tested. The purpose of the *pilot test* is to refine the questionnaire so that respondents will have no problems in answering the questions and there will be no problems in recording the data. In addition, it will enable you to obtain some assessment of the questions' validity and the likely reliability of the data that will be collected. Preliminary analysis using the pilot test data can be undertaken to ensure that the data collected will enable your investigative questions to be answered.

Initially you should ask an expert or group of experts to comment on the representativeness and suitability of your questions. As well as allowing suggestions to be made to the structure of your questionnaire, this will help establish *content validity* (Mitchell, 1996) and enable you to make necessary amendments prior to pilot testing with a group as similar as possible to the final population in your sample. For any research project there is a temptation to skip the pilot tests. We would endorse Bell's (1999:128) advice, 'however pressed for time you are, do your best to give the questionnaire a trial run', as, without a trial run, you have no way of knowing your questionnaire will succeed.

The number of people on whom you pilot your questionnaire and the number of pilot tests you conduct are dependent on your research question(s), your objectives, the size of your research project, the time and money resources you have available and how well you have initially designed your questionnaire. Very large questionnaire surveys such as national censuses will have numerous field trials starting with individual questions and working to larger and more rigorous pilots of later drafts.

For smaller-scale questionnaires, you are unlikely to have sufficient financial or time resources for such testing. However, it is still important that you pilot test your questionnaire. The number of people you choose should be sufficient to include any major variations in your population that you feel are likely to affect responses. For most questionnaires, this means that the minimum number for a pilot is 10 (Fink, 1995b). Occasionally you may be extremely pushed for time. In such instances, it is better to pilot test the questionnaire using friends or family than not at all! This will provide you with at least some idea of your questionnaire's *face validity,* that is whether the questionnaire appears to make sense.

As part of your pilot you should check each completed pilot questionnaire to ensure that respondents have had no problems understanding or answering questions and have followed all instructions correctly (Fink, 1995b). Their responses will provide you with an idea of the reliability of the questions. For self-administered questionnaires, additional information about problems can be obtained by giving respondents a further short questionnaire. Bell (1999) suggests you should use this to find out:

- how long the questionnaire took to complete;
- the clarity of instructions;
- which, if any, questions were unclear or ambiguous;
- which, if any, questions the respondent felt uneasy about answering;
- whether in their opinion there were any major topic omissions;
- whether the layout was clear and attractive;
- any other comments.

Interviewer-administered questionnaires need to be tested with the respondents for all these points other than layout. One way of doing this is to form an assessment as each questionnaire progresses. Another is to interview any interviewers you are employing. However, you can also check by asking the respondent additional questions at the end of their interview. In addition, you will need to pilot test the questionnaire with interviewers to discover whether:

- there are any questions for which visual aids should have been provided;
- they have difficulty in finding their way through the questionnaire;
- they are recording answers correctly.

Once you have completed pilot testing you should write to your respondents thanking them for their help.

Testing for reliability

As outlined at the start of this section the reliability of your questionnaire is concerned with the consistency of responses to your questions. Mitchell (1996) outlines three common approaches to assessing reliability, in addition to comparing the data collected with other data from a variety of sources. Although the analysis for each of these is undertaken after data collection, they need to be considered at the questionnaire design stage. They are:

- test re-test;
- internal consistency;
- alternative form.

Test re-test estimates of reliability are obtained by correlating data collected with those from the same questionnaire collected under as near equivalent conditions as possible. The questionnaire therefore needs to be administered twice to respondents. This may result in difficulties as it is often difficult to persuade respondents to answer the same questionnaire twice. In addition, the longer the time interval between the two questionnaires, the lower the likelihood that respondents will answer the same way. We therefore recommend that you only use this method as a supplement to other methods.

Internal consistency involves correlating the responses to each question in the questionnaire with those to other questions in the questionnaire. It therefore measures the consistency of responses across either all the questions or a sub-group of the questions from your questionnaire. There are a variety of methods for calculating internal consistency, of which one of the most frequently used is Cronbach's alpha. Further details of this and other approaches can be found in Mitchell (1996) and more advanced statistical analysis software manuals such as Norusis (1993).

The final approach to testing for reliability outlined by Mitchell (1996) is *alternative form*. This offers some sense of the reliability within your questionnaire through comparing responses to alternative forms of the same question or groups of questions. Where questions are included for this purpose, usually in longer questionnaires, they are often called *check questions*. However, it is often difficult to ensure that these questions are substantially equivalent. Respondents may suffer from fatigue owing to the need to increase the length of the questionnaire and they may spot the similar question and just refer back to their previous answer! It is therefore advisable to use check questions sparingly.

10.5   Administering the questionnaire

Once your questionnaire is designed, pilot tested and amended and your sample selected the questionnaire can be used to collect data. This final stage is called *administering* the questionnaire. As part of this, you will need to gain access to your sample (Sections 5.2 and 5.3) and to attempt to maximise the response rate. Jobber and O'Reilly (1996) review six techniques used in postal surveys that can raise response rates at this stage, provided that your questionnaire is clearly worded and well laid out. These are summarised in Table 10.7 and, although what happened in these experiments is no guarantee of similar success, the table does at least provide some indication of what you can do and the likely impact.

Table 10.7   **Techniques for raising questionnaire response rates**

Technique	Average impact	Comment
Prior notification, if possible by telephone	+19%	Personal contact raises the perceived importance of the study
Pre-paid monetary incentives	+ 15% to + 26% depending on amount	People feel more obliged to respond if they have received something, the incentive differentiates the questionnaire from others
Non-monetary incentives	+ 12% to +15% depending on incentive	Work for similar reasons to monetary incentives although some evidence suggests that these are not as effective
Stamps on return envelopes	+7%	Stamps raise the importance relative to freepost as the researcher has gone to the trouble of using a stamp
Anonymity	+20% (in company), +10% (external)	Worthwhile along with confidentiality, especially where sensitive information is sought
Follow-up questionnaires	+12%	This may be due to better timing than the first questionnaire, and the fact it raises the perceived importance of the study

Source: Developed from Jobber and O'Reilly, 1996

Which of these techniques you use to help to maximise responses will inevitably be dependent on the way in which your questionnaire is administered. It is the processes associated with administering each of the five types of questionnaire that we now consider.

On-line questionnaires

For on-line questionnaires, it is also important to have a clear timetable that identifies the tasks that need to be done and the resources that will be needed. A good response is dependent on the recipient being motivated to answer the questionnaire and to send it back. Although the covering letter (Section 10.4) and good design will help to ensure a high level of response, the actual administration process is also important.

On-line questionnaires are usually administered in one of two ways: via email or via a web site. The first of these uses email to 'post' and receive questionnaires and is dependent on having a list of addresses. While it is possible to obtain such lists from an Internet-based employment directory or via a search engine (Section 3.5), we would not recommend this approach. If you are considering using the Internet for research, you should abide by the general operating guidelines or *netiquette*. This includes not sending junk emails, often known as *spam*. Failure to do this is likely to result in 'few responses and a barrage of mail informing the researcher of their non-compliance' (Coomber, 1997:10). Despite this, questionnaires can be successfully administered by email within organisations provided that all of the sample have access to and use it. However, unless an anonymous server is used for returning questionnaires then respondents will be identifiable by their email addresses (Witmer *et al.*, 1999). If you choose to use email, we suggest that you:

1 contact recipients by email and advise them to expect a questionnaire – a *pre-survey contact* (Section 5.3);

2 email the questionnaire with a covering letter. For ease of response, the survey should be part of the email message rather than an attached file. You should make sure that this will arrive when recipients are likely to be receptive. For most organisations Fridays and days surrounding major public holidays have been shown to be a poor time;

3 email the *first follow-up* one week after emailing out the survey to all recipients. This should thank early respondents and remind non-respondents to answer (a copy of the survey can be included);

4 email the *second follow-up* to people who have not responded after three weeks. This should include another covering letter and a copy of the questionnaire. The covering letter should be reworded to further emphasise the importance of completing the questionnaire;

5 a *third follow-up* can also be used if time allows or your response rate is low.

Alternatively, the survey can be advertised on the Internet and respondents invited to access a web site and to fill in an on-line questionnaire. Adopting this approach observes netiquette and means that respondents can remain anonymous and, of equal importance, are unable to modify the questionnaire (Witmer *et al.*, 1999). The stages involved are:

1 ensure that a web site which explains the purpose of the research and how to complete the questionnaire has been set up (this takes the place of the covering letter);

2 ensure that the questionnaire has been set up on line and has a direct link (*hyperlink*) from the web site;

3 advertise the web site widely using a range of media (for example a banner advertisement on a page that is likely to be looked at by the target population);

4 when the respondent completes the questionnaire, ensure that it is sent automatically to your designated email address.

Response rates from such an approach are likely to be very low and there are considerable problems of non-response bias as the respondent has to take extra steps to locate and complete the questionnaire (Coomber, 1997). Consequently it is likely to be very difficult to obtain a representative sample from which you might generalise. This is not to say that this approach should not be used as it can, for example, enable you to contact difficult-to-access groups. It all depends, as you would expect us to say, on your research question and objectives!

Postal questionnaires

For postal questionnaires, it is also important to have a well-written covering letter and good design to help to ensure a high level of response. As with on-line questionnaires a clear timetable and well-executed administration process are important.

Our advice for postal questionnaires (developed from deVaus, 1996) can be split into six stages:

1 ensure that questionnaires and letters are printed, and envelopes addressed;

2 contact recipients by post, telephone or email and advise them to expect a questionnaire – a *pre-survey contact* (Section 5.3). This stage is often omitted for cost reasons;

3 post the survey with a covering letter and a return envelope (and fax cover sheet). You should make sure that this will arrive when recipients are likely to be receptive. For most organisations Fridays and days surrounding major public holidays have been shown to be a poor time;

4 post (or email) the *first follow-up* one week after posting out the survey to all recipients. For posted questionnaires this should take the form of a postcard designed to thank early respondents and to remind rather than to persuade non-respondents;

5 post the *second follow-up* to people who have not responded after three weeks. This should contain another copy of the questionnaire, a new return envelope and a new covering letter. The covering letter should be reworded to emphasise further the importance of completing the questionnaire. For anonymous questionnaires, a second follow-up will not be possible as you should not be able to tell who has responded!

6 a *third follow-up* can also be used if time allows or your response rate is low. For this it may be possible to use recorded delivery (post), telephone calls or even call in person to emphasise the importance of responding.

deVaus (1996) also advises placing a unique *identification number* on each questionnaire, which is recorded on your list of recipients. This makes it easy to check and follow-up non-respondents and, according to Salant and Dillman (1994) has little, if any, effect on response rates. However, identification numbers should not be used if you have assured respondents that their replies will be anonymous!

Delivery and collection questionnaires

The administration of delivery and collection questionnaires is very similar to that of postal questionnaires. However, you or field staff will deliver and call to collect the questionnaire. It is therefore important that your covering letter states when the questionnaire is likely to be collected. As with postal questionnaires follow-ups can be used, calling at a variety of times of day and on different days to try to catch the respondent.

A variation on this process which we have used widely in organisations allows for delivery and collection of questionnaires the same day and eliminates the need for a follow-up. The stages are:

1 ensure that all questionnaires and covering letters are printed and a collection box is ready;

2 contact respondents by internal post or telephone advising them to attend a meeting or one of a series of meetings to be held (preferably) in the organisation's time (Section 5.3);

3 at the meeting or meetings hand out the questionnaire with a covering letter to each respondent;

4 introduce the questionnaire and stress its anonymous or confidential nature;

5 ensure that respondents place their completed questionnaires in a collection box before they leave the meeting.

Although this adds to costs, as employees are completing the questionnaire in work time, response rates as high as 98 per cent are achievable!

Telephone questionnaires

The quality of data collected using telephone questionnaires will be affected by the researcher's competence to conduct interviews. These are discussed in Section 9.5. Once your sample has been selected, you need:

1 to ensure that all questionnaires are printed or, for CATI, that the software has been programmed and tested;

2 where possible and resources allow to contact respondents by post, email or telephone advising them to expect a telephone call (Section 5.3);

3 to telephone each respondent recording the date and time of call and whether or not the questionnaire was completed. You should note any specific times that have been arranged for callbacks. For calls that were not successful, you should note the reason such as no reply or telephone disconnected;

4 for unsuccessful calls where there was no reply to try three more times, each at a different time and on a different day and note the same information;

5 to make callback calls at the time arranged.

Structured interviews

Conducting structured interviews uses many of the skills required for in-depth and semi-structured interviews (Section 9.5). Issues such as interviewer appearance and preparedness are important and will affect the response rate (Section 9.4). However, once your sample has been selected you need:

1 to ensure that all questionnaires are printed or, for CAPI, that the software has been programmed and tested;

2 (for probability samples – Section 6.3) to contact respondents by post, email or telephone advising them to expect an interviewer to call within the next week (Section 5.3). This stage is often omitted for cost reasons;

3 (for large-scale surveys) to divide the sample into groups which are of a manageable size (50–100) for one interviewer;

4 to contact each respondent or potential respondent in person recording the date and time of contact and whether or not the interview was completed. You should note down any specific times that have been arranged for return visits. For contacts that were not successful, you should note down the reason;

5 (for probability samples) to try unsuccessful contacts at least twice more, each at a different time and on a different day and note down the same information;

6 to visit respondents at the times arranged for return visits.

10.6 Summary

- Questionnaires collect data by asking people to respond to exactly the same set of questions. They are often used as part of a survey strategy to collect descriptive and explanatory data about attitudes, beliefs, behaviours and attributes. Data collected are normally coded and analysed by computer.

- Your choice of questionnaire will be influenced by your research question(s) and objectives and the resources that you have available. The five main types are on line, postal, delivery and collection, telephone and interview schedule.

- Prior to designing a questionnaire, you must know precisely what data you need to collect to answer your research question(s) and to meet your objectives. One way of helping to ensure that you collect these data is to use a data requirements table.

- The validity and reliability of the data you collect and the response rate you achieve depend, largely, on the design of your questions, the structure of your questionnaire and the rigour of your pilot testing.

- When designing your questionnaire you should consider the wording of individual questions prior to the order in which they appear. Questions can be divided into open and closed. The six types of closed questions are list, category, ranking, scale, quantity and grid.

- Wherever possible closed questions should be pre-coded on your questionnaire to facilitate analysis.

- The order and flow of questions in the questionnaire should be logical to the respondent. This can be assisted by filter questions and linking phrases.

- The questionnaire should be laid out so it is easy to read and the responses are easy to fill in.

- Questionnaires must be introduced carefully to the respondent to ensure a high response rate. For self-administered questionnaires this should take the form of a covering letter; for interviewer-administered questions this will be done by the interviewer.

- All questionnaires should be pilot tested prior to collecting data to assess the validity and likely reliability of the questions.

- Administration of questionnaires needs to be appropriate to the type of questionnaire.

Self check ## Questions

10.1 In what circumstances would you choose to use a delivery and collection questionnaire rather than a postal questionnaire? Give reasons for your answer.

10.2 The following questions have been taken from a questionnaire about flexibility of labour.

    i   Do you agree or disagree with the use of nil hours contracts by employers?

        (please tick appropriate box)

        strongly agree ☐ 4
        agree ☐ 3
        disagree ☐ 2
        strongly disagree ☐ 1

    ii   Have you ever been employed on a nil hours contract?

        (please tick appropriate box)

        yes ☐ 1
        no ☐ 2
        not sure ☐ 3

    iii   What is your marital status?

        (please tick appropriate box)

        single ☐ 1
        married or living in long-term relationship ☐ 2
        widowed ☐ 3
        divorced ☐ 4
        other ☐ 5

        .... (⇐ please describe)

(continued overleaf)

iv   Please describe what you think would be the main impact on
      employees of a nil hours contract?

For each question identify:

a   the sort of data that are being collected;

b   the type of question.

You should give reasons for your answers.

10.3 You are undertaking research on the use of children's book clubs by householders. As
      part of this, you have already undertaken in-depth interviews with households who
      belong and do not belong to children's book clubs. This, along with a literature review,
      has suggested a number of investigative questions from which you start to construct a
      table of data requirements.

Research question/objective: *To establish householders' opinions about children's book clubs*			
Type of research: *Predominantly descriptive, although wish to explain differences between householders*			
Investigative questions	Variable(s) required	Detail in which data measured	Check included in questionnaire ✓	
a. *Do householders think that children's book clubs are a good or a bad idea?*				
b. *What things do householders like most about children's book clubs?*				
c. *Would householders be interested in an all-ages book club?*				
d. *How much do households spend on children's books a year?*				
e. *Do households' responses differ depending on:* i *number of children?* ii *whether already members of a children's book club?*				

a   For each investigative question listed, decide whether you will need to collect data
      on attitudes, beliefs, behaviours or attributes.

b   Complete the table of data requirements for each of the investigative questions
      already listed. (You may embellish the scenario to help in your choice of variables
      required and how the data will be measured as you feel necessary.)

10.4 Design pre-coded or self-coded questions to collect data for each of the investigative
      questions in self-check question 10.3. Note that you will need to answer self-check ques-
      tion 10.3 first (or use the answer at the end of this chapter).

10.5 You work for a major consumer research bureau that has been commissioned by 11 major UK companies to design and administer a telephone questionnaire. The purpose of this questionnaire is to describe and explain relationships between adult consumers' lifestyles, opinions and purchasing intentions. Write the introduction to this telephone questionnaire to be read by an interviewer to each respondent. You may embellish the scenario and include any other relevant information you wish.

10.6 You have been asked by a well-known national charity 'Work for All' to carry out research into the effects of long-term unemployment throughout the UK. The charity intends to use the findings of this research as part of a major campaign to highlight public awareness about the effects of long-term unemployment. The charity has drawn up a list of names and addresses of people who are or were long-term unemployed with whom they have had contact over the past six months. Write a covering letter to accompany the postal questionnaire. You may embellish the scenario and include any other relevant information you wish.

10.7 You have been asked to give a presentation to a group of managers at an oil exploration company to gain access to undertake your research. As part of the presentation, you outline your methodology that includes piloting the questionnaire. In the ensuing question and answer session one of the managers asks you to justify the need for a pilot study arguing that 'given the time constraints the pilot can be left out'. List the arguments that you would use to convince him that pilot testing is essential to your methodology.

Assignment 10

Using a questionnaire in your research

→ Return to your research question(s) and objectives. Decide on how appropriate it would be to use questionnaires as part of your research strategy. If you do decide that this is appropriate note down the reasons why you think it will be sensible to collect at least some of your data in this way. If you decide that using a questionnaire is not appropriate, justify your decision.

→ If you decide that using a questionnaire is appropriate re-read Chapter 6 on sampling and, in conjunction with this chapter, decide which of the five types of questionnaire will be most appropriate. Note down your choice of questionnaire and the reasons for this choice.

→ Construct a data requirements table and work out precisely what data you need to answer your investigative questions. Remember that you will need to relate your investigative questions and data requirements back to the literature you have reviewed and any preliminary research you have already undertaken.

→ Design the separate questions to collect the data specified in your data requirements table. Wherever possible try to use closed questions and to adhere to the suggestions in the question wording checklist. If you are intending to analyse your questionnaire by computer read Section 11.2 and pre-code questions on the questionnaire whenever possible.

→ Order your questions to make reading the questions and filling in the responses as logical as possible to the respondent. Wherever possible, try to adhere to the checklist for layout. Remember that interviewer-administered questionnaires will need instructions for the interviewer.

➡ Write the introduction to your question and where appropriate a covering letter.

➡ Pilot test your questionnaire with as similar a group as possible to the final group in your sample. Pay special attention to issues of validity and reliability.

➡ Administer your questionnaire and remember to send out a follow-up survey to non-respondents whenever possible.

References

Bell, J. (1999) *Doing Your Research Project* (3rd edn), Buckingham, Open University Press.

Bourque, L.B. and Clark, V.A. (1994) 'Processing data: the survey example', *in* Lewis-Beck, M.S., *Research Practice*, London, Sage, pp. 1–88.

Collins, D. and White, A. (1995) 'Making the next census form more respondent-friendly', *Social Survey Methodology Bulletin*, 37, July, 8–14.

Coomber, R. (1997) 'Using the Internet for survey research', *Sociological Research Online*, 2:2 (online)(cited 5 March 1999). Available from <URL:http://www.socresonline.org.uk/socresonline/2/2/2.html>

Cooper, D.R. and Schindler, D.A. (1998) *Business Research Methods* (6th edn), London, McGraw-Hill.

Dillman, D.A. (1978) *Mail and Telephone Surveys: the Total Design Method*, New York, Wiley.

Fink, A. (1995a) *How to Ask Survey Questions*, Thousand Oaks, CA, Sage.

Fink, A. (1995b) *The Survey Handbook*, Thousand Oaks, CA, Sage.

Foddy, W. (1994) *Constructing Questions for Interviews and Questionnaires*, Cambridge, Cambridge University Press.

Ghauri, P., Grønhaugh, K. and Kristianslund, I. (1995) *Research Methods in Business Studies: a Practical Guide*, London, Prentice Hall.

Gill, J. and Johnson, P. (1997) *Research Methods for Managers* (2nd edn), London, Paul Chapman.

Jankowicz, A.D. (1995) *Business Research Projects* (2nd edn), London, Chapman & Hall.

Jobber, D. and O'Reilly, D. (1996) 'Industrial mail surveys: techniques for inducing response', *Marketing & Intelligence Planning*, 14:1, 29–34.

Kervin, J.B. (1999) *Methods for Business Research* (2nd edn), Reading, MA, Addison-Wesley.

Mercator (1999) 'Mercator home page: products' (online)(cited 16 June 1999). Available from <URL:http://www.mercator.co.uk>

Mitchell, V. (1996) 'Assessing the reliability and validity of questionnaires: an empirical example', *Journal of Applied Management Studies*, 5:2 199–207.

Norusis, M.J. (1993) *SPSS for Windows Professional Statistics Release 6.0*, Chicago, IL, SPSS.

Oppenheim, A.N. (1992) *Questionnaire Design, Interviewing and Attitude Measurement* (new edn), London, Pinter.

Robson, C. (1993) *Real World Research*, Oxford, Blackwell.

Salant, P. and Dillman, D.A. (1994) *How to Conduct Your Own Survey*, New York, Wiley.

Saris, W.E. (1994) 'Computer-assisted interviewing', *in* Lewis-Beck, M.S., *Research Practice*, London, Sage, pp. 163–250.

Scolari Sage (1999) 'Research methodology and CD-ROMS' (online)(cited 16 June 1999). Available from <URL:http://www.scolari.co.uk>

deVaus, D.A. (1996) *Surveys in Social Research* (4th edn), London, UCL Press.

Witmer, D.F., Colman, R.W. and Katzman, S.L. (1999) 'From paper and pen to screen and keyboard: towards a methodology for survey research on the Internet', *in* Jones, S., *Doing Internet Research*, Thousand Oaks, CA, Sage, pp. 145–62.

Youngman, M.B. (1986) *Analysing Questionnaires*, Nottingham, University of Nottingham School of Education.

Further reading

Craig, P.B. (1991) 'Designing and using mail questionnaires', *in* Smith, N.C. and Dainty, P., *The Management Research Handbook*, London, Routledge, pp. 181–9. This chapter provides a useful discussion of realities of applying Dillman's total design method to management research.

Salant, P. and Dillman, D.A. (1994) *How to Conduct Your Own Survey,* New York, Wiley. Salant and Dillman's book contains a detailed discussion of how to design postal and telephone questionnaires and structured interviews to maximise response rates. It incorporates many of the ideas from Dillman's seminal work on the total design method.

Foddy, W. (1994) *Constructing Questions for Interviews and Questionnaires,* Cambridge, Cambridge University Press. This contains a wealth of information on framing questions including the use of scaling techniques.

deVaus, D.A. (1996) *Surveys in Social Research* (4th edn), London, UCL Press. Chapters 6 and 7 provide a detailed guide to constructing and administering questionnaires respectively.

Wass, V.J. (1994) 'Minimizing and managing bias in a mail survey: a study of redundant miners', *in* Wass, V.J. and Wells, P.E., *Principles and Practice in Business and Management Research*, Aldershot, Dartmouth, pp. 91–121. This offers an excellent discussion and provides a good case study of the issues of controlling for bias when using a postal questionnaire.

Witmer, D.F., Colman, R.W. and Katzman, S.L. (1999) 'From paper and pen to screen and keyboard: towards a methodology for survey research on the Internet', *in* Jones, S., *Doing Internet Research*, Thousand Oaks, CA, Sage, pp. 145–62. This gives a clear insight into the issues concerning on-line survey methodology.

Case 10 ### The provision of leisure activities for younger people in rural areas

A report from the chairperson of the 'vandalism working party' was the last item on the agenda of the Littlebury town council meeting. Following extensive consultation with representatives of the local population, the group concluded that boredom among the town's 'young people' was a major problem and undoubtedly a contributory factor to the unprecedented rise in vandalism.

A number of preliminary suggestions had been made of projects that might be of interest to young people within the town and help to combat the problem. However, the working party had agreed that, if they were really going to attract the support of the young people, they needed to have concrete information about what the young people wanted to see in the town. They believed that there was a need for a survey.

The chairperson reported that following contact with the business school of the local university, a leisure management undergraduate had expressed interest in carrying out a survey as part of her research project. She was interested in looking at the provision of leisure activities for young people in small rural towns and

▶

had met with him to discuss her preliminary ideas. They had agreed that a survey of the young people in Littlebury could be carried out and that its objectives would be:

- to find out what the town's young people did in their spare time;
- to establish what leisure activities they would like to have available in the town;
- to establish their potential interest in some of the ideas proposed by the working party;
- to compare leisure activities and preferences of different age groups.

The chairperson was able to report that funding such a survey would not be a problem as a group of local business people had agreed to support the costs of reproducing the questionnaires and sending them out. He concluded his report by seeking the council's agreement to proceed with the survey. There was unanimous support and the meeting closed on a very positive note.

The student decided to collect her data using a postal questionnaire. She designed the survey and pilot tested it on five members of the local youth club, all of whom thought that it was fine. (A copy of the questionnaire is included at the end of this case.) Four hundred questionnaires were sent out to young people aged 11–18 living in the town; 187 usable responses were returned. She attributed the relatively high response rate to the high profile given to the survey in the town's local paper.

The results indicated that there was very little support for the existing clubs and societies in the town, with the exception of the youth club and the leisure centre. Membership of the youth club was predominantly from inhabitants of two of the town's housing estates. However, it was not clear which activities held at the leisure centre were patronised by young people. Football and tennis were the most popular sporting activities in all age groups. Shopping and listening to pop music proved to be the most popular out of school pastimes for all ages, while the younger groups preferred to watch videos.

Of the ideas proposed by the working party, the coffee shop and swimming pool proved most popular overall, but especially among younger girls who accounted for 58 per cent of total responses. The younger boys said that the video games centre would be visited most frequently. Working respondents had a different pattern of response, suggesting that their interests were very different from their counterparts at school. Unfortunately these people made up less than 10 per cent of respondents and it was felt that more information was needed here. The answers to question 8 were hardly revolutionary and suggested that the best thing the town could do for all age groups was to attract some of the retail multiples to its high street and to open a night club!

Overall, the working party was disappointed by the results. Although there was a much clearer picture of what the town's young people did with their spare time, the group did not feel any closer to finding out what would capture their interest and reduce the boredom.

Littlebury Leisure Survey

Please answer all of the following questions by ticking the appropriate boxes

1 How often do you use the following in Littlebury:

	more than once a week	once a week	once a month	less than once a month	never
The leisure centre	☐	☐	☐	☐	☐
The youth centre	☐	☐	☐	☐	☐
The library	☐	☐	☐	☐	☐
Church	☐	☐	☐	☐	☐

2 Do you belong to any of the following:

Girl Guides	yes	☐	no	☐
The army cadets	yes	☐	no	☐
The air training corps	yes	☐	no	☐
The theatre club	yes	☐	no	☐
Boy Souts	yes	☐	no	☐
Youth club	yes	☐	no	☐

3 Which of the following sports you play regularly outside school:

Aerobics ☐	Badminton ☐	Basketball ☐	Boxing ☐
Cycling ☐	Cricket ☐	Football ☐	Gymnastics
☐ Riding ☐	Martial arts ☐	Rugby ☐	Self defense
☐ Swimming ☐	Sailing ☐	Table tennis ☐	Tennis ☐

Any other: please state which...

4 Do you belong to any other clubs or societies in Littlebury?

Please state which..
....

5 Which of the following do you do regularly?

Watch videos	☐	Listen to pop music	☐	Go to discos	☐
Play music	☐	Go shopping	☐	Voluntary work	☐

6 Please list up to 3 other things which you do regularly in your spare time

....

....

....

7 If the following were available in Littlebury, how often would you use them?

	more than once a week	once a week	once a month	less than once a month	never
Indoor swimming pool	☐	☐	☐	☐	☐
Drama club	☐	☐	☐	☐	☐
Coffee shop	☐	☐	☐	☐	☐
Video game centre	☐	☐	☐	☐	☐
Sailing club	☐	☐	☐	☐	☐
Karting club	☐	☐	☐	☐	☐

Any other: please state which

.... ☐   ☐   ☐   ☐   ☐

8 Please complete the following sentence:

'The one thing I would really like to be able to do Littlebury in my spare time is

.... ,

9 Please tell us about yourself:

How old are you?............................   Are you   male ☐ or female ☐?

If you're still at school, which school do you attend?...

If you've left school are you: employed full time   ☐
                                    employed part time   ☐
                                    not employed   ☐

10 Please tell us your postcode   GL__ _ _ _

Thank you very much for helping us. Please return this form as soon as possible in the envelope provided. If it reaches us by April 1st, you will be included in the draw for the first prize of £25.00! Good luck.

Questions

1 Why were the working party members 'disappointed with the results'?

2 **a** Design a table that shows which objective(s) are addressed by which questions.

  b What other questions would you include to help to ensure that the data collected could meet the working party's objectives more closely?

3 What other changes would you make to the questionnaire?

4 In what ways could the method used to pilot test the questionnaire be improved?

5 Do you think that a postal questionnaire was the best way of collecting these data?

(Give reasons for your answer.)

Selfcheck   ## Answers

10.1 When you:

- wanted to check that the person whom you wished to answer the questions had actually answered the questions;
- have sufficient resources to devote to delivery and collection and the geographical area over which the questionnaire is administered is small;
- can use field workers to enhance response rates. Delivery and collection questionnaires have a moderately high response rate of between 30 and 50 per cent compared with 30 per cent offered on average by a postal questionnaire;
- are administering a questionnaire to an organisation's employees and require a very high response rate. By administering the questionnaire to groups of employees in work time and collecting it on completion, response rates of up to 98 per cent can be achieved.

10.2 a i Attitude data: the question is asking how the respondent *feels* about the use of nil hours contracts by employees.

ii Behaviour data: the question is asking about the *concrete experience* of being employed on a nil hours contract.

iii Attribute data: the question is asking about the respondent's *characteristics*, in Dillman's (1978:83) phrase '*something they possess*'.

iv Belief data: the question is asking the respondent what they *think* or *believe* would be the impact on employees. It does not imply either good or bad.

b i Scale question using a Likert-type scale in which the respondent is asked how strongly she or he agrees or disagrees with the statement.

ii Category question in which the respondent's answer can fit only one answer.

iii Category question as before.

iv Open question in which the respondent can give her or his own answer in her or his own way.

10.3 Although your answer is unlikely to be precisely the same, the completed table of data requirements below should enable you to check you are on the right lines.

Research question/objective: *To establish householders' opinions about children's book clubs*			
Type of research: *Predominantly descriptive, although wish to explain differences between householders*			
Investigative questions	**Variable(s) required**	**Detail in which data measured**	**Check included in questionnaire** ✓
Do householders think that children's book clubs are a good or a bad idea? (attitude – this is because you are really asking how householders feel)	Attitude to children's book clubs	very good idea, good idea, neither a good nor a bad idea, bad idea, very bad idea	
What things do householders like most about children's book clubs? (belief)	What householders like about children's book clubs	get them to rank the following things (generated from earlier in-depth interviews): monthly magazine, lower prices, credit, choice, special offers, shopping at home	
Would householders be interested in an all-ages book club? (behaviour)	Interest in a book club which was for both adults and children	interested, not interested, may be interested	
How much do households spend on children's books a year? (behaviour)	Amount spent on children's books by adults and children per year by household	(answers to the nearest £) £0 to £10, £11 to £20, £21 to £30, £31 to £50, £51 to £100, over £100	
Do households' responses differ depending on:			
• *number of children?* (attribute)	Number of aged under 16	actual number	
• *whether already members of a children's book club?* (behaviour)	Children's book club member	yes, no	

10.4 a Please complete the following statement by ticking the phrase that matches your feelings most closely . . .

I feel children's book clubs are . . .   . . . a very good idea ☐5

. . . a good idea ☐4

. . . neither a good nor a bad idea ☐3

. . . a bad idea ☐2

. . . a very bad idea ☐1

b Please number each of the features of children's book clubs listed below in order of how much you like them. Number the most important 1, the next 2 and so on. The feature you like the least should be given the highest number.

feature	how much liked
monthly magazine	☐
lower prices	☐
credit	☐
choice	☐
special offers	☐
shopping at home	☐

c Would you be interested in a book club which was for both adults and children?

(please tick the appropriate box)   yes ☐1

no ☐2

not sure ☐3

d How much money is spent in total each year on children's books by all the adults and children living in your household?

(please tick the appropriate box)   £0 to £10 ☐1

£11 to £20 ☐2

£21 to £30 ☐3

£31 to £50 ☐4

£51 to £100 ☐5

over £100 ☐6

e i How many children aged under 16 are there living in your household?

$$\boxed{}\ \text{children}$$

(for example for 3 write:) $\boxed{3}$ children

ii Is any person living in your household a member of a children's book club?

(please tick the appropriate box)   Yes $\square_1$

No $\square_2$

10.5 Although the precise wording of your answer is likely to differ, it would probably be something like this:

Good morning/afternoon/evening. My name is _____ from Saunders and Dawson Consumer Research. We are doing an important national survey covering lifestyles, opinions and likely future purchases of adult consumers. Your telephone number has been selected at random. The questions I need to ask you will take about 15* minutes. If you have any queries I will be happy to answer them (*pause*). Please can I ask you the first question now?

*The total time should not be more than 30 minutes.

10.6 Although the precise wording of your answer is likely to differ it would probably be something like this:

Work for All

Registered Charity No: 123456789

M&D Ltd

M&D Market Research Ltd
St Richard's House
Malvern
Worcestershire WR14 12Z
☎ *01684–56789101*
Fax 01684–56789102

Respondent's name
Respondent's address   *Today's date*

Dear *title name*

Work for All is conducting research into the effects of long-term unemployment. This is an issue of great importance within the UK and yet little is currently known about the consequences.

You are one of a small number of people who are being asked to give your opinion on this issue. You were selected at random from Work for All's list of contacts. In order that the results will truly represent people who have experienced long-term unemployment, it is important that your questionnaire is completed and returned.

All the information you give us will be totally confidential. You will notice that your name and address do not appear on the questionnaire and that there is no identification number.

The results of this research will be passed to Work for All who will be mounting a major campaign to highlight public awareness about the effects of long-term unemployment in the new year.

If you have any questions you wish to ask or there is anything you wish to discuss please do not hesitate to telephone me, or my assistant Dave Dawson, on 01684–56789101 during the day. You can call me at home on 01234–123456789 evenings and weekends.

Thank you for your help.

Yours sincerely

Mark NK Saunders

Dr Mark NK Saunders
Project Manager

10.7 Despite the time constraints, pilot testing is essential to your methodology for the following reasons:

- to find out how long the questionnaire takes to complete;
- to check that respondents understand and can follow the instructions on the questionnaire (including filter questions);
- to ensure that all respondents understand the wording of individual questions in the same way and that there are no unclear or ambiguous questions;
- to ensure that you have the same understanding of the wording of individual questions as the respondents;
- to check that respondents have no problems in answering questions; for example:
  - all possible answers are covered in list questions,
  - whether there are any questions that respondents feel uneasy about answering;
- to discover whether there are any major topic omissions;
- to provide an idea of the validity of the questions that are being asked;
- to provide an idea of the reliability of the questions by checking responses from individual respondents to similar questions;
- to check that the layout appears clear and attractive;
- to provide limited test data so you can check that the proposed analyses will work.

11 Analysing quantitative data

By the end of this chapter you should be able:

- to identify the main issues that you need to consider when preparing quantitative data for analysis and when analysing these data by computer;
- to recognise different types of data and understand the implications of data type for subsequent analyses;
- to create a data matrix and to code data for analysis by computer;
- to select the most appropriate tables and diagrams to explore and illustrate different aspects of your data;
- to select the most appropriate statistics to describe individual variables and to examine relationships between variables and trends in your data;
- to interpret the tables, diagrams and statistics that you use correctly.

11.1 Introduction

Virtually all research will involve some numerical data or contain data that could usefully be quantified to help you answer your research question(s) and to meet your objectives. *Quantitative data* refers to all such data and can be a product of all research strategies (Section 4.2). It can range from simple counts such as the frequency of occurrences to more complex data such as test scores or prices. To be useful these data need to be analysed and interpreted. Quantitative analysis techniques assist this process. These range from creating simple tables or diagrams which show the frequency of occurrence through establishing statistical relationships between variables to complex statistical modelling.

Until the advent of powerful personal computers, data were analysed either by hand or by using mainframe computers. The former of these was extremely time consuming and prone to error, the latter expensive. Fortunately the by-hand or calculator 'number-crunching' and 'charting' elements of quantitative analysis have been incorporated into relatively inexpensive personal-computer-based analysis software. These range from spreadsheets such as 'Excel', 'Lotus 123' and 'SuperCalc' to more advanced data management and statistical analysis software packages such as 'Minitab', 'SAS', 'SPSS for Windows' and 'Statview'. They also include more specialised survey design and analysis packages such as 'Snap' and 'SphinxSurvey'. Consequently, it is no longer necessary for you to be able to draw presentation quality diagrams or to calculate statistics by hand as these can be done by computer. However, if your analyses are to be straightforward and of any value you need:

■ to have prepared your data with quantitative analyses in mind;

■ to be aware of and to know when to use different charting and statistical techniques.

Robson (1993:310) summarises this, arguing that quantitative data analysis is:

. . . a field where it is not at all difficult to carry out an analysis which is simply wrong, or inappropriate for your purposes. And the negative side of readily available analysis software is that it becomes that much easier to generate elegantly presented rubbish.

He also emphasises the need to seek advice regarding statistical analyses, a sentiment that we support strongly.

This chapter builds on the ideas outlined in earlier chapters about data collection. It assumes that you will use a personal computer (with at least a spreadsheet) to analyse all but the most simple quantitative data. It does not focus on one particular piece of analysis software as there are numerous books already published which concentrate on specific software packages (for example Bryman and Cramer, 1999; Morris, 1999; Robson, 1993). Likewise it does not attempt to provide an in-depth discussion of the wide range of graphical and statistical techniques available or to cover more complex statistical modelling as these are already covered elsewhere (for example Fox and Long, 1990; Hays, 1994). Rather it discusses issues that need to be considered at the planning and analysis stages of your research project and outlines analytical techniques our students have found to be of most use. In particular the chapter is concerned with the process of:

■ preparing your data for analysis by computer (Section 11.2);

■ choosing the most appropriate tables and diagrams to explore and present your data (Section 11.3);

■ choosing the most appropriate statistics to describe your data (Section 11.4);

■ choosing the most appropriate statistics to examine relationships and trends in your data (Section 11.5).

11.2 Preparing data for analysis

If you intend to undertake quantitative analysis we recommend that you consider the:

■ type of data (level of numerical measurement);

■ format in which your data will be input to the analysis software;

■ impact of data coding on subsequent analyses (for different data types);

■ need to weight cases;

■ methods you intend to use to check data for errors.

Ideally, all of these should be considered before obtaining your data. This is equally important for both primary and secondary data analysis, although you obviously have far greater control over the type, format and coding of primary data. We will now consider each of these.

Data types

Many business statistics textbooks classify quantitative data into *data types* using a hierarchy of measurement, often in ascending order of numerical precision (Diamantopoulos and Schlegelmilch, 1997; Morris, 1999). These different *levels of numerical measurement* dictate the range of techniques available to you for the presentation, summary and analysis of your data. They are discussed in more detail in subsequent sections of this chapter.

Quantitative data can be divided into two distinct groups: categorical and quantifiable (Fig 11.1). *Categorical data* refer to data whose values cannot be measured numerically but can be either classified into sets (categories) according to the characteristics in which you are interested or placed in rank order. They can be further subdivided into descriptive and ranked. A car manufacturer might categorise the cars they produce as hatchback, saloon and estate. These are known as *descriptive* (or *nominal*) *data* as it is impossible to measure the category numerically or to rank it. For virtually all analyses the categories should be unambiguous and not overlap. This will prevent questions arising as to which category an individual case belongs to. Although these data are purely descriptive, you can count them to establish which category has the most and whether cases are spread evenly between categories (Morris, 1999). *Ranked* (or *ordinal*) *data* are more precise. In such instances you know the definite position of each case within your data set, although the actual numerical measures (such as scores) on which the position is based are not recorded.

Quantifiable data are those whose values you actually measure numerically as quantities. This means that quantifiable data are more precise than categorical as you can assign each data value a position on a numerical scale.[1] Within this group there is, again, a subdivision: continuous and discrete (Fig 11.1). *Continuous data* are those whose values can theoretically take any value (sometimes within a restricted range) provided that you can measure them accurately enough (Morris, 1999). Data such as furnace temperature, delivery distance and length of service are therefore continuous data. *Discrete data* can, by contrast, be measured precisely. Each case takes one of a finite number of values from a scale which measure changes in discrete units. These data are often whole numbers (*integers*) such as number of compact disk players manufactured or customers served. However, in some instances (for example UK shoe size), discrete data will include non-integer values.

Definitions of discrete and continuous data are, in reality, dependent on how your data values are measured. The number of customers served by a large organisation is

---

[1]Some text books (for example Bryman and Cramer, 1999) use an alternative hierarchy of measurement: nominal, ordinal, interval and ratio. Nominal equates to descriptive and ordinal to ranked data. If you have interval data you can, in addition to ranking, state the difference between any two data values. For ratio data, you can also calculate the relative difference between any two data values, that is the ratio.

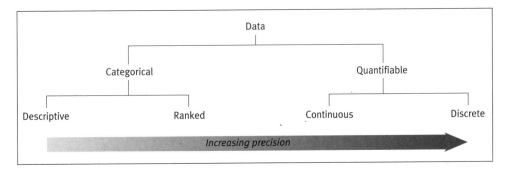

Fig 11.1 **Types of data and levels of numerical measurement**

strictly a discrete datum as you are unlikely to get a part customer! However, for a large organisation with many customers you might treat this as a continuous datum; the discrete measuring units are minute compared with the total number being measured.

The more precise the level of measurement the greater the range of analytical techniques available to you. Data which have been collected and coded using precise numerical measurements can also be regrouped to a less precise level where they can also be analysed. For example, a student's score in a test could be recorded as the actual mark (discrete data) or as the position in their class (ranked data). By contrast, less precise data cannot be made more precise. Therefore if you are not sure about the level of precision you require it is usually better to collect data at the highest level possible and to regroup them if necessary.

Worked example

Levels of numerical measurement

As part of a marketing survey, individual customers were asked to rank up to five features of a new product in order of importance to them. Data collected were therefore categorical and ranked. Initial analyses made use of the ranked data. Unfortunately a substantial minority of customers had ticked, rather than ranked, those features of importance to them.

All responses which had originally been ranked were therefore recoded to 'of some importance'. This reduced the precision of measurement from ranked to descriptive but enabled all responses to be used in subsequent analyses.

Data layout

Some primary data collection methods such as computer-aided personal interviewing (CAPI), computer-aided telephone interviewing (CATI) and on-line questionnaires can automatically enter and save data to a computer file at the time of collection. Survey design and analysis software such as 'Snap' and 'SphinxSurvey' goes one stage further and integrates the analysis software in the same package as the questionnaire design/data input software (Mercator, 1999; Scolari Sage, 1999). Alternatively secondary data (Section 7.3) accessed from CD-ROMS or via the internet can be saved to a file, removing the need for re-entering. For such data, it is often possible to specify a data layout compatible with your analysis software. For other data collection methods, you will have to prepare and enter your data for computer analysis. You therefore need to be clear about the precise data layout requirements of your analysis software.

Virtually all analysis software will accept your data if they are entered in table format. This table is called a *data matrix* (Table 11.1). Once data have been entered into your analysis software, it is usually possible to save them in a format that can be read by other software. Within a data matrix, each column usually represents a single *variable* for which you have obtained data. Each matrix row contains the variables for an individual *case*, that is an individual unit for which data have been obtained. If your data have been collected using a survey, each row will contain the data from one survey form. Alternatively, for longitudinal data such as a company's share price over time, each row (case) will be a different time period. Secondary data that have already been stored in computer-readable form will almost always be held as a large data matrix. For such data sets, you usually select the subset of variables and cases you require and save these on a disk as a separate matrix. If you are entering your own data, they are typed directly into your chosen analysis software one case (row) at a time. We recommend you save your data regularly as you are entering it, to minimise the chances of deleting it all by accident! In addition, you should keep a back-up or security copy on a separate disk.

In Table 11.1, the first variable (id) is the *survey form identifier*. This means that you can link data for each case in your matrix to the survey form when error checking (discussed later). The second variable (age) contains quantifiable data, the age of each respondent (case) at the time of the survey. Subsequent variables contain the remaining data: the third (gender) records this descriptive data using code 1 for male and 2 for female; the fourth (service) records each case's length of service to the nearest year with their most recent employer. The final variable (employed) records whether each case is (code 1) or is not (code 2) currently in employment. Codes can therefore have different meanings for different variables. Larger data sets with more data variables and cases are recorded using larger data matrices. Although data matrices store data using one column for each variable, this may not be the same as one column for each question for data collected using surveys.

Table 11.1   **A simple data matrix**

	id	age	gender	service	employed
case 1	1	27	1	2	1
case 2	2	19	2	1	2
case 3	3	24	2	3	1

If you intend to enter data into a spreadsheet the first variable is in column A, the second in column B and so on. Each cell in the first row (1) should contain a short variable name to enable you to identify each variable. Subsequent rows (2 onwards) will each contain the data for one case. Statistical analysis software follows the same logic although the variable names are usually displayed 'above' the first row, as in Table 11.1.

Worked example

Data input

As part of a marketing interview survey you need to discover which of four products (tomato ketchup, brown sauce, soy sauce, vinegar) have been purchased within the last month by consumers. You therefore need to collect four data items from each respondent:

- tomato ketchup purchased within the last month?   Yes/No
- brown sauce purchased within the last month?   Yes/No
- soy sauce purchased within the last month?   Yes/No
- vinegar purchased within the last month?   Yes/No

Each of these data items is a separate variable. However, the data are collected using one question:

1   Which of the following items have you purchased within the last month?

item	purchased	not purchased	not sure
tomato ketchup	☐1	☐2	☐3
brown sauce	☐1	☐2	☐3
soy sauce	☐1	☐2	☐3
vinegar	☐1	☐2	☐3

The data collected from each respondent will form four separate variables in the data matrix using numerical codes (1 = purchased, 2 = not purchased, 3 = not sure). This is known as multiple-dichotomy coding:

	tomato	brown	soy	vinegar	
respondent	1	1	1	2	

Question 2 (below) could theoretically have millions of possible responses for each of the 'things'. The number that each respondent mentions may also vary. Our experience suggests that virtually all respondents will select five or less. Space therefore has to be left to code up to five responses after data have been collected.

2 List the things you like about your current job	....	for office use only
	....	▢▢▢▢
	....	▢▢▢▢
	....	▢▢▢▢
	....	▢▢▢▢
	....	▢▢▢▢

The *multiple-dichotomy method* uses a separate variable for each different answer. For question 2 a separate variable could be used for each 'thing' listed, for example: salary, location, colleagues, hours, holidays, car and so on. You would subsequently code each variable as 'listed' or 'not listed' for each case. This makes it easy to calculate the number of responses for each 'thing' (deVaus, 1996). The alternative, the *multiple-response method*, uses the same number of variables as the maximum number of different responses from any one case. For question 2 these might be named 'like1', 'like2', 'like3', 'like4' and 'like5'. Each of these variables would use the same codes and could include any of the responses as a category. Statistical analysis software often contains special multiple-response procedures to analyse such data.

Coding

All data types should, with few exceptions, be recorded using numerical codes. This enables you to enter the data quickly and with fewer errors. It also makes subsequent analyses, in particular those that require re-coding of data to create new variables, more straightforward. Unfortunately, analyses of limited meaning are also easier, such as calculating a mean (average) gender from codes 1 and 2! A common exception to using a numerical code for categorical data is where a postcode is used as the code for a geographical reference. If you are using a spreadsheet, you will need to keep a list of codes for each variable. Statistical analysis software can store these so that each code is automatically labelled.

Coding quantifiable data

Actual numbers are often used as codes for quantifiable data, even though this level of precision may not be required. Once you have entered your data as a matrix, you can use analysis software to group or combine data to form additional variables with less detailed categories. This process is referred to as *re-coding*. A UK employee's salary could be coded to the nearest pound and entered into the matrix as 23543 (discrete data). Later, re-coding could be used to place it in a group of similar salaries, from £20 000 to £24 999 (categorical data).

Coding categorical data

Codes are often applied to categorical data with little thought, although you can design a coding scheme that will make subsequent analyses far simpler. For many secondary data sources (such as government surveys), a suitable coding scheme will have already been devised when the data were first collected. However, for some secondary and all primary data you will need to decide on a coding scheme. Prior to this, you need to establish the highest level of precision required by your analyses.

Existing coding schemes can be used for many variables. These include industrial classification (Central Statistical Office, 1997), occupation (Office of Population Censuses and Surveys, 1990a, b), social class (Office of Population Censuses and Surveys, 1991), marital status and ethnic group (Office of Population Censuses and Surveys and General Registrar's Office for Scotland, 1992) as well as social attitude variables (Jowell *et al.*, 1994). Wherever possible we recommend you use these as they:

■ save time;

■ are normally well tested;

■ enable comparisons of your results with other (often larger) surveys.

These codes should be included on your data collection form as *pre-set codes* provided that there are a limited number of categories (Section 10.4), which will be understood by the person filling in the form. Even if you decide not to use an existing coding scheme, perhaps because of a lack of detail, you should ensure that your codes are still compatible. This means that you will be able to compare your data with those already collected.

Coding at data collection occurs when there are a limited range of well-established categories into which the data can be placed. These are included on your data collection form and the person filling in the form selects the correct category.

Coding after data collection is necessary when you are unclear of the likely responses or there are a large number of possible responses in the coding scheme. To ensure that the coding scheme captures the variety in responses (and will work!) it is better to wait until data from the first 50 to 100 cases are available and then develop the coding scheme. This is called the *codebook*. As when designing your data collection method(s) (Chapters 7, 8, 9 and 10) it is essential to be clear about the intended analyses, in particular the:

■ level of precision required;

■ coding schemes used by surveys with which comparisons are to be made.

To create your code book for each variable you:

1 examine the data and establish broad groupings;

2 subdivide the broad groupings into increasingly specific sub-groups dependent on your intended analyses;

3 allocate codes to all categories at the most precise level of detail required;

4 note the actual responses that are allocated to each category and produce a codebook;

5 ensure that those categories that may need to be aggregated together are given adjacent codes to facilitate re-coding.

Coding missing data

Each variable for each case in your data set should have a code, even if no data have been collected. The choice of code is up to you, although some statistical analysis software has a code which is used by default. A *missing data* code is used to indicate why data are missing. deVaus (1996) identifies four main reasons for missing data:

- the data were not required, perhaps because of a skip generated by a filter question in a survey;
- the question was not answered as the respondent had no opinion (a *non-response*);
- the data were not available for some other reason;
- leaving part of a question in a survey blank implies an answer; in such cases the data are not classified as missing.

Statistical analysis software often reserves a special code for missing data. Cases with missing data can then be excluded from subsequent analyses when necessary. For some analyses, it may be necessary to distinguish between reasons for missing data using different codes.

Worked example

Creating a codebook and coding multiple responses

As part of research on vacancy notification procedures Mark collected data from personnel files about how vacancies were notified by the employer. These data specified the precise notification outlets used and can be thought of as the answer to the question: 'Which outlets did you use to notify this vacancy?' The data included over 100 different outlets for over 1500 vacancies, although the maximum number of outlets used for any one vacancy was eight.

Once data had been collected, Mark devised a hierarchical coding scheme based on the type and geographical circulation of each notification outlet. Codes were allocated to each outlet as shown in the extract below.

Notification codes for each vacancy were entered into eight (the maximum number of notification outlets used) variables in the data matrix using the multiple-response method for coding. This meant that any notification outlet could appear in any of the eight variables. When less that eight outlets were used the code 0 was entered in the remaining outlet variables. The first vacancy in the extract below was notified through outlets 1, 90, 91 and 61, the next through outlets 90, 91, 63, 41, 1, 7 and 8, and so on. No significance was attached to the order of variables to which outlets were coded.

outlet 1	outlet 2	outlet 3	outlet 4	outlet 5	outlet 6	outlet 7	outlet 8
1	90	91	61	0	0	0	0
90	91	63	41	1	7	8	0
6	23	22	1	11	0	0	0

Extract from coding scheme used to classify notification outlets

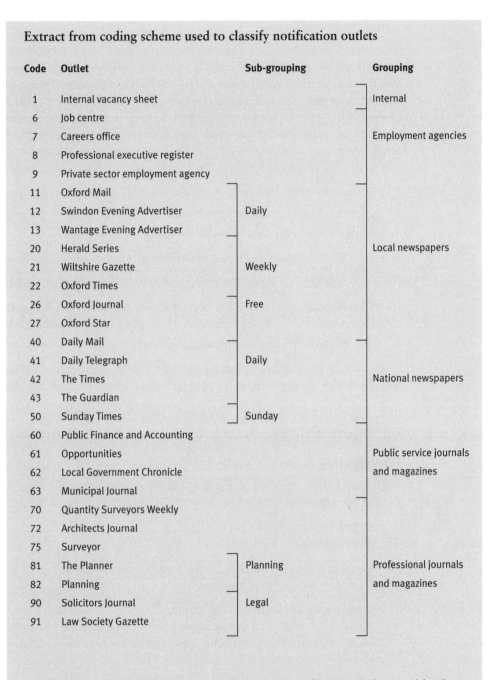

Code	Outlet	Sub-grouping	Grouping
1	Internal vacancy sheet		Internal
6	Job centre		
7	Careers office		Employment agencies
8	Professional executive register		
9	Private sector employment agency		
11	Oxford Mail		
12	Swindon Evening Advertiser	Daily	
13	Wantage Evening Advertiser		
20	Herald Series		Local newspapers
21	Wiltshire Gazette	Weekly	
22	Oxford Times		
26	Oxford Journal	Free	
27	Oxford Star		
40	Daily Mail		
41	Daily Telegraph	Daily	
42	The Times		National newspapers
43	The Guardian		
50	Sunday Times	Sunday	
60	Public Finance and Accounting		
61	Opportunities		Public service journals
62	Local Government Chronicle		and magazines
63	Municipal Journal		
70	Quantity Surveyors Weekly		
72	Architects Journal		
75	Surveyor		
81	The Planner	Planning	Professional journals
82	Planning		and magazines
90	Solicitors Journal	Legal	
91	Law Society Gazette		

The hierarchical coding scheme meant that notification outlets could subsequently be re-coded into groupings such as those indicated above as well as local, regional or national to facilitate a range of different analyses. These were undertaken using statistical analysis software.

Weighting cases

Most data you use will be a sample. For some forms of probability sampling such as stratified random sampling (Section 6.2), you may have used a different sampling fraction for each stratum. Alternatively, you may have obtained a different response rate for each of the strata. To obtain an accurate overall picture you will need to take account of these differences in response rates between strata. A common method of achieving this is to use cases from those strata that have lower proportions of responses to represent more than one case in your analysis. Most statistical analysis software allows you to do this by *weighting cases*. To *weight* the cases you:

1. calculate the percentage of the population responding for each stratum;
2. establish which stratum had the highest percentage of the population responding;
3. calculate the weight for each stratum using the formula:

$$\text{weight} = \frac{\text{highest proportion of population responding for any stratum}}{\text{proportion of population responding in stratum for which calculating weight}}$$

(Note: if your calculations are correct this will always result in the weight for the stratum with the highest proportion of the population responding being 1.)

4. apply the appropriate weight to each case.

Beware, many authors (for example Hays, 1994) question the validity of using statistics to make inferences from your sample if you have weighted cases.

Worked example

Weighting cases

To select your sample for a survey you have used stratified random sampling. The percentage of each stratum's population that responded is given below:

upper stratum: 90%
lower stratum: 65%

To account for the differences in the response rates between strata you decide to weight the cases prior to analysis.

The weight for the upper stratum is: $\frac{90}{90} = 1$

This means that each case in the upper stratum will count as 1 case in your analysis.

The weight for the lower stratum is: $\frac{90}{65} = 1.38$

This means that each case in the lower stratum will count for 1.38 cases in your analysis.

You enter these as a separate variable in your data set and use the statistical analysis software to apply the weights.

Checking for errors

No matter how carefully you code and subsequently enter data there will always be some errors. The main methods to check data for errors are:

■ look for illegitimate codes. In any coding scheme, only certain numbers are allocated. Other numbers are therefore errors. Common errors are the inclusion of letters O and o instead of zero, letters l or I instead of 1, and number 7 instead of 1;

■ look for illogical relationships. For example, if a person is coded to the professional socio-economic group and their social class is unskilled manual an error has occurred.

■ check that rules in filter questions are followed. Certain responses to filter questions (Section 10.4) mean that other variables should be coded as missing values. If this has not happened there has been an error.

For each possible error, you need to discover whether it occurred at coding or data entry and then correct it. By giving each case a unique identifier (normally a number), it is possible to link the matrix to the original data. You must remember to write the identifier on the data collection form and enter it along with the other data into the matrix.

Data checking is very time consuming and so is often not undertaken. Beware, not doing this is very dangerous and can result in incorrect results from which false conclusions are drawn!

11.3 Exploring and presenting data

Once your data have been entered and checked for errors, you are ready to start your analysis. We have found Tukey's (1977) *exploratory data analysis* approach useful in these initial stages. This approach emphasises the use of diagrams to explore and understand your data. As you would expect, we believe that it is important to keep your research question(s) and objectives in mind when exploring your data. However, the exploratory data analysis approach also formalises the common practice of looking for other relationships in data which your research was not initially designed to test. This should not be discounted as it may suggest other fruitful avenues for analysis. In addition, computers make this relatively easy and quick.

Even at this stage, it is important that you structure and label clearly each diagram and table to avoid possible misinterpretation. Table 11.2 summarises the points to remember when designing a diagram or table as a checklist.

We have found it best to begin exploratory analysis by looking at individual variables and their components. The key aspects you may need to consider will be guided by your research question(s) and objectives and are likely to include (Sparrow, 1989):

■ specific values;
■ highest and lowest values;
■ trends over time;
■ proportions;
■ distributions.

Table 11.2	Checklist for diagrams and tables

For both diagrams and tables

✓ Does it have a brief but clear and descriptive title?

✓ Are the units of measurement used clearly stated?

✓ Are the sources of data used clearly stated?

✓ Are there notes to explain abbreviations and unusual terminology?

✓ Does it state the size of the sample on which the values in the table are based?

For diagrams	For tables
✓ Does it have clear axes labels?	✓ Does it have clear column and row headings?
✓ Are bars and their components in the same logical sequence?	✓ Are columns and rows in a logical sequence?
✓ Is more dense shading used for smaller areas?	
✓ Is a key or legend included (where necessary)?	

Once you have explored these you can then begin to compare and look for relationships between variables considering in addition (Sparrow, 1989):

- conjunctions (the point where values for two or more variables intersect);
- totals;
- interdependence and relationships.

These are summarised in Table 11.3. Most analysis software contains procedures to create tables and diagrams. Your choice will depend on those aspects of the data that you wish to emphasise and the level of measurement at which the data were recorded. This section is concerned only with tables and two-dimensional diagrams available on most spreadsheets (Table 11.3). Pictograms and three-dimensional diagrams are not discussed as these can hinder interpretation. Those tables and diagrams most pertinent to your research question(s) and objectives will eventually appear in your research report to support your arguments. You should therefore save a disk copy of all tables and diagrams you create.

Exploring and presenting individual variables

To show specific values

The simplest way of summarising data for individual variables so that specific values can be read is to use a *table (frequency distribution)*. For descriptive data, the table summarises the number of cases (frequency) in each category. For variables where there are likely to be a large number of categories (or values for quantifiable data), you will need to group the data into categories that reflect your research question(s) and objectives.

Table 11.3 **Data presentation by data type: a summary**

	Categorical		Quantifiable	
	Descriptive	*Ranked*	*Continuous*	*Discrete*
To show one variable so that any *specific* value can be read easily	Table/frequency distribution (data often grouped)			
To show the frequency of occurrences of categories or values for one variable so that *highest* and *lowest* are clear	Bar chart (data may need grouping)		Histogram or frequency polygon (data must be grouped)	Bar chart or pictogram (data may need grouping)
To show the *trend* for a variable		Line graph or bar chart	Line graph or histogram	Line graph or bar chart
To show the *proportion* of occurrences of categories or values for one variable	Pie chart (data may need grouping)		Histogram or pie chart (data must be grouped)	Pie chart (data may need grouping)
To show the *distribution* of values for one variable			Frequency polygon, histogram (data must be grouped) or box plot	Frequency polygon, bar chart (data may need grouping) or box plot
To show the *interdependence* between two or more variables so that any *specific* value can be read easily	Contingency table/cross-tabulation (data often grouped)			
To compare the frequency of occurrences of categories or values for two or more variables so that *highest* and *lowest* are clear	Multiple bar chart (continuous data must be grouped, other data may need grouping)			
To compare the *trends* for two or more variables so that *conjunctions* are clear		Multiple line graph or multiple bar chart		
To compare the *proportions* of occurrences of categories or values for two or more variables	Comparative pie charts or percentage component bar chart (continuous data must be grouped, other data may need grouping)			
To compare the *distribution* of values for two or more variables		Multiple box plot		
To compare the frequency of occurrences of categories or values for two or more variables so that *totals* are clear	Stacked bar chart (continuous data must be grouped, other data may need grouping)			
To compare the *proportions* and *totals* of occurrences of categories or values for two or more variables	Comparative proportional pie charts (continuous data must be grouped, other data may need grouping)			
To show the *relationship* between cases for two variables		Scatter graph/scatter plot		

© Mark Saunders, Philip Lewis and Adrian Thornhill, 2000

To show highest and lowest values

Tables attach no visual significance to highest or lowest values unless emphasised by alternative fonts. Diagrams can provide visual clues, although both categorical and quantifiable data may need grouping (Sparrow, 1989). For categorical and discrete data, bar charts and pictograms are both suitable. However, bar charts provide a more accurate representation and are used for most research reports. In a *bar chart*, sometimes called a *column chart*, the heights of the bars represent the frequency of occurrence (Fig 11.2). Bars are separated by gaps, usually half the width of the bars.

Fig 11.2   **Bar chart**

Most researchers use a histogram for continuous data. Prior to being drawn, data will need to be grouped into class intervals. In a *histogram,* the area of each bar represents the frequency of occurrence and the continuous nature of the data is emphasised by the absence of gaps between the bars. For equal width class intervals, the height of your bar still represents the frequency of occurrences (Fig 11.3) and so the highest and lowest values are easy to distinguish. For histograms with unequal class interval widths, this is not the case.

Analysis software treats histograms for data of equal width class intervals as a variation of a bar chart. Unfortunately, few spreadsheets will cope automatically with the calculations required to draw histograms for unequal class intervals. As a consequence, you may have to use a bar chart owing to the limitations of your analysis software.

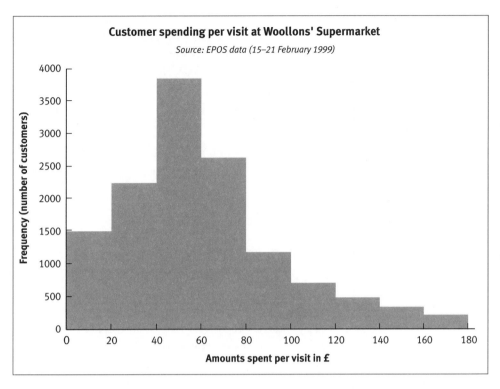

Customer spending per visit at Woollons' Supermarket

Source: EPOS data (15–21 February 1999)

Fig 11.3 **Histogram**

Frequency polygons are used less often to illustrate limits. Most analysis software treats them as a version of a line graph (Fig 11.4) in which the lines are extended to meet the horizontal axis, provided that class widths are equal.

To show the trend

Trends can only be presented for variables containing quantifiable (and occasionally ranked) longitudinal data. The most suitable diagram for exploring the trend is a *line graph* (Sparrow, 1989) in which your data values for each time period are joined with a line to represent the trend (Fig 11.4). You can also use bar charts (Fig 11.2) to show trends between discrete time periods and histograms (Fig 11.3) for continuous time periods. The trend can also be calculated using time series analysis (Section 11.5).

To show proportions

Research has shown that the most suitable diagram to emphasise the proportion or share of occurrences is the pie chart (Sparrow, 1989). A *pie chart* is divided into proportional segments according to the share each has of the total value (Fig 11.5). For continuous and some discrete and categorical data you will need to group data prior to drawing the pie chart, as it is difficult to interpret pie charts with more than six segments (Morris, 1999).

Fig 11.4   Line graph

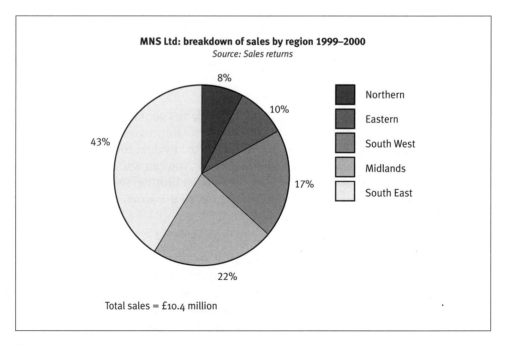

Fig 11.5   Pie chart

To show the distribution of values

Prior to using many statistical tests it is necessary to establish the distribution of values for variables containing quantifiable data (Sections 11.4, 11.5). This can be seen by plotting either a frequency polygon or a histogram (Fig 11.3) for continuous data or a frequency polygon or bar chart for discrete data (Fig 11.2). If your diagram shows a bunching to the left and a long tail to the right as in Fig 11.3 the data are *positively skewed*. If the converse is true, the data are *negatively skewed*. If your data are equally distributed either side of the highest frequency then they are *symmetrically distributed*. A special form of the symmetric distribution, in which the data can be plotted as a bell-shaped curve, is known as the *normal distribution*.

An alternative often included in more advanced statistical analysis software is the *box plot* (Fig 11.6). This diagram provides you with a pictorial representation of the distribution of the data for a variable. The plot shows where the middle value or median is, how this relates to the middle 50 per cent of the data or inter-quartile range, and highest and lowest values or *extremes* (Section 11.4). In this example, we can see that the data values for the variable are positively skewed as there is a long tail to the right.

Fig 11.6   **Annotated sketch of a box plot**

Exploring and presenting data for individual variables

As part of audience research, people attending a play at a provincial theatre were asked to complete a short questionnaire. This collected responses to 25 questions including:

3 How many plays (including this one) have you seen at this theatre in the past year?

___ ___

	strongly disagree	disagree	agree	strongly agree
11 This play is good value for money	☐₁	☐₂	☐₃	☐₄

24 How old are you?

Under 18   ☐₁   35 to 64   ☐₃

18 to 34   ☐₂   Over 65   ☐₄

Exploratory analyses were undertaken using analysis software and diagrams generated. For question 3, which collected discrete data, the aspects that were most important were the distribution of values and the highest and lowest numbers of plays seen. A bar chart was therefore drawn:

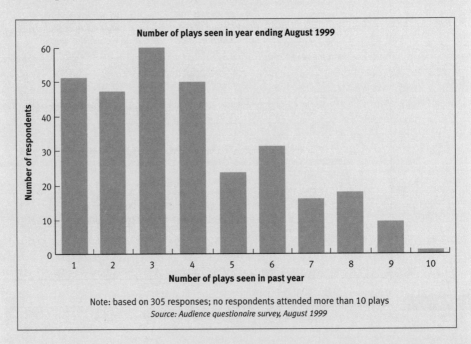

Number of plays seen in year ending August 1999

Number of respondents (y-axis) vs Number of plays seen in past year (x-axis)

Note: based on 305 responses; no respondents attended more than 10 plays

Source: Audience questionaire survey, August 1999

This emphasised that the most frequent number of plays seen by respondents was three and the least frequent 10. It also showed that the distribution was positively skewed towards lower numbers of plays seen.

For question 11 (categorical data), the most important aspect was the proportions of people agreeing and disagreeing with the statement. A pie chart was therefore drawn using the similar shadings for the two agree categories and for the two disagree categories:

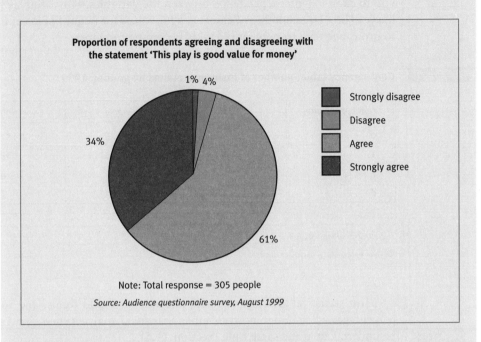

Proportion of respondents agreeing and disagreeing with the statement 'This play is good value for money'

1%   4%

34%

61%

■ Strongly disagree

■ Disagree

■ Agree

■ Strongly agree

Note: Total response = 305 people

Source: Audience questionnaire survey, August 1999

This emphasised that the vast majority (95 per cent) agreed that the play was good value for money. Percentages were included on the chart to emphasise the specific proportions.

Question 24 collected data on each respondent's age. This question had grouped continuous data into four unequal-width age groups. For this analysis, the most important aspect was the specific number of respondents in each age category and so a table was constructed:

Age of respondents

Age group	number
Less than 18	13
18 to 34	63
35 to 64	160
65 plus	64
Total	300

Note: 5 people did not respond

Source: Audience questionnaire survey, August, 1999

Comparing variables

To show specific values and interdependence

As with individual variables the best method of finding specific data values is a table. This is known as a *contingency table* or *cross-tabulation* (Table 11.4) and also enables you to examine interdependence between the variables. For variables where there are likely to be a large number of categories (or values for quantifiable data), you may need to group the data to prevent the table becoming too large.

Table 11.4   **Contingency table: number of insurance claims by gender, 1999**

Number of claims	Male	Female	Total
0	10 032	13 478	23 510
1	2 156	1 430	3 586
2	120	25	145
3	13	4	17
Total	12 321	14 937	27 258

No clients had more than 3 claims

Source: PJ Insurance Services

Most statistical analysis software allows you to add totals, and row and column percentages when designing your table. Statistical analyses such as chi square can also be undertaken at the same time (Section 11.5).

To compare highest and lowest values

Comparisons of variables which emphasise the highest and lowest rather than precise values are best explored using a *multiple bar chart* (Sparrow, 1989). As with a bar chart continuous data, or data where there are many values or categories, need to be grouped. Within any multiple bar chart, you are likely to find it easiest to compare between adjacent bars. Thus, Fig 11.7 has been drawn to emphasise comparisons between years rather than companies.

To compare proportions

Comparison of proportions between variables uses either a *percentage component bar chart* or two or more pie charts. Either type of diagram can be used for all data types provided that continuous data, and data where there are more than six values or categories, are grouped. Percentage component bar charts are more straightforward to draw than comparative pie charts using most spreadsheets. Within your percentage component bar chart, comparisons will be easiest between adjacent bars. The chart in Fig 11.8 has been drawn to compare proportions of each type of response between products. Consumers' responses for each product therefore form a single bar.

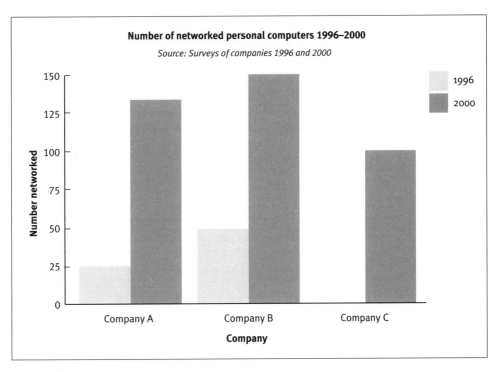

Fig 11.7   **Multiple bar chart**

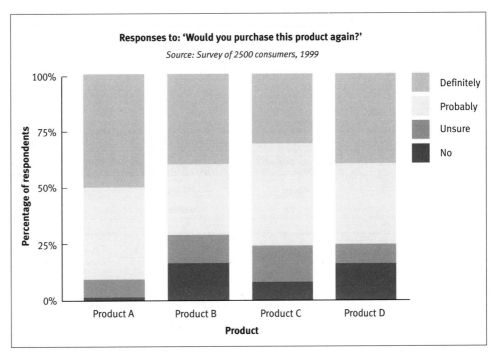

Fig 11.8   **Percentage component bar chart**

To compare trends and conjunctions

The most suitable diagram to compare trends for two or more quantifiable (or occasionally ranked) variables is a *multiple line graph* where one line represents each variable (Sparrow, 1989). You can also use multiple bar charts (Fig 11.7) in which bars for the same time period are placed adjacent.

If you need to look for conjunctions in the trends, that is where values for two or more variables intersect, this is where the lines on a multiple line graph cross.

To compare totals

Comparison of totals between variables uses a variation of the bar chart. A *stacked bar chart* can be used for all data types provided that continuous data and data where there are more than six possible values or categories are grouped. As with percentage component bar charts the design of the stacked bar chart is dictated by the totals you want to compare. For this reason in Fig 11.9 sales for each quarter have been stacked to give totals which can be compared between companies.

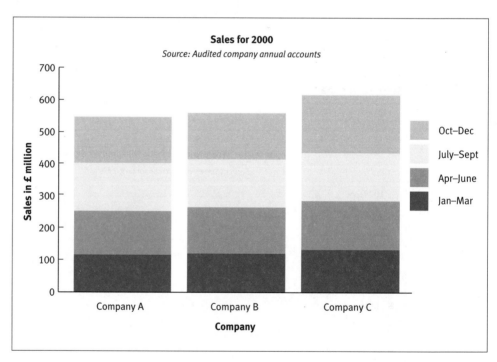

Fig 11.9   **Stacked bar chart**

To compare proportions and totals

To compare both proportions of each category or value and the totals for two or more variables it is best to use *comparative proportional pie charts* for all data types. For each comparative proportional pie chart, the total area of the pie chart represents the total for that variable. By contrast, the angle of each segment represents the relative proportion of a category within the variable (Fig 11.4). Because of the complexity of drawing comparative proportional pie charts, they are rarely used for exploratory data analysis although they can be used to good effect in research reports.

To compare the distribution of values

Often it is useful to compare the distribution of values for two or more variables. Plotting multiple frequency polygons or bar charts (Figs 11.4 and 11.7) will enable you to compare distributions for up to three or four variables. After this your diagram is likely just to look a mess! An alternative is to use a diagram of multiple box plots, similar to the one in Fig 11.6. This provides a pictorial representation of the distribution of the data for the variables in which you are interested. These plots can be compared and are interpreted in the same way as the single box plot.

To show the relationship between cases for variables

You can explore possible relationships between ranked and quantifiable data variables by plotting one variable against another. This is called a *scatter graph* or *scatter plot* and each cross (point) represents the values for one case (Fig 11.10). Convention dictates that you plot the *dependent variable*, that is the variable that changes in response to changes in the other (*independent*) variable, on the vertical axis. The strength of the relationship is indicated by the closeness of the points to an imaginary line. If as the values for one variable increase so do those for the other, you have a positive relationship. If as the values for one variable decrease, those for the other variable increase, you have a negative relationship. Thus in Fig 11.10 there is a negative relationship between the two variables. The strength of this relationship can be assessed statistically using techniques such as correlation or regression (Section 11.5).

Fig 11.10   **Scatter graph**

Worked example

Comparing variables

An independent ice cream manufacturer has kept records of monthly sales of ice cream for 1998 and 1999. In addition, the company has obtained longitudinal data on average (mean) daily hours of sunshine for each month for the same time period from their local weather station. As part of your research project you need to explore data on sales of the three best selling flavours (vanilla, strawberry and chocolate), paying particular attention to:

- comparative trends in sales;
- the relationship between sales and amount of sunshine.

To compare trends in sales between the three flavours you plot a multiple line graph:

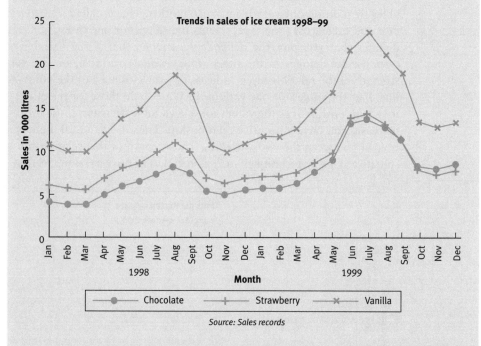

Source: Sales records

This indicates that sales for all flavours of ice cream are following a seasonal pattern but with an overall upward trend. It also shows that sales of vanilla ice cream are highest and that those of chocolate have overtaken strawberry. The multiple line graph highlights the conjunction when sales of chocolate first exceeded strawberry, September 1999.

To show relationships between sales and amount of sunshine you plot scatter graphs for sales of each ice cream flavour against average (mean) daily hours of sunshine for each month. You plot sales on the vertical axis as you presume that these are dependent on the amount of sunshine, for example:

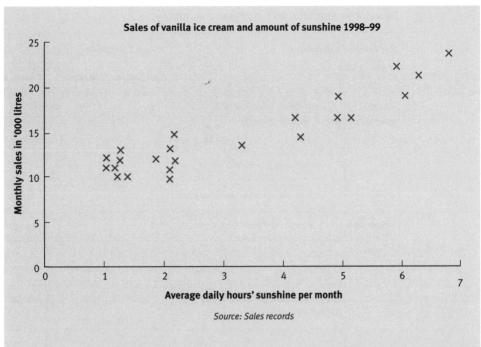

The scatter graph shows there is a positive relationship between the amount of sunshine and sales of vanilla flavour ice cream. Subsequent scatter plots reveal similar relationships for strawberry and chocolate flavours.

11.4 Describing data using statistics

The exploratory data analysis approach (Section 11.3) emphasised the use of diagrams to understand your data. *Descriptive statistics* enable you to describe (and compare) variables numerically. Your research question(s) and objectives, although limited by the type of data (Table 11.5), should guide your choice of statistics. Statistics to describe a variable focus on two aspects:

- the central tendency;
- the dispersion.

These are summarised in Table 11.5. Those most pertinent to your research question(s) and objectives will eventually be quoted in your research report as support for your arguments.

Table 11.5 **Descriptive statistics by data type: a summary**

To calculate a measure of:		Categorical		Quantifiable	
		Descriptive	Ranked	Continuous	Discrete
central tendency which . . .	. . . represents the value which occurs most frequently	Mode			
	. . . represents the middle value			Median	
	. . . includes all data values (average)			Mean	
Dispersion which . . .	. . . states the difference between the highest and lowest values			Range (data need not be normally distributed but must be placed in rank order)	
	. . . states the difference within the middle 50% of values			Inter-quartile range (data need not be normally distributed but must be placed in rank order)	
	. . . states the difference within another fraction of the values			Deciles or percentiles (data need not be normally distributed but must be placed in rank order)	
	. . . describes the extent data values differ from the mean			Variance or more usually the standard deviation (data should be normally distributed)	
	. . . compares the extent data values differ from the mean between variables			Coefficient of variation (data should be normally distributed)	

© Mark Saunders, Philip Lewis and Adrian Thornhill, 2000

Describing the central tendency

When describing data for both samples and populations quantitatively it is usual to provide some general impression of values that could be seen as common, middling or average. These are termed measures of *central tendency* and are discussed in virtually all statistics textbooks. The three ways of measuring the central tendency most used in business research are the:

■ value which occurs most frequently (mode);

■ middle value or mid-point after the data have been ranked (median);

- value, often known as the average, which includes all data values in its calculation (mean).

However, beware; if you have used numerical codes most analysis software can calculate all three measures whether or not they are appropriate!

To represent the value which occurs most frequently

The *mode* is the value that occurs most frequently. For descriptive data, the mode is the only measure of central tendency that can be sensibly interpreted. You might read in a report that the most common (*modal*) colour of motor cars sold last year was red or that the two most common makes were Ford and Vauxhall (it is possible to have more than one mode). The mode can be calculated for variables where there are likely to be a large number of categories (or values for quantifiable data) although it may be less useful. One solution is to group the data into suitable categories and to quote the most frequently occurring or *modal group*.

To represent the middle value

If you have quantitative data it is also possible to calculate the middle or *median* value by ranking all the values in ascending order and finding the mid-point (or *50th percentile*) in the distribution. For variables which have an even number of data values the median will occur halfway between the two middle data values. The median has the advantage that it is not affected by extreme values in the distribution.

To include all data values

The most frequently used measure of central tendency is the *mean* or *average*, which includes all data values in its calculation. However, it is usually only possible to calculate a meaningful mean using quantifiable data.

The value of your mean is unduly influenced by extreme data values in skewed distributions (Section 11.3). In such distributions, the mean tends to get drawn towards the long tail of extreme data values and may be less representative of the central tendency. For this and other reasons Hays (1994) suggests that the median may be a more useful descriptive statistic. However, because the mean is the building block for many of the statistical tests used to explore relationships (Section 11.5), it is usual to include it as at least one of the measures of central tendency for quantifiable data in your report. This is, of course, provided that it makes sense!

Worked example

Measuring the central tendency

As part of your research project, you have obtained secondary data from the service department of your organisation on the length of time for which customers have held service contracts:

▶

Length of time held contract	Number of customers
‹ 3 months	50
3 to ‹ 6 months	44
6 months to ‹ 1 year	71
1 to ‹ 2 years	105
2 to ‹ 3 years	74
3 to ‹ 4 years	35
4 to ‹ 5 years	27
5+ years	11

Your exploratory analysis has revealed a positively skewed distribution (long tail to the right):

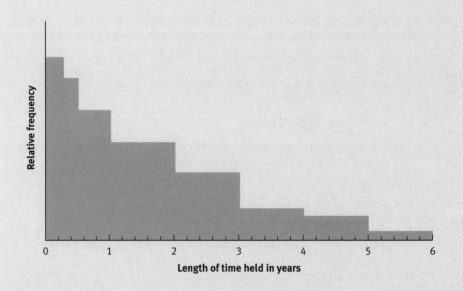

From the table the largest single group of customers is those who have held contracts for 1 to < 2 years. This is the modal time period (most commonly occurring). However, the usefulness of this statistic is limited owing to the variety of class widths. By definition, half the customers will have held contracts below the median time period (approximately 1 year 5 months) and half above it. However, there are 11 customers who have held service contracts for over 5 years. As a consequence, the mean time period (approximately 1 year 9 months) is pulled towards longer times. This is represented by the skewed shape of the distribution.

You need to decide which of these measures of central tendency to include in your research report. As the mode makes little sense you quote the median and mean when interpreting the data:

```
The length of time for which customers have held service
contracts is positively skewed. Although mean length of time is
approximately 1 year 9 months, half of customers have held
service contracts for less than 1 year 5 months (median).
Grouping of these data means that it is not possible to
calculate a meaningful mode.
```

Describing the dispersion

As well as describing the central tendency for a variable, it is important to describe how the data values are dispersed around the central tendency. As you can see from Table 11.5 this is only possible for quantifiable data. Two of the most frequently used ways of describing the dispersion are the:

■ difference within the middle 50 per cent of values (inter-quartile range);

■ extent to which values differ from the mean (standard deviation);

Although these *measures of dispersion* are only suitable for quantifiable data most statistical analysis software will also calculate them for categorical data if you have used numerical codes!

To state the difference between values

In order to get a quick impression of the distribution of data values for a variable you could simply calculate the difference between the lowest and the highest values, that is the *range*. However, this statistic is rarely used in research reports as it only represents the extreme values.

A more frequently used statistic is the *inter-quartile range*. As we discussed earlier, the median divides the range into two. The range can be further divided into four equal sections called *quartiles*. The lower quartile is the value below which a quarter of your data values will fall, the upper quartile is the value above which a quarter of your data values will fall. As you would expect, the remaining half of your data values will fall between the lower and upper quartiles. The difference between the upper and lower quartiles is the inter-quartile range (Diamantopoulos and Schlegelmilch, 1997). As a consequence it is only concerned with the middle 50 per cent of data values and ignores extreme values.

You can also calculate the range for other fractions of a variable's distribution. One alternative is to divide your distribution using *percentiles*. These split your distribution into 100 equal parts. Obviously the lower quartile is the 25th percentile and the upper quartile the 75th percentile. However, you could calculate a range between the 10th and 90th percentiles so as to include 80 per cent of your data values. Another alternative is to divide the range into 10 equal parts called *deciles*.

To describe and compare the extent values differ from the mean

Conceptually and statistically in research it is important to look at the extent to which the data values for a variable are *spread* around their mean, as this is what you need to know to assess its usefulness as a typical value for the distribution. If your data values are all close to the mean, then the mean is more typical than if they vary widely. To describe the extent of spread of quantifiable data you use the *standard deviation*. If your data are a sample (Section 6.1) this is calculated using a slightly different formula than if your data are a population, although if your sample is larger than about 30 cases there is little difference in the two statistics (Morris, 1999).

You may need to compare the relative spread of data between distributions of different magnitudes (for example one may be measured in hundreds of tonnes, the other in billions of tonnes). To make a meaningful comparison you will need to take account of these different magnitudes. A common way of doing this is:

1 to divide the standard deviation by the mean;

2 then to multiply your answer by 100.

This results in a statistic called the *coefficient of variation* (Diamantopoulos and Schlegelmilch, 1997). The values of this statistic can then be compared. The distribution with the largest coefficient of variation has the largest relative spread of data.

Worked example

Describing variables and comparing their dispersion

A bank collects data on the total value of transactions at each of its main and sub-branches. The mean value of total transactions at the main branches is five times as high as that for the sub-branches. This makes it difficult to compare the relative spread in total value of transactions between the two types of branches. Calculating the coefficients of variation reveals that there is relatively more variation in the total value of transactions at the main branches than the sub-branches:

Branch type	Mean total transaction value	Standard deviation	Coefficient of variation
Main	£6 000 000	£1 417 000	23.62
Sub	£1 200 000	£217 000	18.08

This is because the coefficient of variation for the main branches is larger (23.62) than the coefficient for the sub-branches (18.08).

11.5 Examining relationships and trends using statistics

One of the questions you are most likely to ask in your analysis is 'How does a variable relate to another variable?' In statistical analysis you normally answer this question by testing the likelihood of the relationship occurring by chance, that is its significance. The way in which this significance is tested can be thought of as answering one from a series of questions, dependent on the data type:

- are these variables significantly associated?
- are these groups significantly different?
- what is the strength of the relationship between these variables and is it significant?
- if I know the values of the independent variables how well (significantly) can I predict the values of the dependent variable?

These are summarised in Table 11.6 along with statistics to help examine trends.

Table 11.6 **Statistics to examine relationships and trends by data type: a summary**

	Categorical		Quantifiable	
	Descriptive	**Ranked**	**Continuous**	**Discrete**
To test whether two variables are significantly associated	Chi Square (data may need grouping)		Chi Square if variables grouped into discrete classes	
To test whether two groups (categories) are significantly different	Kolmogorov–Smirnov (data may need grouping)		Independent t-test or paired t-test (often used to test for changes over time)	
To test whether three or more groups (categories) are significantly different			Analysis of variance (ANOVA)	
To assess the strength of relationship between two variables		Spearman's rank correlation coefficient	Pearson's product moment correlation coefficient (PMCC)	
To assess the strength of a relationship between one dependent and one or more independent variables			Regression coefficient	
To predict the value of a dependent variable from one or more independent variables			Regression equation	
To compare relative changes over time			Index numbers	
To determine the trend over time of a series of data			Time series: moving averages Regression equation	

© Mark Saunders, Philip Lewis and Adrian Thornhill, 2000.

Testing for significant relationships

Testing the probability of a relationship between variables having occurred by chance is known as *significance testing*. As part of your research project, you might have collected sample data to examine the relationship between two variables. Once you have entered data into the analysis software, chosen the statistic and run the program an answer will appear as if by magic! With most statistical analysis software this will consist of a test statistic, the degrees of freedom and based on these the probability of your test result occurring by chance. If the probability of your test statistic having occurred by chance is very low (usually 0.05 or lower[2]), then you have a significant relationship. If the probability of obtaining the test statistic by chance is higher than 0.05, then you conclude that the relationship is not significant. There may still be a relationship between the variables under such circumstances, but you cannot make the conclusion with any certainty.

The significance of the relationship indicated by the test statistic on sample data is determined in part by your sample size (Section 6.2). As a consequence, it is very difficult to obtain a significant test statistic with a small sample. Fortunately, the impact of sample size declines rapidly for samples over about 30 cases.

To test whether two variables are significantly associated

Often descriptive or quantifiable data will be summarised as a two-way contingency table (such as Table 11.4). The *chi square test* enables you to find out whether the values for the two variables are independent or associated. It is based on a comparison of the observed values in the table with what might be expected if the two distributions were entirely independent. Therefore, you are testing whether the data in your table differ significantly from those which you would expect if the two variables were independent of each other.

The test relies on:

■ the categories used in the contingency table being mutually exclusive so each observation falls into only one category or class interval;

■ no more than 20 per cent of the cells in the table having expected values of less than 5. For contingency tables of two rows and two columns no expected values of less than 10 are preferable (Hays, 1994).

If the latter assumption is not met, the accepted solution is to combine rows and columns.

The chi square test calculates the probability that two variables are independent. Most statistical analysis software does this automatically. However, if you are using a spreadsheet you will usually need to look up the probability in a 'critical values of chi square' table using your calculated chi square value and the degrees of freedom.[3] This table is included in most statistics textbooks. A probability of 0.05 means that there is

---

[2]A probability of 0.05 means that the probability of your test result occurring by chance is 5 in 100, that is 1 in 20.
[3]Degrees of freedom are the number of values free to vary when computing a statistic. Do not worry if you find this concept difficult to grasp; their calculation and application are relatively easy. The number of degrees of freedom for a contingency table is calculated from (number of rows in the table −1) × (number of columns in the table −1).

only a 5 per cent chance that the variables are independent of each other. Therefore, a probability of 0.05 or smaller means you can be at least 95 per cent certain that your two variables are significantly associated.

Worked example

Testing whether two variables are significantly associated

As part of your research, you wish to discover whether there is a significant association between grade of the respondent and gender. Earlier analysis has indicated that there are 760 respondents in your sample with no missing data for either variable. However, it has also highlighted the small numbers of respondents in the lowest grade and very small numbers in the three highest grade categories:

Gender	Grade 1	Grade 2	Grade 3	Grade 4	Grade 5	Grade 6	Grade 7
Male	13	52	100	45	15	3	1
Female	27	233	209	49	12	0	1

Bearing in mind the assumptions of the chi square test you decide to combine categories to give three new grades: lower (grades 1 and 2), middle (grade 3) and higher (grades 4, 5, 6 and 7). The statistical analysis software creates a new data table and provides the following output:

```
                 lower      middle     higher         row
                 grade      grade      grade        totals

male               65        100         64          229
                                                   (30.1%)
         _____

female            260        209         62          531
                                                   (69.9%)
         _____

column            325        309        126          760
totals          (42.8%)    (40.7%)    (16.6%)      (100%)

Chi square = 42.13, degrees of freedom = 2, probability <.001.
```

As can be seen there is an overall chi square value of 42.13 with 2 degrees of freedom. This means that the probability of the values in your table occurring by chance is less than 0.001. You therefore conclude that the variables gender and grade are significantly associated.

To explore this association further, you examine the cell values in relation to the row and column totals. Of males, 27.9 per cent are in higher grades. This is high compared with the column totals, which indicate that only 16.6 per cent of the total sample were in higher grades. The row totals indicate that males in the sample represent 30.1 per cent of the total. Yet column frequencies show that males represented just over half (50.8 per cent) of the higher grades. Thus males are over-represented (and females under-represented) in higher grades.

To test whether two groups are significantly different

Categorical data

Sometimes it is necessary to see whether the distribution of an observed set of values for each category of a variable differs significantly from a specified population, for example whether your sample differs significantly from the population from which it was selected. The *Kolmogorov–Smirnov test* enables you to establish this (Kanji, 1998). It is based on a comparison of the cumulative proportions of the observed values in each category with the cumulative proportions in the same categories for the specified population. Therefore you are testing whether the distribution of your observed data differs significantly from that of the specified population.

The Kolmogorov–Smirnov test calculates a *D* statistic that is then used to work out the probability that the two distributions are significantly different. Although the test and statistic are not often found in analysis software, they are relatively straightforward to calculate using a spreadsheet. A reasonably clear description of this can be found in Tull and Hawkins (1993). Once calculated you will need to look up the significance of your *D* value in a 'critical values of *D* for the Kolmogorov–Smirnov test' table. A probability of 0.05 means that there is only a 5 per cent chance that the two distributions are independent of each other. Therefore a probability of 0.05 or smaller means you can be at least 95 per cent certain that your two distributions do not differ significantly.

Worked example

Testing the representativeness of a sample

Benson's research question was 'To what extent do the espoused values of an organisation match the underlying cultural assumptions?' As part of his research he sent a questionnaire to the 155 employees in the organisation where he worked. Ninety-nine of these responded. The responses from each department were as follows:

		Administration	Consultants	Systems	Trainers	Directorate	Total
Respondents	**Number**	15	49	8	6	21	99
	Cumulative proportion	0.152	0.647	0.728	0.788	1.000	
Total employees	**Number**	31	73	17	10	24	155
	Cumulative proportion	0.200	0.671	0.781	0.846	1.000	
Difference		*0.048*	*0.024*	*0.053*	*0.058*	*0*	

The maximum difference between his observed cumulative proportion (that for respondents) and his specified cumulative proportion (that for total employees) was 0.058. This was the value of his D statistic. Consulting a 'critical values of D for the Kolmogorov–Smirnov test' table for a sample size of 99 revealed the probability that the two distributions were independent of each other was less than 0.01; in other words less than 1 per cent. He concluded that those employees who responded did not differ significantly from the total population in terms of the department in which they were located.

Quantifiable data

If a quantifiable variable can be divided into two distinct groups using a descriptive variable you can assess whether or not these groups are significantly different using an *independent groups t-test*. This compares the difference in the means of the two groups using a measure of the spread of the scores. If the two variables are significantly different this will be represented by a larger t statistic with a probability less than 0.05.

Alternatively you might have quantifiable data for two variables which measure the same feature but under different conditions. Your research could focus on the effects of an intervention such as employee counselling. As a consequence you would have pairs of data that measure work performance before and after counselling for each case. To assess whether or not your two groups (each half of the pair) are significantly different you would use a *paired t-test*. Although the calculation of this is slightly different your interpretation would be the same as for the independent groups t-test.

Although the *t*-test assumes that the data are normally distributed (Section 11.3) this can be ignored without too many problems even with sample sizes of less than 30 (Hays, 1994). The assumption that the data for the two groups have the same variance (standard deviation squared) can also be ignored provided that the two samples are of similar size (Hays, 1994).

Worked example

Testing whether two groups are significantly different

As part of your research project you need to compare the performance of two international companies to see whether there is a significant difference in average (mean) share yield. You decide to use the following secondary data from the financial pages of a national newspaper:

▶

Xofen	Yield	Yffer	Yield
Belgium	5.7	France	6.2
Denmark	6.0	Germany	6.2
Eire	5.7	Italy	5.9
Luxembourg	4.8	Portugal	4.5
Netherlands	6.0	Spain	4.8
Norway	7.2	United Kingdom	5.8
Sweden	5.1		
Switzerland	5.4		

Source: National Newspaper, 1999: 22

After defining the two groups (Xofen and Yffer) using the descriptive variable you use a *t*-test to find out whether there is a significant difference between average yields for the two sectors.

Your statistical analysis software provides you with the means and standard deviations for the two groups as well as the *t* value, degrees of freedom and probability:

```
                         Xofen      Yffer
        Mean             5.74       5.57
        Standard deviation   0.73       0.73

t value = 0.43, degrees of freedom = 12, probability = 0.672
```

As the standard deviations for both sectors are the same the assumption that the two variables have the same variance is satisfied. The *t* value is only 0.43 with 12 degrees of freedom. A probability of 0.672 (much greater than 0.05) indicates that there is no significant difference between the two groups. You conclude in your research report that there is no significant difference in average (mean) yields between Xofen and Yffer.

To test whether three or more groups are significantly different

If a quantifiable variable is divided into three or more distinct groups using a descriptive variable, you can assess whether these groups are significantly different using *one-way analysis of variance* or *one-way ANOVA* (Table 11.6). As you can gather from its name, ANOVA analyses the variations within and between groups of data by comparing means. The *F* ratio or *F* statistic represents these differences. If the means are significantly different between groups this will be represented by a large *F* ratio with a probability of less than 0.05.

Hays (1994) lists the following assumptions which need to be met before using one-way ANOVA:

■ Each data value is independent and does not relate to any of the other data values. This means that you should not use one-way ANOVA where data values are related in some way such as the same person being tested repeatedly;

■ the data for each group are normally distributed (Section 11.3). This assumption is not particularly important provided that the number of cases in each group is large (30 or more);

■ the data for each group have the same variance (standard deviation squared). However, provided that the number of cases in the largest group is not more than 1.5 times that of the smallest group, this appears to have very little effect on the test results.

Worked example

Testing whether three groups are significantly different

Andy and a colleague were interested to discover whether there were significant differences in job satisfaction across three groups of employees (managers, administrators, shop floor workers) within a manufacturing organisation. They decided to measure job satisfaction using a tried-and-tested scale based on five questions that resulted in a job satisfaction score (quantifiable data) for each employee.

After ensuring that the assumptions of one-way ANOVA were satisfied they analysed their data using statistical analysis software. The output included the following:

```
ANALYSIS OF VARIANCE
Source         D.F.    Sum of      Mean       F Ratio    F Prob.
                       Squares     Squares

Between          2     455.7512    227.8756   24.3952    <.0001
Groups

Within         614     5735.3834    9.3410
Groups

Total          616     6191.1345
```

This output shows that the F ratio value of 24.3952 with 2 and 614 degrees of freedom (D.F.) has a probability of occurrence by chance of less than 0.0001 if there is no significant difference between the three groups. Andy and his colleague therefore concluded that there was a significant difference in job satisfaction between managers, administrators, shop floor workers.

Assessing the strength of relationship

As part of your exploratory data analysis you will already have plotted the relationship between cases for two ranked or quantifiable variables using a scatter graph (Fig 11.10). Such relationships might include those between weekly sales of a new product and those of a similar established product, or age of employees and their length of service with the company. These examples emphasise the fact that your data can contain two sorts of relationship:

- those where a change in one variable is accompanied by a change in another variable but it is not clear which variable caused the other to change, a *correlation*;

- those where a change in one or more (independent) variables causes a change in another (dependent) variable, a *cause-and-effect* relationship.

To assess the strength of relationship between pairs of variables

A *correlation coefficient* enables you to quantify the strength of the relationship between two ranked or quantifiable variables. This coefficient (represented by the letter *r*) can take on any value between -1 and +1 (Fig 11.11). A value of +1 represents a perfect *positive correlation*. This means that the two variables are precisely related and that, as values of one variable increase, values of the other variable will increase. By contrast a value of –1 represents a perfect *negative correlation*. Again this means that the two variables are precisely related; however, as the values of one variable increase the other's decrease. Correlation coefficients between +1 and -1 represent weaker positive and negative correlations, a value of 0 meaning the variables are perfectly independent. Within business research it is extremely unusual to obtain perfect correlations.

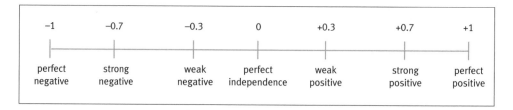

Fig 11.11 **Values of the correlation coefficient**

For data collected from a sample you will need to know the probability of your correlation coefficient having occurred by chance. Most statistical analysis software calculates this probability automatically. As outlined earlier, if this probability is very low (usually less than 0.05) then you have a significant relationship. If the probability is greater than 0.05 then your relationship is not significant.

If both your variables contain quantifiable data you should use *Pearson's product moment correlation coefficient* (PMCC) to assess the strength of relationship (Table 11.6). However, if one of your variables contains rank data you will need to rank the other variable and use *Spearman's rank correlation coefficient*. Although this uses a different formula to calculate the correlation coefficient it is interpreted in the same way.

> **Worked example**
>
> ## Assessing the strength of relationship between pairs of variables
>
> As part of their market research a company has collected data on the number of newspaper advertisements, number of enquiries and number of sales for a product. These data have been entered into their statistical analysis software. They wish to discover whether there are any relationships between the following pairs of these variables:
>
> - number of newspaper advertisements and number of enquires
> - number of newspaper advertisements and number of sales
> - number of enquiries and number of sales
>
> As the data are quantifiable they program the statistical analysis software to calculate Pearson's product moment correlation coefficients for all pairs of variables. The output is provided in the form of a correlation matrix:
>
> ```
> Correlation Coefficients
>
>               advert        enquiry       sales
> advert        1.0000        0.3441*       0.2030
> enquiry       0.3441*       1.0000        0.7002**
> sales         0.2030        0.7002**      1.0000
>
> * significance < .05, **significance < .01
> ```
>
> The matrix is symmetrical because correlation only implies a relationship rather than a cause-and-effect relationship. The value in each cell of the matrix is the correlation coefficient. Thus the correlation between the variable 'advert' and the variable 'enquiry' is 0.3441. This coefficient shows that there is a fairly weak but positive relationship between the number of newspaper advertisements and the number of enquiries. The * indicates that the probability of this correlation coefficient occurring by chance is less than 0.05 (5 per cent). This correlation is therefore significant.
>
> Using the data in this matrix the company concludes that there is a highly significant strong positive relationship between the number of enquiries and the number of sales ($r = 0.7002$) and a significant but weaker relationship between the number of newspaper advertisements and the number of enquiries ($r = 0.3441$). However, there is no significant relationship between the number of newspaper advertisements and the number of sales.

To assess the strength of a cause-and-effect relationship between variables

In contrast to the correlation coefficient the *regression coefficient* (sometimes known as the *coefficient of determination*) enables you to assess the strength of relationship between a quantifiable dependent variable and one or more quantifiable independent variables. For a dependent variable and one (or perhaps two) independent variables you will have probably already plotted this relationship on a scatter graph. If you have more than two independent variables this is unlikely as it is very difficult to represent four or more scatter graph axes visually!

The regression coefficient (represented by r^2) can take on any value between 0 and +1. It measures the proportion of the variation in a dependent variable (amount of sales) that can be explained statistically by the independent variable (marketing expenditure) or variables (marketing expenditure, number of sales staff etc.). This means that if all the variation in amount of sales can be explained by the marketing expenditure and the number of sales staff the regression coefficient will be 1. If 50 per cent of the variation can be explained the regression coefficient will be 0.5 and if none of the variation can be explained the coefficient will be 0. Within our research we have rarely obtained a regression coefficient above 0.8.

The process of calculating a regression coefficient using one independent variable is normally termed *regression*. Calculating the regression coefficient using two or more independent variables is termed *multiple regression*. The calculations and interpretation required by multiple regression are relatively complicated and we advise you to use statistical analysis software and consult a detailed statistics text book or computer manual such as Norusis (1998). Most statistical analysis software will calculate the significance of the regression coefficient for sample data automatically. A very low significance value (usually 0.05) means that your coefficient is unlikely to have occurred by chance. A value greater than 0.05 means you can conclude that your regression coefficient is not significant.

Worked example

Assessing a cause and effect relationship

As part of your research you wish to assess the relationship between all the employees' annual salary and the number of years they have been employed by the organisation. You believe that annual salary will be dependent on the number of years for which they have been employed (the independent variable).

You enter the data into your analysis software and calculate a regression coefficient (r^2) of 0.37.

As you are using data from the population rather than a sample the probability of the coefficient occurring by chance is 0. You therefore conclude that 37 per cent of the variation in employees' salary can be explained by the number of years they have been employed by the organisation.

To predict the value of a variable from one or more other variables

Regression analysis can also be used to predict the values of a dependent variable given the values of one or more independent variables by calculating a *regression equation*. You may wish to predict the amount of sales for a specified marketing expenditure and number of sales staff. You would represent this as a regression equation:

amount of sales = $a + (b_1 \times$ marketing expenditure$) + (b_2 \times$ number of sales staff$)$

Using regression analysis you would calculate the values of a, b_1 and b_2 from data you had already collected on amount of sales, marketing expenditure and number of sales staff. A specified marketing expenditure and number of sales staff could then be substituted into the regression equation to predict the amount of sales that would be generated.

The regression coefficient (discussed earlier) can be used as a measure of how good a predictor your regression equation is likely to be. If your equation is a perfect predictor then the regression coefficient will be 1. If the equation can only predict 50 per cent of the variation then the regression coefficient will be 0.5 and if the equation predicts none of the variation the coefficient will be 0.

Worked example

Forecasting journey time

A mini-cab firm needs to establish the relationship between the time a journey takes (dependent variable) and the distance travelled in towns and the country (independent variables) in order to be able to provide their customers with an estimate of journey time. To do this they have collected data for a sample of 250 journeys on the miles travelled in towns, the miles travelled in the country and the time taken in minutes. The data are entered into statistical analysis software and a multiple regression performed. The output includes the following statistics:

```
R Square = .60459     F = 24.14     Signif F = .0012

Variables in the Equation

Variable          B

town              2.7651
country           1.3453
constant (a)      4.7452
```

The 'variables in the equation' are substituted into the regression equation (after rounding the values of a and b):

journey time = 4.7 + (2.8 × town miles) + (1.3 × country miles)

The time for any journey, such as one of 2 town miles and 3 country miles, can now be estimated:

4.7 + (2.8 × 2) + (1.3 × 3)
= 12.9 minutes

However, care should be taken with these estimates as, while the values in the equation are unlikely to have occurred by chance (significant $F = 0.0012$), they only explain just over 60 per cent ($r^2 = 0.604\ 59$) of the variation in the journey time.

Examining trends

When examining longitudinal data the first thing we recommend you do is to draw a line graph to obtain a visual representation of the trend (Fig 11.4). Subsequent to this statistical analyses can be undertaken. Two of the more common uses of such analyses are:

- to compare trends for variables measured in different units or of different magnitudes;
- to determine the long term trend and forecast future values for a variable.

These are summarised in Table 11.6.

To compare trends

To answer some research question(s) and to meet some objectives you may need to compare trends between two or more variables measured in different units or at different magnitudes. To compare changes in prices of fuel oil and coal over time is difficult as the prices are recorded for different units (litres and tonnes). One way of overcoming this is to use *index numbers* and compare the relative changes in prices rather than actual figures. Index numbers are also widely used in business publications and by organisations. The *Financial Times* share indices and the Index of Retail Prices are well-known examples.

Although such indices can involve quite complex calculations they all compare change over time against a base period. The *base period* is normally given the value of 100 (or 1000 in the case of many share indices) and change calculated relative to this. Thus a value greater than 100 would represent an increase relative to the base period and a value less than 100, a decrease.

To calculate simple index numbers for each case of a longitudinal variable you use the following formula:

$$\text{index number for case} = \frac{\text{data value for case}}{\text{data value for base period}} \times 100$$

Thus if a company's sales were 125 000 units in 1999 (base period) and 150 000 units in 2000 the index number for 1999 would be 100 and for 2000 it would be 120.

To determine the trend and forecasting

The trend can be estimated by drawing a freehand line through the data on a line graph. However, these data are often subject to variations such as seasonal variations (Fig 11.4) and so this method is not very accurate. A straightforward way of overcoming this is to calculate a moving average for the *time series* of data values. Calculating a *moving average* involves replacing each value in the time series with the mean of that value and those values directly preceding and following it (Morris, 1999). This smoothes out the variation in the data so that you can see the trend more clearly. The calculation of a moving average is relatively straightforward using either a spreadsheet or statistical analysis software.

Once the trend has been established it is possible to forecast future values by continuing the trend forward for time periods for which data have not been collected. This involves calculating the *long-term trend*, that is the amount by which values are changing each time period after variations have been smoothed out. Once again this is relatively straightforward to calculate using analysis software. Forecasting can also be undertaken using other statistical methods including regression (Section 11.5).

11.6 Summary

- Data for quantitative analysis can be collected and subsequently coded at different levels of numerical measurement. The data type (precision of measurement) will constrain the data presentation, summary and analysis techniques you can use.

- Data are entered for computer analysis as a data matrix in which each column usually represents a variable and each row a case. Your first variable should be a unique identifier to facilitate error checking.

- All data should, with few exceptions, be recorded using numerical codes to facilitate analyses.

- Where possible you should use existing coding schemes to enable comparisons.

- For primary data you should include pre-set codes on the data collection form to minimise coding after collection. For variables where responses are not known you will need to develop a codebook after data have been collected for the first 50 to 100 cases.

- You should enter codes for all data values including missing data.

- The data matrix must be checked for errors.

- Your initial analysis should explore data using both tables and diagrams. Your choice of table or diagram will be influenced by your research question(s) and objectives, the aspects of the data you wish to emphasise and the level of measurement at which the data were recorded. This may involve using:

  - tables to show specific values;

  - bar charts, multiple bar charts and histograms to show highest and lowest values;

  - line graphs to show trends;

  - pie charts and percentage component bar charts to show proportions;

  - box plots to show distributions;

  - scatter graphs to show relationships between variables.

- Subsequent analyses will involve describing your data and exploring relationships using statistics. As before your choice of statistics will be influenced by your research question(s) and objectives and the level of measurement at which the data were recorded. Your analysis may involve using statistics such as:

- the mean, median and mode to describe the central tendency;
- the inter-quartile range and the standard deviation to describe the dispersion;
- chi square to test whether two variables are significantly associated;
- Kolmogorov–Smirnov to test whether the values differ significantly from a specified population;
- *t*-tests and ANOVA to test whether groups are significantly different;
- correlation and regression to assess the strength of relationships between variables.
- regression analysis to predict values.

■ Longitudinal data may necessitate selecting different statistical techniques such as:

- index numbers to compare trends between two or more variables measured in different units or at different magnitudes;
- moving averages and regression analysis to determine the trend and forecast.

Self check   Questions

11.1 The following secondary data have been obtained from the Park Trading Company's audited annual accounts:

Year	Income (£)	Expenditure (£)
1992	11 000 000	9 500 000
1993	15 200 000	12 900 000
1994	17 050 000	14 000 000
1995	17 900 000	14 900 000
1996	19 000 000	16 100 000
1997	18 700 000	17 200 000
1998	17 100 000	18 100 000
1999	17 700 000	19 500 000
2000	19 900 000	20 000 000

a Which are the variables and which are the cases?

b Sketch a possible data matrix for these data for entering into a spreadsheet.

11.2 a How many variables will be generated from the following request?

Please tell me up to five things you like about the Home Care Service.

for office use
❏❏❏
❏❏❏
❏❏❏
❏❏❏
❏❏❏

....

....

....

....

....

b How would you go about devising a coding scheme for these variables from a survey of 500 Home Care Service clients?

11.3 a Illustrate the data from the Park Trading Company's audited annual accounts (self-check question 11.1) to show trends in income and expenditure.

b What does your diagram emphasise?

c What diagram would you use to emphasise the years with the lowest and highest income?

11.4 As part of research into the impact of television advertising on donations by credit card to a major disaster appeal, data have been collected on the number of viewers reached and the number of donations each day for the past two weeks.

a Which diagram or diagrams would you use to explore these data?

b Give reasons for your choice.

11.5 a What measures of central tendency and dispersion would you choose to describe the Park Trading Company's income (self-check question 11.1) over the period 1992–2000?

b Give reasons for your choice.

11.6 A colleague has collected data from a sample of 103 students. He presents you with the following output from the statistical analysis software:

```
Information technology facilities at this University are....
```

	good	reasonable	poor	row totals
undergraduate	63	18	5	86 (83.5%)
postgraduate	6	4	7	17 (16.5%)
column totals	69	22	12	103
	(67.0%)	(21.4%)	(11.6%)	103

```
Chi square = 18.33, degrees of freedom = 2,  probability <.01.
```

Explain what this tells you about undergraduate and postgraduate students' opinion of the information technology facilities.

11.7 Briefly describe when you would use regression analysis and correlation analysis using examples to illustrate your answer.

11.8 a Use an appropriate technique to compare the following data on share prices for two financial service companies over the past six months using the period six months ago as the base period.

	EJ Investment Holdings	AE Financial Services
Price 6 months ago	10 pence	587 pence
Price 4 months ago	12 pence	613 pence
Price 2 months ago	13 pence	658 pence
Current price	14 pence	690 pence

b Which company's share prices have increased most in the last six months? (Note: you should quote relevant statistics to justify your answer.)

Assignment 11

Analysing your quantitative data

→ Examine the technique(s) you are proposing to use to collect data to answer your research question. You need to decide whether you are collecting any data that could usefully be analysed quantitatively.

→ If you decide that your data should be analysed quantitatively you must ensure that the data collection methods you intend to use have been designed to make analysis by computer as straightforward as possible. In particular you need to pay attention to the coding scheme for each variable and the layout of your data matrix.

→ Once your data have been entered into a computer, you will need to explore and present them. Bearing your research question in mind you should select the most appropriate diagrams and tables after considering the suitability of all possible techniques. Remember to label your diagrams clearly and to keep a copy as they may form part of your research report.

→ Once you are familiar with your data describe and explore relationships using those statistical techniques that best help you to answer your research questions and are suitable for the data type. Remember to keep an annotated copy of your analyses as you will need to quote statistics to justify statements you make in the findings section of your research report.

References

Bryman, A. and Cramer, D. (1999) *Quantitative Data Analysis with SPSS Release 8 for Windows: for Social Scientists*, London, Routledge.

Central Statistical Office (1997) *Standard Industrial Classification of Economic Activities*, London, Stationery Office.

Diamantopoulos, A. and Schlegelmilch, B.B. (1997) *Taking the Fear Out of Data Analysis*, London, Dryden Press.

Fox, J. and Long, J.S. (eds) (1990) *Modern Methods of Data Analysis*, Newbury Park, CA, Sage.

Hays, W.L. (1994) *Statistics* (4th edn), London, Holt-Saunders.

Jowell, R., Curtice, J., Brook, L. and Ahrendt, D. (1994) *British Social Attitudes – the 11th Report*, Aldershot, Dartmouth.

Kanji, G.K. (1998) *100 Statistical Tests* (2nd edn), London, Sage.

Mercator (1999) 'Mercator home page: products' (online)(cited 16 June 1999). Available from <URL:http://www.mercator.co.uk>

Morris, C. (1999) *Quantitative Approaches in Business Studies* (5th edn), London, Pitman.

Norusis, M.J. (1998) *SPSS 8.0 Guide to Data Analysis*, London, Prentice Hall.

Office of Population Censuses and Surveys (1990a) *Standard Occupational Classification, Vol. 1,* London, HMSO.

Office of Population Censuses and Surveys (1990b) *Standard Occupational Classification, Vol. 2,* London, HMSO.

Office of Population Censuses and Surveys (1991) *Standard Occupational Classification, Vol. 3,* London, HMSO.

Office of Population Censuses and Surveys and General Registrar's Office for Scotland (1992) *1991 Census Definitions Great Britain*, London, HMSO.

Robson, C. (1993) *Real World Research*, Oxford, Blackwell.

Scolari Sage (1999) 'Research methodology and CD-ROMS', (online)(cited 16 June 1999). Available from <URL:http://www.scolari.co.uk>

Sparrow, J. (1989) 'Graphic displays in information systems: some data properties influencing the effectiveness of alternate forms', *Behaviour and Information Technology*, 8:1, 43–56.

Tukey J.W. (1977) *Exploratory Data Analysis*, Reading, MA, Addison-Wesley.

Tull, D.S. and Hawkins, D.I. (1993) *Marketing Research: Measurement and Method,* Upper Saddle River, NJ, Prentice-Hall.

deVaus, D.A. (1996) *Surveys in Social Research* (4th edn), London, UCL Press.

Further reading

Bryman, A. and Cramer, D. (1999) *Quantitative Data Analysis with SPSS Release 8 for Windows: for Social Scientists*, London, Routledge. This book offers a formula-free non-technical approach to using 'SPSS for Windows'. It assumes no familiarity with the data analysis software and covers both inputting data and how to generate and interpret a wide range of tables, diagrams and statistics.

Diamantopoulos, A. and Schlegelmilch, B.B. (1997) *Taking the Fear out of Data Analysis,* London, Dryden Press. This is a statistics book which is both humorous and informative. It assumes very little in the way of statistical knowledge and is written for people who do not like data analysis and do not think they can understand numbers!

Hays, W.L. (1994) *Statistics* (4th edn), London, Holt-Saunders. This provides a detailed discussion of statistics emphasising both the theoretical and applied aspects. This book is aimed at the first-year postgraduate student who will probably have already taken an undergraduate statistics module.

Morris, C. (1999) *Quantitative Approaches in Business Studies* (5th edn), London, Financial Times Pitman Publishing. This gives a clear introduction to the use of mathematical and statistical techniques and diagrams in business. Guidance is given on using the 'Excel' spreadsheet and 'Minitab' statistical analysis software.

Robson, C. (1993) *Real World Research*, Oxford, Blackwell. Chapter 11 provides an introduction to quantitative data analysis and guidance on using the 'Statview' statistical analysis software.

deVaus, D.A. (1996) *Surveys in Social Research* (4th edn), London, UCL Press. Chapter 14 contains an excellent discussion on techniques for coding data.

Case 11   ## The marketing of arts festivals

Jemma was interested in utilising secondary data from her placement organisation as part of her undergraduate research project on the marketing of arts festivals. In particular she was interested in:

■ the extent to which audiences associated events with their sponsors;

■ the socio-economic status of those attending;

■ the importance of different media for finding out about events.

Her placement organisation had undertaken a questionnaire survey with attendees at the local arts festival and agreed that Jemma could use the data for her research project. The data had already been entered into a spreadsheet. A copy of a completed questionnaire is included below.

The
Anyshire
Echo

ANYTOWN
FESTIVAL OF ARTS

AUDIENCE QUESTIONNAIRE

Please help us to continue to improve the Arts Festival by completing the questionnaire below.

When you have completed it, please hand it to the Box Office or the Friends Information Desk or send it back to us **by 10th September** and you can enter **a free prize draw** for one of four £30 record tokens.

It takes just five minutes to answer the questions, and your opinions will help us to plan next year's festival.

Please return your completed questionnaire to the address below (NB: no stamp is needed):

FREEPOST 12345
Town Hall
Town Square
Anytown
AN50 2BD

To enter the free prize draw please write your name and address below:

Name: *Mrs Lily Anners* ....

Address: *15, Anytown Road* ....

Anytown ....

Postcode: *AN34 7MS* ....

(NB: this information will not be passed on to any other organisation.)

PART 1: Please answer these questions by putting a <u>circle</u> around the appropriate number

1 Which Festival event have you attended?

Ruskin's Poetry Reading and Arias by Candlelight

2 Where do you live?

In Anytown	①	30 to less than 50 miles away	2
Under 10 miles away	3	50 to less than 100 miles away	4
10 to less than 20 miles away	5	Over 100 miles away	6
20 to less than 30 miles away	7		

3 What age are you?

Under 18	1	35 to 44	3	over 60	5
19 to 30	2	45 to 60	④		

4 Are you . . .

Female ?	①	Male?	2

5 Are you currently . . .

Unemployed?	1	In full-time paid professional employment?	5
Retired?	②	In full-time non-professional employment?	6
A housewife?	3	In part-time paid employment?	⑦
A student?	4	Other? (please say)	8

6 Which of the following organisations do you associate with this festival?

The Anytown Bank	1	Murial's Bookstores	6
Anytown Borough Council	2	Good Deal Records	⑦
The Anyshire Echo	③	Midshire Bank	8
Steven's Computers Ltd	4	Other (please say)	9
VHT Record Stores	5		

7 Did you take advantage of any of the following discounts when booking?

Early booking	1	Poetry pass	4
Friends discount	2	Anyshire Echo pass	5
Group discount	3	Student discount	6 *None of these*

PART 2: Please read the statements below; decide whether you agree, strongly agree, disagree or strongly disagree; then <u>circle</u> the number below your choice:

	strongly disagree	disagree	agree	strongly agree
8 I found it easy to book/buy tickets for the Festival	1	2	3	④

9 The event(s) I came to was/were good value for money	1	② *one*	3	④ *other*

PART 3: Please comment on the following:

10 Is there anything you would like to change to improve the Festival (i.e. the times, the programme, etc.)? *The battle for the best seats nearest the speakers. The middle classes are seen at their most devious here – sneaking in and laying coats on seats etc!!*

11 What did you think of the event you came to? *Good*

12 How did you find out about the Festival? *Programmes available in book shop*

Questions

1 On looking at the questionnaire, Jemma noticed some problems with the way in which some questions had been coded.

   a What were these problems?

   b How might these have been overcome at the survey design stage?

2 a Which of the questions were likely to be most useful to Jemma for her research project?

   b How could Jemma have minimised the impact on her analysis of any coding problems with these questions?

3 Which diagrams, tables and statistics would you recommend Jemma to use to analyse those questions which were useful to her research project? (You should state precisely what your recommended diagrams, tables and statistics will enable Jemma to find out.)

Answers

11.1 a The variables are 'income', 'expenditure' and 'year'. There is no real need for a separate case identifier as the variable 'year' can also fulfil this function. Each case (year)
is represented by one row of data.

b When the data are entered into a spreadsheet the first column will be the case identifier, for these data the year. Income and expenditure should not be entered with the
£ sign as this can be formatted subsequently using the spreadsheet.

	A	B	C
1	year (id)	income	expenditure
2	1992	11 000 000	9 500 000
3	1993	15 200 000	12 900 000
4	1994	17 100 000	14 000 000
4	1995	17 900 000	14 900 000
6	1996	19 000 000	16 100 000
7	1997	18 700 000	17 200 000
8	1998	17 100 000	18 100 000
9	1999	17 700 000	19 500 000
10	2000	19 900 000	20 000 000

11.2 a There is no one correct answer to this question as the number of variables will depend
on the method used to code these descriptive data. If you choose the multiple
response method five variables will be generated. If the multiple dichotomy method is
used the number of variables will depend on the number of different responses.

b Your first priority is to decide on the level of detail of your intended analyses. Your
coding scheme should, if possible, be based on an existing coding scheme. If this of
insufficient detail then it should be designed to be compatible to enable comparisons. To design the coding scheme you need to take the responses from the first
50–100 cases and to establish broad groupings. These can be subdivided into increasingly specific sub-groups until the detail is sufficient for the intended analysis. Codes
can then be allocated to these sub-groups. If you ensure that similar responses receive
adjacent codes this will make any subsequent grouping easier. The actual responses
that correspond to each code should be noted in a code book. Codes should be allocated to data on the data collection form in the 'for Office use' box. These codes need
to include missing data such as when four or less 'things' have been mentioned.

11.3a   Park Trading Company – Income and Expenditure 1992–2000

Source: Audited annual accounts

b Your diagram (it is hoped) emphasises the upward trends of expenditure and to a lesser extent income. It also highlights the conjunction where income falls below expenditure in 1998.

c To emphasise the years with the lowest and highest income you would probably use a histogram because the data are continuous. A frequency polygon would also be suitable.

11.4 a You would probably use a scatter graph in which number of donations would be the dependent variable and number of viewers reached by the advertisement the independent variable.

b This would enable you to see whether there was any relationship between number of viewers reached and number of donations.

11.5 a The first thing you need to do is to establish the data type. As it is quantifiable, you could theoretically use all three measures of central tendency and both the standard deviation and inter-quartile range. However, you would probably calculate the mean and perhaps the median as measures of central tendency and the standard deviation and perhaps the inter-quartile range as measures of dispersion.

b The mean would be chosen because it includes all data values. The median might be chosen to represent the middle income over the 1992–2000 period. The mode would be of little use for these data as each year has different income values.
   If you had chosen the mean you would probably choose the standard deviation as this describes the dispersion of data values around the mean. The inter-quartile range is normally chosen where there are extreme data values that need to be ignored. This is not the case for these data.

11.6 The probability of a chi square value of 18.33 with 2 degrees of freedom occurring by chance for these data is less than 0.01. This means there is a significant association between type of student and their opinion of the information technology facilities.

To explore this association further, you examine the cell values in relation to the row and column totals. Of the postgraduates, 41.1 per cent thought the information technology facilities were poor. This is high compared with the column totals, which indicate that only 11.6 per cent of total students thought the information technology facilities were poor. The column frequencies indicate that undergraduates represent 91.3 per cent of those students who thought information technology facilities were good. Yet only 83.5 per cent of the total students thought information technology facilities were good. Thus, postgraduate students have a poorer opinion of information technology facilities than undergraduate students do.

11.7 Your answer needs to emphasise that correlation analysis is used to establish whether a change in one variable is accompanied by a change in another. In contrast, regression analysis is used to establish whether a change in a dependent variable is caused by changes in one or more independent variables; in other words a cause-and-effect relationship.

Although it is impossible to list all the examples you might use to illustrate your answer, you should make sure that your examples for regression illustrate a dependent and one or more independent variables.

11.8 a These quantitative data are of different magnitudes. Therefore, the most appropriate technique to compare these data is index numbers. The index numbers for the two companies are:

	EJ Investment Holdings	AE Financial Services
Price 6 months ago	100	100.0
Price 4 months ago	120	104.4
Price 2 months ago	130	112.1
Current price	140	117.5

b The price of AE Financial Services' shares has increased by 103 pence compared with an increase of 4 pence for EJ Investment Holdings' share price. However, the proportional increase in prices has been greatest for EJ Investment Holdings. Using six months ago as the base period (with a base index number of 100) the index for EJ Investment Holdings' share price is now 140 while the index for AE Financial Services' share price is 117.5.

12 Analysing qualitative data

By the end of this chapter you should be:

■ able to evaluate the nature and value of qualitative data;

■ aware of a range of approaches to and processes for analysing qualitative data;

■ aware of the use of analytical strategies and procedures related to the use of predicted theoretical explanations and the use of grounded theory;

■ able to consider limitations about quantifying qualitative data as a means of analysis;

■ aware of computer-based text retrievers and text managers.

12.1 Introduction

This chapter is designed to help you to analyse the qualitative data that you collect. However, it commences by considering the nature of qualitative data so that you can recognise the issues associated with attempting to analyse systematically and rigorously this type of data (Section 12.2). Section 12.3 provides an overview of the process of qualitative analysis. In reading this overview you will recognise the interrelated and interactive nature of qualitative data collection and analysis. The stages of the process of qualitative analysis outlined in this overview demonstrate that you will need to undertake your data collection and analysis in a systematic and well-planned manner, in order to be able to analyse your data rigorously and to draw verifiable conclusions from them.

It is possible to approach qualitative data collection and analysis from either a deductive or an inductive perspective (Section 12.4). We therefore consider analytical strategies and procedures which commence with theoretical propositions which can be tested against the data collected (Section 12.5). We also discuss the use of a 'grounded theory' approach and the main implications associated with this particular qualitative research strategy (Section 12.6). The final approach that we consider to help you to analyse some of your qualitative data is the use of quantification (Section 12.7). The advent of powerful personal computers has made a significant impact on the way in which qualitative data can be processed and analysed, and the use of software to facilitate this is therefore also discussed (Section 12.8).

12.2 Understanding qualitative data

A key distinction is drawn between qualitative and quantitative research (for example, Bryman, 1988; Easterby-Smith *et al.*, 1991). However, attempts to define the distinctiveness of qualitative research, and therefore the way in which it can be distinguished from quantitative research, can be problematic (Silverman, 1993). Nevertheless, when we look at the data produced by qualitative research we are able to draw some significant distinctions from those which result from quantitative work. These are helpful in terms of understanding what is necessary in order to be able to analyse these data meaningfully. Table 12.1 highlights three distinct differences between quantitative and qualitative data.

Table 12.1 **Distinctions between quantitative and qualitative data**

Quantitative data	Qualitative data
■ Based on meanings derived from numbers	■ Based on meanings expressed through words
■ Collection results in numerical and standardised data	■ Collection results in non-standardised data requiring classification into categories
■ Analysis conducted through the use of diagrams and statistics	■ Analysis conducted through the use of conceptualisation

Sources: Developed from Dey, 1993; Healey and Rawlinson, 1994; authors' experience

While 'number depends on meaning' (Dey, 1993:28) it is not always the case that meaning is dependent on number. Dey (1993:28) points out that 'The more ambiguous and elastic our concepts, the less possible it is to quantify our data in a meaningful way'. Qualitative data are associated with such concepts and are characterised by their richness and fullness based on your opportunity to explore a subject in as real a manner as is possible (Robson, 1993). A contrast can thus be drawn between the 'thin' abstraction or description which results from quantitative data collection and the 'thick' or 'thorough' abstraction or description associated with qualitative data (Dey, 1993; Robson, 1993).

The nature of qualitative data therefore has implications for both its collection and its analysis. To be able to capture the richness and fullness associated with qualitative data they cannot be collected in a standardised way, like that of quantitative data. During analysis, however, the non-standardised and complex nature of the data which you have collected will need to be classified into categories before they can be meaningfully analysed (discussed later), otherwise the most that can result will be an impressionistic view of what it means. While it may be possible to make some use of diagrams and statistics at this stage, such as the frequency of occurrence of certain categories of data (Sections 11.3 and 11.4), the way in which you are likely to analyse the qualitative data which you collect is through the creation of a conceptual framework. This may be formulated before or during your data collection (discussed later).

The analysis of qualitative data involves a demanding process and should not be seen as an 'easy option'. Yin (1994) refers to those who leave the data that they collected unanalysed for periods of time because of their uncertainty about the analytical process required.

Where you have been through the various stages of formulating and clarifying your research topic (Chapter 2), reviewing appropriate literature (Chapter 3), deciding on a research strategy (Chapter 4), considering access and ethical issues and negotiating the former (Chapter 5) and collecting your data (Chapters 6–10), you clearly do not wish to be halted by an inability to analyse this type of data. Equally you will not wish to be 'marked down' because the analysis of the data collected is perceived to be a weak aspect of your work and one which casts doubt on the thoroughness and validity of the conclusions which you draw from the data.

Indeed, two further aspects spring from this cautionary note. First, you should take the advice of Marshall and Rossman (1999) who include data analysis as one of the issues which you should consider at the time you are formulating a proposal to undertake qualitative research. Second, the act of analysing qualitative data is very likely to occur at the same time as you collect these data as well as afterwards, and this is a matter which we discuss in detail below. This leads us to the next section, which provides an overview of qualitative analysis as a process.

12.3 An overview of qualitative analysis

The features of qualitative data outlined above indicate the problematic nature of qualitative analysis. To add to this, or because of it, there is not a standardised approach to the analysis of qualitative data. There are many qualitative research traditions or approaches with the result that there are also different strategies to deal with the data collected (Dey, 1993; Miles and Huberman, 1994; Tesch, 1990; Robson, 1993). Phenomenologists, for example, resist categorising or coding their data, preferring to work from the transcripts of interviews (Miles and Huberman, 1994). Using the transcripts or notes of qualitative interviews or observations by thoroughly reading and re-reading them is one approach to analysing this type of data. However, this approach may cause you problems in relation to the elements of the numbered list that follows in the next paragraph.

The approach adopted in this Chapter involves disaggregating the mass of qualitative data that you collect, as you collect them, into meaningful and related parts or *categories*. This will allow you to rearrange and analyse these data systematically and rigorously. Adopting this approach essentially means transforming the nature of the data that you collect in order to allow you to:

1 comprehend and manage them;
2 merge related data drawn from different transcripts and notes;
3 identify key themes or patterns from them for further exploration;
4 develop and/or test hypotheses based on these apparent patterns or relationships;
5 draw and verify conclusions (Dey, 1993; Miles and Huberman, 1994).

The process discussed below involves the following activities:

- categorisation;
- 'unitising' data;
- recognising relationships and developing the categories you are using to facilitate this;
- developing and testing hypotheses to reach conclusions.

Categorisation

The first activity involves classifying your data into meaningful *categories*, which may be derived from these data (see Sections 12.5 and 12.6 for a discussion of this aspect) and which should in any case 'fit' what you have revealed. These categories are in effect labels that you will use to re-arrange your data. They provide you with an emergent structure which is relevant to your research project to analyse your data further.

The identification of these categories will be guided by the purpose of your research as expressed through your research question and objectives. Another analyst, for example, with a different purpose, may be able to derive different categories from the same data depending on their research objectives (Dey, 1993). Strauss and Corbin (1998) suggest that there are three main sources to derive names for these categories:

- you utilise terms that emerge from your data;
- they are based on the actual terms used by your participants ('*in vivo*' codes);
- or they come from terms used in existing theory and the literature.

However, the categories which you devise need to be part of a coherent set so that they provide you with a well-structured, analytical framework to pursue your analysis. Dey (1993:96-97) states that 'categories must have two aspects, an internal aspect – they must be meaningful in relation to the data – and an external aspect – they must be meaningful in relation to the other categories'.

'Unitising' data

The next activity of the analytical process will be to attach relevant 'bits' or 'chunks' of your data, which we will refer to as *units* of data, to the appropriate category or categories that you have devised. A unit of data may be a number of words, a sentence, a number of sentences, a complete paragraph or some other chunk of textual data that fits the category.

You may use a computer to help you to process your data (Section 12.8) or you may use a manual approach. Where you use the second approach, you can label a unit of data with the appropriate category (or categories) in the margin of the transcript or set of notes. This may then be copied, cut up and stuck onto a data card, or otherwise transferred, and filed so that you end up with piles of related units of data. An alternative is to index categories by recording where they occur in your transcripts or notes on cards headed with particular category labels (Easterby-Smith *et al.*, 1991). Undertaking this stage of the analytic process means that you are engaging in a selective process guided by the purpose of your research which has the effect of reducing and rearranging your data into a more manageable and comprehensible form.

> ### Worked example
>
> ## Extract of an interview with analytical categories
>
> The categories listed below were initially used to label the following interview extract.
>
> **Some initial categories**
>
> | | |
> |---|---|
> | RED: | Redundancy |
> | RED/STR: | Redundancy strategy |
> | RED/STR/ISS: | Redundancy strategy issues |
> | RED/STR/VOL: | Voluntary redundancy strategy |
> | RED/STR/COM: | Compulsory redundancy strategy |
> | RED/CONS: | Redundancy consultation |
> | RED/MGT: | Redundancy management |
> | RED/MGT/ROLE: | Redundancy management roles |
> | | |
> | SUR: | Survivors |
> | SUR/REAC: | Survivors' reactions |
> | SUR/REAC/PSY: | Psychological reactions |
> | SUR/REAC/BEH: | Behavioural reactions |
> | | |
> | SUR/STR/LINK: | This category was created to denote a link or relationship between other two categories: survivors' reactions and the choice of redundancy strategy |
>
> **Extract**
>
> | | |
> |---|---|
> | *RED/CONS* | The first stage is to find out what particular employees want for themselves and how they want this to happen. |
> | *RED/CONS*

 RED/MGT/ROLE | Staff are seen by their line manager and/or a member of personnel. An employee might want to talk to someone from personnel rather than talk with their line manager – well, you know, for obvious reasons, at least as they see it – and this would be acceptable to the organisation. |
> | *RED/STR/VOL* | This meeting provides them with the opportunity to opt for voluntary redundancy. |
> | *RED/STR/ISS*

 RED/CONS | We do not categorise employees into anything like core or non-core although we will tell a group of employees something like 'there are 4 of you in this particular function and we only need 2 of you, so you think about what should happen'. |
> | *RED/CONS*
 RED/STR/COM | Sometimes when we attempt to give employees a choice about who might leave, they actually ask us to make the choice. This is one such situation where a compulsory selection will occur. |
> | *SUR/STR/LINK*
 SUR/REAC/PSY | We prefer to avoid this compulsory selection because of the impact on those who survive – negative feelings, guilt and so on. |

One way of achieving this reduction and rearrangement of your data, depending on the suitability of the data, is to use one or more of the analytical techniques described by Miles and Huberman (1994). These include a range of different matrices, charts, graphs and networks to use as a means to arrange and display your data. Use of these may allow you to recognise emergent patterns in your data that will provide you with an indication about how to further your data collection. We advise you to consult Miles and Huberman (1994) to see how any of these techniques may assist you in the conduct of your analytical process.

Recognising relationships and developing categories

Generating categories and reorganising your data according to them, or designing a suitable matrix and placing the data gathered within its cells, means that you are engaging in the process of analysing of your data (Dey, 1993; Miles and Huberman, 1994; Yin, 1994). This analysis will continue as you search for key themes and patterns or relationships in your re-arranged data. This may lead you to alter your categories and to continue to re-arrange your data as you search for meaning in your data set. You may decide to 'subdivide or integrate categories as ways of refining or focusing [your] analysis' (Dey, 1993:95).

There may be practical reasons for seeking to divide or join your initial categories. Some categories, for example, may attract large numbers of units of data and prove to be too broad for further analysis without being subdivided. You may also gain new insights within existing categories that suggest new ones. A related piece of advice is to keep an up-to-date definition of each of the categories you are using, so that you can maintain consistency when assigning these to units of data as you continue to under-take interviews or observations (Miles and Huberman, 1994).

> **Worked example**
>
> ### Assigning data to and developing categories
>
> 'After each interview, I transcribed the interview verbatim and filed its material according to the categorisation then in use. The material was typically in the form of paragraphs [that] were cross-classified to several categories. As I filed each statement, I compared it with previous statements in that category and kept running notes on the content of the category. The categories changed over time; some disappeared and were merged under more general titles. Some emerged out of previous categories that became too heterogeneous. Some categories became parts of matched pairs or triads in which any given comment would typically be filed in each constituent category. For example, comments [that] described instances of lax work or bad workmanship also typically mentioned abusive management. Similarly, statements that described devising one's own procedures also typically included statements of satisfaction with the autonomy that provided. This helped to reveal connections between categories.'
>
> *Source: Hodson, 1991, cited in Erlandson et al., 1993: 119.* Journal of Contemporary Ethnography. *Copyright © 1991 by Sage Publications, Inc. Reprinted by permission.*

Developing and testing hypotheses

As you seek to reveal patterns within your data and to recognise relationships between categories you will be able to develop hypotheses in order to test these. Silverman (1993:1) defines a *hypothesis* as 'a testable proposition'. The appearance of an *apparent* relationship or connection between categories will need to be tested if you are to be able to conclude that there is an *actual* relationship.

Worked examples

Research hypotheses

During the process of qualitative data analysis a researcher evaluating the effectiveness of employee communication within a particular organisation formulated the following hypothesis:

- the credibility of employee communication depends on managerial action in the organisation.

A research student exploring mortgage borrowers' decision making drew up this hypothesis:

- potential mortgage borrowers' choice of lending institution is strongly affected by the level of customer service which they receive during the initial inquiry stage.

Another researcher investigating cause-related marketing formulated the following hypothesis:

- companies engaging in cause-related marketing are principally motivated by altruism.

A relationship is evident in each of these hypotheses. Each hypothesis was used to test the relationship within it through the data which had been collected or which were to be collected.

It is important to test the hypotheses that inductively emerge from the data by seeking alternative explanations and negative examples that do not conform to the pattern or relationship being tested. Alternative explanations frequently exist and only by testing the propositions which you identify will you be able to move towards formulating valid conclusions and an explanatory theory, even a simple one (Dey, 1993; Miles and Huberman, 1994). Dey (1993:48) points out that 'the association of one variable with another is not sufficient ground for inferring a causal or any other connection between them'. The existence of an intervening variable may offer a more valid explanation of an association than is apparent in your data.

The impact of an intervening variable

A research project was established to look at legal issues arising from redundancies in organisations in a number of industries. A relationship appeared to emerge between organisations in a particular industry and the frequency of industrial tribunal applications. This could have led the researchers to conclude that managerial competence in relation to this process was lower in this industry when compared with the other industries in the study.

In reality, the firms included in the study from this particular industry had a much higher incidence of using a compulsory approach to declaring redundancies than those organisations in the other industries in the study. These organisations tended to use a voluntary approach to secure redundancies. The use of this compulsory strategy turned out to be highly associated with applications to industrial tribunals, especially when compared with a voluntary approach. The variable of redundancy strategy proved to be a much more valid way of explaining the apparent association that initially emerged, rather than any explanation linked to managerial competence or any other variable.

By rigorously testing your propositions and hypotheses against your data, looking for alternative explanations and seeking to explain why negative cases occur, you will be able to move towards the development of valid and well-grounded conclusions. Thus, the validity of your conclusions will be verified by their ability to withstand alternative explanations and the nature of negative cases. This important aspect of your analysis is considered further in Sections 12.5 and 12.6.

The interactive nature of the process

The course of events outlined above demonstrates that data collection, data analysis and the development and verification of relationships and conclusions are very much an interrelated and interactive set of processes. Analysis occurs during the collection of data as well as after it. This analysis helps to shape the direction of data collection, especially where you are following a grounded theory approach (Section 12.6). As hypotheses or propositions emerge from your data, or if you commence your data collection with a theoretical framework or propositions already worked out (Section 12.5), you will seek to test these as you compare them against the cases in your study (Erlandson et al., 1993; Glaser and Strauss, 1967). The key point here is the relative flexibility that this type of process permits you.

The interactive nature of data collection and analysis allows you to recognise important themes, patterns and relationships as you collect data: in other words, to allow these to emerge from the process of data collection and analysis. As a result you will be able to re-categorise your existing data to see whether these themes, patterns and relationships are present in the cases where you have already collected data. You will also be able to adjust your future data collection approach to see whether they exist in cases where you intend to conduct your research (Strauss and Corbin, 1998). In comparison, the collection of data before their analysis during a quantitative research study may prevent this course of action.

The concurrent process of data collection and analysis also has implications for the way in which you will need to manage your time and organise your data and related documentation. It will be necessary to arrange interviews or observations with enough time between them to allow yourself sufficient time to write up or type in a transcript, or set of notes, and to analyse this before proceeding to your next data collection session (Easterby-Smith *et al.*, 1991; Erlandson, 1993). Where you conduct a small number of interviews in one day you will need time during the evening to undertake some initial analysis on these before carrying out further interviews. You may also be able to find a little time between interviews to carry out a cursory level of analysis. However, there is a clear limit to the value of continuing to undertake interviews or observations without properly analysing these in the manner described above.

Analytical aids

In addition to writing or typing up the recording or notes made of a research session and assigning units of data to appropriate categories, it will also help your analysis if you make a record of additional information. This will help you to recall the context and content of the interview or observation. You may also consider other techniques aimed at helping you to analyse your qualitative data, such as those outlined by Riley (1996). Various researchers have advanced methods to help you to record information that will usefully supplement your written-up notes or transcripts and your categorised data (for example, Glaser, 1978; Miles and Huberman, 1994; Riley, 1996; Robson, 1993; Strauss and Corbin, 1998). We consider the following suggestions:

- summaries, including those for interviews, observations and documents, and also interim ones;
- self-memos;
- a researcher's diary.

Summaries

After you have written up your notes, or produced a transcript, of an interview or observation session, you can produce a *summary* of the key points that emerge from undertaking this activity. At this point you will be conversant with the principal themes which have emerged from the interview or observation and how you would like to explore these further in forthcoming data collection sessions. You may be able to identify apparent relationships between themes that you wish to note down so that you can return to these to seek to establish their validity. It will also be useful to make some comments about the person(s) you interviewed or observed, the setting in which this occurred and whether anything occurred during the interview or observation that might have affected the nature of the data which you collected.

Worked example

The importance of noting an event that affected the nature of data collection

Adrian recalls an interview where the first part was conducted with two participants before their manager joined them. It was noticeable that after this person had joined the interview process the first two deferred and said very little. The interview was considered highly valuable and all the questions asked were answered fully. However, it was worth recording this incident in a post-transcript summary in case any divergence appeared between the nature of the data in the two parts of the interview.

Once you have produced a summary of the key points which emerge from the interview or observation and its context you should attach a copy to the set of your written-up notes or transcript for further reference (Miles and Huberman, 1994; Riley, 1996; Robson, 1993).

Qualitative research may also involve the use of organisational documentation. This may be an important source of data in its own right (for example, using minutes of meetings, internal reports, briefings, planning documents and schedules), or you may use such documentation as a means of triangulating other data which you collect (Section 7.2). Where you use any sort of documentation you can also produce a summary which describes the purpose of the document, how it relates to your work and why it is significant, as well as providing a list of the key points which it contains. This type of summary may be useful when you undertake further analysis if you want to refer to sources of data (i.e. the document) as well as the way in which your categorical data have been categorised into their component parts.

An *interim summary* is an attempt by you to take stock of your progress to date through the production of a written paper that looks at the following aspects:

■ what you have found out so far;

■ what level of confidence you have in your findings and conclusions to date;

■ what you need to do in order to improve the quality of your data and/or to seek to substantiate your apparent conclusions, or to seek alternative explanations;

■ how you will seek to achieve the needs identified by the above interim analysis.

This can become a working document that you make continued reference to as your research project continues to make progress (Miles and Huberman, 1994; Riley, 1996; Robson, 1993).

Self-memos

Self-memos allow you to make a record of the ideas which occur to you about any aspect of your research, as you think of them. Where you omit to record any idea as it occurs to you it may well be lost. The occasions when you will want to write a memo include:

- when you are writing up interview or observation notes, or producing a transcript of this event;
- when you are categorising these data;
- as you continue to categorise and analyse these data;
- when you engage in the process of writing.

Ideas may also occur as you engage in an interview or observation session. In this case you may record very briefly the idea as a margin note and write it as a memo to yourself after the event. Similarly, ideas may occur as you work through a documentary source.

It may be useful to carry a reporter's notebook in order to be able to record your ideas, whenever and wherever they occur. When you are undertaking the production of notes, or a transcript, or any aspect of qualitative analysis, such a notebook can be ready to hand to record your ideas.

These memos may vary in length from a few words to one or more pages. They can be written as simple notes – they do not need to be formally set out. Miles and Huberman (1994) suggest, however, that it will be useful to date them and to provide cross-references to appropriate places in your written-up notes or transcripts, where appropriate. Alternatively, an idea that is not grounded in any data (which may nevertheless prove to be useful) should be recorded as such. Memos should be filed together, not with notes or transcripts, and may themselves be categorised where this will help you to undertake later stages of your qualitative analysis. Memos may also be updated as your research progresses, so that your bank of ideas continues to have currency and relevance (Glaser, 1978; Robson, 1993).

Researcher's diary

An alternative approach to recording your ideas about your research is to maintain a *researcher's diary*. You may of course maintain such a diary alongside the creation of self-memos. Its purpose will be similar to the creation of self-memos: to record your ideas and your reflections on these, and to act as an *aide-mémoire* to your intentions about the direction of your research. However, its chronological format may help you to identify the development of certain ideas (such as data categories or hypotheses) and the way in which your research methodology developed, as well as providing an approach which suits the way in which you like to think (Riley, 1996).

12.4　Strategies for qualitative analysis

In providing an overview of qualitative analysis, it is apparent that there are different approaches to the commencement of this process. These relate to whether you start from a deductive or an inductive perspective. Where you commence your research project from a *deductive* position you will seek to use existing theory to shape the approach which you adopt to the qualitative research process and to aspects of data analysis. On the other hand, where you commence your research project from an *inductive* position you will seek to build up a theory which is adequately grounded in a number of relevant cases. The design of qualitative research requires you to recognise this choice and to devise an appropriate strategy to guide your research project.

Yin (1994) has identified analytical strategies related to these two approaches which you may use to analyse qualitative research:

■ using a theoretical or descriptive framework to analyse qualitative data;

■ exploring qualitative data without a predetermined theoretical or descriptive framework.

Using a theoretical or descriptive framework

Yin (1994) suggests that where you have made use of existing theory to formulate your research question and objectives, you should also use the theoretical propositions which helped you do this as a means to devise a framework to help you to organise and direct your data analysis. This approach demonstrates a preference for commencing with and utilising theory in qualitative research, rather than allowing it to develop from the work.

There is a debate about this approach as applied to qualitative analysis (Bryman, 1988). Bryman (1988:81) sums up the argument against it as follows: 'The prior specification of a theory tends to be disfavoured because of the possibility of introducing a premature closure on the issues to be investigated, as well as the possibility of the theoretical constructs departing excessively from the views of participants in a social setting.' If this occurs when you use a theoretical framework to design and analyse your research you will clearly need to adapt your approach (Section 12.5).

Worked example

Incorporating an inductive approach

Phil commenced a research project by adopting a deductive approach but found that the theoretical framework he adopted did not yield a sufficiently convincing answer to his research questions and objectives. He therefore decided to re-analyse his data inductively. This revealed themes that had not figured prominently in the deductive analysis. A combination of the two approaches generated a more convincing answer to Phil's research questions and objectives.

Even though you may incorporate an inductive approach, commencing your work from a theoretical perspective may have certain advantages. It will link your research into the existing body of knowledge in your subject area and help you to get started and provide you with an initial analytical framework.

To devise a theoretical or descriptive framework you need to identify the main variables, components, themes and issues in your research project and the predicted or presumed relationships between them (Miles and Huberman, 1994; Robson, 1993; Yin, 1994). A descriptive framework will rely more on your prior experience and what you expect to occur, although it is of course possible to develop an explanatory framework based on a mixture of theory and your own expectations. You will use this framework as the means to start and direct the analysis of your data. We advise you to use Miles and Huberman (1994) to consider further how to develop a theoretical or descriptive framework where you believe that this approach will be suitable as a means to approach your research and its analysis.

Exploring without a predetermined theoretical or descriptive framework

The alternative analytical strategy to the previous approach is to start to collect the data and then to explore them to see which themes or issues to follow up and to concentrate on (Glaser and Strauss, 1967; Robson, 1993; Schatzman and Strauss, 1973; Strauss and Corbin, 1998; Yin, 1994). Yin (1994) believes that this may be a difficult strategy to follow and may not lead to success for someone who is an inexperienced researcher. Robson (1993) agrees that this is likely to be the case where you simply go ahead and collect data without examining them to assess which themes are emerging from the data being gathered. However, to use this strategy successfully is likely to involve a lengthy period of time and to be resource intensive.

Where you commence your data collection with this strategy – related initially to an exploratory purpose – you would need to analyse the data as you collect them (Section 12.3) and to develop a conceptual framework to guide your subsequent work. This strategy is referred to as a *grounded* approach because of the nature of the theory or explanation that emerges as a result of the research process. Strauss and Corbin (1990, 1998) emphasise the following aspects of this approach:

- that grounded theory is principally an inductive approach;
- theory emerges from the process of data collection and analysis;
- therefore you do not commence such a study with a defined theoretical framework;
- instead you identify relationships between your data and develop questions and hypotheses to test these.

You will, however, need to commence this strategy with a clear research purpose.

Yin (1994) differentiates between the explanatory and exploratory purposes of research in relation to this type of strategy because his approach to explanation building, which commences with a theoretical proposition (Section 12.5), may appear to be similar to the inductive, 'grounded' theory approach (Section 12.6). Yin states that his hypothesis testing approach is related to *explanatory* case studies, while the hypothesis generating approach developed by Glaser and Strauss (1967) is relevant for *exploratory* studies. If we accept this distinction, it may help us to understand that the suitability of using an emergent, grounded approach is relevant for a particular research purpose, at least in the initial stages of such a research project. However, we feel that the use of this strategy is not suitable where you lack research experience.

The relationship between strategy and process

While the process for analysing qualitative data, which we outlined in Section 12.3, may be applicable to both of the analytical strategies described in this section, its use will vary according to whether you commence from a deductive or an inductive perspective. In the next two sections we therefore go on to describe and discuss specific analytic procedures in relation to these strategies and how these affect the process outlined in Section 12.3.

12.5 Analytical procedures based on predicted theoretical or conceptual explanations

This section will firstly outline the specific analytical procedures described by Yin (1994) which are particularly applicable to qualitative analysis. It will then examine how the process for analysing qualitative data (Section 12.3) is affected by the deductive perspective that underpins these specific analytical procedures.

Theoretically based procedures

Yin's (1994) preference for devising theoretical propositions prior to data collection as a means to analyse data leads to a number of specific analytic procedures to achieve this. These are briefly described and discussed in turn, although you are strongly advised to consult his work (see further reading) to gain a fuller appreciation of these techniques than we are able to provide here.

Pattern-matching

The first analytic procedure is termed *pattern-matching* and essentially involves predicting a pattern of outcomes based on theoretical propositions to explain what you expect to find. Using this approach, you will first need to establish a conceptual or analytical framework, utilising existing theory, and then to test the adequacy of the framework as a means to explain your findings. If the pattern of your data matches that which has been predicted through the conceptual framework you will have found an explanation, where possible threats to the validity of your conclusions can be discounted. Examples are provided in relation to two variations of this procedure which we now describe.

These variations depend on the nature of the variables being considered. The first of these is associated with a set of *dependent* variables where you suggest the likely outcomes arising from another, *independent* variable. For example, based on theoretical propositions drawn from appropriate literature you specify a number of related outcomes (dependent variables) which you expect to find as a result of the implementation of a particular change management programme (independent variable) in an organisation where you intend to undertake research. Having specified these expected outcomes, you then engage in the process of data collection and analysis. Where your predicted outcomes are found then it is likely that your theoretically based explanation is appropriate to explain your findings. If, however, you reveal one or more outcomes that have not been predicted by your explanation then you will need to seek an alternative one (Yin, 1994).

The second explanatory variation is associated with variables that are independent of each other. In this case you would identify a number of *alternative* explanations to explain the pattern of outcomes which you expect to find. As a consequence only one of these predicted explanations may be valid. In other words, if one explanation is found to explain your findings then the others may be discarded. Where you find a match between one of these predicted explanations and the pattern of your outcomes you will have evidence to suggest that this is indeed an explanation for your findings. Further evidence that this is a correct explanation will flow from finding the same pattern of outcomes related to other similar cases (Yin, 1994).

Worked example

Alternative predicted explanations

The objective of your research project is to explain why productivity has increased in a case study organisation even though a number of factors have been held constant (technology, numbers of staff employed, pay rates and bonuses, and the order book) during the period of the increase in productivity. You suggest two alternative explanations based on different theoretical propositions to explain why this increase in productivity has occurred in the organisation. Your explanations are related to the following propositions:

- first, that the increase is due to better management which has been able to generate greater employee commitment, where this proposition is based on theory related to strategic and human resource management;

- second, that the increase is due to fears about change and uncertainty in the future, where this proposition is, in addition, based on theory related to organisational behaviour and change management.

These propositions offer you two possible and exclusive reasons why the described phenomenon has occurred so that where evidence can be found to support one of these the other which does not match your outcomes can be discounted.

Explanation building

Another approach to pattern-matching, which Yin (1994) refers to as a special type, involves an attempt to build an explanation while collecting data and analysing them, rather than testing a predicted explanation as set out above. Yin (1994) recognises that this procedure, which he labels as *explanation building*, appears to be similar to the grounded theory approach, which we discuss later (Section 12.6). However, he differentiates between the two since the explanation building approach is still designed to test a theoretical explanation, albeit in an iterative manner, rather than to generate 'grounded' theory (Section 12.6). This explanation building procedure is designed to go through the following stages (Yin, 1994; Robson, 1993):

1 devising a theoretically based proposition, which you will then seek to test;

2 undertaking data collection through an initial case study in order to be able to compare the findings from this in relation to this theoretically based proposition;

3 where necessary amending this theoretically based proposition in the light of the findings from the initial case study;

4 undertaking a further round of data collection in order to compare the findings from this in relation to the revised proposition;

5 where necessary further amending this revised proposition in the light of the findings from this second case study;

6 undertaking further iterations of this process until a satisfactory explanation is derived.

Impact of a deductive approach on the process

In relation to pattern-matching and explanation building, you will still be able to follow the general process outlined earlier for analysing qualitative data (Section 12.3), with some modification. First, you will be in a position to commence your data collection with a well-defined research question and objectives, and a clear framework and propositions, derived from the theory which you will have used. Second, with regard to sampling (Section 6.3), you will be in a position to identify the number and type of organisations to which you wish to gain access in order to undertake data collection. However, this strategy should not be used as a means to adopt a less than rigorous approach to selecting sufficient cases through which to test the propositions which have been advanced and for you to seek to answer your research question and meet your objectives. Third, the use of this literature and the theory within it will shape the data collection questions which you wish to ask those who participate in your research project (Section 3.2). It is also to be expected that categories for analysis will emerge from the nature of these interview questions. Therefore, you will be able to commence data collection with an initial set of categories derived from your theoretical propositions/hypotheses and conceptual framework linked to your research question and objectives (e.g. Miles and Huberman, 1994).

Of course, these categories may be subject to change depending on their appropriateness for the data which your participants provide (Dey, 1993). However, where your predicted theoretical explanations appear to fit the data being revealed, your predetermined categories may prove to be useful, subject to some revision and development (Miles and Huberman, 1994).

Your use of this analytic strategy will of course also provide you with key themes and patterns to search for in your data. Therefore as you carry out your research and conduct analysis through attaching units of data to categories, and examine these for emergent patterns, your analysis will be guided by the theoretical propositions and explanations with which you commenced. Your hypotheses will still need to be tested with rigour – associated with the thoroughness with which you carry out this analytical process and by seeking alternative explanations and negative examples that do not conform to the pattern or association being tested for.

However, the use of predicted explanations should mean that the pathway to an answer to your research question and objectives is a more defined one. This will of course depend on two factors: first, your level of thoroughness in using existing theory to define clearly the theoretical propositions and conceptual framework which will guide your research project; second, the appropriateness of these theoretical propositions and the conceptual framework for the data that you reveal.

In summary, this section has briefly discussed two of the analytic procedures suggested by Yin (1994) which are particularly relevant to the analysis of qualitative data. The use of these procedures is underpinned by the need to specify theoretical propositions before the commencement of data collection and its analysis. Even in explanation building a theoretically based proposition is initially advanced even though this may be revised through the iterative stages of the process involved. It has also been shown that the general process outlined earlier for analysing qualitative data will be useful to you in carrying out these deductive analytical procedures. However, the stages of this process related to devising categories and identifying patterns should be more apparent, at least initially, because this approach is based on existing theory.

12.6 Analytical procedures to generate 'grounded theory'

There may be a number of good reasons for adopting a grounded theory approach to your research project and the analysis of the data that are produced. First, as we discussed in Section 12.4, you may commence on an exploratory project seeking to generate a direction for further work. Second, the scope of your research may be constrained by adopting restrictive theoretical propositions that do not reflect your participants' views and experience (Bryman, 1988). In this case, the use of a theoretically based approach to qualitative analysis would prove to be inadequate. The use of a grounded theory approach in such a case should allow a good 'fit' to develop between the social reality of the research participants and the theory which emerges – it will be 'grounded' in that reality. This relationship should also mean that those who participated in the research process would understand the theory. Third, the theory may be used to suggest subsequent, appropriate action to be taken because it is specifically derived from the events and circumstances of the setting in which the research was conducted. Finally, the theory's generalisability may also be tested in other contexts (Glaser and Strauss, 1967; Strauss and Corbin, 1990, 1998).

However, you should not draw the conclusion that you may use a grounded approach as a means of avoiding a proper level of preparation before commencing on your research project. Grounded theorists do not jump into a subject area without a competent level of knowledge about that area. Their research will commence with a clearly defined purpose, even though this may be altered by the nature of the data which they collect. For example, Hodson (1991, cited in Erlandson *et al.*, 1993) reported that his initial purpose was focused on organisational sabotage, although the research process led him to develop and seek to verify an hypothesis related to more subtle forms of non-co-operation with an employer. The avoidance of a predetermined theoretical basis to this type of approach is related to the desire to search for and recognise meanings in the data. It is not to avoid the burden of producing this before the process of data collection! You should seek to compare your grounded explanations with existing theory once these have emerged. The use of a grounded theory approach will also involve you in a lengthy period of data collection and concurrent analysis in order to analyse a theme adequately or to derive a well-grounded theory. Strauss and Corbin (1990) suggest that this process is likely to take months to complete.

The procedures related to a grounded approach are therefore designed to develop an explanation or a theory. They are not designed to test existing theory (Strauss and Corbin, 1998). In comparison with the strategy of testing existing theory (Section 12.5), the advocates of grounded theory lay down fairly precise procedures to be adopted in relation to each of the stages of the qualitative analysis process which was outlined in general terms in Section 12.3. Where you do not pay particular attention to the nature of the procedures outlined for grounded theory, you may not produce a research report that is sufficiently rigorous to substantiate the analysis or theory which you are seeking to advance. In the grounded theory approach of Strauss and Corbin (1998) the disaggregation of data into units is called *open coding*, the process of recognising relationships between categories is referred to as *axial coding* and the integration of categories to produce a theory is labelled *selective coding*. We will briefly outline each of these in turn drawing on the work of Strauss and Corbin (1990, 1998).

Open coding

Open coding is essentially the first stage of the process of qualitative analysis outlined in Section 12.3. The data that you collect will be disaggregated into conceptual units and provided with a label. The same label or name will be given to similar units of data. However, because this research process commences without an explicit basis in existing theory, the result may be the creation of a multitude of conceptual labels related to the lower level of focus and structure with which you commence your research. The emphasis in this grounded theory approach will be to derive meaning from the subjects being studied. In Section 12.3, we stated that a unit of data might relate to a few words, a sentence or number of sentences, or a paragraph. The need to understand meanings and to generate categories to encompass these in a grounded theory approach will therefore probably lead you to conduct your early analysis by looking at smaller rather than larger units of data. The resulting multitude of code labels will therefore need to be compared and placed into broader, related groupings or categories. This will allow you to produce a more manageable and focused research project and to develop the analytical process.

Strauss and Corbin (1998) suggest that there are three main sources to derive names for these categories: you utilise terms that emerge from your data; they are based on actual terms used by your participants (*'in vivo'* codes); they come from terms used in existing theory and the literature. However, Strauss and Corbin counsel against names being derived from existing theory and literature in a grounded approach. This is because their use in the written account of your research may lead readers to interpret these according to their prior understanding of such theoretical concepts rather than the particular meaning now being placed on such terms.

The categorisation that you derive from your data will indicate significant themes and issues and help you to consider where data collection should be focused in the future. In conjunction with this, it will also help you to develop a sharper focus in relation to your research question. The nature of this research approach will inevitably mean that your initial research question will be broadly focused, although still within manageable exploratory confines. As you develop a narrower focus through this process you will be able to refine and limit the scope of your research question (Strauss and Corbin, 1998).

Axial coding

This stage refers to the process of looking for relationships between the categories of data that have emerged from open coding. As relationships between categories are recognised, they are re-arranged into a hierarchical form, with the emergence of sub-categories. The essence of this approach is to explore and explain a phenomenon (the subject of your research project, or one of them) by identifying what is happening and why, the environmental factors which affect this (such as economic, technological, political, legal, social and cultural ones), how it is being managed within the context being examined and what the outcomes are of the action which has been taken. Clearly there will be a relationship between these aspects, or categories, and the purpose of your analysis will be to explain this.

Once these relationships have been recognised, you will then seek to verify them against the actual data that you have collected. Strauss and Corbin (1990, 1998) recommend that you undertake this by formulating questions or statements, which can then be phrased as hypotheses, to test these apparent relationships. As you undertake this process you will be looking for evidence which supports these questions and for negative cases which will demonstrate variations to these relationships.

Selective coding

Strauss and Corbin (1990) suggest that after a lengthy period of data collection, which may take several months, you will have developed a number of principal categories and related sub-categories. The stage which follows is called selective coding. This is intended to identify one of these principal categories, which becomes known as the central or core category, in order to relate the other categories to this with the intention of integrating the research and developing a grounded theory (Strauss and Corbin, 1998). In the previous stage, the emphasis was placed on recognising the relationships between categories and their sub-categories. In this stage the emphasis is placed on recognising and developing the relationships between the principal categories which have emerged from this grounded approach in order to develop an explanatory theory. We strongly advise you to consult Strauss and Corbin (1990, 1998) where you are considering the use of this approach in order to familiarise yourself with the procedural steps to achieve this.

Summary implications of using a grounded theory approach

A number of implications have emerged from this brief outline of the main procedures involved in the use of a grounded theory approach. These may be summed up by saying that the use of a grounded theory approach will involve you in a process that will be time consuming, intensive and reflective. You will need to consider the amount of time which you will have to conduct your research project, the level of competence which you will need to use an inductive approach, your access to data and the logistical implications of immersing yourself in such an intensive approach to research, before you commit yourself to this particular approach. There may also be a concern that little of significance will emerge at the end of the research process and this will be an important aspect for you to consider when determining the focus of your research if you use this approach.

12.7 A note on quantifying your qualitative data

There may be occasions when you decide to quantify some of your qualitative data. This is likely to be the case when you wish to count the frequency of certain events, or of particular reasons that have been given or in relation to specific references to a phenomenon. These frequencies can then be shown using a table or diagram (Section 11.3). This form of representation will provide you with the capacity to display a large amount of data which you will be able to discuss through the use of text.

This approach to describing and presenting your data will provide you with a very useful supplement to the principal means of analysing your qualitative data discussed above. It may also enable you to undertake other quantitative analyses such as those discussed in Sections 11.4–11.6. However, it is indeed a supplementary means of achieving this, and there is clearly only limited purpose in collecting qualitative data if you intend to ignore the nature and value of these data by reducing most of them to a simplified form.

Worked example

Recording frequencies of mention

One of our colleagues, Mike, undertook a series of semi-structured interviews with a sample of 12 managers in an organisation to evaluate the extent to which this organisation had adopted its espoused model of managing its human resources. During the analysis of these interviews he recorded which of these human resource initiatives were referred by the managers whom he interviewed. The nature of these data meant that they could be tabulated to show these frequencies clearly. An extract of the table that Mike created is shown below.

▶

HR initiatives	HRM practices identified by senior/line managers (n=12)													
	1	2	3	4	5	6	7	8	9	10	11	12	Total	%
Developing flexible staff base														
Restructuring			✓										1	8
New style (professional) contracts	✓										✓		2	17
Develop a skills mix														
Effective staff development														
Creation of Professional Development Unit	✓			✓									2	17
Appointment of Professional Development Tutor														
Funding staff development at 2% of payroll	✓			✓									2	17
Performance appraisal for all	✓		✓										2	17
Goal-oriented rewarded and appraisal														
Performance-linked pay scheme			✓		✓						✓		3	25
Generating staff commitment														
Ensuring equal opportunity			✓			✓							2	17
High-quality support staff structure														
Introduce quality improvement programme														
Customer care for personnel department														
Harmonisation of staff terms and conditions														
Identification of HR needs from strategic plan														
Targeted appointments														
Development of robust HR MIS System			✓										1	8
Staff development review scheme	✓	✓	✓	✓	✓	✓	✓			✓	✓		9	75
Devolving staff development budgets									✓		✓		2	17
Investors in People		✓						✓					2	17
Induction programme			✓										1	8
Line management training			✓										1	8
In-house training programmes			✓										1	8
Nurturing staff from within			✓										1	8
Devolvement to line managers										✓	✓		2	17
Personnel/Policy Handbook			✓	✓									2	17
Formal structures to support HR function			✓										1	8
Transfer of payroll to personnel														
Harassment policy				✓									1	8
Grading review and promotion policy									✓		✓		2	17
Direct communication										✓			1	8
Communication audit			✓										1	8
Common Interest Groups			✓										1	8

Source: Millmore, 1995

This form of display provides a clear illustration of the level and pattern of references to particular initiatives and is therefore a valuable and concise form of representation. It does not, however, describe the complete data and it might be misleading to attempt to draw conclusions from the table by itself.

12.8 Using a computer for qualitative analysis

The use of computer-assisted qualitative data analysis software (CAQDAS) (Fielding and Lee, 1995) potentially offers a number of advantages in relation to the analytical approaches we have been discussing. However, use of this type of software may be problematic. We briefly summarise some of the current issues related to CAQDAS, before outlining its principal functions. We then highlight internet addresses of some of the CAQDAS available to which you may connect to explore the latest versions of these packages and the features that they offer.

Current issues related to CAQDAS

A number of problems have been recognised in the literature that evaluates CAQDAS. While there are a number of different CAQDAS programs available for purchase, these vary in relation to the type of facilities that they offer and therefore potentially in their usefulness for different analytic situations. In addition, many of these programs may not be available for you to explore and evaluate in your institution. Even where different programs may be accessible your ability to experiment with different software is likely to be impeded by incompatibility. Fisher (1997: 9) summarises this: 'Few researchers are likely to "play" with coding facilities in different programs if each requires the re-entry of original codes.'

One danger is that you will end up using a program that is unsuitable for the analytical procedures that you wish to perform and will abandon the attempt for this reason (Fielding and Lee, 1995). Fielding and Lee (1995) also recognise that many researchers collect data before considering the need for a program to analyse it, rather than first evaluating the nature of their research project and exploring suitable software for its analysis. Where you are commencing as a qualitative analyst you will be confronted by a need to learn how to analyse qualitative data as well as by the need to choose and use appropriate software for this purpose (Fielding and Lee, 1995). This is clearly a far from easy combination given the nature of the resulting data and the purpose of qualitative analysis to explore meaning. The use of CAQDAS may lead some researchers, perhaps, to overlook this purpose, at least in part. Seidel (1991, cited in Fisher, 1997: 26) raises the concern that 'we will be lured into analytical practices and conceptual problems more conducive to breadth analysis than depth analysis'. This is referred to as 'word crunching', where the analyst becomes more concerned with analysis based on quantification than the exploration of meaning (Fisher, 1997).

While the use of CAQDAS may be problematic, it also offers a number of advantages to those who undertake qualitative analysis. Table 12.2 outlines several key functions that will help you in your role as a qualitative analyst. These advantages are clearly related to the suitability of the software that you use for your analysis. Fisher (1997) offers very useful advice to allow qualitative researchers to evaluate the suitability of such software. His criteria for assessing choice of software include consideration of the following aspects:

- whether a particular program will allow you to work between different analytical tasks as you seek to develop your analysis;
- whether it will allow you to maintain a close relationship with your data;
- whether it will allow you to make revisions to your codes and analytical frameworks as your analysis develops.

If you are considering the use of CAQDAS we would recommend that you consult Fisher's (1997) work.

Principal functions

CAQDAS may potentially help you in your role as a qualitative analyst by acting as an aid to:

- project management;
- coding and retrieval;
- data management;
- hypothesis building and theorising.

Table 12.2 summarises these different functions.

Table 12.2	**Functions of CAQDAS**

Project management

Your data need to be organised in such a way that access to them is both quick and accurate. In doing this, a good qualitative analysis program will display an index of documents, with facilities to select and retrieve individual documents. Computer-readable text-based documents can be displayed in full, so that units of text can be selected for operations such as editing, indexing (coding or categorising) or note making (memos), simply by highlighting and without affecting the primary document. One of the most powerful tools in CAQDAS is the ability to search swiftly any number of documents for specified units of data or codes. The software's ability to cluster units of text containing the words you select, and to display the cluster in a window together with reference to the *source document*, replaces the tedious process of multiple photocopying, slicing copies into paper slips and annotating each one before sticking them on to data cards and filing them in piles, or sticking them in appropriate places on a vast 'clipboard'. This process can be undertaken without any damage to your primary data, which are still held in the original primary documents.

Coding and retrieval

If all your data are word processed, or in some other computer-readable form, it will be possible for your primary documents to be accessed directly by the software. The software can search the text itself and allocate codes to specified units of text. More powerful software such as ATLAS/*ti* and NUD.IST can display the documents on screen in your chosen format. Identification of text units is usually by line number, although more powerful software offers you the facility of choosing the most appropriate size of text unit for your type

| Table 12.2 | *Cont.* |

of data (see Section 12.3) simply by highlighting the appropriate section of text in the document window. Data are coded by selecting a unit of text and directing it either to a new or to an existing code 'address'. A text unit may be directed to any number of code addresses. In order that categories (or codes) in a hierarchical system can be readily traced by their location in the hierarchy, they may also be allocated a code number. Some software offers a facility for coding non-computer-readable data such as videotapes, audiotapes, maps, photographs or archive texts.

Data management

As your research project progresses, you will quickly gather more and more data. This needs to be managed in such a way that it can readily be accessed and reviewed. You will have primary data, index codes and memos. The qualitative analysis software will retrieve and display all or any of these individually, in specified groups or clusters, and will indicate cross-references or links between them. Some more powerful software, such as ATLAS/*ti*, incorporates a *linked window system* whereby the selection of a unit of text from the primary document results in the automatic display of its code, any memos associated with it and the text of cross-references from other primary documents. *System closure* is often also available, whereby your notes and memos are themselves open to the same search and retrieve procedures as the primary documents.

Hypothesis building and testing

The foundation of *hypothesis building* lies in discovering links between elements of your data. CAQDAS can help you to discover these links and, with graphic facilities, can display them for you. Two basic ways of organising and linking your data are available. The first of these involves a *hierarchical organisation*. This is where your data may be classified in a few broad themes, then each theme classified into a number of sub-categories, and each of these into sub-sub-categories, and so on. It is similar to the coding used for quantitative data analysis (Section 11.2). For example in Fig 12.1 you may classify your data under the broad themes of 'Values', 'Concepts' and 'Strategies'. On reviewing all the data under 'Strategies', you may wish to divide them into 'Mature' and 'Immature', or 'Long term' and 'Short term'. Your 'Values' theme may fall naturally into, say, 'Internal' and 'External', and then you may identify several sub-categories such as 'Duty', 'Trust' and 'Liking'.

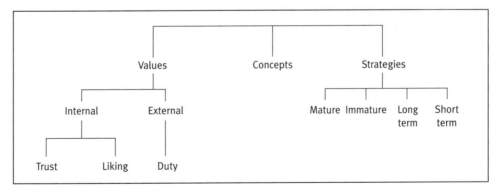

| Fig 12.1 | **Hierarchical organisation and linking of data** |

Table 12.2	*Cont.*

An alternative approach is to code each section of data as you work through it, and later on to discover ways of gathering together like categories that can be grouped together under common headings, which can in turn be grouped together in broad themes, and so on. For example, in the case above you might identify the concepts of 'Duty', 'Trust' and 'Liking' from your reading of the data and then decide to group all these under a common heading of 'Values'. Later you may wish to have distinct sub-headings under 'Values' which you call 'Internal' and 'External', allocating to them your original categories accordingly. The NUD.IST, ATLAS/*ti* and INSPIRATION software, for instance, all offer this style of organisation.

The second way of organising and linking your data involves a *network organisation*. This is where your categories may be more flexibly linked to one another, without the rigidity implicit in the hierarchical structure discussed above. In particular, the ability to represent your data graphically can be a very powerful aid to theory building, and INSPIRATION offers an extremely varied network facility, with publishable quality printing. ATLAS/*ti* has, in addition, a library of code and linkage icons, so that you can see at a glance the nature of the relationships between categories. Networks can be re-arranged in whatever way suits your developing research project. INSPIRATION and ATLAS/*ti* offer both networks and hierarchies, with tools for automatically moving between them.

Source: Summarised from Mark Saunders, Philip Lewis, Adrian Thornhill and John Wilkin in Saunders et al., 1997: 358–60.

Exploring the latest versions of CAQDAS

Published materials about computing and particular programs are likely to become out of date fairly quickly. We would therefore advise you to explore the internet sites of CAQDAS providers to locate details about the latest versions of these packages and the features that they offer. This search may provide you with the opportunity to obtain public domain demonstration disks for some of these programs. The internet addresses for the programs referred to in this section are listed in Table 12.3.

Table 12.3	**Internet addresses for CAQDAS referred to in this chapter**

ATLAS.*ti*

   http://www.atlasti.de/atlasnea.html

   http://www.scolari.co.uk/atlasti/atlasti.html

NUD.IST

   http://www.nudist@qsr.latrobe.edu.au/software/n4/n4.html

   http://www.scolari.co.uk/qsr/qsr.html

INSPIRATION

   http://www.inspiration.com.html

12.9 Summary

- Qualitative data are based on meanings expressed through words. They result in the collection of non-standardised data which require classification and are analysed through the use of conceptualisation.

- The process of qualitative analysis involves the development of data categories, allocating units of your original data to appropriate categories, recognising relationships within and between categories of data, and developing and testing hypotheses to produce well-grounded conclusions.

- The process of data analysis and data collection is necessarily an interactive one.

- There are a number of aids which you may use to help you through the process of qualitative analysis, including interview, observation, document and interim summaries, self-memos and maintaining a researcher's diary.

- Different qualitative analytical strategies can be identified, related to using either predicted theoretical explanations or a grounded theory approach. The use of these strategies has implications for the procedures involved in the analysis of qualitative data.

- Quantifying some categories of qualitative data may help you to analyse this.

- The use of computer software can help you to perform four basic and useful functions during qualitative analysis, related to project management, coding and retrieval, data management, and hypothesis building and theorising.

Self check | **Questions**

12.1 Why do we describe qualitative analysis as an 'interactive process'?

12.2 What types of data will you need to retain and file while you are undertaking qualitative research?

12.3 How would you differentiate between a deductive and an inductive analytic strategy?

12.4 What are the main implications of using a deductive analytical strategy for the way in which you conduct the process of qualitative analysis?

12.5 What are the main implications of using an inductive analytical strategy for the way in which you conduct the process of qualitative analysis?

Assignment 12

Analysing qualitative data

→ Undertake an initial semi-structured or in-depth interview related to your research project, transcribe this interview and make a few copies of your transcript.

→ Where your research project is based on a deductive strategy, develop a provisional set of categories from your research question and objectives, conceptual framework, research themes and initial propositions. Produce a description of each of these categories. Evaluate these categories to see whether they appear to form a coherent set in relation to the aim of your research.

→ Using one of the transcript copies attempt to allocate units of data to appropriate categories by writing their code labels alongside the text in the left-hand margin. Again evaluate this provisional set of categories and modify any that appear to be inappropriate.

→ Where your research project is based on an inductive strategy, work through one of the transcript copies and seek to identify categories related to your research purpose. Write appropriate code labels for these categories alongside the text in the left-hand margin. List these categories and their labels and produce a description for each of the categories that you have devised.

→ Once you have allocated units of data to the set of categories in use cut these out and transfer them to an appropriately labelled index card (reference to the interview, location of the text in the transcript and the date and so forth). Read through the units of data within each category.

→ Commence your analysis of this categorised data by asking questions of it, such as those that follow. What are the points of interest which emerge within each category? How will you seek to follow these up during your next data collection session? How does the material that has been revealed through this interview relate to any theoretical explanation or initial propositions that you commenced your data collection with? Are any connections evident between the categories?

→ Produce a summary of the interview and attach it to a copy of the transcript. Memo any ideas which you have and file these.

→ Repeat the procedure for the remaining qualitative data and revise your ideas as necessary.

References

Bryman, A. (1988) *Quantity and Quality in Social Research*, London, Unwin Hyman.

Dey, I. (1993) *Qualitative Data Analysis*, London, Routledge.

Easterby-Smith, M., Thorpe, R. and Lowe, A. (1991) *Management Research: an Introduction*, London, Sage.

Erlandson, D.A., Harris, E.L., Skipper, B.L. and Allen, S.D. (1993) *Doing Naturalistic Inquiry*, Newbury Park, CA, Sage.

Fielding, N.G. and Lee, R.M. (1995) 'Confronting CAQDAS: choice and contingency', *in* Burgess, R.G. (ed.), *Studies in Qualitative Methodology Computing and Qualitative Research*, Greenwich, CT, JAI Press.

Fisher, M. (1997) *Qualitative Computing: Using Software for Qualitative Data Analysis*, Aldershot, Ashgate.

Glaser, B. (1978) *Theoretical Sensitivity: Advances in the Methodology of Grounded Theory*, Mill Valley, CA, Sociology Press.

Glaser, B. and Strauss, A. (1967) *The Discovery of Grounded Theory*, Chicago, IL, Aldine.

Healey, M.J. and Rawlinson, M.B. (1994) 'Interviewing techniques in business and management research', *in* Wass, V.J. and Wells, P.E., *Principles and Practice in Business and Management Research*, Aldershot, Dartmouth, Chapter 5.

Hodson, R. (1991) 'The active worker: compliance and autonomy at the workplace', *Journal of Contemporary Ethnography*, 20:1, 47–8.

Marshall, C. and Rossman, G.B. (1999) *Designing Qualitative Research* (3rd edn), Thousand Oaks, CA, Sage.

Miles, M.B. and Huberman, A.M. (1994) *Qualitative Data Analysis* (2nd edn), Thousand Oaks, CA, Sage.

Millmore, M. (1995) *HRM in C&GCHE?: Assessing the Current State of Play*, MA dissertation, Cheltenham, Cheltenham & Gloucester College of Higher Education.

Riley, J. (1996) *Getting the Most from your Data. A Handbook of Practical Ideas on How to Analyse Qualitative Data* (2nd edn), Bristol, Technical and Educational Services Ltd.

Robson, C. (1993) *Real World Research*, Oxford, Blackwell.

Saunders, M., Lewis, P. and Thornhill, A. (1997) *Research Methods for Business Students* (1st edn), London, Pitman Publishing.

Schatzman, L. and Strauss, A. (1973) *Field Research: Strategies for a Natural Sociology*, Englewood Cliffs, NJ, Prentice-Hall.

Siedel, J. (1991) 'Method and madness in the application of computer technology to qualitative data analysis', *in* Fielding, N.G. and Lee, R.M. (eds), *Using Computers in Qualitative Research*, London, Sage.

Silverman, D. (1993) *Interpreting Qualitative Data*, London, Sage.

Strauss, A. and Corbin, J. (1990) *Basics of Qualitative Research*, Newbury Park, CA, Sage.

Strauss, A. and Corbin, J. (1998) *Basics of Qualitative Research* (2nd edn), Thousand Oaks, CA, Sage.

Tesch, R. (1990) *Qualitative Research: Analysis Types and Software Tools*, New York, Falmer.

Yin, R.K. (1994) *Case Study Research: Design and Methods* (2nd edn), Thousand Oaks, CA, Sage.

Further reading

Dey, I. (1993) *Qualitative Data Analysis*, London, Routledge. This provides a very thorough discussion of the stages of qualitative analysis without being bound to any of the approaches referred to in the sources below.

Fisher, M. (1997) *Qualitative Computing: Using Software for Qualitative Data Analysis*, Aldershot, Ashgate. This provides a very useful review of this subject area.

Miles, M.B. and Huberman, A.M. (1994) *Qualitative Data Analysis* (2nd edn), Thousand Oaks, CA, Sage. This provides an excellent source of reference to the elements involved in qualitative research as well as offering a number of particular techniques which may help you to analyse your data.

Strauss, A. and Corbin, J. (1998) *Basics of Qualitative Research* (2nd edn), Newbury Park, CA, Sage. This provides a very thorough introduction to the grounded theory approach.

Weitzman, E.A. and Miles, M.B. (1995) *Computer Programs for Qualitative Data Analysis*, Thousand Oaks, CA, Sage. This provides a review of over twenty programs.

Yin, R.K. (1994) *Case Study Research: Design and Methods* (2nd edn), Thousand Oaks, CA, Sage. Chapter 5 very usefully examines analytical strategies and procedures based on a deductive approach.

Case 12 Communicating bad news at Abco

Fiona undertook an interview in an organisation undergoing a period of change. Communicating change was one of the major issues which had to be confronted in the organisation. One of Fiona's research questions was 'How can the communication of bad news be managed to reduce its potentially adverse impact?' The following extract is part of an in-depth interview which relates to this research question.

Does Abco have a close-knit community here in Southtown?

Yes, there is, but there's much more of a community in Northtown, and even more in Easttown, than there is in Southtown. There's a couple of reasons for this: people in Northtown tend to socialise outside of work, after work, and they do in Easttown as well. People live very locally at both sites. People who work in Southtown live all over the place, they can live sixty miles away. There are even people who live in Netherford, which is sixty-five, seventy miles away and they commute every day. So it's not quite so easy for people to intermingle, but yes, they do associate very well. And the industry itself is a very close-knit one. They know people from other companies and there are lots of people who are in dual income relationships, or whatever you call it, whose partners work also in industry or the same company, we've got one whose partner works for Cyco and the other one works in Abco. So there is quite a lot of that going on and people are fairly close and identify very closely.

Do you find that there's a problem with rumours and informal communication?

We did at the beginning, because in a place like Northtown, word just shot around, and people were sometimes – I wouldn't say deliberately – starting rumours but I think when you are frightened and concerned about your job or whatever, you do start reading into things which people say, and sometimes you're reading things that aren't meant to be there or just aren't there. So, there's quite a lot of supposition made.

But these are bright people and it does not take them long to work things out. In most companies, if you've got issues going around the place there are usually a limited number of solutions. And if people think about these issues they will come up with the solutions and they will probably come up with the preferred solution in the same way as management will. So, what happens is people say, well yeah I knew that was going to happen. Well yeah, there is a good likelihood that they will.

That's one of the dangers of being very open about the processes and the solutions, and the options and the issues. You have to just face up to the fact that the grapevine may sometimes work against you. I think that what we've done in our communications has been so good that we've been able to be very sensitive to what the needs and fears will be.

If you're closing somewhere down, like Northtown, with 2000 people and it's the second largest employer in the area, the effect on the infrastructure is huge. It's not just the effect on the individuals who work there – that's bad enough – but there's all sorts of other things that happen, like the retailers who lose business and so on. People in the area also get quite angry about it, because they see the prices of their houses go down.

Was any training given on the delivery of bad news?

Yes, but it was not that sophisticated. It was really just getting people used to the idea that when they get to do this, that they have to think about how they talk to the individual and what they're going to say. It's not the sort of thing when you hand someone a letter in a pub and say you've got to read that and mine's a pint. You know you have to be a bit more sensitive than that.

It was also stressed that it had to be done on an individual basis, and people had to be aware of the support mechanisms that were available. In the United States for example, managers had to be taught about the security angle, because it's not uncommon for disaffected employees who have been fired to come back and shoot the person that did it to them!

Really?

Yeah, it happened at a couple of places in the United States. In one company someone came in and shot four people.

What we learn is put in a manual. This stuff includes the states people go through, like denial and despair; how to prepare, for example don't do it on a Friday; lots of do's and don'ts, whatever; why people are different; the processes people go through. There's also lots of handouts and it gives you all sorts of advice on the logistics of breaking bad news.

But handling some cases is more difficult than most. There have been quite a few people who have been identified as high flyers but we haven't been able to find a job for them and they are so angry about it because they didn't expect the news. So what to do when you meet this situation? Well don't mess about; get to the point straight away; don't come in and go, 'how's the family'; be clear about it.

Try to avoid using words like fire and terminate but don't get into arguments about it. That's one thing you have to make sure the person realises – that the decision has been made, nothing can be done.

You also need to know how people might react, common questions they might ask and how to answer them etc.

Do you think the training was useful in practice?

I think managers realised that it is important and it has been obligatory for them. But I think some of the logistics are quite difficult. Last week, last Thursday in fact, we got everyone in Product Development together in the United States, and what they had done was to tell everyone the previous Monday whether they had a job or not and that created an awful lot of hype and excitement and trepidation among people. Because they had so many people, they had to walk people from one part of the building to the other, I mean it's a big building, so people could see them being walked across and could see how they reacted afterwards so it was a bit public and that's when it's a bit dangerous to do it all at once.

▶

What could be done to improve the training about breaking bad news?

Make it longer, more chance to practise what we tell them as theory. We could test their ability to do it – test them in a realistic situation before we ask them to do it for real. Maybe we could do more about breaking this news to those who have to do this to those they've been working with for years. They're likely to be friends. It's difficult, hard to do this in this situation. We need to recognise the difficulties – evaluate what we do – this should improve this training.

Questions

Given the focus of the research question above conduct the following process to commence the analysis of this qualitative data.

1 Devise categories to label these data and 'unitise' or code these data using these categories.

2 Which passages of text would you avoid categorising, if any, and why?

3 Do any relationships or patterns begin to emerge in the data, and if so what are these?

4 What are the important themes that you feel stand out in your categorisation which you would seek to explore in subsequent interviews?

Self check **Answers**

12.1 There are a number of reasons why we may describe qualitative analysis as an 'interactive process'. Analysis needs to occur during the collection of data as well as after it. This helps to shape the direction of data collection, especially where you are following a grounded theory approach. The interactive nature of data collection and analysis allows you to recognise important themes, patterns and relationships as you collect data. As a result you will be able to re-categorise your existing data to see whether these themes, patterns and relationships are present in the cases where you have already collected data. In addition, you will be able to adjust your future data collection approach to see whether they exist in cases where you intend to conduct your research.

12.2 You will generate three broad types of data that you will need to retain and file as the result of undertaking qualitative research.

The first of these may be referred to as raw data files. These are your original notes and tapes made during the conduct of interviews or observations, or from consulting documentation. In addition, you will also retain transcripts and written-up notes of interviews and observations, although these may also be contained in a computer file.

The second of these is analytical files containing your categorised data. These may of course also be contained in a computer file.

The third of these may be referred to as a supporting file, or indeed it may be different files, containing working papers, self-memos, interim reports and so forth. Again, these may also be contained in a computer file. You are well advised to keep all of this until the end of your research project.

Eventually you will create a fourth file – containing your finished work!

12.3 A *deductive* analytical strategy is one where you will seek to use existing theory to shape the approach that you adopt to the qualitative research process and to aspects of data analysis. An *inductive* analytical strategy is one where you will seek to build up a theory that is adequately grounded in a number of relevant cases. The design of qualitative research requires you to recognise this choice and that you devise an appropriate strategy to guide your research project.

12.4 There are a number of implications of using a deductive analytical strategy for the way in which you conduct the process of qualitative analysis:

- you will be in a position to commence your data collection with a well-defined research question and objectives and a clear framework and propositions, derived from the theory which you will have used;
- with regard to sampling, you will be in a position to identify the number and type of organisations which you wish to gain access to in order to undertake data collection to answer your research question and meet your objectives;
- the use of literature and the theory within it will shape the data collection questions which you wish to ask those who participate in your research project;
- you will be able to commence data collection with an initial set of categories derived from your theoretical propositions/hypotheses and conceptual framework linked to your research question and objectives;
- this strategy will provide you with key themes and patterns to search for in your data and your analysis will be guided by the theoretical propositions and explanations with which you commenced.

12.5 The main implications of using an inductive analytical strategy for the process of qualitative analysis are likely to be related to:

- managing and categorising a large number of code labels which are likely to emerge from the data which you collect;
- working with smaller rather than larger units of data;
- recognising significant themes and issues during early analysis to help you to consider where data collection should be focused in the future;
- recognising the relationships between categories and re-arranging these into a hierarchical form, with the emergence of sub-categories;
- seeking to verify apparent relationships against the actual data which you have collected;
- understanding how negative cases broaden (or threaten) your emerging explanation;
- recognising the relationships between the principal categories which have emerged from this grounded approach in order to develop an explanatory theory;
- being rigorous in your use of the procedures which are advocated by grounded theorists in order to be able to produce a research report which contains findings which are sufficiently 'grounded' to substantiate the analysis or theory which you are seeking to advance.

13 Writing your project report

By the end of this chapter you should be able:

- to view the writing of the final project report as an exciting prospect;
- to write in such a way that you can reflect on all you have learned while conducting the research;
- to write a final project report which presents an authoritative account of your research;
- to adopt an appropriate format, structure and style for the final project report;
- to ensure that your report meets the necessary assessment criteria.

13.1 Introduction

Some of you may view the process of writing your project report as an exciting prospect. However, it is more likely that you will approach this stage of your research with a mixture of resignation and trepidation. This is a great pity. We believe that writing about your work is the most effective way of clarifying your thoughts. This suggests that writing should not be seen as the last stage of your research. It should be thought of as something that is continuous throughout the research process.

Writing is a powerful way of learning (Griffiths, 1993). Most teachers will tell you that the best way to learn is to teach. This is because of the necessity to understand thoroughly something yourself before you can begin to explain it to others. This is the position you are in as the writer of your project report. You have to explain a highly complex set of ideas and facts to an audience that you must assume has little or no knowledge of your subject. There is another problem here which has a parallel with teaching. Often, the more familiar you are with a subject, the more difficult it is to explain it to others with no knowledge of that subject. You will be so familiar with your subject that, like the teacher, you will find it difficult to put yourself in the place of the reader. The result of this is that you may fail to explain something that you assume the reader will know. Even worse, you may leave out important material that should be included.

However, why do most of us view writing with such concern? Veroff (1992) argues that much of this is rooted in the experience we have of writing. Many of us are afraid of exposing our efforts to an audience which we feel will be more likely to criticise than encourage. In our education much of our writing has been little more than rehashing the ideas of others. This has taught us to think of writing as a boring, repetitive process. Some of us are impatient. We are unwilling to devote the time and energy (and inevitable frustration) which are needed for writing.

This fear of criticism is captured perfectly by Richards (1986) who recites the story of being asked by the distinguished sociologist Howard Becker to adopt his method of sitting down and writing what comes into her head about the research she had done without even consulting her notes. Her fears of producing poor-quality material which would be derided by colleagues who saw her work are described vividly. It is a fear most of us experience.

We agree with Phillips and Pugh (1994) who note that writing is the only time when we really think. This suggests that writing your project report is something which should not be left until every other part of your research has been completed. However, there will be more on that in the next section.

13.2 ## Getting started

If writing is synonymous with thinking, it follows that writing is something you should do throughout the whole research process. Chapter 2 emphasises the need for clear ideas in writing about research questions and objectives. If you have done this already you will know the difficulty of committing your vague ideas to paper and amending them continually until they express your ideas with brevity, clarity and accuracy. However, there is no reason why your research proposal and plan should be the last writing you do before you finally write up your research in the project report. We encourage you to write as a continual process throughout the research.

Many researchers find it helpful to write the literature review early on in their research. This has clear benefits. It gets you writing on a part of the research process which necessarily comes early in that process. Also, it focuses your thinking on the way in which the literature will inform the research strategy you adopt. You will be pleased you wrote this part of the report when the time pressure is on as the submission deadline for your report approaches. Do not worry that early writing of the literature review means that later relevant publications are ignored in your review. They can always be incorporated at a later date. This is one of the advantages of using a word processor, a topic that we will cover later in this section.

Having discouraged you from thinking of writing as a process you leave until the end of your research, this section goes on to consider a number of practical hints to assist you to get started.

Create time for your writing

Writing is not an activity that can be allocated an odd half-hour whenever it is convenient. It requires sustained concentration. The amount of time needed to make real progress in your writing is dependent on the way in which you prefer to work. Most people find that it takes a day to write about 2000 words, but we all work in different ways. Once some people have started, they prefer to continue until they drop from exhaustion! Others like to set a strict timetable where three or four hours a day are devoted to writing. Whichever category you are in, make sure that you have time for writing allocated in your diary. We have found that it is helpful to have blocks of time where writing can take place on successive days. This ensures a degree of continuity of ideas which is not as easy if you keep having to 'think your way back' into your research.

Write when your mind is fresh

We have emphasised so far in this chapter that writing should be a highly creative process. It is important, therefore, that you write at the time of day when your mind is at its freshest. All of us have jobs to do during the day which require little or no creativity. Arrange your day so the uncreative jobs are done in the time when you are at your least mentally alert.

Find a regular writing place

Most of us have one place where we do our writing. It is so important that we often cannot write in unfamiliar surroundings. If this is the case with you it is essential that you combine this psychological comfort with a few practical features of your writing place which will enhance your productivity. One of the most important of these is to ensure that you are not interrupted. A simple 'do not disturb' sign on the door usually works wonders. You may, like Phil, find a telephone-answering machine a useful investment. Remove all distractions, such as television, magazines and computer games from the room. It may be that you need background noise, even your personal stereo, to help you concentrate. One person's distractions are another person's necessities. What is important is to know what distracts you and to remove those distractions.

Set goals and achieve them

This is the height of self-discipline. Most writers set themselves targets for the period of writing. Usually this is a set number of words. It is better to be realistic about these goals. If you are too ambitious the quality of your work may suffer as you rush to meet the goal. You may be as self-disciplined as Mark who sets himself sub-goals during the day and rewards the achievement of these goals with coffee breaks. What is important is that you see this as entering into a contract with yourself. If you break this contract by not meeting your goal you are the one who should feel guilty. You may like to enter into a similar arrangement with a close friend on the understanding that each of you will insist on the other meeting your goals.

Use a word processor

The word processor has revolutionised writing. There are still some who prefer to write long-hand before word processing the final report. However, for those of us who 'think on to the screen', the main advantage of the word processor is that it enables us to keep amending copy without having to fill the waste paper basket with numerous unsatisfactory attempts. In addition, the word processor enables you to keep updating your project report as you develop new ideas or become dissatisfied with old ones. There is, however, a potential problem here. The ease with which you can keep inserting and deleting text means that relevant *'flagging'* material will need to be changed. At its simplest this may be the contents page or the announcement at the beginning of a chapter that the chapter will cover certain ground. However, it is just as likely to be an obscure reference buried in the text to a table that you have deleted, thus making the reference redundant.

Worked example

Using the word processor to transcribe field notes to the final project report

Phil made interview notes in long-hand during the interviews which he conducted with managers about the pay system in their organisations. He was particularly careful to note verbatim especially relevant comments from the managers.

Phil ensured that he word processed these notes, either on the return train journey at the end of the day or at home in the evening.

When writing the project report Phil found the word-processed notes invaluable. He wanted to use some of the verbatim quotes to illustrate key arguments that he was developing from the data. He was able to insert many of these into the report, thus saving time and ensuring accuracy of transcription.

One other advantage of the word processor may have occurred to you. Most packages have a word count facility. You can use this to check your progress towards the word goal you have set yourself for the writing session.

The necessity to keep back-up copies of your work should go without saying. However, do learn from the experience of one of our students who lost all his research material as a consequence of not keeping adequate back-up copies. This led to him having to abandon completely his research project.

Generate a plan

Few of us can sit down and write without a lot of thought and planning. We all have our own systems for doing this. However, most people find it essential to construct a plan before they start writing. Veroff (1992) describes the 'clustering' method. This may be familiar to you. The method's stages are:

1 write the main topic in the middle of a sheet of paper;
2 jot down the other ideas which occur to you at other points on the page;

3 as the page begins to fill, relationships between the ideas suggest themselves and lines between the ideas may be drawn;

4 this allows you to group the ideas into discrete but related 'chunks' which enables you to devise an outline structure for a section, or chapter.

This chapter started out as just such a pencilled plan written on four pieces of A4 held together with sticky tape. It is essential to get your ideas into some form of order at the outset. This will give you encouragement to start writing.

Finish the writing session on a high point

Many writers prefer to finish their writing session while they are in the middle of a section to which they will look forward to returning. This eases the way in next time. The worse thing you can do is to leave a complex part half-way through. It will be difficult to pick up the threads.

Get friends to read your work

Writing is creative and exciting but checking our work is not. The importance of getting someone else to read through your material cannot be over-emphasised. Your project tutor should not be the first person who reads your report, even in its draft form.

Ask your friend to be constructively critical. Your friend must be prepared to tell you about things in the text that are not easy to understand; to point out omissions, spelling, punctuation and grammatical errors. Overall, your friend must tell you whether the piece of writing makes sense and achieves its purpose.

This is not an easy process for you or your critical friend. Most of us are sensitive to criticism, particularly when the consequence of it is the necessity to do a lot more work. Many of us are also hesitant about giving criticism. However, if your project report does not communicate to the reader in the way it should you will get it back for revision work in the long run. It is much better to try and to ensure that this does not happen.

13.3 Structuring your project report

Suggested structure

Most writers agree with Robson (1993) on the general structure to adopt for a project report that is the end product of your research. This is:

- Abstract
- Introduction
- Literature review
- Method

- Results
- Conclusions
- References
- Appendices

However, this suggested structure should not inhibit you from adopting something different. The structure outlined above fits the deductive approach particularly closely. It assumes that the literature was reviewed to establish the current state of knowledge on the topic and this informed the method adopted. Reporting the findings in a factual manner gives rise to a detailed consideration of what these findings mean to the specific piece of research that has been conducted and to the current state of knowledge on the topic. However, if your research is essentially inductive, it may be that you prefer to structure the report in a different way. You may prefer to tell your story (i.e. to explain your conclusions) in the early part of the report. This may include a clear explanation of how this story relates to the existing literature on the topic. This could be followed by a detailed explanation of how you arrived at these conclusions (a combination of an explanation of method adopted and findings established). The precise structure you adopt is less important than the necessity for your reader to be absolutely clear what you are saying and for you to meet the assessment criteria.

Phillips and Pugh (1994) note that these general sections can be sub-divided into one or more relevant chapters depending on the topic and the way in which you want to present your particular *storyline*. This is a vital point. Your structure should have a logical flow. Your readers should know the journey on which they are being taken and should know at all times the point in the journey that has been reached. Above all, the structure you adopt should enable your reader, having read the report, to identify clearly the storyline.

We will now explain how to distinguish between these broad sections by outlining their purpose and content.

The abstract

The *abstract* is probably the most important part of your report because it may be the only part that some will read. It is a short summary of the complete content of the project report. This enables those who are not sure whether they wish to read the complete report to make an informed decision. For those who intend to read the whole report the abstract prepares them for what is to come. It should contain four short paragraphs with the answers to the following questions:

1 What were my research questions and why were these important?

2 How did I go about answering the research questions?

3 What did I find out in response to my research questions?

4 What conclusions do I draw regarding my research questions?

Smith (1991) lists five principles for the writing of a good abstract. He argues that:

1 It should be short. Try to keep it to a maximum of two sides of A4.

2 It must be self-contained. Since it may be the only part of your report that some people see it follows that it must summarise the complete content of your report.

3 It must satisfy your reader's needs. Your reader must be told about the problem, or central issue, which the research addressed and the method adopted to pursue the issue. It must also contain a brief statement of the main results and conclusions.

4 It must convey the same emphasis as the report with the consequence that the reader should get an accurate impression of the report's contents from the abstract.

5 It should be objective, precise and easy to read. The project report contents page should give you the outline structure for the abstract. Summarising each section should give you an accurate résumé of the content of the report. Do ensure that you stick to what you have written in the report. The abstract is not the place for elaborating any of your main themes. Be objective. You will need to write several drafts before you eliminate every word that is not absolutely necessary. The purpose is to convey the content of your report in as clear and brief a way as possible.

Writing a good abstract is difficult. The obvious thing to do is to write it after you have finished the report. We suggest that you draft it at the start of your writing so that you have got your storyline abundantly clear in your mind. You can then amend the draft when you have finished the report so that it conforms to the five principles above.

The introductory chapter

The *introduction* should give the reader a clear idea about the central issue of concern in your research and why you thought that this was worth studying. It should also include a full statement of your research question(s) and research objectives. If your research is based in an organisation, we think that it is a good idea to include in this chapter some details of the organisation, e.g. its history, size, product and services etc. This may be a general background to the more specific detail on the research setting you include in the method chapter. It is also important to include in this chapter a 'route map' to guide the reader through the rest of the report. This will give brief details of the content of each chapter and present an overview of how your storyline unfolds.

This will usually be a fairly brief chapter, but it is vitally important.

The literature review

Chapter 3 deals in detail with the writing of a literature review. All that it is necessary to comment on here is the position of this chapter in the project report. We suggest that this is placed before the methodology chapter.

The main purpose of your literature review is to show the reader how your study supplements the work that has already been done on your topic. The literature review, therefore, may inform directly any specific hypotheses that your research was designed to test. These hypotheses will also suggest a particular research approach, strategy and data collection methods. If, on the other hand, you are working inductively (i.e. from data to theory) your literature review may serve the purpose of illuminating and enriching your conclusions.

The title of your literature review chapter should reflect the content of the chapter. It may draw on one of the main themes in the review. We recommend that you do not call it simply 'literature review'. It may be that your literature is reviewed in more than one chapter. This would be the case, for example, where you were using more than one body of literature in your research.

Worked example

Using the literature review to inform the research questions

Paul was fascinated by the way in which organisations pursued policies of rewarding their employees on the basis of individual merit because the literature showed that these policies often seemed not to produce the results which the organisations wanted.

Much of the literature which Paul covered in his review was American psychological studies which paid no attention to the organisational context in which merit pay policies were pursued. Paul used his literature review to argue that there was a gap in the literature which his research could fill.

Paul wanted to explore his theory that the success of merit pay schemes was dependent on an organisational context which was consistent with the aims of the scheme.

The method chapter

This should be a detailed chapter giving the reader sufficient information to make an estimate of the reliability and validity of your methods. Table 13.1 is a useful list of the points that you should include in the method chapter.

Table 13.1   **Points for inclusion in the method chapter**

Setting

- What was the research setting?
- Why did you choose that particular setting?

Participants

- How many?
- How were they selected?
- What were their characteristics?
- How were refusals/non-returns handled?

▶

Table 13.1	*Cont.*

Materials

- What tests/scales/interview or observation schedules/questionnaires were used?

- How were purpose-made instruments developed?

- How were the resulting data analysed?

Procedures

- What were the characteristics of the interviewers and observers and how were they trained?

- How valid and reliable do you think that the procedures were?

- What instructions were given to participants?

- How many interviews/observations/questionnaires were there; how long did they last; where did they take place?

- When was the research carried out?

Source: Developed from Robson, 1993.

The results chapter(s)

It may well be that your report will contain more than one results chapter. The question you should ask yourself is, 'is more than one results chapter necessary to communicate my findings clearly?'

The results chapter is probably the most straightforward chapter to write. It is your opportunity to report the facts that your research discovered. These may be in the form of either quantitative or qualitative data analysis or a combination of both. This is where you will include such tables and graphs that will illustrate your findings (do not put these in the appendices). The chapter may also contain verbatim quotes from interviewees or sections of narrative account which illustrate periods of unstructured observation. This is a particularly powerful way in which you can convey the richness of your data. It is the qualitative researcher's equivalent of tables and graphs. Often, a short verbatim quote can convey with penetrating simplicity a particularly difficult concept that you are trying to explain. Do not be afraid to capture precisely what the interviewee said. Slang and swear words are often the most revealing and provide amusement for the reader!

There are two important points to bear in mind when writing your results. The first is to stress that the purpose is to present facts. It is normally not appropriate in this chapter to begin to offer opinions on the facts. This is for the following chapter. Many of us become confused about the difference between findings and conclusions. One way of overcoming the confusion is to draw up a table with two columns. The first should be headed 'what I found out' and the second 'what judgements I have formed as a result of what I found out'. The first list is entirely factual (for example, 66 per cent of respondents indicated they preferred to receive paper memos than email messages) and therefore the content of your findings chapter. The second list will be your judgements based on what you found out (for example, it appears that traditional forms of communication are still preferred to electronic) and therefore the content of your conclusions section.

The second point links to the first. Drawing up a table will lead you to a consideration of the way in which you present your findings. The purpose of your project report is to communicate the answer to your research question to your audience in as clear a manner as possible. Therefore, you should structure your findings in a clear, logical and easily understood manner. There are many ways of doing this. One of the simplest is to return to the research objectives and to let these dictate the order in which you present your findings. Alternatively, you may prefer to report your findings thematically. You could present the themes in descending order of importance. Whichever method you choose should be obvious to the reader. As with the literature review, the chapter(s) devoted to research should be titled in an interesting way which reflects the content of findings.

The conclusions chapter(s)

Logically, for each finding there should be at least one conclusion. This suggests that the *conclusions* chapter(s) (which is often called discussion) should be at least as long as the findings chapter(s). This is certainly the case. Findings presented without reflective thought run the risk of your reader asking 'so what?'

The conclusions chapter (which, again, should have a more interesting title than 'conclusions') is where you have the opportunity to shine. It is your conclusions that will demonstrate whether you have answered the research question and show the degree of insight that you exhibit in reaching your conclusions. However, it is the part of the report which most of us find difficult. It is the second major opportunity in the research process to demonstrate real originality of thought (the first time being at the stage where you choose the research topic). Because of that, we urge you to pay due attention to the conclusions chapter. Often students do little more than write a conclusions section which is a re-hash of their findings. It is essential that you give the content of this chapter careful thought over a long period of time. Ask yourself questions about your findings such as 'so what?, 'what does this mean?', 'what are the implications for the organisation?', 'what are the implications for the current state of knowledge of the topic?' and 'how does it add to the literature?'

You may find that the clearest way to present your conclusions is to follow a similar structure to the one used in your findings section. If that structure reflects the research objectives then it should make certain that your conclusions will address the research question(s). Drawing up a matrix similar to that in Fig 13.1 may help you in structuring your findings and conclusions.

An alternative approach to the matrix is to draw a 'mind map' which places the findings randomly on a blank page and links conclusions to these findings by way of lines and arrows. For some of you this may be a more creative approach which enables you to associate groups of findings with conclusions and vice versa.

Answering the research question(s), meeting the objectives and, if appropriate, supporting or otherwise the research hypotheses is the main purpose of the conclusions chapter. This is where you will consider the findings presented in the previous chapter. You should also return to your literature review and ask yourself 'what do my conclusions add to the understanding of the topic displayed in the literature?'

Research questions	Results (what factual information did I discover in relation to the specific research questions?)	Conclusions (what judgements can I make about the results in relation to the specific research questions?)
What are the operational differences between different shifts in the production plant?	Cases of indiscipline in the last six months have been twice as frequent on the night shift as on the day shift	The night shift indiscipline problems may be due to the reluctance of operators to work on this shift

Fig 13.1 **Using a matrix in the planning of the content for the results and conclusions chapters**

It may be that there are practical implications of your findings. In a management report this would normally form the content of a chapter specifically devoted to recommendations. We suggest that you check with your project tutor whether this is expected. In the reports which students are required to prepare on some professional courses this is an important requirement. For academic degree programmes this is often unnecessary.

Even if you do not specify any practical implications of your research you may comment in the conclusions chapter on what your research implies for any future research. This is a logical extension of a section in the conclusions chapter which should be devoted to the limitations of your research. These limitations may be the size of sample, the snapshot nature of the research or the restriction to one geographical area of an organisation. Virtually all research has its limitations. This section should not be seen as a confession of your weaknesses but a mature reflection on the degree to which your findings and conclusions can be said to be the 'truth'.

References

A range of conventions is used to reference the material of other writers' material which you have cited in your text. Appendix 2 illustrates the most popular of these, the Harvard system. However, we suggest that you consult your project tutor about the system which is appropriate for your report.

It is a good idea to start your references section at the beginning of the writing process and to add to it as you go along. It will be a tedious and time-consuming task if left until you have completed the main body of the text. If you do leave this until the end, the time spent on compiling the reference section is time which will be better spent on checking and amending your report.

Appendices

In general, *appendices* should be kept to the minimum. If they are so important that your reader's understanding of the points you are making in the text makes their inclusion in the report necessary, then they should be in the main body of the text. If, on the other hand, the material is 'interesting to know' rather than 'essential to know' then it should be in the appendices. Often we feel tempted to include appendices to 'pad out' a project report. Resist this temptation. Your readers will not be reading your report for leisure reading. They will be pressed for time and will probably not look at your appendices. Your report will stand or fall on the quality of the main text. However, your appendices should include a blank copy of your questionnaire, interview or observation schedule.

The management report

You may have wondered why we made no reference to recommendations in the report structure. In the typical *management report* this may be the most important section. The hard-pressed executive reading your report may turn to your recommendations first to see what action needs to be taken to tackle the issue.

Whether you include a recommendation section depends on the objectives of your research. If you are doing exploratory research you may well write recommendations among which will be suggestions for the pursuit of further research. However, if your research is designed to explain or describe, recommendations are less likely. For example, the research question 'why do small engineering companies in the UK re-invest less of their profits in their businesses than their German counterparts?' may imply clear points for action. However, strictly speaking, recommendations are outside the scope of the research question which is to discover 'why?', not 'what can be done about it?' The message is clear. If you want your research to change the situation that you are researching, then include the need to develop recommendations in your research objectives.

Length of the project report

You will probably have guidelines on the amount of words your project report should contain. Do stick to these. However interesting your report, your tutors will have others to read so they will not thank you for exceeding the limit. Indeed, if you can meet your research objectives fully in a clear and absorbing report which is significantly shorter than the word limit, the good mood in which you put your tutors may be reflected in a higher grade. Reports which exceed the word limit are usually excessively verbose. It is more difficult to be succinct. Do not fall into the trap of writing a long report because you did not have the time to write a shorter one.

13.4   Organising the project report's content

Choosing a title

This is the part of the project report on which most of us spend the least time. Yet it is the only knowledge that many people have of the project. Day (1995:15) describes a good *title* as one that has 'the fewest possible words that adequately describe the content of the paper'. Try choosing a title and then ask a colleague who knows your subject what she/he thinks the title describes. If her/his description matches your content then stick with your title.

Tell a clear story

Be prepared for your project tutor to ask you 'what's your main *storyline*?' Your storyline (your central argument or thesis) should be clear, simple and straightforward. It should be so clear that you can stop the next person you see walking towards you and tell that person what your project report's storyline is and he or she will say 'yes, I understand that'. This is where writing the abstract helps. It forces you to think clearly about the storyline because you have to summarise it in so few words.

A simple format for developing the storyline is shown in Fig 13.2.

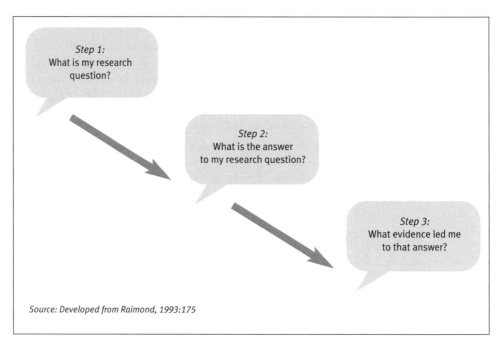

Source: Developed from Raimond, 1993:175

Fig 13.2   **A format for developing the storyline**

Helping the reader to get all the information out

Dividing your work

One of us once received the first draft of a 20 000-word project report which had virtually no divisions except the chapters. It was like looking at a road map of Britain which did not illustrate any road numbers or towns. It was just as difficult to find your way around that report as it would be to journey from Southampton to Harrogate using a townless road map. The content of the project report seemed fine. However, it was hard to be sure about this because it was so difficult to spot any gaps in the ground it covered. What was needed were some signposts and some town names. Do not think about how you can put in all your information. Instead, concentrate on helping the reader to get all the information out.

> **Worked example**
>
> ## Developing a storyline
>
> ### Step 1
> I wanted to know whether, as the literature suggested, organisational structures are determined by their strategies.
>
> ### Step 2
> The answer is that organisation structures are in part determined by strategies and in part by *ad hoc* factors which owe little to strategy considerations.
>
> ### Step 3
> I based this answer on interviews with senior managers in three large UK organisations and examination of the minutes of meetings at which structural issues were discussed. The particular focus was on the removal of management positions.

The message is simple. Divide your work in such a way that it is easy for readers to find their way round it and for them always to be clear where they are, where they have come from and where they are going.

To do this you may find it helpful to return to the matrix idea in Fig 13.1. You will see that each column of the matrix represents the broad content of a chapter. The cells indicate the way in which the chapters may be divided. Each division may have a sub-division.

We hope that you have noticed that we have employed a similar system in this book. However, this is two-colour. The equivalent would be that each chapter section is identified by bold upper-case letters. The sub-headings are bold lower case and further divisions of the sub-section content are denoted by bold, lower-case italics. Smith (1991) explains various ways of organising and sign-posting text. It is not important which way you do this as long as your approach is consistent and it helps the reader around the report and matches the ways specified by your examining institution.

Previewing and summarising chapters

A further way in which you can sign-post your work is to 'top and tail' each chapter. This is to include a few words at the beginning of the chapter (Smith, 1991) which provide a description of how the chapter is to contribute to answering the research question, the methods used in this part of the study and the points that are covered. At the end of each chapter it is useful if the reader has a brief summary of the content of the chapter and a very brief indication of how this content links to the following chapter. This may seem like repetition. However, it helps the reader on her/his journey through your report and ensures that you, the writer, are on the correct road.

Tables and graphics

Your reader will find your project report more accessible and easier to read if you present some of your data and ideas in *tables* and *graphics*. It is not only numerical data which can be presented in tables. You can also present ideas which can be easily compared. Table 13.1 is an example of this.

Do not be tempted to put your numerical tables in the appendices. They will probably be some of your most important data. Include them and comment on them in the text. Your commentary should note the significance of the data in the tables. It should not simply describe the table's contents.

Section 11.3 has detail on the presentation of tables and graphics.

A final note of caution should be sounded. To avoid confusing your reader, do make sure that wherever possible you have introduced the table or graphic before it appears in the text.

One report or two?

Many researchers of management topics face the dilemma of having to write for two audiences: the academic audience who possibly will mark and grade the report for a degree or a diploma and the organisation's managers who will be interested in the practical benefit which the report promises. This raises the thorny question, 'for whom should the report be written?'

Many people have resolved this dilemma by writing two reports: one for each audience. The academic report will usually be much longer and contain contextual description which the organisational audience does not require. Similarly, those managers reading the report will probably be less interested in the literature review and the development of theory than the academic audience. If the research question did not imply the necessity for recommendations for future action, these may need to be written for the organisational version.

Fortunately, the advent of word processors makes this job easy. Some careful cutting and pasting will be necessary. However, what should always be kept in mind is the audience each specific report is addressing. Take care not to fall between two stools. Write each report for its audience in style and content.

13.5 Developing an appropriate writing style

Much of your concern in writing your project report will be about what you write. In this section of the chapter we ask you to think about the way you write. Your writing style is just as important as the content, structure and layout of your report. Good writing cannot cure bad thought (Phillips and Pugh, 1994:66). In fact, the clearer the writing the more bad thought is exposed. However, bad writing can spoil the effect of good thought.

Clarity and simplicity

> The . . . lack of ready intelligibility [in scholarly writing], I believe, usually has little or nothing to do with the complexity of the subject matter, and nothing

at all to do with profundity of thought. It has to do almost entirely with certain confusions of the academic writer about his own status . . . To overcome the academic prose you first of all have to overcome the academic pose . . .

Wright Mills (1970:239–40)

Each Christmas Mark accompanies his Christmas cards with a family newsletter. It is written in a simple, direct and friendly manner which is easy and enjoyable to read. Few of the project reports we read are written in such a simple, direct manner. They are more elaborate in their explanation: they use difficult words where Mark's family newsletter would use simple ones. They adopt the academic pose.

Phil tells a story which reinforces the point made by Wright Mills in the above quotation. He was asked by a student to comment on her thesis in progress which was about the impact of a particular job advertising strategy. He thought that it was written in an over-elaborate and academic way. After many suggestions for amendments Phil came across a sentence which explained that the strategy his student was studying 'was characterised by factors congruent with the results of a lifestyle analysis of the target market'. Phil thought that this was too wordy and academic. He suggested making it simpler. His student examined the sentence at length and declared she could see no way of improving it. Phil thought that it could say 'it was a strategy which matched the lifestyles of those at which is was aimed'. His student protested. She agreed it was shorter and clearer but protested that it was less 'academic'. We think that clarity and simplicity are more important than wishing to appear academic. Your project report is a piece of communication in the same way as Mark's Christmas newsletter.

Phillips and Pugh (1994) advise that you should aim to provide the reader with a report that she/he cannot put down until 2.00 a.m. or later for fear of spoiling the flow. (If you are reading this chapter at 2.30 a.m. we have succeeded!)

Write simple sentences

A common source of lack of clarity is the confusing sentence. This is often because it is too long. A simple rule to adopt is, one idea – one sentence. Mark reads his work out loud. If the sentences are too long he runs out of breath! This is another useful guide to sentence length.

Worked example

Writing clearer sentences

While it is true to say that researchers have illusions of academic grandeur when they sit down to write their project report, and who can blame them because they have had to demonstrate skill and resilience to get to this point in their studies, they nonetheless must consider that writing a project report is an exercise in communication and nobody likes reading a lot of ideas which are expressed in

▶

such a confusing and pretentious way that nobody can understand them, let alone the poor tutor who has to plough through it all to try and make some sense of it.

There appear to be at least six separate ideas in this sentence. It contains 101 words (when marking, we sometimes come across sentences with over 150!). In addition, it contains a common way of introducing multiple ideas into a sentence: the embedded clause. In the sentence above the embedded clause is '..., and who can blame them because they have had to demonstrate skill and resilience to get to this point in their studies, ...'. The give-away is the first word in the sentence: 'While'. This invites an embedded clause. The point here is that potentially rich ideas get buried away in the literary undergrowth. Dig them up and re-plant them. Let them breathe in a sentence of their own.

The sentence needs to be clearer and simpler. However, it should not lose any of its meaning. Halving the amount of words and dividing up the sentence into smaller clearer sentences results in the following:

> Researchers have illusions of academic grandeur when they write their project report. This is understandable. They have demonstrated skill and resilience to reach this point in their studies. However, writing a project report is an exercise in communication. Nobody likes confusing and pretentious writing which is difficult to understand. Pity the tutor who has to make sense of it.

Avoid jargon

Jargon should not be confused with technical terminology. Some technical terms are unavoidable. To assist your reader, it is best to put a glossary of such terms in the appendices. However, do not assume that your reader will have such a full knowledge as you of the subject and, in particular, the context. Here, and in all cases, try to put yourself in the position of the reader. Phil makes this point to MBA students who use their organisations as vehicles to write assignments. He asks them to 'mark' past (anonymous) assignments. They are usually horrified at the assumptions that their fellow students make about the tutor's prior knowledge.

What can be avoided is the sort of jargon which the Oxford dictionary defines as 'gibberish' and 'debased language'. You will know the sort of phrases: 'ongoing situation'; 'going down the route of'; 'at the end of the day'; 'the bottom line'; 'at this moment in time'. It is not just that they are ugly but they are not clear and simple. For example, 'now' is much clearer and simpler than 'at this moment in time'.

Beware of using large numbers of quotations from the literature

We believe that quotations from the literature should be used infrequently in your project report. Occasionally we receive draft projects which consist of little more than a series of quotations from books and journal articles which a student has linked together with a few sentences of her or his own. This tells us very little about the student's understanding of the concepts within the quotations. All it shows is that he or she has looked at the book or journal article and, it is hoped, can acknowledge sources correctly! In addition, by using quotations in this way the student's line of argument tends to become disjointed and less easy to follow. It is therefore usually better to explain other people's ideas in your own words.

That is not to say that you should never use quotations. As you have seen, we have used direct quotations from other people's work in this book. Rather we would advise you to use them sparingly to create maximum impact in supporting your storyline.

Check your spelling and grammar

Spelling is still a problem for many of us, in spite of the word processor's spelling check. It will not correct your 'moral' when you wished to say 'morale' or sort out when you should write 'practise' rather than 'practice'. This is where the friend who is reading your draft can help, provided that friend is a competent speller. Tutors tend to be more patient with errors of this kind than those which reflect carelessness. However, the point remains that spelling errors detract from the quality of your presentation and the authority of your ideas.

The ten commandments of good writing

Day (1995:160) provides a useful checklist for those of us who make the sort of *grammatical errors* which threaten the credibility of our writing. He demonstrates cleverly the error in each of the points which are listed in Table 13.2.

Table 13.2   **Common grammatical errors**

Often we write	*The correct way is*
1 Each pronoun should agree with **their** antecedent	Each pronoun should agree with **its** antecedent.
2 Just between you and **I**, case is important	Just between you and **me**, case is important.
3 A preposition is a poor word to end a sentence **with**.	A preposition is a poor word **with which** to end a sentence.
4 Verbs **has** to agree with their subject.	Verbs **have** to agree with their subject.
5 Do not use **no** double negatives	Do not use double negatives.
6 Remember **to never split** an infinitive.	Remember **never to split** an infinitive.
7 When dangling, do not use participles.	Do not use dangling participles.
8 Avoid clichés like the plague.	To avoid clichés like the plague!
9 Do not write a run-on sentence it is difficult when you got to punctuate it so it makes sense when the reader reads what you wrote.	Do not write a run-on sentence. It is difficult to punctuate it so that it makes sense to the reader.
10 About sentence fragments.	What about sentence fragments? (!)
11 The data **is** included in this section.	The data **are** included in this section.

Source: Developed from Day, 1995:160

It is not our intention here to conduct an English grammar lesson. Some of the common errors in Table 13.2 are self-explanatory.

You may argue that the *split infinitive* is not often thought of as an error these days. However, 'to boldly go' ahead with your project report ignoring this rule risks irritating your reader – something you can ill afford to do. You want the reader to concentrate on your ideas.

Day's '*dangling participle*' warning is amusingly illustrated by the draft questionnaire shown to us by a student. This asked for 'the amount of people you employ in your organisation, broken down by sex'. We wrote on our copy: 'we haven't got people in that category: they've not got the energy when they work here!' (Remember that when writing your questionnaire!)

Some of the more obvious grammatical errors you can spot by reading your text aloud to yourself. You need not know the grammatical rules; they often just sound wrong.

Person, tense and gender

Traditionally, academic writing has been dry and unexciting. This is partly because the convention has been to write impersonally, in the past *tense* and in the *passive voice* (e.g. 'interviews were conducted following the administration of questionnaires').

The writer was expected to be distanced from the text. This convention is no longer as strong. It is a matter of preferred style rather than rules. The research approach which dominates your methods may dictate your choice of *personal pronoun*. Section 4.1 lists 'the observer is independent of what is being observed' as one feature of positivism. It follows from this that an impersonal style is more appropriate. By contrast, Section 8.2. notes that the participant observer 'participates in the daily life of people under study'. The researcher is an intrinsic part of the research process. Use of the first person seems more logical here. However, style is important. Use of the term 'the author' sounds too impersonal and stilted. Excessive use of 'I' and 'we' may raise questions in your readers' minds about your ability to stand outside your data and to be objective.

Day (1995:160) identifies rules for the use correct use of tense. He suggests that 'you should normally use the present tense when referring to previously published work (e.g. Day identifies) and you should use the past tense when referring to your present results (e.g. I found that . . .)'. Although he notes exceptions to this rule, it serves as a useful guide.

Day (1995) and Becker (1986) both stridently attack the passive voice (e.g. it was found that) and champion the use of the *active voice* (e.g. I found that). Certainly it is clearer, shorter and unambiguous. It is a good idea to check with your project tutor here which is most likely to be acceptable.

Finally, a note about the use of language which assumes the *gender* of a classification of people. The most obvious example of these is the constant reference to managers as 'he'. Not only is this inaccurate in many organisations but it gives offence to many people of both sexes. Those offended will probably include your readers! It is simple enough to avoid (e.g. 'I propose to interview each executive unless he refuses' becomes 'I propose to interview each executive unless I receive a refusal') but often less easy to spot. The further reading section in the first draft of this chapter referred to Becker as a 'master craftsman'. These notes on language and gender prompted us to change it to 'an expert in the field'. Appendix 6 gives more detailed guidance on the use of non-discriminatory language.

Preserving anonymity

You may have given the participants (and the organisations) from whom you collected data an undertaking that you would not disclose their identity in anything you write. In this case you will need to conceal their identity in your project report. The usual way of doing this is to invent pseudonyms for organisations and not to name individual participants. This should not detract from the impact of your report.

Similarly, your sponsoring organisation(s) may have requested sight of your report before it is submitted. Should there be misgivings about the content of the report you should be able to alleviate these by the use of pseudonyms. This is usually a better option than significant text changes.

13.6 ■ The need for continual revision

Adrian recently asked a group of undergraduate students how many of them did more than one draft of their assignment papers. He did not expect that many would reply that they did. What he did not predict was that many of them had not even thought that this was necessary.

Submitting the first attempt is partly due to the heavy assessment loads on many courses which means that students are constantly having to 'keep up with the clock'. On part-time courses, students these days have so many demands in their daily work that writing an assignment just once is all that is possible. Becker (1986) argues that this is the way most of us learned to write at school. The paper is usually only seen by the teacher. The arrangement is a private one.

However, project reports are different. They will be seen by an audience much wider than one tutor. They will usually be lodged in the library to be read by succeeding students. You will be judged on the quality of your work. For that reason we urge you most strongly to polish your work with successive drafts until you are happy that you can do no better.

The final version of this chapter (which, incidentally, was read by five people and is the last of seven or eight drafts) contains guidelines that you can use to evaluate your first draft. These are summarised in the checklist in Table 13.3.

Having been through this checklist you may decide to make minor alterations to your text. On the other hand you may re-write sections or move sections within chapters to other chapters. Keep asking yourself 'how easy can I make the reader's task?'

After each successive draft do leave a space of time for your thoughts to mature. It is amazing how something you wrote a few days before will now make no sense to you. However, you will also be impressed with the clarity and insight of some passages.

Table 13.3	**Checklist for evaluating your first draft**

✓ Is there are a clear structure?

✓ Is there are a clear storyline?

✓ Does your abstract reflect accurately the whole content of the report?

✓ Does your introduction state clearly the research question(s) and objectives?

✓ Does your literature review inform the later content of the report?

✓ Are your methods clearly explained?

✓ Have you made a clear distinction between findings and conclusions in the two relevant chapters?

✓ Have you checked all your references and presented these in the required manner?

✓ Is there any text material which should be in the appendices and vice versa?

✓ Does your title reflect accurately your content?

✓ Have you divided up your text throughout with suitable headings?

✓ Does each chapter have a preview and a summary?

✓ Are you happy that your writing is clear, simple and direct?

✓ Have you eliminated all jargon?

✓ Have you eliminated all unnecessary quotations?

✓ Have you checked spelling and grammar?

✓ Have you checked for assumptions about gender?

✓ Is your report in a format which will be acceptable to the assessing body?

Having completed a second draft you may now feel confident enough to give it to your colleague or friend to read. Ask your reader to use the checklist above to which you can add specific points which you feel are important (e.g. are my arguments well-reasoned?).

13.7   Meeting the assessment criteria

Your readers will be assessing your work against the assessment criteria which apply to your research programme. Therefore, it is essential that you familiarise yourself with these criteria. Easterby-Smith *et al.* (1991) cite Bloom's (1971) well-known taxonomy of educational objectives to illustrate the level which project reports should meet. At the lower levels project reports should show *knowledge* and *comprehension* of the topic covered. At the intermediate levels they should contain evidence of *application* and *analysis*. Application is thought of as the ability to apply certain principles and rules in particular situations. Your methodology section should be the principal vehicle for demonstrating application. Analysis may be illustrated by your ability to break down your data and to clarify the nature of the component parts and the relationship between them. Whatever your assessment criteria, it is certain that you will be expected to demonstrate your ability at these lower and intermediate levels.

The higher levels are *synthesis* and *evaluation*. Rowntree (1987:103) defines synthesis as 'the ability to arrange and assemble various elements so as to make a new statement or plan or conclusion – a unique communication'. The emphasis put on conclusions and, in particular, the development of a storyline in your project report suggests that we feel that you should be showing evidence of synthesis. Evaluation refers to 'the ability to judge materials or methods in terms of internal accuracy and consistency or by comparison with external criteria' (Rowntree, 1987:103). You have the chance to show this ability in the literature review and in the awareness of the limitations of your own research (see Section 13.3).

In summary, we think that each of the levels of educational objectives should be demonstrated in your project report.

13.8   Summary

- Writing is a powerful way of clarifying your thinking.

- Writing is a creative process which needs the right conditions if it is to produce successful results.

- Your project report should have a clear structure which enables you to develop a clear storyline.

- Your report should be laid out in such a way that your reader finds all the information readily accessible.

- You should try to develop a clear, simple writing style which will make reading the report an easy and enjoyable experience.

- Spelling and grammatical errors should be avoided.

- Do not think of your first draft as your last. Be prepared to re-write your report several times until you think it is the best you can do.

Self check   **Questions**

13.1 Your project tutor has returned your draft project report with the suggestion that you make a clearer distinction between your results and your findings. How will you go about this?

13.2 Why is it considered good practice to acknowledge the limitations of your research in the project report?

13.3 Look again at the quote from Wright Mills cited early in Section 13.5. Re-write this so that his idea is communicated to the reader in the clearest way possible.

13.4 There are other problems that must be avoided when re-positioning sections of your report in the re-drafting processes. What are they?

Assignment 13

Writing your research report

➡ Design a clear structure for your report which fits broadly the structure suggested in section 13.3. Ensure that the structure that you design accommodates a clear storyline.

➡ Write the report's abstract. Remember that you will need to re-write this when you have finished your first draft.

➡ Compile the main body of the report. How will you ensure that the literature review relates to the following chapters? What method will you adopt to make the distinction between result and conclusions?

➡ Give your report the 'reader-friendly' test to ensure that the style is easy to read and free from avoidable errors.

References

Becker, H. (1986) *Writing for Social Scientists*, Chicago, IL, University of Chicago Press.

Bloom, B. (ed.) (1971) *Taxonomy of Educational Objectives: Cognitive Domain*, New York, McKay.

Day, R. (1995) *How to Write and Publish a Scientific Paper* (4th edn), Cambridge, Cambridge University Press.

Easterby-Smith, M., Thorpe, R. and Lowe, A. (1991) *Management Research: an Introduction*, London, Sage.

Griffiths, M. (1993) 'Productive writing', *The New Academic*, Autumn.

Phillips, E. and Pugh, D. (1994) *How to Get a PhD (2nd edn)*, Buckingham, Open University Press.

Raimond, P. (1993) *Management Projects: Design, Research and Presentation*, London, Chapman & Hall.

Richards, P. (1986) 'Risk', *in* Becker, H., *Writing for Social Scientists*, Chicago, IL, University of Chicago Press.

Robson, C. (1993) *Real World Research: a Resource for Social Scientists and Practitioner–Researchers*, Oxford, Blackwell.

Rowntree, D. (1987) *Assessing Students: How Shall we Know Them?* (revised edn), London, Harper and Row.

Smith, C.B. (1991) *A Guide to Business Research*, Chicago, IL, Nelson-Hall.

Veroff, J. (1992) 'Writing', *in* Rudestam, K. and Newton, R. *Surviving your Dissertation*, Newbury Park, CA, Sage.

Wright Mills, C. (1970) 'On intellectual craftsmanship', *in The Sociological Imagination*, London, Pelican.

Further reading

Becker, H. (1986) *Writing for Social Scientists*, Chicago, IL, University of Chicago Press. This is a highly readable book, full of anecdotes, from an expert in the field. It is rich in ideas about how writing may be improved. Most of these have been developed by Becker from his own writing and teaching. Such is the emphasis that Becker puts on re-writing that the title would more accurately be 'Re-writing for Social Scientists'.

Day, R. (1995) *How to Write and Publish a Scientific Paper* (4th edn), Cambridge, Cambridge University Press. This takes the reader through the whole process with a host of useful advice. It is funny and irreverent but none the less valuable for that!

Smith, C.B. (1991) *A Guide to Business Research*, Chicago, IL, Nelson-Hall. Chapters 7–10 provide an excellent introduction to writing for business and management researchers.

Case 13 Writing Lata's project report

Lata had worked hard on her research. She was pleased with the project report she had submitted and was quietly confident it would receive a good grade. However, this was not to be. She was horrified when she received a note from Louise, her course tutor, telling her that her report had been referred back for substantial re-working. Lata went to see Louise immediately. She told the story of how her research had developed from the time she had first discussed it with Eddie, her project tutor, to the time her report was submitted. This is that story.

> My research question was, 'what have been the effects of office automation on the social relations between staff?' I was conducting a case study in Midshire, a large local authority. My data collection methods were questionnaire and semi-structured interviews.
>
> I was enthusiastic about my research. In the early days I had frequent meetings with Eddie. I wanted to start collecting data immediately. However, Eddie counselled caution. He was concerned that I should think through more thoroughly my research objectives and the questions I was going to ask in my questionnaire. To be honest, I became impatient with Eddie's approach which I thought was too fussy.
>
> I went ahead and collected the data. I had piloted the questionnaire with friends whom I met when working in Midshire's education department. I was pleased with the response rate of over 60 per cent. I then went ahead and conducted my interviews. I interviewed those people I was friendly with and who would be more likely to give up their time. I suppose that by the time I had finished my data collection I had not seen Eddie for several months.
>
> I had taken Eddie's advice not to leave all my writing until the last minute. I was determined to write up my research as I went along. Early on in my research I had written a literature review which was current and comprehensive. I was pleased with this and decided that this would form a part of the final report. I was also writing up my data as I went along. My questionnaire analysis formed a major part of this writing. My results were in the form of computer-generated tables related to each question. I wrote an extensive commentary on these tables. I also wrote a separate section on my

▶

interview data, reporting in some detail what each interviewee had said. The result was that I had a major section on my data which I was satisfied would form the bulk of my report.

Meanwhile I had a meeting with Eddie to report progress. He seemed pleased that I had collected so much data. He said he was in the annual process of chasing some students who seemed to have done little, despite the fast approaching deadline for handing-in. I had done a lot. However, I think that Eddie felt I was rather complacent about what I had done. He asked to see of a copy of my draft report. I said that a little more time was needed to get it up together. We agreed that it would be with Eddie in two weeks' time.

I must admit that the deadline passed and the draft report did not arrive. I had been hit with the normal rush to finish assignments for other parts of my course. I was pleased that I had gone ahead with writing my project report because it meant that I was able to hand in all my work. I also thought there was not much I could do to the report since I had already hit the word limit. I sent Eddie a note to explain the problems I had experienced. I told him that I would 'polish up' what I had written and submit that for examination.

Louise went to see Eddie to report on her meeting with Lata. This was Eddie's reaction.

To be honest I am not surprised it turned out like this. The report is far too descriptive. It is good at the description, but that is about all. There is no attempt to link the data to the literature review and not really much connection between the data and the research questions. It reads a bit like two separate reports. One of these is a review of the literature in the field and the other a report of what Lata found out in Midshire. Both, in their own right, are quite good but as a project report it simply doesn't come together. However, my main criticism is that it does not actually say anything . . . you know, it does not draw any conclusions. When I finished reading it I could not help saying: 'so what?'

The material is there for Lata to write a decent report. However, I am afraid that she has a lot more work to do.

Questions

1 Where do you think Lata went wrong in her approach to the process of preparing her research report?

2 How do you think Lata could have overcome Eddie's criticism that 'it reads a bit like two separate reports'?

3 How may Lata have approached the writing of her results section?

4 How could Lata have prevented Eddie saying 'so what?' to himself after he had finished reading her report?

Self check **Answers**

13.1 This is easier said than done. Start by going through your results chapter continually asking yourself 'did I find this out?' You will probably weed out a lot of things which you have thought about which are related to points you found out. These belong in the conclusions (or discussion) chapter.

Now turn to the conclusions chapter asking yourself the same question. You will probably find fewer results in the conclusions chapter than vice versa.

13.2 It shows that you have thought about your research design. It demonstrates that you have insight into the various ways of pursuing research. Remember that there is no perfect research design. Look again at Section 4.4. This asked the question 'How do you know that the answer to the research question(s) is the correct one?' The answer, of course, is that in the literal sense of the question you cannot know. All you can do is to reduce the possibility of getting the answer wrong.

13.3 Academic writing is often difficult to understand. This is not usually because the subject matter is complex or the thoughts profound. It is because the writer thinks it necessary to write in an 'academic' way.

13.4 The 'road map' you announced in the introduction may not now be correct. The previews and summaries at the beginning and end of the relevant chapters may need changing. A more serious potential problem is that the storyline may be altered. This should not be the case. Nonetheless, it is important to re-read the whole report to ensure that the re-positioning does not alter its sense of coherence.

Bibliography

Ackroyd, S. and Hughes, J. (1992) *Data Collection in Context* (2nd edn), London, Longman.

Adams, G. and Schvaneveldt, J. (1991) *Understanding Research Methods* (2nd edn), New York, Longman.

Barnett, V. (1991) *Sample Survey Principles and Method*, London, Edward Arnold.

Barrow, M. (1998) *The Times 1000 1998*, London, Times Books.

Becker, H. (1986) *Writing for Social Scientists*, Chicago, IL, University of Chicago Press.

BECTA (1997) 'Information sheet on internet searching' (online)(cited 1 January 1999). Available from <URL:http://www.becta.org.uk/info-sheets/intsearch.html>.

Bell, J. (1999) *Doing Your Research Project* (3rd edn), Buckingham, Open University Press.

Bennett, R. (1991) 'What is management research', *in* Smith, N.C. and Dainty, P., *The Management Research Handbook,* London, Routledge, pp. 67–77.

Bloom, B. (ed.) (1971) *Taxonomy of Educational Objectives: Cognitive Domain,* New York, McKay.

Bouma, G., and Atkinson, G. (1995) *A Handbook of Social Science Research: a Comprehensive and Practical Guide for Students* (2nd edn), Oxford, Oxford University Press.

Bourque, L.B. and Clark, V.A. (1994) 'Processing data: the survey example', *in* Lewis-Beck, M.S., *Research Practice* London, Sage, pp. 1–88.

Branscomb, H.E. (1998) *Casting Your Net: a Student's Guide to Research on the Internet,* Boston, Allyn and Bacon.

British Psychological Society. (1988) 'Guidelines for the use of non-sexist language', *The Psychologist,* 1:2, 53–4.

Bryman, A. (1988) *Quantity and Quality in Social Research*, London, Unwin Hyman.

Bryman, A. (1989) *Research Methods and Organisation Studies*, London, Unwin Hyman.

Bryman, A. and Cramer, D. (1999) *Quantitative Data Analysis with SPSS Release 8 for Windows: for Social Scientists*, London, Routledge.

Bryson, B. (1995) *Made in America*, London, Minerva.

Buchanan, D., Boddy, D. and McAlman, J. (1988) 'Getting in, getting on, getting out and getting back', *in* Bryman, A. (ed.), *Doing Research in Organisations*, London, Routledge, 53–67.

Buzan, T. with Buzan, B. (1995) *The Mind Map Book* (revised edn), London, BBC Books.

Campbell, D. and Campbell, M. (1995) *The Students' Guide to Doing Research on the Internet*, Reading, MA, Addison-Wesley.

Carroll, L. (1989) *Alice's Adventures in Wonderland*, London, Hutchinson.

Central Statistical Office (1997) *Standard Industrial Classification of Economic Activities*, London, Stationery Office.

Cheltenham & Gloucester College of Higher Education (1999) 'Setting out your bibliography using Harvard' (online) (cited 6 April 1999). Available from <URL:http://www.chelt.ac.uk/is/mjenkins/reference/bibliography.htm>.

Clausen, H. (1996) 'Web information quality as seen from libraries', *New Library World*, 97: 1130, 4–8.

Collins, D. and White, A. (1995) 'Making the next census form more respondent-friendly', *Social Survey Methodology Bulletin*, 37, July, 8–14.

Coomber, R. (1997) 'Using the internet for survey research', *Sociological Research Online*, 2:2 (online)(cited 5 March 1999). Available from <URL:http://www.socresonline.org.uk/socresonline/2/2/2.html>.

Cooper, D.R. and Schindler, P.S. (1998) *Business Research Methods* (6th edn), Boston, MA, Irwin McGraw-Hill.

Cowton, C.J. (1998) 'The use of secondary data in business ethics research', *Journal of Business Ethics*, 17:4, 423–34.

Creswell, J. (1994) *Research Design: Quantitative and Qualitative Approaches*, Thousand Oaks, CA, Sage.

Cunningham, J.B. (1995) 'Strategic considerations in using action research for improving personnel practices', *Public Personnel Management*, 24:2, 515–29.

Dale, A. (1993) 'Fieldwork and data processing', *in* Dale, A. and Marsh, C. (eds), *The 1991 Census User's Guide*, London, HMSO, pp. 84–110.

Dale, A., Arber, S. and Procter, M. (1988) *Doing Secondary Research*, London, Unwin Hyman.

Davis, S.M. and Saunders, M.N.K. (1997) 'Freedom of movement for professionals: an assessment of the European Union policy and the barriers that remain', *Journal of Applied Management Studies*, 6:2, 199–218.

Day, R. (1995) *How to Write and Publish a Scientific Paper* (4th edn), Cambridge, Cambridge University Press.

Deci, E.L. (1972) 'The effects of contingent and non-contingent rewards and controls on intrinsic motivation', *Organisational Behaviour and Human Performance*, 8, 217–9.

Delbridge, R. and Kirkpatrick, I. (1994) 'Theory and practice of participant observation', *in* Wass, V. and Wells, P. (eds), *Principles and Practice in Business and Management Research*, Aldershot, Dartmouth, pp. 35–62.

Dennis, G, Pearson, N. and Ukueku, C. (eds). (1995) *Annual Abstract of Statistics*, London, HMSO.

Denscombe, M. (1998) *The Good Research Guide*, Buckingham, Open University Press.

Denzin, N. (1989) *The Research Act: a Theoretical Introduction to Sociological Methods* (3rd edn), Englewood Cliffs, NJ, Prentice-Hall.

Dey, I. (1993) *Qualitative Data Analysis*, London, Routledge.

Diamantopoulos, A. and Schlegelmilch, B.B. (1997) *Taking the Fear out of Data Analysis*, London, Dryden Press.

Dillman, D.A. (1978) *Mail and Telephone Surveys: the Total Design Method*, New York, Wiley.

Ditton, J. (1977) *Part-Time Crime: an Ethnography of Fiddling and Pilferage*, London, Macmillan.

Dunkerley, D. (1988) 'Historical methods and organizational analysis', *in* Bryman, A. (ed.), *Doing Research in Organisations*, London, Routledge, pp. 82–95.

Easterby-Smith, M., Thorpe, R. and Lowe, A. (1991) *Management Research: an Introduction*, London, Sage.

Economist, The (1997) *The Economist Numbers Guide: the Essentials of Business Numeracy* (3rd edn), London, Profile Books.

Eden, C. and Huxham, C. (1996) 'Action research for management research', *British Journal of Management*, 7:1, 75–86.

Ellsworth, J.H. and Ellsworth, M.V. (1996) *The New Internet Business Book* (2nd edn), New York, Wiley.

Erlandson, D.A., Harris, E.L., Skipper, B.L. and Allen, S.D. (1993*) Doing Naturalistic Inquiry,* Newbury Park, CA, Sage.

ESRC Data Archive (1995) *The ESRC Data Archive: Sharing and Preserving Research Data* Colchester, ESRC Data Archive.

Fenwick, D. and Denman, J. (1995) 'The monthly claimant unemployment count: change and consistency', *Labour Market Trends,* November, 397–400.

Fielding, N.G. and Lee, R.M. (1995) 'Confronting CAQDAS: choice and contingency', *in* Burgess, R.G. (ed.), *Studies in Qualitative Methodology Computing and Qualitative Research*, Greenwich, CT, JAI Press.

Fink, A. (1995) *How to Analyze Survey Data*, Thousand Oaks, CA, Sage.

Fink, A. (1995) *How to Ask Survey Questions*, Thousand Oaks, CA, Sage.

Fink, A. (1995) *The Survey Handbook*, Thousand Oaks, CA, Sage.

Fisher, M. (1997*) Qualitative Computing: Using Software for Qualitative Data Analysis*, Aldershot, Ashgate.

Foddy,W. (1994) *Constructing Questions for Interviews and Questionnaires,* Cambridge, Cambridge University Press.

Fox, J. and Long, J.S. (eds) (1990) *Modern Methods of Data Analysis*, Newbury Park, CA, Sage.

Gall, M.D., Borg, W.R. and Gall, J.P. (1996) *Educational Research: an Introduction* (6th edn), New York, Longman.

Ghauri, P.N., Grønhaug, K. and Kristianslund, I. (1995) *Research Methods in Business Studies: a Practical Guide*, London, Prentice Hall.

Gibb, F. (1995) 'Consumer group accuses lawyers of shoddy service', *The Times*, 5 October.

Gill, J. and Johnson, P. (1997) *Research Methods for Managers* (2nd edn), London, Paul Chapman.

Glaser, B. (1978*) Theoretical Sensitivity: Advances in the Methodology of Grounded Theory,* Mill Valley, CA, Sociology Press.

Glaser, B. and Strauss, A. (1967) *The Discovery of Grounded Theory*, Chicago, IL, Aldine.

Griffiths, M. (1993) 'Productive writing', *The New Academic,* Autumn.

Grummitt, J. (1980) *Interviewing Skills*, London, The Industrial Society.

Gummesson E. (1991) *Qualitative Methods in Management Research,* Newbury Park, CA, Sage.

Hakim, C. (1982) *Secondary Analysis in Social Research*, London, Allen & Unwin.

Hakim, C. (1987) *Research Design: Strategies and Choices in the Design of Social Research*, London, Allen & Unwin.

Hays, W.L. (1994) *Statistics* (4th edn), London, Holt-Saunders.

Haythornthwaite, J. (ed.) (1990) *The Business Information Maze: an Essential Guide,* London, ASLIB.

Haywood, P. and Wragg, E.C. (1982) *Evaluating the Literature: Rediguide 2*, Nottingham, University of Nottingham School of Education.

Healey, M.J. (1991) 'Obtaining information from businesses', *in* Healey, M.J. (ed.), *Economic Activity and Land Use: the Changing Information Base for Local and Regional Studies,* Harlow, Longman, pp. 193–250.

Healey, M.J. and Rawlinson, M.B. (1994) 'Interviewing techniques in business and management research' *in* Wass, V.J. and Wells, P.E., *Principles and Practice in Business and Management Research*, Aldershot, Dartmouth, Chapter 5.

Healey, M.J. and Rawlinson, M.B. (1993) 'Interviewing business owners and managers: a review of methods and techniques', *Geoforum, 24*:3, 339–55.

Hedrick, T.E., Bickmann, L. and Rog, D.J. (1993) *Applied Research Design*, Newbury Park, CA, Sage.

Henry, G.T. (1990) *Practical Sampling,* Newbury Park, CA, Sage.

Higgins, R. (1996) *Approaches to Research: a Handbook for Those Writing a Dissertation*, London, Jessica Kingsley.

Hodson, R. (1991) 'The active worker: compliance and autonomy at the workplace', *Journal of Contemporary Ethnography, 20*:1, 47–8.

Hofstede, G. (1991) *Cultures and Organisations*, London, McGraw-Hill.

Hoinville, G., Jowell, R. and Associates (1985) *Survey Research Practice*, Aldershot, Gower.

Hussey, J. and Hussey, R. (1997) *Business Research: a Practical Guide for Undergraduate and Postgraduate Students*, Basingstoke, Macmillan Business.

Jacob, H. (1994) 'Using published data: errors and remedies', *in* Lewis-Beck, M.S., *Research Practice*, London, Sage and Toppan Publishing, pp. 339–89.

Jankowicz, A.D. (1995) *Business Research Projects* (2nd edn), London, Chapman & Hall.

Jobber, D. and O'Reilly, D. (1996) 'Industrial mail surveys: techniques for inducing response', *Marketing & Intelligence Planning, 14*:1, 29–34.

Johnson, G. (1996) 'The debate begins', *BAM News*, 6, 1–2.

Johnson, J.M. (1975) *Doing Field Research,* New York, Free Press.

Jowell, R., Curtice. J, Brook, L. and Ahrendt, D. (1994) *British Social Attitudes – the 11th Report*, Aldershot, Dartmouth.

Kahn, R. and Cannell, C. (1957) *The Dynamics of Interviewing*, New York and Chichester, Wiley.

Kanji, G.K. (1998) *100 Statistical Tests* (2nd edn), London, Sage.

Kerlinger, F. (1973) *Foundations of Behavioral Research* (2nd edn), New York, Holt, Rinehart and Winston.

Kervin, J.B. (1999) *Methods for Business Research* (2nd edn), Reading, MA, Addison-Wesley.

King, J. (ed.) (1996) *Family Spending – a Report on the 1995–96 Family Expenditure Survey*, London, Stationery Office.

Kingsbury, P. (1997) *IT Answers to HR Questions*, London, Institute of Personnel and Development.

Lewin, P. (1997) *Economic Trends Annual Supplement* (1997 edn), London, Stationery Office.

Mackintosh, N. (ed.). (1995) *Cyril Burt: Fraud or Framed?*, Oxford, Oxford University Press.

Marsh, C. (1993) 'An overview', *in* Dale, A. and Marsh, C. (eds), *The 1991 Census User's Guide*, London, HMSO, pp. 1–15.

Marshall, C. and Rossman, G.B. (1999) *Designing Qualitative Research* (3rd edn), Thousand Oaks, CA, Sage.

Marsick, V.J. and Watkins, K.E. (1997) 'Case study research methods', *in* Swanson, R.A. and

Holton, E.F. (eds), *Human Resource Development Research Handbook*, San Francisco, CA, Berrett-Koehler, pp. 138–57.

McGuinness, K. and Short, T. *Research on the Net*, London, Old Bailey Press.

McNeill, P. (1990) *Research Methods* (2nd edn), London, Routledge.

Mercator. (1999) 'Mercator home page: products' (online)(cited 16 June 1999). Available from <URL:http://www.mercator.co.uk>.

Meyer, H., Kay, E. and French, J. (1965) 'Split roles in performance appraisal', *Harvard Business Review*, 43:1, 123–9.

Miles, M.B. and Huberman, A.M. (1994) *Qualitative Data Analysis* (2nd edn), Thousand Oaks, CA, Sage.

Millmore, M. (1995) *HRM in C&GCHE?: Assessing the Current State of Play*, MA Dissertation, Cheltenham, Cheltenham & Gloucester College of Higher Education.

Millward, N., Stevens, M., Smart, D. and Hawes, W.R. (1992*) Workplace Industrial Relations in Transition*, Aldershot, Dartmouth.

Mintzberg, H. (1973) *The Nature of Managerial Work*, New York, Harper & Row.

Mintzberg, H. and Waters, J. (1989) 'Of strategies, deliberate and emergent', *in* Asch, D. and Bowman, C. (eds), *Readings in Strategic Management*, Basingstoke, Macmillan Education, pp. 4–19.

Mitchell, V. (1996) 'Assessing the reliability and validity of questionnaires: an empirical example', *Journal of Applied Management Studies*, 5:2, 199–207.

Moody, P.E. (1983) *Decision Making: Proven Methods for Better Decisions*, London, McGraw-Hill.

Morgan, M. (1995) 'The case of the dubious data', *The Guardian*, August 4, second section, pp. 10–11.

Morris, C. (1999) *Quantitative Approaches in Business Studies* (5th edn), London, Financial Times Pitman Publishing.

Morris, T. and Wood, S. (1991) 'Testing the survey method: continuity and change in British industrial relations', *Work Employment and Society*, 5:2, 259–82.

Mort, D. (1992) *UK Statistics – a Guide for Business Users*, Aldershot, Ashgate.

Moser, C.A. and Kalton, G. (1986) *Survey Methods in Social Investigation* (2nd edn), Aldershot, Gower.

Mullins, L. (1999) *Management and Organisational Behaviour* (5th edn), London, Financial Times Pitman Publishing.

Naipaul, V.S. (1989) *A Turn in the South*, London, Penguin.

Neuman, W.L. (1997) *Social Research Methods* (2nd edn), London, Allyn and Bacon.

New Riders. (1997) *New Riders Official Internet Directory* (revised edn), Indianapolis, IN, New Rider Publishing.

North, D.J, Leigh, R. and Gough, J. (1983) 'Monitoring industrial change at the local level: some comments on methods and data sources', *in* Healey, M.J. (ed.), *Urban and Regional Industrial Research: the Changing UK Data Base*, Norwich, Geo Books, pp. 111–29.

Norusis, M.J. (1993) *SPSS for Windows Professional Statistics Release 6.0*, Chicago, IL, SPSS.

Norusis, M.J. (1998) *SPSS 8.0 Guide to Data Analysis*, London, Prentice Hall.

Office for National Statistics. (1996) *30 Years of Regional Trends*, London, Stationery Office.

Office of Population Censuses and Surveys (1990) *Standard Occupational Classification, Vol. 1*, London, HMSO.

Office of Population Censuses and Surveys (1990) *Standard Occupational Classification, Vol. 2*, London, HMSO.

Office of Population Censuses and Surveys (1991) *Standard Occupational Classification, Vol. 3*, London, HMSO.

Office of Population Censuses and Surveys and General Registrar's Office for Scotland (1992) *1991 Census Definitions Great Britain*, London, HMSO.

Oppenheim, A.N. (1992) *Questionnaire Design, Interviewing and Attitude Measurement* (new edn), London, Pinter.

Owen, F. and Jones, R. (1994) *Statistics* (4th edn), London, Pitman.

Partington, J. and Mayell, C. (1998) 'Revision of the annual employment survey results for 1995 and 1996', *Labour Market Trends*, 106:7, 387–97.

Patton, M.Q. (1990) *Qualitative Evaluation and Research Methods* (2nd edn), Newbury Park, CA, Sage.

Patzer, G.L. (1996) *Using Secondary Data in Market Research: United States and Worldwide*, Westport, CT, Quorum Books.

Peters, T. and Waterman, R. (1982) *In Search of Excellence*, New York, Harper & Row.

Phillips, E. and Pugh, D. (1994) *How to Get a PhD* (2nd edn), Buckingham, Open University Press.

Pointon, G. (no date) *Disability and Television: Guidelines on Representation for Producers*, London, Channel 4.

Powney, J. and Watts, M. (1987) *Interviewing in Educational Research*, London, Routledge and Kegan Paul.

Pullinger, J. (ed.) (1998) *Regional Trends 33* (1998 edn), London, Stationery Office.

Punch, M. (1993) 'Observation and the police the research experience', *in* Hammersley, M., *Social Research Philosophy Politics and Practice*, London, Sage, pp. 181–99.

Raimond, P. (1993) *Management Projects: Design, Research and Presentation*, London, Chapman & Hall.

Reichman, C.S. (1962) *Use and Abuse of Statistics*, New York, Oxford University Press.

Remenyi, D., Williams, B., Money, A. and Swartz, E. (1998) *Doing Research in Business and Management: an Introduction to Process and Method*, London, Sage.

Richards, P. (1986) 'Risk', *in* Becker, H., *Writing for Social Scientists*, Chicago, IL, University of Chicago Press.

Riley, J. (1996) *Getting the Most from your Data. A Handbook of Practical Ideas on How to Analyse Qualitative Data* (2nd edn), Bristol, Technical and Educational Services Ltd.

Robson, C. (1993) *Real World Research: a Resource for Social Scientists and Practitioner–Researchers*, Oxford, Blackwell.

Rogers, C.R. (1961) *On Becoming a Person*, Constable, London.

Rokeach, M. (1979) *Understanding Human Values: Individual and Society*, USA, Free Press.

Rosen, M. (1991) 'Breakfast at Spiro's dramaturgy and dominance', *in* Frost, P., Moore, L., Louis, M., Lundberg, C. and Martin, J. (eds), *Reframing Organisational Culture*, Newbury Park, CA, Sage 77–89.

Rowntree, D. (1987) *Assessing Students: How Shall we Know Them?* (revised edn), London, Harper & Row.

Roy, D. (1952) 'Quota restriction and goldbricking in a machine shop', *American Journal of Sociology*, 57, 427–42.

Salant, P and Dillman, D.A. (1994) *How to Conduct your own Survey*, New York, Wiley.

Saris, W.E. (1994) 'Computer-assisted interviewing', *in* Lewis-Beck, M.S., *Research Practice*, London, Sage, pp. 163–250.

Saunders, M.N.K. (1993) 'Vacancy notification and employee mobility', *International Journal of Manpower* 14:6, 39–57.

Saunders, M.N.K. and Lewis, P. (1997) 'Great ideas and blind alleys? A review of the literature on starting research', *Management Learning*, 28:3, 283–99.

Schatzman, L. and Strauss, A. (1973) *Field Research: Strategies for a Natural Sociology*, Englewood Cliffs, NJ, Prentice-Hall.

Schein, E. (1992) 'Coming to a new awareness of organisational culture', in Salaman, G., *Human Resource Strategies*, London, Sage.

Scolari Sage (1999) 'Research methodology and CD-ROMS' (online)(cited 16 June 1999). Available from <URL:http://www.scolari.co.uk>.

Sekaran, U. (1992) *Research Methods for Business: a Skill-Building Approach* (2nd edn), New York, Wiley.

Sharp, J.A. and Howard, K. (1996) *The Management of a Student Research Project* (2nd edn), Aldershot, Gower.

Siedel, J. (1991) 'Method and madness in the application of computer technology to qualitative data analysis', *in* Fielding, N.G. and Lee, R.M. (eds) *Using Computers in Qualitative Research*, London, Sage.

Silverman, D. (1993) *Interpreting Qualitative Data*, London, Sage.

Smith, C.B. (1991) *A Guide to Business Research*, Chicago, IL, Nelson-Hall.

Smith, H. (1975) *Strategies of Social Research: the Methodological Imagination*, Englewood Cliffs, NJ, Prentice-Hall.

Smith, N.C. and Dainty, P. (1991) *The Management Research Handbook*, London, Routledge.

Sparrow, J. (1989) 'Graphic displays in information systems: some data properties influencing the effectiveness of alternate forms', *Behaviour and Information Technology*, 8:1, 43–56.

Stewart, D.W. and Kamins, M.A. (1993) *Secondary Research: Information Sources and Methods* (2nd edn), Newbury Park, CA, Sage.

Strauss, A. and Corbin, J. (1990) *Basics of Qualitative Research*, Newbury Park, CA, Sage.

Strauss, A. and Corbin, J. (1998) *Basics of Qualitative Research* (2nd edn), Thousand Oaks, CA, Sage.

Swanson, R.A. and Holton, E.F. (eds) (1997) *Human Resource Development Research Handbook*, San Francisco, CA, Berrett-Koehler, pp. 138–57.

Sykes, W. (1991) 'Taking stock: issues from the literature in validity and reliability in qualitative research', *Journal of Market Research Society*, 33, 3–12.

Tesch, R. (1990) *Qualitative Research: Analysis Types and Software Tools*, New York, Falmer.

Thomas, M, Walker, A, Wilmot, A. and Bennett, N. (1998) *Living in Britain: Results from the 1996 General Household Survey*, London, Stationery Office.

Torrington, D. (1991) *Management Face to Face*, London, Prentice Hall.

Tranfield, D and Starkey, K. (1998) 'The nature, social organization and promotion of management research: towards policy', *British Journal of Management*, 9, 341–53.

Tukey, J.W. (1977) *Exploratory Data Analysis*, Reading, MA, Addison-Wesley.

Tull, D.S. and Hawkins, D.I. (1993) *Marketing Research: Measurement and Method*, Upper Saddle River, NJ, Prentice-Hall.

deVaus, D.A. (1991) *Surveys in Social Research* (3rd edn), London, UCL Press and Allen & Unwin.

Veroff, J. (1992) 'Writing', *in* Rudestam, K. and Newton, R., *Surviving your Dissertation,* Newbury Park, CA, Sage.

Walker, R. (1985) *Doing Research: a Handbook for Teachers,* London, Methuen.

Wass, V.J. (1994) 'Minimizing and managing bias in a mail survey: a study of redundant miners', *in* Wass, V.J. and Wells, P.E., *Principles and Practice in Business and Management Research,* Aldershot, Dartmouth, pp. 91–121.

Wass, V. and Well, P. (1994) 'Research methods in action: an introduction', *in* Wass, V.J. and Wells, P.E., *Principles and Practice in Business and Management Research,* Aldershot, Dartmouth, pp. 1–34.

Weitzman, E.A. and Miles, M.B. (1995) *Computer Programs for Qualitative Data Analysis,* Thousand Oaks, CA, Sage.

Wells, P. (1994) 'Ethics in business and management research', *in* Wass, V.J. and Wells, P.E. (eds), *Principles and Practice in Business and Management Research,* Aldershot, Dartmouth, pp. 277–97.

Whyte, W. (1955) *Street Corner Society* (2nd edn), Chicago, IL, University of Chicago Press.

Wisniewski, D. (ed.) (1998) *Annual Abstract of Statistics 1998,* London, Stationery Office.

Witmer, D.F, Colman, R.W. and Katzman, S.L. (1999) 'From paper and pen to screen and keyboard: towards a methodology for survey research on the internet', *in* Jones. S., *Doing Internet Research,* Thousand Oaks, CA, Sage, pp. 145–62.

Wright Mills, C. (1970) 'On intellectual craftsmanship', in *The Sociological Imagination,* London, Pelican.

Yin, R.K. (1994) *Case Study Research: Design and Methods* (2nd edn), Thousand Oaks, CA, Sage.

Youngman, M.B. (1986) *Analysing Questionnaires,* Nottingham, University of Nottingham School of Education.

Zikmund, W.G. (1997) *Business Research Methods* (5th edn), Fort Worth, TX, Dryden Press.

Zuber-Skerritt, O. (1996) 'Emancipatory action research for organisational change and management development', in Zuber-Skerritt, O. (ed.), *New Directions in Action Research,* London, Falmer, pp. 83–105.

Example research project titles

The following titles are included to help stimulate possible research ideas. You should not take the inclusion of a title as an indication of the quality of the title or any associated research project.

Accountability of accountants

Competitor strategies in the mortgage market

Do the new direct methods of selling financial services pose a major threat to existing providers and, if so, what impact will this have in the future?

Does activity-based costing give companies a competitive edge?

FRSI : are cash flow statements a useful vehicle for conveying relevant and clear information about a business's liquidity and financial viability?

Has the introduction of the self-regulatory organisation (PIA) brought about better advice for the public?

How do financial services market to the 'youth' market?

In 1995 England had a total of 80 building societies. In 20 years time, how many will still exist?

Insider dealing: the development of the criminal law and an evaluation of alternative approaches

Is the demand for pension products increasing from the female sector, and if so how are life assurance companies reacting to this change?

An assessment of the potential of a major domestic and industrial food manufacturer within the children's confectionery market

The acquisition of mortgage books – managing change

The cashless society – imminent reality or impossible dream?

The change of banks and building societies to public companies

The changing face/future of banks and building societies with regards to products and services

The impact of developments in IT on financial services

The impact on the financial management of NHS hospitals with the granting of 'trust' status: case study

The implementation of principles of sound corporate governance within organisations

The implications of introducing compulsory competitive tendering to white collar services within local government: a critical evaluation

The importance of group personal pensions to individual employees at an organisation compared with company pension schemes

The use and application of purchasing within the organisation

With ever-increasing improvements in modern technology, will a career in accountancy become a thing of the past?

Commercial organisations and the green consumer phenomenon

Has the National Lottery had a detrimental impact on the fund raising of charitable bodies?

Global warming. What does it mean for commercial insurers?

Green revolution in the consumer goods market – a consumer-led phenomenon or the marketing industry's profit-making creation?

The impact of ozone depletion and the greenhouse warming effect on the marketing policies of the domestic refrigeration industry in recent years

The relationship between tobacco advertising and sport on television – can it be justified?

Why is there a need for a standard definition of cruelty free and to what extent does the cosmetic and toiletry industry's definition correspond to the consumer's preferred interpretation?

A comparison of recruitment and selection procedures used in the UK and elsewhere in Europe

A study of the role of human resources today and its effectiveness – is there a real future for it?

Age discrimination in the workplace

An investigation into how skills are acquired on an outdoor management development course and transferred to the workplace

Corporate strategy and planning: the role of the personnel department in its formulation

Disability awareness training within leisure organisations: a case study

Equal opportunities: a marketing and recruitment concept or a reality?

From job interview to promoting a business – how effective is marketing yourself?

Graduates' job attribute preferences: to what extent can they be explained by Maslow's hierarchy of needs?

Internal communications – what role does it have within the organisation of the future?

Investors in people – an investigation into how IIP is introduced in organisations in order to gain staff support for IIP

Is personality testing a valid tool in the recruitment and selection process?

Honesty and integrity testing and the security industry

How important is employee communication today?

Performance appraisal: a review of the benefits

Psychometric testing – an effective way for selection

Racial discrimination in recruitment and selection

Recruitment on the Internet – is this a step forward in the recruitment process or just the new fad?

Stress – the cost to employers

The armed forces, equal opportunities and equality

The changing role of HRM

The effectiveness of middle management on a culture change

The extended interview technique and its validity as a method of selection

To what extent can 'tele-working' benefit the re-locating organisation?

Human resource management and outsourcing

Workplace harassment and bullying: causes and effects and the need for organisations to protect their employees from behavioural excesses

A critical review of the prospects for interactive services to the home and the implications for marketing strategy

A study of the influence of information technology on management development – implementation of IT policy

Has modern technology destroyed customer services within the financial services sector?

How can information technology aid marketing communications?

Preparing for the worst – an investigation into the need for and methods of backing up business computer files

RSI in the workplace: a study of causation and management

The development and relationship of office automation, information technology strategies and their impact on the use of information technology: a case study

A woman's place – an investigation of the factors that facilitate the achievement of equal opportunities

Great British culture versus women in manufacturing

Women in management – the glass ceiling

Opportunity 2000 addressing the barriers to women's progress in organisations. A critical evaluation of current theories and practice

The rise in the number of female entrepreneurs: why is it happening and what problems are they facing?

A comparative study of marketing techniques adopted by body-building supplement manufacturers

A consideration of the promotional strategies and tools used in achieving greater sales in retail organisations

A critical evaluation of strategic planning and marketing techniques used in the public sector recreation provision

A study of global brands : what makes them and what can break them?

A study on the evolution of the use of target marketing in the media, entertainment and ·show business

Airline marketing – is there a difference between what business travellers want and what is promoted to them?

An analysis into the marketing methods employed by a professional football club

An investigation into branding within the new premium bottled lager market

An investigation into marketing activity aimed at children

An investigation into the market segmentation. Has social group E developed from previous ideas?

An investigation into the marketing techniques employed by the motor industry in the UK

Marketing by general practitioner fund holders

Marketing in the NHS – is it an alien concept?

Marketing is an essential aspect of successful tourism. How can competitive analysis of similar companies improve one's product and maximise sales?

Marketing of non-profit-making organisations

Marketing the changing face of licensed premises

Marketing tourism in urban areas – a comparison of Gloucester and Bradford

The role of loyalty schemes in grocery retailing and their effectiveness as part of a relationship marketing strategy

Benefits and disbenefits of press and radio advertising to small businesses

Brands marketing, positioning – launching of new brands

Can a leading retailer rely on their name to sell pensions?

Do marketers exploit customers through manipulative marketing?

Measurement of results within the marketing mix. Can public relations be accurately compared with the other marketing disciplines?

Employee rights in the event of transfers of undertakings: an examination of local government

Global advertising: a review?

How can small businesses produce an effective marketing plan given the limited resources available?

How effective is bill-board advertising within the UK?

How have Eurotunnel advertised and has this been successful in affecting people's perceptions of cross channel travel?

How marketers use sex to sell advertising

Justification for marketing in the food industry

Niche marketing in the service industry – when a niche market ceases to become a niche market!

The effectiveness of marketing and PR in the manufacturing industry and the place of PR in marketing mix

What are the problems of marketing a 'services' product such as insurance, compared with that of a tangible product?

Why do businesses sponsor sport?

Are quality assurance and total quality management a cost or a benefit for professional service firms?

Bench-marking: a critical evaluation

Is it possible to achieve total quality management and a high level of customer service within a commercial vehicle supplier?

Is there a link between bench marking and total quality management (TQM)?

Quality initiatives within the insurance industry

Quality management and BS5750 in small to medium manufacturing enterprises

The digital revolution – a case study examining the Xerox corporation in the light of the digital explosion

A study of the industrial branch, examining its past, its present and its future

An evaluation of the extent to which language training equips managers to better understand foreign business cultures

An investigation into how the management of technical and cultural change can have an effect on the organisation

An investigation into management buy-outs/buy-ins within the UK economy

A comparative analysis of off-shore companies in Cyprus and the Isle of Man

Can JIT be successfully implemented within service organisations?

Compulsory competitive tendering in local government

Could UK export capabilities in the Asian region be improved by gaining an understanding of their national cultures?

Competition in the parcel delivery industry

Funding of NHS and private health care

How beneficial is management consultancy to the manufacturing industry?

How have the theories of the quality gurus developed into the standards employed by a pharmaceutical printing firm?

Britain's future within the EC: is full economic and monetary union in the national interest?

Is the British film industry beyond recovery?

Japanese investment and economic regeneration in South Wales

Quality systems in the insurance industry

Selling to the Japanese: a critical evaluation of current theories and practice for successful market entry

The brewing industry – why did the investigation by the Monopolies and Mergers Commission have such a big impact on the industry?

The development of mail order/home shopping: a case study

The flexible organisation. Is it a myth or reality?

The impact of charging for sport for 'fun'

Strategy for shareholder value

Survival of the fittest: a comparison between local independent and national/international music outlets

What are the consequences of the trade war in the yellow fat market?

Will a single European currency benefit British business?

The Harvard and footnotes systems of referencing

Three points are important when referencing:

- credit must be given when quoting or citing other work;
- adequate information must be provided in the bibliography to enable a reader to locate each reference;
- references must be consistent and complete.

The Harvard System

Referencing in the text

The Harvard system, which we use in this book, usually uses the author's name and year of publication to identify cited documents within the text. The system for referencing work in the text is outlined in Table A2.1.

Table A2.1 **Using the Harvard system to reference in the text**

To refer to	Use the general format	For example
A single author	(Surname, date)	(Saunders, 1993)
Dual authors	(Surname and Surname, date)	(Saunders and Cooper, 1993)
More than two authors	(Surname *et al.*, date)	(Slack *et al.*, 1996)
Work by different authors generally	(Surname, date; Surname, date) in alphabetical order	(Baker, 1996; Lewis, 1998; Thornhill, 1997)
Different authors with the same surname	(Surname, Initial., date)	(Smith, J., 1998)
Different publications by the same author	(Surname, date, date) in ascending date author	(Lewis, 1991, 1998)
Different publications by the same author from the same year	(Surname, date), make sure the letter is consistent throughout	(Forster, 1991a)

Table A2.1 *Cont.*

To refer to	Use the general format	For example
An author referred to by another author where the original has not been read (*secondary reference*)	(Surname, date, cited by Surname, date)	(Granovetter,1974; cited by Saunders, 1993)
A corporate author	(Corporate name, date)	(Hanson Trust Plc, 1990)
A newspaper article with no obvious author	(Publication name, date)	(Guardian, 1999)
Another type of publication with no obvious author	(Publication name, date)	(Labour Market Trends, 1999)
An internet site	(Site title, date)	(Advertising Association, 1999)
A publication for which the year of publication cannot be identified	(Surname or Corporate name, nd) where 'nd' means no date (Surname or Corporate name, c. date) where 'c.' means circa	(Woollons, nd) (Hattersley, c. 1977)
A direct quotation	(Surname or Corporate name, date: page) where 'page' is the page in the original publication on which the quotation appears	'. . . the Harvard method of referencing provides a simple way of coping with the main text and also bibliographies' (Bell, 1993: 28)

Referencing in the references or bibliography

In the references or bibliography the publications are listed alphabetically by author's name and all authors' surnames and initials are listed in full. If there is more than one work by the same author, these are listed chronologically. The system for referencing work in the references or bibliography is outlined in Table A2.2. While it would be impossible for us to include an example of every type of reference you might need to include, the information contained in this table should enable you to work out the required format for all your references.

Remember to include a, b, c etc. immediately after the date when you are referencing different publications by the same author from the same year. Do not forget to ensure that these are consistent with the letters used for the references in the main text.

Table A2.2 Using the Harvard system to reference in the references or bibliography

To reference		Use the general format	For example
Books and chapters in books	Book (first edition)	Surname, Initials. and Surname, Initials. (date) *Title*, Place of publication, Publisher.	Saunders, M.N.K. and Cooper, S.A. (1993) *Understanding Business Statistics*, London, DP Publications Ltd.
	Book (other than first edition)	Surname, Initials. and Surname, Initials. (date) *Title* (? edn), Place of publication, Publisher.	Morris, C. (1999) *Quantitative Approaches to Business Studies* (5th edn), London, Financial Times Pitman Publishing.
	Book (no obvious author)	Corporate name or Publication name (date) *Title*, Place of publication, Publisher.	Mintel Marketing Intelligence (1998) *Designerwear: Mintel Marketing Intelligence Report*, London, Mintel International Group Ltd.
	Chapter in a book	Surname, Initials. and Surname, Initials. (date) *Title*, Place of publication, Publisher, Chapter ?.	Robson, C. (1993) *Real World Research*, Oxford, Blackwell, Chapter 3.
	Chapter in an edited book	Surname, Initials. (date) 'Chapter title', *in* Surname, Initials. and Surname, Initials. (eds), *Title*, Place of publication, Publisher, page numbers.	Craig, P.B. (1991) 'Designing and using mail questionnaires' *in* Smith, N.C. and Dainty, P. (eds), *The Management Research Handbook*, London, Routledge, pp. 181–9.
Journal articles	Journal article	Surname, Initials. and Surname, Initials. (date) 'Title of article', *Journal name*, volume number, part number, pages.	Storey, J., Cressey, P., Morris, T. and Wilkinson, A. (1997) 'Changing employment practices in UK banking: case studies', *Personnel Review*, 26:1, 24–42.
	journal article (no obvious author)	Corporate name or Publication name (date) 'Title of article', *Journal name*, volume number, part number, pages.	Local Government Chronicle (1993) 'Westminster poised for return to AMA fold', *Local Government Chronicle*, 5 November, p. 5.
Government publications	Parliamentary papers including acts and bills	Country of origin (date) *Title*, Place of publication, Publisher.	Great Britain (1994) *Criminal Justice and Public Order Act 1994*, London, HMSO.
	Others (with authors)	As for books	As for books

Table A2.2

Cont.

To reference		Use the general format	For example
Newspapers, including CD-ROM databases:	Others (no obvious authors)	Department name or Committee name (date) *Title*, Place of publication, Publisher.	Department of Trade and Industry (1992) *The Single Market: Europe Open for Professions, UK Implementation*, London, HMSO.
	Newspaper article	Surname, Initials. and Surname, Initials., (date) 'Title of article', *Newspaper name*, day, month, pages.	Roberts, D. (1998) 'BAe sells property wing for £301m', *The Daily Telegraph*, London, 10 October, p. 31.
	Newspaper article (no obvious author)	Newspaper name (date) 'Title of article', *newspaper name*, day, month, pages.	Guardian (1992) 'Fraud trial at Britannia Theme Park', *The Guardian*, Manchester, 5 February, p. 4.
	Newspaper article (from CD-ROM database)	Newspaper name or Surname, Initials. (date) 'Title of article', *Newspaper name*, (CD-ROM), day, month, pages.	Financial Times (1998) 'Recruitment: lessons in leadership: moral issues are increasingly pertinent to the military and top corporate ranks', *Financial Times*, (CD-ROM), London, 11 March, p. 32.
Other CD-ROM publications		Title of CD-ROM or Surname, Initials, (date) (CD-ROM), Place of publication, Publisher.	Encarta 98 Encyclopaedia (1997) (CD-ROM) Redmond, WA, Microsoft Corporation.
Unpublished conference papers		Surname, Initials. and Surname, Initials. (date) 'Title of paper', *paper presented at the Conference name*, days, month, location of conference.	Saunders, M.N.K. and Thornhill, A. (1998) 'The development and application of a diagnostic tool to help manage survivors of change over time', *paper presented at the Fifth Annual International Conference on Advances in Management 8–11 July*, Lincoln.
Letters, personal emails and electronic conferences/ bulletin boards	Letter	Surname, Initials. and Surname, Initials. (date) *unpublished letter: subject matter.*	MacClelland, S. (1998) *Unpublished letter: Reviewer's feedback.*
	Personal email	Surname, Initials. (date) *subject matter* (email to the author) (online).	MacClelland, S. (1998) *Reviewer's feedback* (email to the author) (online).
	Electronic conference/ Bulletin Boards	Surname, Initials. (date) subject matter, *name of electronic conference/bulletin board* (online).	Jones, K. (1999) 101 reasons why we need the pound, *Britain and European Monetary Union* (online).

▶

Table A2.2 *Cont.*

To reference		Use the general format	For example
Internet items excluding emails	Journal published on the Internet	<URL:http://www. remainder of full Internet electronic conference/bulletin board>	<URL:http://.stingray.ivision.co.uk/groups/emu/frindex.htm>
		Surname, Initials. and Surname, Initials. (date) 'Title of article', *journal name*, volume number part number (online)(cited day month year). Available from <URL:http://www. remainder of full Internet address>.	Jenkins, M. and Bailey, L. (1995) 'The role of learning centre staff in supporting student learning', *Journal of Learning and Teaching* 1:1, Spring (online) (cited 29 March 1996). Available from <URL:http://www.chelt.ac.uk/cwis/pubs/jolt/issue1.1/page2.htm>.
	Internet site	Site title (date) 'Title of page within site where applicable' (online) (cited day month year). Available from <URL:http://www. remainder of full Internet address>.	Institute of Personnel and Development (online)(cited 14 October 1988). Available from <URL:http://www.ipd.co.uk>.

Footnotes

Referencing in the text

When using *footnotes*, sometimes referred to as the *Vancouver system*, references within the research report are shown by a number. This number refers directly to the references and it means it is not necessary for you to include the authors' names or date of publication:

'Recent research[1] indicates that . . .'

Referencing in the references

These list sequentially the referenced work in the order they are referred to in your research report. This can be useful as it enables you to include comments and footnotes as well as the references (Jankowicz, 1995). It does, however, mean that the references are unlikely to be in alphabetical order. When using the footnotes system you need to ensure that:

- the layout of individual references is the same as that for the Harvard system (Table A2.2), other than that they are preceded by a number, for example:

  1   Ritzer, G. (1996) *The McDonaldization of Society* (revised edn), Thousand Oaks, CA, Pine Forge Press.

- the publications referred to only include those you have cited in your report. They should therefore be headed 'References' rather than 'Bibliography';
- you refer to the same item more than once using standard bibliographic abbreviations to save repeating in full the reference (Table A2.3).

Table A2.3   **Bibliographic abbreviations**

Abbreviation	Explanation	For example
op. cit. (*opere citato*)	Meaning in the work cited. This refers to a work previously referenced and so you must give the author and date and if necessary the page number.	Robson (1993) *op. cit*. pp. 23–4
loc. cit. (*loco citato*)	Meaning in the place cited. This refers to the same page of a work previously referenced and so you must give the author and date.	Robson (1993) *loc. cit.*
ibid. (*ibidem*)	Meaning the same work given immediately before. This refers to the work referenced immediately before and replaces all details of the previous reference other than a page number if necessary.	*ibid.*

Further reading

Cheltenham & Gloucester College of Higher Education (1999) 'Setting out your bibliography using Harvard' (online) (cited 6 April 1999). Available from <URL:http://www.chelt.ac.uk/is/mjenkins/reference/bibliography.htm>. This provides a thorough, up-to-date, discussion of the layout required for a wide range of information sources using the Harvard system.

Branscomb, H.E. (1998) *Casting Your Net: a Student's Guide to Research on the Internet*, Boston, MA, Allyn and Bacon. Appendix 2 provides a detailed discussion of documenting a wide range of sources from the internet.

Ethical principles and guidelines for research with human participants

Documentation concerning ethics and ethical codes produced by the British Sociological Association and the British Psychological Society is gratefully acknowledged, as is information supplied by Jonathan Elcock.

1   Introduction

These principles and guidelines relate to social research undertaken with human participants and should be followed by all researchers within the College, whether they are members of staff, postgraduate or undergraduate students. Faculties or Departments may operate their own specific guidelines or codes of practice, and researchers are advised to check with their Faculty Office.

2   Process of approval

2.1   *Members of staff*

The appropriate Faculty Research Committee is responsible for ensuring that staff are aware of, and agree to abide by the guidelines.

2.2   *Research students*

All research students are required to signal their adherence to the College's ethical guidelines on the registration form RD1, as is the supervisory team for each research degree programme. The Faculty Research Director signs the form to confirm that student and supervisors are aware of, and agree to abide by the guidelines.

2.3   *All taught students*

The Course Tutor is responsible for ensuring that all taught students are aware of, and agree to abide by the guidelines.

3 General responsibilities

3.1 Towards research participants

Researchers have a responsibility to ensure as far as possible that the physical, social and psychological well-being of their research participants is not detrimentally affected by the research, and research relationships should be characterized, whenever possible, by trust.

3.2 Towards other researchers

Researchers should avoid, wherever possible, actions which may have deleterious consequences for other researchers or which might undermine the reputation of their discipline. Research directors should bear in mind their responsibilities towards members of their research teams and should aim to anticipate and guard against the possible harmful consequences of the research for team members.

4 Informed consent

4.1   Research should be based, as far as possible and practicable, on the freely given informed consent of those under study. However, it is recognised that in some cases it may be necessary to employ covert methods should these constitute the only means to obtain the required data, in which case the researcher should refer to section 5 below.

4.2   It is the responsibility of the researcher to explain as fully as possible, and in terms meaningful to the participants: the aims and nature of the research, who is undertaking it, who is funding it, its likely duration, why it is being undertaken, the possible consequences of the research, and how the results are to be disseminated.

4.3   The power imbalance between researcher and researched should be addressed. Care should be taken to ensure that as far as possible the latter are not pressurised into participation. Research participants should be aware of their right to refuse participation whenever and for whatever reason and should not be given the impression that they are required to participate. It should also be recognised that research may involve a lengthy data-gathering period and that it may be necessary to regard consent not as obtained once and for all, but subject to renegotiation over time.

4.4   The researcher should explain how far research participants will be afforded anonymity and confidentiality and participants should have the option of rejecting the use of data-gathering devices such as tape-recorders and video cameras.

4.5   If there is a likelihood of data being shared with or divulged to other researchers, the potential uses of the data should be discussed with the participants and their agreement to such use should be obtained.

4.6   Where access to a research setting is gained via a 'gatekeeper', researchers should also obtain the informed consent of research participants, while at the same time taking account of the gatekeeper's interests. It should be borne in mind that the relationship between research participant and gatekeeper may well continue long after the research has been undertaken.

4.7   Where research participants are young children or other vulnerable groups such as elderly, disabled or sick people or people with learning difficulties, whose understanding is impaired in some way so that they are unable to give full informed consent, it may be necessary to use a proxy in order to gather data. In this case great care must be taken not to intrude upon the privacy of the vulnerable participants. The researcher should consult relevant professionals, parents/guardians and relatives, as appropriate. Researchers should attempt to obtain the informed consent of children and their parents and in relation to schoolchildren those *in loco parentis*.

4.8   In addition to obtaining the informed consent of those under study, researchers should attempt to anticipate and guard against the possible harmful consequences of their research for participants.

5   Covert research

5.1   While it is recognised that there is a continuum of covert–overt research and therefore difficulty in defining research as entirely covert or overt, researchers should endeavour, wherever possible and practicable to avoid the use of deception in their research methods, as this violates the principle of informed consent and may invade the privacy of those under study, particularly in non-public spaces. If it appears that the employment of covert research methods is the only means to obtain the required data, the researcher should seek to assure her/himself that no other non-deceptive research methods could be employed to achieve the research objectives.

5.2   Covert research in non-public spaces or experimental manipulation of research participants without their knowledge should be a last resort when it is impossible to use other methods to obtain the required data. It is particularly important in such cases to safeguard the anonymity of participants.

5.3   If covert methods are employed and informed consent has not been obtained prior to the research, every attempt should be made to obtain this *post hoc*.

6   Confidentiality and anonymity

6.1   The anonymity and privacy of research participants should be respected and personal information relating to participants should be kept confidential and secure. Researchers must comply with the provisions of the Data Protection Act (see

Annex 1 for a précis of principles) and should consider whether it is proper or appropriate even to record certain kinds of sensitive information.

6.2   Where possible, threats to the confidentiality and anonymity of research data should be anticipated by researchers and normally the identities and research records of participants should be kept confidential, whether or not an explicit pledge of confidentiality has been given.

6.3   Whilst the researcher should take every practicable measure to ensure the confidentiality and anonymity of research participants, s/he should also take care not to give unrealistic assurances or guarantees of confidentiality. Research participants with easily identifiable characteristics or positions within an organisation should be reminded that it may be difficult to disguise their identity totally without distorting the data.

J A Collinson

Calculating the minimum sample size

In some situations, such as experimental research, it is necessary for you to calculate the precise *minimum sample size* you require. This calculation assumes that data will be collected from all cases in the sample and is based on:

- how confident you need to be that the estimate is accurate (the *level of confidence* in the estimate);
- how accurate the estimate needs to be (the *margin of error* that can be tolerated);
- the proportion of responses you expect to have some particular attribute.

Provided that you know the level of confidence and the margin of error it is relatively easy to estimate the proportion of responses you expect to have a particular attribute. To do this ideally you need to collect a pilot sample of about 30 observations and from this to infer the likely proportion for your main survey. It is therefore important that the pilot sample uses the same methods as your main survey. Alternatively you might have undertaken a very similar survey and so already have a reasonable idea of the likely proportion. If you do not, then you need to either make an informed guess or assume that 50 per cent of the sample will have the specified attribute – the worst scenario. Most surveys will involve collecting data on more than one attribute. deVaus (1991:72) argues that for such multi-purpose surveys you should 'play safe' and determine the sample size on the basis of those variables where there is likely to be 'greatest diversity in the sample'.

Once you have all the information you substitute it into the formula:

$$n = p\% \times q\% \times \left[\frac{z}{e\%} \right]^2$$

where n is the minimum sample size required
$p\%$ is the proportion belonging to the specified category
$q\%$ is the proportion not belonging to the specified category
z is the z value corresponding to the level of confidence required (see Table A4.1)
$e\%$ is the margin of error required

Where your population is less than 10 000 a smaller sample size can be used without affecting the accuracy. This is called the *adjusted minimum sample size*. It is calculated using the following formula:

$$n' = \cfrac{n}{1 + \left[\cfrac{n}{N}\right]}$$

where n' is the adjusted minimum sample size

           n is the minimum sample size (as calculated above)

           N is the total population

Table A4.1   **Levels of confidence and associated z values**

Level of confidence	z value
90% certain	1.65
95% certain	1.96
99% certain	2.57

Worked example

Calculating the minimum sample size

To answer a research question you need to estimate the proportion of a total population of 4000 home care clients who receive a visit from their home care assistant at least once a week. You have been told that you need to be 95 per cent certain that the 'estimate' is accurate (the level of confidence in the estimate); this corresponds to a z score of 1.96 (Table A4.1). You have also been told that your 'estimate' needs to be accurate to within plus or minus 5 per cent of the true percentage (the margin of error that can be tolerated).

You still need to estimate the proportion of responses who receive a visit from their home care assistant at least once a week. From your pilot survey you discover that 12 out of the 30 clients receive a visit at least once a week, in other words that 40 per cent belong to the specified category. This means that 60 per cent do not.

These figures can then be substituted into the formula:

$$n = 40 \times 60 \times \left[\frac{1.96}{5}\right]^2$$

$$= 2400 \times (0.392)^2$$

$$= 2400 \times 0.154$$

$$= 369.6$$

Your minimum sample size is therefore 370 returns.

As the total population of home care clients is 4000 the adjusted minimum sample size can now be calculated:

$$n' = \cfrac{369.6}{1 + \left[\cfrac{369.6}{4000}\right]}$$

$$= \frac{369.6}{1 + 0.092}$$

$$= \frac{369.6}{1.092}$$

$$= 338.46$$

Because of the small total population you only need a minimum sample size of 339. However this assumes a response rate of 100 per cent.

Reference

deVaus, D.A. (1991) *Surveys in Social Research* (3rd edn), London, UCL Press and Allen & Unwin.

Random sampling numbers

78 41	11 62	72 18	66 69	58 71	31 90	51 36	78 09	41 00
70 50	58 19	68 26	75 69	04 00	25 29	16 72	35 73	55 85
32 78	14 47	01 55	10 91	83 21	13 32	59 53	03 38	79 32
71 60	20 53	86 78	50 57	42 30	73 48	68 09	16 35	21 87
35 30	15 57	99 96	33 25	56 43	65 67	51 45	37 99	54 89
09 08	05 41	66 54	01 49	97 34	38 85	85 23	34 62	60 58
02 59	34 51	98 71	31 54	28 85	23 84	49 07	33 71	17 88
20 13	44 15	22 95	98 97	60 02	85 07	17 57	20 51	01 67
36 26	70 11	63 81	27 31	79 71	08 11	87 74	85 53	86 78
00 30	62 19	81 68	86 10	65 61	62 22	17 22	96 83	56 37
38 41	14 59	53 03	52 86	21 88	55 87	85 59	14 90	74 87
18 89	40 84	71 04	09 82	54 44	94 23	83 89	04 59	38 29
34 38	85 56	80 74	22 31	26 39	65 63	12 38	45 75	30 35
55 90	21 71	17 88	20 08	57 64	17 93	22 34	00 55	09 78
81 43	53 96	96 88	36 86	04 33	31 40	18 71	06 00	51 45
59 69	13 03	38 31	77 08	71 20	23 28	92 43	92 63	21 74
60 24	47 44	73 93	64 37	64 97	19 82	27 59	24 20	00 04
17 04	93 46	05 70	20 95	42 25	33 95	78 80	07 57	86 58
09 55	42 30	27 05	27 93	78 10	69 11	29 56	29 79	28 66
46 69	28 64	81 02	41 89	12 03	31 20	25 16	79 93	28 22
28 94	00 91	16 15	35 12	68 93	23 71	11 55	64 56	76 95
59 10	06 29	83 84	03 68	97 65	59 21	58 54	61 59	30 54
41 04	70 71	05 56	76 66	57 86	29 30	11 31	56 76	24 13
09 81	81 80	73 10	10 23	26 29	61 15	50 00	76 37	60 16
91 55	76 68	06 82	05 33	06 75	92 35	82 21	78 15	19 43
82 69	36 73	58 69	10 92	31 14	21 08	13 78	56 53	97 77
03 59	65 34	32 06	63 43	38 04	65 30	32 82	57 05	33 95
03 96	30 87	81 54	69 39	95 69	95 69	89 33	78 90	30 07
39 91	27 38	20 90	41 10	10 80	59 68	93 10	85 25	59 25
89 93	92 10	59 40	26 14	27 47	39 51	46 70	86 85	76 02
99 16	73 21	39 05	03 36	87 58	18 52	61 61	02 92	07 24
93 13	20 70	42 59	77 69	35 59	71 80	61 95	82 96	48 84
47 32	87 68	97 86	28 51	61 21	33 02	79 65	59 49	89 93
09 75	58 00	72 49	36 58	19 45	30 61	87 74	43 01	93 91
63 24	15 65	02 05	32 92	45 61	35 43	67 64	94 45	95 66
33 58	69 42	25 71	74 31	88 80	04 50	22 60	72 01	27 88
23 25	22 78	24 88	68 48	83 60	53 59	73 73	82 43	82 66
07 17	77 20	79 37	50 08	29 79	55 13	51 90	36 77	68 69
16 07	31 84	57 22	29 54	35 14	22 22	22 60	72 15	40 90
67 90	79 28	62 83	44 96	87 70	40 64	27 22	60 19	52 54
79 52	74 68	69 74	31 75	80 59	29 28	21 69	15 97	35 88
69 44	31 09	16 38	92 82	12 25	10 57	81 32	76 71	31 61
09 47	57 04	54 00	78 75	91 99	26 20	36 19	53 29	11 55
74 78	09 25	95 80	25 72	88 85	76 02	29 89	70 78	93 84

Source: Morris (1993), reproduced by permission

Guidelines for non-discriminatory language

Writing in a non-discriminatory manner is important in all areas of business and management. For example in Section 13.5 we noted how the use of language which assumes the gender of a group of people, such as referring to a clerical assistant as 'she', is not only inaccurate but gives offence to people of both sexes. Similar care needs to be exercised when using other gender-based terms, referring to people from different ethnic groups and writing about people with disabilities. Without this, the language used may be prejudiced, oppressive, offensive, unfair or even incorrect. The impact of this is summarised clearly by Bill Bryson (1995: 425) in his book *Made in America* when he observes '. . . at the root of the bias-free language movement lies a commendable sentiment: to make language less wounding or demeaning to those whose sex, race, physical condition or circumstances leave them vulnerable to the raw power of words.'

Therefore, although the task of changing the language you use may seem difficult at first, it is important that you do so in order that your communication is accurate, unbiased and does not cause offence.

Guidelines for gender

When referring to both sexes using the terms 'men' or 'women' and their gender-based equivalents is inappropriate. Some of the more common alternatives are listed in Table A6.1.

Guidelines for ethnicity

Attention needs to be paid when referring to different ethnic groups. This is especially important where the term used refers to a number of ethnic groups. For example, the term 'Asian' includes a number of diverse ethnic groups that can be recognised with the terms 'Asian peoples' or Asian communities'. Similarly, the diversity of people represented by the term 'Black' can be recognised by referring to 'Black peoples' or 'Black communities'. Where possible the individual groups within these communities should be identified separately.

'Black' as a term used to be regarded as offensive. More recently it has acquired connotations of unity against racism and been reclaimed as a source of pride and identity. 'Afro-Caribbean' is a term that is also associated with a commitment to anti-racism and is used to describe black people from the Caribbean islands.

Table A6.1	Gender-specific terms and gender-neutral alternatives

Gender-specific term	Gender-neutral alternative
Chairman	Chair, chair person
Forefathers	Ancestors
Foreman	Supervisor
Layman	Lay person
Man	Person
Mankind	Humanity, people
Man-made	Manufactured, synthetic
Manning	Resourcing, staffing
Manpower	Human resources, labour, staff, workforce
Master copy	Original, top copy
Policeman	Police officer
Policewoman	Police officer
Women	People

Source: Developed from British Psychological Society, 1988

Other terms that are regarded as offensive include 'coloured', 'half-caste', 'mixed race', 'Negress', 'Negro' and 'West Indian'.

If you are unsure of the term to use then ask someone from the appropriate community for the most acceptable current term. In addition, you need to try to ensure that the language you are using is not inadvertently reinforcing racism or xenophobia.

Guidelines for disability

Disability is an area where terminology is constantly changing as people voice their own preferences. Despite this, guidelines can be offered for the more common terms. These are summarised in Table A6.2. However, if you are unsure of the term to use ask someone from the appropriate group for the most acceptable current term.

Table A6.2 **Disability language – what to avoid and preferences**

Avoid	Preference	Comment
The disabled	Disabled people, people with disabilities	Individuals often have strong preferences so ask
The blind	Blind people, people who are blind, people with a visual impairment	'Blind' on its own is dehumanising and distancing
The deaf	Deaf people, people who have a hearing impairment, the deaf community	'Deaf' and other collective names on their own are dehumanising and distancing
The handicapped	People with impairments, disabled students, employees with disabilities	'Handicapped' is regarded as outdated by many
Mentally handicapped	Person with learning difficulties	'Mentally handicapped' is regarded as offensive and inaccurate
An epileptic, epileptics	Person who has epilepsy	'Epileptic' implies a medical condition rather than a person
Spastic	Person who has cerebral palsy	'Spastic' is both inaccurate and offensive
Dumb/mute	Unable to speak, having a speech impairment	'Dumb' implies stupid
Wheelchair-bound	wheelchair user	Conveys helplessness when wheelchair aids mobility
Victim of, afflicted by, suffering from	Person who has	Makes assumption of tragedy, reinforces ideas of dependence or frailty

Source: Developed from Pointon, G. (no date)

References

British Psychological Society (1988) 'Guidelines for the use of non-sexist language', *The Psychologist*, 1:2, 53–54. This offers useful advice about the use of non-sexist language.

Bryson B (1995) *Made in America*, London, Minerva.

Pointon, G. (no date) *Disability and Television: Guidelines on Representation for Producers*, London, Channel 4.

Index